Very Young Children with Special Needs

A Formative Approach for Today's Children

Third Edition

Vikki F. Howard

Betty Fry Williams
Whitworth College

Cheryl Lepper

PEARSON

Merrill
Prentice Hall

Upper Saddle River, New Jersey
Columbus, Ohio

Library of Congress Cataloging-in-Publication Data

Howard, Vikki F.
  Very young children with special needs: a formative approach for the twenty-first
century/Vikki Howard, Betty Fry Williams, Cheryl Lepper.—3rd ed.
  p. cm.
  Rev. ed, of: Very young children with special needs/Vicki F. Howard . . . [et al.]. 2nd ed. c2001.
  Includes bibliographical references and indexes.
  ISBN 0-13-112795-0
  1. Children with disabilities—Education (Early childhood) 2. Child development. 3. Special education.
I. Williams, Betty Fry. II. Lepper, Cheryl. III. Title.
  LC4019.3.V47 2005
  371.9'0472—dc22   2004003502

Vice President and Executive Publisher: Jeffery W. Johnston
Acquisitions Editor: Allyson P. Sharp
Editorial Assistant: Kathleen S. Burk
Associate Editor: Martha Flynn
Production Editor: Linda Hillis Bayma
Production Coordination: Emily Hatteberg, Carlisle Publishers Services
Design Coordinator: Diane C. Lorenzo
Illustrations: Cheryl Lepper
Cover Designer: Harold Leber
Cover Image: Spokane Guilds' School and Neuromuscular Center
Production Manager: Laura Messerly
Director of Marketing: Ann Castel Davis
Marketing Manager: Autumn Purdy
Marketing Coordinator: Tyra Poole

This book was set in Garamond by Carlisle Communications, Ltd. It was printed and bound by R.R. Donnelley & Sons Company. The cover was printed by Phoenix Color Corp.

Photo Credits: pp. 164, 193, 242, 321, 375, courtesy of the Berke family; p. 59, courtesy of the DeWolf family; pp. 81, 91, 138, 142, 191, 199, 202, 217, 218, 222, 224, 412, Betsy Downey; pp. 28, 93, 115, 367, 447, 513, courtesy of the Finkel family; pp. 85, 119, 183, 265, courtesy of the Holden family; pp. 128, 207, 411, courtesy of the Moore family; pp. 1, 51, 103, 155, 231, 275, 329, 389, 441, 483, courtesy of the Spokane Guilds' School and Neuromuscular Center; pp. 395, 435, 455, courtesy of the Shafer family; p. 355, courtesy of the Simpson family; p. 66, Anne Vega/Merrill; pp. 8, 281, 346, 505, courtesy of the Waritz family; pp. 187, 249, 314, 317, courtesy of Kathy Werfelmann; pp. 117, 190, Randy Williams.

Pearson Education Ltd.
Pearson Education Singapore Pte. Ltd.
Pearson Education Canada, Ltd.
Pearson Education–Japan

Pearson Education Australia Pty. Limited
Pearson Education North Asia Ltd.
Pearson Educación de Mexico, S.A. de C.V.
Pearson Education Malaysia Pte. Ltd.

PEARSON
Merrill
Prentice Hall

10 9 8 7 6 5 4 3 2 1
ISBN: 0-13-112795-0

DEDICATION

IN MEMORY OF PAT PORT, A BELOVED FRIEND TO US AND TO CHILDREN EVERYWHERE

This book is dedicated to the many children, students, colleagues, parents, and family members who have taught us well throughout our personal and professional lives. They set high standards for themselves and others, respected individual differences and needs, and committed themselves unselfishly to advocate for the care and education of children. It is their lessons we have tried to share in this text and from which we continue to learn.

PREFACE

This text is a collaborative effort, not only on the part of the authors, but also because of the contributions of the many parents, professionals, researchers, and students who have added to the growing body of knowledge about how to best serve very young children with disabilities and their families. It was our intention to synthesize perspectives and information from the fields of medicine, education, intervention, psychology, law, sociology, and family life for use by those who will work with infants, toddlers, and preschoolers with special needs. It was also our goal to challenge our readers to consider the future of early intervention and their role in shaping the field of early childhood special education. We hope this text is a relevant and long-lasting resource.

The purpose of this text is to provide an introduction to early childhood professionals who plan to engage in providing services and intervention to very young children with disabilities. It is not intended as a methods text, but rather as a foundation regarding the philosophy, history, family impact, legal issues, and medical concerns that are most relevant to early services to children with exceptional needs. Though early childhood special education teachers may make up the majority of readers who use this text, the term *early childhood professional* is also used to address individuals in many disciplines, including health care, social work, physical and occupational therapy, child care, and those who are involved in interagency services to young children and their families.

Chapter 1 presents an overview of the guiding philosophies of the text, which will be applied and reiterated throughout the chapters. Chapter 2 reviews the history of the care of young children, and Chapter 3 focuses on the growth of special services for those with disabilities and their families. Chapters 4 to 8 provide detail on typical child development and the etiology of disabling conditions that affect the very young child with exceptional needs. Chapters 9 and 10 address how intervention and support are provided to young children and their families.

Very young children with special needs are the focus of this text, but to thoroughly understand and serve a child with disabilities, one must be knowledgeable about typical development, understand how health and genetics affect potential, and recognize the influence of the child's family and environment on realizing that potential. Throughout the book, the stories of families will be provided through case studies, and special issues will be identified through close-ups, in order to provide real-life examples. The text is interdisciplinary, inclusive, and family-focused.

ACKNOWLEDGMENTS

The authors wish to extend their deepest gratitude to the following people for their insight, inspiration, and encouragement. We are especially grateful to Pat

Port, our collaborator and co-author on the original text and our dear deceased friend. Though every person listed was extremely busy, they all gave generously of their time and talents. There are no words adequate to express our thanks.

Editors: Allyson P. Sharp and Martha Flynn

The parents who shared their family histories and advice: David and Priscilla DeWolf, James and Judy Holden, Marsha and James Moore, Ann and Tom Simpson, Tammy and Mike McCauley, Kim and Mark Shafer, Amy and Michael Finkel, and Sarah and Terry Berke.

Photographers: Betsy Downey, Kathy Werfelmann, and Randy Williams

Organizations that permitted our photographers to do their work: Gonzaga University's School of Education Preschool, Martin Luther King Center, Shriners Hospital, and the Spokane Guilds' School and Neuromuscular Center.

Reviewers who kindly read our manuscript and provided constructive comments: Ida Bailey, Shaw University; Barbara A. Beakley, Millersville University; and Rebecca J. Cook, Eastern Illinois University.

DISCOVER THE COMPANION WEBSITE ACCOMPANYING THIS BOOK

THE PRENTICE HALL COMPANION WEBSITE: A VIRTUAL LEARNING ENVIRONMENT

Technology is a constantly growing and changing aspect of our field that is creating a need for content and resources. To address this emerging need, Prentice Hall has developed an online learning environment for students and professors alike—Companion Websites—to support our textbooks.

In creating a Companion Website, our goal is to build on and enhance what the textbook already offers. For this reason, the content for each user-friendly website is organized by topic and provides the professor and student with a variety of meaningful resources. Common features of a Companion Website include:

FOR THE PROFESSOR—

Every Companion Website integrates **Syllabus Manager**™, an online syllabus creation and management utility.

- ◆ **Syllabus Manager**™ provides you, the instructor, with an easy, step-by-step process to create and revise syllabi, with direct links into Companion Website and other online content without having to learn HTML.
- ◆ Students may log on to your syllabus during any study session. All they need to know is the web address for the Companion Website and the password you've assigned to your syllabus.
- ◆ After you have created a syllabus using **Syllabus Manager**™, students may enter the syllabus for their course section from any point in the Companion Website.
- ◆ Clicking on a date, the student is shown the list of activities for the assignment. The activities for each assignment are linked directly to actual content, saving time for students.
- ◆ Adding assignments consists of clicking on the desired due date, then filling in the details of the assignment—name of the assignment, instructions, and whether it is a one-time or repeating assignment.

- In addition, links to other activities can be created easily. If the activity is online, a URL can be entered in the space provided, and it will be linked automatically in the final syllabus.
- Your completed syllabus is hosted on our servers, allowing convenient updates from any computer on the Internet. Changes you make to your syllabus are immediately available to your students at their next logon.

FOR THE STUDENT—

- **Overview and General Information**—General information about the topic and how it will be covered in the website.
- **Web Links**—A variety of websites related to topic areas.
- **Content Methods and Strategies**—Resources that help to put theories into practice in the special education classroom.
- **Reflective Questions and Case-Based Activities**—Put concepts into action, participate in activities, examine strategies, and more.
- **National and State Laws**—An online guide to how federal and state laws affect your special education classroom.
- **Behavior Management**—An online guide to help you manage behaviors in the special education classroom.
- **Message Board**—Virtual bulletin board to post and respond to questions and comments from a national audience.

To take advantage of these and other resources, please visit the *Very Young Children with Special Needs,* Third Edition, Companion Website at

www.prenhall.com/howard

EDUCATOR LEARNING CENTER:
AN INVALUABLE ONLINE RESOURCE

Merrill Education and the Association for Supervision and Curriculum Development (ASCD) invite you to take advantage of a new online resource, one that provides access to the top research and proven strategies associated with ASCD and Merrill—the Educator Learning Center. At **www.EducatorLearningCenter.com** you will find resources that will enhance your students' understanding of course topics and of current educational issues, in addition to being invaluable for further research.

How the Educator Learning Center will Help Your Students Become Better Teachers

With the combined resources of Merrill Education and ASCD, you and your students will find a wealth of tools and materials to better prepare them for the classroom.

Research

- More than 600 articles from the ASCD journal *Educational Leadership* discuss everyday issues faced by practicing teachers.
- A direct link on the site to Research Navigator™ gives students access to many of the leading education journals, as well as extensive content detailing the research process.
- Excerpts from Merrill Education texts give your students insights on important topics of instructional methods, diverse populations, assessment, classroom management, technology, and refining classroom practice.

Classroom Practice

- Hundreds of lesson plans and teaching strategies are categorized by content area and age range.
- Case studies and classroom video footage provide virtual field experience for student reflection.
- Computer simulations and other electronic tools keep your students abreast of today's classrooms and current technologies.

Look into the Value of Educator Learning Center Yourself

A four-month subscription to Educator Learning Center is $25 but is **FREE** when used in conjunction with this text. To obtain free passcodes for your students, simply contact your local Merrill/Prentice Hall sales representative, and your representative will give you a special ISBN to give your bookstore when ordering your textbooks. To preview the value of this website to you and your students, please go to **www.EducatorLearningCenter.com** and click on "Demo."

Brief Contents

CONTENTS

Note: Every effort has been made to provide accurate and current Internet information in this book. However, the Internet and information posted on it are constantly changing, and it is inevitable that some of the Internet addresses listed in this textbook will change.

SPECIAL FEATURES

CASE STUDIES

CLOSE-UPS

1

Philosophy of Early Education

The potential possibilities of any child are the most intriguing and stimulating in all creation.

(Ray L. Wilbur)

With the first cry in the delivery room, the sudden pause in what has been a growing frenzy of action and emotion, like a long exhalation of relief and joy; a baby is born. Parents beam, laugh, and cry; attendants share smiles and swing into action;

and baby, bewildered and naked, draws in the first breath of life. Whatever this little one's life will be, it is begun totally dependent on family, caregivers, educators, and the community. One new life, whose potential is determined not only by genetics, environment, and accidents of fate, but by the larger value and support society provides, begins its journey.

For children born with disabilities and those whose conditions place them at developmental risk, the journey has built-in roadblocks. At the same time, these children and their families can expect far greater support than has been the case in the past. Early education for infants and children with special needs offers both promise and challenge. Though the field is relatively young and establishing its knowledge-base, it is also accepted enough to be considered a necessary and important part of the educational system. Today, to a much greater degree than in the past, society acknowledges the need for early childhood services and values the quality of care and education provided for young children. Professional educators recognize the legitimacy and importance of education and treatment during early development. Consequently, Congress has mandated the provision of services to preschool-aged children with disabilities and has encouraged states to meet the needs of infants and toddlers with and at risk for developmental delays. Families can expect to become advocates for their children by providing continuous input into the manner of care received in child-care, early intervention, and preschool services.

Exciting opportunities open in the field of early childhood **special education** bring serious responsibilities as well. Much is expected of early educators today. Professionals must be knowledgeable in issues important to families, must demonstrate skill in providing direct services to children, and can contribute to the growing body of knowledge about early development and care. The recent, impressive growth of early childhood special education is a legacy that professionals can advance only by understanding the philosophy and knowledge base of disciplinary best practices. A **best practice** is a dynamic concept, changing in content as the technologies of service and education are extended through research and application. Early childhood educators should expect to be lifelong learners, keeping abreast of evolutionary changes and, at the same time, actively taking part in these changes. The current assumptions of best practice most important in the field of early childhood special education include the following:

1. A growing professional treats the field with an **attitude of science.** That is, individuals respect data-based information and evaluate the effects of new procedures, materials, or interventions by their impact on children and families being served.

2. An early childhood professional **personalizes** services to children with disabilities across a continuum of placements, recognizing the value of treatment in natural settings, while also

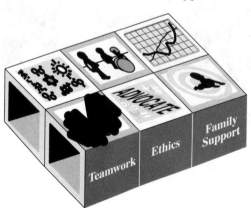

Building blocks of our philosophy for early childhood education.

respecting the specific treatment needs of individuals and the desires of their families. Early intervention is comprehensive care, not a predetermined method or place.

3. An effective professional is **culturally sensitive,** prepared to work with various populations and cultures in respectful and supportive ways.

4. A professional in early childhood education recognizes that very young children are a part of their larger family support systems and the environments that surround them. Such a professional may provide direct services to children, but only within the context of family needs and environmental demands, and in ways that will **empower** families.

5. An early childhood professional works in **collaboration** with experts from other disciplines to develop and provide the comprehensive services very young children need.

6. Finally, early childhood special educators must practice their profession with the highest **ethical standards.** Moreover, professionals must serve as advocates for parents and children, politically and professionally, as well as through service to their communities.

Professionals now entering early childhood special education are in the position of launching their careers equipped with skills and attitudes others have taken decades to identify and develop. This chapter will explore these key concepts in terms of their value to professionals. These concepts also will be woven throughout the content of the text.

THE IMPORTANCE OF AN ATTITUDE OF SCIENCE

Many professionals consider teaching to be an art; that is, a natural aptitude or ability granted a person at birth, which flowers with opportunity and experience. Some of this may be true; certainly most professionals in early childhood education were drawn into the field by the pleasure they found in working with young children and their families. Some gifted individuals possess talents that seem especially suited to working with infants, toddlers, and preschoolers. They display tolerance, playfulness, and a keen intuition for teaching. Others may be adept at communicating with children and parents, they may be more sensitive to others' needs, or they may be more skilled at working with diverse personalities and backgrounds. However, in all fields, the factor separating hobby artists from professional artists is the quality of study and effort they put into developing their natural gifts, whether they be painting, dance, drama, or teaching. Inspiration comes not from spontaneity, but from a combination of knowledge, talent, and experience.

Professional artists enhance their talents by a reflective study of the work of other artists. They strive to identify principles that will improve their craft and advance the field for others. An artful teacher who relies on raw ability alone may take years to become skillful and helpful for a variety of students. Another artful teacher who reads the professional literature, experiments with and evaluates recommended materials and procedures, and holds an attitude of science builds on natural talent to efficiently become a versatile and effective teacher.

WHAT IS AN ATTITUDE OF SCIENCE?

An attitude of science deals with what is parsimonious and empirical. **Parsimony** is the adoption of the simplest assumption in the formulation of a theory or in the interpretation of data. That is, one would look for a simple explanation before investigating more complicated possibilities. For example, if a small infant awakens crying in the middle of the night, one would first see if the child were hungry or wet. One would not immediately jump to the conclusion that the child is suffering separation anxiety or is ill with an intestinal infection.

> Parsimony does not guarantee correctness—because the simplest explanation may not always be the correct one—but it prevents our being so imaginative as to lose touch with the reality of observed data. (Alberto & Troutman, 1990, p. 4)

Often, what is simplest is not the most interesting. For years, psychologists told mothers of children with autism that the latter were uncommunicative and developmentally delayed because the mother's relationship with her child during infancy had been cold and rejecting. This was an intriguing theory that grew from a complicated Freudian explanation based on psychotherapy with verbal adults, but it was not the most parsimonious. A great deal of mental suffering on the part of mothers, as well as misspent therapy, might have been saved if a parsimonious explanation had been investigated earlier. Though there is still no explanation for the etiology of autism, parsimony might have led professionals to investigate biochemical or physical causes earlier if complex theories of attribution had not been so appealing to earlier psychologists.

In special education, many methods of intervention have evolved from complicated theories. Some theories, because they make assumptions about activities in the brain that can neither be seen nor measured easily, are untestable. One example of such a method is patterning or neural training developed by Dolman and Delacato. Patterning was a regimen that prescribed physical exercises that were purported to retrain the brain in a "normal" neural pattern which could cure motor, language, and cognitive disabilities. Thousands of parents were trained to use patterning techniques for several hours per day, often using a team of volunteers to guide precise movement exercises. Later, this method was declared to be ineffective, and a distraction from more practical and effective methods (American Academy of Pediatrics, 1982; Novella, 1996). In fact, recent research suggests that much of early education, including physical movement exercises, should be conducted within the context of natural daily routines (Mallory & New, 1994). The latter offers a more parsimonious solution to families and children.

An attitude of science is also a "disposition to deal with the facts rather than with what someone has said about them. . . . Science is a willingness to accept facts even when they are opposed to wishes" (Skinner, 1953, p. 6). An attitude of science requires one to be **empirical** (that is, to rely on observation or experimentation) and to be guided by practical experience rather than theory alone. A professional who is empirical tries new materials and procedures with careful observation to determine their effect on children or families using them. Based on the outcomes of such experiments, professionals decide to continue or discontinue the use of individual procedures. For example, theory (or trend) may indicate that pastel colors have a warm and calming effect on infants, encouraging their attention. To evaluate this recommendation, an empirical professional might place an infant in a plain crib with a pastel yellow, pink, and blue mobile and observe carefully to see how much the infant vocalizes, kicks, looks at the mobile, and so on. This professional would then compare the same infant's behavior when the baby is placed in the same crib and room with a mobile of contrasting white and black. Scientific professionals experiment to find out if a theory really applies in a particular situation, rather than accepting a theory without a verifiable demonstration.

Of course, a professional cannot function efficiently if every piece of advice must be directly tested or experienced before it is adopted. Fortunately, "science is more than the mere description of events as they occur. Rather, empiricism is an attempt to discover order, to show that certain events stand in lawful relations to other events" (Skinner, 1953, p. 6). Other professionals and researchers work to **replicate** results, that is, to demonstrate the same results with other children and in other settings. A scientific professional can then review research to identify data-based procedures that have been verified repeatedly through experimentation and that are likely to work, with and without adaptation, in the professional's own situation.

When the same results can be replicated consistently, and when there is a well-documented literature base, the theory or principle has **predictive utility.** Such a theory provides accurate forecasts regarding how a child might respond in certain circumstances, thereby giving professionals a useful tool for supporting or modifying a child's behavior. This is not to say the data-based method selected will work with all children. However, the likelihood is increased that this method will work more often or effectively than an untested or unverified method. For example, the principle of **reinforcement** states that if a stimulus is a reinforcer, the behavior it follows is likely to increase in frequency. A professional might find that giving requested items (a music box, for example) to Amy when she says "please" increases the rate of Amy's saying "please." The professional might then use those items as consequences for Amy when she takes a step independently, predicting with some confidence that the music box (for example) will act as a reinforcer to increase Amy's independent walking.

> As the principle is tried over and over again and continues to produce the same results, we gain faith in it and the probability that it is indeed true for all behavior. (Whaley & Malott, 1971, p. 444)

When a body of knowledge is advanced enough to provide a set of principles based on extensive research and experimentation, it becomes a **conceptual system.** A conceptual system shows researchers and professionals how similar procedures may be derived from basic principles.

> This can have the effect of making a body of technology into a discipline rather than a collection of tricks. Collections of tricks historically have been difficult to expand systematically, and when they were extensive, difficult to learn and teach. (Baer, Wolf, & Risley, 1968, p. 97)

Look again at the example of Amy's saying "please." Using the music box as a consequence seems like a pretty good trick to Ms. Johnson, who is visiting that day. When she returns to her classroom, she tries the music box as a consequence for Joey to see if it will increase his babbling. Nothing happens. Ms. Johnson would have been more successful if she understood the principle behind the use of the music box. If she had the *concept* of reinforcement in her repertoire, she would have looked for some consequence that was already effective in increasing the rate of Joey's behavior. A brief observation might show that Joey reaches for a toy more frequently when the toy is squeezed to make a noise each time Joey reaches for the toy. Squeezing the toy as a consequence to increase Joey's babbling has a higher probability of success than playing the music box. Or, if Ms. Johnson recognized the concept that a child's frequently chosen activities or materials often act as reinforcers, she might have found that marshmallows, bouncing, or clapping would also be predictable reinforcers. Ms. Johnson's skills would have been much improved if she had a data-based conceptual system from which to work, and not just a set of tricks. Applied behavior analysis offers one data-based conceptual system that is of great value to educators. Behavioral approaches are parsimonious because they deal with observable relationships between environmental stimuli, behavioral responses, and contingent consequences.

> For a behaviorist, all learning principles are defined on the basis of what actually happens, not what we think is happening. (Alberto & Troutman, 1990, p. 23)

The basic principles of behavior analysis were developed through extensive empirical testing and were replicated in thousands of classroom, clinic, and home applications. Therefore, the principles and procedures have a high degree of predictive utility, and many successful interventions have been developed based on this conceptual system. Though it is not within the scope of this text to teach the principles of behavior analysis, a few behavioral examples will help to illustrate elements of a conceptual system (see Table 1–1). The basic principles of behavior analysis include reinforcement, punishment, and extinction, though these simple principles have been extended to dozens of procedures that help children learn. Yet this conceptual system, like all others, must be challenged by scientific educators to build on and improve their ability to match intervention to the needs of children and families served. The scientific professional builds on natural talent for working with children, families, and professionals by drawing from a knowledge base of concepts that work because they are parsimonious, empirically derived, and replicable.

> Educational research is the way in which one acquires dependable and useful information about the educative process. Its goal is to discover general principles or interpretations of behavior that can be used to explain, predict, and control events in education situations. (Ary, Jacobs, & Razavich, 1996, p. 22)

Gallagher (1998) questioned whether the field of special education is at a point where its knowledge base can be considered scientific. Certainly, to reach this goal, we must aspire to achieve two things: (1) to identify generalizations that allow us to explain, predict, and control the outcomes of our interventions, and (2) to advance progressively, that is, to lay some questions to rest as we work to solve others. Gallagher cautioned that science must never replace values as a part of the professional conversation. We hasten to add, however, that values must also not replace empiricism; it is essential that professionals balance the two. We must

Table 1–1   Basic Principles of Applied Behavior Analysis

Basic Principle	Contingent Consequence	Effect on Future Rate of Behavior	Example
Reinforcement	When a stimulus is presented (positive) or removed (negative) contingent upon a response,	the future probability of that response **increases.**	A child who chews his carrot carefully before swallowing is given ice cream immediately after, and in the future he chews carefully more often. (positive reinforcement)
Punishment	When a stimulus is presented or removed contingent upon a response,	the future probability of that response **decreases.**	A child who hits his play partner is removed from the play activity and told to watch for 5 minutes before he is returned to the play activity, and in the future he hits less often.
Extinction	When the contingent stimulus for a previously reinforced response is no longer presented,	the future probability of the behavior **decreases.**	A child who takes toys away from others has in the past been allowed to keep playing with the stolen toys and her rate of stealing toys increased. Now the teacher makes sure she must return any toy taken from another child and her rate of stealing decreases.

embrace a philosophy of moral advocacy that also determines, explains, and makes effective our course of action.

PERSONALIZATION

Personalization is a new term used to capture a philosophy of care that recognizes the multiple, comprehensive services that are often needed by very young children with disabilities, while accommodating for the diverse priorities and needs of their families. Personalization emphasizes the "person-first" attitude of disability advocates who serve *children* with mental retardation rather than *mentally retarded* children, using language which gives more importance to category. Personalization seeks to create a community where services are tailored to fit the goals and aspirations of each child and his family and to provide support for each child to reach his potential.

Personalization is a logical progression in the development of disability rights and services, moving beyond the recent prevailing philosophy of **inclusion,** generally applied to educating students with and without disabilities together within regular classes in neighborhood schools. In order to understand how personalization differs from inclusion, we must return to the roots of inclusion, the political struggle for establishing rights for those with disabilities.

Case Study

FAMILY HARDSHIP: INTERVIEW WITH TAMMY WARITZ

In my job as a parent advocate, I see families with many difficulties to overcome. One of the biggest problems for families of children with disabilities is finding financial resources. There are a lot of families who don't have insurance and their incomes are not low enough to meet the federal guidelines to get medical assistance, so they're really struggling to figure out how they're going to pay for the services their children need.

For a number of years, our family has made sacrifices that no family should ever have to make. Some of the things that Jennifer requires are common needs for a child with disabilities and we had to be flexible enough to ensure she received what she needed. The cost of her equipment is incredible. For example, the braces that she has on her feet have to be replaced at least once a year, sometimes twice a year, and it costs $700 each time. We just got a brand new seat and back for her wheelchair, and it was $1,000. Jennifer's chair alone cost $3,500.

Our family got to a point of desperation, and my husband and I separated so that our income could be low enough to receive state funding for Jennifer's needs. At the time Jennifer had been

Jennifer in her wheelchair.

denied state funding, we were only $147 over the monthly eligibility limit on our income. We were stuck; we were struggling just to make enough money for food, shelter, and clothing; even with two blue-collar people working. It wasn't like we had a lot of money and we were

THE HISTORY OF DISABILITY RIGHTS

Disability rights have been a part of the larger civil rights movement in the United States and in many ways mirrored or echoed the history, actions, and achievements of better-known activists who fought for racial equality in the United States (see Figure 1–1). During the 18th and 19th centuries, exclusion and segregation of both people of color and people with disabilities predominated. It took a civil war to eliminate slavery, but even into the 20th century, people of color were still not guaranteed the right to vote, the right to an education, access to political office, or economic security. At the same time, people with disabilities were locked away from society in asylums, hospitals, workhouses, and prisons, and were often abused (Malhotra, 2001).

trying to cheat the system out of something. We felt like we were being punished, because we had this child with special needs, and we didn't have jobs that paid $20 an hour.

Finally, our situation reached a point where I had to break down publicly. I knew there were income waiver programs available and that Jennifer met the federal criteria for such a waiver, but the state agency would not approve one. I was crying uncontrollably one day, and I told them on the phone, "My family cannot continue to live like this. We can't afford to have a single-parent household. Furthermore, it's not right that I have to continue turning down raises at work to keep the financial assistance we have. If my family cannot access a waiver, you're going to have to place Jennifer because we cannot continue to live the way that we're living."

The need for medical funding literally put us in the position to choose between Jennifer and our family, though she is part of our family. I begged, "Please don't make us make that choice." I don't know how many lawyers we saw, on a consultation kind of basis, and they never charged us anything, but they all said: "There's nothing your family can do, you just don't have an option."

Finally, the state granted an exception to policy to give us a waiver for Jennifer. Jennifer is now deemed an individual household of one, so that our income no longer counts against her eligibility for Social Security Supplementary Income (SSI) and Medicaid. For us, the SSI, which is the check that she gets, wasn't important. It didn't matter to us whether she got one penny of financial assistance as long as she got the medical help she needed.

I think that it was fortunate I was well informed, assertive, and articulate, and I also think that's why I do the work that I do. Outside my job as a parent advocate, I'm very active legislatively, and I'm thankful that I've had a supportive husband who recognized that's a need I have. We are better off because I've learned to be politically active. It's my crusade. I don't want other families to have to experience what we've gone through. I can help to lessen that hardship because I've impacted the system in changes that go beyond Jennifer to reach other families in need.

This year my husband and I filed for divorce. The stress on the family for the last 9 years has taken its toll. Certainly not all of our marital difficulties were caused by challenges in state agencies, but a family can only endure so much hardship before its foundation is eroded. I believe my family has now paid the ultimate sacrifice to a system that was set up to help and support but fell short in doing so.

At the end of the 1880s, rates of institutionalization actually increased, and the growth of social Darwinism and the eugenics movement brought forced sterilization of persons with disabilities. Between 1927 and 1964, more than 63,000 persons with disabilities had been sterilized (Malhotra, 2001). Early in the years building up to the Holocaust, children with disabilities under Nazi control were exterminated by lethal injection, starvation, withholding of treatment, and poisoning. By 1945, 5,000 children had been murdered, and when the program was extended to adults with disabilities, hundreds of thousands were killed (Malhotra, 2001).

Figure 1–1 Phases in the Development of Disability Rights, an Echo of the Civil Rights Movement and the Bridges That Led to Progress

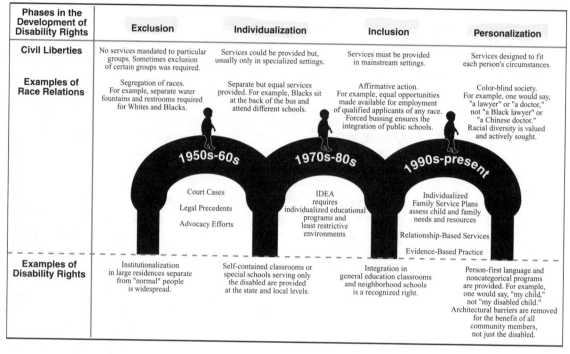

Phases in the Development of Disability Rights	Exclusion	Individualization	Inclusion	Personalization
Civil Liberties	No services mandated to particular groups. Sometimes exclusion of certain groups was required.	Services could be provided but, usually only in specialized settings.	Services must be provided in mainstream settings.	Services designed to fit each person's circumstances.
Examples of Race Relations	Segregation of races. For example, separate water fountains and restrooms required for Whites and Blacks.	Separate but equal services provided. For example, Blacks sit at the back of the bus and attend different schools.	Affirmative action. For example, equal opportunities made available for employment of qualified applicants of any race. Forced bussing ensures the integration of public schools.	Color-blind society. For example, one would say, "a lawyer" or "a doctor," not "a Black lawyer" or "a Chinese doctor." Racial diversity is valued and actively sought.
	1950s–60s	1970s–80s	1990s–present	
	Court Cases Legal Precedents Advocacy Efforts	IDEA requires individualized educational programs and least restrictive environments	Individualized Family Service Plans assess child and family needs and resources Relationship-Based Services Evidence-Based Practice	
Examples of Disability Rights	Institutionalization in large residences separate from "normal" people is widespread.	Self-contained classrooms or special schools serving only the disabled are provided at the state and local levels.	Integration in general education classrooms and neighborhood schools is a recognized right.	Person-first language and noncategorical programs are provided. For example, one would say, "my child," not "my disabled child." Architectural barriers are removed for the benefit of all community members, not just the disabled.

INDIVIDUALIZATION

Following World War II, years of fighting racial segregation in public schools resulted in victory in 1954 as Special Counsel Thurgood Marshall and the NAACP won in the case of *Brown v. the Board of Education,* assuring that no child could be excluded from public education. The Supreme Court stated: " . . . in these days it is doubtful that any child may reasonably be expected to succeed in life if he is denied access to education, such an opportunity, where a state has undertaken to provide it, is a right which must be available to all on equal terms . . . equal facilities are inherently unequal." In determining that exclusion from education violated the due process clause of the 14th Amendment of the Constitution, the court established a right to an equal opportunity to education.

This victory was a catalyst for the African American civil rights movement and a major inspiration to the disability rights movement at a time when the political climate was equally supportive. Former presidents John F. Kennedy and Lyndon B. Johnson, both strong forces for progress in civil rights and racial equality, also were essential in increasing federal involvement in the care and treatment of people with disabilities. Kennedy had a personal interest, because his sister had been institutionalized with mental retardation. Consequently, Kennedy established programs to improve the care of persons with disabilities. It was he who proposed funding for training personnel to serve people with disabilities, to increase research in the area of disabilities, and to provide incentives for community-based services. Johnson's Great Society initiated a "war on poverty" which also sought improved educational services for all children. During his administration, Title I of the Elementary and Secondary Education Act of 1965, the Elementary and Secondary Education Act of 1966, and the Federal Assistance to State Owned and Operated Schools for the Handicapped (1965) were passed. The era of separate or private facilities for children with disabilities gave way to state and federal provisions for individualized services in less-restrictive settings. From this point on, the federal role in early childhood special education and early intervention was to provide access to services and to improve the quality of services (Smith & Strain, 1988).

One example of this federal vision is seen in the development of Head Start (Smith, 2000). Head Start was begun in the mid-1960s to provide early education for children in poverty, but in 1972, the program specifically set aside 10% of its enrollment slots for children with disabilities. Thus, federal funds could be used in local communities to initiate services to young children with disabilities. Another example is the Handicapped Children's Early Education Program (HCEEP) which was established in 1968 and continued for 30 years in the business of promoting research and development efforts aimed at improving assessment, instruction, and service delivery for preschoolers with disabilities. In this way, the federal government was able to generate a knowledge base that supported state and local programs (Smith, 2000).

Parent groups and professional associations united in advocating for children with disabilities at a time when many were totally excluded from any educational services. From 1972 though 1974, court cases regarding the right to education were heard in 28 states (Crockett & Kauffman, 1998). When Congress was finally persuaded to act, it approved the original 1975 legislation of the Individuals with Disabilities Education Act (IDEA); it called for the free, appropriate education of children in the **least restrictive environment** (LRE). Prior to IDEA's passage, 1 million children were excluded from public school because of their disabilities (Yell, 1995). Those who attended public school often received inadequate services in isolated settings.

The LRE

Least restrictive environment is the legal term used to define the rights of children with disabilities to be educated in settings where they are not segregated from children without disabilities. The law states (Education for All Handicapped Children's Act, 1975):

> 1. That to the maximum extent appropriate, children with disabilities are educated with children who are nondisabled; and 2. That special classes, separate schooling, or other removal of children with disabilities from the regular educational environment occurs only when the nature or severity of the disability is such that education in regular classes with the use of supplementary aids and services cannot be achieved satisfactorily. (Section 34 C.F.R. 300.55o([b])

The legal provisions for the LRE never supported an immutable rule of placement, but rather a preference for including children in regular classrooms and allowing specialized (separated) services as needed by individuals (Yell, 1995). When asked if placement of a child with a disability in the regular classroom clearly constituted the LRE, the courts responded with the ambiguous answer, "It depends" (Crockett & Kauffman, 1998; Zirkel, 1996). One was advised to consider how well the child was progressing in the regular setting, the preference of the parents, the availability and need for special **related services,** and other highly individualized factors.

INCLUSION

This movement toward greater provision of services in regular school settings has been referred to as inclusion. Fuchs and Fuchs (1998) defined inclusion as a **continuum of services** that depends on the regular classroom and a variety of options in terms of special education placements and related services. "In principle, each special education placement on the continuum (from residential facility to special day school to self-contained classes and resource rooms) offers specialized, differentiated, individualized and intensive instruction, all of which are continuously evaluated for effectiveness" (Fuchs & Fuchs, 1998, p. 3). Within this system, teachers and students work on the general education curricula and all have the understanding that the goal of special education instruction outside the regular classroom is to move students closer to being successful in the regular classroom.

Despite the federal role in providing incentives for states to serve very young children with disabilities, by the mid-1980s, only 25 states had passed laws to serve children from 3 to 5 years of age (Smith, 2000). Advocates, becoming discouraged with the lack of state response to these incentives, went to Congress and successfully argued for an extension of IDEA to mandate services for 3- to 5-year-olds and to provide incentives for services for children birth to 3 years old with disabilities (Smith, 2000). By 1994, all states had mandated services for preschoolers and established early intervention policies. The number of infants and toddlers receiving services had increased by more than 100,000.

Natural Environments

With the 1997 revision of the Individuals with Disabilities Education Act, early intervention regulations stressed "natural environments" for providing services to very young children within an inclusion model. This meant that as much as is appropriate, given individual child and family needs, infants and toddlers should be served in homes, day-care centers, and preschools where children without disabilities would be naturally present. But, in defense of center-based services as viable options, one parent pointed out, "Having a child with a disability is never 'natural' and the most important thing is to meet that child's needs," (J. Gately, personal communication, 1999). Perhaps what is most important about the inclusion effort, is to think of special education with its related therapies as a service, not a place.

Preschool programs, due to their ecology, may provide an ideal context for inclusion. According to Mallory and New (1994), preschool classrooms are predicated on social activity. Most early childhood programs are language- and social-skills based and have multiple daily activities in which children are encouraged to learn from contextually relevant and problem-based curricula. Inclusion is not considered as simply a child's placement, but inclusion also has to do with the integrity of the placement. When a child with a disability is placed in a regular setting without the delivery of the specialized services that define special education, everyone in the system loses—the teacher, the other students, the parents, and the children with disabilities themselves (Fuchs & Fuchs, 1998).

Challenges for Inclusion and the Natural Environments Approach
With several years of implementation of inclusion in natural environments, it has become clear that certain dimensions are still troubling. These elements include professional specialization, intensity of service delivery, appropriate response to individual needs, respect for family needs and priorities, lack of quality settings, and lack of community resources and support.

Professional specializations. As we begin to use early childhood educators and early childhood special educators in the same settings, sharing the work of serving children with disabilities, it is important that we continue to see not only how their roles are similar but also how their roles differ (McCollum, 2000). General educators must be prepared for work with children with disabilities, and special educators must have a solid grounding in child development and general curriculum, but they should not necessarily receive identical training and certification. Children with disabilities (even those enrolled in natural environments) still require specialized services that can be provided only by specialists in early childhood special education. Likewise, therapists in physical and occupational therapy, speech and language development, mental health, and other related services struggle with how to best provide treatment in settings that have not been designed for specialized services.

Intensity of services. Though the natural environment seems to be a good fit at the preschool level, a great deal of debate has surfaced when the concept is applied to early intervention for children from birth to 3 years of age (Shelden & Rush, 2001). The early detection of problems and the provision of appropriate intervention can improve outcomes for an infant or toddler with disabilities, but the quality of the intervention that is actually delivered is of fundamental importance (Fenichel, 2001). The ultimate impact of any intervention is dependent on both the expertise of the person delivering the intervention and the personal relationship that person has established with each child's family (Fenichel, 2001). An individualized approach that works toward well-defined goals as to the specific needs and resources of children and their families is demanded; there is little support for a "one-size-fits-all" model of early intervention. Some critics question whether the zeal applied to treatment in natural environments gives sufficient consideration to these factors.

Bricker (2001) pointed out that some professionals have interpreted natural environments to exclude settings that are operated solely for children with disabilities or are specialized laboratory settings where research and training take place. She cautioned against interpreting the setting as more important than the activities and supports present in each setting. It is absolutely necessary to ensure the delivery of specialized and individualized services that enhance development and learning for very young children with disabilities. It is also necessary to insist that these services are consistent with the family's values, priorities, and needs. Clearly children with disabilities require services above and beyond those provided to nondisabled peers. Goals such as teaching within natural routines, in familiar settings, and with nondisabled peers are important but should not take precedence over the child's needs.

Individual needs. Such a perspective may be particularly important for children from birth to 3 years of age. "This is a critical time in the history of the field of early intervention. There now exist unprecedented numbers of vulnerable children and families confronted with a remarkably diverse and challenging array of risk factors and developmental disabilities" (Guralnick, 2001, p. 1). Approximately 230,800 infants and toddlers received early intervention in 2001 (National Early Childhood Technical Assistance Center, 2001). This represented only 2% of all children 0 to 3, compared to the nearly 13% of school-aged children served in special education. These children tended to be the most severely disabled and multiply disabled (see Table 1–2).

Many other children received early intervention because of developmental problems, rather than health per se. Two thirds of infants and toddlers served in early intervention programs were identified because of developmental delays and began early intervention by about 21 months of age. Their delays were most prevalent in the domains of language and behavior (see Table 1–3). However, of 56 states and territories reporting on early intervention services, most required a developmental delay of 25% in one or more areas (scoring two standard deviations below the mean on standardized measures), 7 states served children only if they presented at least a 50% delay in development, and only 9 states served children who were at risk biologically or environmentally. In general, children from birth to 3 who are receiving early intervention present significant developmental delays (Shackelford, 2002).

Table 1–2   Characteristics of Children from Birth to 3 with Disabilities

Proportion of Population	Risk Factor
40% (of children beginning early intervention before 12 months of age)	presented prenatal and or perinatal abnormalities
33%	were born at low birth weight
17%	were born at very low birth weight
37%	had been in neonatal intensive care
44%	were required to stay in the hospital after birth
19%	stayed in the hospital more than a month after birth
25%	continued to take prescription medication for chronic conditions

Table 1–3   Characteristics of Children from Birth to 3 with Developmental Delays

Proportion of Population	Area of Delay
66–70%	were somewhat or very hard to understand and could not communicate their needs as well as other children their age
25%	were reported as having a lot of trouble with communication
50%	presented behavior difficulties
10–40%	were described as having behavioral challenges
19%	could not pay attention and stay focused
25%	startled easily
39%	were very active and excitable
11%	were often aggressive

Table 1–4   Characteristics of Families of Children Receiving Early Intervention

Proportion of Children	Risk Factors of Families
41%	had incomes of less than $25,000 a year (compared to only 20% of families in the general population)
33%	received Welfare or food stamps in the previous year
33%	were in households that did not include the child's biological or adoptive father (given that these children were under 3 years of age, this number was likely to increase over time)
4%	were born to teenaged mothers
4%	were born to mothers over age 40

Family needs. A number of the families of infants and toddlers receiving early intervention also presented factors which may have placed their children at risk (see Table 1–4). Unfortunately, as state agencies change the way personnel deliver services, particularly moving toward fee-for-service structures often tied to Medicaid or other insurance systems, there is a tendency to fragment services at the family level. This tends to reduce collaboration among professionals, to make it more difficult to embed interventions within the context of families' lives, to reduce the integration of interventions with those of other professionals, and to make it much more difficult to be "family-centered" (McCollum, 2000). The reality of funding may cause agencies to dictate limited or no choices to families of very young children with disabilities, thus losing the options provided by a continuum of services.

Quality of community settings. At the same time advocates have been striving for early intervention services and inclusion in typical environments, communities are faced with the decline in availability of quality of child care. There is the dilemma of advocating for inclusion into poor-quality settings or turning to the few natural environments that are of high quality for very young children (Smith, 2000). Bricker (2001) suggested that "when possible and appropriate, services should be delivered to children in their natural environment; however, the individual needs of some children may supersede blanket policy and require that other placements be considered. The bottom line is that services should meet the individual needs of children and families" (p. 2). In other words, natural environments should be broadly defined to mean any setting that a family chooses for its child and should include specialized settings when they are necessary and appropriate for a child to prosper. Child and family needs vary tremendously and require a high quality of service that can meet standards of best practice.

PERSONALIZATION: A WAY TO MOVE INTO THE NEXT CENTURY

Many gains for people with disabilities were made through civil-rights-based strategies that resulted in state and federal laws providing entitlement programs to those with disabilities. At the same time, these entitlements were contingent on being able to define an individual as disabled. This meant that though opportunities were guaranteed, persons had to identify themselves as "abnormal" and apart from their peer communities to take advantage of such programs (Clapton & Fitzgerald, 2002). Today, advances in genetic technology and reproductive science further emphasize the differences of those with diagnosed disabilities. Therefore, it becomes increasingly critical that society embrace a new conception of disability. We need to understand disability as part of the gradient of the human condition, one that can affect any of us any time in our lives, that can be a part of any family, and that is a natural condition found in any community. We need to value disability as we have come to value diversity (Clapton & Fitzgerald, 2002).

It is the responsibility of professionals to advance high-quality, effective early childhood special education and early intervention in two ways. First, we must protect and expand the federal gains that have been made, and second, we need to strengthen state, and perhaps more importantly, local commitment (Smith, 2000). There is an ever-present threat that federal measures may be rescinded. When former president Ronald Reagan tried to repeal IDEA in 1980, a groundswell of protest stopped his attempt. Yet the Early Education Program for Children with Disabilities (formerly HCEEP) was repealed in 1997 to reduce federal bureaucracy, despite 30 years of proven effectiveness (Smith, 2000). Before it was repealed, HCEEP provided $25 million annually to research and development in early childhood education and services. The unlimited number of public needs vying for limited public resources make the job of adequately funding early childhood services more difficult.

It would be wise at this time in our history to rebuild a sense of local community and its responsibilities in providing services to young children with special needs (Smith, 2000). All citizens need to understand that, as we fight for early intervention services, we also need to ensure high-quality services for all young children and their families. The real change in how young children are cared for in our society relies on that which is in the hearts and minds of individual citizens (Smith, 2000). This change is best accomplished by building communities that are family friendly, that care enough about children to increase taxes, to restructure jobs so families can spend more time at home, to value early childhood professionals, and to attract the best and brightest for serving young children.

WHAT IS MEANT BY PERSONALIZATION IN EARLY EDUCATION AND INTERVENTION?

Personalized intervention is based on several important principles (Williams, 2003):

1. ***Each child's abilities and needs are unique and specific to that individual.*** A child's program of goals and treatment should depend on that child's developmental progress, therapeutic needs caused by the type and severity of the disabling condition, risk factors and supports present within the environment, and family strengths and concerns. This requires comprehensive, interdisciplinary assessment and planning. No child should be placed or treated based solely on age, economic level, type of diagnosis, or preference of the service providers or third-party payers. The individual outcomes identified for a child must drive where and what supports are provided, and all eligible children must have access to comprehensive services.

2. ***Each child's success is dependent on the quality of interaction, therapy, and education provided by caregivers, family, and professionals.*** The level of care must be consistent with a child and family's level of need. "The ultimate impact of any intervention is dependent on both staff expertise and the quality and continuity of the personal relationship established between the service provider and the family that is being served" (National Research Council and Institute of Medicine, 2000, p. 365). High standards for professional training and delivery of services must be met and positive relationships established. Of most importance is the quality of parent–child transactions which should reflect sensitivity, reciprocity, affective warmth, and other positive traits (Guralnick, 2001). Also of great importance are the relationships among all members of the service team, the professionals, and the family. Coordination of services and collaboration in planning and delivery are critical to teaming (Hanson & Bruder, 2001). It is also critical that families have the opportunity to connect to each other.

3. ***A full spectrum of services and placement options must be available in order to appropriately serve each child's needs.*** IDEA, Part C, stipulates that services may encompass a wide range of options, including family training, counseling, home visits, special instruction, speech and language and audiology services; occupational and physical therapy, psychological services, medical services, health services, social work services, vision services, assistive technology, transportation, and other supports. Early intervention may be provided in a range of locations, including hospitals, homes, child care centers, special schools, clinics, and other settings. Not all services have to be provided at the same location, and settings may change over time as a child or family's needs change (Hanson & Bruder, 2001). When appropriate, all children should have the opportunity to interact with nondisabled and disabled peers, but service providers should be able to customize services and placements to meet individual needs.

4. ***The focus of intervention must be on achieving goals identified for each individual child and family by maximizing all learning opportunities.*** Research-based practices that are determined to be most likely to profit each child must be implemented and the child's progress evaluated on an ongoing basis. Evidence-based practice presents a sound model for serving very young children with disabilities. A child's goals and expected outcomes are defined, a review of relevant research is undertaken to identify the treatments most likely to be effective, and

data are collected as the interventions are implemented so that the treatment can be changed or modified depending of the qualify of the outcomes (Law, 2000). Authentic, meaningful, and functional educational and therapeutic activities must take center stage, regardless of the setting in which they are provided, and outcomes must be monitored to maximize progress (Bricker, 2001).

5. *The primacy of parent decisions must be respected, and their family values, priorities, and needs honored.* Parents and caregivers should be real partners on assessment, intervention, and evaluation teams (Bricker, 2001). Families are to be treated with dignity and with sensitivity to their cultural and socioeconomic differences (Hanson & Bruder, 2001). Information would be fully disclosed and a range of community resources offered so that families can make good choices for their children. In addition, practices that allow families to become more knowledgeable and confident would be used to assist the families' growth and self-determination. Stressors that affect the quality of family interaction and effectiveness, such as information needs, interpersonal distress, resource needs, and confidence threats, would be assessed and addressed to ensure families' optimal functioning (Guralnick, 2001).

6. *Comprehensive care requires full community commitment.* In order to provide a full spectrum of options for families and their very young children with disabilities, the whole community must be aware of local needs and must participate in providing the resources necessary for support. Child care providers who are capable and willing to accept children with disabilities, neighbors and extended family who are supportive and understanding, and employers who recognize legitimate family demands on an employee's time would be available. There would also be a range of professionals and treatment settings available to provide alternatives that most closely meet the needs of children and families. A collaborative spirit among these professionals and a sense of responsibility throughout the community would be present. There would be a commitment to provide the best possible services to all children and thereby raise the standards for the care and education of all children. Local stakeholders would be informed about the importance of quality services and know how to access them (Smith, 2000).

THE IMPLICATIONS OF PERSONALIZATION

A professional commitment to a philosophy of personalization requires a good deal of groundwork in order to be effectively operationalized. A number of associated activities must be undertaken to make such an approach a reality:

1. Services to very young children with disabilities require full funding. It is incumbent upon Congress to finally commit to immediately appropriate promised funds to IDEA (U.S. Commission on Civil Rights, 2002). By creating a federal safety net to support service providers who educate children with extraordinary needs and require more resources, states would have adequate funds to implement services for preschoolers and the mandate to provide early intervention to those from birth to 3.

2. There must be priorities set for personnel training in order to fill positions in short supply with highly qualified personnel. In 2002, nearly 600,000 special education students were being taught by unqualified special education teachers

(Consortium for Citizens with Disabilities, 2002). Further shortages in pediatric therapies abound and make it difficult to provide alternative placements and comprehensive services to children.

3. Well-documented, evidence-based best practices in early intervention should be implemented on a wider, regular basis. In addition, information about advancements in the technology of early intervention areas must be developed and disseminated for ease in accessing information and planning treatment. The process is a complex one and is complicated by the lack of time available to professionals and families who are directly involved in child intervention. Resources must be made available that will allow speedy response to immediate needs.

4. Advocacy on behalf of individuals with disabilities must continue. Membership in advocacy groups such as the Council for Exceptional Children has decreased in recent years (Smith, 2000). Vigilance is required to protect rights that have been hard won, or we risk losing them. We also must find ways to impassion grassroots groups who have always achieved the greatest gains for the disabled to seek higher quality services now. Access to poor-quality services will make little difference in children's lives (Smith, 2000). It is critical that advocates recognize that real change in how young children are viewed and cared for in this society should not rest on federal or even state laws, but must be founded on local citizens' concern for the children within their midst. "You can't mandate everything that matters!" (Smith, 2000, p.13).

THE IMPORTANCE OF BEING CULTURALLY SENSITIVE

The United States is the most ethnically diverse country in the world, including at least a hundred racial, ethnic, and cultural groups (Taylor, 1998). In recent years, however, trends in birthrates, immigration, family structures, and economics have greatly altered national **demographics** and will continue to do so in the future. Since the 2000 census question asking racial origin was worded differently from the 1990 census, one cannot accurately interpret changes in the racial composition of the U.S. population; respondents were able to select categories for mixed racial origin for the first time (U.S. Census Bureau, March 2001). Still, much diversity was revealed: those of Spanish/Latino or Hispanic origin accounted for 12.5% of the population, those of Black or African American descent made up 12.3%, Asians reported in at 3.6%, American Indian and Alaska Natives made up .9%, and 2.4% reported mixed racial origins. Caucasians made up 75.1% of the population. The population of the United States was 281.4 million, an increase of 32.7 million from 1990 to 2000 and the largest increase in history (U.S. Census Bureau, April 2001). Each percentage point in the population statistics represents about 2.8 million people. Children under the age of 5 were in much larger proportions for the Black, American Indian, Native Hawaiian, and Hispanic groups than for Asians or Whites (U.S. Census Bureau, April 2001). In the 2000 census, 39% of children under age 18 were from racial minorities. In fact, minority children accounted for 98% of the growth in the child population in the 1990s, and that decade saw the largest increase in children in the United States since the 1950s (O'Hare, 2001).

Such diversity has often led to conflict because of a lack of receptiveness to differences (Taylor, 1998). Interpersonal reactions to others may be negative due to a number of factors:

1. **Assumed similarity.** We assume our beliefs and values are the same as others.
2. **Ethnocentrism/denigration of differences.** We hold the attitude that our own culture/origin is superior.
3. **Anxiety/tension.** We are uncomfortable when our basic values are opposed.
4. **Prejudice.** We hold a hostile attitude toward people who belong to a different group.
5. **Stereotyping.** We make assumptions about people based on their ethnic or cultural group.
6. **Comfort with the familiar.** We are drawn to people who share similar interests and values and exclude others.

Early childhood educators must overcome the tendency to not acknowledge and respond to the importance of a child's home language and culture. We must respect and preserve this diversity (National Association for Education of Young Children [NAEYC], 1996), celebrate our shared beliefs and traditions, and honor that which is distinctive in the many groups that make up our nation (National Council of Teachers of English [NCTE], 1996).

Professionals serving diverse children and families must become culturally competent, able to transform knowledge and cultural awareness into interventions that support healthy relationships within the appropriate cultural context (McPhatter, 1997), and identify knowledge that is critical in becoming culturally competent (see Table 1–5).

The challenge of becoming culturally competent begins with an honest assessment of how one deals with those who are different (McPhatter, 1997). Questions to

Table 1–5   Essential Knowledge for Cultural Competence

1. Knowledge of diverse cultures, histories, traditions, values, religions, languages, and so forth.
2. Knowledge of social problems and issues related to minority communities, such as poverty, unemployment, health concerns, and community violence.
3. Familiarity with the formal and informal resources available in diverse neighborhoods and communities, such as churches and community centers.
4. Understanding of the dynamics of oppression, racism, sexism, classism, and other forms of discrimination.
5. Knowledge of the contributions of people of color, current service issues, and obstacles to providing service.
6. Knowledge of the diversity of family structure and how these families survive and excel over time.
7. Knowledge about family functioning, such as childrearing practices, methods of discipline and nurturing, and how health needs are met. Knowing "what works" within family cultures.
8. Knowledge of alternative interventions that are culturally relevant. What might be viewed as manipulative behavior might be reframed as problem solving within the demands for survival faced by minority groups.
9. Value for the long-standing informal foster/adoption/kinship care practiced in families of color.
10. Respect for the strengths and resilience of minority families.

Source: From "Cultural Competence in Child Welfare: What Is It? How Do We Achieve It? What Happens Without It?" by A. R. McPhatter, 1997, *Child Welfare, 76* (1), pp. 255–278.

be asked include: How much time do I spend with people who are culturally different from me? How comfortable am I in immersion experiences? What is my commitment to being culturally competent? Negative answers to these questions help identify new experiences that should be sought out to improve **cultural competence.**

POPULATION TRENDS

In the first census of the 21st century, Hispanic Americans overtook African Americans to become the country's largest ethnic minority (U.S. Census Bureau, March 2001), and are expected to account for 25% of the U.S. population by 2050 ("Hispanic Population," 1997). People of Hispanic origin include immigrants from many countries and cultures connected to Spain, Mexico, Central and South America, and the Caribbean. Asian Americans encompass an astounding variety of people, languages, religions, and cultures with many differences among them (Lee, 1998). Though relatively small, the Asian American population is growing at a rapid pace, nearly doubling between 1980 and 1990 and expected to double again by 2010 (Lee, 1998). By the year 2050, it is predicted Caucasians will shrink to only 50% of the total U.S. population (Martin & Midgley, 1994). In many of the largest urban counties and in some nonmetropolitan counties, the shift has already occurred, with no single ethnic or racial group maintaining a majority (Allen & Turner, 1990). Thirty-three states have K–12 minority enrollments of 20% or more, with minority enrollment increases in 44 states in recent years. All 25 of the nation's largest city school systems have "majority minorities" (Wehrly, 1988).

A major factor influencing ethnic **demographics** is immigration, with Hispanics comprising the fastest growing minority (Martin & Midgley, 1994). Today's immigrants are less well-educated, poorer, and more likely to be unemployed than past immigrants. Every year, nearly two thirds of Hispanic immigrants live and work in the United States illegally before being granted legal status. Other factors contributing to demographic shifts are the birthrate, which is slightly higher in foreign-born families than for native-born citizens, and the fact that the average age of immigrant females is younger than the average age of native-born women (Martin & Midgley, 1994).

Hispanics, like most recent immigrant groups throughout history, suffer from the highest rates of poverty, have the highest school dropout rates, and are educated in the most highly segregated schools. In 1992, 26% of families of Hispanic origin lived below the poverty line; in 1993, 23% of Hispanic families were headed by a female, and 72% of Hispanics held unskilled or semiskilled jobs. About 50% of Hispanics will not finish high school, 38% are held back at least one grade, and 50% are overage at grade 12. Hispanics were placed in special education six times more often than the general population. Ninety percent of Hispanic students are in urban districts, and 82% attend segregated schools (Garcia, 1997).

Following a similar trend, African American enrollment in public schools increased 3% between 1972 and 1992, while Caucasian enrollment dropped 14% (Orfield, Schley, Glass, & Reardon, 1994). In the 1990 census, 32% of African American families reported living below the poverty level; more than 57% of those lived in urban areas (Russo & Talbert-Johnson, 1997). It is predicted that by the year 2020, children of color will make up 46% of the school population, yet fewer than 5% of teachers will be African American (Russo & Talbert-Johnson, 1997).

Unfortunately, special education services are not proportionately representative of minority populations (Rounds, Weil, & Bishop, 1994). Hispanics, African Americans, and American Indians tend to be overrepresented in special education. For example, during the 2001–2002 school year, Black students accounted for 14.8% of the general population of students, but made up nearly 20% of the special education population (U.S. Commission on Civil Rights, 2002). In addition, Black students were diagnosed as mentally retarded at a rate more than twice their national proportion in the general population, and representation in the categories of developmental delay and emotional disturbance were nearly two thirds higher (U.S. Commission on Civil Rights, 2002). Black students are also more likely than White students to be placed outside the regular classroom in residential facilities, separate schools, and correctional facilities.

These racial discrepancies are probably due to many confounding factors that tend to correlate with minority status: low educational attainment, language differences, lack of economic resources, and lack of health insurance, all of which may contribute to an endless cycle of educational disadvantage (Smart & Smart, 1997). Though difficult to estimate precisely, the discriminating impact of institutional biases in testing, curriculum, social expectations, and teaching strategies on the appropriate education of minority children is also apparent. In addition, poor-quality "regular" education triggering more referrals, poorly trained teachers and diagnosticians, lack of adequate school resources, and use of special education as discipline add to the problem (U.S. Commission on Civil Rights, 2002).

ECONOMICS

From 1950 until 1969, the average family's economic situation was improving; the poverty rate for children dropped to about 14% (Mitchell, 1995). The 1980s saw a dramatic increase in the number of children living in poverty in the United States; by the early 1990s, about 20% of all children lived below the poverty line; and by 1993, the figure for children under age 6 who lived in poverty reached 26% (Guo, 1998). An estimated 7 million children under the age of 6 live in poverty in the United States, and two thirds of these children live in working families who are not on welfare (Lewis, 1997). Very young children are the most likely to be poor; the poverty rate for American children under age 3 (2.1 million of them in 2000) is about 80% higher than the rate for adults or the elderly (Song & Lu, 2002). Another 2.6 million children under age 3 lived in near poverty (calculated at 200% the federal poverty level) which made them eligible for Medicaid and State Child Health Insurance (Song & Lu, 2002). In the last decade, the largest increases in the child population were in five states (California, Texas, Florida, Georgia, and New York) that rank poorly in terms of comprehensive measures of child well-being (O'Hare, 2001).

The consequences of childhood poverty are multiple. Poor children are more likely to have a low birth weight, more likely to die in the first year, more likely to suffer hunger or abuse, and less likely to have adequate medical care. Children from poor homes start off at a disadvantage, with less access to prenatal and early health care, quality day care as infants, and quality early childhood programs (Slavin, 1998).

In this century, the number of single-parent and working poor families increased, and more and more mothers of young children were compelled to enter the labor force (Olmsted, 1992). In 1940, 87% of young children had a nonemployed parent who could provide full-time care (Hernandez, 1995). By 1989, only 48% of children under 6 had a parent who didn't work outside the home. The number of children who spend a significant amount of each day in professional care places greater responsibility on early educators to provide appropriate experiences for these children and their families.

The likelihood that a child will live in poverty tends to parallel the data on children from minority families. While 18% of Caucasian children are poor, 46% of African American children live in poverty; this proportion has not been lower than 40% since 1959, when the Census Bureau first started measuring childhood poverty (Mitchell, 1995). More than two out of three African American children in single-mother households are poor (Montgomery, Kiely, & Pappas, 1996). As with other trends, a disproportionate percentage of African Americans and people of Hispanic origin are among the homeless (Williams & DeSander, 1999). For children under age 3, young African American and Hispanic children are three times more likely to live in poverty (Song & Lu, 2002). For those under age 3 who lived with single mothers, the poverty rate for African American children was 52% and for Hispanic children, 45%.

Children also make up the fastest-growing segment of the homeless population (Williams & DeSander, 1999). Families with children represented 36% of those in homeless shelters (Children's Defense Fund, 1998). By 1997, more than a million American children were homeless, 250,000 of those were below school age (Nunez & Collignon, 1997). These children displayed a wide range of social, emotional, and academic difficulties typically seen in children who qualify for special education (Walther-Thomas, Korinek, McLaughlin, & Williams, 1996). These deficiencies include poor personal/emotional development, reduced gross motor and fine motor skills, and fewer interaction skills. Poor children also have significantly higher rates of lead poisoning, which contributes to neurological damage and long-term behavior problems.

Early educators must be especially sensitive to the needs of poor and homeless children when designing programs (McCormick & Holden, 1992). That is, programs for young homeless children must be maximally flexible about scheduling, opening at earlier times and closing later, and providing respite care for parents. Programs should provide transportation or funds to cover transportation expenses. They should provide social and case-management services and emphasize special attention for specific developmental delays and emotional problems that poor and homeless children may exhibit. Staff of such programs must be sensitive to the support and encouragement needed by parents.

FAMILY COMPOSITION

Most people recognize that the traditional nuclear family of "Ozzie and Harriet" is neither predominate today, nor did it ever truly exist, but perhaps many do not fully comprehend how much diversity exists. In 1992, for every 100 children born, 58 entered a broken family (Fagan & Coontz, 1997). By 1993, the proportion of young children living with one parent in the home was 21% for Caucasians, 66% for African Americans, and 34% for Hispanics (Hernandez, 1995). These statistics are significant, because research indicates that children in families headed by both parents, biological or adoptive, tend to do better in terms of social adjustment and academic performance than children in either **blended families** or those headed by a single parent (Thomson, Hanson, & McLanahan, 1994). The single-parent family is a much riskier place for a child (Fagan & Coontz, 1997). Being born out of wedlock increases the risk of infant mortality and of ill health in early infancy; the rates of abuse are 13 times higher in single-mother families and 20 times higher in single-father families (Fagan & Coontz, 1997).

Most of the differences in children's outcomes are, however, explained by economic disadvantage. In other words, adoptive families and those headed by two biological parents tend to be more economically stable; though it is the resources, not the family configuration, that places children at social and academic risk. Interestingly, Thomson et al. (1994) found that in most cases, parental childrearing behaviors had much less to do with children's outcomes than family income and parents' educational levels. Unfortunately, among very poor families making less than $15,000 a year, marriage has all but disappeared, and among working class families with incomes between $15,000 and $30,000 a year, married parents don't exist for 45% of children.

The sharp rise in childhood poverty since the mid-1970s is accounted for in large part by the increased proportion of children living in families headed by single mothers (Montgomery et al., 1996). Between 1970 and 1994, the percentage of children living in single-mother households rose from about 13% to about 31% (Florsheim, Tolan, & Gorman-Smith, 1998). There is substantial evidence that children growing up in single-mother families are at greater risk for developing achievement-related problems which may be due to the consequences of being financially disadvantaged (Florsheim et al., 1998). The poverty rate for children in single-mother families is five times higher than that for children in two-parent families. Over 55% of children in single female-headed families live in poverty. The majority of these single mothers are divorced or separated, but the number of never married mothers is increasing.

Adolescents in single-parent families are more likely to become adolescent parents (Moore, Manlove, Glei, & Morrison, 1998). Birthrates among teenagers in the United States are substantially higher than in other Western industrialized countries. There were 89,900 teen pregnancies in 1995; fortunately, the rate has declined in recent years (Shelton, 1998; Wetzstein, 1998). Low **socioeconomic** status for the family has also been correlated with higher risk of adolescent childbearing.

Divorce, remarriage, and never-married parenting has greatly affected the composition of American families. The term *stepfamily* is now used to include households in which there is an adult couple, at least one of whom has a child from a previous relationship (Kelley, 1996). By 1990, 20% (about 5.3 million) of married-couple households cared for at least one stepchild (Kelley, 1996). Children in stepfamilies tended to have higher rates of behavioral, health, and education problems (Kelley, 1996).

Divorce, however, does not account for all family diversity. Children may be living with grandparents, in foster care, or in residential facilities. Since the late 1980s, foster care systems in the United States have been overwhelmed by the numbers of children who need assistance (Hegar & Scannapieco, 1995). This is partly because the total number of foster families dropped from 147,000 to 100,000 between 1984 and 1990 (National Commission on Foster Family Care, 1991). Many infants and young children spend the early part of their lives in "boarder" nurseries, temporary shelters where shift changes and high ratios of children to caretakers decrease the possibility of healthy attachments (Griffith, 1992). Children lucky enough to be placed in foster care may find untrained foster parents overwhelmed by the demands of caring for children with special needs and may consequently be returned to institutional placement (Griffith, 1992).

An emerging family option, developed out of necessity, is **kinship care** (Hegar & Scannapieco, 1995). Defined broadly, **kin** may include extended family, such as grandmothers and aunts, as well as other members of a community who are close to a family. This type of informal care is also referred to as "kith & kin" care and accounts for about 30% of out-of-home placements (Brown-Lyons, Robertson, & Layzer, 2001). Parents using kinship care are more likely to be less educated than the general population, to have lower income, and to tend toward having larger families. For example, high rates of such care came from families receiving Aid to Families with Dependent Children funds (Brown-Lyons et al., 2001). Minority families are also most likely to use kinship care. Parents tend to choose kinship care for its affordability, safety, flexible scheduling, lack of other available care, and because a child has special needs.

However, the primary reasons for full-time kinship care are parental drug abuse and neglect. Yet, full-time living arrangements with kin tend to have significant advantages over traditional foster care options. Children who stay with kin tend to be more stable and are associated with fewer behavioral problems than those in foster care, even though most kinship caregivers live in poverty themselves (Iglehart, 1994). Multigenerational family relationships, the sharing of childrearing and economic relationships across household boundaries, and the use of unrelated household members and parent surrogates have added greatly to the complexity of children's lives, particularly within the inner city (Hunter, Pearson, Isalongo, & Kellam, 1998).

What can professionals do to assist children whose lives are complicated by divorce or separation, who are surviving with a single parent, or whose lives in some other way no longer fit the "traditional" image? Several actions may be appropriate (Carlile, 1991), though empirical research is meager. Teachers should use instructional activities that teach children about the many different types of family structures in today's society. Numerous books deal with divorce, single parenting, grandmothers as guardians, and so on, and can be used to show different kinds of families. Teachers should modify their language and actions to match existing family patterns—inviting a grandparent to Open House, making a Mother's Day card for an aunt, speaking with foster parents at child conferences. Professionals need to make special efforts to keep communication open with both parents or other appropriate guardians. This may mean adjusting conference times, making evening telephone calls when working parents are home, or sending out multiple copies of announcements. Finally, professionals need to recognize they can provide a kind of safety net of consistency and support as children go through transitions in family situations. Yet, none of these expectations are as simple as they might appear.

SUMMARY ON DIVERSITY

This nation is rapidly becoming a people of color, with significant growth in minority populations, who are disproportionately poor and more likely to be single-parent families, in virtually every region of the country. Though the United States has moved forward in defining equity, justice, and multiculturalism, the country has done a poor job in translating these attitudes into improved educational achievement (Wells, 1988). In fact, due to significant political shifting during the 1980s, culturally-diverse families have drifted further behind the mainstream economically and educationally and suffer considerable social inequity in the education system (Slavin, 1998).

To conclude that educational underachievement and other social problems are caused by racial characteristics would be inaccurate and dangerous. The correlation between race and educational disadvantage is far more complicated, as multiple factors influence members of racial minorities in this country (Williams, 1992). Educators need greater preparation in working with families who are at risk. Family service planning and case management must become a natural part of all educational planning. Early childhood professionals need to be familiar with local resources and be able to empower families to identify and access community services. Special service delivery must reach beyond the traditional services of the school building to locations on the streets, in shelters, and within community centers. Traditionally delivered services are unlikely to reach those in greatest need if they are offered only within the agency setting. Likewise, such services will provide only part of what is needed unless they are given in conjunction with social services support. Team management and social support should include family counseling, financial assistance, job training, family planning, and housing.

As educators address the needs of the increasing numbers of children who are at risk, more comparisons will be made between minority children and children of the dominant culture. Because race is certain to be emphasized, these comparisons may unfairly foster a view that minority students are inferior and incompetent, particularly when cultural differences are viewed as deficits (McLoyd, 1990). Early childhood professionals must be careful to document the ways in which minority children achieve educationally and find methods to promote the ecological, situational, and cultural factors that encourage success. Professionals must also collaborate with other service providers to work constantly for the elimination of bigotry and discrimination, which may limit opportunities available to all children and families within this diverse population.

Slavin (1998) suggested we reduce the social inequity of education through several means. First, we need to constantly remind ourselves to think of all children as being a promise. We must identify and build on cultural and personal strengths and accept nothing less than outstanding performance and design high-quality education that is sensitive to students' needs from the beginning. Second, start early by providing early childhood programs that enhance children's preparation for elementary school while children are highly motivated and confident in their abilities to learn. Finally, overdetermine success by working on many fronts at once—addressing the multitude of needs children in poverty face.

THE IMPORTANCE OF SERVING CHILDREN IN THE CONTEXT OF A FAMILY

Empowerment is a term widely used in social science fields. According to Koren, DeChillo, and Friesen (1992), various definitions have been offered for empowerment over the past 20 years: "the reduction of powerlessness . . . gaining, developing, seizing, enabling or giving power . . . the ability to influence people, organizations, and the environment affecting one's life . . . attaining control over one's life and democratic participation in the life of one's community" (p. 306). Empowerment means increasing one's control over one's life and taking action to get what one wants (Turnbull & Turnbull, 1997). Within organizations, such as early childhood programs, one should attempt to provide families with three levels of empowerment:

1. The personal level, where individuals feel a sense of self-efficacy;
2. The interpersonal level, which is the ability to influence others; and
3. Political empowerment, the ability to effect social change and engage in social action. (Gutierrez & Ortega, 1991)

Like inclusion, the term empowerment has become a cliché, empty and scorned by those who are wary of passing fads and those who might agree with the principle, but have observed empty promise (Brinker, 1992). Still, early childhood professionals are challenged by law to be more inclusive of families in intervention for young children with disabilities (Sass-Lehrer & Bodner-Johnson, 1989). Bailey, Huntington, Simmeonson, and Yoder (1992) found, however, that professionals across disciplines are ill-prepared for this responsibility. Moreover, Brinker (1992) claimed the field's current knowledge base regarding family dynamics is so weak that early childhood professionals are likely to fail in most situations when exploratory empowerment practices are attempted. In fact, Brinker (1992) was so cynical that, like opponents of full inclusion, he believed family empowerment philosophy to be motivated more by "political correctness" than by sound pedagogical practice. Even parents sometimes have rejected the term empowerment, which to them infers that professionals are condescendingly "granting" them power that belonged to them in the first place (Healy, Keesee, & Smith, 1989).

The fact that federal law requires families in early intervention to be assessed for the purpose of establishing goals for intervention implies an intent to "fix" families so they can become capable, caregiving units. Though recent literature cautions against such clinical intrusiveness in families, current practices for older school-age children might be used to predict the challenge (Bailey, 1989). Twenty years after IDEA first mandated schools to include parents as equal partners in the educational process, parents largely remain either passive or adversarial in planning their children's education (Benson & Turnbull, 1986; Goodman & Bond, 1993; Turnbull & Turnbull, 1990). In fact, a study by Yanok and Derubertis (1989) found little difference between the level of participation by parents of children in regular and special education.

These findings indicate those parents who are involved in special education would be so with or without the law. A similar pattern has already been acknowledged in early intervention programs. For example, Minke and Scott (1993)

LIVING WITH AUTISM: INTERVIEW WITH AMY FINKEL

Autism is the third most common developmental disability, more common than Down syndrome, but the research dollars are 1% of almost any other disability. Someday, I'd like to get on the lecture tour and educate people about what autism is, because there are many misperceptions. First you get the scornful looks, like "What's wrong with you? Boy, you have a real brat!" A lot of autistic children are beautiful children and you would never guess in a million years that there was anything wrong with them because they look fine physically. When your autistic child acts out in public, you learn to develop a thick skin.

When people hear the word autism, this look of horror comes across their faces. Usually two things come to mind. Often all people know about autism is from having seen the movie *Rainman*. They think your child is like the man in *Rainman*. "Wow, I bet he knows all those dates!" Or, the other thing they envision is a child sitting in a corner banging his head against the wall; a child who refuses to be touched. Both of these visions scare people, so they treat you and your family like you have the plague.

You lose friends. Some people are fearful their child will "catch it." Certain peers don't want to come over and play with the child's sibling. You just know that the parents have thought that maybe it's not a good idea that their child develop a friendship with yours. You have to deal with that.

I would like to educate people and be more politically active. I'm currently trying to get a seat on the state advisory committee for disabilities. There

Josh Finkel on a swing.

are some openings coming up and I'm going to put my application in. I think school districts need to do better for these children in terms of intensity, in terms of appropriateness, and it needs to start at the federal level. I'm going to try to be more politically active. I'm going to try to speak at conventions and conferences and help families get started with their own home programs.

There needs to be an autism protocol for physicians. Speech therapists need to be able to diagnose autism, because typically they are the first professionals to see these kids. Early intervention is so important, that if speech/language consultants could suggest a diagnosis and refer children, that would be a help. So many physicians are scared to diagnose with the "A-word" because they don't know how to treat it. They may cop out and diagnose pervasive developmental delay (PDD) instead, but in the long run, that really does parents a disservice. There needs to be a protocol where parents can be told, this treatment works 50% of the time, this treatment is effective 47% of the time. This may work or may not work, these are the risks, these are the potential benefits, these are your options. Parents need a guide.

There is so much bad information out there. A lot of parents early on tried infusions of gamma globulin that is usually used for severe immuno-deficiency disorders. The downside to that treatment is that some autistic kids who received those infusions died of anaphylactic shock. The recent hysteria over Secretin is another example of why a protocol guide is needed. So many parents tried Secretin without knowing any of the potential negative side effects, and there are quite a few. We tried it for Josh, but we tried it knowing all the potential risks.

Applied behavior analysis (ABA) needs to be right at the top of the list of any recommended treatments, because right now it is the only thing that makes a real impact of any significance at all. ABA and visual communication systems both work. But, a lot of parents don't know that and they'll start out with the quick, easy fixes that are cheap but that have little impact, and they'll waste valuable years with auditory integration training (AIT), they'll fly to Hawaii to swim with the dolphins, they'll go to Disneyland hoping that their child will respond like one autistic boy did who suddenly started talking when he saw the Wolfman there. That was just a fluke, but parents are so desperate for something.

Parents need solid information about ABA and need to get started with it while they try other peripheral interventions on the side as money, time, and energy permit. That's what we did. We used ABA as the cornerstone of Josh's therapy, but we've also tried megavitamins, dimethyl glycine, Secretin infusion, Vitamin B_6 and magnesium coupled with folic acid, and AIT. We have a friend who is from Hawaii, and if we ever have an opportunity to have a vacation, I'll swim with the dolphins, you betcha! But we'll do the ABA at home first, because that, by far, has made the difference.

It helps me helping other families because it gets me off my own pity pot. One of the ways I've dealt with my despair and my anger and sadness over this is to just get busy and stay active and try to channel those negative feelings into trying to do positive things for other people. My biggest fear, though, is what the future holds for my son when I'm gone. I'm hoping that his siblings will step in and make sure that he's living in a good place, that his fingernails are clipped, that he's not dirty, and that his clothes are clean. But I can't count on that. You never know what life holds. You do the best you can for your kids, but you never know what they're going to grow up and end up being.

That's why I decided to get started in the specialty adult family home business. I want to make an impact in this community. I want to establish really high-quality adult family homes of which Joshua will end up being a trustee, so that he'll always have one of his own homes to live in. If I make a successful business out of it, there is no reason why maybe his brother or his sister wouldn't want to step in at some point and take over the directorship of that.

Before autism, I had a normal life. I had a career in international marketing. The ironic thing is that my bachelor's degree was in liberal arts with an emphasis in marketing. I had so many interests that I was never able to focus on any one thing. I knew a little bit about everything. What Josh has done for me personally is to give me that focus and that passion. I got started a little late in life, but better late than never. I try to look at the positive. Maybe this is God's way of giving me something so I can help more people. I try not to get too philosophical about it. I'd rather not have focus if it meant I didn't have a disabled child. But I am very focused now on my career and education.

(continued)

It's been tough too, in the marriage department. It's been a real struggle and I think that finally, this past 6 months to a year, we've finally gotten past it. Frankly, I think we had one foot into divorce court there for a couple of years. I think the only reason we didn't get divorced was that we were so busy and so devastated that neither one of us had the time to go file the papers! I guess that was good because we worked through it and we are past the worst of it now. It's forced both of us to really reach inside and be honest. It forced us to deal with a lot of stuff that most married couples don't ever have to deal with.

Josh's autism has had a huge impact on everybody. One thing I don't like is when people say, "God gave you this disabled child, because He knew your son would have a good home." I find that patronizing. One of the comments I hear a lot is, "Oh Amy, you're so terrific with Josh's autism!" I think, oh sure, drug addicts have normal children. Me, I don't do any drugs, I don't drink, I don't smoke, I exercise, but I'm the one with the disabled child. Why? "Because you have such a good home for him. God knew!" Please!

---

found that parents rarely suggested goals in Individualized Family Service Plan (IFSP) meetings, and when they did, those goals sometimes did not appear in the final document. Even when intensive efforts were made to involve parents, there tended to be a disturbing lack of participation (Fallon & Harris, 1992).

Harry (1992) concluded that the very fact that professional behavior is prescribed by legal mandate precludes spontaneous, honest, and effective interactions. Ironically, early childhood special education law may achieve the opposite effect intended by Congress. The precise structure of special education, including clinical eligibility, written documentation of standardized tests and instructional plans with their related jargon, and "written notification" to parents, places educators and parents in two different worlds: an objective-clinical one for educators and a personal-subjective one for parents. Hence, early interventionists are at great risk of concentrating on the "letter of the law" rather than on the "spirit of the law."

WHAT IS A FAMILY?

One of the most significant shifts in special education, particularly in early childhood, is the move from focusing on the child to focusing more broadly on the child within the family system (Turnbull & Turnbull, 1997). This model recognizes that each family member is affected by other family members and events that might influence those persons. For example, if a child with a disability requires extraordinary medical attention, other siblings may be affected by loss of parental attention, perhaps by loss of financial support once available for activities or things, and by more responsibilities around the home. Similarly, the amount of involvement in programs associated with a child with a disability will be affected when caregivers are required to work extra hours to make rent payments, when they lose a job because of the need to take time off, or if they experience marital conflict. Professionals, ignorant or neglectful of the family system, will likely become frustrated when concentrating solely on the needs of a child who has been identified for services. This child-centered model (see Figure 1–2), though convenient and compatible with most professionals' training, has not been terribly effective for families who do not already possess considerable self-efficacy.

Definitions of family are influenced by culture, politics, economics, and religion. Consequently, in early childhood professions there is no consensus on criteria for membership in families (Brinker, 1992). Yet, the issue is not moot; the scope of early childhood work relies on such a definition. For example, a broad definition of family (e.g., parents, siblings, grandparents, child-care providers, involved relatives, and close friends of the family, all of whom influence the development of the child in question) would require that all these persons be considered in the development of a family service plan. A more narrow definition

Figure 1–2 Ecological Mapping of the Child and Family
Source: Adapted from *Enabling and Empowering Families: Principles and Guidelines for Practice,* by C. Dunst, C. Trivette, and A. Deal, 1988, Cambridge, MA: Brookline.

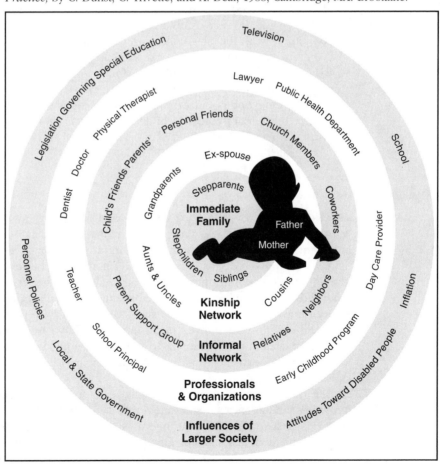

(e.g., blood relatives who live in the child's dwelling) reduces the scope of intervention required but may also limit possible benefits for children with special needs.

Clearly, a traditional definition of family as a nuclear construct will not suffice. According to Healy et al. (1989), a family is comprised of parents and any family or nonfamily members who have an important caregiving responsibility. This simply stated definition is consistent with the *family systems model*, which acknowledges all important influences on individuals within families. Still, society struggles with "moral" issues related to the "goodness" or "rightness" of diverse family structures (Ingrassia & Rossi, 1994). However, early childhood educators can little afford to be exclusive or negative when defining families. Family configurations include foster families, adoptive families, nuclear biological families, single-parent families, extended families, and same-gender-parents families.

Though it is difficult to define families, the next step—involvement of all family members—is even more difficult. For example, the parent in parent–professional interactions has almost exclusively referred to mothers (Davis & May, 1991). In recent history, society has engaged in practices that fail to prepare men for the role of involved father, focusing on paternal attributes incompatible with the best childrearing practices (Lillie, 1993). Morgan (1993) claimed that mothers are, in part, responsible for exclusion of fathers, as women attempt to protect this one domain over which they tend to possess more power than men. Again, early educators can be most effective when they move beyond popular opinion in interactions with families. A true "family-centered" approach to early childhood compels professionals to find ways to permit fathers to be involved in decision making and child care (Davis & May, 1991; Lillie, 1993; McBride & McBride, 1993).

EMPOWERMENT

Families are empowered when their needs are met, and most of the credit goes to the families themselves. When a professional can boast, "Look, they don't need me to make decisions for them, locate information, or access services," then a family is empowered. Fostering empowerment will require that educators practice in a way that they never have before. As Buysse and Wesley (1993) acknowledged, these changes cause substantial *disequilibrium* for early childhood educators whose roles are being reformed. Social service professionals, in particular, feel useful, wanted, even necessary when they can do things "for" families. It is not unusual for professionals to "need to feel needed." Yet, this very practice of apparent benevolence builds in paternalism and dependency (Dunst, Trivette, & Deal, 1988).

The desire to feel needed eventually leads to behavior that supports service providers, and agencies begin to feel that it is families' responsibility to serve the agencies' goals rather than the needs of the families. Agencies can become didactic and judgmental, labeling families as "good" or "dysfunctional" based on the agencies' definitions of what is best for children with disabilities and their families. It is not uncommon for educators and even other parents to prescribe how each family should feel, how long they should "grieve," what steps they should take to become "involved," and how they should serve professionals' needs (McGill-Smith, 1992).

Changes in the verbal behavior of service providers can reflect a new philosophy based on the preservation of families' dignity. For example, one might do away with the psychology of "death" as it relates to families with members with disabilities (Bragg, Brown, & Berninger, 1992). Professionals often label a parent who refuses to accept the opinions of professionals as "in denial," or families who seek another opinion as "bargainers," and perhaps most often label parents who express their rights as "angry." Learning the "stages of grief" and thinking that all family behavior can fit into this model of inferred maladjustment brings one no closer to understanding individual family members. In fact, Hodapp and Zigler (1993) found that families of children with severe disabilities face problems that are "the same, only more so" than other families.

Furthermore, there is increasing evidence that families with children with disabilities exude considerable resilience, and that family resources quickly "kick in" to compensate for their new stress (Krausse, 1991). Treating families as if they are disabled because their child is disabled "undermines the intent and the effect" of family centered services (Bailey, 1989). Krausse (1991) proposed an alternative view of families, which he refers to as the "family adaptation hypothesis." This hypothesis rejects the concept of pathological maladaptation associated with the presence of a child with a disability (grief model) and acknowledges the hardiness of families to cope both initially and over time. The fundamental assumption of empowerment is that families are the center. All decisions move from the center outward; all action by the periphery is to serve the center (see Figure 1–2).

The goal of empowerment is to enable families to make decisions and take action serving their self-selected needs. According to Dunst et al. (1988):

> To the extent that professionals do not recognize and explicitly consider empowerment of families as the goal of intervention, they are more likely to fool themselves into believing they have done a good job when in fact they have lost an opportunity to enable and empower the family and perhaps even created dependencies by engaging in noncontingent helping. (p. 7)

Noncontingent helping is defined as providing services or support for families while expecting no proactive behavior on the part of families. While seemingly "helping" families, professionals actually usurp opportunities for empowerment when family members are given no responsibility. Dunst et al. (1988) further contended that empowerment requires the fulfillment of three criteria:

1. Taking a **proactive stance;** enabling experiences and attribution of change to help the seeker. A proactive stance is one in which professionals assume that families are either competent or capable of becoming competent. Assuming that some families are incompetent and unable to change renders a professional useless for those children and their families.

2. Creating opportunities for families to display their strengths in order to gain new competencies is the responsibility of helping systems. "A failure to display competencies is not due to deficits within the person but rather failure of the social system to create opportunities" (Dunst et al., 1988, p. 4).

3. The third empowerment criterion is met when professionals enable families to acquire a sense of personal control over family affairs. "It is not simply a matter of whether or not family needs are met, but rather the manner in which needs are met that is likely to be both enabling and empowering" (Dunst et al., 1988, p. 4).

Building a climate for parent–professional partnerships is perhaps the field's greatest challenge. There is still much unknown. Most discouraging is the fact that those families who may benefit the most from family empowerment (i.e., minorities and low-income families) are the least likely to receive empowering services (Rueda & Martinez, 1992). Research efforts in the 21st century should be devoted to identifying methods of supporting the philosophy of empowerment and the spirit, finally, of IDEA (Nelson, Howard, & McLaughlin, 1993).

CLOSE-UP

RESPITE FROM STRESS AND OTHER SERVICE NEEDS OF HOMELESS FAMILIES

Families with children make up the fastest growing segment of the homeless population, representing almost 43% of those who are homeless. Many obstacles stand in the way of homeless parents and affect the well-being of these families. Among these are mental health problems, domestic violence, substance abuse, and lack of family support. About half of the parents have not completed high school, and many have a long way to go to even become literate. Many need job training, education, and work to help them become self-sufficient and residentially stable.

When families live in shelters under strict rules and crowded conditions, "public parenting" occurs. This is the situation when other mothers and shelter staff interfere with the discipline of children. This can be very stressful for parent/child relationships, and even a short respite can help mothers apply better parenting skills (such as positive reinforcement for appropriate behavior) and empathy toward their children's needs.

A camp program designed to give temporary relief from some of the stress associated with homelessness and shelter living was very successful. The program was aimed at providing outdoor camping experiences for homeless children and families and to strengthen parental skills. Rather than directly teaching parenting skills, groups of mothers met to share and validate their experiences with parenting that were common to families who live in shelters. Older mothers tended to assume teaching roles in the groups, leading lively discussions about effective ways to talk to children, to get their attention, and to help them discover the world around them. They talked about how to make children "mind," particularly without using physical punishment. Individuals were also interviewed to identify specific supports they needed for obtaining jobs, education, and so forth.

The program helped families engage in more activities together and to be more in tune with ways to keep children occupied to prevent acting out under shelter conditions. Modeling of positive adult/child interactions by caring counselors helped increase the playful interactions between children and their parents. Many of the parents possessed skills in child management, but the stressful conditions in which they lived affected their relationships with their children. Even a brief respite and sharing support from other parents enhanced their functioning as families.

Source: From "Respite from Stress and Other Service Needs of Homeless Families," by K. Kissman, 1999, *Community Mental Health Journal, 35*(3), 241–249.

THE IMPORTANCE OF WORKING COLLABORATIVELY

An infant or toddler whose medical condition, developmental delay, or physical disability is so severe that it comes to the attention of caregivers and service providers at an early age is likely to present more complex needs than a child who does not demonstrate a disability until he or she is of school age. Very young children with medical, cognitive, or physical complications are typically at risk for developing disabilities in related developmental areas. For example, a child with abnormal muscle tone may have trouble learning to walk, may have motor problems related to eating difficulties, may not develop necessary motor movements to produce intelligible speech, and, with poor tools for communication, may be unable to demonstrate her cognitive abilities. This child has one primary disabling condition, poor muscle tone, yet the intervention services of a physical therapist, occupational therapist, speech therapist, special educator, and parents are all necessary.

Though it was common practice in the past, it is unlikely that any one professional could serve this child well. Consequently, very young children with special needs are likely to have a team of specialists attending to different aspects of their care and development. An **interdisciplinary** approach combines expertise from many disciplines to scrutinize a child's various aspects of development, combining interpretation, synthesis, planning, and practices to design a plan that will promote a child's overall development (Healy et al., 1989).

When a number of professionals collaborate with a family, careful teamwork becomes absolutely necessary. Without careful coordination, there might be unnecessary duplication of services and paperwork, lack of communication with important parties, an increase in confusion and contradiction, and resultant poorer services to children and their families. A successful team approach must be organized to produce timely and accurate assessment, comprehensive and effective intervention, clear and inclusive communication, and regular evaluation and review. An effective team approach is reached only through mutual trust and respect, practice, and hard work.

Several approaches to teaming have worked well, as long as fundamental guidelines are respected. First, **consensus building** is more effective than an authoritative structure. When various professionals gather with parents, each comes with differing levels of professional status and biases. It is hard to set priorities unless each participant is willing to listen carefully to all parties and to "give and take" in regard to their particular areas of expertise. In situations with a breakdown of give and take, team coordination is at an impasse.

One father described his experience as a member of his son's individualized education planning (IEP) team (McCauley, personal communication, January 25, 1994). He requested that the team include toilet training on Sean's IEP, even though the teacher reported that his son had not had any "accidents" at school. Mr. McCauley acknowledged this observation but contended that Sean continued to have difficulty at home, and wanted to have his toileting routine continued at school. The educators refused to listen to Mr. McCauley's priorities (including the toileting training) and the IEP process eventually reached an impasse. This conflict might have been avoided had members of the team valued the input of all members and tried to accommodate as many priorities as possible from each member.

Each professional must be flexible and willing to share roles as well as information. Consider a child who presents a language delay; the teacher, the physical therapist, and the parents must all work to develop the child's language whether that is within that person's area of expertise or not. This team approach requires that each member has some working understanding of other disciplines or at least a willingness to implement suggestions made by other professionals. For example, both the speech therapist and the teacher should learn how to position a motor-involved child in the most appropriate way during all aspects of the child's home or school day. This will require some instruction and modeling by the physical therapist.

Finally, effective **group process** is essential for ensuring a positive team experience. Group process includes making all participants comfortable in sharing their concerns and desires, listening carefully to all members of the team, valuing the input of all members of the team, and making decisions based on consensus. For example, parents are often intimidated when meeting with a large group of professionals and may hesitate to speak honestly and clearly regarding their priorities. If coerced into silence by intimidation or lack of opportunity, parents may leave a meeting unhappy with the planning and uncommitted to the work a plan involves. To decrease anxiety, parents should be greeted when they arrive, perhaps offered refreshments and comfortable seating, and introduced to all members of the team. These practices may seem overly zealous to some. As one educator put it, "This is not a social gathering! Do you get refreshments when you go to a law office or a dental office?" Though this objection is reasonable, the goals of early childhood special education may be incompatible with the client-expert practices of many other professions. Certainly one would want to avoid the intimidation and sterility of legal and dental visits.

Professionals should refrain from using technical jargon or should take care to explain terminology carefully to other members of the team. Written plans should never be formally completed ahead of time, nor should parents be expected to sign-off at the time of the meeting. Soliciting parent suggestions and input before decisions are made is a necessary (and legally required) component of the group process. One person should act as a facilitator to make sure a meeting begins promptly, to keep the discussion on task, to see that all members have a chance to give input or to object when appropriate, and to restate or summarize when agreement has been reached. Before a meeting ends, everyone present should know what will happen next, who is responsible for each part of a plan, and when the team will meet again to review progress.

TEAMING MODELS

There are three basic team models or arrangements, and they vary in the degree to which team members are able to work together. **Multidisciplinary** teams are made up of members who work independently in providing assessment and direct services to a child and meet to share their goals and progress reports, though there is little direct coordination of efforts. For example, the psychologist may meet with a child to test intelligence and achievement levels, then meet with the team to report his results and recommendations for treatment. Members in an **interdisciplinary model** may conduct their assessments and plan goals together, but continue to provide direct services on an independent basis. For example, the speech therapist may observe while the psychologist is testing a child and check-off speech sounds, or phonemes, that the child can say, rather than duplicating the testing in a separate speech session. In a **transdisciplinary model,** professionals share roles and may combine their assessment and treatment tasks so that any one individual may be carrying out the responsibilities of a different professional. For example, the classroom teacher may be using a phoneme check-off instrument to obtain information for the speech therapist or may carry out a language program the speech therapist has recommended.

Of particular benefit to a child served by a team approach is that each team member sees the child's problem from his or her own perspective. "Early childhood education has always been an interdisciplinary field with a commitment to the education of the whole child; an understanding of the child as a complete human being is basic to the development of a program concerned with each area of development and learning" (Spodek, Saracho, & Lee, 1986). Sometimes a teacher may be intimidated by the knowledge of other specialized team members; however, the generalist perspective that a teacher brings is a necessary part of team dynamics. Specialists have in-depth knowledge of their discipline, but teachers are better able to see the whole child as he or she functions in a variety of settings, both socially and physically.

The team configuration used in a particular situation will depend on the administrative policy of the school and service agencies involved and on the comfort and cohesiveness of the professionals serving a particular child. There is no question, however, that teaming across disciplines is a necessary part of services to young children. The greater the ability of the team to interact, to share roles, and to inform each other across disciplines, the more unified and complete a child's services are likely to be. Table 1–6 summarizes the strengths and weaknesses of each of these models.

Table 1–6 Team Models

Team Model	Strengths	Weaknesses
Multidisciplinary Team	• Involves more than one discipline in planning and services • Pools expertise for decision making • Reduces mistake and biases	• May not promote a unified approach to intervention • May lack team cohesion and commitment
Interdisciplinary Team	• Activities and goals complement and support other disciplines • Allows commitment to unified service plan • Information flow is coordinated through a case manager	• Professional "turf" may be threatened • Inflexibility by professionals may reduce efficiency • Role of case manager may be ambiguous, case manager may become autocratic
Transdisciplinary Team	• Encourages interaction within many disciplines • Encourages role sharing • Provides a unified, holistic plan for intervention • Allows a more complete understanding of the child • Leads to professional enhancement and increased knowledge and skill	• Requires participation by many experts • Places largest responsibility on the teacher as case manager • Requires a high degree of coordination and interaction • Requires more time for communication and planning

COLLABORATION IN EARLY INTERVENTION

Collaboration with other professionals is apparently not as easy as it seems. In fact, many teachers report that their jobs are made most difficult by lack of co-operation among their peers and themselves. A study of teachers' and prospective teachers' preferences for collaboration may aid understanding of issues involved in planning (Morrison, Walker, Wakefield, & Solberg, 1994). Teachers with the highest level of self-efficacy were the most amenable to collaborative problem solving. Ironically, those teachers who most believed they were capable of teaching a broad range of skills in the classroom were the most willing to work collaboratively. For example, the student teachers in this study were less willing than the practicing teachers to work with and gain assistance from other professionals. One might conclude from this study that an important barrier to collaboration is a lack of self-confidence. Yet, collaboration by all professionals, with other professionals as well as with parents, is a necessary prerequisite to an effective program.

In early intervention, the challenge of integrating services for families demands the most of collaborative efforts. As family needs increase, the need for increased services increases—as does the need for greater coordination of disciplines (see Figure 1–2). For example, families with multiple needs cannot be well served by autonomous narrowly defined programs. Take the following example:

> Paulette is a young 28-year-old mother and about-to-be grandmother living on Aid to Families with Dependent Children (AFDC), with four children by three fathers, none of whom is part of the household physically or financially.

Paulette never finished high school. Her son, Mark, 14 years old, was a chronic truant in school, and in and out of trouble in the neighborhood, which finally earned him a sentence to the Maryland Training School for Boys. Since his release, his caseworker has been trying to place him in a suitable school but without success. Her oldest daughter, Tessie, is pregnant at age 13, repeating her maternal family pattern. She wants to drop out of school, but a neighbor told her about a special school for pregnant girls, and Paulette is trying to get admission. The 8-year-old daughter, Marie, is doing satisfactory school work, but Paulette has noticed her late returns from school with unexplained spending money. There is a real concern that Marie is earning her money as a "spotter" for neighborhood drug dealers. The 2-year-old baby of the family has started exhibiting symptoms of lead paint poisoning, caused by nibbling on flaking paint chips in their apartment. Unchecked and untreated, this could result in permanent brain damage. This is a family beset with behavioral, health, educational, housing, and financial problems. At least five different public agencies in five separate locations have some knowledge of and contact with this family. Fourteen different workers in those agencies have attempted to offer assistance during the past two years, each concerned with the specialized service agency but with little or no knowledge of efforts by the other professionals. (Levitan, Mangum, & Pines, 1989, p. 21)

This family's needs can be viewed from an ecological systems model described by Bronfenbrenner (1986). The most immediate needs, schooling for Tessie and Mark, supervision for Marie, and prevention of paint eating for the baby, are at the **microsystem** level. At the **mesosystem** level, there is a linkage between microsystems, such as a linkage between Paulette and the schools, or between the schools and the juvenile justice system. The **exosystems** are those affecting families, but with no direct relationship with agencies, such as church and neighbors. Finally, families are influenced by **macrosystems,** broad social values and belief systems of cultures and subcultures. Interdependency of agencies serving families from these multiple perspectives is a crucial philosophy. A formal link between professionals/agencies and early childhood programs serving Paulette and her family should be the service coordinator. This person is responsible for assessment of family and child needs, coordination of planning for intervention and delivery of services, as well as monitoring of services delivered.

Programs that are successful at integrating these services are correlated with such broad-based family needs as decreased birthrates in adolescents, lower incidences of low birth weight babies, increased school participation by parents, decreased drug abuse and behavior problems, increased financial self-sufficiency, and higher IQ and test scores (Voydanoff, 1994). Clearly, one professional or agency cannot possibly address all these areas. In a *meta-analysis,* Schorr and Both (1991) concluded that successfully integrated systems had the following attributes:

1. Comprehensive, flexible, and responsive
2. Child is part of family and family is part of community
3. Well-trained staff, who are accepting enough to build trusting relationships
4. Persistent and responsive to the needs of those families at greatest risk
5. Well-managed, with energetic and committed professionals whose attitudes and skills are well-defined. Professionals are willing to take risks, tolerate

ambiguity, work with diverse populations, and operate with a collaborative management style

6. Client centered

In summary, collaboration as a philosophy is possible only when professionals are able to separate their own needs from those of clients and are nonjudgmental, open-minded, and committed to providing families with the very best services possible.

CLOSE-UP

INFANTS AND TODDLERS WITH DISABILITIES: RELATIONSHIP-BASED APPROACHES

For the past 15 years, intervention for very young children has focused on traditional discipline-based provision of activities and therapies, and services requested by parents. Service providers focused on their own disciplines, acting as experts and parents functioned as recipients who were instructed in recommendations they were to carry out. Treatment was based on child deficits with some consideration for family strengths.

In contrast, the recent emphasis on family-centered service delivery emphasizes the need for families to be major planners in treatment and for professionals to operate using transdisciplinary approaches. This goes beyond simple collaboration and requires all members of a planning and treatment team to share their expertise. To do so requires a high level of communication among disciplines assessing and treating young children. Relationships become very important, and relationship-based approaches are a new organizing principle in early intervention.

One outcome of this perspective is new attention to parent-child relationships and their important effects on the development of children. It appears that increases in maternal-child responsivity have as many positive effects on child outcomes as does the presence of an intervention itself. Three components were key (1) sensitivity to a child's interests and engagement in the child's interest, (2) consistency and appropriateness of parental responses to a child, and (3) how well the parent engages a child in turn-taking.

A second important relationship is that between the parents and the service providers. Rather than dwelling on deficits, good relationships focus on family strengths and respect parents as experts on their child. Service providers highlight the family's strengths and assist in identifying and locating necessary supports to make the most of those. Professionals join parents in creative problem solving to design services that meet a family's needs and desires while relieving identified stressors.

Families consistently identify competent and caring, supportive, and trustworthy professionals as the most essential part of successful early intervention. Respectful, responsive listening is highly valued. But professionals need help in balancing a friendly relationship with boundary issues, paying attention to their own and the parents' emotional needs, and dealing with conflict. Diversity of cultural backgrounds also represent a challenge in relationship-based approaches. It is also important for service providers to reflect on how interventions can be congruent with family beliefs and values.

Early childhood professionals need to understand basic principles of infant mental health:

- ◆ The baby's primary relationships need to support developmental needs—That is the core of a baby's capacity to love well and grow well.
- ◆ Each parent and each baby is unique in many ways including temperament, interaction style and emotional makeup. This effects the "goodness of fit" of any relationship.
- ◆ The particular environmental context in which a baby and parent reside deeply affects functioning.

Service providers can understand parents' behavior only by trying to walk in parents' shoes. They need to know about parents' feelings, dreams, desires, and perceptions.

Service providers must be aware of their own feelings and how their behavior affects their relationships with parents. Supported parents are more likely to nurture and support their children.

The perfect relationship-based organization does not exist. It is the ongoing striving toward that ideal that distinguishes quality organizations.

Source: From "Infants and Toddlers with Disabilities: Relationship-Based Approaches," by Atkins-Burnett S. and P. A. Meares, 2000, *Social Work, 45* (4), 371–379.

The Importance of Ethical Conduct and Advocacy

What do **ethical conduct** and **advocacy** have to do with philosophy? Many decisions educators make, including their daily activities in a classroom, are based on a set of personal ethics or personal philosophy. Professionals, charged with working with families of very young children with disabilities, should be held to the highest ethical standards. First, educators should know and follow the ethical standards of their profession. Second, educators should actively advocate for issues that will encourage society to respond to the needs of families and children with disabilities in an ethical fashion.

Ethical professional behavior means that one will be the best early childhood professional that one can be and will support others in providing quality services with the highest ethical standards. Professional organizations serving children have already articulated high ethical and accreditation standards for those who provide services to young children. A prime example is the Code of Ethical Conduct developed by the National Association for the Education of Young Children

(1989). These standards for ethical behavior in early childhood education describe professional responsibilities in regard to children, families, colleagues, the community, and society. The first principle presented in the Code expresses its ideals well:

> Above all, we shall not harm children. We shall not participate in practices that are disrespectful, degrading, dangerous, exploitative, intimidating, psychologically damaging, or physically harmful to children. This principle has precedence over all others in this Code. (National Association for the Education of Young Children, 1989)

ADVOCACY ISSUES

An advocate is someone who takes up another person's cause (Alper, Schloss, & Schloss, 1995). For what should one advocate? The president of the Association of Child Advocates, Eve Brooks, suggested getting involved with what is closest to one's heart (Himelfarb, 1992). For an early childhood professional, that may mean working and playing with one's own children or helping others in need. It may mean voting regularly and intelligently, writing one's congressman, or participating on state councils or research projects. *Putting People First* (Clinton & Gore, 1992) identified national priorities for children that few could argue against. These goals included the following:

1. Guarantee affordable quality health care through maternal and child networks and programs.
2. Revolutionize lifetime learning by fully funding Head Start, improving the K–12 education systems, and providing opportunities for college and vocational experience.
3. Make homes, schools, and streets safer for children by reducing violence and providing drug education.
4. Support pro-family and pro-children policies through tax credits for families, family and medical leaves, child-care networks, and tough child-support legislation.

Obtaining good child care is a nationwide problem due to short supply, lack of affordability, poor regulation, frequent staff turnover, and little staff training (Ryan, 1992). An estimated 23 million children in the United States require child care. Of this number, only 8.3 million attend licensed day-care settings required to meet minimum standards for health, safety, and curriculum; the remaining 14.7 million are placed in unlicensed settings that may or may not provide adequate care. Many other children are left with friends and relatives, or even left unsupervised (Ryan, 1992). The consequences of poor child care are often troubling, leaving very young children at risk for molestation, physical injury, and even death (Hoyt & Schoonmaker, 1991). Though an enormous population of children require child care while their parents work, society must take responsibility for insuring the well-being of children in child care (Hoyt & Schoonmaker, 1991).

Although the federal government sets standards for many aspects of daily life, the regulation of child care is left to state governments. Consequently, there is tremendous variability among state laws and enforcement levels (Hoyt & Schoonmaker, 1991). In fact, the Children's Defense Fund (1993, December) reported that nearly half the children in child care outside their own homes are not protected by any state regulations at all. Even when states have regulations on the books, many are not able to properly inspect centers and enforce these regulations (Hoyt & Schoonmaker, 1991). In any case, as many as 80% to 90% of day-care settings are unlicensed. Yet, even a license on the wall does not guarantee appropriate care is being provided, and eight states reported that they could not even respond to all the parent complaints they received.

Who should monitor the quality of child care provided? Who should insist on high standards for programs for young children, and who should police the enforcement of these standards? Parents are often ill-equipped to do so because they are victims of a provider's market; the short supply of openings available and the high cost of quality day care tend to make parents settle for availability and affordability (Hoyt & Schoonmaker, 1991). It is absolutely essential that early childhood professionals advocate for appropriate, high-quality services to very young children. Professionals have the education, the commitment, and the voice to insist that standards for child care be adequate and that society contribute to the health, safety, and education of all children regardless of race, disabling condition, or economic status. This is not a new role or futile use of energy, because educators have (hand in hand with parents) accomplished extraordinary changes in terms of legal, pedagogical, financial, practical, and ethical practices in the past few decades.

Another issue that will have an impact on early childhood special education is the reform of public assistance policies at state and federal levels that require single mothers (and families) on public assistance to work and limit the length of time for which families are eligible. Such policies will most assuredly increase the need for low-cost child care and place a further burden on a system already in crises.

To date, policymakers have not addressed this need. Therefore, it is possible that the lack of child care will result in higher rates of child neglect, homelessness, and need of special services. A professional should be an informed citizen and participate in advocacy for families through voting, writing, or using e-mail to contact congressional representatives, sending letters to the editor of the local newspaper, and using other effective ways to inform the public of issues important to families of young children with disabilities.

HOW TO GET INVOLVED IN ADVOCACY

Advocacy is a dynamic and continuous process that begins with the recognition of an unmet need and does not end until that need is met (Alper et al., 1995). An advocate's work progresses in two directions at once; as the advocate supports and obtains services for an individual, his work promotes changes across the system, eventually applying to large numbers of children. Effective advocacy can begin within a family, within a classroom, or within a community.

Within the local context, children with disabilities have many immediate needs, including the need for friendships, need for support in extracurricular activities, need for community access, and need for appropriate curriculum (Alper et al., 1995). Parents of children with disabilities need healthy communication between the many professionals with whom they deal, they also need emotional support, economic supports, respite care, legal protection, and information about the future. Your advocacy may begin with connecting parents with each other, arranging "buddy" systems within your class, or providing informational brochures.

On a broader level, there are numerous ways one can become involved in child advocacy (Himelfarb, 1992). Many community organizations have an interest in child issues—from Parent Teacher Associations to Kiwanis Clubs, Junior Leagues, and religious charities. Every state now has at least one organization devoted to child advocacy. These organizations may track state legislation, monitor voting records of elected officials, lobby for child issues, and fund research and education aimed at improving children's circumstances. A phone call or letter will put one in contact with a number of national organizations working on behalf of children.

A number of national professional, parent, and citizen organizations specialize in advocacy for young children and those with disabilities. Information about membership, mission, activities and goals for most of these can be found easily on the Internet and many have local groups that meet regularly. Among these are:

◆ The Arc
◆ American Association on Mental Retardation
◆ American Occupational Therapy Association
◆ American Speech–Language–Hearing Association
◆ Child Welfare League
◆ Council for Exceptional Children
◆ Disability Rights Education and Defense Fund Inc.
◆ Division for Early Childhood of the Council for Exceptional Children
◆ Down Syndrome Congress
◆ Easter Seals
◆ National Association for the Education of Young Children
◆ National Association of School Psychologists
◆ TASH (formerly The Association for the Severely Handicapped)
◆ The Neuro-Developmental Treatment Association
◆ Tourette Syndrome Association
◆ Zero to Three

A profession is more than a job. It is a long-term commitment to a field. In early childhood education, that commitment is to the well-being of children, and that well-being cannot be insured if efforts are confined to one's classroom, playground, or home. The health, safety, and education of children are dependent on society and its efforts to protect children from discrimination, poverty, disease, abuse, violence, and ignorance. Marian Wright Edelman, President of the Children's Defense Fund, gave this advice on life: "Hang in with your advocacy for children and the poor. The tide is going to turn. . . . Don't think you have to be a big dog to make a difference. You just need to be a persistent flea. . . . Enough committed fleas biting strategically can make even the biggest dog uncomfortable and transform even the biggest nation, as we will transform America. . . . " (Edelman, 1991).

IN CONCLUSION

This chapter has summarized the major assumptions of early childhood special education. Over the past three decades, since early childhood education seriously began its business of serving children with special needs and their families, an increasingly liberal philosophy has evolved, in sharp contrast with the social changes in an increasingly conservative society. Already, this clash in direction has meant the closure of many early intervention programs and the reduction of funds for preschool special education programs. An assumption not discussed in this chapter is that of efficacy. There is little doubt as to the efficacy of early childhood services for very young children with special needs (Baer, 1987). Years of research have demonstrated that money and time spent in the first year of life save money and reduce the effects of developmental delays later in life (White & Castro, 1985). This is especially true of children with mild delays or those who are at risk for delays. An analogy to automobile maintenance can be made. If a problem is detected early and repaired quickly, the cost and effort are small. However, if the problem is allowed to persist, the automobile will suffer extensive damage that will subsequently be more costly and difficult to repair.

Professionals in early intervention are at a crossroads where diminishing resources are available to serve increasing needs. Society must recognize the considerable benefits that can be gained by early investment in our children, and it is up to those professionals who know this best to advocate for cultural values that prioritize children and families.

STUDY GUIDE QUESTIONS

1. What are the two important elements of an attitude of science?
2. What is the value of a conceptual system?
3. How does applied behavior analysis meet the criteria for a good conceptual system?
4. What is meant by personalization of intervention? What are its basic premises?
5. What is needed in order to make the philosophy of personalization a reality?
6. How has the population of the United States changed in regard to racial distribution?
7. What impact do changing demographics have on education?
8. State two reasons sensitivity to cultural differences is important in early childhood education.
9. What are the detrimental effects of childhood poverty?
10. How have families changed in recent years?
11. What can teachers do to support children from nontraditional families?
12. Why is it inappropriate to conclude that minority children are abnormal or incompetent?
13. What problems accompany a philosophy of empowerment?
14. How is family defined within a family systems model?
15. Why is noncontingent helping not helpful?
16. Describe how a professional effectively relates to empower a family.

17. What can professionals do to ensure that a team works well together?
18. Describe the differences among the three primary team models.
19. Give examples of how you could relate to a single mother of a child with Down syndrome that would contribute to a successful collaborative team.
20. Give an example of how early childhood special education could demonstrate each of the following: accountability, flexibility, and parent empowerment.

REFERENCES

Alberto, P. A., & Troutman, A. C. (1990). *Applied behavior analysis for teachers* (3rd ed.). Upper Saddle River, NJ: Merrill/Prentice Hall.

Allen, J. P., & Turner, E. (1990). Where diversity is. *American Demographics, 12*(8), 34–38.

Alper, S., Schloss, P. J., & Schloss, C. N. (1995). Families of children with disabilities in elementary and middle school: Advocacy models and strategies. *Exceptional Children, 62*(3), 261.

American Academy of Pediatrics. (1982). The Doman-Delacato treatment of neurologically handicapped children (RE2709). *Pediatrics, 70*(5), 810–812.

Anderson, E. A., & Koblinsky, S. A. (1995). Homeless policy: The need to speak to families. *Family Relations, 44,* 13–18.

Ary, D., Jacobs, L., & Razavich, A. (1996). *Introduction to research in education.* Fort Worth, TX: Harcourt Brace College.

Atkins-Burnett, S., & Meares, P. A. (2000). Infants and toddlers with disabilities: Relationship-based approaches. *Social Work, 45*(4), 371–379.

Baer, D. M. (1987, March). A behavior-analytic query into early intervention. Paper presented at the 19th Banff International Conference on Behavioral Science: Early Intervention in the Coming Decade. Banff, Alberta.

Baer, D. M., Wolf, M. M., & Risley, T. R. (1968). Some current dimensions of applied behavior analysis. *Journal of Applied Behavior Analysis, 1,* 91–97.

Bailey, D. B. (1989). Case management in early intervention. *Journal of Early Intervention, 13,* 120–134.

Bailey, D., Huntington, G., Simmeonson, R., & Yoder, D. (1992). Preparing professionals to serve infants and toddlers with handicaps and their families: An integrative analysis across eight disciplines. *Exceptional Children, 10,* 26–34.

Benson, H. A., & Turnbull, A. P. (1986). Approaching families from an individualized perspective. In R. H. Horner, L. H. Meyers, & H. D. Fredericks (Eds.), *Educating learners with severe handicaps: Exemplary service strategies* (pp. 127–157). Baltimore: Paul H. Brookes.

Bragg, R. M., Brown, R. L., & Berninger, V. W. (1992). The impact of congenital and acquired disabilities on the family system: Implications for school counseling. *The School Counselor, 39,* 292–299.

Bricker, D. (2001). The natural environment: A useful construct? *Infants and Young Children, 13*(4), 21–31.

Brinker, R. P. (1992). Family involvement in early intervention: Accepting the unchangeable, changing the changeable, and knowing the difference. *Topics in Early Childhood Special Education, 12*(3), 307–332.

Bronfenbrenner, U. (1986). Ecology of the family as a context for human development. *Developmental Psychology, 22,* 732–752.

Brown-Lyons, M., Robertson, A., Layzer, J. (2001). *Kith and kin—Informal child care: Highlights from recent research.* New York: The National Center for Children in Poverty.

Buysse, B., & Wesley, P. W. (1993). The identity crisis in early childhood education: A call for professional role clarification. *Topics in Early Childhood Special Education, 13,* 418–429.

Carlile, C. (1991, Summer). Children of divorce: How teachers can ease the pain. *Childhood Education,* 232–234.

Children's Defense Fund. (1993, December). Family support. *CDF Reports,* pp. 5–9.

Children's Defense Fund. (1998). *The state of America's children. Yearbook 1998.* Washington, DC: Author.

Clapton, J., & Fitzgerald, J. (2002). The history of disability: A history of 'otherness.' *New Renaissance Magazine, 7*(1), 8 pages.

Clinton, B., & Gore, A. (1992). *Putting people first.* New York: Times Books, 47–51.

Consortium for Citizens with Disabilities (2002). Letter to Thomas Irvin, Office of Special Education and Rehabilitation Services. Retrieved July 10, 2002 from *http://www.c-c-d.org/childideacomments.htm*

Crockett, J. B., & Kauffman, J. M. (1998). Taking inclusion back to its roots. *Educational Leadership, 56*(2), 74–77.

Davis, P. B., & May, J. E. (1991, Spring). Involving fathers in early intervention and family support programs: Issues and strategies. *CHC,* 87–91.

Dunst, C., Trivette, C., & Deal, A. (1988). *Enabling and empowering families: Principles and guidelines for practice.* Cambridge, MA: Brookline.

Edelman, M. W. (1991). Ten lessons to help us through the 1990s: The state of America's children. *The Measure of Our Success.* Beacon Press, 13–15, 19, 20.

Education for All Handicapped Children Act. (1975). 20 USC [sections] 1401 et Seq.

Fagan, P., & Coontz, S. (1997). Q: Are single-parent families a major cause of social dysfunction? *Insight on the News, 13*(45): 24–27.

Fallon, M. A., & Harris, M. B. (1992). Encouraging parent participation in intervention programs. *The Transdisciplinary Journal, 2*(2), 141–146.

Fenichel, E. (2001). *From neurons to neighborhoods: What's in it for you?* Washington, DC: Zero to Three: National Center for Infants, Toddlers, and Families.

Florsheim, P., Tolan, P., & Gorman-Smith, D. (1998). Family relationships, parenting practices, the availability of male family members, and the behavior of inner-city boys in single-mother and two-parent families. *Child Development, 69*(5), 1437–1447.

Fuchs, D., & Fuchs, L. S. (1998). Competing visions for educating students with disabilities: Inclusion versus full inclusion. *Childhood Education, 74*(5), 309–316.

Gallagher, D. J. (1998). The scientific knowledge base of special education: Do we know what we think we know? *Exceptional Children, 64*(4), 493–502.

Garcia, E. E. (1997). The education of Hispanics in early childhood: Of roots and wings. *Young Children, 53*(3): 5–14.

Gately, J. (personal communication).

Goodman, J. F., & Bond, L. (1993). The Individualized Education Program: A retrospective critique. *The Journal of Special Education, 26,* 408–422.

Griffith, D. R. (1992, September). Prenatal exposure to cocaine and other drugs: Developmental and educational prognosis. *Phi Delta Kappan,* 30–34.

Guo, G. (1998). The timing of the influences of cumulative poverty on children's cognitive ability and achievement. *Social Forces, 77*(1): 257–287.

Guralnick, M. J. (2001). A developmental systems model for early intervention. *Infants and Young Children, 14*(2), 1–14.

Gutierrez, L., & Ortega, R. (1991). Developing methods to empower Latinos: The importance of groups. *Social Work with Groups, 14*(2), 23–43.

Hanson, M. J., & Bruder, M. B. (2001). Early intervention: Promises to keep. *Infants and Young Children, 13*(3), 47–58.

Haring, N. G., & McCormick, L. (1990). *Exceptional children and youth.* Upper Saddle River, NJ: Merrill/Prentice Hall.

Harry, B. (1992). *Cultural diversity, families, and the special educational system: Communication and empowerment.* New York: Teachers College Press.

Healy, A., Keesee, P. D., & Smith, B. S. (1989). *Early services for children with special needs: Transactions for family support.* Baltimore: Paul H. Brookes Publishing.

Hegar, R., & Scannapieco, M. (1995). From family duty to family policy: The evolution of kinship care. *Child Welfare, 75*(1), 200–217.

Hernandez, D. J. (1995). Changing demographics: Past and future demands for early childhood programs. *The Future of Children,* 145–160.

Himelfarb, S. (1992, November). You can make a difference for America's children. *Parents,* pp. 221–224.

Hispanic population to become largest U.S. minority. (1997). *Population Today, 25*(11), 1–2.

Hodapp, R. M., & Zigler, E. (1993). Comparison of families of children with mental retardation and families of children without mental retardation. *Mental Retardation, 31*(2), 75–87.

Hoyt, M. & Schoonmaker, M. E. (1991, October 15). The day care delusion: When parents accept the unacceptable. *Family Circle,* pp. 81–87.

Hunter, A. G., Pearson, J. L., Isalongo, N. S., & Kellam, S. G. (1998). Parenting alone to multiple caregivers: Child care and parenting arrangements in black and white urban families. *Family Relations, 47*(4), 343–353.

Iglehart, A. P. (1994). Kinship foster care: Placement, service, and outcome issues. *Children and Youth Services Review, 16*(1–2), 107–121.

Ingrassia, M., & Rossi, M. (1994, February). The limits of tolerance? *Newsweek,* p. 47.

Kelley, P. (1996). Family-centered practice with stepfamilies. *Families in Society, 77*(9), 535–544.

Kissman, K. (1999). Respite from stress and other service needs of nameless families. *Community Mental Health Journal, 35*(3), 241–249.

Koren, P. E., DeChillo, N., & Friesen, B. J. (1992). Measuring empowerment in families whose children have emotional disabilities: A brief questionnaire. *Rehabilitation Psychology, 37*(4), 304–321.

Krausse, M. W. (1991). Theoretical issues in family research. Paper presented at the Annual meeting of the American Association on Mental Retardation, Washington, DC (ERIC Document Reproduction Service No. ED 337 923).

Law, M. (2000). Strategies for implementing evidence-based practice in early intervention. I*nfants and Young Children, 13*(2), 32–40.

Lee, S. M. (1998). Asian Americans: Diverse and growing. *Population Bulletin, 53*(2), 2–40.

Levitan, S. A., Mangum, G. L., & Pines, M. W. (1989). *A proper inheritance: Investing in the self-sufficiency of poor families.* Washington, DC: The George Washington University.

Lewis, A. C. (1997). The price of poverty. *Phi Delta Kappan, 78*(6), 423–424.

Lillie, T. (1993). A harder thing than triumph: Roles of fathers of children with disabilities. *Mental Retardation, 31,* 438–442.

Malhotra, R. (2001). The politics of the disability rights movements. *New Politics, 8*(3), 10 pages.

Mallory, B. L., & New, R. S. (1994). Social constructivist theory and principles of inclusion: Challenges for early childhood special education. *Journal of Special Education, 28*(3), 322–337.

Martin, P., & Midgley, E. (1994). Immigration to the United States: Journey to an uncertain destination. *Population Bulletin, 49*(2), 2–47.

McBride, B. A., & McBride, R. J. (1993). Parent education and support programs for fathers. *Childhood Education, 70,* 4–8.

McCollum, J. A. (2000). Taking the past along: Reflecting on our identity as a discipline. *Topics in Early Childhood Special Education, 20*(2), 79–86.

McCormick, L., & Holden, R. (1992). Homeless children: A special challenge. *Young Children, 47*(6), 61–67.

McGill-Smith, P. (1992). Can't get on the train without a ticket. *Teaching Exceptional Children, 25,* 49.

McLoyd, V. C. (1990). Minority children: Introduction to the special issue. *Child Development, 61,* 263–266.

McPhatter, A. R. (1997). Cultural competence in child welfare: What is it? How do we achieve it? What happens without it? *Child Welfare, 76*(1), 255–278.

Minke, K. M., & Scott, M. M. (1993). The development of Individualized Family Service Plans: Roles for parents and staff. *The Journal of Special Education, 27,* 82–106.

Mitchell, S. (1995). The next baby boom. *American Demographics,* 22–27, 30–31.

Moore, K. A., Manlove, J., Glei, D. A., & Morrison, D. R. (1998). Nonmarital school-age motherhood: Family, individual, and school characteristics. *Journal of Adolescent Research, 13*(4), 433–457.

Montgomery, L. E., Kiely, J. L. & Pappas, G. (1996). The effects of poverty, race, and family structure on U.S. children's health: Data from the NHIS, 1978 through 1980 and 1989 through 1991. *American Journal of Public Health, 86*(10), 1401.

Morgan, R. (1993). *The word of a woman.* New York: W. W. Norton.

Morrison, G. M., Walker, D., Wakefield, P., & Solberg, S. (1994). Teacher preferences for collaborative relationships: Relationship to efficacy for teaching in prevention-related domains. *Psychology in the Schools, 31,* 221–231.

National Association for the Education of Young Children. (1989). *Code of Ethics.* Washington, DC: Author.

National Association for the Education of Young Children. (1996). NAEYC position statement: Responding to linguistic and cultural diversity—recommendations for effective early childhood education. *Young Children, 51*(2): 4–12.

National Commission on Family Foster Care. (1991). *The significance of kinship care: Blueprint for fostering infants, children, and youths in the 1990s.* Washington, DC: Child Welfare League of America.

National Council of Teachers of English and International Reading Association. (1996). *Standards for the English language arts.* Urbana, IL: NCTE.

National Early Childhood Technical Assistance Center. (2001). *Annual appropriations and number of children under part C of IDEA Federal Fiscal Years 1987–2000.* Retrieved July 2, 2002 from *http://www.nectas. unc.edu/partc/partcdata.asp*

National Research Council and Institute of Medicine. (2000). *From neurons to neighborhoods: The science of early childhood development.* Committee on Integrating the Science of Early Childhood Development. Jack P. Shonkoff and Deborah A. Phillips, eds. Board on Children, Youth, and Families, Commission of Behavioral and Social Sciences and Education. Washington, DC: National Academy Press.

Nelson, D., Howard, V. F., & McLaughlin, T. F. (1993). Empowering parents to become advocates for their own children with disabilities. *B. C. Journal of Special Education, 17*(1), 62–72.

Novella, S. (1996). Psychomotor patterning. *The Connecticut Skeptic, 1*(4), 6.

Nunez, R. C., & Collignon, K. (1997). Creating a community of learning for homeless children. *Educational Leadership,* 56–60.

O'Hare, W. P. (2001). *The child population: First data from the 2000 census.* The Annie E. Casey Foundation and The Population Reference Bureau.

Olmsted, P. P. (1992). Where did our diversity come from? *High/Scope ReSource, 11*(3), 4–9.

Orfield, G., Schley, S., Glass, D., & Reardon, S. (1994). The growth of segregation in American schools: Changing patterns of separation and poverty since 1968. *Equity and Excellence, 27*(1), 5–8.

Rounds, K. A., Weil, M., & Bishop, K. K. (1994). Practice with culturally diverse families of young children with disabilities. *Families in Society, 75,* 3–15.

Rueda, R., & Martinez, I. (1992). Fiesta Educativa: One community's approach to parent training in developmental disabilities for Latino families. *Journal of the Association for the Severely Handicapped, 17*(2), 95–103.

Russo, C. J., & Talbert-Johnson, C. (1997). The overrepresentation of African American children in special education: The resegregation of educational programming? *Education and Urban Society, 29*(2), 136–148.

Ryan, M. (August 30, 1992). "Who's Taking Care of the Children?" *Parade Magazine,* pp. 3–5.

Sass-Lehrer, M., & Bodner-Johnson, B. (1989). P. L. 99–457: A new challenge to early intervention. *American Annals of the Deaf, 134*(2), 71–77.

Schorr, L. B., & Both, D. (1991). Attributes of effective services for young children: A brief survey of current knowledge and its implications for program and policy development. In L. B. Schorr, D. Both, & C. Copple (Eds.), *Effective services for young children: Report of a workshop* (pp. 23–47), Washington, DC: National Academy.

Shackelford, J. (2002). State and jurisdictional eligibility definitions for infants and toddlers with disabilities under IDEA. *NECTAC Notes, 5,* 1–14.

Shelden, L. L., & Rush, D. D. (2001). The ten myths about providing early intervention services in natural environments. *Infants and Young Children, 14*(1), 1–13.

Shelton, D. L. (1998). Downward public health statistics show upbeat trends. *American Medical News, 41*(42), 35.

Skinner, B. F. (1953). *Science and human behavior.* New York: Macmillan.

Slavin, R. E. (1998). Can education reduce social inequity? *Educational Leadership, 55*(4), 6–10.

Smart, J. F., & Smart, D. W. (1997). The racial/ethnic demography of disability. *Journal of Rehabilitation, 63*(4): 9–15.

Smith, B. J. (2000). The federal role in early childhood special education policy in the next century: The responsibility of the individual. *Topics in Early Childhood Special Education, 20*(1), 7–13.

Smith, B. J., & Strain, P. S. (1998). Early childhood special education in the next decade: Implementing and expanding P. L. 99–457. *Topics in Early Childhood Special Education, 8*(1), 37–47.

Song, Y. and Lu, H. (2002). *Early childhood poverty: A statistical profile.* National Center for Children In Poverty. Retrieved July 25, 2002 from *http://cpmcnet.columbia.edu/dept/ nccp/ecp302.html*

Spodek, B., Saracho, O. N., & Lee, R. C. (1986). *Mainstreaming young children.* Newton, MA: Allyn & Bacon.

Taylor, R. (1998). Check your cultural competence. *Nursing Management, 29*(8), 30–32.

Thomson, E., Hanson, T. L., & McLanahan, S. S. (1994). Family structure and child well-being: Economic resources vs. parental behaviors. *Social Forces, 73*(1), 221–242.

Turnbull, A., & Turnbull, R. (1990). *Parents, professionals, and exceptionality.* Upper Saddle River, NJ: Merrill/Prentice Hall.

Turnbull, A., & Turnbull, R. (1997). *Parents, professionals, and exceptionality, A special partnership.* Upper Saddle River, NJ: Merrill/Prentice Hall.

U.S. Census Bureau (March, 2001). *Overview of race and Hispanic origin. Census Brief.* U.S. Department of Commerce.

U.S. Census Bureau (April, 2001). *Population Change and Distribution.Census Brief.* U.S. Department of Commerce.

U.S. Commission on Civil Rights. (2002). *Recommendations for the reauthorization of the Individuals with Disabilities Education Act.* Retrieved July 10, 2002 from *http://www.usccr.gov/pubs/idea/recs.htm*

U.S. Conference of Mayors. (1993). *A status report on hunger and homelessness in America's cities: A 26-city survey.* Washington, DC: Author.

Voydanoff, P. (1994). A family perspective on services integration. *Family Relations, 44,* 63–68.

Walther-Thomas, C., Korinek, L., McLaughlin, V., & Williams, B. (1996). Improving educational opportunities for students with disabilities who are homeless. *Journal of Children and Poverty, 2*(2), 57–75.

Wehrly, B. (1988). *Toward a multicultural partnership in higher education.* Macomb, IL: Western Illinois University. (ERIC Document Reproduction Service No. ED 308 731)

Wells, A. S. (1988). *Urban teacher recruitment programs.* New York: Columbia University, Institute for Urban and Minority Education. (ERIC Document Reproduction Service No. ED 312 318)

Wetzstein, C. (1998). Teen births decline. *Insight on the News, 14*(44), 40.

Whaley, D. L., & Malott, M. E. (1971). *Elementary principles of behavior* (2nd ed.). Upper Saddle River, NJ: Prentice Hall.

White, K., & Castro, G. (1985). An Integrative review of early intervention efficacy studies with at-risk children: Implications for the handicapped. *Analysis and Intervention in Developmental Disabilities, 5,* 7–31.

Williams, B. F. (1992). Changing demographics; Challenges for educators. *Intervention in Schools and Community, 27*(3), 157–163.

Williams, B. F. (Ed.). (2003). *Directions in early intervention and assessment.* Spokane, WA: Spokane Guilds' School.

Williams, B. T., & DeSander, M. K. (1999). Dueling legislation: The impact of incongruent federal statutes on homeless and other special-needs students. *Journal for a Just and Caring Education, 5*(1), 34–50.

Yanok, J., & Derubertis, D. (1989). Comparative study of parental participation in regular and special education programs. *Exceptional Children, 56,* 195–199.

Yell, M. L. (1995). Least restrictive environment, inclusion, and students with disabilities: A legal analysis. *Journal of Special Education, 28*(4), 389–415.

Zirkel, P. (1996). Inclusion: Return of the pendulum? *The Special Educator, 12*(9), 1, 5.

2 Early Childhood Services— Yesterday, Today, and Around the World

During the 30 or so years that I have been involved in child care research and administration, the field has been plagued with claims and counterclaims, praise and denunciation, acceptance and rejection. Even so, child care has come a long way. From an obscure service that most people had never heard of or thought about, it has risen to a position of national prominence and makes every list of key issues for the present and future of our nation and the world.

(Caldwell, 1997, p. 35)

The first organization of child-care providers was established in the United States in New York City just 30 years after this country declared its independence (Neugebauer, 1990). The history of organized services to very young children began much earlier and has evolved through a variety of forms to become what we know as day care, preschool, kindergarten, early intervention, and other names. By examining these roots and those of other cultures, we develop an informed perspective on where services to very young children have been and where they might be going. We also better understand and pay tribute to many caring individuals who sought to genuinely improve the quality of early childhood education.

A HISTORICAL PERSPECTIVE

This chapter explores the history of Western culture in terms of its beliefs about the rights of young children and their families and subsequent practices that have changed as those beliefs changed. Though it would seem to be egalitarian and therefore preferable to be global in this analysis, it is undeniable that Western civilization, because of worldwide colonization since the 16th century, has dominated the evolution of educational services provided in most parts of the world today (Woodill, 1992). Still, some examination of various cultural perspectives on raising and educating children, which have changed over time, gives insight into how cultures have attempted to solve both the economic and civil rights problems. Recently, theory and research in early childhood development and education have provided the blueprints for practices and policy. Many challenges remain, despite considerable accomplishments. As with most fields, progress is rarely linear, but as this chapter will reveal, there is much to celebrate.

THE HISTORY OF CHILDHOOD IN WESTERN CIVILIZATION

This text is sensitive to the ethnocentricity of describing the history of early childhood education from the viewpoint of Western culture. However, study of this discipline reveals that to know the history of European education (and in particular that of very young children) is to understand educational practices worldwide (Woodill, Bernhard, & Prochner, 1992). Western-style cultural infusion in early education has become the dominant global model.

Lloyd deMause (1974) described the history of childhood as a series of stages in which the concept of childhood in Western civilization evolved over the last 2,000 years (see Table 2–1).

Each stage was marked by great changes in society—changes in the way people were governed, changes in religious beliefs and customs, and changes in the way wealth was distributed (Day, 1983). In general, children in ancient times were treated with indifference, with no apparent conception of childhood as a distinct human experience. Not until the period from the 14th to the 17th century did

Table 2–1 A History of Childhood

Stages	Date	Problem	Solution
Stage 1: From Bad to Worse No apparent conception of childhood	To the 4th century A.D.: infanticide mode The 4th to 13th century: abandonment mode	Survival depends on pleasing the gods, controlling population, and maintaining a physically strong community	Eliminate extra mouths to feed, ensure that only the strongest are raised from childhood
Stage 2: Children Will Be Children The emergence of the idea of childhood as a special period	The 14th to 17th century: ambivalent mode	Rampant disease and hardship kill many young children	Remain detached from young children, have many but don't form bonds until they survive early childhood
Stage 3: Church and State Mix Parents begin to feel a responsibility for the soul of the child	The 18th century: intrusive mode	Everlasting salvation of the soul is highest priority, heavenly life beyond this earthly toil is the final reward	Provide an early education so that children can learn of god's redemption
Stage 4: Parents Know Best Parents become responsible for training the child; a recognition of independence	The 19th to the mid-20th century: socialization mode	Industrialization requires an increasing labor base; immigrant parents work long hours and neglect their children	Provide early childhood care and education to promote productive citizenship among children
Stage 5: Children Know Best Children know better than the parents what they need and involve parents in fulfilling those needs	The mid-20th century, current: helping mode	Resources are abundant enough that all people should have equal opportunity, including children	Provide early educational services to children who are poor or disabled

there emerge some notion that childhood was a special time. Even then, economic struggle and survival were so prominent that children tended to be treated with ambivalence and emotional distance.

In the 18th century, when Christian belief systems developed strongly, parents were expected to be responsible for the souls of their children, and thus formal education for children grew more important. During the 19th century and through the early part of the 20th century, the concept of childhood evolved to a point that parents were seen as responsible for training their children to be independent and to follow the rules and values of society.

**??BC –
1200 A.D.**
ABANDONMENT MODE

STAGE 1: FROM BAD TO WORSE

From ancient civilization until the 4th century A.D., many cultures of Western civilization were characterized by their struggles to survive. The solution to crises was often ritualistic sacrifice of children to supplicate the gods or abandonment of children to ensure the survival of the strongest or perhaps to control population density (Day, 1983).

Until well into the 4th century, children were also murdered in great numbers for nonreligious reasons. Cultures in Greece and Rome, among others, abandoned babies on hillsides to die, threw them into the sea or rivers to drown, and even entombed them in large pots. It is clear that children were not generally treated protectively or held in special regard.

Children who were born infirm, sickly, or premature were almost always destroyed. Political states like Sparta killed all but the most fit children in order to maintain strength in their society. Though infanticide became a punishable crime by the 4th century, the practice lingered in some places until the 18th and 19th centuries (deMause, 1974). In traditional patriarchal societies, the role of women was very different from that in today's Western culture. Women who protested or cried at the slaughter of their children were subjected to fines (Greenleaf, 1978). Perhaps if mothers had possessed more control over their own destinies they could have influenced the treatment of their children as well.

In ancient times, a child was considered to be an adult by age 7 (Gordon & Browne, 1993). Formal education of children began at about this same age, though Plato and Aristotle both spoke of the need to educate younger children. Greek education, and virtually all classical European schooling that followed this model, was provided for boys of wealthy families, while girls and children of working class families were trained for domestic work or trades (Gordon & Browne, 1993). A few insightful ancient Romans provided education at home beginning as soon as a child could talk; some even used systems of rewards for their children's educational gains (Hewes & Hartman, 1974).

The fall of the Roman Empire was followed by centuries of lawlessness and anarchy; people left their villages for the protection of a local baron or king, and formal schooling ceased to exist (Gordon & Browne, 1993). With no educational system to speak of, even members of the ruling class were seldom taught to write their names or to read. Only monastery schools were available, and these were open only to those entering the priesthood. In medieval times (5th through 13th centuries), childhood was viewed as a period beginning with birth and lasting just beyond infancy. Adults assumed that, in their natural state, children were basically evil and needed to be directed, punished, and corrected in order to learn to follow social rules. Youth were expected to take up the responsibilities of adulthood as quickly as possible, learning the necessary skills of a trade mostly through their parents or through apprenticeship. Survival was the primary goal.

Excerpts from the Domostroi (Excerpts, 2002) written in the mid-16th century, illustrate this prevailing sentiment well:

How to Teach Children and Save Them Through Fear

Punish your son in his youth, and he will give you a quiet old age, and restfulness to your soul. Weaken not beating the boy, for he will not die from your striking him with the rod, but will be in better health: for while you strike his body, you save his soul from death. If you love your son, punish him frequently, that you may rejoice later. Chide your son in his childhood and you will be glad in his manhood, and you will boast among evil persons and your enemies will be envious. Bring up your child with much prohibition and you will have peace and blessing from him. Do not smile at him, or play with him, for though that will diminish your grief while he is a child, it will increase it when he is older, and you will cause much bitterness to your soul. Give him no power in his youth, but crush his ribs while he is growing and does not in his willfulness obey you, lest there be an aggravation and suffering to your soul, a loss to your house, destruction to your property, scorn from your neighbours and ridicule from your enemies, and cost and worriment from the authorities.

STAGE 2: CHILDREN WILL BE CHILDREN

1200 – 1600 A.D.
AMBIVALENT MODE

Well into the 17th century, children were commonly beaten, sexually abused, sold into slavery, and abandoned. Even children who were valued by their families were commonly sent away from home to be raised by wet nurses or other families. It was clear that parents were generally ambivalent toward their children.

It could be that the lack of attachment was a psychological survival technique. The rate of infant mortality was so high that more young children were lost to illness or injury than survived childhood. Consequently, it was common practice to have many children in order to ensure that a few children would live. For many years, there were no pictures made of young children, nor were formal names given until children had passed the toddler stage.

The shift to a more compassionate approach to childhood began in French cities among more affluent families. The gentry of France found enjoyment and amusement in their children. Philosophers began to theorize about the effect that adult care and nurturance could have on the well-being of children. At the same time, Christian beliefs were spreading, and people began to think about the immortality of a child's soul.

In 1658, Comenius, a Czech educator, wrote *Orbis Pictus* (The World of Pictures), the first picture book for children (Gordon & Browne, 1993). The book was a guide for teachers and emphasized sensory awareness and the study of nature. Comenius believed that education should follow the natural order of things, and he referred to the "school of the mother's lap." His ideas were later reflected in Montessori's and Piaget's theories of the stages of development.

As an English philosopher of the 1600s, John Locke theorized that children are born neutral, rather than evil, and possess a moral and behavioral "clean slate," or *tabula rasa,* to be written upon by parents, society, education, and the world (Gordon & Browne, 1993). He was one of the first Europeans to promote the idea of taking the individual learner into account when planning instruction and evaluating progress. Locke recommended pleasant instruction in business and the Bible. Though Locke's influence was minimal during his life, his ideas were later refined and popularized by Rousseau (Gordon & Browne, 1993).

In 1647, the Massachusetts Bay Colony enacted a law by which all communities of 50 households had to hire a teacher and open a school. If a community had more than 100 families, a Latin grammar school was required. There was no political or moral separation of Christian churches and Christian schools at this time. Indeed, the principle purpose of education was to teach children to read in order to understand the Bible and to study Christian doctrine.

Early life in New England was difficult and, though conditions had improved over the medieval period, as many as 60% to 70% of children under age 4 died in colonial towns during the "starving season" (Gordon & Browne, 1993). Puritan families showed little overt affection, and children were seen as important economic tools, working the land and apprenticed into trades early (Gordon & Browne, 1993). Discipline was harsh, and children were expected to obey without question.

By the beginning of the 1700s, most towns provided schooling. However, formal education was still considered unnecessary for children under the age of 6 or 7 years. It was the general belief that young children should stay in the care of their mothers until middle childhood.

The charity school movement began in England in 1698 (Cahan, 1989). It was one of the earliest attempts to educate poor children through an organized community effort. The charity school movement was intended to combat social problems, including the decay of religion and the rise of ignorance among the poor. Children were to be educated for the honor of God and also to learn to be content with their rank and station in society. Similar schools spread throughout the rest of Great Britain and Europe.

STAGE 3: CHURCH AND STATE MIX

1600 – 1700 A.D.

INTRUSIVE MODE

By the mid-1700s, there was a realization that childhood was developmentally connected to adulthood (Day, 1983). This encouraged consideration of childrearing practices, and society began to place value on disciplined activity and tasks that would foster an appropriate spirit, a fear of God, and a respect for elders. Puritan beliefs supported the idea that children possessed souls that could be saved through devotion to God. Hence, it was expected that parents ensure the education of their children so the children could begin their studies of Christian doctrine early in life. Moral and spiritual goodness were often inspired with the birch whip; children were thrashed to drive out evil spirits and to ensure their well-being (Day, 1983; deMause, 1974).

Such beliefs continued in some Christian communities. More than a hundred years later, John Wesley still warned against indulgence in one of his sermons on child rearing (Wesley, 1872 edition):

> To let them take their own way, is the sure method of increasing their self-will sevenfold. . . . To humour children is, as far was in us lies, to make their disease incurable. A wise parent, on the other hand, should begin to break their will the first moment it appears. In the whole area of Christian education there is nothing more important than this. The will of the parent is to a little child in the place of the will of God. Therefore studiously teach them to submit to this while they are children, that they may be ready to submit to his will when they are men. . . . you must never intermit your attention for one hour; otherwise you lose your labour.

Providing an altogether different view of education, the French scholar Rousseau (1712–1778) became an outspoken champion for children. Rousseau departed from the view that children were simply miniature adults (Williams,

1992). In his book, *Emile,* in which he raised a hypothetical child to adulthood, Rousseau argued that children should be treated with gentle care early in life and that play and childhood experiences contributed to learning (Day, 1983; Gordon & Browne, 1993; Rousseau, 1969). Rousseau dismissed the idea that children were inherently evil, concluding, on the contrary, that they were naturally good (Gordon & Browne, 1993). The importance of beginning a child's education at birth and treating children with sympathy and compassion was stressed, providing the philosophical basis for early childhood education (Cook, Tessier, & Klein, 1992). He stood against harsh, physical punishment of children and also against education that stressed memorization and recitation. Like others, however, Rousseau was considered a radical by his contemporaries, and his ideas had little impact on educational practices during his life.

Still, by the late 1700s, several authors extolled similarly humane ways to educate children. For example, Johann "Papa" Pestalozzi, an Italian-Swiss school teacher, formulated his theory regarding children's ability to learn through self-discovery (Cook et al., 1992). He felt that education should be consistent with the natural development of children, that mothers were the best teachers for very young children, and that the home should be the basic model for teaching and learning. Pestalozzi's ideas were much like Rousseau's, though he was more pragmatic and included principles on how to teach basic skills and the concept of caring for, as well as educating, children (Gordon & Browne, 1993).

Pestalozzi founded the first European school to acknowledge the developmental characteristics of children (Williams, 1992). "Papa" Pestalozzi prescribed parental guidance, strong morality and work ethic, and high-intensity work training (Pestalozzi, 1915; Williams, 1992). It was Pestalozzi who coined the phrase, "education should be of the hand, the head, and the heart of the child" (Gordon & Browne, 1993). His humane attitude was a source of present day philosophy in special education where caregivers focus on unique characteristics of children in planning and conducting educational programs.

In 1799, Jean-Marc Itard undertook the first documented efforts to educate a child with special needs (Day, 1983; Itard, 1962). A child, approximately 12 years old, was found living in isolation in the forest near Aveyron, France. Victor, labeled the "Wild Boy of Aveyron," was thought to have been raised by animals, and was described as an "incurable idiot." Itard undertook the task of humanizing the boy, and though claiming failure, Itard's methods showed that specialized instruction could improve the abilities of children with significant developmental delays.

By the early 1800s, the Industrial Revolution had transformed much of Europe (Cahan, 1989). Working class families were increasingly crowded into urban areas, and their infants died in alarming numbers. Infant schools were created to protect poor young children and to encourage good character formation while allowing adults to labor in the factories. Robert Owen, a utopian socialist, defined the scope of his infant schools:

> . . . the Institution has been devised to afford the means of receiving your children at an early age, as soon almost as they can walk. By this means many of you, mothers of families, will be enabled to earn a better maintenance or support for your children; you will have less care and anxiety about them; while the children will be prevented from acquiring any bad habits, and gradually prepared to learn the best. (cited in Cahan, 1989, p. 9)

Case Study

LIVING NATURALLY: INTERVIEW WITH DAVID DEWOLF

It's an important thing for our teachers to recognize the need for disabled children to have natural lives and not to be pushed too hard too early. From my perspective, one of the mistakes that you can make is to try so hard to overcome the disability that you push too hard. A parent or a professional can become a little bit like the doctor whose job it is to fight sickness. The doctor views the disease as an enemy and as sort of a matter of pride, decides he is not going to let this thing take his patient. The doctor uses all his ingenuity and energy to figure out ways to beat the disease.

In dealing with children with disabilities, it is healthy and appropriate to try to ameliorate the effects. Perhaps if the child has a hearing impairment one thinks, "How can I provide a hearing aid?" or, "What new technology or breakthroughs in terms of electronics or whatever can I offer that will compensate and allow the child as normal an experience as possible?"

I think, particularly for kids with a learning disability or a cognitive disability like Down syndrome, there is an impulse to accelerate the educational process, as though you saw a hill coming up ahead of you and you jammed on the accelerator to get up enough momentum so when you get to the hill your momentum will kind of carry you over the top before you've lost your steam. I think some of that is a good idea, but if you're not careful, you can make the child's academic accomplishments overshadow their right to be a child.

Children with disabilities ought to be able to kind of go at their own speed, at their own rate in what feels good to them in the same way that children without disabilities are allowed to develop whatever talents and abilities they have. That's a difficult balance to strike. I think it's the same balance you have to strike with a normal child. Do I teach my kid to play the violin at the age of 4? Suppose I have a tradition in my family of violin players, can I pass that along to my child at the age of 4 by encouraging him and keeping at him to do this because of the great benefit that I see at the end of the process? He may resent it now, but he'll thank me for it later when they can see the fruits of all this effort. On the other hand, I can sit back and say, if he wants to, that's great, but I'm not going to push it on him. I think many of the same dynamics are present with a kid who has a disability.

The most important thing is to be sure that what you're doing is really for the child's benefit rather than for your own psychological benefit. I think that parents who have kids with disabilities are subject to the same kind of competitive streak as everybody else. Some parents want their kid to make the varsity team because it will help them get ahead. We're similarly tempted to think well, maybe most kids with this condition can only sit there and babble, but by golly, my kid is going to be able to recite the alphabet. That's not all bad, the ambitions that you have for your children to help them achieve, that's part of the reasons that kids do achieve.

But, I think you have to take stock of it periodically to say, is this really for my ego gratification or is this really because I think my child will genuinely be better for this? Also, it is very important to avoid a denial process. Just like the doctor who appropriately enough is engaged in the fight against disease and death, you can kid yourself into thinking that if you just work hard enough and do enough research in the lab you can beat it.

There is a risk that you get so infatuated with all of the compensatory mechanisms that you think if you just work hard enough and are a devoted enough parent, you can compensate for the disability so that your kid will be just like everybody else. I think that people who work with parents have to be prepared for the parent who won't allow any discussion of the child's limitations, as though it were a kind of sabotage or disloyalty if you ever suggested that something less than normal milestones was acceptable.

In the same way, the doctor occasionally has to tell the patient, "I'm sorry, but there's nothing more we can do for your father [child or husband]." There are times, I think, when you have to say, "Your child is only going to be able to do this and that's just because of the condition that he has." There was a time in which people had unrealistically low expectations of children with Down syndrome. They just wanted to warehouse these kids, or get rid of them. Children with Down syndrome were denied basic opportunities to prove what they could do. So it has become unfashionable to speak discouraging words, to say, "Hey, because your kid has this condition, this is all you should expect."

I think now there is more risk of denial. Both parents and the people who work with children who have disabilities need to accept the fact that their efforts—as worthy as they may be—may be unsuccessful, or may prove to be disappointing. They need to understand that you don't have to win this. I think it is particularly important to communicate to the child that whatever they do is acceptable. Just as the parent who wants his kid to play the violin can subconsciously—or not even subconsciously, but overtly—communicate to the kid, "Hey, if you don't do this, if you can't make the varsity team, or accomplish this particular thing which I think is so important, well, you're not really a member of this family, or you're not really worth much, or you must not be trying hard enough." A child with wonderful gifts can be destroyed by the fact that the gifts they have don't measure up to some parent's arbitrary idea of what it is to be a great kid.

Parents who want their kids to be normal have to watch that they don't place such high expecta-

Robin DeWolf.

tions on their child, that the child is taught in essence "I'm only good to the extent that I outperform my disability expectations." If I'm just a normal handicapped kid, then it's not good enough. I suppose that's a form of equal treatment for parents who push their other kids to be extraordinary. Some parents want their kid with a disability to be extraordinary too. Just as a matter of parenting style, I think that parents have to be gently helped to accept their kids for who they are.

Teachers and other people who work with these kids can help parents see their children through fresh eyes. Parents of both normal kids and kids with disabilities get stuck with their own perceptions. They don't see their kids the way

(continued)

other people see them, and sometimes it's very important for the teacher to say, "Gee, here's the way this kid looks to me, here's the way I perceive him or her. Maybe you're stuck on something here that doesn't really fit." No parent likes to hear that. Those are tough words to speak to any parent, but I think you can do it if you really care about the child, and if you establish some credibility with the parent. You can do it in a subtle and nonjudgmental way, and if you can help the parent get a fresh perspective, that's one of the most important things that I think that a teacher can do.

There's nothing wrong with the impulse to "save" a child; it's just that it has to take place within a context of acceptance. Life is limited and we can't have all we want all the time. A disability is a forced example of learning to accept what you're given rather than always thinking that life's going to be a series of pleasant experiences.

The first early childhood teachers in America ran "dame schools." These 17th- and 18th-century "schools" have only recently been researched, as feminist historians have studied the journals and diaries of women who ran the schools (Wyman, 1995). To make ends meet, widowed or young unmarried women held school for very young children in their homes. According to Wyman (1995), dame schools provided a transitional education to students whose mothers had too many children to care for, too many tasks, or too little time. Though no curriculum was available for children of any age, preschoolers at the dame schools were often taught fine motor skills, sewing, knitting, bread making, and rhyming songs. Because the Bible was typically the only reading material available, children learned to read from this text, mostly through rote recitation. It is interesting to note that dame teachers, because they were female, were rarely permitted to attend school themselves after completing their education in a dame school. Therefore, the academic skills taught in dame schools were rudimentary.

1800 – 1950 A.D.

SOCIALIZATION MODE

STAGE 4: PARENTS KNOW BEST

By the 19th century, the American and French revolutions had changed the way Western society thought about human rights. It was believed the common person should expect freedom, and concerns were gradually raised about paternalistic treatment of women, children, peasants, and the infirm, who were often treated as property (Day, 1983). Slavery, child labor, and harsh punishment were now considered inhumane. There was movement toward social reform and new voices encouraged parents to raise their children to live self-determined and productive lives. Ellen G. White (2002) articulated this well in her essay on discipline:

The object of discipline is the training of the child for self-government. He should be taught self-reliance and self-control. Therefore as soon as he is capable of understanding, his reason should be enlisted on the side of obedience. . . . Children and youth are benefited by being trusted. Many, even of the little children, have a high sense of honour; all desire to be treated with confidence and respect, and this is their right . . . Lead the youth to feel that they are trusted, and there are few who will not seek to prove themselves worthy of the trust.

Like their European counterparts, American cities were becoming more industrial and great numbers of immigrants flocked to this country to seek a better life. Rapidly growing cities were heavily populated with foreigners who could barely scratch out an existence. The cities teemed with children whose parents had little time for child-rearing activities. Still, parents were expected to guide their children to good citizenship; children were viewed as the product of parents' competence and attention. Yet, a growing conviction that the government should intervene in raising the neglected children of immigrants was fueled by an inspired movement to maintain cultural integrity (Day, 1983).

Child-care centers and public schools developed in response to the needs of working families. By 1828, the Boston Infant School was established as a service to working mothers. The school cared for children from 18 months to 4 years of age. It was open for 13 hours daily in the summer and for 9 hours daily in the winter to accommodate work schedules (Day, 1983). Some historians point to the early infant schools as the first American attempt to establish poverty track educational institutions in the belief that lower income families were incapable of properly socializing their children (Cahan, 1989). Following the lead of European infant schools, these institutions were used as a means to teach morality to the children of poverty. As articulated by the Infant School Society of Boston (cited in Cahan, 1989), the children "would be removed from the unhappy association of want and vice, and be placed under better influences . . ." (p. 11).

Not long after their establishment, the American tide turned against the infant school movement, and the child's home was deemed the most appropriate environment for early development and the child's mother the best teacher (Cahan, 1989). Educators argued that the bond between a mother and her child was weakened by spending a great deal of the day away from home. Some went so far as to claim that early mental stimulation would cause physical illness and even insanity. Donations that supported infant schools diminished. Curiously, at about the same time, day nurseries and kindergartens flourished, taking up where infant schools left off, serving the working poor and more affluent families, respectively.

The quality of day nurseries varied widely, though they were typically intended to be simple, quiet, and clean settings for children during the day (Cahan, 1989). Some offered employment services for mothers to encourage work rather than charity. Most fed children three meals a day, though they were commonly meager offerings. One matron might cook, clean and supervise as many as 30 to 50 preschool children. It should be noted that day nurseries were a form of social welfare that helped keep children out of institutions and families intact (Cahan, 1989). Like other forms of social welfare at the time, African Americans were virtually excluded. Therefore, leaders in the African American communities established their own orphanages, old folks' homes, day nurseries, and kindergartens.

In 1837, the German educator Froebel created kindergartens (literally translated as "children's garden") and the early childhood education model quickly spread throughout the world (Day, 1983; Froebel, 1895). Froebel had studied with Pestalozzi, and though he agreed that play should be the medium for children's learning, he altered Pestalozzi's theory to encompass the "self-actualization" of children as a legitimate goal of early childhood (Williams, 1992). Consistent with his desire to build a moral society, Froebel idealistically assumed the potential for perfection in each child. Froebel felt the role of the teacher was to bring a child's inborn capabilities to fruition. He emphasized the use of manipulatives and introduced handiwork projects for children (Williams, 1992).

Froebel started his German kindergarten with children age 2 to 6 years, focusing on self-directed activities, self-esteem, and self-confidence. Kindergarteners were encouraged to play in school, had toys as learning tools, and were educated by trained teachers who joined in the games with playful attitudes (Gordon & Browne, 1993). Furthermore, Froebel pushed the radical idea that both men and women should teach young children by being friendly facilitators rather than stern disciplinarians. "Play is the highest phase of child development—the representation of the inner necessity and impulse." (In Froebel's 1826 *Education of Man* [Gordon & Browne, 1993].)

Unfortunately, at the time of his death in 1852, Froebel's methods were still being developed, leaving no written guide to explain his ideas (Gordon & Browne, 1993).

Kindergarten in the United States

In 1856, Margaretha Schurz, a German emigrant who had studied under Froebel, opened the first kindergarten in the United States for German-speaking children (Gordon & Browne, 1993). It was Schurz's inspiration that led Elizabeth Palmer Peabody to open Boston's first kindergarten for English-speaking children in 1860.

Early kindergartens for children age 3 and older were intended to supplement nurturance in the home environment. The goals of these early programs were moral and social growth for children. Women were hired to assist as both teachers and mother-surrogates, even though teaching had traditionally been a male-dominated profession before this time. By now, society had embraced the need for kindergartens, and as with other forms of early education, it was affluent families who were the first able to take advantage of these services (Cook et al., 1992). However, because Froebel's underlying philosophy was poorly translated from German to English, most American kindergartens were quite different from what Froebel had intended, and few maintained a spirit of joyous play (Gordon & Browne, 1993).

Social Reform

Following the American Civil War, the view that parents were obligated to provide good child rearing was strong enough that parent manuals were developed to outline a family's responsibilities to its children. There was an increasing emphasis on safe custodial care that could meet children's nutritional, physical, and health needs. Day-care services expanded rapidly with the support of philanthropic women and carried on the philosophy of social reform for poor or neglected children that had begun with the charity schools (Day, 1983). The growth of kindergartens from 1880 to 1900 was phenomenal. Free kindergartens were established in Boston in 1877, and St. Louis superintendent William Harris (influenced by Elizabeth Peabody) established public-school kindergartens districtwide before going on to serve as United States commissioner of Education from 1889 to 1906. As commissioner, Harris continued to advocate for public funding of kindergartens.

Every dollar spent at the Nursery means from one to three dollars earned by the mother while her little one is in our care. But that is not all. Every mother receives her child at night happy, clean and in excellent physical condition. The influence toward cleanliness and thrift is strong, and every mother has felt it. (From the 1888 *Second Annual Report of the South Side Day Nursery,* St. Louis, Missouri [Neugebauer, 1990, p. 6])

A parallel but independent movement among African American women turned particular attention to day nurseries and kindergartens (Cahan, 1989). Because of prevailing racial segregation of the times, few nurseries in the Northeast would accept African American children. African American women trained in churches and clubs established their own day nurseries to serve poor African American families.

In the United States, the 1890s were known as the "progressive era" and in some ways served as a turning point for early childhood education. There was a growing national concern for the means by which the poor and immigrants living in cities were forced to exist. Considerable efforts were made to enact child labor laws, establish clean milk distribution centers, and provide for the nurturance of children whose parents needed to work. Kindergartens became an instrument of social reform. These early childhood programs became known as charity kindergartens and included a day-care function (Gordon & Browne, 1993).

To teach morality and social order was considered good, but there was also a systematic movement away from early Puritanical (community-serving) motives to more benevolent child-centered motives. All were with the same purpose, to give children the best chance for success in society. At the same time, it was generally recognized that some people had greater knowledge and expertise in child development than others.

G. Stanley Hall began the American Child Study Movement, and though he was criticized by his peers, other child advocates and psychologists soon added to the momentum (Day, 1983; Williams, 1992). In 1892, *Children's Rights* was published by Kate Douglas Wiggen; in it she pressed for children's freedom. About the same time, William James, a noted psychologist, argued (like those before him) that children must be active participants in their education process. John Dewey echoed James as an advocate for school reform, insisting that children needed to be actively engaged in order to learn. Dewey emphasized children's direct experience with the natural world and the goal of socializing children as builders of social order and democracy. He believed children should be trained as social beings and should participate in role playing and problem solving that might prepare them to handle societal problems as adults (Gordon & Browne, 1993; Williams, 1992).

By the early 1900s, there was almost universal acknowledgment that some form of education for 3- to 5-year-olds was beneficial. Many nursery schools and daycare programs were created, and kindergartens underwent a second evolution. Kindergarten proponents diverged into two groups. Patty Smith Hill, a student and later a colleague of Dewey at Teachers College, Columbia University, was a prominent leader of the Progressive Movement, which emphasized child-oriented rather than regimented kindergarten curricula (Gordon & Browne, 1993). (Patty Smith Hill wrote the song "Happy Birthday" and founded the National Association for Nursery Education, now known as the National Association for the Education of

Young Children.) She infused new ideas in the kindergarten model, such as scheduling free play, providing larger blocks, introducing dolls and doll houses, and giving more freedom for creative play. She also introduced the use of workbenches and tools, as well as curricula for music and dance. By 1925, kindergarten had been transformed. Practical curricula were now more concerned with conformity than morality—a class-related value system was substituted for universal values, and an emphasis was placed on punctuality, cleanliness, responsibility, and sharing.

Patty Smith Hill also promoted nursery schools for children too young for kindergarten and maintained Froebel's belief that young children should learn by doing in a nurturing environment (Gordon & Browne, 1993). Today, teachers in centers and homes across the country practice the belief that early education should be a garden where adults plant ideas and materials for children to use as they grow at their own pace (Gordon & Browne, 1993). Over 90% of the eligible population in the United States now attends kindergarten. For all practical purposes, kindergarten is a universal educational practice in the United States (Warger, 1988).

Yet, some critics continued to insist that the time children spent away from home contributed to the decline of family life (Cahan, 1989). Even Jane Addams, who had spent many years sponsoring a day nursery at Hull House to care for the children of working mothers, became disillusioned (Cahan, 1989). She wondered if the provision of such a service tempted mothers to "attempt the impossible." It was pointed out that mothers were not only working away from home during the day, but also spending their nights cleaning, mending, ironing, and more; "overwork is slowly killing the mother" (p. 18).

The Advent of Child Psychology

In the early 1900s there was a growth of child psychology, as many scholars emerged with advice regarding child-rearing and educational practices. In 1907, Maria Montessori, the first female physician in Italy and a noted educator, opened the *Casa De Bambini* for children of lower income, working class, Roman citizens (Gordon & Browne, 1993). She had been commissioned by the Italian government to serve the educational needs of children living in the tenements. Children from age 3 attended for 6 to 8 hours each day. The purpose of the preschool was to prepare children for common school and to train them in self-care. Many of the children were labeled mentally retarded, though Montessori sensed that they really lacked proper motivation and environment (Gordon & Browne, 1993).

Montessori believed that education begins at birth and that the early years are the most important for fostering intellectual and social development. She hypothesized what she called "sensitive periods," in which children's natural curiosity makes them especially ready to acquire certain skills and knowledge (Gordon & Browne, 1993). Montessori also believed that any task could be reduced to a series of small steps suitable for a child's learning. Therefore, she developed materials graded in difficulty and emphasizing self-help skills. She emphasized a "prepared environment," meaning that by purposefully engineering the resources and materials available in a classroom, children could be encouraged to explore certain materials and to engage in activities specifically intended to foster problem solving and concept formation. She also designed materials, classrooms, and a teaching procedure to prove her points (Gordon & Browne, 1993).

Montessori's curriculum had three major components:

1. *Exercises in practical life*—hygiene, care of clothing and living space, and skills for self-management.
2. *Sensorial experiences*—didactic materials that would instruct children, such as stacking blocks, series of rods, and wooden cylinders.
3. *Language development*—training on articulation, dialect, and precision in usage. (Montessori, 1964)

From 1910 to 1915, Montessori gathered attention in the United States, but her methods were criticized by progressive educators as too rigid and constraining. Her work was seemingly forgotten, until interest in Montessori's methods reemerged in the early 1960s. Now, this scholar and teacher should be viewed as one of the most influential child psychologists of the 20th century.

In 1914, behavioral psychologists Watson and Thorndike introduced the idea that child development resulted almost entirely from environmental influence (Thorndike, 1913; Watson, 1914). They were convinced that heredity was an inadequate and misleading explanation of human behavior. Thorndike explained that habits were formed by conditioning in which appropriate behavior was rewarded and unwanted behavior stopped because it was either no longer reinforced or was punished (Day, 1983). John Watson emphasized the contribution of specific environmental influences, proposing that parents could make of their children what they wished (Cook et al., 1992). B. F. Skinner, who was the intellectual force behind behavior analysis, proposed a natural science approach to human behavior, moving it away from its early mechanistic focus (Pierce & Epling, 1995). Skinner outlined his theory of operant behavior, discussing basic operant principles and their application to human behavior. He addressed self-control, thinking, the self, and social behaviors. Applied behavior analysis extended the application of behavioral principles to socially important problems. Today, behavioral psychology offers a vast array of effective procedures for the education and training of young children.

Gesell, a developmental psychologist, wrote *The Preschool Child* in 1923. In it, he too emphasized the importance of the early years. Gesell stated that the preschool period "is biologically the most important period in the development of an individual for the simple but sufficient reason that it comes first in a dynamic sequence; it inevitably influences all subsequent development." He created a normative developmental approach based on keen observation of children at various ages. However, Gesell warned that his "ages and stages" concept could not be interpreted too literally. His norms were not rigid prescriptions, but rather indices of behavior likely to occur (Cook et al., 1992).

Day Care. Throughout the early 1900s, day cares were considered a component of social welfare and were designed to serve "pathological" families who were incapable of providing proper care for their children. Day care was offered selectively and restrictively to families in hardship and was seen as temporary assistance until families could care for their own children.

*Young children
in day care.*

During the Great Depression, the demand for jobs was considerable, and the federal government provided Works Progress Administration (WPA) nursery schools, which hired unemployed teachers, custodians, cooks, and nurses in the United States (Gordon & Browne, 1993). Six million dollars was earmarked for nursery schools, with the primary intention to provide work to unemployed adults (Cahan, 1989). The objective of serving needy young children was only secondary to creating jobs. Any child between the ages of 2 and 5 whose family was on relief was eligible to attend an emergency nursery school. In 1937, there were 1900 WPA day cares serving 40,000 children in the United States; however, this was a fraction of the 10 million preschoolers with unemployed fathers (Cahan, 1989). These schools were generally not progressive nursery schools; they were poverty track institutions designed to provide sustenance to impoverished children during hard times of economic crisis (Cahan, 1989).

When World War II started, the number of working women increased by more than 50% to a total of more than 6 million (Cahan, 1989). As the country became dependent on women to support the war effort at home, absenteeism and job turnover became significant problems (a great deal of absenteeism was due to the need to supervise infant and school age children). The 1941 Lanham Act (Community Facilities Act) gave communities funds to provide support for the war effort; by 1942, the Lanham Act was interpreted to include funding for day care. By 1945, government-funded day care was being provided for 1.5 million children across the United States. Unlike previous programs, child enrollment was based solely on whether the mothers were employed, not on the presence of family pathology. Still, because of child care's long, stigmatizing association with welfare relief, as few as

5% of women placed their children in these nursery schools; most made arrangements with relatives or neighbors to care for their children (Cahan, 1989).

Sadly, Lanham funds were withdrawn in 1946 when the war ended, and the schools were either turned over to the states or closed (Gordon & Browne, 1993). This decision reflected the government's ambivalence about providing child care (Cahan, 1989). A return to normalcy was sought after the war; mothers returned home from work and fathers returned from war. Protest against the curtailment of child-care services was sufficient to convince President Harry Truman to extend federal money for child care, but only for a few more months as local communities were encouraged to take over this responsibility. Even so, group child care remained mostly unpopular with the public, a position that was strengthened when Dr. Benjamin Spock, a well-known pediatrician, urged mothers to give up employment to spend the preschool years at home with their children (Cahan, 1989).

Europe emerged from the rubble of the Second World War to rebuild its communities. In Italy, mothers in the village of Reggio Emilia teamed with a young teacher named Loris Malaguzzi to build a school for young children. They believed that all children had a natural ability to learn about their world and that the teacher's job was to help them explore their ideas in a myriad of ways, including art, drama, and music. The approach featured community commitment, supportive, amiable relationships, preparation of the environment for learning, an emphasis on art, project-based curriculum, collaboration, multiple languages of intelligence, and documentation of conceptual development (Abramson, Robinson, & Ankenman, 1995). Babies napped in floor-level "nests" so they could crawl out and explore when they awakened. Preschoolers spent weeks on projects, producing artwork and analytical thinking to solve problems they had chosen for themselves.

The Reggio preschools were later taken over by the government in the 1960s and expanded to include infant-toddler centers in the 1970s. By the 1980s, the rest of the world was taking notice and incorporating these ideas (Edwards, Gandini, & Foreman, 1993).

CLOSE-UP

THE BEST DAY CARE THERE EVER WAS

The "best day care that ever was" arose in response to the urgent need to meet production requirements during World War II. In 1943, in Portland, Oregon, 25,000 women were employed to carry out a massive undertaking: the production of tankers and cargo ships desperately needed for the war in Asia. These massive ships were completed, from start to finish, in an unbelievable 4 days in shipyards that operated day and night, 7 days a week. Five thousand women, working as welders, secretaries, chippers, and burners, were mothers who required day care for their children.

Hence, Edgar Kaiser, general manager of the yards, set about building the finest facilities for a child-care program. Mr. Kaiser began by hiring the best architects to design two children's centers which would each serve 1,125 children a day and would be open 24 hours a day, 364 days a year. The buildings were huge, with round wheel-like plans containing 15 large rooms in the spokes and a protected playground at the central hub. Classrooms were placed at the plant entrances so that every worker passed by and mothers could drop their children off in the most convenient way.

Kaiser hired only the best professionals—teachers with degrees in child development and 3 or more years' experience. The educators were recruited from every major teacher-training institution in the country. When Kaiser learned what the going pay rate was for nursery-school work, he exploded, "You can't pay college graduates that!" The pay was raised to match that of other shipyard workers. One hundred teachers, 6 group supervisors, 10 nurses, 5 nutritionists, and 2 family consultants formed an astonishing concentration of experts in child care.

The classrooms were large and each had storage space and a bathroom with child-sized sinks and toilets. Windows on two sides gave the children views of the shipyards. Two bathtubs were added, high enough that adults did not have to bend over and big enough for children to splash and play in the water. The rooms were filled with carloads of nonbreakable juice glasses, self-feed bibs, cots, sheets, blocks, puzzles, easels, and play equipment.

Kaiser's day-care centers were designed for the needs of working mothers. Each child went through a health test every morning before being admitted. Children who were mildly sick attended an infirmary where nurses and a consulting pediatrician took care of the children in isolated class cubicles and infirmary teachers provided quiet bed play. The nurses also immunized the children. Three meals and two snacks were provided each day, and the chief nutritionist sent parents a weekly list of meals served and suggestions for additional food to complete an adequate day's diet. Also helpful was the Home Service Food, precooked and packaged meals mothers could purchase and pick up at the center's kitchen.

The centers cared for children from 18 months to 6 years of age and expanded services for school-age children to after school, on Saturdays, and during summer vacations. A commissary provided necessary items like toothbrushes and shoelaces. For a short while, a Lending Service was also in operation and parents could borrow children's books from the center's library. As James Hymes, Jr., the on-site manager put it, "We thought that anything that saved the working [mother] her time and energy meant she would have more to give to her child."

The Kaiser Centers were in operation for only 2 years, closing in 1945 when the war in the Pacific was winding down. When the staff separated, they hoped their work would provide a model for excellent day-care programs, but the Kaiser Centers were never to be replicated. Though the Kaiser Centers demonstrated that day care could be good for children and mothers, it took a special set of circumstances to bring about full support for working mothers.

Source: "The Best Day Care There Ever Was," by C. Zinsser, 1984, October, *Working Mother*, pp. 76–78.

1950 – 2000 A.D.
HELPING MODE

STAGE 5: CHILDREN KNOW BEST

In the mid-20th century, new psychological theories regarding childhood became popular in the United States. Freud's psychotherapy concentrated on the affective development of individuals and its connection to early childhood experiences. This view revived a pessimistic attitude toward childhood that had been dormant since the 1700s. According to Freud, childhood was ambiguous, incoherent, and filled with conflict (Freud, 1953). Freud advocated parental permissiveness in order to free children of possible causes of conflict and subsequent neuroses (Cook et al., 1992).

Early childhood education was seen as critical to the social and emotional development of children (Day, 1983).

It was also during the 1950s that Jean Piaget's work became popular in America. Providing an antidote to Freud's pessimism, Piaget proposed that children have an inborn tendency toward adaptation and that through their encounters with the environment they develop categories of knowledge that are remarkably similar among all humans. Piaget, a cognitive psychologist, suggested the purpose of education should be to provide opportunities that allow children to combine experiences into coherent cognitive systems constituting knowledge. He insisted children are active learners and initiators and should direct their own play and learning. The Perry Preschool Project, developed in the late 1950s in Ypsilanti, Michigan, is the most notable Piagetian (cognitive) program (Cook et al., 1992). However, there is no doubt that Piaget's observations of young children, their translation to theory, and subsequent recommendations for practitioners are the most significant influence of this century on early childhood education policy and practices.

Poverty and Child Development

Similar to efforts at the turn of the century to address issues of parental neglect, an interest in poverty and its effect on child development reemerged in the 1950s. During the 1950s, the term "cultural deprivation" was coined. This theory assumed that poor children suffered from a dearth of experiences necessary to meet the demands of a complex and changing world (Day, 1983). A subsequent revolution in early education occurred in the United States, as curricula were specifically designed for the enrichment of poor children. In 1962, the Baltimore Early Admissions project established preschool programs in public schools explicitly for poor children (Day, 1983). In the same year, the New York City schools arranged an experimental enrichment program for preschool-aged children in three Harlem schools (Day, 1983).

Such remedial efforts were bolstered by scholars like J. M. Hunt, who published *Intelligence and Experience* (1961), arguing against the concept of fixed intelligence and predetermined development. Similarly, William Fowler (1962) suggested that concept formation began during infancy, based on evidence that early verbal stimulation helped the development of memory and knowledge acquisition. This research contradicted Freud's warning that challenging young children's intellect might damage their psychological development (Day, 1983). In 1964, Benjamin Bloom published *Stability and Change in Human Characteristics* in which he claimed that 70% of a person's intellectual aptitude and 50% of the reading skill of young adults was established before the age of 9. Combined, these educators provided ample justification for systematic early intervention (Day, 1983).

Head Start

In 1964, the United States government passed the Economic Opportunity Act (EOA), which launched President Lyndon Johnson's ambitious War on Poverty campaign. Eventually, the showcase project for the War on Poverty, the Head Start program, was initiated in 1965 (Bailey & Wolery, 1992). Head Start was the first federally funded enrichment program of preschool education in the United States. It began as a summer program for 560,000 children whose admission was based on their poverty status. As a community action program, Head Start was designed to address the health, nutrition, and education needs of poor families, with the goal of preventing later school failure. Two key features of Head Start are parental participation and health care services.

The Head Start effort was supplemented by the 1965 Elementary and Secondary Education Act, which provided funding to support the creation of preschools for poor children to be directed by public school districts (Day, 1983). It is interesting to note that, until 1965, the Federal Children's Bureau still held the position that day care would be disruptive for healthy family relations and that it should be provided only to those families who were not capable of providing adequate care for their children.

Both a strength and a weakness of Head Start were flexible guidelines that allowed individual programs to develop along a wide range of educational approaches (Zigler & Muenchow, 1992). By 1968, there were 14 different variations of Head Start in implementation across the nation. The Westinghouse Learning Corporation and Ohio University conducted an evaluation of the effectiveness of summer and full-year Head Start programs (Cicirelli, Evans, & Schiller, 1969). When the independent evaluators released the Westinghouse Report, it was very damaging to the Head Start effort (Day, 1983).

These researchers found that, despite early gains, summer programs did not produce cognitive or affective gains that persisted into the early elementary grades and that full-year programs had only marginal effects on cognitive development that could still be detected in grades 1, 2, and 3 (Smith & Bissell, 1970). Head Start was judged a failure. At the same time, Arthur Jensen (1969), a noted psychological researcher, claimed compensatory education had been tried and had failed. This fueled tremendous debate and controversy.

However, this political and philosophical controversy stimulated early educators to do more to solve the problem of equalizing educational opportunities. It became more socially acceptable to recognize that various cultures are different, not deficient (Cole & Bruner, 1972; Labov, 1972) and by the 1970s, the concept of cultural deprivation was discredited (Day, 1983).

Researchers focused on identifying which early education approaches might have the most success and extending those interventions to poor children in elementary school "Follow Through" programs. By 1969, there were 21 alternative preschool and primary grade curricula being researched under the Head Start Planned Variation program and 20 educational models under Follow Through programs, which served poor children from kindergarten through third grade. In 1970, the Head Start summer programs were discontinued and replaced with full-time, year-round programs serving about 400,000 children. The long-term data on well-run model preschool programs and Follow Through programs revealed positive effects on school performance, special education placement, grade retention, teen pregnancy, delinquency, welfare participation, and employment (Haskins, 1989).

Since 1965, Head Start has provided services to more than 13 million children (Head Start: A Child Development Program, 1998). By 1993, its Congressional appropriation reached $2.8 billion a year. Head Start enrolled hundreds of thousands of children across all 50 states, the District of Columbia, and the U.S. territories. It also served migrant and American Indian children. Approximately 1,400 community agencies supported Head Start through their non-federal share of 20% of cost or services. Head Start provided parent involvement, educational, medical, dental, nutritional, mental health, and social services to children and their families. Ten percent of Head Start's enrollment slots were reserved for children with disabilities. Studies have indicated that Head Start children scored higher than non-Head Start children on preschool achievement tests, that they performed equal to or better than their peers when they entered school, and that there were fewer grade retentions and special class placements later in their school careers (Head Start: A Child Development Program, 1998).

Early Head Start

Early Head Start began with 68 programs in 1995 and today extends high-quality child and family development services to more than 55,000 low-income pregnant women and families with infants and toddlers each year (Administration for Children and Families, 2002). Comprehensive child development services are offered through center-based, home-based, and combination programs. A rigorous evaluation of the first program cohorts showed that the program had significant and positive effects on a wide range of parent and child dimensions, including increased cognitive, language, and social-emotional development of the children and improved parenting skills, participation in education, and job training for the adults.

Recent Day Care Efforts

In 1971, advocates for national day-care services for all families suffered a serious blow. The National Organization for Women (NOW) had argued for publicly supported, 24-hour on-demand day care as a necessary service for women if they were ever to achieve equitable freedom of opportunity. Though initially supportive, then-president Richard Nixon, in his first term, vetoed the Comprehensive Child Development Bill, asserting that day care would ruin the American family (Day, 1983). Since that time, the United States has failed even to establish national standards for child care, despite the increasing numbers of children who are cared for outside of the home.

Though inadequate, the majority of public funds that supported child care and early education in recent years came from the federal government. In addition to

Head Start and Early Head Start, a number of public programs supported child care in some small part (Key Facts, 1999):

◆ The Child Care and Development Block Grant gave assistance to low-income families and those working to get off welfare (serving about 1.5 million children in 1998).
◆ The 21st Century Community Learning Centers program made $450 million available in 2000 for local school districts to offer after-school care.
◆ The Child and Adult Care Food Program supported 2.6 million children with free or reduced-price food through child care and after-school programs in 1999.
◆ The Dependent Care Tax Credit allowed tax credits for child-care expenses.

THE "TRILEMMA" OF CHILD CARE

A "trilemma" has been created by the large numbers of children for whom care is neither available, affordable, nor of sufficient quality (Culkin, Morris, & Helburn, 1991). An estimated 13 million children under the age of 6 spend some or all of their day being cared for by someone other than their parents. Many begin this care by the age of 11 weeks and stay in some form of child care until they enter school (Key Facts, 1999). Seventy-three percent of infants and toddlers of employed mothers are cared for by someone other than a parent while their mother is working (Ehrle, Adams, & Tout, 2001).

Perhaps the most pressing of these problems is affordability (Culkin et al., 1991). Full-day child-care costs from $4,000 to $10,000 a year, about the same as college tuition at a public university (Schulman & Adams, 1998). At the same time, one third of families with young children earned only $25,000 a year and a family with both parents earning minimum wage earned only $21,400 a year (U.S. Census Bureau, September, 1999).

The average family spent almost 11% on child care, the same proportion as they spent on food (Culkin et al., 1991). Low-income families spent as much as 20% to 25% of their budget on child care (Hofferth & Phillips, 1991). Families paid almost 60% of child-care costs (with government assistance paying the rest) in contrast to the 23% of the cost of a public college education that comes from families (with public funds and private donors covering three fourths of the real costs; U.S. Census, September, 1999).

Further, affordability is directly related to quality of service because a primary means of reducing costs is to increase child-to-staff ratios and to offer low pay (Culkin et al., 1991). In the late 1990s, child-care workers averaged only about $200 a week in earnings. Certified preschool teachers in public schools fared much better with wages and benefits, averaging salaries of about $750 per week (U.S. Department of Labor Women's Bureau, 1997).

> "When you look at the whole concept of putting your children in someone else's hands, you think money is not an object," said Monaghan, who manages the hair salon at the Hudson's Southland store. "But then it adds up. It's amazing what you end up paying. . . . It's kind of a contradiction, and I don't know what the answer is." (Kresnak, 1999)

A study of the quality of child-care centers in the United States found that the majority rated poor to mediocre, and 12% provided less than minimal care, to the point of jeopardizing the health, safety and development of children. Only 14% were rated as good quality. Centers that cared for infants and toddlers were of particularly poor quality, with 40% judged to be at a less than minimal quality and only 8% receiving a good quality rating (Helburn, et al., 1995). One third of family- and home-based settings were also found to be inadequate, meaning that they could actually harm child development (Galinsky, et al., 1994).

THE FUTURE OF CHILD CARE

A careful look at the history of child care reveals at least three generalizations that can be applied to the future of early childhood programs (Caldwell, 1989). The issue of early child care has always been conflicted about its potential risks and benefits and will continue to be so. Though scientists and educators have assured us that early education and formal training can enhance learning and character building, opponents have warned that early child care outside of the home would weaken the family unit. It was this kind of opposition that caused former president Richard Nixon to veto the first Child Development Act.

Secondly, there has always been a two-tiered child-care system, one for the poor and one for the affluent. These programs have differed markedly in their objectives. Care for the children of low income families has really been intended to help working mothers, not children, and has often been poorly staffed and equipped and met minimum standards. Child care for the disadvantaged has been a function of social welfare and reform and has stigmatized child care by the stamp of poverty (Cahan, 1989). When child care for low income families has been supported by the federal government, it was usually deemed a temporary emergency measure and its support fell away when each crisis ended. Most often child care for the poor was given in response to patterns of maternal employment, and many objections to child care actually are related to objections to women working.

Care for the children of affluent families has been designed to enhance child development and typically uses teachers, curriculum, and activities that are of the highest quality. Child care for the affluent rose out of the nursery school and kindergarten movements whose primary focus was to supplement the enrichment these children received at home (Cahan, 1989). Such care supports the home environment by providing educational experts.

Finally, progress in early child care has always depended on the convergence of three critical conditions: (1) child development theory that stresses the importance of early experiences, (2) a knowledge base that provides guidance about what can be accomplished through early intervention, and (3) a social climate that is receptive to applying this knowledge to relieve existing social problems. We've always needed the theory and knowledge base to suggest progress was possible, but only when economic and social needs coincided with this knowledge has the field been propelled forward.

Still, progress has been slow (Caldwell, 1989). Historically, we see several reasons for this incremental evolution. One reason is abundantly clear; early childhood programs have a long history of underfunding, and many modern programs are no better supported today. We have been consistently satisfied with meeting only minimal standards. Another factor that has slowed progress has been the resistance of the field to use innovative and experimental teaching techniques and to evaluate programs and their effectiveness. It is time for professionals to push diligently for such evaluation, and indeed this is happening with more purpose today.

Despite the ambivalence that has characterized the history of child care, modern families have made it clear that they will raise their children collaboratively with others in their communities (Caldwell, 1989). "Child care, early education and school-age care are part of the daily lives of millions of American families," (National Center for Education Statistics, October, 1996). Two thirds of women with children under age 6 (and three quarters of women with children ages 6 to 17) were in the labor force (Bureau of Labor Statistics, December, 1998). Nearly 60% of all children under the age of 6 (about 13 million each day), regardless of whether their mothers were working, were in some form of nonparental care (National Center for Education Statistics, October, 1996). As many as 45% of children less than age 1 were in nonparental care, while 84% of children age 5 were in nonparental care. Half of these children are cared for in child-care centers or family child-care homes. "The question is no longer, Is it good for the children? but, How can it be done, and be done well?" (Caldwell, 1989).

Developmentally Appropriate Practice

Perhaps the height of the era of "Children know best" was met with the National Association for the Education of Young Children's (NAEYC) endorsement of developmentally appropriate practice (DAP) in 1987 (Bredekamp, 1987). The paper maintained that highly structured, adult-directed activities are counterproductive to learning for very young children. The message was that children are intrinsically motivated and capable of understanding and interpreting their environment. This approach to preacademic instruction for preschoolers was widely adopted by Head Start and other child-care providers as the acceptable method for teaching skills to very young children. Greenberg (1990) aptly described DAP:

> It is characterized by active learning within enriched free play with teachers who are responsive and expand upon children's interests . . . Emphasis is equally on all aspects of each child's development. Intellectual learning is fostered, but is not given priority over physical, social, and emotional learning. (p. 72)

Program standards and characteristics would include the following (Bredekamp & Copple, 1997; NAEYC, 1991): a clean indoor environment that is not overcrowded and has access to a fenced outdoor play area; age-appropriate toys on low shelves with child-sized furniture; adult to child ratio no greater than 1 to 3 for infants and 1 to 5 for toddlers; supervised daily activities including flexible time for active play, naps, snacks; prompt responses to child distress with caregiver time to hold, talk to, sing and read to young children; and parents welcome at any time. To encourage cognitive development, a DAP environment allows children to freely explore through group play, and little emphasis is placed on structured lessons with "correct" answers. Caretakers follow a child's lead by using materials and activities in which the child first demonstrates interest.

Developmentally and Individually Appropriate

As children with disabilities were integrated into Head Start and other child-care settings, the DAP philosophy and the more structured approach of early intervention and early childhood special education (ECSE) often conflicted. Both approaches embrace standards for healthy care, respect for individual growth, and the value of interaction with the environment and other children (Sandall, McLean, & Smith, 2000). These programs diverge significantly, however, in terms of how teacher-directed and how intensely structured early special education should be. Carta, Schwartz, Atwater, and McConnell (1991) provided a succinct justification for special education's more systematic approach:

> While DAP has focused primarily on preventing attempts to artificially accelerate the progress of children who are developing normally, the explicit mission of ECSE is to produce outcomes that would not occur in the absence of intervention or teaching. (p. 4)

This apparent incompatibility has created tension in how programs for young children with disabilities should be managed and evaluated, especially when children with disabilities are integrated into programs designed primarily for typically developing children. The challenge is to provide both developmentally and individually appropriate programming. The rationale and basic premises of early childhood special education are specific to needs created by a disability (Carta et al., 1991):

1. Early intervention and special education programs must offer a range of services that vary in intensity based on the needs of the children they serve. Both what is taught and how it is taught must be in response to children's needs. Many children with disabilities do not have prerequisite skills that would allow them to explore and interact with the environment in the same way typical children do. For these children, adults must guide behavior and structure interactions in order to enhance their development.
2. Early intervention and special education programs must plan individualized instruction based on a child's unique strengths and weaknesses and what is needed to be successful in future environments. A certain amount of precision is necessary to be as efficient as possible in helping children with delays to catch up and to function appropriately in new settings.
3. In special education, assessment must come from many sources, be carried out across settings, and happen frequently in order to effectively monitor a child's progress and to adjust to a child's needs. Continuous (daily) measurement is most appropriate for accommodating for individual differences and promoting development of skills.
4. Instructional methods for children with disabilities must be effective, efficient, functional, and normalized to make a significant difference in a child's development. The goal of intervention is to acquire new skills, to efficiently make the most progress in the shortest time, to promote use of new skills across settings, and to minimize intrusiveness as much as possible.
5. Instruction must provide for high levels of active child involvement and participation in activities. This may require substantial teacher assistance in order for engagement to occur.

6. Programs for children with disabilities must focus on strengthening the abilities of families to encourage their own child's development and community integration. Family needs must also be taken into consideration so that resources, training, and support can be provided as necessary.

7. Early intervention and special education programs are required to be outcome-based, with specific criteria, procedures, and timelines in order to determine if these outcomes are met. Accountability is part and parcel of the legislation and funding that support these programs. Families, schools, and communities expect early special education to make significant gains for each child served.

In sum, it would be dangerous for the field of early intervention to adopt a DAP approach to the exclusion of the premises and principles that are critical to the success of ECSE (Carta et al., 1991). It is important that those involved in ECSE and early intervention find ways to integrate the best normalizing philosophies of DAP while continuing to advocate for the instructional strategies and structures that are as effective, efficient, and functional as necessary for young children with disabilities.

THE HISTORY OF SPECIAL EDUCATION

Special education and early intervention are relatively recent phenomena in the historical sense. Just as the history of child care is marked by stages that reflect the popular philosophies of the day, so the history of special education for children with disabilities might also be demarcated by phases. Rutherford Turnbull (1997) suggested the following stages in the history of care for those with mental retardation. These might be more broadly interpreted in the same way for those with disabilities in general.

FAMILIES BEAR ALL

During colonial days, the burdens of cost, care, social stigma, and emotional strife belonged to the family. There was no sense of community, and indeed, a person with a disability was often banished from a colony or town.

A shift in responsibility for the disabled began in the early 1900s with the seeding of services for children with special needs through the initiation of a variety of programs both in the United States and in Europe. In the last years of the 19th century, Alexander Graham Bell, inventor of the telephone and a strong advocate of oral education for the deaf, petitioned the National Education Association to establish a division for the needs of persons with disabilities. The approved division was called the Department of Education of the Deaf, Blind, and the Feebleminded, later shortened to Department of Special Education (Cook et al., 1992).

In 1904, Alfred Binet was commissioned by France's minister of public instruction to design a test to determine which children could succeed in the public schools and which children needed special attention. The philosophy of the time was to keep children with disabilities in the regular classroom, while creating a method of identification so that teachers would avoid the problem of prejudice that might occur if these children were mistaken for "slackers" or "lazy students" (Cook et al., 1992).

In 1922, the International Council for Exceptional Children was formed. Its members were an influential advocacy group who worked on behalf of children with special needs (Cook et al., 1992). The 1930 White House Conference on Child Health and Protection marked the first time special education had received national recognition in the United States. However, prior to World War II, parents were still inclined to isolate children who had severe disabilities, to institutionalize them, or to be unwilling to admit their children needed special services. At the same time, children with mild disabilities received no special services though many were placed in regular classrooms in neighborhood schools (Cook et al., 1992).

THE ASYLUM MOVEMENT

Early in the 20th century, the "asylum" movement dominated. Communities regarded those with disabilities with more enlightened beneficence. Asylums were established, presumably to help families protect and care for the disabled. However, asylums were quickly perverted from a place of safety to a place of horror where people with disabilities were mistreated and degraded. Contributing to this perversion was the new science of intelligence testing, originally developed by Binet to help identify and provide services to children who learned more slowly. Instead, IQ testing was used to label "abnormal" individuals; those disabled who scored the lowest on intelligence measures were involuntarily institutionalized, sterilized, and denied civil liberties. Except for some children who were deaf or blind, almost no children with disabilities received public education.

SOCIAL DARWINISM

Prior to World War II, the science of evolution set the stage for the eugenics era. The prevailing theme of survival of the fittest proved dangerous and even deadly for those with disabilities. It was recommended that the disabled be removed from their families and segregated in institutions so that those with undesirable traits could not reproduce and dilute the gene pool for generations to come. Some even pursued the humane euthanization of the disabled, an agenda Hitler actively implemented from the beginning of his genocidal Holocaust.

In the worst and most extreme form of eugenics, Hitler began with compulsory sterilization for people with disabilities in 1933, with the Law for the Prevention of Genetically Diseased Offspring (Forgotten Crimes, 2001). In 1939, Hitler authorized "mercy deaths" for the incurably "sick" that grew into a formal killing program known as Aktion T-4, exterminating more than 275,000 people with disabilities (not counting those in concentration camps).

In addition to Aktion T-4, the "Children's Program" specifically targeted children with disabilities for disposal. All newborns and infants under the age of 3 who were suspected of having serious hereditary diseases (such as Down syndrome, deafness, blindness, and others) were deemed unfit to live and were killed, most commonly by lethal injection. By 1941, physicians were required to register any minors with disabilities and child killing was expanded to minors up to the age of 17 (Forgotten Crimes, 2001). Older people with disabilities were herded into concentration camps and exterminated when deemed unable to work.

FIRST GENERATION MODERN ERA

The horrors uncovered in Nazi Germany and the return of war-injured and maimed adults contributed to a growing public conscience regarding the disabled that flourished in the 1950s and 1960s. At the same time, the growth of professions serving the disabled, including physical therapy, occupational therapy, and psychology, provided promise for effective rehabilitation and training for those with disabilities.

By the late 1940s a number of prominent individuals such as author Pearl Buck, entertainers Roy Rogers and Dale Evans, and the political Kennedy family were visibly calling for better education of individuals with special needs. Parents in the 1950s were beginning to question the practice of keeping children with disabilities hidden at home, and advocacy groups such as the United Cerebral Palsy Association, the National Association for Retarded Citizens, and the American Foundation for the Blind demanded alternatives to institutionalization (Cook et al., 1992). Between 1953 and 1958, there was a 260% increase in enrollment in special education classes (Cook et al., 1992). At about the same time, the civil rights movement became a force to be reckoned with. Together, these groups accomplished an enormous change in the public philosophy. Thus, the age of public support of children with special needs had begun.

As special education services for older children grew during the 1950s and 1960s, a few key pieces of federal legislation laid important groundwork that supported the later extension of services to very young children with special needs (Office of Special Education and Rehabilitative Services [OSERS], 2002). Among these were:

1. The Training of Professional Personnel Act of 1959, which helped train leaders to educate children with mental retardation;
2. The Teachers of the Deaf Act of 1961, which trained personnel for children who were deaf or hard of hearing; and
3. The Elementary and Secondary Education Act and State Schools Act of 1965, which provided states with grant assistance to educate children with disabilities.

By 1968, more than 30,000 special education teachers and related specialists had been trained through support from the federal government (OSERS, 2002). Captioned films were viewed by more than three million deaf people. Education was being provided for some children with disabilities from preschool through secondary levels (only one out of five by 1970). State institutions still housed 200,000 people with significant disabilities and too often these settings provided only the minimal food, clothing, and shelter. Many states actually had laws that prohibited public education for certain children, including those who were deaf, blind, emotionally disturbed, or mentally retarded (OSERS, 2002).

Turnbull (1997) referred to this period as the "First Generation Modern Era," a time when the doctrine of equal protection called for integration and equal access for all. *Brown v. the Board of Education* set a new tone for education (and subsequently also for special education):

> In these days, it is doubtful that any child may reasonably be expected to succeed in life if he is denied access to an education, such an opportunity, where a state has undertaken to provide it, is a right which must be available to all on equal terms.

Turnbull (1997) also called this time the "Age of Aquarius," when political and legal progress combined to seek community inclusion and equality in human services. Prior to 1975, more than one million children with disabilities were excluded entirely from the education system, and half of all children with disabilities had only limited access to education and were thus denied an appropriate education (OSERS, 2002). During the 1970s, *normalization,* the inclusion of the disabled in the normal activities of the nondisabled, grew. Deinsitutionalization moved at a frenetic pace, and people with disabilities were returned to smaller community settings and family homes. Landmark federal legislation, the Education for All Handicapped Children Act in 1975 (Public Law 94-142, now IDEA), opened all local schools to children with disabilities.

Four purposes of Public Law 94-142 were articulated in the Education for All Handicapped Children Act of 1975:

1. to assure that all children with disabilities have available to them . . . a free appropriate public education which emphasizes special education and related services designed to meet their unique needs
2. to assure that the rights of children with disabilities and their parents . . . are protected
3. to assist States and localities to provide for the education of all children with disabilities
4. to assess and assure the effectiveness of efforts to educate all children with disabilities.

SECOND GENERATION OF THE MODERN ERA

The "Second Generation of the Modern Era" began with the inauguration of President Ronald Reagan in 1981 (Turnbull, 1997). Reagan sought to reduce government regulations and to defederalize human services; he proposed the elimination of the U.S. Department of Education. This was a highly "individualistic" philosophy that threatened the disabled with a reduction in only recently gained rights and services. The public responded with an explosion of disability litigation to firmly establish and refine the rights of the disabled. Arguments were made not just for equal treatment, but for "more equal" treatment. "Rights bearers" sought to not only strengthen existing rights, but to establish community responsibility and care for those who had much less.

COMMUNAL PERSPECTIVE

Where does special education need to go? Turnbull (1997) argued for a communal perspective that recognizes the government is one part of a collective effort to support the disabled; the government provides programs for those who are most vulnerable as a part of the common good. But a communal perspective is bigger than just government; it sets a moral tone for the country, emphasizing the interdependence of all of us, those with disabilities and those without. This calls for mutuality and reciprocity. Disability is a natural part of the human condition; we are all vulnerable, therefore, we contribute when we can so that others will contribute to us when we can't. In addition to recognizing and protecting one's rights, a communal perspective creates a reliable circle of friends and support around any person with a disability.

When operational, a communal perspective means more than just inclusion and equal opportunity. It means special supports that allow real opportunities—more than equal treatment. Disability is by its very definition a distinction that makes a difference, and therefore requires more than just equal access, it requires advocacy, prevention, early intervention, effective educational outcomes, meaningful employment, community presence, and long-term care.

EARLY EDUCATION FOR CHILDREN WITH DISABILITIES

Services to young children with special needs was the last piece of an elaborate early childhood puzzle. All the other pieces—education, universal education, and education of children with disabilities in public schools—had to come first.

One of the earliest and most dramatic demonstrations of the importance of early intervention was reported in 1939. Skeels and Dye (1939) removed two "hopeless" babies from an orphanage and placed them under the care of adult women with mental retardation who also resided in an institution. After living on the women's ward for 6 months, the babies' IQs rose by 40 points; a few more months in this setting and their IQs rose to the mid-90s. Skeels and Dye then convinced state authorities to move 13 more children (all but two of whom were classified as mentally retarded and unsuitable for adoption) to the one-on-one care of teenage girls with mental retardation who lived at the institution.

The teenage girls were trained in simple mothering skills, and the children also attended a half-morning kindergarten program at the institution. Twelve other children under age 3 who remained in the orphanage were used as a comparison group. After 2 years, the experimental group in the care of the teenage "mothers" averaged a gain of 28 IQ points, whereas the comparison group that stayed with the orphanage lost an average of 26 IQ points. A follow-up 25 years later by Skeels (1966) showed the experimental group had almost all completed high school, married, and had normal children. By contrast, four of the control children were still institutionalized, and the average education of the group was only third grade. These studies provided substantial support for theories that early environmental experiences influence child development.

It was still not until 1968 that the first federal law written exclusively for services to preschoolers with special needs, the Handicapped Children's Early Childhood Assistance Act (P.L. 90-538), was passed. This act constituted landmark legislation, because it represented the first major federal recognition of the importance of early childhood special education. The purpose of the bill was to develop model early educational programs for children with disabilities from birth through age 8. These model programs were funded as 3-year demonstration grants, called First Chance projects. First Chance directors were required to include parents, to provide inservice training, to evaluate the progress of children served in the program, to coordinate with public schools, and to disseminate information (Cook et al., 1992).

The First Chance Network began in 1969 with 24 programs funded for a total of one million dollars. Of those 24 projects, 84% continued past their original 3-year

Integrated population of children at school.

funding (Fallen & Umansky, 1985). By 1985, there were 173 different First Chance programs throughout the country, and by 1987, over 500 programs had been funded. These projects have developed screening and assessment devices, curriculum materials, parent training programs, and thousands of other print, audiovisual, and support materials for early childhood intervention (Heward & Orlansky, 1992).

As state and federal support for early childhood special education grew, the professionals involved also became more organized. The passage of the HCEEP projects brought together many of the same researchers who had promoted projects for compensatory education for young children in poverty during the 1960s (McCollum, 2000). These included a range of professionals from psychology, child development, medicine, and social work. In 1973, the Council for Exceptional Children formed the Division for Early Childhood (DEC). In 1979, DEC published its first journal (now the *Journal of Early Intervention*). A body of work about young children with special needs began to grow and interest in the preparation of personnel specialized in early childhood special education as a separate field also grew.

The Economic Opportunity and Community Partnership Act of 1974 required that Head Start programs in each state reserve 10% of their enrollment slots for children with disabilities (Fallen & Umansky, 1985). By 1977, 13% of all children enrolled in Head Start programs were classified as disabled, a total of over 36,000 children ("HEW reports," 1978; Heward & Orlansky, 1992). Later, Head Start developed 14 regional Resource Access Projects which provided training and technical assistance to personnel serving children with disabilities in Head Start programs (Fallen & Umansky, 1985).

IDEA OF 1975 AND IMPLICATIONS FOR EARLY CHILDHOOD

Head Start's inclusion of children with disabilities was only the first step in extensive federal legislation to provide services to all children with disabilities.

The Individuals with Disabilities Education Act (IDEA), as Public Law 94-142 was later renamed, has evolved through several revisions. At the time, its passage provided landmark legislation that ensured the free and appropriate education of all children with disabilities. Its impact was primarily on school-aged children, but the law contained language and funding that encouraged states to further develop services for preschoolers with disabilities (McCollum, 2000). Public Law 94-142 linked services to young children with disabilities to public education and brought the field of early childhood special education into public awareness.

Even in its first stages, IDEA recognized the importance of early intervention. IDEA was intended to apply to children ages 3 to 21, unless an individual state's law did not allow services to children starting at this young age. Financial incentives were built into IDEA to encourage the provision of services to preschoolers; by 1985, 31 states had passed some form of preschool legislation (Bailey & Wolery, 1992).

In 1986, Congress amended IDEA, reauthorizing it under Public Law 99-457. The big surprise of the revised law was that it extended all the act's mandated rights and protections to preschoolers and encouraged states to serve children with disabilities from birth through age 2. When the newly revised IDEA was put in place in 1986, fewer than half the states had mandates for the education of preschoolers with disabilities; but soon all states established such a mandate ("DEC holds IDEA reauthorization hearing," January 1994). Almost 400,000 preschool children were served through IDEA programs and Chapter 1 funding in the 1990–1991 school year (OSERS, 1992). By IDEA's 25th anniversary, almost 200,000 infants and toddlers under age 3 were receiving early intervention through the assistance of federal funds (OSERS, 2002).

At the same time, intensive efforts were initiated to prepare personnel to work with the birth through age 2 population. The unusual degree of caregiver and professional collaboration required meant that training had to be extended to fields beyond special education and early childhood, including mental health, medicine, and the therapies (McCollum, 2000).

Provisions of IDEA did much to encourage the collaboration of parents and community agencies, including schools, in serving infants and toddlers with disabilities. The law made clear that services were the responsibility of an interagency system and that resources should be shared ("DEC holds IDEA reauthorization hearing," 1994). Its emphasis was on delivery of services within the context of the family and in natural settings, which should encourage community-based, culturally sensitive, and family-driven services ("DEC holds IDEA reauthorization hearing," 1994). In addition, the revised law provided an incentive to states to address the early intervention needs of children who were born at-risk for developing later disabilities and delays. Table 2–2 summarizes recent legislation, up to IDEA 1997.

Though its evolution, IDEA became increasingly preschool friendly, and early childhood personnel development became closely tied to federally funded demonstration or university programs (McCollum, 2000). Early on, these programs

Table 2–2 Recent Landmarks in Early Intervention Services

Date	Landmark Description
1965	Project Head Start was established to serve 3- and 4-year-olds living in poverty
1968	Handicapped Children's Early Education Program established to fund model preschool programs for children with disabilities
1972	Economic Opportunity Act required Head Start to reserve 10% of its enrollment for children with disabilities
1975	P.L. 94-142, The Education for All Handicapped Children Act, provided incentive funding for programs serving preschoolers with disabilities ages 3 to 5 years
1986	P.L. 99-457 amends P.L. 94-142 to require services to children age 3 to 5 with disabilities and to provide incentives for programs serving infants and toddlers who are developmentally delayed or at risk of developmental delay
1990	Head Start Expansion and Quality Improvement Act reauthorized and expanded Head Start programs through 1994
1997	P.L. 105-17, the 1997 amendments to IDEA, renew early intervention efforts

Source:Teaching Infants and Preschoolers with Disabilities (2nd ed.), by D. Bailey and M. Wolery, 1992. Adapted by permission of Pearson Education, Inc., Upper Saddle River, NJ.

developed early childhood personnel training based on effective instructional procedures for children with severe disabilities (whose needs were similar to those of very young children with disabilities). Several common points of consensus emerged. First, the instructional method of choice in special education was systemic instruction; a structured technology for intervention was developing. Second, young children at risk for academic failure were also a target for state programs. Third, early childhood personnel roles went beyond instruction and included establishing relationships with families, teaming with other disciplines, and providing services in environments other than classrooms. Finally, attention was being given to younger and younger children. Preschool special education was being extended to infants and toddlers.

The 1997 revisions brought even greater attention to educating young children with disabilities in settings with nondisabled children (McCollum, 2000). Equal emphasis was placed on serving infants and toddlers in their natural environments and providing treatment and education appropriate for their needs. For some families this has meant services brought to their homes or to a child's day-care setting. For those children with greater need for more intensive therapies or specialized equipment, justification could be made to provide services in center-based programs for children with disabilities. It also meant that care must be given in transitioning 3-year-olds. IDEA continues to support best practices in early childhood special education and early intervention (OSERS, 2002):

1. State-of-the-art models of appropriate programs and services for young children with disabilities (birth to 5 years) and their families;
2. Individualized Family Service Plans (IFSPs) to identify and meet the unique needs of each infant and toddler with a disability and her family;
3. Effective assessment and teaching practices and related instructional materials for young children and their families;

A NATIVE AMERICAN PERSPECTIVE: INTERVIEW WITH JAMES HOLDEN

We know by many of the various demographics available today what's happening to Native American students. They are overrepresented in remedial programs and badly underrepresented in gifted and talented programs. Unfortunately, the reality is, a lot of that, in my opinion, is because of stereotypic beliefs on the part of the educational community. That's part of it, but another part of it is how we as Native Americans look at ourselves. We tend to think, sometimes, we've lost the ability to know who we are.

Our Indian children today, and our Indian parents, are struggling with who they are. We're dealing with second, third, fourth, and fifth generation children off the reservation, and parents off the reservation. The circle of life on the reservation is pretty real, but it's also pretty short. The circle of life is you're born, you go to school if you can, you play some sports, often you drink, and you get a job. It seems to repeat itself over and over again across generations.

Unemployment's high; alcoholism is extremely high; emotional, sexual, and physical abuse is extremely high. A lot of Indians believe if they get off the reservation, that will fix them. We get off the reservation, and we run smack into this whole wall of misinformation.

If you want to see a third world country, go to a reservation, but don't make a judgment about what it is you see, unless you understand what it is.

Somehow, we as a group, need to get the idea that we must and can walk in two worlds. I want to be able to work and compete in the White man's world. That's fine, there's nothing wrong with that. But I also must have the other foot firmly planted in my roots, my beliefs, and my customs. You know, if you look at the whole warrior society idea, many male Indians are still stuck in that. What's a warrior? All those stereotypes that Whites have about savage warriors have some truth, because that's how we were. Do we treat females differently than our White counterparts? What do you think? Some of us are still stuck back with the warrior mentality.

So, what do we do for children? That's really what it's all about, what do we do for children, because if the water of life is our children, and I believe it is, then what are we doing for our children? We must somehow teach them it is right and just to be proud of being Indian. But we also must tell them what being an Indian is. We can't just say it's living on the reservation. It is who and what we are as a people; our old ways, our

4. National network of professionals dedicated to improving early intervention and preschool education at the state and local levels; and

5. Collaboration with other federal, state, and local agencies to avoid duplication of efforts in providing early intervention and preschool education.

CURRENT PHILOSOPHY OF EARLY INTERVENTION

Three broad historical themes led to the current status of early intervention (Bailey & Wolery, 1992). First, society became concerned about the care and welfare of young children, as evidenced in the passage of legislation to protect and provide services to young children. Second, society demonstrated concern about the rights

oral traditions, our celebrations, and the history of how we have been treated by the dominant culture. A lot of it is just traditional views of Mother Earth getting us back to the basics.

I think you should start with the smallest of the small. As soon as they're in preschool, what do we teach them? Do we teach them that the girls play with the dolls, and the boys play with the blocks and all the dolls are White? Or, do we teach them it is all right, for the teacher, who is male, to put on an apron to cook, and it's okay for the girls to put on the construction outfit in play time. That's the way it should be.

Reuben Holden.

Deeper than that, we have to somehow reach them with the idea that diversity is a way of life, and where your place is in that structure of diversity. Our children don't have that sense, when they go back to visit grandfather on a reservation and he's still stuck. Grandfather is still stuck with the idea that it's a White man's school system. Grandmother is stuck with showing her girls the old way because the old way's getting lost. The children today are saying, "What are you talking about, old way? If it's not video and microwave,

I'm not sure I want to know it." But many of us believe there is tremendous value to honoring and understanding the old customs and ideas as a bridge to our past.

Unfortunately, one major problem of Native Americans today is that our agenda is not put on the front burner by many districts, because that spot is often already taken by African Americans or other minority groups. We do not seem to have those powerful speakers and activists who can engage the system in a meaningful way to bring about change.

and needs of individual citizens and minority groups. Changes in advocacy for civil rights, individual rights, women's rights, and disability rights have set the stage for establishing legal rights and improved services for children with disabilities. Third, focus increased on support for individuals and families as a primary goal of human service programs.

These themes have supported diversity in the population and the ways in which services are delivered. Heterogeneity in the kinds of children served has expanded with the inclusion of newborns and infants, the improving survival rate of medically fragile infants, the advent of children with AIDS, and the increasing numbers of children who have been affected *in utero* by exposure to alcohol, cocaine, or other drugs (Bailey & Wolery, 1992). Likewise, the families of these children show greater diversity than in years past.

Despite this increasing diversity, professionals in the field of early childhood share assumptions based on the accumulated knowledge of the profession, knowledge derived from research, theory, cultural values, and clinical experiences. Bailey (1989) summarized the principles of early intervention that have become generally accepted across the profession. Among these shared principles are the following:

1. The quality of a child's physical and social environment has a significant influence on the child's behavior and long-term development
2. Early intervention is effective in reducing the impact of disabling conditions
3. Parent involvement is essential for appropriate early intervention
4. Early intervention is most effective when professionals work together as an interdisciplinary team
5. Clinicians should teach to a child's strengths rather than focusing on the child's deficits
6. Intervention must be developmentally based [and individually appropriate]
7. Individualized assessment is a necessary prerequisite to effective intervention
8. Skills taught to children with disabilities do not generalize to other contexts unless specific planning and training is designed for such carryover

The history of IDEA reflects a uniquely American approach to serving children with disabilities, and this Western attitude has had substantial impact on the rest of the world. But there is also much we can learn about best serving young children by looking at both the traditional and modern approaches present in other cultures around the world.

CROSS-CULTURAL HISTORY OF CHILDHOOD EDUCATION

Rising preschool enrollments and use of child care are cross-cultural trends (Boocock, 1995). Economic pressures have caused employment of more mothers worldwide, but there is also an international recognition of the value of early developmental experiences. Other factors, such as dwindling family size and disappearing extended-family support are worldwide phenomena that influence the need for early childhood services (Olmsted, 1989). We include these brief descriptions of models for early education in various nations, not simply to illustrate diversity and understanding, but to cultivate ideas for the evolution of preschool education in decades to come.

Because Western civilizations inhabited and colonized all corners of the globe during the same interval that childhood education in Western culture was evolving, and because Western industrialization has influenced almost every culture, there are distinct commonalties among early childhood services in most countries. Unfortunately, Western practices have supplanted traditional educational activities in so many cultures that knowledge and understanding of heritage and customs of various cultures has often been lost, and with their absence, the possibility of learning new and potentially powerful principles of teaching and learning are gone forever. Nevertheless, Woodill et al. (1992) compiled brief analyses of early educational practices across the world. Table 2–3 reviews some of these summaries and provides a sample of cultural histories that reflect heritage different from that of Western culture.

Table 2–3 Early Education in Non-Western Cultures Reflects the Unique Heritage of Each Culture

Country	Unique Educational Heritage
	A "collective" means has been used to educate young children since the Illyrian tribe. Children were given over to the state for their education at the age of 5, where they learned a love of work and were given military training (Dedja, 1992).
	Traditionally, families, including extended family members, have been responsible for the education of their own children (Monau, 1992). Grandparents and older siblings are responsible for basic survival needs including health, education, and socialization.
	The two primary foci of preschool education in China are morality (love of motherland, its people, and family) and language. Morality includes teaching children a love of collective work and values of altruism, modesty, ability to accept criticism, honesty, respect of adults, use of social manners, hospitality, and a sense of optimism and confidence (Laing and Pang, 1992).
	In the 1940s, Tarabai Modak adapted Montessori education for tribal children. Her *anganwadi* (courtyard centers) literally meant to take education to the doorsteps of tribal children. The preferred teaching method in India is "playway," in which activities are largely child-directed (Kaul, 1992).
	According to Noguchi, Ogawa, Yoshidawa, and Hashimoto (1992), primitive Japan regarded children as precious, and they were reared within the protection of their tribe. In the dynasty periods (794–1185 A.D.) children of noble families were reared to be cultured women and men. Samuri warriors took charge of the state in the Middle Ages and boys were trained to become warriors, whereas girls were trained to become "womanly" for the sake of the family.
	Even today, boys are educated in *poros* and girls are educated in *sandes*. In early childhood, boys are secluded from females and noninitiates in groves where they remain for their cultural education and where they will learn the responsibilities placed on them by society. Similarly, girls are isolated in a sande, away from males and noninitiates. Girls are taught to perform the roles of females in society, to be loyal and faithful wives (Gormuyor, 1992).
	Education in Nigeria has been traced to preliterate times when children's teachers were the mothers or grandmothers who cared for them while others worked on the farm or elsewhere (Aghenta & Omatseye, 1992). Children learned practical skills. Oral tradition constituted instruction, in which children learned through songs, folk tales, and legends. An emphasis was also placed on community belonging and achievement through hard work.
	Children of both genders were served throughout the Sultanate of Oman in *kuttab* (Al-Barwani, 1992). Teaching in the privately owned kuttabs took place under the shade of a tree, in a mosque, in a teacher's home; or in the courtyard. The teachers themselves were appointed, based on their age, their knowledge of Quaran, and their reputations as good citizens of the community. Even now, these private schools are held during summer sessions and after school in many communities.

CLOSE-UP

WHO CARES FOR THE CHILDREN?
DENMARK'S UNIQUE PUBLIC CHILD-CARE MODEL

Valerie Polakow reminds us that today's anti-tax sentiment may be costing us dearly. "We might do well to pause and think about what we have lost by failing to create a publicly subsidized day care system and a generous set of family support policies." Her article presents her first-hand account of Denmark's high-quality child-care system.

Denmark has a long tradition of public support for families and universal equity which are reflected in its social policies. The country provides a multitiered system of universal support policies for families, such that chronic family and child poverty has been eliminated. There is a statutory paid maternity leave of 4 weeks prior to birth and 14 weeks after birth followed by a paid paternal leave that may be taken by one or both parents for up to 52 weeks. In addition, a monthly stipend is provided, as well as housing subsidies, generous unemployment benefits, and universal health care.

A comprehensive, subsidized public day-care system serves children from 6 months of age, guarantees a slot for all 1-year-olds, and gives single parents priority placement. A variety of care options are available for children through age 6 at which time they normally begin public school. Neighborhood family day care serves three to five children in a licensed home, and substitute caregivers are provided if the day-care mother falls ill. Several types of day-care centers are available, each run by teachers and paraprofessionals who are paid as unionized municipal employees. The *vuggestuer* are infant/toddler centers serving children from 6 months to 3 years of age. Usually 30 to 40 children populate a center, and are organized into smaller groups of about 10 each. The *bornehaver* are preschool centers for children from 3 to 6 years old, enrolling 20 to 80 students, again organized into smaller teams. The *aldersintegrerede institutioner* are age-integrated centers for children from 6 months to 14 years of age, which developed in the 1970s.

Danish centers provide high-quality care which is flexible, play-based, and developmental, with a strong focus on child-centered, child-initiated learning. The Reggio Emilia approach is key to intellectual learning, and music and movement are a part of daily activity. Cooperative play and socially inclusive group activities are emphasized, with a strong bias against any form of exclusion, even for difficult children. There are also strong feelings against teaching reading or math readiness. All intervention for children who were at risk or have disabilities is carried out within the child's center where social workers and a psychologist are regularly available.

There is a national crisis in the United States in terms of available, quality, child care for both low-income and middle-class families. Yet, our public consciousness resists providing support for families. Polakow suggests we consider "Who cares for the children?" and use Denmark as a model for popular, accessible, affordable, quality care and family policy.

Source: "Who Cares for the Children? Denmark's Unique Public Child-Care Model," by V. Polakow, 1997, April, *Phi Delta Kappan,* 604–610.

INTERNATIONAL RESEARCH ON EARLY CHILDHOOD PROGRAMS

Boocock (1995) examined 15 major international studies of early childhood programs and came to the following conclusions. The overall availability and quality of early childhood programs is much higher in industrialized countries, but there are large differences even between similar nations. For example, almost 100% of French and Belgian children are in preschools at age 3, but only 28% of Spanish and Portuguese children and only 6% of Swiss children are active in preschool at the same age. Generally, urban areas are more widely served than rural areas, and children from upper- and middle-income levels are more likely to participate in preschool programs than are poor children. The following summarizes findings for Western cultures and developing nations.

NORTH AMERICA

Canada's social welfare policies and programs were more inclusive than those in the United States, though less generous than those in Europe. Family care regulated by even minimal standards was of better quality than that offered in unlicensed homes. Children in child-care centers tended to have higher levels of language development and more highly developed play and activity patterns than children in family care. Across Canadian settings, the quality of care influenced the development of lower income children more than those of middle or higher income. However, as in the United States, many children receive the "worst of both worlds"—they come from low-income families and attend low-quality family care (Goclman & Pence, 1987).

WESTERN EUROPE

Nations comprising the European Community and those in Nordic areas offered the most highly developed early childhood programs in the world. The French *e'cole maternelle,* or nursery school, is attended by nearly 100% of all 3- to 5-year-olds. French preschool teachers were paid as well as primary teachers, and their programs emphasized academic activities, though adult-child ratios were higher than those in the United States. The *e'cole maternelle* system was expanded during the 1970s and 1980s, when research revealed that every year of preschool attended reduced the likelihood of school failure, particularly for those from disadvantaged homes (McMahan, 1992).

The United Kingdom had a more diverse early childhood system than France (Boocock, 1995). About 44% of 3- and 4-year-olds attended public or private nursery school, and many children entered the public school system at age 4. Most families used individual caregivers called childminders, and many of those with parents at home attended organized play groups several times a week. Longitudinal research on 9,000 children found that those who had any preschool or organized play group experience displayed higher cognitive development and school achievement than those who had none (Curtis, 1992). Again, disadvantaged children gained the most from such experiences. However, preschool experience did not improve social development.

In the former West Germany, about 65% to 70% of children between 3 and 6 years of age attended half-day kindergartens. Research results corroborated that of studies done in France and the United Kingdom; attending preschool improved children's readiness for school and promoted their educational success (Tietze, 1987).

Swedish child care is considered the most advanced system in the world and has been carried out since the mid-1960s (Boocock, 1995). Swedish mothers of preschool-aged children are mostly employed (86%), and full-time child care is the centerpiece of the Swedish system. Local governments provide supervised, subsidized child care through centers and family homes to almost half of children between birth and age 7, although many parents care for their infants during paid parental leaves. Swedish research found distinct advantages to children participating in early nonparental child care. Children in such care before age 1 had greater verbal facility and were rated as more persistent and independent, less anxious, and more confident than children placed at a later age (Andersson, 1992). However, research also found that the quality of care in children's own homes was a better predictor of later development than socioeconomic status or preschool experience.

Boocock (1995) cited research in Ireland that focused on impoverished children in Dublin who were provided a 2-year, half-day preschool program much like Head Start. Later measures of cognitive development, school achievement, and parent involvement showed significant improvements on early standardized tests, but most of the initial gains were not maintained. By secondary school, however, the participants were more likely to stay in school and to take examinations required for further education. Data on later employment and trouble with the law showed no differences between those who had the early childhood program and those who did not (Kellaghan & Greaney, 1993).

THE PACIFIC RIM

Australia and New Zealand, though very similar to the United States, are considered Pacific Rim countries in Boocock's analysis (1995). Both countries have experienced sharply increased demands for early childhood programs. In New Zealand, 81% of young children attend some kind of organized child-care or play program. About 52% of Australian children ages 3 to 5 are similarly engaged. In addition to finding benefits for children in preschool programs, research in both countries documented parents' improved satisfaction with their lives when children spent time in nonmaternal care (Ochiltree & Edgar, 1990; Wylie, 1994).

DEVELOPING NATIONS

Preschool programs have been promoted in the developing nations of Latin America, Asia, and Africa by outside sources such as private foundations, the World

Early education in non-Western cultures reflects the unique heritage of each culture.

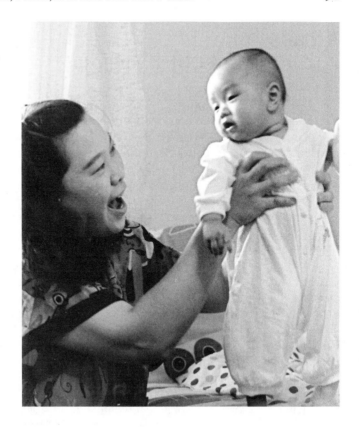

Bank, UNESCO, and UNICEF (Boocock, 1995). These early childhood programs often include nutrition and health education, as well as educational intervention. Overall, however, preschool education is limited. Research has been conducted only on specific intervention programs. The following are two examples.

The Cali project in Cali, Colombia focused on malnourished, low-income children and provided nutrition supplementation, health surveillance, child care, and education. Researchers found that the magnitude of a child's cognitive gains was related to the length of the child's experience in the program (McKay & McKay, 1983). All children receiving nutritional supplementation made gains in height and weight but did not gain intellectually until they also participated in preschool education. Gains in IQ persisted to age 8, and children who had preschool were more successful in school.

In Turkey, only about 2% of children under 6 years old attended preschool programs (Boocock, 1995). During the late 1980s, a program for home enrichment was offered that trained mothers to work with their preschool children on educational activities. Children whose mothers received this training surpassed others in cognitive measures. The mothers also enjoyed higher status in the family and participated more in decision making and determining child discipline (Kagitcibasi, 1991).

Case Study ADVOCATING FOR JOSH: INTERVIEW WITH AMY FINKEL

Josh started out in a self-contained preschool, and that was the impetus that got me to go back for further training. The public school system is actually responsible for me being in graduate school today. When Josh began in the self-contained preschool, I used to go a lot to observe and one of the teachers started to get upset because, even though I showed up all the time, I wasn't volunteering with the other kids or helping Josh with things. I sat and did nothing, but that was my intention. I didn't want to facilitate; I just wanted to see how things were managed with the level of staffing that was available. I felt uncomfortable helping with the other children because I didn't have access to their IEPs. I didn't know what their issues were. I knew that I didn't want someone else working with my son without my permission, so I told the teacher, "I'm sorry, I'm not here to volunteer. I'm just here to observe."

I think that made her mad, because pretty soon I got a letter in the mail from the principal stating that from now on if I wanted to come observe in the classroom, I would need to call in advance and schedule a time. The school principal continued on to say that she and the teacher would hold a meeting to decide if I could come and visit my son. I came home and became physically ill. I was throwing up, I had diarrhea, and it just hit me like a brick. "My God! Is this what I'm up against? How can this be? How can they prevent me from coming and popping in to see

how my nonverbal, disabled son is doing?" I was devastated!

In the past, I've always had nothing but positive experiences with public schools. I'm a product of public schools, my other children went through public schools. My daughter was in the Able Learners Program for gifted learners, my other son barely missed Ables. I just couldn't believe my treatment. I was in shock, and physically ill.

Once I was done throwing up, I got mad. I thought, "No, this isn't right!" That's when I got a copy of IDEA. Most people would go to bed at night and read their favorite novel. I would go to bed at night and read federal legislation. I was living on 2 hours of sleep a night during that period of time. I was drinking a lot of coffee and I was reading legislation night, after night, after night.

It took me about 2 weeks to recover from that letter. I made a call to the Office of Civil Rights (OCR). I got hooked up with our local parent advocacy group, Parents Are Vital in Education (PAVE). I was mad! I put on my best suit and I marched over to the school and barged right into the principal's office. I was very professional, and I was pinching myself the whole time so I wouldn't lose my temper. I told her, "If you are going to require that I have to call in advance, and that you will have a meeting with the teacher to determine if the time I want to visit my son is appropriate, you had better damn well do that with every parent in the district, special education and regular educa-

SUMMARY OF WORLD CULTURES

These brief descriptions of educational history around the world illustrate the pervasive adoption of Western culture, even in some of the most remote places on Earth. Christian religious groups, who dispatched missionaries and priests to colonies in Africa, Asia, and South America, were instrumental in converting indigenous educational methods to Western-style schooling. In most cases, traditional

tion. Because if you don't, that's discrimination, and I'll file an OCR complaint."

I said, "Furthermore, my son is nonverbal. He can't tell me if he is being physically abused, emotionally abused, or sexually abused. He can't come home from school and tell me what he had for lunch or how his day was. Therefore, I feel I have even more reason to pop in unannounced to see how things are going. My son is incapable of communicating his school day to me."

From that point on, every time I showed up at school, it was, "Oh, Mrs. Finkel, how pretty you look in pink. Oh my! Doesn't your hair look nice today!" It wasn't a problem after that.

That was when it hit me. That was when I first discovered that knowledge is power. If I wanted to be able to advocate for my son, I needed to know what the laws were and I needed to understand the world of special education. I didn't even know what an IEP was at that time. So I got busy and I started going to every one of the PAVE meetings. After going to many of their clinics and workshops, they asked me if I wanted to be a community liaison and of course, I said I would love to. I flew all over the country attending conferences on the topic of autism and advocacy. It was really hectic trying to keep the home program running, coordinating with the school and being gone.

I'd have to schedule the red-eye flight home, because at that time I didn't feel comfortable being gone from the house overnight because Josh was so dependent on me for his routine and stability. So I'd catch the early flight, attend the conference, go like crazy getting all the information

Josh and brother David at the lake.

I could that day and then take the last flight out to go back home that night.

The school district is actually responsible for the success I have achieved now. It was a defining moment for me when I realized what I was up against and that I had better learn how to protect my son. The only way to do that is with knowledge.

teaching methods were so effectively supplanted that knowledge of the methods themselves is lost or obscure. The industrial age that created a global economy and infiltration of Western culture to all parts of the world helped to institutionalize efforts begun by religiously motivated educators. Now, the information age will surely contribute to an ever-increasing uniformity of educational practices worldwide, in spite of the multicultural emphasis on valuing cultural integrity.

Boocock (1995) made the following generalizations from international research on early childhood programs:

1. There is widespread evidence that participating in a preschool program promotes cognitive development in the short term and prepares children to succeed in school.
2. There is no strong or consistent evidence that the form of preschool experience (pedagogic approach, daily schedule, or setting) influences long-term outcomes for children.
3. Preschool experience appears to be a stronger force in the lives of low-income than more advantaged children.
4. Preschool attendance can narrow the achievement gaps faced by disadvantaged children though most of these effects diminish over time.
5. Maternal employment and participation in out-of-home child care, even during infancy, appear not to harm children and may yield benefits if the child care is regulated and of adequate quality.

As in the United States, public preschool education in most countries is valued but not universally available. The education of preschool children with disabilities, if available, is usually conducted in separate school facilities that emphasize functional skill development and offer little in integration with other children. Finally, services to young children are constantly challenged to do more with fewer resources. Though the field has a substantial history and cross-cultural basis, many issues remain to be addressed.

POLITICAL MODE

ISSUES AND CHALLENGES IN EARLY INTERVENTION

Early intervention has reached its adolescence, but there are issues and challenges that must be confronted before it can emerge into adulthood. (Thurman, 1993, p. 303)

Children and their parents are pioneers in a world where there are no precedents for such simultaneous trends as high mobility, dual-earner parents, minimal extended-family support, single-headed households, and early academic expectations. All these disruptive factors converge on the American family, regardless of its particular form or makeup (Stegelin, 1993, p. 6).

As governments at local, state, and national levels determine policies for the coming century, they must consider a vast array of possibilities and plan for the necessary flexibility to best serve children and families. They will make decisions regarding a number of salient early childhood issues identified by Stegelin (1992), all of which have numerous permutations:

1. Child care for children at all age levels from infancy through school age, both its quality and accessibility
2. Delivery systems for a variety of quality programs such as home-based, center-based, nonprofit, for-profit, school-based, and community-based sites, all requiring extensive collaboration among agencies

3. Funding mechanisms and wage equity—determining ways to pay for services through parent fees, family support and social welfare, employer sponsored benefits, tax credits, public vouchers, purchase of services, federal funds or subsidies, state funds or subsidies, or open enrollment in programs with sliding scales for payment dependent on family incomes
4. Accountability and standards—deciding how outcomes should be measured in terms of child gains and cost effectiveness
5. Programs for impoverished and special needs children that must address family needs as well and determine long-term gains
6. Public school early childhood programs and universal access to early education
7. Developmentally appropriate curriculum and related research in early childhood education
8. Family support systems

None of these issues is easy to resolve, particularly in a time of limited economic and human resources. Such scarcity may lead to the conclusion that only certain children and their families will be able to receive services. Programs find themselves competing for a piece of a dwindling, finite pie. Therefore, decisions must be made wisely, and eligibility criteria must be seen as aspects of a continuum that has as its basis the degree of risk to which an infant or family is exposed. An intervention model that is flexible enough to provide the degree of intervention that is necessary for different situations must be developed and supported. All of these challenges may also be seen as future goals. Advocates for early childhood care, education, and intervention have a full agenda ahead of them that might include the following:

1. *Prevention programs.* Whatever can be done, must be done to expand efforts to prevent risk to young children and their families prior to birth (Thurman, 1993). Efforts might include the provision of child-rearing and birthing classes, greater access to prenatal care, increased economic security for families, genetic counseling, and family planning.

2. *Family assessment.* Professionals need to develop more extensive ways to assess and intervene with families in greater depth (Paget, 1992). For example, it is necessary to involve family members beyond the mother, who has been a traditional focus of services; early childhood professionals may be working more directly with fathers, siblings, and grandparents. It may be wise to assess the informal support provided by friends, neighbors, and relatives.

3. *Family context.* An increasing awareness of how children with disabilities may disrupt normal family functioning and impede parental effectiveness is needed (Paget, 1992). Early childhood professionals must do a better job of working within the context of particular environmental stressors, such as poverty, unemployment, the death of a parent, family discord, divorce, single-parenting, child maltreatment and abuse, and parental deviance (Pianta & Nimetz, 1992).

4. *Transition.* Professionals need to pay more attention to transitions all along the continuum of childhood and develop deliberate and effective procedures for easing stress at times of transition (Thurman, 1993).

5. *Integration with personalization.* Ultimately, children are truly included only when they develop friendships—mutual child preferences characterized by reciprocity and positive affect (Howes, Droege, & Phillipsen, 1992). This cannot occur without access to nondisabled peers, but it also requires sufficient support for children with disabilities to be functional and active in the typical settings. This implies a rethinking of how professional services are funded and provided, how parent expectations, resources, and needs are assessed and honored, and how the community as a whole accepts the concept of disability as part of the human condition.

6. *Microcomputer technology.* Professionals must be prepared to use computers in the best way possible to benefit young children. Computers can be used to enhance social interactions, improve attitudes toward learning, provide intrinsic motivation, facilitate cognitive development, and increase children's sense of competence. However, there is much to be learned about what support and guidance is necessary, how to select appropriate software, how to structure computer activities, and how to encourage independent work (Clements & Nastasi, 1992).

CLOSE-UP

CARING FOR OUR YOUNGEST: PUBLIC ATTITUDES IN THE UNITED STATES

A recent poll of public opinion regarding parent and government roles and responsibilities with respect to child care revealed (1) the American public believes parents should be the primary influence on their children and thus it is best if mothers stay home with their young children; (2) families have to be self-sufficient and low-income families may need public assistance to balance child care and employment; and (3) the public is skeptical about government involvement in providing or improving child care. These opinions demonstrate a clash in American's core values. At a time when parents are felt to be critical to the early development of their children, society believes families must be self-supporting; and, despite believing in self-sufficiency, we think it is appropriate for the government to subsidize families in order to ensure good child care, but we don't feel government involvement is a healthy solution!

The nation seems to be caught up in inconsistencies both between our values and in conflict with reality. Almost 69% of both mothers and fathers felt that fathers should work outside the home and mothers should stay home with the children. At the same time, another poll found that most women preferred to work, at least part time, outside the home rather than staying full time with their children. The 2000 Census Bureau report found that 59% of women with babies younger than age 1 were employed.

The debate over welfare for poor families was renewed in the mid 1990s; some advocates for welfare said mothers should not be required to work so that they could stay home with their children. But the public rejected this arrangement, supporting the ideal that fairness requires all welfare recipients to work. Some states exempted new mothers from working until their children reached age 1, but others made mothers go back to work when their children were 12 weeks old. Under these circumstances, most Americans felt it would behoove us to increase funding for child care for low-income families.

While parents and the public support the idea of the government helping to defray the costs of child care for parents, they don't want government to become the babysitter. More than 54% of Americans felt the government is doing too many things that should be left to individuals and private enterprise. In fact, Americans believed that religious, charitable, and community organizations can do the best job of providing services to people in need.

What does this mean for the field of child care? First, we must respect the rights of parents to raise children as they see fit. Second, we must help families balance their obligations to work and to their children. Third, the government should support community-based assistance, but not directly provide child care. A couple of programs have done this well.

The Smart Start Initiative in North Carolina sought to increase the quality of center-based programs by training staff so that parents would have more options available to them if they chose to put their children in organized child care. At the same time, Smart Start also provided subsidies to needy families so they could choose to have their children cared for by family, neighbors, or in a center.

In Vermont, the Success by Six program offered home visits for every family with a new child. New parents received a welcome bag with diapers, books, and toys. Home visitors answered questions regarding child development and referred families to available community services. Because home visitors were from the community, their presence was not perceived as government intrusion.

In conclusion, parents want choices for their children from among quality options. The government can best ensure this by making sure parents have good child-care services nearby and that families have the support to pay for the services they choose while continuing to support themselves. Our most acceptable public goals are to make sure that child care is adequate, affordable and available.

Source: "Caring for Our Youngest: Public Attitudes in the United States," by K. Sylvester, 2001, *The Future of Children, 11*(1), pp. 53–61.

IN CONCLUSION

The direction of early childhood special education is shaped by its past, but what each of us does today, as a professional, also influences that future. We must commit ourselves to the humane and dignified treatment of all children, whether they are disabled or not, and to the empowerment of their parents. We must work wisely to develop policies and programs that contribute to improved education and well-being of the next generation and to their acceptance and assistance of each other. To make wise choices, we must be informed on diagnoses and treatment, knowledgeable of best educational practices, sensitive to individual needs and contexts, and open to examining evidence of effective new developments and those of other cultures.

STUDY GUIDE QUESTIONS

1. Why is an understanding of Western civilization essential for understanding other world cultures in regard to how very young children are treated?
2. Ancient Western culture was not benevolent toward children. Why? How were children treated?
3. What rationale justified the lack of attachment to children by their parents in medieval culture?
4. What motivated the educational efforts of early American colonists? Why was this purpose so important?
5. Summarize the philosophy of Rousseau and explain how his approach differed from Puritan philosophy.
6. How did social changes in industrial America change child care? What was the larger purpose of child care at this time?
7. Compare Froebel's notion of kindergarten with the practices of today in America.
8. What influence did social reformers have on early education in the late 1800s?
9. Identify the fundamental elements of Montessori's model.
10. Explain why the Skeels and Dye (1939) study was so important to early education advocates.
11. In your opinion, why is it impossible to re-create "the best day care that ever was"?
12. In what way was Freud's theory a step backwards in child psychology?
13. How do the major conclusions of Piaget's theory reflect that of some earlier educators?
14. What were the documented long-term benefits of Head Start and Follow Through?
15. In what ways have First Chance projects influenced early education?
16. What is the relationship between provisions of IDEA legislation of 1975 and IDEA legislation of 1986 in terms of encouraging early childhood services to children who are disabled?
17. What assumptions regarding early intervention are accepted today?
18. What factors do you believe drive the current demand for qualified personnel in the field of early intervention?
19. Explain how Western notions of child care and early childhood became an influence globally.
20. What are the important issues that face early intervention today?

REFERENCES

Abramson, S., Robinson, R., & Ankenman, K. (1995, Summer). Project work with diverse students: Adapting curriculum based on the Reggio Emilia approach. *Childhood Education,* 197–202.

Administration for Children and Families. (2002). U.S. Department of Health and Human Services. June 2002 Early Head Start evaluation reports. Retrieved July 7, 2002 from *http://www.acf.dhhs.gov/programs/core/ ongoingresearch/ehs intro.html*

Aghenta, J. A., & Omatseye, J. N. (1992). Preschool and primary education in Nigeria. In G. A. Woodill, J. Bernhard, & L. Prochner (Eds.), *International handbook of early childhood education* (pp. 399–406). New York: Garland.

Al-Barwani, T. (1992). Early childhood education in the Sultanate of Oman. In G. A. Woodill, J. Bernhard, & L. Prochner (Eds.), *International handbook of early childhood education* (pp. 407–416). New York: Garland.

Andersson, B. E. (1992). Effects of day-care on cognitive and socioemotional competence of thirteen-year-old Swedish schoolchildren. *Child Development, 63,* 20–36.

Bailey, D. B. (1989). Issues and directions in preparing professionals to work with young handicapped children and their families. In J. J. Gallagher, P. L. Trohanis, & R. M. Clifford (Eds.), *Policy implementation and P. L. 99–457: Planning for young children with special needs* (pp. 97–132). Baltimore: Paul Brookes.

Bailey, D. B., & Wolery, M. (1992). *Teaching infants and preschoolers with disabilities* (2nd ed.). Upper Saddle River, NJ: Merrill/Prentice Hall.

Bloom, B. (1964). *Stability and change in human characteristics.* New York: Wiley.

Boocock, S. S. (1995). Early childhood programs in other nations: Goals and outcomes. *The Future of Children, 5*(3).

Bredekamp, S. (Ed.). (1987). *Developmentally appropriate practice in early childhood programs serving children from birth through age 8.* Washington, DC: NAEYC.

Bredekamp, S., & Copple, C. (Eds.) (1997). *Developmentally appropriate practice in early childhood programs* (rev. ed.) Washington, DC: National Association for the Education of Young Children.

Bureau of Labor Statistics, (December, 1998). *Marital and family characteristics of the labor force from the March 1998 current population survey* (unpublished data). Washington, DC: U.S. Department of Labor.

Cahan, E. D. (1989). *Past caring:. A history of the U.S. preschool care and education for the poor, 1820–1965.* Columbia University: National Center for Children.

Caldwell, B. M. (1989). Foreword: Prologue to the past. In E. D. Cahan, *Past caring: A history of U.S. preschool care and education for the poor, 1820–1965.* (pp. 4–6). Columbia University: National Center for Children.

Caldwell, B. M. (1997). Child care research comes of age. *Child Care Information Exchange,* 35–39.

Carta, J. J., Schwartz, I. S., Atwater, J. B., & McConnell, S. R. (1991). Developmentally Appropriate Practice: Appraising its usefulness for young children with disabilities. *Topics in Early Childhood Special Education. 11*(1), 1–20.

Cicirelli, V. G., Evans, J. W., & Schiller, J. S. (1969). The impact of Head Start: An evaluation of the effects of Head Start on children's cognitive and affective development. *Report to the U.S. Office of Economic Opportunity by Westinghouse Learning Corporation and Ohio University.* Washington, DC: Government Printing Office.

Clements, D. H., & Nastasi, B. K. (1992). Computers and early childhood education. In M. Gettinger, S. N. Elliott, & T. R. Kratochwill (Eds.), *Preschool and early childhood treatment directions* (pp. 113–150). Hillsdale, NJ: Lawrence Erlbaum Associates.

Cole, M., & Bruner, J. S. (1972). Preliminaries to a theory of cultural differences. In I. J. Gordon (Ed.), Early childhood education. *The seventy-first yearbook of the National Society for the Study of Education, Part II.* Chicago: University of Chicago Press.

Cook, R. E., Tessier, A., & Klein, M. D. (1992). *Adapting early childhood curricula for children with special needs* (3rd ed.). Upper Saddle River, NJ: Merrill/Prentice Hall.

Culkin, M., Morris, J. R., & Helburn, S. W. (1991). Quality and the true cost of child-care. *Journal of Social Issues, 47*(2), 71–86.

Curtis, A. (1992). Early childhood education in Great Britain. In G. A. Woodill, J. Bernhard, & L. Prochner (Eds.), *International handbook of early childhood education* (pp. 231–249). New York: Garland.

Day, D. E. (1983). *Early childhood education.* Palo Alto, CA: Scott, Foresman.

DEC holds IDEA reauthorization hearing. (1994, January). *Early Childhood Report, 1*(1), 8–11.

Dedja, B. (1992). The development of preschool and primary education in People's Socialist Republic of Albania. In G. A. Woodill, J. Bernhard, & L. Prochner (Eds.), *International handbook of early childhood education* (pp. 21–30). New York: Garland.

deMause, L. (Ed.). (1974). *The history of childhood.* New York: The Psychohistory Press.

Edwards, C., Gandini, L., & Foreman, G. (Eds.). (1993). *The hundred languages of children: The Reggio Emilia approach to early childhood.* Norwood, NJ: Ablex.

Ehrle, J., Adams, G., & Tout, K. (2001). *Who's caring for our youngest children? Child care patterns of infants and toddlers.* Washington, DC: The Urban Institute.

Excerpts from the Domostroi (mid-16th century). (2002). Retrieved July 30, 2002 from *http://www.dur.ac.uk/~dm10www/domstroi.html.*

Fallen, N. H., & Umansky, W. (1985). *Young children with special needs* (2nd ed.). Upper Saddle River, NJ: Merrill/Prentice Hall.

Forgotten Crimes. (2001). Retrieved October 5, 2001 from *http://www.butchcc.edu/dept/4/insight/disable/docs/*

Fowler, W. (1962). Cognitive learning in infancy and early childhood. *Psychological Bulletin, 59,* 116–152.

Freud, S. (1953). Three essays on sexuality. In *Standard edition, 7.* London: Hogarth.

Froebel, F. (1895). *Pedagogics of the kindergarten*. Translated by Josephine Jarvis. New York: Appleton.

Galinsky, E., et al. (1994). *The study of children in family child care and relative care: Highlights of findings*. New York: Families and Work Institute.

Gesell, A. L. (1923). *The preschool child*. New York: Macmillan.

Goelman, H., & Pence, A. (1987). Effects of child care, family, and individual characteristics on children's language development: The Victoria Day Care Research Project. In D. Phillips (Ed.), *Quality in child care: What does research tell us?* (pp. 89–104). Washington, DC: National Association for the Education of Young Children.

Gordon, A., & Browne, K. W. (1993). *Beginnings and beyond*. Albany, NY: Delmar.

Gormuyor, J. N. (1992). Early childhood education in Liberia. In G. A. Woodill, J. Bernhard, & L. Prochner (Eds.), *International handbook of early childhood education* (pp. 337–342). New York: Garland.

Greenberg, P. (1990, January). Why not academic preschool? *Young Children, 45*(2), 70–80.

Greenleaf, B. K. (1978). *Children through the ages: A history of childhood*. New York: McGraw-Hill.

Haskins, R. (1989). Beyond metaphor: The efficacy of early childhood education. *American Psychologist, 44,* 274–282.

Head Start: A Child Development Program. (1998, November). Retrieved November 9, 1998 from *http://www.head-start.lane.or.us/public/information/federal/HHS-brochure.html*

Head Start quality, expansion guidelines released. (1994, February). *Early Childhood Report, 5*(2), 1–3.

Helburn, S., Culkin, M. L., Howes, C., Bryant, D., Clifford, R., Cryer, D., Peisner-Feinberg, E., Kagan, S. L. (1995). *Cost, quality, and child outcomes in child care centers*. Denver, CO: University of Colorado. Executive Summary.

HEW reports 13 percent of Head Start children are handicapped. (1978). *Report of Preschool Education, 10.*

Heward, W. L., & Orlansky, M. D. (1992). *Exceptional children* (4th ed.). Upper Saddle River, NJ: Merrill/Prentice Hall.

Hewes, D., & Hartman, B. (1974). *Early childhood education: A workbook for administrators* (2nd ed.). San Francisco: R & E Associates.

Hofferth, S. L., & Phillips, D. A. (1991). Child care policy research. *Journal of Social Issues, 47*(2), 1–13.

Howes, C., Droege, K., & Phillipsen, L. (1992). Contribution of peers to socialization in early childhood. In M. Gettinger, S. N. Elliott, & T. R. Kratochwill (Eds.), *Preschool and early childhood treatment directions* (pp. 113–150). Hillsdale, NJ: Lawrence Erlbaum Associates.

Hunt, J. M. (1961). *Intelligence and experience*. New York: Ronald Press.

Itard, J. M. G. (1962). *The wild boy of Aveyron*. New York: Appleton-Century-Crofts.

Jensen, A. R. (1969). How much can we boost I.Q. and scholastic achievement? *Harvard Educational Review, 39,* 1–123.

Kagitcibasi, C. (1991, February). *The early enrichment project in Turkey*. Paris: UNESCO-UNICEF-WFP.

Kaul, V. (1992). Early childhood education in India. In G. A. Woodill, J. Bernhard, & L. Prochner (Eds.), *International handbook of early childhood education* (pp. 275–292). New York: Garland.

Kellaghan, T., & Greaney, B. J. (1993). *The educational development of students following participation in a preschool programme in a disadvantaged area*. Dublin: St. Patrick's College, Educational Research Center.

Key Facts. (1999). *Essential information on child care, early education, and school age care*. Washington, DC: Children's Defense Fund.

Kresnak, J. (1999, January 12). *Clinton's child-care plan wins praise*. Detroit: Detroit Free Press. Retrieved October 5, 2001 from *http://www.freep.com*

Labov, W. (1972). *Language in the inner city*. Philadelphia: University of Pennsylvania Press.

Laing, Z., & Pang, L. (1992). Early childhood education in the People's Republic of China. In G. A. Woodill, J. Bernhard, & L. Prochner (Eds.), *International handbook of early childhood education* (pp. 169–174). New York: Garland.

McCollum, J. A. (2000). Taking the past along: Reflecting on our identity as a discipline. *Topics in Early Childhood Special Education, 2*(2), 79–86.

McKay, A., & McKay, H. (1983). Primary school progress after preschool experience: Troublesome issues in the conduct of follow-up research and findings from the Cali, Colombia Study. In K. King & R. Myers, (Eds.), *Preventing School Failure* (pp. 36–41). Ottawa, Canada: International Development Research Center.

McMahan, I. D. (1992). Public preschool from the age of two: The e'cole maternelle in France. *Young Children, 47*(5), 22–28.

Monau, R. (1992). Early childhood education in Botswana. In G. A. Woodill, J. Bernhard, & L. Prochner (Eds.), *International handbook of early childhood education* (pp. 111–118). New York: Garland.

Montessori, M. (1964). *The Montessori method*. Cambridge, MA: Robert Bentley.

National Association for the Education of Young Children. (1991). *Accreditation criteria and procedures of the National Academy of Early Childhood Programs* (rev. ed.). Washington, DC: Author.

National Center for Education Statistics. (1996, October). *Child care and early education program participation of infants, toddlers, and preschoolers* (NCES 95-824). Washington, DC: U.S. Department of Education.

Neugebauer, R. (1990, December). Child care's long and colorful past. *Child Care Information Exchange,* 5–9.

Noguchi, I., Ogawa, S., Yoshidawa, T., & Hashimoto, S. (1992). Early education in Japan: From ancient times to the present. In G. A. Woodill, J. Bernhard, & L. Prochner (Eds.), *International handbook of early childhood education* (pp. 317–326). New York: Garland.

Ochiltree, G., & Edgar, D. (1990). *The effects of nonmaternal care in the first twelve months of life on children in the first year of school. Preliminary findings from a two stage study (The Early Childhood Study).* Melbourne: Australian Institute of Family Studies.

Office of Special Education and Rehabilitative Services (OSERS). (2002). *23rd annual report to Congress on the implementation of the IDEA.* Retrieved September 9, 2003 from *http://www.ed.gov/about/reports/annual/osep/2001/index.html*

Olmsted, P. P. (1989). *A look at early childhood education in the United States from a global perspective.* Paper commissioned by the National Center for Educational Statistics.

Paget, K. D. (1992). Parent involvement in early childhood services. In M. Gettinger, S. N. Elliott, & T. R. Kratochwill, (Eds.), *Preschool and early childhood treatment directions* (pp. 89–111). Hillsdale, NJ: Lawrence Erlbaum Associates.

Pestalozzi, J. H. (1915). *How Gertrude teaches her children.* (L. E. Holand, & F. C. Turner, Trans.) Syracuse, NY: C. W. Bordeen. (Originally published 1801).

Pianta, R. C., & Nimetz, S. L. (1992). Development of young children in stressful contexts: Theory, assessment, and prevention. In M. Gettinger, S. N. Elliott, & T. R. Kratochwill, (Eds.), *Preschool and early childhood treatment directions* (pp. 151–185). Hillsdale, NJ: Lawrence Erlbaum Associates.

Pierce, W. D., & Epling, W. F. (1995). *Behavior analysis and learning.* Upper Saddle River, NJ: Prentice Hall.

Polakow, V. (1997, April). Who cares for the children? Denmark's unique public child-care model. *Phi Delta Kappan,* 604–610.

Rousseau, J. J. (1969). *Emile.* (A. Bloom, Trans.). New York: Basic Books. (Originally published 1762).

Sandall, S., McLean, M. E., & Smith, B. J. (2000). *DEC recommended practices in early intervention/early childhood special education.* Longmont, CO: Sopris West.

Schulman, L., & Adams, G. (1998). *Issue Brief: The high cost of child care puts quality care out of reach for many families.* Washington, DC: Children's Defense Fund.

Skeels, H. M. (1966). Adult status of children with contrasting early life experiences. *Monographs of the Society for Research in Child Development, 31,* (Serial No. 105).

Skeels, H. M., & Dye, H. B. (1939). A study of the effects of differential stimulation on mentally retarded children. *Convention Proceedings, American Association of Mental Deficiency, 44,* 114–136.

Smith, M. S., & Bissell, J. S. (1970). Report analysis: The impact of Head Start. *Harvard Educational Review, 40,* 51–104.

Stegelin, D. A. (1993). Early childhood policy: An introduction. In D. A. Stegelin (Ed.), *Early Childhood education: Policy issues for the 1990s* (pp. 1–18). Norwood, NJ: Ablex Publishing.

Sylvester, K. (2001). Caring for our youngest: Public attitudes in the United States. *The Future of Children, 11*(1), 53–61.

Thorndike, E. L. (1913). *The psychology of learning.* New York: Teachers College Press, Columbia University.

Thurman, K. S. (1993). Some perspectives on the continuing challenges in early intervention. In W. Brown, S. K. Thurman, & L. F. Pearl (Eds.), *Family-centered early intervention with infants and toddlers: Innovative cross-disciplinary approaches* (pp. 303–316). Baltimore: Paul H. Brookes.

Tietze, W. (1987). A structural model for the evaluation of preschool effects. *Early Childhood Research Quarterly, 2*(2), 133–153.

Turnbull, R. (1997). *New ways of serving and supporting people with mental retardation in the new century—policy directions.* Paper presented at The Arc's National Leadership Training Conference. Retrieved October 23, 2002 from *http://thearc.org/misc/arc.2000.html*

U.S. Census Bureau. (September, 1999). *Money and income in the United States: 1998 Current Population Reports, 60–206.* Washington, DC: U.S. Government Printing Office.

U.S. Department of Labor Women's Bureau. (1997, November). *Facts on Working Women.* No. 98–1. Washington, DC: U.S. Department of Labor.

Warger, C. (Ed.). (1988). *A Resource Guide to Public School Early Childhood Programs.* Alexandria, VA: Association for Supervision and Curriculum Development.

Watson, J. B. (1914). *Behavior.* New York: Henry Holt.

Wesley, J. (1872). *Sermon 95: On the education of children.* Retrieved July 30, 2002 from *http://www.ccel.org/w/wesley/sermons/sermons-html/serm-095.html*

White, E. G. (2002). *Education.* Retrieved July 30, 2002 from *http://elenwhite.org/sl/ed34.htm*

Williams, L. R. (1992). Determining the curriculum. In C. Seefeldt (Ed.), *The early childhood curriculum; A review of current research* (2nd ed., pp. 1–15). New York: Teachers College Press.

Woodill, G. A. (1992). International early childhood care and education: Historical perspectives. In G. A. Woodill, J. Bernhard, & L. Prochner (Eds.), *International handbook of early childhood education* (pp. 3–10). New York: Garland.

Woodill, G. A., J. Bernhard, & L. Prochner (Eds.). (1992). *International handbook of early childhood education* (pp. 3–10). New York: Garland.

Wylie, C. (1994). *What research on early childhood education/care outcomes can, and can't, tell policymakers*. Wellington: New Zealand Council for Educational Research.

Wyman, A. (January, 1995). The earliest early childhood teachers: Women teachers of America's dame schools. *Young Children*, 29–32.

Zigler, E., & Muenchow, S. (1992). *Head Start: The inside story of America's most successful educational experiment*. New York: Basic Books.

Zinsser, C. (October, 1984). The best day care there ever was. *Working Mother*, 76–78.

3 Relationship-Based Teaming with Families

Our daughter at age three fell into our family pool. As she lay in critical condition for three days, my thoughts and my prayers were that she would live. After three days, we were told that our daughter would survive. Then the words I dreaded came. But more horrifying than I ever imagined. My daughter would never walk again. I would never hear her little voice. Severely brain damaged, they said. I was so alone. I wasn't a nurse, nor a doctor and had little experience. Yet I wanted to take this medically fragile child home and care for her. But how? Who would help me?

(Beach Center on Families and Disability, Summer 1998)

The poet Maya Angelou captured our concern for families, "At our best level of existence, we are parts of a family, and at our highest level of achievement, we work to keep the family alive." This may be the best definition of family-centered practice (Beach Center on Families and Disability, Summer 1997). Perhaps the most extraordinary outcome of legislation supporting services for very young children with disabilities and their families has been the requirement of interdisciplinary and interagency cooperation with families. Our nation has matured considerably from days, not too distant past, when parents were shamefully considered the cause of their children's disabilities to a point where families are now viewed as partners or collaborators in the decision making and treatment of their children's special needs (Turnbull & Turnbull 1996). In recent years, all education legislation passed by Congress has strengthened a commitment to collaboration (Dettmer, Dyck, & Thurston, 1999).

Family-centered practice and philosophy embrace the following key components (Beach Center on Families and Disability, 1998):

1. Focus on the family, not just the child
2. Emphasis on mutual respect and teamwork
3. Organized assistance according to individual family needs
4. Consideration of family strengths, talents, resources, attributes, and aspirations
5. Actions that address family needs holistically (not focusing on one member)
6. Information given to families in a supportive manner
7. Recognition that there are similar family reactions to exceptional circumstances
8. Delivery of services structured to make them accessible without undue disruption of the family integrity and routine

Family-centered principles encourage delivering services in natural, least-restrictive settings while honoring child needs and family preferences. They encourage identifying both formal and informal family supports in the home and in the community. These principles require professionals to be culturally sensitive, competent, legally accountable, and well-trained. Family-centered also means being cost-efficient and working to support in-home and community placements. Finally, to be "family first" is to speak people-first language that refers to the person before the disability. In short, these principles increase family empowerment (Beach Center for Families and Disability, 1999).

Family empowerment is "a process through which people become more able to influence those people and organizations that affect their lives and the lives of those they care about" (Vanderslice, 1984). Those who foster empowerment promote access to resources, competence, and self-efficacy (Heflinger & Bickman, 1997). Most importantly, a relationship exists in which professionals view families as part of an equal, reciprocal partnership (Swick, 1996). One of the most important functions of empowerment is to provide skills that promote self-sufficiency. Empowerment may grow through a family's changes in self-perception, increased self-confidence, ability to set goals, acquisition of skills to attain goals, and the opportunity for supported practice (Dunlap, 1997). Families may transition from isolation to independence, from feeling alienated to feeling a part of the solution (Dunlap, 1997). Strategies that promote family empowerment include:

1. Involving families in developing plans to address critical needs
2. Personalizing contacts between helpers and families where there is mutual trust and support
3. Networking with other families for problem solving and enrichment
4. Enabling action through provision of services such as child care and transportation
5. Offering a variety of meaningful activities, such as home visits, group meetings, individual conferences
6. Focusing on prevention of risk factors
7. Advocating for collaborative community services

When parents of children with developmental disabilities were asked to identify the most important aspects of support programs, they identified empowerment among their highest ratings (Herman, Marcenko, & O'Hazel, 1996). They said services should be guided by the principles of family-centered care and should result in families and individuals who are integrated into their community, carry out the tasks of family life independently and autonomously, and make productive contributions to society. They also emphasized the need to be connected with other parents and stressed the importance of healthy interpersonal relationships with staff.

CLOSE-UP

PARAEDUCATOR EXPERIENCES IN INCLUSIVE SETTINGS: HELPING, HOVERING, OR HOLDING THEIR OWN

The role of paraeducators has grown in recent years as more special education students attend regular programs with one-on-one assistance. In an effort to meet both the needs of the students and the teachers in inclusive settings, paraeducators have been hired to assist with behavioral and physical challenges specific to individual children. These staff members often become a child's personal "specialist" but hold a position on the teaching team that is poorly defined, presenting difficult challenges for the paraeducator. Interviews with 20 paraeducators revealed the following responsibilities: (1) keeping a student from being a bother to the teacher, (2) meeting a student's immediate needs, (3) being the "hub" and the "expert" on a child, and (4) representing inclusion to other team members. The following excerpts from these interviews illustrate each of these challenges.

Paraeducators felt their most pressing responsibility was making sure regular teachers were not "burdened" by an inclusion student; that is, to make sure the inclusion experience was a positive one for all involved. More than half the para-educators felt their role was to address immediate daily needs of the student, which most often meant adapting an activity for the student's participation. One paraeducator noted, "It would take a lot of modifications so the child can participate more in the class. . . . And it was left for me to initiate, and they would say, 'Oh that sounds like a great idea'. . . . And I would end up doing it, and trying it" (p. 321).

Paraeducators felt they were the "hub" for a child, the liaison between all the various individuals who were involved with the inclusion child. This often meant they had to be the one to see that everyone's suggestions were implemented and were, in fact, the "expert" on the child. "I felt like . . . I was very much the hub, with the spokes coming in' " (p. 322).

Sometimes the paraeducators felt they were responsible for representing the whole idea of inclusion to the rest of the school and community. They felt that how their students actually did would be a reflection on the inclusion movement. " . . . it's a lot of education, talking to people about the student, 'Well you know she is very capable, she learns at a slower rate because of her disability, but she is quite capable of functioning . . . With adaptations, of course'" (p. 322).

Paraeducators want to be a part of the child's team, from planning through implementation. They need teaming as a way to share their expertise, to clarify their roles, and to plan for a student's increased independence. They also need more training on accommodations and the support of other team members.

Source: "Paraeducator Experiences in Inclusive Settings: Helping, Hovering, or Holding Their Own," by S. U. Marks, C., Schrader, and M. Levine, 1999, *Exceptional Children, 65*(3), 315–328.

RELATIONSHIP-BASED SERVICES TO FAMILIES

To be genuinely "family friendly," early intervention and preschool practitioners need to pay attention to the emotional experience of family members (Hirshberg, 1997/1998). A capacity for empathy is especially essential when helping families facing multiple challenges, such as dealing with a child's medical condition, obtaining funding for needed treatment, finding respite care in order to continue working, and providing support to nondisabled siblings. Though empowerment requires a focus on a family's strengths, it does not mean the professional should ignore the family's vulnerability and pain. Frequently there are barriers to a family's effective use of the help offered by early intervention and special education professionals due to complex attitudes, feelings, expectations, and behavior. Effective collaboration in serving a child with a disability is most likely when the parents and professionals involved have established a trusting relationship.

Fraiberg and her colleagues (Fraiberg, L., 1980; Fraiberg, S. 1996) described the importance of family relationships across four modalities: concrete assistance, emotional support, developmental guidance, and insight-oriented psychotherapy. Each term indicates increasing levels of psychological support thought of as points along a continuum. The first point concerns helping parents identify basic needs (**concrete assistance**) a team could provide or refer to appropriate providers, such as housing, childcare, and transportation. **Emotional support** involves encouraging, eliciting, listening to and thinking about parents' descriptions of their experiences. Is a parent afraid for the future, exhausted by the demands of caring for her child, or feeling guilty about causing a disabling condition?

> Shepherding a child through infancy and toddlerhood is a process that shakes all parents to the core at certain moments, no matter how many resources and how much support they have. The simple act of someone else knowing, bearing witness to, and normalizing this fact can make the difference between a parent feeling like the most horrible person on earth at such a moment, and feeling like one in the number of parents populating the planet (St. John & Pawl, 2000, p. 4).

Developmental guidance involves providing information about age-appropriate behaviors, interests, concerns and conflicts, and suggesting positive parental responses based on their developmental understanding of their child. For example, a typical 2-year-old would be exploring his environment by opening doors, banging toys, and making messes around the house. It might be suggested that parents of a 2-year-old with a disability find ways their nonmobile child could also explore, encouraging and even celebrating the resulting messes rather than getting angry when they occur.

Psychotherapy, on the other hand, involves understanding a parent's reactions to the child in the context of his or her own early experience, current circumstances or psychological conflicts. For example, a parent of a child with Down syndrome may remember having an uncle with Down syndrome who was institutionalized and who frightened the parent as a young child on one of the rare occasions when the uncle joined a family get-together. That early experience may make the parent feel unaccountably sad for his own child and pessimistic about the child's future. The level of psychological support that might be appropriate in this situation would be the specialty of a mental health professional, such as a social worker or counselor, and would be explored only in those cases when there are complicated emotional needs. An early interventionist or special education preschool provider who has an empathetic relationship with a parent should recognize the need for referral for such services.

A relationship-based approach seeks to establish and maintain partnership, attention, and connectedness between a parent and child (St. John & Pawl, 2000). Professionals are required to be flexible and active in noticing and responding to new information coming from parents and their children in terms of their experiences. Noticing the unique way each parent and child fit together, helping parents find their own solutions to problems and being comfortable with the results they reach is another aspect of such relationships. Relationships are built in order to use them as instruments for change and growth. Early intervention and special education professionals should share observations about the infant's or preschooler's growth and development, offer anticipatory guidance to the parent that is specific to the child, alert the parent to the child's individual accomplishments and needs, and help the parent find pleasure in his relationship with the child (Weatherston, 2000).

The early childhood professional's role in this relationship is to offer parents multiple opportunities to nurture, protect, steady, and enhance their understanding about their very young children. Team members can use spontaneous events as "teachable moments" to provide information that should help parents understand their child's temperament, behavior, and development (Kaplan-Sanoff, Lerner, & Bernard, 2000). Observing parents and children together, noticing what is happening, inviting the parent's comments, and reinforcing what is going well helps a team make useful suggestions. As professionals and parents grow comfortable with each other, it becomes possible to discuss both pleasurable and painful aspects of the parent/child relationship. Professionals should create opportunities for interaction between a parent and child, allow parents to take the lead in interacting with the child or determining what to talk about, and identify and enhance the capacities that each parent brings to the care of his child (Weatherston, 2000).

As advocates, professionals should help parents voice their feelings about their relationships with their children and to understand these feelings. This may mean identifying and discussing early negative as well as positive parent experiences with a child. This will require listening; allowing emotions and conflicts to be expressed; attending to and responding to parent concerns; and collaborating with others if needed, to provide treatment in those situations where there may be serious family dysfunction, such as drug abuse, mental illness, or violence (Weatherston, 2000).

The relationship-based approach in an early intervention or preschool program describes a framework for the delivery of many kinds of services that may be described as promotion, preventive intervention, and treatment (Heffron, 2000). Promotion stresses wellness, which is important in the early years for supportive, nurturing interactions between parents and children. Public education and information about how to optimize child development would be considered promotion. Public health nurses, child-care providers, or pediatricians, for example, might put colorful posters on their walls describing typical development.

Relationship-based preventive intervention is a way of delivering a variety of services to infants, toddlers, and their families that includes a focus on the importance of parent-child interaction, and how a staff–family relationship influences family–child interaction. For example, a speech and language specialist might help a parent understand the kinds of cues and signals a child is giving when overstimulated, and thus help a parent to know when to speak slowly and softly or to end a practice session. At the same time, the speech and language specialist might notice that the parent is frowning while listening to this advice and should then take time to ask if the parent is concerned about the child's low tolerance for interaction. At the point such a conversation takes on a "therapy feel," the professional should recognize that a mental health specialist should be consulted (Heffron, 2000).

Families with difficulties that include mental health needs beyond those involving interaction with their children need specialized treatment. Such problems might include diagnosed mental illness, serious drug use, or persistent marital problems, for example. Not every member of an early intervention or special education team can or should attempt to intervene when mental trauma or pathology is present. It is unlikely a special education teacher or a physical therapist, for example, has been trained in dealing with serious psychological trauma. However, a social worker, counselor, or psychologist might be specifically identified by a team as the most appropriate member to address these issues. Of course, the parents themselves would have to be willing to participate in any mental health treatment that might be recommended and should have options from which to choose a level of intervention that is most comfortable for their family.

UNDERSTANDING FAMILIES

In order to establish a trusting relationship between families and professionals, early childhood providers may need to first calibrate their own attitudes and perspectives. Special education services have a history of stereotyping parents in ways that have not been productive. Stereotyping or generalizing about families is not confined to educators, but this practice creates an especially serious barrier to treatment objectives in early childhood services. The challenge for practitioners is to overcome these tendencies. From 1960 through 1980, a large body of research was compiled that indicated families of children with disabilities, as compared to families of children without disabilities, were at increased risk for stress (Kazak, 1986) and depression (Cox, Rutter, Newman, & Bartak, 1975), had different family coping strategies or styles (McCubbin et al., 1982), had less family cohesion (Darling, 1979), had more family strain (Roth, 1982), and experienced greater social isolation (Breslau, 1983). Subsequently, both researchers and theorists assumed that these families had an increased risk of family dysfunction. Research in the 1990s, which focused less on the pathology of deficiency, has been more expansive and indicates that many of the early research assumptions should be questioned. It now appears that the psychosocial functioning of families of children with disabilities is more similar to that of families of children without disabilities than it is different. Though extensive needs are expressed by all families, those with children who have disabilities face different, though not necessarily extraordinary, obstacles.

Like other families with facing crises, the impact of a disability may be negative, positive, or mixed (Turnbull & Turnbull, 1996). Some early studies indicated that divorce or disruption of marriage was disproportionately high when there was an exceptional child in the family (Gath, 1977; Murphy, 1982; Reed & Reed, 1965), but more recent studies have indicated that the divorce rate is not higher for these families (Benson & Gross, 1989) and that these marriages are sometimes strengthened because of a shared commitment for their child (Kazak & Marvin, 1984). Singer and Nixon (1996) found that exceptionality can simultaneously strengthen and impair a couple's relationship. On the other hand, some researchers found no differences in personal relationships between families who had exceptional children and those who didn't (Abbott & Meredith, 1986; Young & Roopnarine, 1994).

One mother shared how her daughter's disability changed her life:

> In my house there is an eight-by-ten picture of me taken on my wedding day. It is just my face, looking somewhat seriously into the camera. When I am in a particularly melancholy frame of mind, it is sad for me to see it, for the woman in that picture is gone. . . . I was 23, my husband Jim had just turned

22 and we knew little about anything then. Eleven months later, . . . Maggie
was born. She was not a planned child, and I do not think much else in my
life has been since that day. As my husband peered into the nursery he saw
Maggie turn, in his words, "navy blue." He came running into my room yelling,
"There's something wrong with the baby!" and my life changed forever. . . . I
wish that the woman in that picture could have left me less suddenly, less
painfully. But the person she left behind is smarter, wiser, more confident. . . .
She has tested the love of her family and friends and has found it to be strong
and enduring. She knows there is little life can put in her path that she will not
be able to face and conquer head on. (Klemm & Schimanski, 1999, pp.
109–110)

Not surprisingly, mothers typically assume the responsibility for caring for their
family needs, including the special needs of a child with a disability (Traustadottir, 1991). Fathers tend to spend a comparable amount of time in child care
whether their children are disabled or not (Turbiville, 1995), about two-thirds less
than mothers (Young & Roopnarine, 1994). However, when fathers engage in
greater participation, there is improved marital satisfaction for both parents
(Willoughby & Glidden, 1995). It's important, therefore, that efforts to empower
a family are directed to both parents when both are present (Turnbull & Turnbull,
1996). Yet, fathers tend to feel left out for several reasons: (1) services are often
scheduled during the day when they are at their place of employment; (2) professionals in early intervention and preschool tend to be overwhelmingly women,
making a male uncomfortable in communicating; and (3) service providers may
discourage a father's interest unintentionally by coming to expect mothers to be
the main family spokesperson (Beach Center on Families and Disability, 1995).

Research is similarly mixed on siblings in families with children who are disabled. Some studies showed that siblings have a higher incidence of emotional
and behavioral problems (Orsillo, McCaffrey, & Fisher, 1993) such as lower self-
esteem (McHale & Gamble, 1989), but other researchers have not found greater
problems (Gath & Gumley, 1987). Carr (1988) found siblings of children with disabilities actually had fewer behavioral problems than the siblings of children without disabilities. Opportunities for positive contributions by siblings are apparent:
enhanced maturity, social competence, insight, tolerance, pride, advocacy, and
loyalty are all attributes that might evolve from growing up with children who
have special needs (Meyer & Vadasy, 1994).

Thirteen-year-old Matthew (Fennel, 1999) wrote this about his sibling:

My brother Alex and I used to roll around on the ground for hours while I tick-
led him. We had so much fun. As we got older, I realized that Alex was different from other kids. It never changed my love for him, but we could not
share in things as much as we used to. Because of his autism, Alex cannot
speak. Nor can he understand many words that are said. . . . Though Alex is
unable to speak, he is able to tell us things in other ways. His autism has
shown me how to love. In a way, autism could help the world to be rid of ha-
tred and anger. (p. 132)

Extended family members may also be an important part of the family unit as
well as a source of support; this is truer in some cultures than in others (Turnbull
& Turnbull, 1996). Grandparents often participate in a wide range of everyday tasks

related to family care (Able-Boone, Sandall, Stevens, & Frederick, 1992). In African American families, for example, grandmothers are commonly the family matriarchs who provide shelter, care, and advice on a daily basis. When there is a child with a disability, the whole family may be called into action; grandmother may accompany the parents to planning meetings and doctor's visits, an aunt may arrange transportation, and cousins may babysit siblings left at home. This kind of support makes economic sense and encourages the well-being of the parents and the child with a disability; more people care and advocate for the child with special needs.

Whether discussion focuses on families of children with disabilities or families of children without disabilities, the reality is that many family units are not composed of two parents. Though statistics vary, it is now probable that professionals supporting families will be working with many families that consist of one parent with one or two children, headed by either a mother or father. Furthermore, in two-parent households, it is likely that families will consist of a blend of children from at least one previous marriage and will consequently include multiple family systems. Other family configurations include:

◆ Extended family members as primary caregivers (grandmother, grandfather, aunt, or uncle)
◆ Same-sex parenting partners
◆ Families without homes
◆ Families built through adoption or foster care

Each of these family configurations adds to the complexity of interactions between families and professionals. Table 3–1 highlights some of the factors that

Table 3–1 Variables That Make Family-Professional Interaction Challenging

Situation	Impact
Family structure	loyalties, power, complex and varying rules under similar conditions, transitions between dwellings, availability of equipment
Child-care requirements	availability of child care for infants, toddlers and young children with disabilities, debates with child-care providers about the realities of serving children with disabilities, financial burdens
Single -parent families	time and resource management, single-parent income, transportation issues, ill child responsibilities, possible conflict with personal goals, increased need for respite care
Nontraditional partnerships	prejudice of service providers and local community, debates over "proper parenting authority," legal authority issues
Poverty	prejudice of service providers toward poor persons, lack of transportation to get to and from services, possible lack of phone services, possible lack of a permanent address
Substance abuse	immediate impact on the person suffering the abuse, subsequent impact on immediate and extended family members, inability to keep priorities in desired order, secondary health issues, guilt, shame
Foster care	no long term goals or personal authority, lack of accurate history

may be involved in diverse family structures and the impact of these variations on family relationships with professionals.

Though family service programs have historically been based on a traditional, albeit somewhat fictional, family model, it is realistic to define families more broadly today. Dettmer and colleagues (1999) recommend an inclusive definition of family that was articulated at the Second Family Leadership Conference:

> A family is a group of people who are important to each other and offer each other love and support, especially in times of crisis. In order to be sensitive to the wide range of life styles, living arrangements, and cultural variations that exist today, family . . . can no longer be limited to just parent/child relationships. Family involvement . . . must reach out to include mothers, fathers, grandparents, sisters, brothers, neighbors, and other persons who have important roles in the lives of people with disabilities. (Family and Integration Resources, 1991, p. 37, as cited in Dettmer et al., 1999)

Census data support such an inclusive definition. Although married-couple families still represent the majority of family households in the United States, there have been substantial increases in postponed marriages, divorces, and nonmarital births that have contributed to a rise in single-parent families, mostly headed by women (Leslie & Morton, 2001). Single women headed 23% of all families, while single men headed 5% in 1997. Cohabitation has become so commonplace that 40% of all children will spend some time in such an arrangement before age 16. A survey of gay and lesbian adults who considered themselves unmarried partners revealed that as many as 27% of these partners cared for children in a family situation.

The last U. S. census also found that more than 2 million grandparents were guardians for their grandchildren (Bauer & Shea, 2003). Many other children were in non-relative foster care, and a high percentage of them received special education services. Likewise, almost half of homeless children living in shelters qualified for special education with at least one disability. These families present particularly challenging risks.

PARENTAL RESPONSES TO THE DIAGNOSIS OF A DISABILITY

For many families, life becomes more difficult from the first moments a child's disability is diagnosed. After a review of the literature, Moore, Howard, and McLaughlin (2002) concluded that all families have needs; it just so happens that for families of children with disabilities, the obstacles are those of a child with special needs. Other families must deal with issues such as poverty, mental illness, child abuse, divorce, drugs, or death of family members, but not of a child with a disability. According to Moore et al., these factors do not make families special, unusual, dysfunctional, or, least of all, homogeneous. There are, however, some shared reactions to crisis that should be recognized.

Parents unexpectedly faced with the loss of "typical child" hopes and expectations often proceed through several common stages, ranging from total disbelief and bewilderment to the ability to grasp and control the situation. Even so, every parent or couple responds to a diagnosis of a disability in accord with their own external and internal resources. Dr. Elizabeth Kubler-Ross, in her classic research with cancer patients over three decades ago (Kubler-Ross, 1969), first identified the general progression people in grief follow; these stages are referred to as the grief cycle.

Professionals working with parents of at-risk infants or infants in crisis recognized that many, though not all, parents of children with disabilities proceed through the same or similar phases (Featherstone, 1980; Turnbull & Turnbull, 1985). Today, many early childhood professionals refer to Kubler-Ross's reaction cycle as **stage theory response**.

Stage theory response is useful primarily to parents who find that naming their complex emotions helps order them and facilitates communication with others who have similar experiences. Knowledge of stage theory response also helps professionals validate parental emotions. However, when used to label parents or to associate a pathology with a particular stage, stage theory response is potentially harmful.

Consider two conversations as samples of appropriate and inappropriate use of grief stage theory. A parent may say, "Sometimes when I'm told about all my child's problems, I get so angry I feel like throwing things." A professional conscious of stage theory may appropriately respond, "That's not unusual. I've known other parents who felt the same way. Do you suppose your anger is a part of how you are coping emotionally?" On the other hand, if a parent says, "I feel like screaming sometimes, because I am treated like a bystander and no one asks my opinion about my child's treatment!" and the professional inappropriately thinks, "That woman is clearly in the anger stage!" and ignores the parent's perception of the relationship, then stage theory is being applied inappropriately. It is necessary to realize that passage through grief, like any other life passage, is not a sign of dysfunction but of normalcy.

The stages, or phases, described are neither sequential nor of equal duration, intensity, or frequency in reoccurrence, either within or across families. Parents often report that the stages overlap and almost always reoccur, often at periods of significant transition. Studies by Allen and Affleck (1985) indicated that for some parents, a stage may last one day or one year. What is important to know and remember about the grief or adjustment process is that knowledge of the process often helps parents to understand that these common emotional behaviors are shared by many others in similar circumstances. The key components of the stage theory, or grief process, as described by Kubler-Ross and subsequent researchers (Francis & Jones, 1984; Seligman & Darling, 1989) are shock and denial, anger and frustration, volatile emotions (hope, isolation, depression), bargaining, and, finally, acceptance or reestablishment. Cook, Tessier, and Klein (1992) outlined several ways in which early childhood professionals can support parents through each of these stages (see Table 3–2).

Anderegg, Vergason, and Smith (1992) studied the grief process with 130 parents. Their work led to the development of a slightly different model, though it is still supportive of earlier work. This later research indicated that parents and extended family members pass through three phases:

1. Confronting (denial, blame/guilt, shock)
2. Adjusting (depression, anger, bargaining)
3. Adapting (life-cycle changes, realistic planning, adjusting expectations)

Table 3–2 Stage Theory Response and How Professionals Should Support Parents

Stages and Responses	Support Needed
Shock, Disbelief, and Denial: May be accompanied by feelings of shame, guilt, and unworthiness. Parents may try to deny the existing problems. Parents may go from doctor to doctor seeking opinions. Some may refuse to accept guidance.	Convey to parents that these feelings are appropriate. Listen with acceptance. Help parents focus on ways professionals can work with them to benefit the child. Become active listeners through patience and practice.
Anger and Resentment: Parents may direct anger at the very professionals who are trying to help and be suspicions about a professional's motives. Verbal abuse is common and parents try to prove the professional to be wrong about their child.	Professionals must be understanding, compassionate, and gently caring. They should get parents busy with child activities that cannot fail. Refuse to blame or react to unreasonable demands.
Bargaining: Parents may work diligently as if to say, "If I do everything you tell me to do, then this problem will go away." If progress is not rapid, they may become severely depressed.	Be empathetic, recognize and accept the natural feelings of parents. Convey an attitude of interest and caring.
Depression and Discouragement: Hopelessness overtakes parents but may make them more likely to request assistance. Parents may be saying "good-bye" to the normal image of the child they held. Parents can begin to focus on productive solutions.	Focus on the positive but avoid over-eagerness to get on with the intervention. Give parents activities that will be successful to avoid self-doubt. Avoid all criticism as well as unwarranted praise. Provide access to parent support groups.
Acceptance: Parents have an increasing willingness to do practical, useful activities. The child's needs are recognized, not denied. There may be a conviction that much needs to be done and will make a difference.	Encourage the parents to be patient and set realistic goals. Help parents read their child's cues. Praise the parents for the child's progress. Focus on positive interaction techniques.

Source: Adapting Early Childhood Curriculum for Children in Inclusive Settings, 6/E, by Ruth E. Cook and Diane M. Klein, ©2004. Reprinted by permission of Pearson Education, Inc., Upper Saddle River, NJ.

A number of factors account for a family's ability to reach a point of adjustment and acceptance. Among the most significant factors are the characteristics of a child's exceptionality, the degree of exceptionality, and, in particular, the demands of an exceptionality (Turnbull & Turnbull, 1996). Werner and Smith (1982) found that family configuration (e.g., single-parent family, blended family), family size, and socioeconomic status also affected a family's ability to cope and adjust.

The passage from diagnosis to adaptation is cyclical and complex. Some parents feel they never really move out of a low-grade sadness that seems to permeate their lives. However, shifts usually do take place. The early panic that follows a diagnosis of an infant in crisis usually changes and develops according to healthy patterns of adaptation.

Case Study JOSH'S FAMILY: INTERVIEW WITH AMY FINKEL

That first year, Josh's older brother, David, was essentially neglected. I had so much to do focusing on my disabled child. I started to see by the end of the year that David was starting some attention-getting behaviors. It woke me up to the fact that I had two other children who also needed me. So we've made a real effort to do things just with David, and just with Josh's older sister Rebecca. Rebecca is a musician, so we get a babysitter and go to her concerts and do things just for her. We enrolled David in soccer, summer camp, and different things that are just for him. I try to go out of my way to give quality one-on-one time with each of them. That's helped a lot.

I think the largest impact of Josh's disability has been on David because Josh and David are so close in age (the boys are only 18 months apart). One of our biggest fears in the future for Josh is, what's going to happen to him when we are gone? David has heard us go through the early diagnosis. He was here when all the crying and the screaming was going on because we were in such despair. One night we were lying in bed watching a movie and David said, "Mom, I don't know how to hire a therapist. How do I hire a therapist? What do I tell them to do?" He had internalized some of our fears. He felt responsible for his brother.

Another time, David had a friend spend the night and Josh started making some strange sounds. David's little friend started mocking Josh, by making the same sounds and teasing him. David told him to stop it and his friend started to cry. David, matter of factly, said, "It's okay. You have to understand my brother is disabled. You need to be nice to him. But it's okay, everybody makes mistakes." It was so sweet. Some of his

friends come over and they ask questions about Josh. After a while they warm up to him and it's okay. I think David is going to grow up to be a real champion of the disabled. He has a compassionate heart. We talk to him a lot about issues involving people who are disabled.

I know also the time will come when David is 15 or 16 that he will be at an age when it is uncool to have a disabled brother. He'll have some friends over and he is not going to want his disabled brother around. It wouldn't be normal if that didn't happen. He'll go through that stage where he is trying to impress a girl and he won't want to admit that he has a disabled brother. We'll deal with that when the time comes and hopefully we'll have a solid foundation. I think he's already learned a lot of valuable lessons in life that a lot of kids and a lot of adults unfortunately never learn.

David once said, "Mom, I promise you when I grow up, I'll make sure my wife will let Josh live with us. I'll find a wife that understands about my brother."

David (left) and Josh (right) Finkel at home playing.

Stage theory response has a distinct psychiatric flavor, which may imply that parents are maladjusted and need counseling when, in fact, they are responding normally (Roos, 1985). Therefore, it is necessary to be cautious in applying stage theory response to any particular parent or family. Parents arrive at adjustment in many ways, and the sequence and time needed are different for every parent (Allen & Affleck, 1985; Bradley, Knoll, & Agosta, 1992; Schell, 1981).

FAMILY HARDINESS

In addition to the basic needs or desires of all families, researchers have identified stressors that may be prominent in families of children with disabilities. **Acute stressors** occur as periodic incidents related to a child's disability; **chronic stressors** include concerns about the future, financial limitations, and society's acceptance of human differences; and last, **transition stressors** are linked to significant milestones, such as entry into school, that occur throughout a child's lifespan. Put in the context of need, Failla and Jones (1991) concluded that, based on these unique stressors, there is a need for **family hardiness**. Hardiness was defined as a constellation of three dimensions that includes:

1. A sense of control or the ability to influence events rather than being controlled by them
2. A commitment to becoming actively involved in events and viewing them as meaningful
3. Recognition of life changes as opportunities for growth and development, not a burden to bear (Kobasa, Maddi, & Puccetti, 1982; Pollack, 1986)

Throughout the course of a child's life, services and providers will come and go. The primary functions and needs of a family may vacillate. Cultural and community norms may expand or contract, and society's acceptance of exceptional persons is uncertain. Funding and research in the area of early childhood education and intervention will undoubtedly pass through highs and lows. What will remain constant in all this will be the children and their families, formed.

Family hardiness might best be fostered through connections with other parents who have however had similar experiences. These parents can teach others about professionals they never knew existed, words and acronyms that are unfamiliar, and reactions from friends and families that can't be anticipated (Klemm & Schimanski, 1999). Other parents provide information and emotional support as a family learns about a disability and what it will mean. There are important resources that help connect parents:

◆ Beach Center on Families and Disability
   3111 Haworth Hall
   University of Kansas
   Lawrence, KS 66045
   website: *http://www.beachcenter.org*
   e-mail: beach@dole.lsi.ukans.edu

- ◆ National Parent Network on Disabilities
  1130 17th Street NW, Suite 400
  Washington, DC 20036
  website: *www.npnd.org*
- ◆ National Information Center for Children and Youth with Disabilities
  (NICHCY)
  P.O. Box 1492
  Washington, DC 20013
  (800) 695–0285 – voice and TTY
  (202) 884–8441 – fax
  website: *http://www.nichcy.org*
- ◆ The Fathers Network
  website: *http://www.fathersnetwork.org/page.php?page=564&*

BARRIERS TO RELATIONSHIPS

It is essential that professionals remember that just about all families care for their children and want the best for them, but barriers to collaboration may exist that will have to be overcome before success is possible (Dettmer et al., 1999). Many parents fear and mistrust school and agency personnel because of their own negative experiences as children or because of unpleasant experiences with other professionals. Overburdened by economic and personal hardships that create work schedule, transportation, and child care concerns, parents may find early childhood services to be one more challenge in their overtaxed lives. Some parents may fear being blamed for their child's condition or stereotyped because of their culture or lifestyle. Such cultural differences can make parents feel uncomfortable or feel misunderstood. Hence, collaboration requires respect, trust, and cooperation, and it is the professional's responsibility to cope

Case Study   ADVICE FOR TEACHERS: INTERVIEW WITH JAMES HOLDEN

The most important thing is to try to treat the child with a disability with as much similarity to other children as possible. Hold them, in so far as possible, to similar expectations: behavioral, cognitive, and emotional. Your instinct is to compensate for their disability, and you think the way to show concern is by doing special things for them to show that you really care. On the other hand, one of the greatest gifts to a child, particularly a child with a disability who may be separated from other children by the physical limitations of their disability, is to really give them a sense of inclusion, that they are really part of a group of children. You have to find the commonalty and the points of similarity which may involve getting past some superficial difference in order to tap into the point at which they're a child no different from any other child. That is an important gift.

As far as treating parents, my advice would be, to be brave in addressing issues. Sometimes, people are afraid to step on toes and so they tend to leave things unsaid or unspoken. That leads to confusion or may inadvertently commu-nicate a lack of concern or caring or thought. I know I do this myself; if someone has had a death in the family, I talk about other things, thinking I'm being a good person by keeping their mind off this painful subject, when some-times what they want to do is talk about that very thing. It requires a bit of courage to address is-sues in a very straightforward fashion. There is certainly the risk that the parent may be offended or you may inadvertently touch a sensitive nerve, and you're going to make some mistakes and say the wrong thing. But I think you're better off in the long run taking some risks, making some mistakes and getting better at it, than being too cautious about being direct. Even when it's painful, I think that the truth is more healing in the long run than euphemisms.

At the same time, I think that it is important to treat the child's disability in context. This is a child with a disability rather than a disability at-tached to a carrier. Sometimes you can get like a doctor; you get so tied up with the disease and forget that a real live person is connected to it.

with and value differences in positive ways. Dettmer and colleagues (1999) ad-vise the following mindset in working in this sensitive field:

1. Remember that a professional's place is on a parent's side as a team member working for the common goal of each child's success
2. Be aware of feelings of defensiveness, take a deep breath and put those feelings aside
3. Remember the focus is on the needs and interests of families and their children, not their values—attack the problem, not the person
4. Accept people as they are and stop wishing they were different
5. Remember that most families are doing the best they can
6. Respect family rights to values and opinions—even when they differ from yours
7. Demonstrate open-mindedness and flexibility

You may think you're being good by devoting all your professional energy to the disability, but sometimes, you need to pull back and see the disability as a small part of a much larger person. Parents need to be reassured that you love their child. One of the most important things is for them to feel their child is in the hands of someone who really does care about the child.

This may be tough to do. It's hard to like your own children all of the time. But if you can do that and communicate it, that is what parents really appreciate. The bonds between you and the parents are much closer when you make a friend of a child with a disability. Parents can appreciate a teacher or a coach, but they really appreciate those people who can see in their child that special quality that lots of other people look away from. There are a lot of parents with a child whose disability causes other people to look away. Think of how much that must hurt and how desperately they want somebody to really like their child and see their child's good qualities.

It's hard to do it all the time, but if you can find the strength to engage at that level, that's the most important thing for a parent. I think that it's far more important than any of the technical skills, though there are many wonderful techni-

The Holden children.

cal skills that you can learn. As a parent, I would rather have a person who knew nothing about the technical skills, but liked my kid and liked to play with him or work with her. I would pick that person any day over someone who had all of the technical skills in the world, but didn't care.

Even though family collaboration is mandated and challenging, its rewards are many (Dettmer et al., 1999). Children benefit from family involvement through more success in school, higher achievement, and more positive attitudes (Christenson & Cleary, 1990). Family members report greater feelings of self-worth, self-satisfaction, and increased motivation for enhancing the educational environment of the home (Hoover-Dempsey & Sandler, 1997; Murphy, 1981). Finally, professionals learn more about the children in their care and improve communication and advocacy in their communities.

COMMUNICATION BETWEEN PARENTS AND PROFESSIONALS

Communication, in its most basic form, is the ability of two or more people to send and receive messages. Of all the skills expected of early childhood professionals, communication skills rank among the most necessary. When Linda Davern (1996) interviewed parents regarding their suggestions for improving the quality of home-school relationships, they recommended the following:

1. Convey a clear, consistent message regarding the value of a child. See aspects aside from achievement and focus on the children's progress, rather than comparing them to other children.
2. Walk in parents' shoes. Try to understand what it is like to have a child with a disability. Understand their frustration.
3. Expand awareness of cultural diversity. Be aware of the cultural lenses through which judgments about children and families are made.
4. See individuals, and challenge stereotypes. Don't make assumptions about parents and their skills just because their child has a disability. Don't lump all parents together.
5. Persevere in building partnerships. Consider this a long-term commitment that takes time and flexibility.
6. Demonstrate an authentic interest in the parent's goals for the child. Work to diminish distance between professionals and parents while establishing connections. Avoid sending the message that professionals are the experts and parents know nothing.
7. Talk with parents about how they want to share information. Ask parents which school person they want to communicate with, how often, and through what means.
8. Use everyday language. Avoid jargon that confuses understanding.
9. Create effective forums for planning and problem solving. Formal meetings can be very intimidating, so schedule regular, less formal meetings where parents can be more comfortable.

Several basic communication concepts or skills can enhance relationships between parents and professionals. These involve active listening, **perception checks**, and ways to accurately state needs.

ACTIVE LISTENING

Active listening means that listeners (receivers of information) are attentive to a speaker on multiple levels: hearing, interpreting, sorting, and analyzing (see Table 3–3). It is the opposite of passive listening, in which the recipient hears without understanding the intended message and without responding appropriately to the speaker. Table 3–4 illustrates the problems that can develop between an active and passive listener, and ultimately, the effect this has on communication and learning.

Table 3–3 Active Listening

Skills	Description
Hearing:	Understands and comprehends the words (spoken or written)
Interpreting:	Is attentive to nuances, the larger context of the statement, and the political, cultural and emotional dimensions of comments
Sorting:	Categorizes information with other like information to increase the meaning or clarify intent
Analyzing:	Compares information with other knowledge about the topic and draws conclusions

Table 3–4   Example of Interaction When Only One Party Is Actively Listening

Actively listening parent:	Passively listening preschool teacher:
"I would very much like to have my child use his communication board on a more regular basis. Currently, he becomes very frustrated because he can't tell us what he needs." The parent frowns and looks sad.	"All the students in my class are able to speak. We will have the speech language pathologist work with Andy so that he can speak as well." The teacher is fiddling with papers she needs for her next parent conference.
"Perhaps you didn't read Andy's file carefully. His cerebral palsy is so involved that he is not able to make any understandable speech sounds. We have already had him evaluated by a speech therapist at St. Luke's and they created the communication board for him so he could develop his language skills." The parent shakes her head and pushes a catalogue of language devices toward the child-care provider.	(Still looking at her other papers.) "We have an excellent speech language pathologist. She will have Andy talking in no time. Andy can work with her during circle time since that is oral and Andy wouldn't be able to participate."
"We don't want Andy to miss out on circle time. He loves to be a part of the group. We can choose appropriate pictures to put on his communication board so he can respond with the rest of the children. He gets very frustrated when he is not allowed to be with the rest of the students." The parent's shoulders tighten and she leans forward, thumping the catalogue of language devices to emphasize the use of the communication board.	"Oh, we don't let the children bring toys to the circle. He has to be able to speak up like everyone else. Also, I've been meaning to talk to you about his behavior. He has been refusing to cooperate with our group activities. I'd like to send him to time out when this happens."
(She gives a big sigh.) "As I said, he gets very frustrated when he isn't able to communicate and when he isn't a part of the group. I don't think time out would be the right answer for this problem."	"Well, if you don't allow us to control his behavior, I don't know how Andy is ever going to be able to be a part of our class." She looks at her watch, ready to end the meeting.
"We seem to have a different understanding of Andy's problems. Perhaps we need to meet as a team again, so the speech language pathologist can also be involved. I'm concerned that you are not addressing Andy's communication needs." The parent's face is red, her hands are shaking as she pulls the catalogue back to her bag. The parent takes a deep breath, pulls her bag over her shoulder, and leaves, shaking her head as she goes.	"That would be fine, because I have another parent coming now and can't talk any longer. It has been a pleasure meeting with you today." The child-care provider smiles and shakes the parent's hand as she shuffles her papers together and heads toward the door to greet the next parent.

When active listening is done well, relationships develop between the sender and the listener: partners hear and can respond to what their counterpart is saying; parents and children learn that what they have to say is important and respected; and professionals increase the probability that the right supports will be given parents. Unlike passive listening, which involves only one sender, active listening is an inclusive engagement between and among people. Table 3–5 presents an example where both parties are actively listening.

Table 3–5   Example of Interaction When Both Parties Are Actively Listening

Actively listening preschool teacher:	Actively listening parent:
"We didn't address this in our last IEP meeting, but I think Cherise has matured in her language and self-help skills enough that she is ready to start toilet training. What do you think about this?" The teacher leans forward, looking the parent directly in the eye.	"Do you really think she could learn to go by herself? It would be such a relief to not have her in diapers, now that we are expecting another child." The parent smiles.
The teacher nods enthusiastically. "I just want to explain what this would involve and make sure we can work on this at both home and school. I'd like to check her every 15 minutes to see if there is a pattern to when she is wet and then start putting her on the potty at those most likely times each day. Can you do the same thing when she is at home with you in the afternoon and evening?" The teacher watches the parent's face and notices that her mouth falls a little.	"I don't think I could check every 15 minutes. We have the two older ones you know, so I'm always driving them to soccer or dance lessons; and Cherise's therapy sessions usually run at least 45 minutes and I don't like to disturb her once she is started in those." The parent sits back in her chair, pushing away from the table.
"Of course, you are probably on the go so much there isn't a lot of down-time where you could stop and do this every 15 minutes. Is there any period of time, like maybe the hour just before bed that you could work on this? I find kids learn toileting so much faster when we work on it at school and at home." The teacher raises her eyebrows in a hopeful gesture.	"Maybe I could ask my husband to watch Cherise when I take her older sister off to dance. That way she'd be home for the 2 hours before bed. Would that be enough to make a difference?" The parent leans on the table.
"I appreciate you rearranging your hectic schedule. I think that could make a big difference, and once Cherise is out of diapers, you'll have a little more free time with the new baby."	"I'm so glad you think we can do this. It would make a huge difference not to have two in diapers. Cherise will be happier too if she can be like the big girls." She hesitates. "But what if I can't carry through at home? What if she doesn't learn?"
"I know it's harder to do these things at home when your hands are full. We'll keep working on it at school, and we might brainstorm another way to accomplish it at home. Cherise might not learn right away, but I've got some ways to motivate her. Perhaps we could use a buzzer that will let us know when she starts to wet, so we don't have to watch the clock. You just let me know if you don't think it's going well at home and we'll go back to the drawing board."	"Thank you for being so understanding. I'll give it my best shot." She rises and extends her hand. "I'm so glad you thought to work on this. It's like you read my mind."

COMMUNICATING WELL

Several specific communication strategies can be employed to become a more effective communicator. The following suggestions may improve relationships with other professionals and with family members.

Avoid Binding Statements

Binding communications are habits of interaction that generally close or diminish the probability of continued conversation. By contrast, freeing communications are those habits of interaction that actually encourage expanded dialogue. The following examples illustrate a few habits that often lead to **binding communications**:

◆ Giving overly enthusiastic responses that are generally based on what would be best for the professional
◆ Changing the subject without explanation
◆ Explaining others' behavior by interpreting their history (You act this way because your mother acted this way.)
◆ Providing direct advice and even persuasion (If I were you, this is what I would do.)
◆ Setting up expectations that bind the speaker to the past; this disallows change and innovation (You've never acted this way before; what's wrong?)
◆ Communicating expectations that bind the speaker to the future (I'm sure you'll figure this out and do such and such.)
◆ Denying feelings (You really don't mean that! Or, You really don't feel that way, do you?)
◆ Overgeneralizing (Everyone feels that way.); this diminishes the other; makes one feel like one's feelings or experiences really do not matter much
◆ Approving on personal grounds: praising the other for thinking, feeling, or acting in ways that agree with, or conform to a professional's standards
◆ Disapproving on personal grounds: blaming or censuring the other for thinking, feeling, or acting in ways you do not like
◆ Commanding and ordering: telling the other what to do (including, Tell me what to do)
◆ Obligating emotionally: controlling through arousing feelings of shame and inferiority (How can you do this to me when I have done so much for you?)

In summary, binding statements are those comments that diminish the listener's desire to continue the conversation.

Use Freeing Statements

Freeing statements, such as "go on," "tell me more," "how do you feel about that?" actually increase the speaker's desire to continue and increase both personal autonomy and power. As a note of caution, professionals must use these statements sincerely and avoid assuming a therapeutic tone.

Avoid Killer Phrases

Killer phrases range from those comments that discourage further comment to those that break a person's spirit. Appropriately named for the effect they have on communication, killer phrases are generally (though not always) uttered in

Table 3–6 Examples of Killer Phrases

• That's a swell idea, but . . .	• I haven't the time.
• Good idea, but your family is different.	• I'm not ready for it. (You're not ready for it.)
• It's too academic (or it's too medical).	• There are better ways than that!
• We're rural (or we're too large).	• You haven't considered . . .
• It's too simplistic.	• Let's not step on anyone's toes.
• It needs more study.	• Why start anything now?
• We've never done it that way.	• The agency won't understand.

moments of frustration, anger, or depression. Examples are: "It won't work," or "It's all right in theory, but can you put it into practice?" Early childhood professionals should recognize killer phrases and attribute no more to them than indications of weariness. As for the language of professionals, to the greatest extent possible, it should be void of killer phrases. Table 3–6 gives more examples of killer phrases to avoid.

It is much easier for a professional to impose hurt on a parent than vice versa since professionals are generally supported in several ways by the power visited on them through training, social norms, and organizational structure. Therefore, the playing field is never level. In consideration of this relationship, professionals should prepare to weather killer phrases aimed at them without bowing to the temptation to respond in kind.

Allow and Respect "No"

Most novice professionals find themselves eager to pass on what they know and to support parents' decisions. Professionals simply do not set out to be offensive or to get in a family's way; yet it happens. It happens, against all intentions, because service providers fail to recognize the more basic needs of families, one of which is to not need a professional support person! In the course of each family or family system, there comes a time when parents and other members of the family wish to be left alone. Families may grow weary of professional conversations and interactions; they may well have priorities not shared by professional support persons.

Not wanting to discourage or seem ungrateful, parents will find various and subtle ways to say "Stay away for now." For a shy parent, avoidance may begin by simply canceling meetings or calling in ill. Others will tell a professional that the timing is bad and reschedule for some distant date. In such situations, it is the responsibility of a professional to analyze the communication as carefully as possible and to draw and confirm a conclusion. When it becomes apparent that a parent is asking for some free space from professionals, support for that request needs to be forthcoming. If professionals are unclear about a parent's actual intent, they need only ask parents directly: "Would you like my assistance? Please feel free to say no." If the parent answers "no," that answer must be accepted with the same dignity afforded the opposite response. In short, parents and caregivers need to be allowed to say "no" to support or services, (after all, it is their legal right to do so), and then be respected for saying it.

Use Perception Checks

Sometimes, despite best efforts, it is difficult to draw an accurate conclusion regarding the intent of a speaker. When this happens, it is possible to draw on a communication skill called a **perception check**. A perception check means that listeners check their perception or understanding of what was said (e.g., the parent doesn't want to waste the specialist's Saturday morning) against what the speaker was actually thinking (e.g., "My oldest child was sick all night, and I'm exhausted. Please leave me alone!"). A perception check is executed not by asking the speaker to repeat what was just said, but by saying, "This is what I understand you to mean. . . . " This pattern allows the initial speaker to confirm or deny the perception.

Perception checks are especially important to use when more than two people are engaged in an interaction. During assessment sessions, in planning meetings, or in family consultations, early childhood professionals may find there is often a good deal of confusion about the intent or content of transactions or interactions. By using any of the following phrases, professionals can help keep the communication lines clear and open.

- ◆ I was listening to what you just said. Is (give explanation) what you mean?
- ◆ So many people have been offering comments. I'm a bit unsure of your position on (name the issue). Is (give explanation) what you meant?
- ◆ You just said, "no." Are you trying to accommodate my schedule, or is there really a better time for us to get together?

These three statements ask for clarification without judging the effectiveness or ability of the speaker.

Use Paraphrasing

Paraphrasing is another technique by which confirmation is obtained by restating the essence of the comment or conversation. In paraphrasing, listeners put into words what they think they have just heard. Though a perception check seeks clarification (Is this what you meant?), paraphrasing seeks right direction. In the latter, the listener accepts responsibility for interpretation (e.g., "Another way to say what you just said is . . . " or "So what you just said is . . . "). Paraphrasing conclusions or using paraphrasing to confirm what is to be done next are the two most commonly used and highly productive forms of paraphrasing.

Use Descriptions of Behavior Rather Than Descriptions of Feelings

There are a number of ways that parents, siblings, and professionals avoid participating in difficult or sensitive conversations. On one end of a continuum, people avoid engagement in difficult topics by withdrawing. On the other end of the continuum, people avoid a topic by engaging in unrelated conversations or behaviors. Though these postures are perhaps admirable during a poker game, they generally complicate family discussions, interdisciplinary work, and most social interactions. When behaviors occur that range from withdrawal to unrelated engagement, there are two issues that must be confronted by listeners. First, what is the person indicating through her or his actions and words, or lack of action or words? Second, what is the parent, sibling, or professional really feeling?

Early childhood professionals working with parents and family members need to be especially aware of words, communication styles, and the feelings that ought to correspond to those words or gestures. For example, it is not uncommon to find a parent or professional colleague nodding "yes," only to find out later they did not agree at all. Because human beings sometimes experience a dissonance between their logical conclusions and their actual feelings, professionals must be aware of discrepancies between descriptions of behaviors and descriptions of feelings.

Someone wishing to make clear the intent of a participant who suddenly pushes her chair back and withdraws from a discussion can interject, "I've noticed that you pulled out of the conversation [description of behavior]. Would you like to talk about what's going on for you at this time? [asking for description of feelings]." The person may well choose to say nothing because his feelings are still too close to the surface. In this case, the professional may return to the individual after a short while and ask again. It is more productive to rest comfortably with a description of behavior (which is something that can be seen, touched, or heard) and refrain from making assumptions about feelings based on behavior (only an interpretation). An accurate description of behavior can come from an observer; an accurate description of feelings can come only from the person experiencing those feelings.

SPECIAL SKILLS FOR COMMUNICATING WITH PARENTS AT THE TIME OF DIAGNOSIS

In 1972, Korsch and Negrete investigated typical problems in communication between parents and physicians when difficult news needed to be delivered. Studying the pediatrician–parent interactions in a large urban hospital, Korsch and Negrete found that 76% of parents felt satisfied with the communication at the time the information was delivered (usually diagnostic information). Yet, follow-up 10 and 30 days later revealed unsettling repercussions:

◆ 20% of the parents had no idea what was wrong with their child.
◆ 50% of the parents had no idea of the cause of the illness or disability.
◆ 26% of the parents had not mentioned their greatest concern about the child because they felt they were not encouraged to do so.
◆ 38% of the parents complied only in part with the physician's recommendations.
◆ 11% of the parents did not comply at all with any of the physician's recommendations.

Thirty years have passed since the Korsch and Negrete study. During that time, researchers have taken seriously the importance of determining how best to deliver difficult information to family members. Important recommendations (Turnbull & Turnbull, 1990) for this unique situation include:

◆ Provide full and honest information about the condition of a child.
◆ Repeat information in many different ways and at many different times.
◆ Try to tell both parents at the same time.
◆ Avoid a patronizing or condescending attitude.

CONFLICT WITH THE SCHOOL: INTERVIEW WITH MARSHA MOORE

Case Study

It was important to us to live in a school district large enough to provide special education services to Michael, so just before his second birthday, we made the decision to look for employment in a larger town. After a year's search, we moved to Washington state. We focused our search for a home in an area where Michael could be served at a neighborhood school. We contacted the Association for Retarded Citizens to get recommendations for special education preschools. We visited the schools, talked with teachers and administrators, and finally made what we thought to be an informed decision. Two or three days after moving into our new home, and in the middle of unpacking, I called the school district to get information on how I would go about enrolling Michael in preschool. It was mid-August and I felt I didn't have much time to waste.

I was told that no decision would be made until Michael's developmental level could be evaluated by the school psychologist. Several days later, Mike and I drove out to the special education administration building for his assessment. I had dressed Michael in a little "preppy" outfit: short pants, knee socks, saddle shoes. I really had him "spiffed" up. The school psychologist took one look at him and commented that probably the only thing Michael needed was some interaction with some other children. I felt as if I'd just been told that the only problem Michael had was the lack of a stimulating environment, as if I had kept him in a closet all his life. The psychologist never told me outright that I was not providing Michael with the proper early childhood setting, but he clearly insinuated that school would "cure" everything. He also purposefully ignored the medical evaluations from Denver Children's Hospital and stated in a very patronizing manner that Michael was definitely

not "autistic," as reported in his medical records. The psychologist "played" with Michael for almost 2 hours, and never managed to get him to respond. Michael was found eligible for special education preschool because he was two standard deviations below the mean in every domain.

From his office, I was sent over to meet Michael's preschool teacher who, at that point, was already setting up her classroom. We had left home at 9 in the morning and it was now almost noon. Mike was getting cross. He was tired, he was hungry, and he was hot. The teacher sat Mike in the middle of the floor. He immediately stiffened and he threw himself back, banging his head on the carpet, howling loudly. He would not be comforted. She looked at him as if to say, "This is definitely not the kind of child we have in this classroom." She didn't say that, but that was the feeling I got. I was trying so hard to carry on a conversation, trying to be so polite, trying to get a rapport going with this teacher.

As I got up to leave, Michael was still crying. "We'll see you on the first day of school and you will bring him, right?" she instructed. I told her that he probably wouldn't ride the bus for the first few days, and that I had planned to bring him to school until he could get adjusted. The teacher continued, "And you will stay with him?" Well, I stayed every day for at least 2 weeks and then every other day for another month or two, because he just hated that new and strange environment. He had never been around other small children and he cried and cried, and wanted me to hold him.

Several months into school, right after Halloween, the director of special education phoned me and suggested that another program might be more suitable for Mike. This program was "specifically designed for children like

(continued)

Michael." She arranged to meet me at another school. I went, having no idea what the classroom would be like. When we opened the door, I found a large classroom with 8 or 10 children ranging in ages from about 3 to 12 or 13. Only one child could walk, a big boy who was taller than I was. Several children were lying on the floor on mats. One little girl was rocking back and forth on the floor; another was sitting in a rocker and shaking her head. I wondered what program was available for each of these children. Later I found that the room

Mike in school with classmates.

was called the "Severe and Profound Room," whatever that must mean!

It didn't take me long to realize that all of these other children should be in their own classes and not grouped together; it didn't seem appropriate to me that 3-year-olds would be with 12- or 13-year-olds. Whether they were developmentally on the same plateau or not, I just didn't think that was right. I remember feeling my cheeks and my ears getting very flushed. I had never had to fight a school system. I had never even thought about challenging anything that went on in school with my other children. My job as parent had been to support the school. I was a room mother, PTA officer, school carnival chairman. If our children had any problems academically, I had always been able to collaborate with the teacher and often helped my child put in extra time at home. Discipline worked the same way. "So she's talking too much in class, we will see what we can do to take care of that right away." These simple problems were not even considered problems. Now how could I even think of taking a different path than the school suggested?

We visited the room for no more than 20 minutes when I stated that I would not allow Michael to be placed in this environment. The director wanted me to give it a trial run, but I held my ground and flatly refused. I told her I

expected her to make the current placement work. I knew nothing of LRE then, but I soon would.

We completed an IEP for the original placement. Mike received a lot of help from an experienced physical therapist who worked for the school district. We were so pleased because by November of that same school year, Mike was up on his hands and knees, ready to crawl. Within a month he was actually pulling himself to stand, and by January he was crawling around. Soon, Mike was able to sit quietly and join circle time, and he was learning to eat finger-food at snack time. His teacher, although hesitant towards Michael in the beginning, structured her class in ways that allowed each child to work and learn at their own pace and towards their own goals. Well as you know, all good things must come to an end, and in February, she left school to have a baby. It's sad to say, but a program is only as good as the teacher.

When Mike started school the next year, the classroom situation was not good. After several conferences with the teacher, I started looking for help from specialists in the community. They recommended many things to facilitate Mike's progress, but the school did not provide what I was convinced he needed. For example, the school refused to work on toilet training although Michael had all the prerequisite skills. Because he did not interact with the other children, he was often left to sit in the corner and watch the other children play, as if he would learn how to play from watching them. The most frustrating thing for me was that the school district disregarded Mike's diagnosis of infantile autism. In fact, they not only disregarded it, but during an IEP meeting, they brought in another school psychologist to tell me that she was an expert on autism and Mike didn't have autism. I realize now that she didn't know what she was talking about, but at the time I didn't know as much and felt very intimidated by her professional expertise. I only felt angry and frustrated that they continually reminded me that I did not know my child as well as they knew him. In reality, they did not have a program for children with autism, so therefore, Michael was not autistic.

As the year progressed, I went to school once a week, sometimes twice a week. I was very quiet. If I participated in the circle time, it was only to help Mike do what the other children were doing. I held my tongue and never interrupted any classroom activity, no matter how inappropriate I felt it was. I called the teacher on a monthly basis to check on Mike's progress and ask questions that I felt were pertinent to his program. I often expressed my exasperation that Michael's program was not individualized to meet his needs. I was reminded that the "other" program was the individualized program!

When Michael started preschool the third year in the same classroom, I conferenced with the principal about what I had learned from the community specialist. I felt Mike needed more individual instruction. Mike seemed not to pay any attention to the other children in the classroom, and they were too socially delayed to interact effectively with him. I asked about bringing some kindergarten children into the classroom to act as appropriate role models for all of the children. The principal would not agree to any arrangement I suggested. There was absolutely no room for negotiation. I became more and more assertive, maybe even aggressive. I just got downright ornery.

I invited one of Michael's community autism specialists to visit his classroom in hopes that his recommendations would not fall on deaf ears. He met with the teacher, principal, and special education director and recommended one-on-one assistance, direct instruction, behavioral intervention, and other specifics. All recommendations were totally disregarded. No explanation was given. It was obvious to me that the district had a program and my child needed to fit that program. It didn't matter that the program was inappropriate for my child. What made me most angry was the reality that there were no data taken during the entire 3 years that Michael was in the preschool. There was no method to track Michael's progress or lack of progress. To me, that very fact indicated that Michael did not matter much.

Several weeks after the specialist had come in, the principal informed me that I made the teacher uncomfortable and that I was no longer allowed free access to the classroom. I obeyed the rules, but often would watch through the classroom door window until one day, the window blind was pulled. The principal met me in the hallway and asked me please to stay outside the school building unless I was there for a purpose other than to "harass" the teacher.

I was furious! I wrote various certified letters to the teacher, principal, and special education director to document Michael's inappropriate program as well as the unfair and illegal way I had been treated as a parent. I made a request to schedule an IEP meeting, and I listed the goals and objectives that I believed were appropriate for Michael to work towards. I repeated the recommendations of the specialists I had used as consultants. In the meantime, I shared with the school staff an excellent book on IEP development, underlining everything I was requesting. I took a video to the principal about inclusion in the classroom. My information was politely refused. The school never responded to any of my half dozen certified letters.

Michael's IEP meetings were very tense and very stressful. Communication was terse and every one of my requests for Michael was met

(continued)

with blank stares, simply no response. I think the school staff thought that if they ignored me, I would go away or perhaps just give up. We must have had at least a dozen meetings, dozens of revised IEPs, and finally, Jim and I went to the Superintendent of our school district. We spent less than an hour with him and gave him copies of all the information and documentation we had concerning Michael's program.

Apparently he must have thought that we had some valid concerns. The district hired an aide to work with Michael and after continued advocacy for an integrated setting, we were finally given a 6-week trial placement in a regular classroom. We got lucky. Mike had a wonderful first-grade teacher who made the placement a successful one, not only for Mike, but for everyone in the classroom. That year marked the beginning of a very different educational path which Michael and our family would follow over the next several years.

- ◆ Provide parents with time to filter the information. Always schedule a follow-up meeting.
- ◆ Understand that parents may respond with anger. The anger is about the diagnosis—not about the informant.
- ◆ Discuss and practice strategies for informing brothers, sisters, and other family members.

CONFERENCING WITH PARENTS

Formal conferences between families and professionals are often structured around a child's individualized education program or arise from a particular concern on the part of the parent or the school or agency. Meetings such as these can be a source of considerable apprehension, especially for parents, if they are viewed as an unpleasant obligation rather than an opportunity to strengthen the cooperative ties between home and school (Perl, 1995). As a professional, the important objective is to bring out the best in people—to empower them, not to be overly directive or to "do for" them (Perl, 1995). Monitoring reactions to parents and learning to communicate a genuine caring for families and their children by displaying a sincere sense of warmth and caring supports parent empowerment.

Building rapport is an important part of conferencing (Perl, 1995). Parents may be put at ease when a meeting begins with pleasant informal conversation—"small talk," and an offer of coffee, a soft drink, or other refreshment. Holding the meeting around a table rather than on opposite sides of a desk also relaxes the participants. Using "door-opening statements" helps to encourage the parents to talk and to promote one's own listening. Encouraging parents to express concerns and make suggestions, even to "blow off steam" if they are upset or angry is appropriate (Perl, 1995).

Empathizing with the parent's situation and reflecting the affect that is behind another person's words encourages communication (Perl, 1995). Restating a parent's feelings in words or with facial expressions conveys understanding. Clarifying a parent's statement to ensure it is understood and noticing nonverbal cues help demonstrate careful listening. Responding to and acting on the concerns that are expressed are essential.

RESPONDING TO FAMILY PRIORITIES

Though a professional's role in the past may have been one of dispensing expertise, today's professional is responsive to the priorities of the family. Above all, families and professionals join in a partnership that is truly collaborative in nature. In its best form, members are mutually engaged in the work to be accomplished and recognize the constraints placed on each other.

CONSTRAINTS AND CONFLICTS

An area of considerable constraint and a possible area for conflict between families and professionals that deserves special attention is time and the level of stress that time demands place on a family. Within the last decade, a number of researchers focused attention on the use of time as a critical resource of families with young children with disabilities. McLinden (1990) described time as the critical resource. Indeed, the amount of time demanded by caregiving responsibilities was the stressor most often mentioned by parents of children with disabilities. Brotherson and Goldstein (1992) described the availability of time within families in the following manner:

> Time is an example of a fundamental resource to family well-being that families can only partially generate and control themselves. To a large extent, a family's time is controlled externally by people, institutions, and events that impose expectations and requirements on the family. Time is a resource when it is available and when it can be negotiated and used; as with other resources, its absence often redefines time as a constraint. (p. 509)

Though issues of time literally cross thousands of activities, the research of Brotherson and Goldstein (1992) and Brotherson and Martin (1992) found that most critical time issues fell into five categories:

1. Meeting the needs of the whole family
2. Decision making in partnerships
3. Working with the health care system
4. Professional demonstration of respect and sensitivity to families
5. Issues of working within service delivery systems across a variety of programs and agencies

Parents noted four supports that would help them in their use of time. The first of these is a need to fit therapy and education activities into the family's daily routine and environment. Brotherson and Goldstein (1992) wrote that parents' time was used more effectively when therapists integrated activities into the family's daily routines and home environment. Several parents stated that for professionals to know how to truly integrate activities into home life, the professionals had to spend time in their homes. No single prescription can fit different family demands. Some parents also used time to frame the issue of transfer of knowledge from clinic to home. In part, this is a time issue, but it is also the issue of effective transferability of skills to the home environment and the material conditions of families' lives. Brotherson and Goldstein (1992) quoted a parent on this issue:

> In the past, the therapist would show me how to do this exercise on a nice round ball and wedges and then she turns around and says, "But you can do this with a dish towel and a beach ball." How am I going to get this together when I go home and try to do the exercises she's just told me about? This year we have been getting home PT and that has been very helpful, because they've got what you've got to work with and can show me how to work on the living room floor between the TV and stereo. (pp. 515–516)

It is also critical that professionals listen to what parents know about their child and family. Perhaps the most common frustration of parents is when professionals "discover" what families have already told them. Having to repeat information or wait for the results of clinical assessments only to confirm what families already know frustrates parents and undermines professional legitimacy. Parents feel (whether it is true or not) they were not taken seriously and the information they offered was less than credible. This frustration frames the broader questions: (1) what information, provided by parents, needs to be reaffirmed by a professional, and what can be assumed to be factual? and (2) how can both parents and professionals learn to share information that results in the best use of time by both parties?

Today, professionals must learn to use technology for therapy and education activities as a way to work more efficiently. The Internet, conference call capabilities, cell phones, faxes, e-mail, and 800-number phone lines provide communication modes with families that were not possible in the past. It is certainly consistent with professional obligation for early childhood educators to teach parents how to access and use those technologies that will free their time and lead to more consistent and less stressful communication.

Professionals must provide time and consistency to develop trusting relationships with parents. Professionals who believe they can quickly meet with a family, assess their needs, and immediately participate in the development of an appropriate IFSP or IEP are badly mistaken. Time must be invested to develop and to maintain a relationship, even though an IFSP or IEP cannot be delayed beyond legal time limits. Services may begin while the process of association continues and a partnership is built.

Parents have also reported at least four common impositions on their time: (1) lack of coordination among professionals, (2) being overwhelmed with therapy and educational activities, (3) trying to access services not available in the community, and (4) lack of flexible and family-centered scheduling. In order to respond to these complaints, professionals need to address the lack of flexibility within the structures of their organizations and the inherent difficulty in meeting all the needs of a whole family.

CULTURAL CONSTRAINTS

Early childhood special education and intervention are envisioned as partnerships between professionals and families for serving young children with special needs and their families (Hains, Lynch, & Winton, 2000). This partnership means both professionals and families bring their culture to the table as they develop and deliver services. The challenge is to provide child and family programs that are consistent with best practices based on research while respecting the culture of the families who are served.

Anne and Rutherford Turnbull (1996) offer a definition of culture that is especially relevant to professional relationships with families:

> Culture refers to many different factors that shape one's sense of group identity, including race, ethnicity, religion, geographical location, income status, gender, sexual orientation, disability status, and occupation. It is the framework within which individuals, families, or groups interpret their experiences and develop their visions of how they want to live their lives. (p. 56)

It is important that professionals are aware of their own cultural perceptions so that these do not unduly affect the way they interact with diverse families. A key element of professional development is to be knowledgeable of others' cultural values so the basis on which family decisions are made is understood. Professionals must deal with stereotyping by recognizing that their cultural preferences are not superior; that making assumptions based on ethnicity can be quite misleading. Early educators must be sensitive to cultural differences that may be of concern to specific culturally diverse groups (Heward, 1996). Consider these examples of cultural tendencies (but be careful not to stereotype):

◆ Caucasian educators generally place a high value on eye contact when talking with a student, but many African Americans engage in conversation without making eye contact at all times; some may participate in unrelated activities while still paying attention to a conversation.

◆ Hispanic children may be reluctant to ask for help because they are accustomed to families that respond to nonverbal cues when help is needed. Hispanic children may work well in group projects but may not be motivated to strive for individual gain.

◆ Asian American parents may be reluctant to seek help for a child with disabilities, preferring instead to handle a child's abnormal development within the family.

◆ American Indian children with disabilities may be so absorbed by family and community that it is difficult to identify and provide services to these children and their families.

These and many other differences may interfere with a professional's understanding of the family and communication between school or agency and home unless early educators work hard to learn about a child's culture and customs. However, responding to family members as individuals and making no assumptions, but allowing each to "be himself" is the most productive approach. Whether a family is culturally different from a professional or not, personalization is the key to successful interaction. A professional should never expect a family to fit into a particular cultural "box."

Hispanic Families

For many Hispanics or Latinos (a broad ethnic group which can include people whose families originally came from South and Central America, Mexico, Spain, and the Caribbean), children are the most important and valued assets, even when the family is in poor economic straits (Gonzales Alvarez, 1998). Having many children is considered a blessing, but having a child with a disability (as in most cultures) is very difficult. That child may always be viewed as sick, and if the disability is severe, may always be considered a child. Parents tend to feel sad about these children. Religion, often a strong influence within this culture, affects their perspective on a disability. Sometimes a child with a disability is seen as a punishment or curse from God, in which case the family may feel it is pointless to seek out services because that would go against God's will. A growing number of Hispanic families view the disability as fate, something that happened for a purpose. Mothers are more likely to seek services, since mothers are the main caretakers. But fathers are the decision makers and often must be consulted on setting appointments and agreeing to intervention (Gonzales Alvarez, 1998).

Hispanic families typically include extended family members and have a great deal of respect for their elderly members (Belmonte, 1996). Interpersonal relationships, interdependence and cooperation are emphasized. Family structure is patriarchal, and it is courteous to speak to the husband before speaking to the wife when both are present. A father's decisions regarding recommendations should be acknowledged, even when the father is not present.

To be effective for Hispanic families, service providers must become close to the family. Hospitality is important, and home visits may begin with food and conversation. Providers must be open to family invitations and become someone the family learns to trust. Speaking Spanish helps, but Spanish differs depending on the country of origin, so one should recognize there may be difficulties communicating. Hispanics tend to respect authority and may say they agree with recommendations when in fact they are not comfortable with the suggestions (Gonzales Alvarez, 1998). Therefore, it is especially useful to be open-ended about opportunities to help and encourage families to contribute their own ideas for collaboration.

Hispanic families may be reluctant to send their children to preschool because school is not believed to be more beneficial than home (Bauer & Shea, 2003). Since an extended and nurturing family is often involved, parents may be hesitant to turn over care-giving to a school. Hispanic families rely on nuclear and extended family for support, loyalty, and solidarity. School services tend to be less satisfying for Hispanic families because of language barriers and the uninviting formal nature of school relationships.

Asian Families

Asian (another broad and varied ethnic group encompassing Chinese, Japanese, Korean, Vietnamese, Thai, Indonesian, and often other Pacific Islanders) families may consider matters involving a child with a disability to be private concerns, not to be openly discussed with others (Hyun & Fowler, 1995). For this reason, choosing an interpreter, when appropriate, can be a critical, though difficult, decision, because the interpreter must be trusted and respected by the family; a community leader or clergyman, for example, may be a wise choice in this capacity. Unlike the Hispanic family which may dislike formality, an Asian family should be treated formally; use Mr., Mrs., or Miss with the family name, learn simple greeting words, and use written materials prepared in the family's language. Many Asian families convey information through nonverbal communication such as silence or eye contact. Silence may mean respect or disagreement, direct eye contact is viewed as disrespectful. Encourage Asian families to bring people who are important to them to conferences and to choose a setting that is comfortable for them. When making a home visit, it is usually common courtesy to remove one's shoes when entering. Greet older persons with a slight bow, and avoid sitting with legs crossed. It is likely that food will be offered. If a meeting is in a public place, try to choose a private, quiet area.

Families with Asian roots may embrace a heart-oriented philosophy that stresses stoicism, patience, tradition, self-discipline and spiritualism (Belmonte, 1996). They place great value on the group welfare, responsibility, obligation and independence. Status centers around birthright, inheritance, family name, age, gender, and role rigidity; the roles of men and women are clearly defined. The parent-child bond is very important, and children are viewed as extensions of their parents. However, parents provide authority and make decisions for their children. Asians may be perceived as more formal and emotionally controlled than other cultures. Some may be so polite as to be perceived as overly submissive (Bauer & Shea, 2003).

In planning interventions, differing Asian childrearing practices may alter approaches and goals. For example, often young children do not self-feed but are assisted during mealtime. Infants rarely sleep alone, and children under school age often sleep with their parents. Because teachers are often revered, parents may feel it is appropriate to be dependent rather than active partners. Still, Asian origins are very diverse; each family is different and one must never assume something about a family based on cultural stereotype. Many Asians are newly immigrated and may be additionally challenged by their refugee status (Bauer & Shea, 2003). Educators will be most effective if they are willing to learn about different people each time they meet a new family (Hyun & Fowler, 1995).

African American Families

African American families have great diversity in their family living arrangements (Hunter, Pearson, Ialongo, & Kellam, 1998). Kinship is highly valued, and extended families are supportive. There may be multigenerational family relationships, the sharing of child rearing and economic relationships across household boundaries, and a much greater role for fictive kin and parent surrogates (such as a friend who lives with the family). A great deal of respect is given to the elderly and their role in the family (Belmonte, 1996). Grandparents, particularly grandmothers, are more likely to be actively involved in parenting children than in Anglo cultures. Extended kin and nonrelatives play a significant role in child care, child management, rule setting, and discipline. When planning services, it is important to ask: How do parents and other caregivers organize child care and parenting tasks? Who partic-ipates in the provision of care? and What is the role of parenting agents inside and outside of the household? (Hunter et al., 1998).

African American families may also have greater value for communal and movement-expressive attitudes and practices. Dubbed as "verve," this quality em-phasizes liveliness, variability, and stimulation (Bauer & Shea, 2003). These fam-ilies may prefer group activities that allow for music, movement, and high energy. An emphasis on time management, quietness, and low energy activities (typical in school settings) may not be compatible with family values.

Native American (American Indian) Families

Native Americans also value group life and respect their elders, experts, and spir-itual leaders (Belmonte, 1996). Grandparents may be viewed as the primary par-ents with others as the disciplinarians. Customs and traditions are very important, and service providers will want to be careful not to infringe on these social mores. Children with special needs may have fewer demands placed on them because these children are believed to suffer enough challenges. Native American families tend to accept "what is" and seek harmony with their situations. As with any eth-nic group, the term Native American encompasses many different Indian nations and customs that vary greatly; there are more than 600 officially recognized and unrecognized tribal groups with more than 300 indigenous languages in the United States (Stubben, 2001). Likewise, Native Americans living on reservations or in rural areas face different stressors than those in urban areas who are more isolated from their traditional communities. Urbanization of Native Americans has often disrupted extended family supports (Stubben, 2001).

Though cultural pride remains strong in most American Indian families, many also have suffered a long history of challenges: loss of tribal identities, removal to boarding schools and foster homes, high rates of alcohol and drug abuse, high in-cidence of suicides, and poverty (Bauer & Shea, 2003; Stubben, 2001). They may feel alienated from school settings and service providers and may respond de-fensively. Some American Indians consider themselves bicultural, which can cre-ate dissonance in either a traditional or a mainstream way of life; others observe that American Indians who try to be bicultural seem stranded between two cul-tures (Stubben, 2001).

When possible, a service provider should become known to and by the tribal community and should work to understand the particular tribal community that is being served; its values, history and even language (Stubben, 2001). Most Na-tive American families prefer a Native American service provider; such a person can be useful in communicating with elders and sharing personal information. Spirituality is a key factor in American Indian life and can be applied to help re-solve family problems. For example, a medical doctor may work with a tribal healer prior to treating a member of the family (Stubben, 2001).

Caucasian (Anglo) Families

The majority of professionals providing services in early intervention and early childhood special education (and many of the families they serve) have Anglo-European (Caucasian) roots. This culture values personal control over the environment, human equality, individualism, self-help and competition (Belmonte, 1996). Clearly, these values conflict with those of many other cultures. Anglos tend to be oriented toward the future and act more directly, openly, and informally. Time management is valued and punctuality is highly regarded. It is customary to treat men and women with equal respect and courtesy.

Cultural differences also abound even within "mainstream" America. One must be aware that a rural family may have different traditions and resources than an inner-city or suburban family. Regions of the United States may also vary in the way they relate family matters to professionals. Northeasterners may have different expectations than families from the deep South, for example.

In fact, low income levels may create greater cultural differences than ethnic origin (Harry, 2002). Researchers have found that families of low socioeconomic status tend to (a) be less verbal, (b) use more coercive discipline, (c) hold less positive beliefs regarding the effectiveness of early education, (d) feel a disability has less impact on their expectations than do others, and (e) have fewer resources available such as space, transportation, and childcare. These challenges may require additional resources and interaction with the family to ensure the family's access to and comfort with a plan for quality child services and support.

Each Family Is Unique

Despite these examples of cultural differences among various ethnic groups, one must always be aware that in the United States each family comes with its own unique experience and distance from traditional beliefs and practices. A family's educational level, history within the mainstream culture, socioeconomic status, and geographic location will make a great deal of difference in how closely or how differently they mirror a particular cultural profile (Harry, 2002). Rather than generalizing from what a given ethnic culture is supposed to look like, it is better to consider each family within its personal "activity setting." That is, the family context is the basis for consideration: Who is present? What is the physical setting for the family's daily routines? What is the script for conduct within this family? (Harry, 2002). Such questions, with careful listening to parents, permits one to work within a family's "zone" and identify goals for a child and preferences for services. It is always critical to get to know each individual family for its own heritage and immediate circumstances.

When working with families, one must also consider the ecological context for the family, which may create different needs, varying with the child's type of disability and the family's resources (Duis, Summers, & Summers, 1997). For example, families with more cohesion tend to have less stress, as do families with higher incomes, while single-parent families are the most stressed regardless of income. Higher embarrassment ratings are linked with higher stress as is poor relationships between siblings (Duis et al., 1997). Sometimes, the needs of other family members take precedence over the specific needs of the child with a disability, for example, when a parent becomes sick or loses a job. Often, educational needs may be a lower priority for families when compared to needs for such basics as food, shelter, child care, and health care (Bosch, 1996).

Financial needs can be a significant concern. Beyond hospitalization, families may also accumulate expenses for specialized equipment, transportation, time off

The family-centered approach ensures that each family receives the unique set of services it requires.

work, therapy services, medications, and dietary supplements (Bosch, 1996). Sometimes private and public insurance coverage, such as Medicaid or the Supplemental Security Income program, helps, but there are many gaps. Even relatively small out-of-pocket expenses can create a significant burden if a family has few resources to spare (Lukemeyer, Myers, & Smeeding, 2000). In fact, families with children who are disabled tend to be economically worse off than families with healthy children, even before the extra costs associated with the disability are taken into account. Families caring for children with special needs were 2–8% more likely to be living in poverty. Due to extraordinary medical and therapy costs, families with severely affected children are particularly hard hit.

Young children with disabilities often have unusual or special caregiving needs that demand significant time and energy from their parents and contribute to fatigue (Bosch, 1996). Feeding difficulties or behavioral disturbances can add significant stress. A lack of communication skills, difficult temperaments, or the need for constant supervision adds to the strain. This creates stress on the usual routines of family life and makes finding respite difficult (Guralnick, 1998).

Emotional needs, including grieving and reactions to stress, are also important to consider (Bosch, 1996). Not all parents react in the same way, and their reactions may change as the family life cycle changes. Often sadness reappears when developmental milestones are missed, and the sadness can be more intense than the impact of the original diagnosis (Bosch, 1996). Cultural values may inhibit a family from discussing personal issues with "outsiders" or prohibit their reliance on help outside the family (Bosch, 1996).

The greatest need perceived by parents is the requirement of information (Bosch, 1996). When a diagnosis is made, families face an immediate "crisis of information" in regard to their child's current and anticipated health and development (Guralnick, 1998). Parents of very young children with disabilities seek medical and diagnostic information. Those with older children want to know how to teach them, what services are currently available, and what their children might need in the future.

Parents need to establish their own priorities and choose the appropriate level and type of intervention that suits their family's needs (Bosch, 1996). However, the following must always be considered in planning for family needs. Adequate economic and institutional supports should be available to help families provide for their children with disabilities. Access to appropriate services should be facilitated through coordination among agencies. Informal supports may be as important as formal support. Extended family, friends, neighbors, and community should be assessed as resources. Professionals must behave competently, and this implies having a team of persons with different expertise available to provide information, resources, and support.

FORMING COLLABORATIVE TEAMS

Clearly, parental involvement in the education of children with disabilities produces academic, developmental, and social benefits, yet professionals have not been especially successful in facilitating such involvement or in promoting collaboration as much as possible (Pruitt, Wandry, & Hollums, 1998). Parents are a key source for information about their children, because of their firsthand knowledge of their children's physical, social, emotional, and cognitive traits (Hedrick, 1997). By working together, everyone benefits: parents, professionals, and children; and programs comply with the spirit of the federal law, not just the letter of the law (Duckworth & Kostell, 1999). There are specific steps that can be taken to strengthen partnerships with families, such as increasing communication, using parent networks, and learning to understand family views and strengths in shared decision making (Turnbull & Turnbull, 1996). Collaborative strategies, including one-on-one conferences, home visits, and parent panels are useful (Duckworth & Kostell, 1999), but the most important strategy may be the use of an effective collaborative team for planning, carrying out, and monitoring programs for young children.

Collaborative teams should be made up of all those who are essential in serving a young child with disabilities. This includes parents (and extended family as appropriate); teachers (both regular and special educators); specialists and therapists who work directly with a child, such as an occupational or physical therapist; a family advocate, if desired; an administrator or designee who can commit program services; and someone who can interpret evaluation results as needed.

Others who might be invited would include an interpreter, if needed, paraprofessionals who provide one-on-one aid to a child, and perhaps related medical personnel, such as the visiting nurse or pediatrician. Families may also decide to include support persons of their choosing, such as a disability advocate or friend.

Collaborative teaming has been implemented and researched in both regular and special education since the early 1970s (Johnson & Johnson, 1987; Kagan, 1991). "Teamwork is not magic, and simply 'getting along' or communicating information to one another does not constitute collaboration" (Hinojosa et al., 2001). Though researchers lack agreement as to the essential components of collaborative teaming, at least five elements, or attributes, are common to most models of collaborative, or cooperative, teaming:

1. There is a common goal or set of goals to which all parties agree. The first order of business in team conduct is to determine the primary goal of the team. All other decisions, personal and team, should be measured against this fundamental intent.

2. There is an agreed-upon strategy for achieving each goal or set of goals (responsibilities). Members of a team collectively determine the most efficacious method(s). Even when the goal is quite clear, however, finding common ground on a method for achieving the goal can be a challenge.

3. There is a commitment to dignified and meaningful interactions, individual skill development, and task completion. In short, professional conduct is fundamental to team success.

4. There is a commitment to dependence on each other. In other words, teamwork cannot be completed if any one member fails in his or her responsibility. On the other hand, the entire team celebrates together when success is achieved because it was achieved collectively.

5. Individuals commit to a shared system of decision making and accountability. Components such as leadership, role assignments, agendas, and evaluation are determined together.

In addition, several other factors have been discussed in the literature and are believed necessary if a team is to function successfully and assert that they are indeed co-laboring. Trust building is essential. Smith and Auger (1986) contended that teams must have a way of building and maintaining trust. This trust is generated only over a period of time and, once developed, is the basis for mutual respect and security (Friend & Cook, 1990).

Face-to-face interactions must occur. It is relatively simple today to communicate ideas without actually seeing our colleagues. One can usually e-mail, fax, phone, and voice mail ideas more quickly than scheduling and attending a meeting. However, these types of "interactions" are often not effective as a primary means of communicating. The sacrifice of time and effort made in order to hold meetings will eliminate many misunderstandings and conflicts that can set the team back unnecessarily (Thousand, Villa, & Nevin, 1994). Prolonged engagement with one another is essential for bonding, reflecting, and carrying on in-depth discussions (Hinojosa, et al., 2001).

Team members must acquire, refine, and practice small-group interpersonal skills. Most professional educators would agree that committee work can be torturous if decision makers lack basic skills to conduct small-group work. Collaboration should be voluntary. Though individuals can be mandated through policy to work together, collaboration cannot be coerced from individuals (Friend & Cook, 1990). Collaboration requires equity among participants. Each member of a team must be equally valued, even though certain members may become more pivotal at different points in the process (Friend & Cook, 1990; Morgan, 1985). In collaboration, all members of a team are considered "experts" and may serve as consultant and/or consultee at different points in time.

As early interventionists and preschool providers seek to become vital and reliable members of teams, the following strategies should prove helpful:

1. Be clear about what is known and what is not known. One professional is not expected to know other professional orientations, philosophies, and content as well as they know their own and should not pretend otherwise.

2. Listen. And listen some more. Think carefully about what has been heard and be careful to analyze it correctly. Do not screen out information at an early stage based on past experiences or personal biases.

3. Consider both the short- and long-term consequences of a position and the short- and long-term consequences of the other possibilities placed before the group.

4. Insist upon clarification. If a goal statement is ambiguous or unclear to one person, it may be unclear to others.

5. Check all assumptions underlying a goal before agreeing to support or reject it.

6. In setting goals on behalf of an infant or young child, be creative. Develop habits of conscience and imagination in order to move beyond personal experiences or the limits of one's education.

Haroutunian-Gordon (1991) identified four rules of conversation that need to be understood and practiced in group problem solving.

1. Offer ideas that are supported by data (research or experience).
2. Ensure that individuals are listening carefully to one another.
3. Uncover and discuss contradictory evidence.
4. Allow members to build on one another's knowledge and comments and to validate new associations of information.

These skills require individual members to find value in collaboration itself. According to Kagan (1991), "Valuing collaboration means valuing empowerment, growth, and diversity. It means moving from programmatic to systematic thinking, from short- to long-term visions" (p. 93).

If collaborative teams are truly going to serve well, a practice of personal responsibility within a culture of shared and mutual responsibility must be developed. For example, members of teams must learn not to let minor issues, which they find contrary to their own thinking or judgment, go unresolved. Differences must be addressed at the time the differences are first identified. Team members must not be allowed to accept the long ramblings and dominating behaviors of certain members. Members should acknowledge the source of their input— whether they are speaking from opinion, fact, experience, intuition, or research.

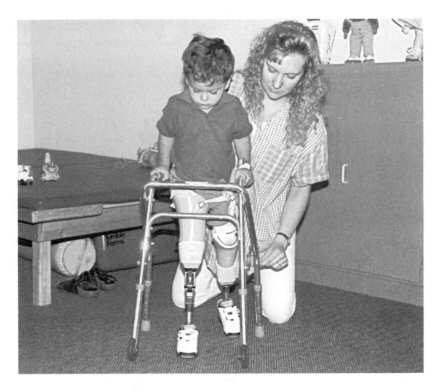

Members should confront, with compassion, those individuals or group behaviors that are obstructing the work and direction of the group. Likewise, feedback about tasks or responsibilities done well is equally necessary.

Despite an almost universal acceptance of the importance of collaborative teaming in relationship-based, family-centered early intervention and special education, collaborative teaming is not easy (Hinojosa, et al., 2001). Those in early intervention and special education need to be aware of pitfalls and be prepared to work around them. Among these are conflicts in philosophy and practice among different disciplines, conflicts with family values, system boundaries such as lack of space and time in a schedule to have formal and informal exchanges, and determining who gives and who takes advice. Therapists and educators profess to value collaborative decision making but seem most comfortable with their own autonomy. "The one thing I love about my job is that I have a lot of freedom, and I can do what I want and it helps build my confidence, and it helps build my communication. It helps me build my little world," (Hinojosa, et al., 2001). People tend to define themselves by their roles, and this tendency is counterproductive to teamwork and collaboration. Team collaboration may be hard to achieve in an environment that limits time together, reduces communication opportunities, and does not build trust. These factors must be considered first before mutually satisfying and effective collaboration can take place.

Collaboration is much easier for individuals who remain flexible, retain a sense of humor, communicate effectively, demonstrate tolerance for ambiguity, respect others' input, and have confidence in their own professional ability and the integrity of other team members. Such an atmosphere encourages a "trusting team" not only in planning, but also in service provision, problem solving, and management of programs.

TEAMING AND IDEA

Federal law requires that early intervention and preschool special education services provided to children with disabilities or who are at risk be coordinated by a team of professionals and parents. Team members are expected to assist a child eligible for early intervention or school services and the child's family in receiving the rights, procedural safeguards, and services that are authorized to be provided (Roberts-DeGennaro, 1996). The team must draw together relevant professionals from various disciplines to share their expertise, decision making, and intervention skills with parents. To do so successfully requires trust in each other's competencies, trust in each other's opinions, and reliance on each other's skills (Roberts-DeGennaro, 1996). An attitude like this does not develop magically; it requires a great deal of time and energy devoted to working collaboratively. As professionals work together, they should be going through a series of steps that bring them closer and closer to a transdisciplinary, or role-sharing approach. Roberts-DeGennaro (1996) outlines these progressive stages well:

> Step 1—**Unidisciplinary:** Believing that (even alone) one's own discipline can make an important contribution to children with disabilities or at risk of disabling conditions.
>
> Step 2—**Intradisciplinary:** Recognizing that other disciplines have important contributions to make.
>
> Step 3—**Multidisciplinary:** Recognizing that coordinated and comprehensive services must be made available to all who are disabled or at high risk of disabling conditions.
>
> Step 4—**Interdisciplinary:** Being willing and able to work with other disciplines in the development of jointly planned programs for children and being willing to assume responsibility for providing needed services as part of the total program.
>
> Step 5—**Transdisciplinary:** Committing oneself to teaching, learning, and working together with other providers of services who are also comfortable in crossing traditional disciplinary boundaries.

In practice, this progression toward increased collaboration requires a number of regular activities. Here are a few guidelines for working on collaborative teams (Stump & Wilson, 1996).

1. Set a clear team purpose and identify what each individual brings to the team. Identify talents and abilities and how they can best be used collaboratively. Set expectations for each team member.

2. Establish schedules. Be consistent in when meetings are held, and set a specific amount of time for meetings. Plan to spend a lot of time when first working collaboratively.

3. Conduct meetings. Set a specific purpose for each meeting and stick to it until a plan is developed. List who is going to do what and set dates for task completion.

4. Share workload and responsibilities. Vary assignments so that members are not always doing the same thing. Be flexible about each member's time demands.

5. Share expertise. Identify shared and unique expertise. Share knowledge and skills.

6. Follow through. Check in to be sure that things agreed on have been completed.

7. Celebrate successes and shoulder failures together.

8. Keep the lines of communication open.

Early intervention and preschool teams coordinate several important components necessary for serving very young children with disabilities and their families; these include resource supports, social supports, and information and services (Guralnick, 1998). Resource supports include providing awareness of, access to, and coordination of services. Providing supplemental supports, such as financial assistance or respite care, are additional components. Social supports involve parent-to-parent groups, family counseling, and mobilization of family, friend, and community networks. Information and services include the formal intervention program (in home or center), parent–professional relationships (problem solving, decision making), and individual therapies.

If early intervention and special education systems are working well, then services will be individually matched to the needs of the child and family (Guralnick, 1998). Some children and their families will require only surveillance or minimal supports, whereas others will require highly intensive, long-term programs. This diversity of need implies that professionals must have a great deal of knowledge and the will to use that expertise flexibly, according to the needs of individual families.

RESPONSIBILITIES OF COLLABORATIVE TEAMS

Though these tasks are detailed in later chapters in this text, there are primary responsibilities for which collaborative teams must be prepared because of the special skills required at each stage in a family's adjustment to having a child with a disability. These stages include points at which a team determines eligibility for special services, informs parents of their rights, plans and provides treatment and education across a continuum of settings, evaluates outcomes of these services, and prepares for transitions to other educational placements.

At Diagnosis or Determination of Eligibility

Guralnick (2001) asserted that a child's developmental outcomes are governed by the quality of a family's interactions: the relationship between parents and child, the kind of child experiences a family can orchestrate for their child, and the level of health and safety a family can provide. It makes sense, then, for collaborative teams to begin interacting with a family as soon as possible after a family receives a diagnosis of a disability or a determination that a child is eligible for special services. Early interaction supports positive family adaptation to having a member with a disability (Bauer & Shea, 2003). Among the initial tasks the team performs are: providing information the family needs to understand the disability and the child's unique development; responding to interpersonal distress experienced as the family adjusts its expectations toward the child; identifying resources that might reduce family stressors, such as respite care; and promoting confidence in the family's ability to carry out their new parenting roles under atypical circumstances (Guralnick, 2001).

Informing Parents of Their Rights

It is critical that collaborative teams inform families of young children with disabilities of all their legal rights. A large majority of parents of children with special needs said their children lost out because their families were "in the dark about the services they are entitled to" (Public Agenda, 2002, p. 11). Families reported that information about how special education works, what it offers, and what their child was entitled to was difficult to obtain. More than half of families surveyed by Public Agenda (2002) said they had to find out on their own what was available to their children because the school would not volunteer the information.

Families need their legal rights explained in simple language rather than jargon, and in their dominant language if it is not English. Important rights parents should know are these:

- A wide range of special services, from audiology to transportation, are to be provided if the child's assessment indicates they are necessary.
- A family's records are to be kept confidential but are open to the family's inspection.
- The intervention or educational plan is developed by the team including the parents and other persons the parents would like to include.
- Meetings should be held at a time and place convenient to the family and in their native language or mode of communication; if the parents chose not to attend, written parental consent is still required before a program can begin.
- A service coordinator or school staff responsible for implementing the plan must be identified.
- The educational or treatment plan must be developed within 45 days of referral and reviewed regularly (every 6 months for children from birth to 3, or every year for children from 3 to 21 years of age).
- A family may disagree with a team's educational or treatment plan and appeal for mediation or a hearing to review the appropriateness of the plan.

Planning and Providing Treatment and Education Across a Continuum of Settings.

After assessing both a child's and family's needs, a plan for intervention or education is developed. It is important to recognize that early intervention can be provided across a wide range of settings, including in a hospital, special center, child-care setting, the home, or elsewhere (Hanson & Bruder, 2001). Not all services have to be provided in the same location, and services may change over time as needs change. A wide breadth of professionals may be involved and they should all be a part of the collaborative team as long as a family does not feel over-whelmed by dealing with too many individuals. It is helpful if parents have a choice of who their service coordinator or main contact person will be. Parent choice should also be honored in terms of the model for services they desire for their child; such services should fit into the routines and demands of the family's life. Likewise, parents tend to be more engaged in their child's education if they are actively involved in developing the objectives targeted, are able to prioritize objectives they feel should have immediate attention, and can make an informed decision about the best way to provide treatment and education (Bauer & Shea, 2003).

Objectives should be identified in an open discussion of the services needed, how intense the services should be, who would deliver the services, and what the family's role would be; all this should be recorded in a family-friendly document (Guralnick, 2001). The information that was most helpful to families surveyed was what they could do to help a child meet the next milestone (McWilliam & Scott, 2001). Determining next steps can be facilitated through routines-based assess-ment by talking about a family's daily routines and identifying where difficulties arise.

Family constraints should also be recognized and strengths built on as part of how services are organized. The team should consider what a family needs in the way of material support, such as resources to meet basic needs, adaptive materi-als or equipment for their child, and financial support (often through state and federal assistance programs). Emotional support, through professionals or other parents, is one of the most important factors in reducing family stress and pro-moting well being (McWilliam & Scott, 2001). Connections to parent groups and information about how to build support networks with friends and extended fam-ily are important.

Evaluating Outcomes

Though a family service plan or individualized education plan should be reviewed to determine if goals, outcomes, and specific objectives for the child are being re-alized, other outcomes are also important to families and providers and should be considered. Priorities for early intervention include not only improved child de-velopment and functioning, but also a better quality of life for the child and en-hanced parenting competence and confidence (Dunst & Bruder, 2002). All those involved should know how the child and family is progressing and what should be adjusted. From time to time, stressors will also change as major life events oc-cur, or because of a child's transitions, and these events will require adjustments in a plan (Guralnick, 2001).

Planning for Transitions

Transitions occur at several different points in the early life of a child with a dis-ability. The move from a hospital to home, entry into an early intervention pro-gram, transition to a preschool special education program and then graduation into the primary grades of an elementary program disrupt a family's routines and create turmoil (Guralnick, 2001). These transitions cause stress for parents, often renewing anxieties about adjusting to new patterns and expectations. Advanced team planning for transitions has been long underestimated as an important stage for helping both the child and the family make these moves smoothly. The team must make a conscious effort to communicate to staff in the new program so that information can be shared about the child's progress, program, and priorities. A visit to the new environment can help allay fears and may allow for planning needed accommodations ahead of time.

CLOSE-UP

ADDRESSING THE CHALLENGES OF FAMILIES WITH MULTIPLE RISKS

The shifts and realities that American families face today reflect growing social concerns that have profound implications for professionals who provide educational, health, and social services. Families have changed dramatically in composition and size, with growing numbers of single-parent households and blended families. Both parents are more likely to be in the workforce, though it has become more difficult for families to stay out of poverty. Parental age is shifting, with more later childbearing at one end of the spectrum and more teen pregnancies at the other. Substance abuse leads to family problems and poses serious threats to caregiving for children. Children across the country are exposed to more violence in their communities and within their own homes. Many of today's families face not just one of these factors but live under the stress of multiple risks.

The stress associated with these many risks can sap parents' physical energy, undermine their sense of competence, and reduce their sense of control over their lives. Parents may find they are so overwhelmed in meeting basic needs that they cannot respond to specific developmental needs of their children. They may find it difficult to follow through, or they may lack knowledge, resources, or motivation to even access services. When these families must turn to schools or agencies for assistance, they bring the impact of this stress with them. Children from these families may suffer the multiple stresses of poverty, risks from inadequate prenatal care, and deficits from the lack of nurturance, structure, and stimulation that would prepare them for life. Finally, these children may see little hope or success for the future.

Social support within the larger community may be a key factor to reducing parents' emotional strain and coercive parenting behavior. However, professionals must understand how to provide this support in effective ways. First, they must recognize that family problems do not come from single causes and, thus, single interventions will probably not be effective. It is helpful in reaching out to multiple-risk families to: (1) provide a wide range of educational, health, and social services; (2) use family associates and paraprofessionals to assist families in gaining access to services; and (3) to employ home visitors to enhance contact with children's parents and caregivers. Such comprehensive services require a coordinated interagency response.

Service providers and educators who to engage in effective interaction approaches provide the most appropriate family support. They give support at the earliest point for children and parents to establish positive and mutually satisfying relationships with one another. They shift their focus from deficits to an emphasis on child and family strengths such as cognitive skills, goal-setting behaviors, family stability, and belief systems. Effective professionals help build and encourage natural support systems from neighbors, friends, coworkers, and others within the family's community. Service providers who are respectful of cultural differences are able to listen and clearly hear families as they express their needs, even though they may differ widely from that of the professional.

Service delivery that is comprehensive and coordinated provides a continuum of options that are community-based and valued by the community members who are being served. Service providers should be advocates for all children, not just those labeled with specific needs. Educators and service providers who are willing to regularly cross traditional professional boundaries offer options and individualize interventions to meet families' and children's needs. They do not provide an inflexible, uniform, or routine kind of service to all families. Finally, professionals must also go beyond bureaucratic limitations to work with representatives from other agencies and outside the jurisdiction of their own areas.

Only an interactive, multilevel, coordinated approach can address the many challenges of families who experience multiple risks. A broad range of resources and services must be mobilized to counteract these risk factors. One must remember the African proverb, "It takes a whole village to raise a child."

Source: From "Addressing the Challenges of Families with Multiple Risks," M. J. Hanson and J. J. Carta, 1995, *Exceptional Children, 62*(3), 201–212.

SUMMARY OF BUILDING COLLABORATIVE TEAMS

Because of the unique mandate given to early childhood professionals to collaborate with and for families, it has been said that these service providers have "the potential to be a guiding light to collaborators as they grapple with the complex issues inherent in today's unique social, political, and ideological context" (Kagan, 1991, p. 60). Still, Kagan labeled the collectivism effort as "naive idealism." She claimed that, as a whole, the movement is unlikely to be a panacea for our country's social ills. On a more modest level, however, she hoped that early childhood special education would be a beacon in the collaboration effort and that collaboration itself will be one necessary tool in efforts to improve care and education for young children with special needs.

Collaboration is the future (Dettmer et al., 1999). It is essential for achieving school reform, for responding to changing students' needs, and for ensuring the development of global, economic, and technological productivity. The work each professional does as a part of a collaborative team adds to the framework for continued collaboration throughout the global village (Dettmer et al., 1999). A personal plan for today's small collaborative efforts may have an impact on the future. Consider the following suggestions for encouraging collaboration on a wider scale (Dettmer et al., 1999):

1. Be a guest speaker about collaboration at community clubs and service organizations.
2. Develop a networking system that delivers positive "strokes" to school staff and families.
3. Inform colleagues of legislative and judicial activity.
4. Host sessions at conferences for school policymakers and administrators.
5. Have an open house and invite school board members.
6. Send summer postcards to school personnel saying, "I am looking forward to working with you this year."
7. Serve as an officer and committee member to organizations that support valued goals.

Bringing together all the team members of a special education student's program takes considerable effort and time, but it is extremely important (Marks, Schrader, & Levine, 1999). However, collaboration is more than just meeting together; a group's power lies in a team's capacity to merge its members' unique skills, to foster feelings of positive interdependence, to develop creative problem-solving skills, and to hold one another personally responsible for a student's success (Wood, 1998). It is only when individual members open themselves to each other's influence that the behaviors and attitudes necessary for collaboration can emerge. Those who effectively serve young children with disabilities and their families must be informed, caring, skilled, and flexible. They must believe in diversity, meeting individual needs, and supporting shared decision making. They must seek to strengthen alliances with parents and peers rather than achieving professional status by insulating themselves from those they serve (O'Shea, Williams, & Sattler, 1999). In short, effective teaming requires a commitment to children and families first, using multiple resources and skills to support our best efforts to their success.

STUDY GUIDE QUESTIONS

1. How would you describe family-centered practice to someone who is not in early intervention or preschool special education?
2. What would be the final measure of whether a family was empowered? What might you see that family doing?
3. Describe the different levels of relationship-based teaming. What kind of assistance is given at each level?
4. What common negative assumptions about families of children with disabilities have grown from past research on these families? How has that changed in more recent years?
5. In your own words, how would you define "family"?
6. Describe the typical stages of the grief process and how they might be misused by professionals.
7. What is meant by family hardiness, and what are the three dimensions of family hardiness?
8. Give your own examples of specific communication skills that should be used and pitfalls that must be avoided when working with families.
9. How should one deliver difficult diagnostic information to families?

10. What have researchers learned about time as a family resource? What are the implications for early childhood professionals?
11. Give an example of how one's ethnic culture might affect the way a family treated a child with a disability.
12. What are some of the unique needs faced by families of children with disabilities?
13. What are five elements that are desirable, if not key elements, in collaborative teaming? State these in your own words.
14. What guidelines should direct the regular activities of a collaborative team?

REFERENCES

Abbott, D. A., & Meredith, W. H. (1986). Strengths of parents with retarded children. *Family Relations, 35,* 371–375.

Able-Boone, H., Sandall, S. R., Stevens, E., & Frederick, L. (1992). Family support resources and needs: How early intervention can make a difference. *Infant-Toddler Intervention, 2*(2), 93–102.

Allen, D. A., & Affleck, G. (1985). Are we stereotyping parents? A postscript to Blacker. *Mental Retardation, 23*(4), 200–202.

Anderegg, M. L., Vergason, G. A., & Smith, M. C. (1992). A visual representation of the grief cycle for use by teachers with families of children with disabilities. *Remedial and Special Education, 13,* 17–23.

Bauer, A. M. & Shea, T. M. (2003). *Parents and schools: Creating a successful partnership for students with special needs.* Upper Saddle River, NJ: Merrill/Prentice Hall.

Beach Center on Families and Disability. (1995). Dads feel left out. *The Beach Center Newsletter, 6*(3). Retrieved August 9, 1999 from *http://www.lsi.ukans.edu/beach/html/dis2.htm*

Beach Center on Families and Disability. (Summer 1997). Family-centered service delivery. *The Beach Center Newsletter, 8*(2). Retrieved August 9, 1999 from *http://www.lsi.ukans.edu/beach/ html/fc1.htm*

Beach Center on Families and Disability. (1998). Quality Indicators of Exemplary Family-Centered Programs. Retrieved August 9, 1999 from *http://www.lsi.ukans.edu/ beach/html/f19.htm*

Beach Center on Families and Disability. (Summer 1998). Family stories. *The Beach Center Newsletter, 9*(1). Retrieved August 9, 1999 from *http://www.lsi.ukans. edu/beach/html/sfam2.htm*

Beach Center on Families and Disability. (1999). Quality Indicators of Exemplary Family-Centered Legislation. Retrieved August 9, 1999 from *http://www.lsi.ukans. edu/beach/html/17.htm*

Belmonte, T. (1996). Developing cross-cultural sensitivity. *Family Childcare Connections, 6*(2), 2–3.

Benson, B. A., & Gross, A. M. (1989). The effect of a congenitally handicapped child upon the marital dyad: A review of the literature. *Clinical Psychology Review, 9*(6), 747–758.

Bosch, L. A. (1996). Needs of parents of young children with developmental delay: Implications for social work practice. *Families in Society, 77*(8), 477–487.

Bradley, V. J., Knoll, J., & Agosta, J. M. (Eds.). (1992). *Emerging issues in family support.* Washington, DC: American Association on Mental Retardation.

Breslau, N. (1983). Care of disabled children and women's time issue. *Medical Care, 21,* 620–629.

Brotherson, M. J., & Goldstein, B. (1992). Time as a resource and constraint for parents of young children with disabilities: Implications for early intervention services. *Topics in Early Childhood Special Education, 12,* 508–527.

Brotherson, M. J., & Martin, L. H. (1992). *Building successful partnerships with families with young children with disabilities: Family, early interventionist, and physician perspectives.* Paper presented at the Annual Conference of the Association for the Care of Children's Health, Atlanta.

Carr, J. (1988). Six-weeks to twenty-one years old: A longitudinal study of children with Down syndrome and their families. *Journal of Child Psychology and Psychiatry, 29*(4), 407–431.

Christenson, S. L., & Cleary, M. (1990). Consultation and the parent-educator partnership: A perspective. *Journal of Educational and Psychological Consultation, 1,* 219–241.

Cook, R. E., Tessier, A., & Klein, M. D. (1992). *Adapting early childhood curricula for children with special needs.* Upper Saddle River, NJ: Merrill/Prentice Hall.

Cox, A., Rutter, M., Newman, S., & Bartak, L. (1975). A comparative study of infantile autism and specific developmental receptive language disorders: Parental characteristics. *British Journal of Psychiatry, 126,* 146–159.

Darling, R. (1979). *Families against society: A study of reactions to children with birth defects.* London: SAGE.

Davern, L. (April, 1996). Listening to parents of children with disabilities. *Educational Leadership,* 61–63.

Dettmer, P., Dyck, N., & Thurston, L. P. (1999). *Consultation, collaboration, and teamwork*. (3rd ed.). Boston: Allyn & Bacon.

Duckworth, S. V., & Kostell, P. H. (1999). The parent panel: Supporting children with special needs. *Childhood education, 75*(4), 199–203.

Duis, S. S., Summers, M., & Summers, C. R. (1997). Parent versus child stress in diverse family types: An ecological approach. *Topics in Early Childhood Special Education, 17*(1), 53–73.

Dunlap, K. M. (1997). Family empowerment: One outcome of cooperative preschool education. *Child Welfare, 76*(4), 501–519.

Dunst, C. J., & Bruder, M. J. (2002). Valued outcomes of service coordination, early intervention, and natural environments. *Exceptional Children, 68*(3), 361–375.

Failla, S., & Jones, L. (1991). Families of children with developmental disabilities: An examination of family hardiness. *Research in Nursing and Health, 14,* 41–50.

Featherstone, H. (1980). A difference in the family: *Living with a disabled child*. New York: Penguin.

Fennel, M. (1999). The boy who could not speak. *Exceptional Parent, 29*(9), 132.

Fraiberg, L. (1980). *Clinical studies in infant mental health: The first year of life*. New York: Basic Books.

Fraiberg. S. H. (1996). *The magic years: Understanding and handling the problems of early childhood*. (Paperback Reissue edition). New York: Fireside.

Francis, P. L., & Jones, F. A. (1984). Interactions of mothers and their developmentally-delayed infants: Age, parity, and gender effects. *Journal of Clinical Child Psychology, 13*(3), 268–273.

Friend, M., & Cook, L. (1990). Collaboration as a predictor for success in school reform. *Journal of Educational and Psychological Consultation, 1*(1), 69–86.

Gath, A. (1977). The impact of an abnormal child upon the parents. *British Journal of Psychiatry, 130,* 405–410.

Gath A., & Gumley, D. (1987). Retarded children and their siblings. *Journal of Child Psychology and Psychiatry, 28,* 715–730.

Gonzales Alvarez, L. I. (1998). A short course in sensitivity training. *Teaching Exceptional Children, 1,* 73–77.

Guralnick, M. J. (1998). Effectiveness of early intervention for vulnerable children: A developmental perspective. *American Journal on Mental Retardation, 102*(4), 319–345.

Guralnick, M. J. (2001). A developmental systems model for early intervention. *Infants and Young Children, 14(2)*. Retrieved January 10, 2002 from *http://proquest, umi.com/pdqweb?TS=1010712433&RQT=309&CC=2&Dtp=1&Did=000000086092740&*

Hains, A. H., Lynch, E. W., & Winton, P. J. (2000). *Moving toward cross-cultural competence in lifelong personnel development: A review of the literature. Technical Report #3*. Culturally and Linguistically Appropriate Services. Retrieved February 24, 2003 from *http://class. uiuc.edu/techreport/tech3.html*

Hanson, M. J., & Carta, J. J. (1995). Addressing the challenges of families with multiple risks. *Exceptional Children, 62*(3), 201–212.

Hanson, M. J. & Bruder, M. B. (2001). Early intervention: Promises to keep. *Infants and Young Children, 13*(3), 47–58.

Haroutunian-Gordon, S. (1991). *Turning the soul: Teaching through conversation in the high school*. Chicago: University of Chicago Press.

Harry, B. (2002). Trends and issues in serving culturally diverse families of children with disabilities. *The Journal of Special Education, 36*(3), 131–138.

Hedrick, L. (1997). Parents and professionals working together. In L. L. Dunlap (Ed.), *An introduction to early childhood special education* (pp. 118–136). Boston: Allyn & Bacon.

Heflinger, C. A., & Bickman, L. (1997). A theory-driven intervention and evaluation to explore family caregiver empowerment. *Journal of Emotional & Behavioral Disorders, 5*(3), 184–192.

Heffron, M. C. (2000). Clarifying concepts of infant mental health—Promotion, relationship-based preventive intervention, and treatment. *Infants and Young Children, 12*(4), 14–21.

Herman, S. E., Marcenko, M., & O'Hazel, K. L. (1996). Parents' perspectives on quality in family support programs. *Journal of Mental Health Administration 23*(2), 156–164.

Heward, W. L. (1996). *Exceptional children*. (5th ed.). Upper Saddle River, NJ: Merrill/Prentice Hall.

Hinojosa, J., Bedell, G., Buchholz, E. S., Charles, J., Shigaki, I. S., & Bicchieri, S. M. (2001). Team collaboration: A case study of an early intervention team. *Qualitative Health Research, 11*(2), 206–220.

Hirshberg, L. M. (December 1997/January 1998). Infant mental health consultation to early intervention. *Zero to Three, 18*(3). Retrieved March 5, 2003 from *http://www.zerotothree.org/sample.html*

Hoover-Dempsey, K., & Sandler, H. (1997). Why do parents become involved in their children's education? *Review of Educational Research, 67*(1), 3–42.

Hunter, A. G., Pearson, J. L., Ialongo, N. S., & Kellam, S. G. (1998). Parenting alone to multiple caregivers: Childcare and parenting arrangements in black and white urban families. *Family Relations, 47*(4), 343–353.

Hyun, J. K., & Fowler, S. A. (1995). Respect, cultural sensitivity, and communication. *Teaching Exceptional Children*, 25–28.

Johnson, D. W., & Johnson, F. P. (1987). *Joining together*. (3rd ed.). Upper Saddle River, NJ: Prentice Hall.

Kagan, S. L. (1991). *United we stand: Collaboration for childcare and early childhood services.* New York: Teacher's College Press.

Kaplan-Sanoff, M., Lerner, C., and Bernard, A. (2000). New roles for developmental specialists in pediatric primary care. *Zero to three, 21*(2). Retrieved March 5, 2003, from *http://www.zerotothree.org/sample.html*

Kazak, A. E. (1986). Families with physically handicapped children: Social ecology and family systems. *Family Process, 25,* 265–281.

Kazak, A. E., & Marvin, R. S. (1984). Differences, difficulties and adaptation: Stress and social networks in families with a handicapped child. *Family Relations, 33,* 67–77.

Klemm, D., & Schimanski, C. (1999). Parent to parent: The crucial connection. *Exceptional Parent, 29*(9), 109–112.

Kobasa, S., Maddi, S., & Puccetti, M. (1982). Personality and exercise as buffers in the stress–illness relationship. *Journal of Behavior Medicine, 5,* 391–403.

Korsch, B. M., & Negrete, V. F. (1972). Doctor-patient communication. *Scientific American, 227,* 66–74.

Kubler-Ross, E. (1969). *Locus of control: Current trends in theory and research.* Hillsdale, NJ: Lawrence Earlbaum Associates.

Leslie, L. A., & Morton, G. (2001). Family therapy's response to family diversity: Looking back, looking forward. *Journal of Family Issues, 22*(7), 904–921.

Lukemeyer, A., Myers, M. K., & Smeeding, T. (2000). Expensive children in poor families: Out-of-pocket expenditures for the care of disabled and chronically ill children in welfare families. *Journal of Marriage and the Family, 62*(2), 399–415.

Marks, S. U., Schrader, C., & Levine, M. (1999). Paraeducator experiences in inclusive settings: Helping, hovering, or holding their own. *Exceptional Children, 65*(3), 315–328.

McCubbin, H. L., Nevin, R. S., Cauble, A. E., Larsen, A., Comeau, J. K., & Patterson, J. M. (1982). Family coping with chronic illness: The case of cerebral palsy. In H. I. McCubbin, A. E. Cauble, & J. M. Patterson (Eds.), *Family stress, coping, and social support* (pp. 169–188). Springfield, IL: Thomas.

McHale, S. M., & Gamble, W. C. (1989). Sibling relationships of children with disabled and nondisabled brothers and sisters. *Developmental Psychology, 25*(3), 421–429.

McLinden, S. E. (1990). Mothers' and fathers' reports of the effects of a young child with special needs on the family. *Journal of Early Intervention, 14,* 249–259.

McWilliam, R. A. & Scott, S. (2001). A support approach to early intervention: A three-part framework. *Infants and Young Children, 13*(4), 55–66.

Meyer, D. J., & Vadasy, P. F. (1994). Sibshops: *Workshops for siblings of children with special needs.* Baltimore: Brookes.

Morgan, S. R. (1985). *Children in crisis: A team approach in the schools.* Austin, TX: PRO-ED.

Moore, M. L., Howard, V. F., & McLaughlin, T. F. (2002). Siblings of children with disabilities: A review and analysis. *International Journal of Special Education. 17*(1), 49–64.

Murphy, A. T. (1981). *Special children, special parents: Personal issues with handicapped children.* Upper Saddle River, NJ: Prentice Hall.

Murphy, A. T. (1982). The family with a handicapped child: A review of the literature. *Developmental and Behavioral Pediatrics, 3*(2), 73–82.

O'Shea, D. J., Williams, A. L., & Sattler, R. O. (1999). Collaboration across special education and general education: Preservice teachers' views. *Journal of Teacher Education, 50*(2), 147–157.

Orsillo, S. M., McCaffrey, R. J., & Fisher, J. M. (1993). Siblings of head-injured individuals: A population at risk. *Journal of Head Trauma Rehabilitation, 8*(1), 102–115.

Perl, J. (1995). Improving relationship skills for parent conferences. *Exceptional Children, 27*(1), 29–31.

Pollack, S. (1986). Human responses to diabetes mellitus. *Western Journal of Nursing Research, 11,* 265–280.

Pruitt, P., Wandry, D., & Hollums, D. (1998). Listen to us! Parents speak out about their interactions with special educators. *Preventing School Failure, 42*(4), 161–167.

Public Agenda. (2002). *When it's your own child; A report on special education from the families who use it.* New York: Author.

Reed, E. W., & Reed, S. C. (1965). *Mental Retardation: A family study.* Philadelphia: Saunders.

Roberts-DeGennaro, M. (1996). An interdisciplinary training model in the field of early intervention. *Social Work in Education, 18*(1), 20–30.

Roos, P. (1985). Parents of mentally retarded children—misunderstood and mistreated. In A. P. Turnbull & H. R. Turnbull (Eds.), *Parents speak out: Views from the other side of the two-way mirror* (2nd ed., pp. 245–257). Upper Saddle River, NJ: Merrill/Prentice Hall.

Roth, W. (1982). Poverty and the handicapped child. *Children and Youth Services Review, 4,* 67–75.

Schell, G. C. (1981). The young handicapped child: A family perspective. *Topics in Early Childhood Special Education, 1,* 21–27.

Seligman, M., & Darling, R. B. (1989). *Ordinary families special children: A systems approach to childhood disability.* New York: The Guilford Press.

Singer, G. H. S., & Nixon, C. (1996). A report on the concerns of parents of children with acquired brain injury. In G. H. S. Singer, A. Glang, & J. Williams (Eds.), *Children with acquired brain injury: Educating and supporting families* (pp. 23–52). Baltimore: Brookes.

Smith, S. D., & Auger, K. (1986). Conflict or cooperation? Keys to success in partnerships in education. *Action in Teacher Education, 7*(4), 1–9.

St. John. M. & Pawl, J. H. (February/March 2000). Inclusive interaction in infant-parent psychotherapy. *Zero to Three*. Retrieved October 10, 2002 from *http://www.zerotothree.org/vol20–4.html*

Stubben, J. D. Working with and conducting research among American Indian families. *The American Behavioral Scientist, 44*(9), 1466–1481.

Stump, C. S., & Wilson, C. (1996). Collaboration: Making it happen. *Intervention in School & Clinic, 31*(5), 310–313.

Swick, K. J. (1996). Building healthy families: Early childhood educators can make a difference. *Journal of Instructional Psychology, 23*(1), 75–82.

Thousand, J. S., Villa, R., & Nevin, A. (1994). *Creativity and collaborative learning*. Baltimore: Paul H. Brookes.

Traustadottir, R. (1991). Mothers who care: Gender, disability, and family life. *Journal of Family Issues, 12*(2), 211–228.

Turbiville, V. P. (1995). Fathers, their children, and disability. *Infants and Young Children, 7*(4).

Turnbull, A. P. & Turnbull, H. R. (Eds.). (1985). *Parents speak out: Views from the other side of the two-way mirror* (2nd ed., pp. 245–257). Upper Saddle River, NJ: Merrill/Prentice Hall.

Turnbull, A. P., & Turnbull, H. R. (1990). *Families, professionals, and exceptionality: A special partnership.* (2nd ed.). Upper Saddle River, NJ: Merrill/Prentice Hall.

Turnbull, A. P., & Turnbull, H. R. (1996). *Families, professionals, and exceptionality: A special partnership* (3rd ed.). Upper Saddle River, NJ: Merrill/Prentice Hall.

Vanderslice, V. (1984). Empowerment: A definition in progress. *Human Ecology Forum, 14*(1), 2–3.

Weatherston, D. J. (2000). The infant mental health specialist. *Zero to Three, 21*(22). Retrieved March 5, 2003 from *http://www.zerotothree.org/sample.html*

Werner, E., & Smith, R. (1982). *Vulnerable but invincible: A study of resilient children*. New York: McGraw-Hill.

Willoughby, J. C., & Glidden, L. M. (1995). Fathers helping out: Shared childcare and marital satisfaction of parents of children with disabilities. *American Journal on Mental Retardation, 99*(4), 399–406.

Wood, M. (1998). Whose job is it anyway? Educational roles in inclusion. *Exceptional Children, 64*(2), 181–195.

Young, D. M., & Roopnarine, J. L. (1994). Fathers' childcare involvement with children with and without disabilities. *Topics in Early Childhood Special Education, 14*(4), 488–502.

4 *Human Development*

The wonder of nature, responsible for the changes that take place between human conception and the first years of school, largely awaits scientific explanation. Our understanding of human development is confined to describing the surprisingly predictable processes and stages through which the human species matures. Psychologists, linguists, biologists, geneticists, sociologists, educators, and other researchers continue to study this fascinating phenomenon. Even without complete answers, however, our present knowledge of human growth is vital to fields serving families with very young children.

IMPORTANCE AND USE OF KNOWLEDGE OF HUMAN DEVELOPMENT

A thorough understanding of human development is fundamental to the competency of early childhood professionals. Without basic knowledge of the principles and stages through which infants and preschoolers pass, educators would be unable to communicate with parents, identify and assess children, design instruction, set expectations, select intervention strategies, or evaluate child and program progress. Parents turn to early childhood professionals for information and assistance, thus expecting them to be experts in normal development. To satisfy this need, educators must have at least a knowledge of developmental patterns for physical growth, as well as of cognitive, language, and social/emotional growth.

Perhaps the greatest use of our knowledge of human development is in the identification of appropriate intervention objectives and the selection of related intervention strategies. Because human development is largely predictable, it is possible to note a child's present behavior and identify the probable emerging behavior. Selecting a target behavior that is too simple or too difficult for a child would constrain that child's success, and, consequently, lessen the professional's effectiveness.

Intervention strategies must also be appropriate for a child's developmental abilities. Professionals should be capable of matching materials to children's cognitive levels, giving instructions to match a child's understanding of language, determining how long a child can be expected to pay attention, and knowing the degree of social interaction that can be expected.

Knowledge of normal human development, paired with a knowledge of conditions that may lead to developmental disabilities, enables professionals to estimate the potential effects of a particular disability on a child. For example, an educator might anticipate that a child with a moderate degree of athetoid cerebral palsy will experience difficulties in expressive language and motor development. The probability of such problems should prompt this child's team to focus on intensive communication intervention and physical and occupational therapy, as well as to consider assistive devices as the child matures.

The need to cultivate a thorough understanding of how humans develop is underscored by the difficulty of such an undertaking. It often takes professionals years to master this knowledge. Fortunately, many resources regarding development are available to assist in making day-to-day and long-term decisions. While these resources are no substitute for mastery, they provide a useful supplement to a soundly established basic understanding of human development. Some basic principles of development are well established in the literature, and knowledge of these guidelines assists professionals in making daily decisions.

PRENATAL GROWTH AND DEVELOPMENT

By the time children are born, they have already undergone an average of 38 weeks of development. This period is divided into three stages: ovum, embryo, and fetus. For 2 weeks following the time of conception, the ovum, or fertilized egg, travels down one of the fallopian tubes and eventually attaches to the wall of the uterus, where it remains throughout the prenatal period.

The **embryonic stage** begins in the 3rd week, when cell differentiation permits the emergence of a central nervous system and a circulatory system. The stage is completed by the end of the 8th week, when ossification of the bones begins. During the embryonic phase, the heart, lungs, digestive system, and brain develop from unspecified cells to well-defined structures. Muscular and nervous system development accompanies these structural changes. At the extremeties, hands, feet, fingers, and toes are formed, as well as facial features such as eyelids and ears.

The embryonic period is the most vulnerable stage of pregnancy. First, many women are unaware of their pregnancies at this point, and they may inadvertently cause harm to the fragile embryo. Many embryos spontaneously abort when they detach from the uterine wall and are expelled. During this early period, harmful substances (e.g., cigarette smoke, radiation) or trauma can also disrupt the structural development taking place in an embryo. Hence, embryonic damage may result in spontaneous abortion, miscarriage, or development of a birth defect.

Supporting the developing embryo, and later the fetus, are the **placenta**, umbilical cord, and **amniotic sac** (see Figure 4–1). The placenta is a fleshy mass made up of villi or projectiles that insert themselves into the lining of the uterus. The largest and most important of these is the **umbilical cord**, which joins the bloodstream of the embryo at the site of the child's abdomen to the bloodstream of the mother via the uterine lining. This connection permits the exchange of life-sustaining substances between the maternal bloodstream and the fetus. Though the fetal and maternal blood do not mix, it is the passage of nutrients, oxygen, and other gases through the umbilical cord to the fetus that allows the unborn baby to survive. At the same time, fetal waste products such as carbon dioxide and other metabolites pass back through the umbilical cord to be excreted by the mother. Though the placenta also serves as a barrier to large molecules and potentially harmful substances, it is not infallible. The placenta, unable to differentiate healthy

Figure 4–1 Developing Fetus in Prenatal Environment

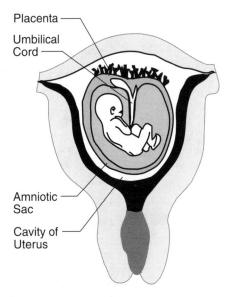

Placenta

Umbilical Cord

Amniotic Sac

Cavity of Uterus

from damaging chemicals, permits some dangerous drugs (including alcohol), hormones, and bacterial and viral organisms to cross into the bloodstream of the developing human.

Another important structure is the amniotic sac, which contains liquid amniotic fluid and surrounds the embryo. This sac, made pliable by the encapsulated fluid, protects the vulnerable embryo from physical shocks a mother might experience and maintains a constant temperature for the fetus.

The final and longest stage of development is the **fetal stage**, which begins in the 9th week and lasts through the 9th month. While each system was primitively developed during the embryonic stage, these systems undergo rapid growth and increase in complexity through differentiation during the final period (see Figure 4–2). At 12 weeks, a fetus resembles a human figure, and spontaneous movement of the limbs may be observed. By 16 weeks a mother can usually feel movement in the infant, referred to as "the quickening." At 16 weeks, a fetus can also open and close its mouth and eyes and grows fingernails and hair.

The age at which a fetus is considered viable, or would have the potential to live outside the womb, is about 24 weeks. To permit independent survival, a fetus must have developed reflexes such as sucking and swallowing, and the lungs must be sufficiently developed to produce surfactant, which allows breathing without collapse of the lungs. During the final 2 months of pregnancy, the central nervous system, including the brain, continues to develop greater differentiation, and the fetus grows rapidly in height and weight.

Figure 4–2
Phases of Fetal Development
Source: Adapted from *Before We Were Born: Basic Embryology and Birth Defects* (2nd ed.), by K. L. Moore, 1983, W. B. Saunders. Reprinted with permission.

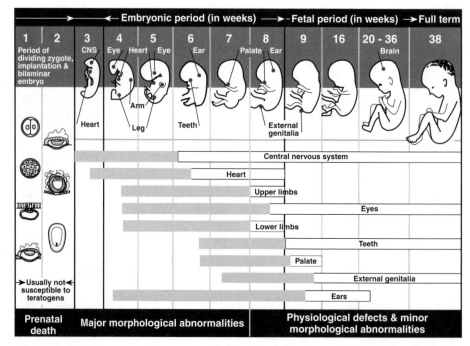

THE NEIGHBORHOODS THEY LIVE IN

A comprehensive review of literature regarding the effects of a child's neighborhood charactertistics on their social and cognitive outcomes revealed that a constellation of factors influence the immediate and long-term well-being of individuals within our society. Although family-level factors tend to outweigh neighborhood factors in strength of influence on children's outcomes, it is clear that neighborhoods do matter.

ACHIEVEMENT

The most consistent finding was that high-income neighbors have a positive influence on a child's readiness for school as well as specific achievement outcomes. Powerful effects accrue when a neighborhood is comprised of a high percentage of affluent (income over $30,000), well-educated, and/or professional residents. Increases in IQ, verbal ability, reading recognition, and general educational attainment have been found in early childhood, early education, and adolescent beneficiaries. These benefits tend to be more significant for European American and male children.

Neighborhood ethnic diversity has also been studied, though less rigorously. It appears that heterogenous neighborhoods may be beneficial for some children and associated with higher risk for other children. Male minority children tend to benefit from ethnically diverse communities, with lower drop-out rates. Yet, for younger children, racial/ethnic diversity was found to be negatively related to school readiness.

BEHAVIORAL/EMOTIONAL PROBLEMS

Having a high percentage of managerial/professional residents in a neighborhood, greater socioeconomic resources, ethnic and racial heterogeneity, and residential stability were all related to lower rates of behavioral and social problems. On the other hand, children raised in low-income neighborhoods and those who moved into low-income neighborhoods (as opposed to those who were raised in public housing) engaged in higher rates of crime, truancy, runaways, and disruptiveness. Furthermore, repeated studies have found that children who grow up in heterogenous environments are more likely to engage in criminal behavior and to be labeled with oppositional behavior or conduct disorder.

SEXUALITY AND CHILDBEARING

The presence of economic and social resources for girls in neighborhoods with higher incomes and a few professional/managerial residents seems to mitigate the rate of nonmarital childbearing. Conversely, communities associated with high levels of poverty are associated with high rates of teen intercourse and having impregnated someone and low rates of contraceptive use. Neighborhoods with a high percentage of unemployed persons are related to increased teen sexuality and childbearing.

EARLY DEVELOPMENT

For young children, neighborhood composition is more indirectly related to development than for older children, in that income, education, employment status, ethnicity, and so on influence the availability of resources that support parents of young children. Three mechanisms of support are important to families of young children: institutional, relational, and normative/collective efficacy.

Institutional community support comes in the form of learning, recreational and social activities, child care, schools, medical facilities and employment opportunities. Libraries, museums, and literacy programs can all influence school readiness and achievement. Likewise, the availability and quality of child care available in a neighborhood have implications for a child's learning and behavioral and physical well-being. Obviously the quality of schools and accessibility to health care directly affect a child's development.

Relationships within the family, intergenerational support, and interpersonal associations influence a parent's mental health, irritability, coping skills, and efficacy. The quality and quantity of neighborhood networks between families assist parents in seeking and finding resources important to themselves and to the well-being of children within families. Such relationships also inform families regarding parent styles, healthy family routines, and quality and structure of home environments.

Finally, normative or collective efficacy is the degree to which neighbors within a community agree (explicitly or implicitly) to a set of acceptable behavioral standards and monitor this behavior with the goal of supervising children and maintaining order. Informal control and social cohesion are manifest through implementation of informal and formal institutions to monitor the activities of children and youth. As early as preschool, children are negatively influenced by violent behavior within peer groups—a condition which is exacerbated in unstructured and unsupervised play. To date, limited research is encouraging regarding the positive influence of collective efficacy in mediating problem behaviors in youth.

To summarize, neighborhood constitution does influence child development and adolescent behavior. Demographic factors, such as income, educational levels, and ethnic diversity, that are related to school readiness, achievement, behavior, and sexuality can be mitigated by family-level influences as well as community-based institutions, social networks, and families working together to provide safe and structured environments for children to play and go to school.

Source: "The Neighborhoods They Live In: The Effects of Neighborhood Resience on Child and Adolescent Outcomes," by T. Leventhal and J. Brooks-Gunn, 2000, *Psychological Bulletin, 126,* pp. 309–337.

CHILD GROWTH AND DEVELOPMENT

After birth, development continues as the system just described unfolds into the biological and behavioral traits that define individual children. Others may observe signs of a child's genetic inheritance through changes in physical and behavioral characteristics. Though some of these characteristics are solely determined by genetic code (e.g., eye color), others are influenced to some, as yet unknown, degree by other factors. Characteristics that are determined by both genetic and environmental factors tend to progress, though variant in rate, in a continuous and predictable pattern.

Maturation is the universally observed sequence of biological changes that take place as one ages. Maturation permits the development of psychological functions. For example, as the brain develops in the early months of life and becomes capable of understanding and producing language, infants who are exposed to language gradually develop this ability. If either language stimulation or neurological growth is missing, language cannot develop. Along with physical development is a maturation of perceptual abilities including sight, hearing, and balance (see Table 4–1). Each of these senses interacts with the other and with other developmental areas to foster normal patterns and rates of development.

Normal development refers to a sequence of physical and psychological changes that are very similar for all children. Within individual children, the extent to which environment is likely to influence this sequence, or the extent to which children will realize their potential, has been referred to as **range of reaction** (Zigler & Stevensen, 1993). Favorable conditions enable children to reach the high end of their potential, while unfavorable conditions can depress development.

Major indexes of developmental accomplishments, such as "Casey just took his first step yesterday" or "Adam just learned to say 'mama'!", are used to measure developmental progress. These indexes, which are identified across developmental

Table 4–1 Patterns of Percepual Development

Sense	Ability at Birth	Patterns of Development
Vision	Research indicates range from 20/800 to 20/150; discriminates colors; shows preference for patterns & three-dimensional images; 20/20 at 5 years	20/100 at 1 year; 20/60 at 2 years; 180 visual arc at 3 mo; adult-like focus at 4 mo; discriminates age & gender at 5–1/2 mo; recognizes face from different angles at 7 mo
Hearing	40 dB (decibel) threshold; startle response; habituation to sound; soothe to rhythmic music	discriminate speech sounds (ba/pa) at 4–14 weeks; 20 db threshold at 3–8 mo; localize to sound and show preference for female voices at 4–6 mo
Gustatory	little research; prefers sugar solution to water	
Olfactory	little research; appears to respond differentially to odors	
Tactile	reflexive responses to touch; differential sensitivity by body parts; discriminates warm and cold	decrease response threshold across first 5 days; by three days learns to habituate and is conditioned to tactile stimulation; thermal regulation at 1–1/2 wks; discriminates objects tactually by 10-12 mo

Source: Adapted from "Behavioral Competencies and Outcomes: The Effects of Disorders," by M. J. Hanson, and M. F. Hanline, 1984, in M. J. Hanson (Ed.), *Atypical Infant Development* (pp. 109–142), Austin, TX: PRO-ED.

areas (e.g., language or social skills) and across years, are referred to as **developmental milestones**. Established milestones are based on the average age at which children acquire skills or pass through stages. For example, an average child begins to take the first step at 12 months and begins to say "mama" at 9 months. The milestones at which children are expected to achieve skills are determined by taking a representative sample of children and determining the average age at which they acquire those skills.

Norms are statistically determined standard (normal) age levels for developmental milestones. For example, the norm for independent sitting is 6 months. Some children sit earlier, and others take longer than 6 months to acquire this skill, but on the average, infants learn to sit by themselves about midway through their first year. It is important to stress, however, that norms are simply averages, around which there is a **range of normalcy**. For example, slight deviations in development are known to be related to infants' sleeping posture. Since the early 1990s parents have been advised to place sleeping infants on their sides or backs to reduce the possibility of Sudden Infant Death. Recent research indicates that 6-month-old infants who sleep face down are more developed in motor and other skills than infants who sleep on their backs or side (Davis, Moon, Sachs, & Ottolini, 1998). However, by the time these infants reach 18 months, there are no developmental differences. This research shows how prevailing is nature on child development.

Typically developing children who acquire developmental skills earlier or later than the norm will still be considered normal. It is when acquisition of developmental milestones occurs sometime beyond the range of normalcy that parents and educators should be concerned about a child's progress. For example, if a child is not sitting independently (norm is 6 months; range is 4–8 months) by 10 months of age, parents should seek professional advice. Children who exceed the norms in several areas or the expected ranges in a few areas may be **at risk** for **developmental delays**. Significant delays in acquisition of developmental milestones in one or more developmental areas would indicate developmental delay and eligibility for early childhood special education.

PATTERNS OF GROWTH

From conception throughout early adulthood, humans experience physical growth. The most obvious index of growth is in size, as measured by changes in height and weight. Height and weight measures increase rapidly during fetal development and early childhood. An increase in birth weight of 300% is expected by the time a child is 12 months of age, while height is expected to increase 200% by 24 months of age. This rate of growth slows after the first year to an almost linear rate until adolescence. While some children grow in spurts, others appear to grow steadily throughout childhood. In addition to individual genetic differences in rate and pattern of development, factors such as nutrition and health influence growth outcomes. Children from economically advantaged families tend to grow faster than children from poorer families who tend to have poor nutrition and more frequent illnesses.

SIZE

Body proportion also changes as a child ages. At birth, a child's head accounts for approximately one fourth of the total body height and weight. Gradually, the proportion of the head to the body decreases, while the proportion of the legs gradually increases. Ossification or hardening of the bones is another function of growth, beginning during the prenatal period. This skeletal development is necessary for posture and strength. During early infancy, the bones of the legs and arms are fragile and unable to support an infant's weight. As hardening of the bones takes place, the extremities straighten, and 1-year-olds are able to bear weight in standing and walking.

DEVELOPMENTAL PATTERNS

Three universal patterns of physical growth govern motor development. **Cephalo-caudal** is the sequence in which growth and development of motor skills occurs progressively downward from head and neck, to the trunk, hips, and legs, and finally to the feet and toes. Children first gain head and neck control, which enables them to hold their heads steady and look around; then they gain trunk control, which allows infants to turn from back to tummy, to sit, and so on. A second principle, **proximo-distal** sequencing, refers to development that progresses from the center of the body outward toward the extremities. Legs and arms, being closer to the midline of the body, can be controlled earlier than toes and fingers, as seen by gross movements of extremities in the play of young infants. A child will reach (arm movement) before grasping because the hands are farther from the center of the body, and finger control comes later.

Refinement is a third principle that is also referred to as simple-to-complex or gross-to-fine development. A child's motor development is initially concentrated on large muscle groups for sitting and walking, and then on small muscle group control for such things as scribbling and writing with a crayon. Understanding these three principles helps adults predict a child's development so that intervention is appropriately concentrated on present and emerging stages of development.

PHYSICAL GROWTH

At birth, an infant should be capable of independent functioning that is separate from its mother. Even though organ systems are not all fully developed, they should function well enough to permit growth and development. Deviations from the normal progression of growth may indicate a health problem, but more often they are normal variations that relate to genetic predisposition. Again, though the normal sequence of growth and development is known, the individual timing of certain milestones is not always predictable.

Physical growth implies a biological change in the structure and mass of a person through increases in weight and size. In each of us, growth is a reaction to a predetermined, but idiosyncratic, plan. Events and relationships influence growth, though they rarely completely stop advancement. Finally, because of the nature of human growth, behavior observed and accepted during one stage of development may be considered abnormal during another stage of development.

Case Study   THE DIARY OF ESTHER ANNA BERKE: MONTH 1

November 15–22, 1998: Esther Anna was born on November 15 at the Huang Baby Clinic in Taiwan after a 12-hour labor. The Taiwanese doctors and nurses were amazed at her size, 4.5 kg (10 lbs) and 52 cm (21") long. She was a "blue baby" and had to be rushed to the ICU at Shinlao Christian Hospital in Taiwan. After clearing her lungs she breathed normally and was released after 2 days. Mother and daughter went home on Day 3.

November 23–30: Esther Anna sleeps most of the time and appears normal, although she "quivers" occasionally. Our pediatric guide says this happens occasionally in newborn babies, so we ignored it. We weighed her at her 2-week checkup; she lost 400 g (~1 pound).

December 1–7: Esther Anna had more episodes of "quivering," so we started to record time, date, circumstance, and so on, and we started weighing her at home to monitor her condition more closely.

December 8–15: Esther Anna started having more pronounced seizures, including one where she just "froze" for 30 seconds. We started checking for her pulse when she suddenly came out of it and appeared normal. We had several neurological tests done, including an EEG and a brain ultrasound. The neurologist said she has agenesis of the corpus callosum. At her 4-week checkup, she only weighed 3.8 kg.

Esther Anna was diagnosed with Aicardi Syndrome on December 15, "Black Tuesday." The neurologist examined her eyes and said he is 97% sure she has Aicardi Syndrome, a rare genetic disorder characterized by seizures, retardation, eye problems, and death by age 20. To be sure, he referred us to an eye specialist, who confirmed his diagnosis (the disease is characterized by certain peculiar lesions on the retina) and said that Esther Anna may be partially or completely blind. We start her on Depakine, an anti-seizure medication.

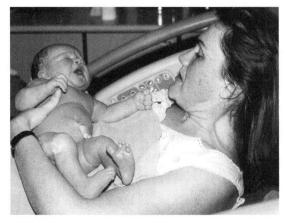

Esther Anna 20 minutes old.

Major organ systems develop at different rates and at different times. All of the major systems are established during fetal life and, by birth, have developed to the point where adaptation of the systems to extrauterine life can occur. Major organ systems include the respiratory, cardiovascular, gastrointestinal, renal, neurological, skeletal, and integumentary systems. Each of these systems controls different activities of normal physiological functions that are critical to a normal life.

The **respiratory system** is made of many complex structures that enable human beings to both take in oxygen, essential for cellular life, and give off carbon dioxide (a by-product of cellular function). The lungs are the main organs of the respiratory system, though healthy cardiovascular functioning is critical to normal functioning of the lungs. Adequate nutrition is necessary for normal lung growth. This factor can be very important when dealing with certain infants and children, such as those with cerebral palsy, who suffer from diseases that affect either the lungs themselves or a child's ability to sustain adequate caloric intake.

The **cardiovascular system** is comprised of the heart and the blood vessels that extend throughout the body connecting all cells to their source of nutrition. A fetal heart begins to beat at approximately four weeks of gestation. This development provides the link necessary for the placenta to adequately provide oxygen and nutrition to a fetus. These nutritional elements (oxygen, glucose, etc.) are then carried to the fetus and circulated throughout the body by the fetal circulatory system.

After birth, the act of independent respiration changes the normal blood flow. This transition occurs when the lungs expand, changing the pathway of blood to the lungs for oxygenation. Newborns consequently become self-reliant in the physiology of oxygen and carbon dioxide exchange. Deviations in development of heart structure or of the pathways for blood flow can have significant effects on the growth of a child.

The **gastrointestinal system** (GI system) both processes and absorbs nutrients taken in with food to maintain metabolism and to support growth. The system includes the mouth, esophagus, stomach, and small and large intestines. The GI system also is involved with excretion of both digestive residue and waste products absorbed from the blood as it passes through the intestinal tract. A functioning GI system is essential for life. Failure to develop this system, or malformation, can produce significant problems related to malnutrition and failure to thrive.

Prior to birth, the **neurological system** is the fastest growing system. Rapid brain growth occurs between 18 and 20 weeks of gestation and again at about 30 weeks through the first 12 months of postnatal life. Typically, measurements of the head change rapidly during the first year of life then slow down during subsequent years.

During the first 6 months of life, the brain cortex increases in size and function, as **neurons** (cells responsible for receiving and sending messages) of the brain increase in number and connectedness to other neurons. Immediately after birth, the brain's cortex has little control over neonates' activities. Primitive reflexes, controlled by peripheral nerves and the brain stem, generally guide the activity of very young infants. As growth and development occur, the brain, through its developing pathways, exerts increasing control over the reflex activity of infants, facilitating the acquisition of more complex abilities. Cortical control requires the development of a **myelin sheath** on the nerves. This sheath permits electrical impulses to move quickly along the nerve fiber or axon (see Figure 4–3). That is, the more myelinization there is, the more efficient or rapid the nervous system becomes at sending/receiving messages. Hence, myelinization of the nervous system is required before complex motor skills can be developed. Lack of myelinization or damage to the myelin sheath leads to motor disorders such as cerebral palsy. Myelinization is also required before visual discrimination can be accomplished.

Figure 4–3 Neural Transmission of Myelinated Axon

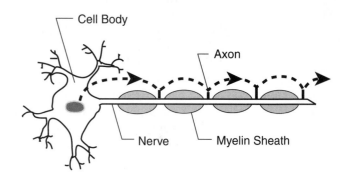

Increases in body size require both new bone growth and the maturation of existing bone structures. The development of new skeletal cells and connective tissue leads to this linear growth. Through maturation, tissues consolidate into a permanent shape that provides structure for the body. Bone growth follows a genetic plan that continues for up to 20 years after birth (Beck, et al., 1973). Many diseases that affect children may affect bone growth. For example, chronic lung disease in premature infants increases the possibility for decreased food intake leading to poor nutrition that can adversely affect bone growth.

Muscle growth also has a role in childhood development. Muscle fibers, which have been laid down in fetal life, remain constant in number throughout the lifespan, but increase in size at varying times. Growth periods are probably most apparent during adolescence, when hormonal changes in puberty stimulate the muscle fibers to increase in size. By contrast, muscles that are unused in childhood will shrink in size, ultimately leading to atrophy with eventual loss of muscle function.

Dentition (tooth formation) is another process of growth. Primary and secondary tooth formation can be categorized into stages that consist of growth, calcification, eruption, and tooth loss. Ages at which teeth erupt are inconsistent among children, but the order in which they erupt is fairly constant (see Figure 4–4). With the exception of the first molar, the teeth erupt from the incisors, or front teeth, backward in order to the molars. Still, significant delays in eruption may be indicative of nutritional factors or other health problems.

Weight is a growth variable that is influenced by many factors. Heredity, gestational age, maternal conditions, and environmental influences all affect weight. Weight and height, in combination, make it possible to determine normal ranges of growth for different populations. Periodic measurements of weight and height are monitored using standard charts to determine an individual child's rate of growth according to the norm (see Figure 4–5). This information is useful in determining where a particular child stands in relation to other children of the same age. Children who deviate from the norm are categorized as "large for age" or "small for age." These deviations give information related to the overall health of a particular child and indicate potential or real problems.

Growth parameters follow age-related guidelines. However, age stages are arbitrarily determined and do not generally take into account individual differences. Therefore, it is more important to follow the weight gain in a particular child than

Figure 4–4
Sequence of
Eruption and
Loss of Primary
Teeth and
Permanent
Teeth

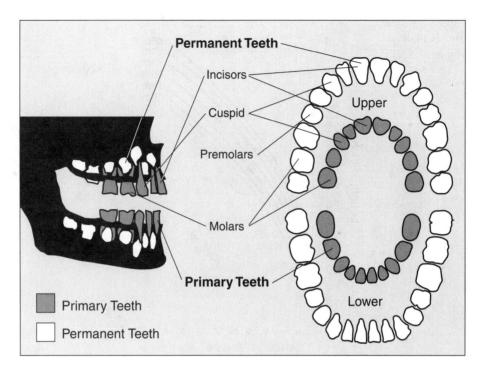

to make assumptions about health based solely on where a child lies on the standard growth curve.

Typical stages of growth include the **prenatal** period (from conception to birth), the **neonatal** period (from birth to 30 days of age), the **infancy** period (from 30 days to 12 months), the **toddler stage** (from 1 year to 3 years), the **early childhood stage** (from 3 years to 6 years), the **middle childhood stage** (from 6 years to 12 years), and the **adolescent stage** (from 13 years to 18 years). As mentioned, the prenatal growth period consists of the embryonic and the fetal stage of development. During prenatal care, obstetricians can determine if growth complications that may lead to problems during the neonatal period are present. During the neonatal period, babies attain stability from intrauterine to extrauterine life. Infants must transition completely from fetal circulation patterns, during which they relied on their mothers for all their metabolic needs, to assuming much of the responsibility for meeting their own needs.

An average newborn weighs between 7 and 7½ pounds (3175 to 3400 grams), is usually 18–21 inches long, and has a head circumference of 12–15 inches (Allen & Marotz, 1989). These newborns generally lose about 7% to 10% of their body weight during the first 2 to 3 days of life, but gradually regain that weight and stabilize their ongoing weight gain to approximately an ounce per day. **Neonates** have poor temperature control, requiring external heat management, such as extra blankets, to maintain a normal temperature of 98.6°F (37°C). Poor heat control is related to the insufficient fat stores under the skin, which produce fuel for maintaining body temperature (Dahn & James, 1972). Neonates also have a rapid heart rate and a fast but somewhat inconsistent breathing pattern. Because of their

Figure 4–5
Typical Growth
Charts for Male
and Female
Infants

Girls from Birth to 18 Months

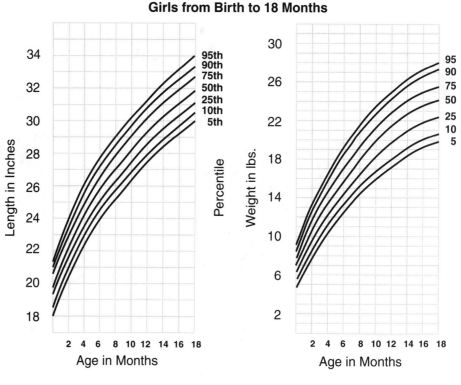

Boys from Birth to 18 Months

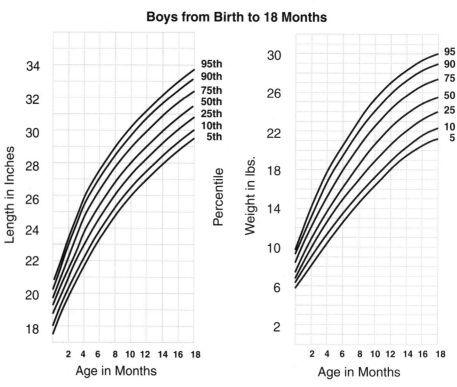

small stomach size, neonates eat small amounts frequently. Breastfed infants may eat as often as every hour.

The infancy period (from 30 days to 12 months) is also a time of very rapid physical growth. By 1 year, normally progressing infants have tripled their birth weights and are approximately one-and-a-half times their birth heights. The head and chest circumferences have equalized. Heart rates continue to be elevated but are less rapid, and the respiratory pattern is well established. By this time (2 to 3 months), infants can maintain temperature stability, and fat stores are sufficient to preserve heat. Skeletal and muscle growth has also occurred, enabling infants to progress through the developmental tasks that are appropriate for this age, especially those related to gross motor skills. Primary tooth eruption usually occurs, and by 12 months infants have an established pattern of three meals daily with an additional feeding before going to bed for the night. Most infants sleep approximately 12 hours each day.

Toddlers (from 12 to 36 months) generally weigh four times their birth weight (26–32 pounds) and are about 32 to 33 inches tall at the end of this stage. Head circumference is increasing, though more slowly now, and primary dentition is usually complete (Allen & Marotz, 1989). Toddlers have food preferences and may not exhibit much of an appetite. In spite of this, many toddlers' abdomens protrude and their extremities appear to have an excess of fat. Toddlers' heart rates may continue to be slightly elevated, though heart rate is decreasing to an average of about 100 beats per minute. The respiratory rate continues at about 25 breaths per minute with use of the abdominal muscles. Many toddlers have inconsistent sleep patterns and are reluctant to go to bed.

Early childhood is the period between 3 and 6 years of age. It is during this time that children begin a steady linear growth rate that will continue until adolescence. Three-year-olds will have attained about 50% of their adult height. Weight gain also continues on a steady curve, though growth may be slowed due to an enormous amount of physical activity. This increased physical activity and the increase in linear growth both require calories that are diverted away from weight gain. Brain growth has achieved approximately 90% of its total, with the head circumference reaching approximately 90% of the adult size. Organ growth continues along the same steady curve as external physical growth. The average heart rate continues at about 100 beats per minute, with the average respiratory rate between 21 and 23 breaths per minute. Young children may begin to lose their primary teeth in early childhood.

THEORIES OF DEVELOPMENT

A spectrum of theories regarding the human development lend direction to research and practice in the fields of early intervention and preschood education. Some of developmental theories are so broad they are diciplines in themselves. Though others may be less weighty, it would be difficult to fully comprehend the elements of each theory in the brief space allowed in this text. Nevertheless, it is useful to review the dominant theories. These theories fall into several general categories which are often associated directly with a dominant theorist: psychodynamic, psychosocial, maturationist, environmental/behavioral, cognitive, social developmental, or attachment/ethological.

Sigmund Freud was perhaps the first pyschologist to attempt to acknowledge the relationship between childhood and adult behavior (Gay, 1998). Specifically, his theory suggested explanations for anomalies of early childhood that led directly to adult mental illnesses. According to Freud, individual personality develops from three aspects of the psyche. A person's id directs their need for pleasure, is present at birth, and is unconsciously responsible for all individual energy. Much later in childhood, between 3 and 6 years of age, a child begins to develop a superego. As children internalize the moral teaching of their parents and culture, the superego drives individuals unrealistically to seek perfection. At the awareness level, and developing in early infancy is a person's ego, or sense of reality. In other words, the ego balances an individual's competing drives for pleasure and perfection. Prominent in Freud's theory of childhood experiences are psychosocial stages, where too much or too little gratification by parents can lead to "fixation" deviancy. For example, adults who act compulsively may have an "anal fixation" that can be blamed on an overly rigid toilet training regimen; premature weaning can lead to an "oral fixation" in the form of compulsive smoking or overeating. In the decades since Freud's theories were postulated, many professionals have debated their relevance to child development.

Like Freud, *Erik Erikson's* psychosocial theory of child development provided a hypotheses for understanding the genesus of adult mental health problems (Erikson, 1963; 1968; 1980). According to this theory, all babies are believed to be born with basic capabilities and temperaments which are gradually differentially shaped through eight stages of development. Each stage is characterized by a different psychological "crisis" that must be resolved before moving on to the next stage; a failure to resolve each crisis leading to specific social maladaption in adulthood. The following is a brief description of the first four stages of Erickson's theory, which cover the first 12 years of life.

a. Between birth and 12 months, infants must resolve the basic **trust/mistrust crisis**. If infants are provided with essential food, security and affection, they should develop secure attachment and become trusting children/adults. If not, infants will become distrustful of others' behavior.

b. The **autonomy/doubt crisis** is normally resolved between 1 and 2 years of age where the issues surround walking, toilet training—all of which require a degree of self-control. Parents who encourage initiative will foster confidence, self-control, and independence. On the other hand, if parents are too overprotective and/or disapproving, their children will develop self-doubt, shame, and a sense of dependency.

c. The remaining preschool years (2–6 years of age) are devoted to resolving the issue of **initiative/guilt**. A child needs to be provided a balance of adventure and responsibility. Encouraging risk-taking with limits helps children self-manage while possessing an imagination. Again, discouraging parents will cause their children to be plagued by guilt and to be overly dependent.

d. Elementary-aged youth are challenged by the **competence/inferiority** crisis, a crucial stage where individuals acquire the skills necessary to become a worker or provider. Success in school leads to enjoyment of learning and consquently competence, whereas failure will lead to an enduring sense of inferiority.

The key maturationist theorist was *Arnold Gesell*, who explained development as a biological process that occurs across time and along a predictable—and sequential—timeline (Gesell & Thompson, 1934). Developmental milestones are based upon this prominent description of childhood. Gesell theorized that skills are acquired naturally and automatically with little deviation unless a child has some serious biological interruption.

By contrast, environmental/behavioral theory credits a child's environment with playing a key role in the rate and direction of development. Broadly explained by prominent behaviorist *B.F. Skinner*, a child's biological endowment is gradually influenced by differential consequences for behavior. Through rigorously controlled laboratory and clinical research, Skinner developed principles of human behavior which were based upon repeatedly observed phenomenon. This scientific approach was based upon the contention that what is unobservable/unmeasurable cannot be known and therefore is not helpful in developing methods of teaching that might be relied upon to work. Two key behavioral principles of learning, reinforcement and punishment, shape behavior across time—gradually developing a child's repertoire of behavior (Skinner, 1953). Reinforcing consequences increase the likelihood that a behavior will be repeated under similar circumstances. Conversely, punishing consequences decrease the likelihood that the behavior will be produced again. The strength or predictability of a behavior is determined by both the conditions under which a behavior is learned, as well as the schedule, timing, and type of consequences delivered. Of special interest to Skinner was the development of language; his book, *Verbal Behavior*, led to a great deal of reseach and intervention practices for children with language delays (Skinner, 1957).

Albert Bandura, categorized variously as a behaviorist, a cognitivist, and a social learning theorist, began his research with aggressive adolescents in the 1950s. Bandura suggested that the relationship between behavior and one's environment were interrelated—not unidirectional—as some believe behavioral theory to be (Bandura, 1971). This theory of reciprocal determinism separates Bandura from other behaviorists, because he believed that a person's psychological processes—specifically language and imagery—interact with their environment and behavior. Bandura's most significant theoretical contribution was the importance of modeling to learning. Through observation of children, steps for learning through modeling were defined:

1. Attention: Factors that heighten (e.g., attractiveness or prestigiousness) or diminish (e.g., tired, sick or distracted) a person's ability to attend to a model will influence a child's ability to learn from that model.
2. Retention: Imagery and/or language is the medium through which incoming information is converted to memory.
3. Motor reproduction: Physically replicating a model's behavior and being able to judge the accuracy of the reproduction are necessary to learning.
4. Motivation: External, vicarious and self-reinforcement provide both motivation and consequences that maintain behavior.

Russian theorist, *Lev Vygotsky* authored the social/development theory (Vygotsky, 1962; 1978). Positing that social and cultural indicators play a key role in cognitive development, Vygotsky believed that every human function is first exercised/learned in the context of an interpersonal interaction. That is, all higher functions of language and cognition (attention, memory, logic, conceptual formation, etc.) originate from actual relationships between individuals. Furthermore, the limits of cognitive development are determined by zones of proximal development (ZPD), which are critical time periods for maximal learning efficiency of certain cognitive skills—and which are dependent upon social interactions. In early childhood, teaching children "what" and "how" to use cognitive skills evolves from problem solving *with* someone else. Gradually, the responsibility for problem solving transfers from others to the child. Placing particular emphasis on the role of language in socialization, Vygotsky explained that a child's internal tool for self-directed behavior is through the medium of language. As children age, intellectual development is constantly dependent upon the integrity of social interactions.

One of the most influential developmenal theorists was French psychologist *Jean Piaget* (Piaget, 1963). A biologist, philosopher, and psychologist, Piaget was perhaps the first psychologist to suggest that children think and process information differently than adults. Simply put, Piaget's theory provided a description of intellectual stages of child development (sensorimotor, preoperational, concrete operations, formal operations). Piaget created his theory by intensively observing the learning patterns of his own children over a number of years. Intelligence was viewed by Piaget as the ability to assimilate (take in new information and mentally organize the new data within an already existing framework of related knowledge) and accomodate (incorporate new information within an existing cognitive framework or scheme modified to adjust to new elements). Therefore, child development is viewed as an increasingly complex ability to process, based upon primitive foundations laid in earlier stages of development. Piaget was one of the first theorists to place special emphasis on the active role that children have in their own intellectual development. That is, Piaget noted that a child may neither be prematurely "taught" out of one stage into another, nor can a child develop increasingly complex schemes without interacting with the environment. Accordingly, nature and nurture are interdependent forces on development.

Bridging social learning theory and psychoanalysis were *John Bowlby's* important contributions regarding attachment or ethnological theory (Bowlby, 1958; 1960; 1969). Attachment, it seemed to Bowlby, serves a biological purpose in providing a child with physical security necesary for exploration of the environment. The quality of a child's early separation events with her mother may have long-term consequences. Bowlby identified three phases of separation response that represent important transitions: protest (separation anxiety), despair (grief and mourning), and detachment/denial (defense mechanism). Bowlby stressed the importance of early and active mother-and-infant bonding relationships. Repeated or prolonged separation might lead to feelings of abandonment or rejection. The consequences of disturbances to attachment would be psychological maladjustment. In sum, separation angst is created when attachment is breached and cannot be alleviated until reunion is restored.

Urie Bronfrebrenner placed children in an ecological perspective (Bronfrenbrenner, 1977; 1979). His ecological theory emphasized the importance of a reciprocal relationship between individuals and their subsequent behavior. Individuals experience a set of "nested structures," one within the other, including:

1. Microsystem: This relationship system starts with the family where intense and enduring relationships evolve. If this circle of influence is large, there is a greater positive influence on child development.
2. Mesosystem: The connectivity between/across settings (e.g., between home and caretaker) determines the power of influence of each system on a child's development.
3. Exosystems: The degree of parental involvement across settings (e.g., school parent organization, social service agencies, etc.) determines the quality of relationships between these settings and a developing child.
4. Macrosystems: Broad societal indices (economy, political climate and funding, technology, etc.) generally influence the political/organization and ideological patterns of childrearing and other important interrelationships with a child.

This brief description of the array of theories of child development does not do justice to the great effort made by the aforementioned theorists and the many important corrollary contributions of devotees to the respective bodies of knowledge. Theories range from unverifiable (psychoanalytic) to completely scientifically dependent (behavioral). While contemporary psychologists and practitioners place less confidence in some of these threories than in others, each has had an important role in our current understanding of child development. Still, there is much that is not known. In fact, none of these theories, either alone or put together, adequately explain the mechanisms of child development. It is possible that emerging biological research will provide the missing links. What seems increasingly clear is the important role of human relationships to cognitive, linguistic, and social development. This claim, first championed by Bronfenbrenner, is now supported by neurophysical research. For example, when infants respond to their parents' initiatives in positive ways, a hormone is released in the adult's brain that influences those adults' future interactions. Other research shows that fetal and infant brains are endowed with excessive neurological stuctures (e.g., dendrites, neurons). Those that are unused are sloughed off, while those that are repeatedly used grow, forming the "hardwiring" or structure of the brain. In short, the "soft" science of developmental psychology is about to collide with the "hard" sciences of neurology and endocrinology—leading to ever-evolving theories of child development.

PRINCIPLES AND PATTERNS OF DEVELOPMENT

Several principles of normal development have been derived from decades of observation of infants and young children. These principles represent our current knowledge and beliefs about human patterns of physical and behavioral development. These principles probably will be revised or replaced in the future as our understanding of very young children grows. Still, what we now know allows early childhood professionals to plan intervention and to advise parents. Assessment

Case Study

THE DIARY OF ESTHER ANNA BERKE: MONTH 2

December 16–23, 1998: Esther Anna's seizures decreased, but so did her appetite (one of the side-effects). She refused to eat at times, clenching her lips together and turning away when we tried to feed her. We weighed her at 6 weeks and she is down to 3.6 kg (she went from 10 lbs. at birth to 8 lbs. at 6 weeks old).

December 24–31: She had an MRI on Dec. 31 to assess her brain condition. The MRI revealed at least three different brain abnormalities, including agenesis of the corpus callosum (the area which joins the left and right sides of the brain is missing). These abnormalities are due to the dominant mutation on the X chromosome which causes Aicardi Syndrome. We weighed her at 7 weeks and she was down to 3.5 kg.

January 1–7, 1999: The doctor inserted a feeding tube down her right nostril Jan. 4 at the doctor's office (fortunately we didn't have to go to the hospital for it, and we can feed her at home). She did NOT like having a tube shoved down her nose, and she had a Grand Mal seizure (her second one in 2 days!) after they inserted the feeding tube. We injected formula and/or breast milk down her nose directly into her stomach 6x a day. The feeding tube was somewhat successful, she stopped losing weight but didn't gain any weight either. It extended about 12" out of her nose, and she sometimes batted it with her hand. The kids called her "baby elephant."

January 8–15: I traveled to California Jan. 9 to consult with a pediatric neurologist, Dr. Berg, at UCSF Medical Center, and check out job opportunities with some private vegetable seed companies. The feeding tube falls out on Monday so the doctor re-inserts it, a very painful process. Esther Anna starts to spit up 2–3x a day, and then chokes and turns blue. She has to be watched almost constantly, and Sarah brushes up on her CPR techniques. She becomes physically exhausted preparing formula (what a pain), feeding Esther Anna every 2 hours (takes 20 to 30 min.), and then holding her upright for a half hour afterward to try to prevent the reflux. The most exhausting part, however, is the emotional toll. I talked to Dr. Berg but Esther's medical records (which we mailed and faxed to him 3 days in advance) never reached him so he couldn't tell us much. He is interested in her case and promises to pursue it. I return to Taiwan on Jan. 15.

---

tools, instructional strategies, and curricular materials are based on the principles of development that follow.

INFANTS ARE HIGHLY COMPETENT ORGANISMS

As research emerges on child development, it becomes increasingly clear that even newborns possess complex skills. Young infants are capable of learning new behaviors, solving problems, and adapting to changes in their environment. Abilities that enable neonates to use perceptual and cognitive abilities to acquire vast knowledge were unrecognized by early researchers. For example, a wind-up mobile was once thought to be appropriate stimulation for a "passive" infant. Now mobiles that jingle or turn only when the infant touches the mobile are considered more appropriate, since they help infants establish cause-and-effect and encourage them to take control of their environments.

INFANTS ARE SOCIALLY INTERACTIVE

Recently, educators have recognized that not only is social interaction a critical area of development, but it also influences development in intellectual growth. In fact, it is possible that social competencies may be a more accurate predictor of later abilities than cognitive abilities. Evidence suggests that the need for social attachment is a biological drive. For example, positive social interactions stimulate the release of endorphins in a baby's brain, stimulating pleasure and excitement (Lipari, 2000).

According to MacDonald (1992), human affection provides motivation for children to be compliant and accepting, and it correspondingly encourages adults to invest in their children. For example, in the past, parents were sometimes advised to feed a child on a fixed schedule at 3-hour intervals. Considering the interactive nature of development, parents are now trained to respond to a child's cues to feed or stop feeding based on the child's facial expressions, vocalizations, or activity levels. Parents try to read a child's intent and respect the child's social communication. A child who has not experienced such interactions on a regular basis may learn to be a passive participant.

INFANTS ARE ACTIVE LEARNERS

Developmentalists believe infants are not merely passively modified by the goings-on around them, but play an active, if not always intentional, role in their own development. Early give-and-take interactions between infants and caregivers provide the context for a child to learn control over the environment. In fact, a child may be biologically programmed to engage in behaviors (i.e., cooing, smiling, etc.) which elicit parental responses (i.e., communication, proximity, smiling, etc.) that are optimal for brain development (Reis, Collins, & Berscheid, 2000).

INFANT DEVELOPMENT IS MULTIDIMENSIONAL

The process by which infants' skills become more complex and integrated is a nonarbitrary sequence. Rather, this highly organized process unfolds predictably as children simultaneously grow physically and develop cognitively and socially. Behaviors in each area have an impact on behaviors in other domains, as skills develop across domains at the same time. The following example illustrates the interdependency of developmental domains. Children with Down syndrome often have cognitive delays. Their ability to problem-solve is complicated by poor language development, which is also typically delayed. Articulation difficulties may further compound the communication problems. Consequently, when this child needs help in solving a problem, she may not be able to request it in an understandable way. As a consequence, social interactions are affected.

DEVELOPMENTAL SEQUENCING IS UNIVERSAL

Developmental milestones describe a universal sequence of steps through which children progress (see Figure 4–6). Though not all children progress through the steps at precisely the same age, the pattern of development is very reliable. When there are significant deviations in this pattern of development, a child may be at risk of developmental disability.

SKILLS BECOME MORE SPECIALIZED

As children develop, they are able to integrate more refined skills in one area with newly acquired skills in another to perform coordinated behaviors. For example, infants learn to recognize an adult's voice as their auditory discrimination improves. At the same time, facial muscle control increases to the point where a child can smile voluntarily. The result is a specialized ability to smile at "mom" when she is speaking. This acts as a way to enhance social relationships. In early childhood, children scribble nondiscriminately. Gradually, they refine this skill so that they can copy lines and circles. As children near school age, they integrate their emerging cognitive knowledge of alphabet letters with their newly refined fine motor skills. Thus, the specialization of these two domains results in handwriting.

Figure 4–6 Typical Motor Development Sequence
Source: From Mussen et al., *Child Development and Personality,* Sixth Edition. Published by Allyn & Bacon, Boston, MA. Copyright ©1984 by Pearson Education. Reprinted by permission of the publisher.

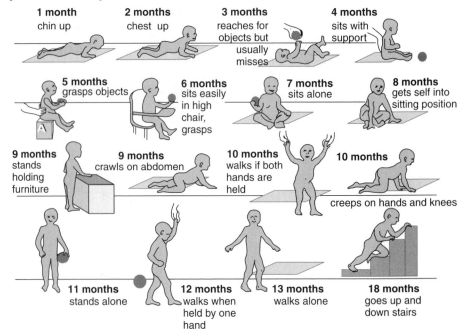

PLASTICITY

One of the remarkable aspects of development is the **plasticity** of the human brain, by which alternate neural pathways can be formed to compensate for deficits in other portions of the brain. Damage to a specific area of the brain (e.g., language) often results in another portion of the brain developing the function of the damaged section. Another example of this flexibility is seen in infants who are blind or deaf but who acquire necessary developmental skills by focusing on alternate channels of understanding.

CRITICAL LEARNING PERIODS

Interactional and developmental theorists contend that critical sensitive periods, during which a child is biologically most ready to learn certain new behaviors, occur throughout human development. When environmental events provide the right conditions for a particularly sensitive period, developmental progress can be maximized. However, when experiences fail to match a child's predisposition for learning, the window of opportunity is missed. Though a child will not necessarily fail to acquire the new skills, learning will take much longer than otherwise possible.

Paired with the theory of "peak" periods of learning is the need to provide diverse learning experiences involving all sensory systems. Many factors can upset the formula of optimal development. For example, Guo (1998) found that poverty experienced in early childhood had a signficant and lasting effect on cognitive aptitude. Another example of missed opportunity is in children who have chronic ear infections during a critical period when children learn to discriminate sounds used by others in conversations; those children may have difficulty acquiring the sounds necessary for speech.

INFANT RELATIONSHIPS ARE THE KEY TO COGNITIVE DEVELOPMENT

In contrast to some current practices, where parents go to great effort to teach babies complex cognitive skills at an early age (words, numbers, shapes, colors, etc.), the optimal stimulation for cognitive growth is actually the emotional quality of parent–infant relationships (Lipari, 2000). Neurobehavioral researchers are finding that the emotional quality of relationships directly activate the brain's neural connections and form a network of neural pathways. These neural structures within areas of the brain form the foundation for higher level mental functioning, such as memory, language, emotion, representation, and states of mind (Reis et al., 2000).

CHILDREN UNDERGO SEVERAL TRANSITIONS

It is typical for children to undergo stages of **transition** when there are spurts of growth and development that may be followed by unpredictable behavior or regression. For example, changes in a daily pattern, such as beginning at a new daycare center, may result in behavior problems that are generally short lived. As children cognitively become more inquisitive, more mobile, and more verbal in the latter half of their second year, their behavior also becomes more unpredictable.

The resolution of these problems, referred to as **consolidation**, occurs when the disorganized behavior is replaced by more advanced developmental skills. For example, a child may become better behaved when babbling is replaced by the more sophisticated means of communication, conventional words.

INDIVIDUAL DIFFERENCES AMONG CHILDREN

Children differ in such characteristics as **temperament** and gender, making each child unique. Temperament, or one's adaptation to everyday events, is partially innate and partially learned. Thomas and Chess (1981) concluded that temperament is a relatively constant trait throughout life. Differences in temperament affect the manner in which adults interact with infants and children and often result in such labels as "difficult" or "easy" baby. These responses, in turn, influence the development of a child's temperament. For example, if a cuddly, active, and smiling infant is reinforced by similar adult behaviors, the child is likely to continue being a socially rewarding companion.

Expectations of infants according to gender are obvious, even in newborns, as adults handle and talk to infants differently based on a child's sex (Rheingold & Cook, 1975). This social training appears to be so powerful that children learn to label their own and other's gender before they are able to label objects or tasks that are nongender related (Bussey & Bandura, 1992). Evidence of the influence of childhood experiences is found in studies of hand coordination, where research consistently finds that men have greater fine motor control than women. Yet, in childhood, no such differences are found, suggesting that it is the types of activities in which males and females engage that result in significant differences as adults (Gabbard & Hart, 1995). Influences such as toy selection, play activities, playmates, adult-modeled behavior, and exposure to television all affect the degree of children's compliance to sex-role expectations.

FACTORS INFLUENCING DEVELOPMENT

There is little argument that children born into this world are at the mercy of their genetic endowments, as well as the capriciousness of the world around them in terms of the rate of their development across domains. Though the search to determine the relative degree of these two factors continues, it can be assumed that to some large extent, children's development can be altered by the manipulation (intentional or not) of environmental factors (see Figure 4–7). For example, poverty, maternal income and education, family size, culture, and race are all factors that influence both opportunity and motivation and consequently child development (Guo, 1998). Several factors have known risk for cognitive, social, and language development (maternal mental health, maternal anxiety, unresponsive mother–child interactions, mother's education, head of household, semiskilled or unskilled occupation, minority ethnic status, father absent, many stressful life events, and large household size), but when multiple risk factors exist, developmental potential is more likely to be diminished (Burchinal, Roberts, Hooper, & Zeisel, 2000). The following is a discussion of important factors that affect every child's growth and development.

Figure 4–7
Pathways
Leading from
Poverty to
Childhood
Disabilities
Source: Adapted
from *Wasting
America's future:
The Children's
Defense Fund
Report in the
Costs of Child
Poverty* (p. 12),
by A. Sherman,
1994, Boston:
Beacon.

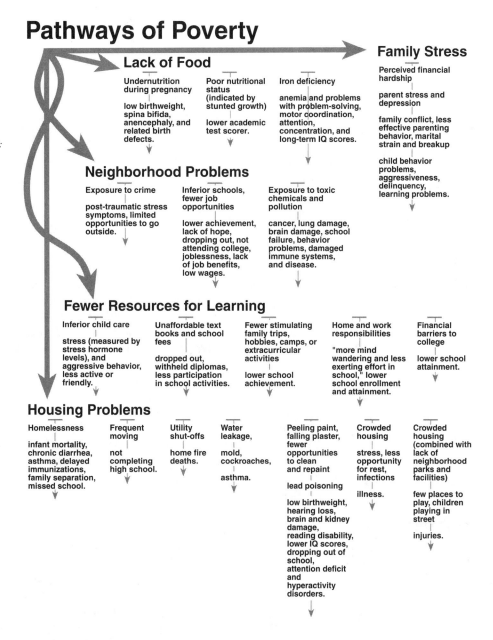

Pathways of Poverty

Family Stress

Perceived financial hardship

parent stress and depression

family conflict, less effective parenting behavior, marital strain and breakup

child behavior problems, aggressiveness, delinquency, learning problems.

Lack of Food

Undernutrition during pregnancy

low birthweight, spina bifida, anencephaly, and related birth defects.

Poor nutritional status (indicated by stunted growth)

lower academic test scorer.

Iron deficiency

anemia and problems with problem-solving, motor coordination, attention, concentration, and long-term IQ scores.

Neighborhood Problems

Exposure to crime

post-traumatic stress symptoms, limited opportunities to go outside.

Inferior schools, fewer job opportunities

lower achievement, lack of hope, dropping out, not attending college, joblessness, lack of job benefits, low wages.

Exposure to toxic chemicals and pollution

cancer, lung damage, brain damage, school failure, behavior problems, damaged immune systems, and disease.

Fewer Resources for Learning

Inferior child care

stress (measured by stress hormone levels), and aggressive behavior, less active or friendly.

Unaffordable text books and school fees

dropped out, withheld diplomas, less participation in school activities.

Fewer stimulating family trips, hobbies, camps, or extracurricular activities

lower school achievement.

Home and work responsibilities

"more mind wandering and less exerting effort in school," lower school enrollment and attainment.

Financial barriers to college

lower school attainment.

Housing Problems

Homelessness

infant mortality, chronic diarrhea, asthma, delayed immunizations, family separation, missed school.

Frequent moving

not completing high school.

Utility shut-offs

home fire deaths.

Water leakage,

mold, cockroaches,

asthma.

Peeling paint, falling plaster, fewer opportunities to clean and repaint

lead poisoning

low birthweight, hearing loss, brain and kidney damage, reading disability, lower IQ scores, dropping out of school, attention deficit and hyperactivity disorders.

Crowded housing

stress, less opportunity for rest, infections

illness.

Crowded housing (combined with lack of neighborhood parks and facilities)

few places to play, children playing in street

injuries.

FAMILY STRUCTURE

American families are diverse in family structure, with a large number of families either in transition or headed by a single parent. The absence of either a dominant female or male adult figure in a child's life influences patterns of development, particularly in social and personal areas. Between 1970 and 2000, the number of children living in two-parent families decreased from 85% to 69%. Much of this change can be attributed to the rate of births by unmarried women, which rose from 5.3% in 1960 to 33.2% in 2000. These data are important, because family structure is directly related to family income, which influences children's health. Female-headed families earn only 47% of that earned by two-parent families (65% of two parents-one working families), and female-headed families are five times more likely to live in poverty than married-couple families. The reconstitution of divorced families in blended or extended families results in socialization patterns that may affect children's loyalty to others, values, adaptability, and self-esteem. Research indicates that divorce has a variable influence on children, depending on such factors as age and gender of children, the presence of siblings, the psychological status of custodial parents, the intensity and outcome of custody battles, and the reconstitution of families in subsequent marriages (Monahan, Buchanan, Maccoby, & Dornbusch, 1993).

CHILD CARE

Raising children while working full time places stress on both parents, especially when the working mothers are expected to fulfill all their traditional responsibilities (Schor, 2003). An assumption underlying research comparing stay-at-home versus nonmaternal child care is that it will lead to insecure attachment. Yet, research has consistently shown that child development is neither postively nor negatively associated with type of child care *per se* (Erel, Oberman, & Yirmiya, 2000). The only caveat to these findings was the observation that children placed in child care after the age of 30 months showed less secure attachment than children placed in child care prior to 30 months of age.

Vandell and Ramanan (1992) made a longitudinal analysis of work patterns of low-income women and related factors. These authors found that the earlier women went to work after childbirth and the more recently (relative to the time of the study) they worked, the better off was the family. These women were more educated and more intelligent, the family was less likely to exist in poverty, and the quality of home life was higher; finally, their children were more likely to do well in school academics.

PSYCHOLOGICAL FACTORS

The maintenance of a nurturing environment is as important to child development as health care and nutrition. From the first days of life, adults begin to nurture children through breastfeeding, eye contact, smiling, kissing, and vocalizations, which in turn establish an attachment between infant and caregiver referred to as bonding (Siegel, 1982). Unlike other species, however, human babies resiliently retain the capability of bonding, even if parents miss opportunities in the first days and weeks of life. As infants grow, other psychological factors begin to influence development. Erikson (1963) wrote that one of the primary tasks of infants in their first year of life was to develop a sense of trust, which comes out of predictable and positive responses of caregivers and siblings. Although responsiveness in parenting early in life is critical to social and cogntive development, it also appears that parents must be vigilant across time (Landry, Swank, Assel, Smith, & Vellet, 2001). It was observed by

Landry et al. (2001) that a failure to consistently provide responsive caregiving resulted in a deceleration in cogntive growth after age four.

It seems that children not only require secure social attachments but may also need intermittent solitude as a condition of normal growth (Buchholz, 1997). Buchholz contended that greater emphasis on social interactions may actually deplete opportunities that infants have to self-regulate, organize information, and take a "psychological rest"; this may actually prove harmful if taken to an extreme. Research citing the physiological benefits of solitude includes improvements in the immune system and general functioning.

Parental style is important to nurturance of children. Adults who use warm and gentle tones to give directions and provide frequent positive feedback supporting appropriate behaviors develop the strongest levels of attachment (Reis et al., 2000). Kennedy (1992) analyzed the childrearing strategies of parents whose children were rejected by their peers and found that mothers had spent less time teaching social skills to their children, were more likely to use punishment, and used less reasoning to explain discipline. At the same time, the fathers and mothers of these children did not value or spend time in child-centered activities.

Environmental deprivation and/or environmental chaos can affect social and cognitive development (Coll, Buckner, Brooks, & Wei, 1998). When homeless and low-income infants and toddlers were assessed at 9 months and 18 months of age, there was a significant drop in motor and cognitive developmental scores. These findings suggest that poverty has a cumulative negative effect on development, increasing the longer children are exposed to conditions of poverty, including single parenting, violence, maternal depression, and substance abuse.

Infants and young children must also be given the freedom to explore their environments and to experiment and play with appropriate toys or materials (Allen & Marotz, 1989). For decades it has been recognized that the absence of stimulation or deprivation of experiences negatively affects development (Skeels, 1942; 1966). In Skeels's original research, 25 infants were selected from an overcrowded orphanage; 13 of them were sent to an institution to be cared for by adult women with mental retardation who provided the children with a stimulating and responsive environment. Though initially testing an average of 22 IQ points lower than the 12 infants remaining in the orphanage, a year and a half after placement in the institution, the children raised by women with mental retardation gained an average of 28 IQ points. Meanwhile, the children who remained in the overcrowded orphanage lost an average of 26 IQ points in the same interval of time.

In the past decade, more concern has been paid the rising "stress" exerted upon families related to such factors as: longer work days and longer commutes to/from work, need for day care—and unavailability of quality child care, feelings of isolation, commercial/moral pressure exerted on children by society/media, perception of increasing danger in the world, obligation of caring for multigenerational family members, and intrusion of television and computers into family life (Schor, 2003). That these stress factors may be related to a sharp increase in pediatric behavioral problems means that early intervention professionals will be best able to assist families in meeting the needs of their children by addressing families as a whole.

Case Study

WORKING WITH THE FOSTER CARE SYSTEM: INTERVIEW WITH JAMES HOLDEN

I have been an early childhood special education teacher, and now I teach a regular sixth grade, but my wife and I started taking foster children before I was ever trained in education. We've probably had a couple of hundred foster children over the course of our marriage. We did foster care for years, when our family was smaller but as our own family increased to seven children, we retired from foster care for a while. At the time, we didn't feel we had a voice in what was happening to the foster children. When foster children were placed, the decisions on what was going to happen with them were pretty much controlled and dictated by the state.

For example, when we first started, in the mid-1960s, there was not a lot of emphasis on disabilities. All the children were just foster children and there wasn't really a thought given to the special needs a lot of those children had. The only special service I can remember being considered was the notion that counseling would fix whatever was wrong with foster children. Many of the children we dealt with, even then, were of mixed ethnic backgrounds, or coming out of divorce situations, so there were some emotional needs which got in the way of education. When you would have children like that you'd have a hard time.

We had not had foster children for some time when I went back to school and became a certified special education teacher. I took a teaching position on an Indian reservation and that was when we got back into the foster system. These children would show up at our house anyway. Sometimes parents would get to the point where they didn't feel like they could take care of their children, so they would bring them to our house and we'd watch over them a few days. Usually this was in a crisis situation. The school district superintendent's wife worked for the Department of Social and Health Services on the reservation, so in an emergency situation she would always place a few children with us. Finally, someone at the tribe said, "Well you're doing it anyway, you might as well get a license"; so that's what we did.

All the foster children from the reservation were high-needs children. Many had parents who had used drugs or alcohol during pregnancy; the children were chemically effected, fetal alcohol syndrome, or alcohol-impacted children. All kinds of differing abilities go with these problems. We no longer live on the reservation and now the children we receive tend to have health impairment or emotional problems.

Medical care is paid for through the foster care system, which is a big bonus. The difficulty is making sure you get children with special needs to the right people. The treatment can be more traumatic than just leaving them alone. For example, taking Rueben and April to an office for physical therapy is more traumatic than trying to do it yourself at home because you're taking them off of their schedules and they're being exposed to a lot of people. You also expose them more to illness and they're already medically fragile, so they can become undone by then. Doing something in an unfamiliar setting can be very stressful for these children.

Many times you get children with problems that have not been diagnosed, so you're starting from ground zero. Each child is so individual, the evaluation process can be overpowering. I know a lot of foster parents just say, "Hey, it's not worth the effort," or "I just don't have the time to do it." As the children get older you're often looking at some kind of counseling or therapy as well. Getting services is very time intensive and distracting from a normal life, whatever that is.

We often have had five foster children at one time. With the kinds of high-needs children we have, that's about all a family can handle. Right now we have two children who have cystic fibrosis and fetal alcohol effect, and the other three we're adopting are all chemically impacted from crack cocaine. My wife and I are a team. I try to deal with the bureaucracy, arrange the medical treatment and the diagnostic testing, but she does the everyday nitty gritty care of the children.

Holden children dressed in costume for Halloween.

Right now, the foster care system is overloaded with these kinds of children, and many of them are not in appropriate homes. Many of the foster parents are simply not trained adequately to deal with high-needs children. When they hit school, many foster parents are going to feel, "Hey, we've done our job, now do yours." If the evaluation process doesn't start until then, the child has already lost three years before we do anything with them.

Foster parents in this area have organized to try to make changes in the system. They would like to see ongoing training about ways to identify suspected abuse or neglect, and continuing training with substance abuse impacted children.

AIDS is another huge part of what we're going through right now. The system will put a child with AIDS or suspected AIDS in your home and will not give you that information. I've also had a couple children who had hepatitis and they did not tell us. Those can be scary things because you're really in jeopardy. Family contact is very intimate at that level, there's no way to avoid it— so something needs to be done. Again we're balancing confidentiality rights with the rights of the caregiver and we as a society haven't come to grips with that.

All in all, I feel the foster parent association and the state foster care workers work very well together to try to provide for the best care available. But this will be an ongoing and important battle to win for the children. If we don't fight for these children, who will?

EDUCATION

A child's educational opportunities, when good, can compensate for some disadvantages and, when economically disadvantaged, serve to exacerbate the environmental disadvantage of children and their development. The following list represents some educationally related factors that have been found to differentially influence a child's development (McLaughlin & Vacha, 1992):

1. Opportunity for preschool educational services, especially for children who are raised in poverty
2. Educational level of parents
3. Structure and curriculum focus of educational program
4. Safety of child in school
5. Opportunity for success and positive experiences in school
6. Consistency of school attendance and mobility
7. Value of a child's education to parents
8. A parent's knowledge of the educational system

Evidence is mounting in support of early educational child care for infants and preschoolers. For example, a longitudinal study of economically disadvantaged minority children compared the long-term effects of a full-time, high-quality educational program from infancy to age 5 across those who attended the program and a control group of children who did not receive early education (Campbell, Pungello, Miller-Johnson, Burchinal, & Ramey, 2001). Those who received early education performed far better on long-term **indexes** of development: though both groups gradually declined in IQ, the control group had a significantly lower average IQ; those children who received early intervention scored significantly higher on measures of math and reading than the control. The observed cognitive advantages for recipients of early intervention, though continuously dropping for both groups when compared to national averages, persisted into adulthood.

CULTURE

Although cross-cultural research is in its infancy, it has revealed that universality exists in many aspects of development, just as differences have been observed in the rates of that development. For example, infants within the same culture seem to behave similarly, while behaving as a group differently than children from other cultures (Lester & Brazelton, 1982). In the past, educators tended to evaluate the development of all children according to the norms established with White, middle-income children. Similarly, educational priorities favor the values of the dominant culture. For example, cooperative group behavior is highly valued in most minority groups, whereas Caucasians tend to value independence and competition. More recently, it has been realized that this practice gives undue priority to a single culture, while simultaneously and arbitrarily devaluing the practices of other cultures that may differentially affect child development.

TECHNOLOGY

Two major influences of the technological expansion in the last half of the 20th century are television and the computer. While these have become household tools for both adults and children, the long-term influence of this technology on child development is undetermined. Television, on the other hand, has been the center of controversy for decades. The potential influence of television cannot be underestimated, as it has been found that no other activity consumes as much time for American children as watching television (Nielson, 1988).

Of particular concern to parents and child advocates has been the correlational findings linking programming and commercials on television to aggression in children (Huesmann, Moise-Titus, Podolski, & Eron, 2003), alcohol and tobacco use, increased high-risk behaviors, and accelerated onset of sexual activity (Villani, 2001). A reduction in children's academic capacity when greater than 3 hours per day were spent watching television was identified by Beentjes and VanderVoort (1988). However, Henggeler, Cohen, Edwards, Summerville, and Ray (1991) concluded that family contexts (maternal life events, stress, and paternal marital satisfaction), when correlated with television viewing time, might be interrelated with academic performance of children (support for and active participation in studying). Though computers and television are sources of concern when overused to entertain, as in computer and video games and in many television forums, both obviously have the potential to be valuable learning tools.

MILESTONES OF DEVELOPMENT

Understanding the principles of human development is prerequisite to interpreting the milestones that mark the developmental progression of infants and young children, including those with and at risk for developmental disabilities. Maturation across developmental domains is characterized by behavioral markers or key milestones. For practitioners working with young children with disabilities, this knowledge should be constantly at the ready—available for ongoing assessments of the headway children are making. In the absence of this knowledge, an educator's barometer of normalcy tends to drift. For example, early childhood special educators often admit that when they have an opportunity to observe typically developing children, they are reminded of the severity of their own students' delays. While the point is not to highlight individual differences, misinterpretation of development can lead to lowered expectations, oversight of potential problems, inaccuracy in educational programming, and miscommunication with families and other professionals. Since drift is possible, even for well-trained professionals, early childhood professionals should continuously recalibrate by revisiting developmental milestones.

In this chapter, our descriptions in each of five areas of development—motor, cognitive, language, social, and self-help—are accompanied by little theory. The absence of theory is intentional but is not meant to diminish its importance to the field of early childhood special education. Entire courses, indeed entire disciplines, have been devoted to these theories. This text's purpose, however, is to provide the elementary basis for making judgments about a child's performance in relation to typical developmental patterns and rates.

MOTOR DEVELOPMENT

Motor development provides the physical basis for movement, posture, and balance, which are critical prerequisites for acquiring concrete knowledge, producing speech, exploring the environment, carrying out daily self-help activities, and socializing with others. Normal development allows children to accomplish organized, purposeful, and efficient movement. This movement is dependent on the integration of the central nervous system and the muscular system acting together on skeletal structures (Bigge, 1991). Delayed or dysfunctional motor development can greatly influence when and how well children reach expected milestones. For example, chronic middle ear infections can disrupt functioning of the vestibular system that controls posture and balance against gravity. Delays in gross motor skills are observed in excessive falling, clumsiness, and collisions with objects, and may also be related to language development (Orlin & Effgen, 1997). In fact, motor delays can signal later developmental problems, such as learning disabilities, mental retardation, and attention deficit disorder (Festschrift, 1994). Consequently, it is important that early childhood professionals understand motor development, recognize deviations from norms, and know appropriate intervention services that may support a child's individual motor needs.

GROSS MOTOR DEVELOPMENT

A review of the principles of physical development will provide a means for understanding the progress of gross motor development. It has been noted that children's muscle control progresses from head to toe (cephalo-caudal), from gross to fine, and from the center of the body toward the extremities (proximo-distal). The first of these, head to toe, is most useful in determining which skills one would expect to emerge next, based upon the present level of maturity.

Head Control

A newborn has very little intentional body control, yet it does move its arms, legs, head, fingers, and toes reflexively. Because newborns are unable to independently support the weight of their heads, caregivers provide these babies with substantial head support. Soon, neck muscles develop sufficient strength and tone for turning the head from side to side in a **supine** (lying on the back) position and for greater ability to hold the head up in an upright or horizontal position. This head control becomes stronger until, eventually, infants raise their heads off a surface from a supine position and turn their heads from side to side in a **prone** (on the tummy) position. An infant is said to have gained good head control when,

Typical prone propping position.

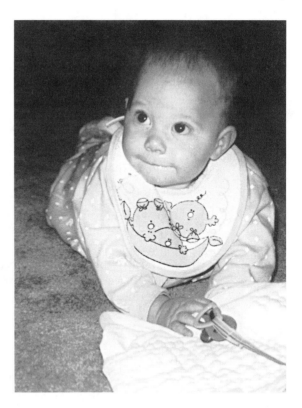

as the infant is tilted side to side and front to back, there is no head lag and the posture of the head remains upright. A test for head control is the facilitated sit-up. A caregiver places a child supine and, taking the arms, pulls the child to a sitting position. If an infant is able to raise its head independently so the head stays parallel to the trunk, there is no head lag.

Shoulder Control

Though overlap exists in the development of neck and shoulder control, the latter cannot fully develop without an infant first achieving complete head control. At approximately 2 to 3 months of age, infants begin to assist themselves in turning their heads from side to side by propping their chests on their forearms. As muscle control is gained, infants are able to prop themselves higher and for a longer time, eventually pushing up on fully extended arms and hands (proximo-distal principle in effect). Prone propping is paralleled by supine use of the arms, in which children begin to reach, first a few inches and then with fully extended arms. At this age, infants will begin to play with mobiles hung over their beds and to reach for near objects while lying on their tummies. When infants have well-developed shoulder control, they are able to turn themselves from prone to supine and back the other way. Usually, it is the front to back roll that emerges first since infants get an assist from their extended arms. However, by the fourth or fifth month, most infants are able to do both well since trunk control is also emerging.

Trunk Control

A neonate placed in a sitting position will droop from the waist to the head, exhibiting little resistance to gravity. At 2 months, an infant can hold its head upright in a sitting position and, at four months, it can hold its upper body upright but will fall over when a caregiver releases support of the waist. By 6 months, most infants will be able to sit independently, though they may not be able to catch themselves in a fall because protective extension reflexes are still immature. A strong sitter at 8 months will independently get in and out of a sitting position, will reach for objects on the floor without falling over, and can stay upright when pushed gently in all directions. The last protective reaction to develop is extension to the rear, and even at eight months, an infant is vulnerable to head injuries from falls backward.

Hip Control

When an infant is independently able to get in and out of a sitting position, it is because some hip control has developed. At this time, an infant in a prone position will begin to crawl by coordinating its arms and legs to move across the floor or other surface. Later, weight bearing at the hips permits infants to resist gravity by raising their heads and lifting their trunks off the floor on their hands and knees (some infants go straight to hands and feet in a "bear crawl"). By coordinating movement of the extremities, infants of 9 to 10 months creep from this elevated position.

Lower Body Control

The final major gross motor stage is upright mobility. Once hip control is fully developed, infants are capable of balance and stability on extended legs. Initially, standing may be possible only when knee joints are hyperextended. By 10 to 12 months though, most children can stand upright while holding onto a support. This evolves into cruising, or stepping sideways while holding onto furniture or some structure for support. Before long, a competent cruiser can be expected to transfer short distances between furniture by taking short steps without holding on. Finally, a child begins to take first a few, and then several, independent steps.

Refinement

Once a child has learned to walk independently, the remainder of gross motor movement can be considered a refinement of the most critical skills of this domain. In fact, early childhood professionals tend to place relatively less emphasis on this domain (see Table 4–2) and more on cognitive and language skills after a child has begun to walk well. Refinement includes walking up and down stairs, running, standing on one leg, skipping, jumping, and development of recreation skills. While a child could be quite functional in life without most of these skills, a delay in development of gross motor coordination could be an early signal of generalized developmental problems later in life.

FINE MOTOR SKILLS

Like gross motor skills, fine motor development follows a predictable pattern. The most relevant principle is gross-to-fine motor skill maturation. For example, you would not expect a child to be capable of grasping objects intentionally until the

Table 4–2 Refinement of Gross Motor Development

12 to 18 months	• Creeps up and down stairs
	• Runs
	• Throws ball overhand
	• Pulls toy behind when walking
	• Walks backward
18 to 24 months	• Kicks a ball
	• Squats
	• Bends at waist to pick something up without falling
	• Walks up stairs alone with both feet on each step
3 years	• Rides a tricycle by pedaling with alternating feet
	• Catches a large bounced ball
	• Broad jumps two feet
	• Runs smoothly with changes in speed
4 years	• Catches a thrown playground ball against body w/arms
	• Walks up and down stairs alternating feet holding rail
	• Jumps over a string held slightly off the floor
	• Walks to the rhythm of music
5 years	• Catches bounced ball
	• Skips alternating feet
	• Jumps rope 2–3 consecutive times
	• Rides a bike with training wheels
	• Skates forward a few feet
	• Hits a ball with a bat or stick

Source: Adapted from "Behavioral Competencies and Outcomes: The Effects of Disorders," by M. J. Hanson and M. F. Hanline, 1984, in M. J. Hanson (Ed.), *Atypical Infant Development* (pp. 109–142). Austin, TX: PRO-ED.

child had gained shoulder control and was reaching with some accuracy. It can also be predicted that control of grasping progresses from the palm of the hand to the fingertips (proximo-distal).

Eye Contact and Facial Expression

In conformity with head-to-toe development, fine muscle control of the eyes is one of the first observable fine motor skills to begin developing. Within the first few days of life, neonates may be observed matching maternal eye movement. Yet, neonates have difficulty tracking, following moving objects with their eyes, and they lose contact once an object has been moved away from their midline. In just a few weeks, however, infants begin to track objects that are moved gradually from side to side and, eventually, they will track 180 degrees by moving their heads to prevent loss of eye contact. Both range and duration of eye contact are important to mobility, fine motor coordination, and language development.

Reaching

At birth, an infant's reach and grasp are entirely reflexive. Intentional reaching from a supine position begins at about 2 months, after an infant has gained some control at the shoulders. Infants will initially reach toward objects with minimal

Achieving independence.

coordination and may bat or swing at an object but do not grasp it. Instead, a predominant flexor pattern holds the hands in a fisted position. By 4 months, an infant's reach has become more coordinated, and the infant will unhesitatingly move its arm and hand in the direction of a desired object.

Grasping

At the point where reaching has become a refined movement, grasping becomes intentional, now permitting infants to acquire and hold objects. Still, the unintegrated grasp reflex does not permit infants to intentionally release objects. The most primitive grasp is referred to as the palmar grasp (see Figure 4–8), in which a child acquires an object by scooping it into the palm with all fingers extended. Obviously, this grasp prevents an infant from manipulating an object in any precise fashion, and play with the object is unsophisticated. Later, infants will be able to pick up and hold an object by opposing the palm with the tips of all fingers. Still there is no differentiation of finger use. A major milestone is reached when infants are able to grasp by opposing their thumbs with other fingers. This development, the prehensile grasp, is a feature unique to humans and other primates. First the thumb opposes all the fingers, then the second and third fingers, and finally a fine pincer grasp is achieved.

Handedness

Handedness, or the tendency to be more skillful at using one hand/foot over the other, is a reflection of the dominance of one hemisphere of the brain over the

Figure 4–8
A. Palmar Grasp
B. Pincer Grasp

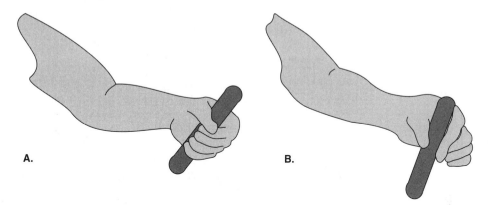

A.   B.

A predominant flexor pattern: the infant holds its hands in a fisted position and swipes at objects.

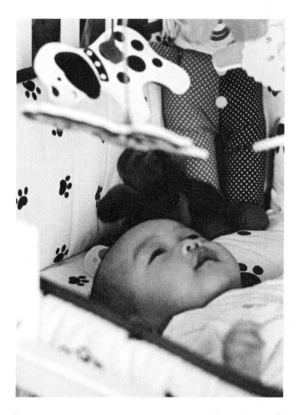

other. In infancy, most children do not show a preference but use both hands with equal coordination. Later, as children begin to perform more specialized hand movements, the majority show a preference for right handedness. In spite of beliefs to the contrary, right handers are not better coordinated than left handers or children who are "inconsistent" left handers (Gabbard & Hart, 1995).

Table 4–3   Refinement of Fine Motor Development

12 to 18 months	• Holds crayon, with crayon held from radial side of hand • Turns pages of a cardboard book • Places a peg in a pegboard • Builds a tower with two blocks • Places a round form in a formboard
18 to 24 months	• Imitates a crayon stroke • Imitates vertical and circular stroke • Completes puzzle with circle, square, triangle
2 years	• Builds tower with several blocks (4–6) • Turns door knobs or TV handles by twisting wrist • Unscrews nesting toys • Turns pages one at a time • Holds a crayon with thumb and forefinger
3 years	• Cuts with scissors on a line • Holds pencil with adult-like tripod grasp (resting on third finger) • Folds paper • Winds up toys
4 years	• Completes puzzle of 3–5 pieces • Moves paper and cuts out simple shapes (e.g., triangle) • Draws a person with two body parts • Makes crude objects with 2–3 parts with clay • Screws together threaded objects
5 years	• Prints first name • Completes 11–15 piece puzzle • Copies small case letters • Colors within lines • Opens lock with a key • Hits a nail with hammer

Refinement of fine motor abilities is observed throughout the preschool years (see Table 4–3). The gradual refinement is facilitated by increased speed, strength, and coordination of small muscle groups. This ability is closely integrated with cognitive and perceptual development. Infants learn to pick up small objects and use their index finger to point to and probe objects. Toddlers begin to put simple puzzles together and to scribble with a crayon. Later on, preschoolers learn to draw, to cut with scissors, and to form objects with clay.

LANGUAGE DEVELOPMENT

One of the most amazing phenomena of human life is the development of language. In just 3-years' time, infants progress from almost total reflexive responding to the development of adult-like speech. Yet, even in the first few days, infants communicate; they send messages that are understood by caregivers. For most children, this **communication** will later conform to a set of rules that guide how ideas are formed into words and put together in

Case Study

THE DIARY OF ESTHER ANNA BERKE: MONTH 3

The doctor orders Esther Anna admitted to NCKU Hospital in Taiwan on Wed. Jan. 27. She is dehydrated and anemic and the doctor puts her on an IV and re-inserts the nasal feeding tube. A nurse asks us why we didn't abort her! GRRR!!! Esther's right lung collapsed and she was put into the ICU. After 16 days in the hospital, Esther celebrated her 3-month birthday at home; she weighs 4.1 kg and measures 55 cm long.

February 16–21: This is New Year's Day on the Chinese lunar calendar, Happy Chinese New Year, the Year of the Rabbit! Esther is eating well and staying healthy. Our colds are slowly improving, and Esther weighs 4.4 kg. On Feb. 21 she weighed 4.5 kg, finally back to her birth weight after 14 weeks! She is at the 25th percentile for weight and height for girls her age. We hope we can put some fat on her.

February 22–March 1: Sunday Feb. 28: She weighs 4.75 kg today, and is eating well. Esther's seizures are still a problem; she has two new types we have not seen before, and their frequency is much higher than before. Other than her seizures, she is doing well—she rolled over from her stomach to her back for the first time. We took her to a physical therapist to begin strengthening her neck muscles which are weak. We appreciate a relatively calm week!

March 2–8: Sunday March 7: She weighs 5.0 kg, and started a new drug this week—Rivotril in addition to the Sabril. We are investigating a diet called the ketogenic diet, it is a high-fat, low-protein, ultra-low carbohydrate diet that has helped many people with seizures, including at least one

Aicardi girl. One baby was started on it at 4 1/2 months old, using a special formula. The Johns Hopkins Medical Center in Baltimore is the world's expert on this diet. We are also investigating a holistic therapy program prescribed by the National Academy of Child Development in Ogden, Utah. They try to treat the entire child (5 senses and mental and emotional aspects) in order to stimulate the brain to grow new connections between the brain cells. People have written us dramatic stories of how they helped their children.

March 9–15: Esther celebrated her 4-month birthday March 15 by hiking in Yu Shan (Jade Mountain) National Park. Actually she didn't hike, she and Mom stayed in the car because it was pretty cold up there for us "tropicalized" people, all of 5 degrees Celsius (that's 40 degrees Fahrenheit for you metrically-challenged people out there). She weighed 5.2 kg and measured 63.5 cm; her weight is only in the 15th percentile for her age, but her length is in the 70th percentile. We need to put some more fat on that baby!

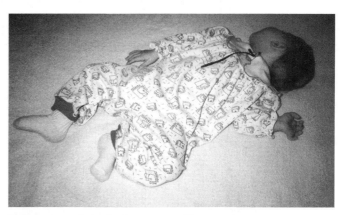

Esther Anna's typical prone position.

sentences. These symbolic systems, known as languages, differ across cultures. Furthermore, language can be communicated in writing, orally through speech, and manually (e.g., American Sign Language). All these systems have something in common. Individuals who share the language conform to the standard rules, enabling them to communicate very efficiently. However, humans do not send and receive messages through language alone. Unconventional language—body language, facial expressions, grunts, laughter, wincing, and so on—all communicate powerful messages that are "read" by the listener.

Just as musculoskeletal movement is reflexive at birth, so is the majority of neonatal communication. A newborn communicates basically in two ways—crying and not crying. Within 2 years, however, this child will have developed all the basic constructs of human adult language. Several theories attempt to explain the nature of linguistic development. The various theories can be viewed as complementary, contradictory, or supplemental. In fact, our current understanding of language seems to borrow from each of the most prominent theories (McCormick & Schiefelbusch, 1990). The following principles of language development are generally agreed upon by linguists.

◆ Humans are born with a certain capacity to acquire language (McCormick & Schiefelbusch, 1990).
◆ Children acquire language according to a universal pattern, which is observed across children of different languages, cultures, families, and disabilities (Chaudhary & Supama, 1991).
◆ Children generally develop an understanding of the meaning of concepts before they learn to use the corresponding words. Moreover, a child's **receptive language** (words they understand) is almost always more highly developed than a child's **expressive language** (words they use).
◆ Social exchanges are a necessary context for language development (McDonald, 1989).
◆ Children's language development is facilitated through modeling by adults, repeated practice of sounds and words, and differential reinforcement (i.e., attending to understandable language and not attending to incomprehensible language).

The remainder of this section will be a description, rather than an explanation, of language development in children from birth to 6 years of age. Interactional theorists describe language as three interrelated components: form, content, and use. The *form* of language refers to its structure: phonology, syntax, and morphemes. Language *content* refers to a child's knowledge of the words and the interrelationship between words. Both receptive and expressive language are considered in language content. Finally, language *use*, or *pragmatics,* is the way in which children communicate in social contexts.

LANGUAGE FORM

Three aspects of language are generally considered when discussing language form. **Phonology** is the study of speech sounds. When considering the linguistic development of infants, the evolution of phonemes (speech sounds) follows a predictable pattern. The rules that govern structural patterns of language utterances and sentence grammar are referred to as **syntax**. Finally, **morphological development** refers to the evolution of word structure and word parts such as prefixes and suffixes.

Phonological Development

The sounds made by neonates are nonspecific crying, grunting, and gurgling. Without training or direction, caregivers are typically able to differentiate types of crying sounds to determine if an infant is wet, tired, hungry, or otherwise uncomfortable. Infants begin to make vowel sounds within the first few months. Vowel sound production is referred to as **cooing**. Vowels are physically the easiest sounds to make since they require little motor control or use of the articulators (tongue, lips, palate, and teeth).

Infants begin to **babble** by about 4 months of age as they gain greater oral motor control. Babbling is a combination of consonant (C) and vowel (V) sounds (C–V and V–C) and progresses from simple to complex sound production. In the early babbling stages, infants produce a variety of sounds, some of which are not a part of their native language. Later, sounds not used in children's native language(s) drop from their repertoire and may be very difficult to acquire at an older age. By the end of the first year, infants' first words begin to appear; many of these are monosyllabic C–V or V–C combinations, for example "up" or "ma-ma." Thereafter, consonant sound production progresses along a continuum of easy to hard, relative to oral–motor complexity (see Table 4–4).

Children produce words that increase in understandability as initial sounds, ending sounds, and middle sounds of words are put together with precision. The transition to real words is remarkably fleet. At 18 months, only about 25% of infant's language is intelligible. By 2 years, when toddlers begin to produce two-word utterances, it should be approximately 65% intelligible. At 4 years of age, children have acquired most phonetic sounds and are producing almost totally intelligible sentences.

Syntax

Without direct instruction, children acquire the rules of spoken syntax with surprising accuracy. It is not until after children already speak with correct syntax

Table 4–4 Sequence of Phonological Acquisition*

Age	Sounds Produced
By age 3	p, m, h, n, w
By age 4	b, k, g, d, f, y
By age 6	t, ng, r, l, s
By age 7	ch, sh, j, voiced th (as in thick)
By age 8	s, z, v, unvoiced th (as in this)
Later	zh

*The age of acquisition may vary by as much as 3 years.
Source: From McCormick et al., *Early Language Intervention.* Published by Allyn & Bacon, Boston, MA. Copyright ©1984 by Pearson Education. Adapted by permission of the publisher.

that the rules of grammar are specifically taught. Initially, infants rely primarily on one-word utterances, and toward the end of their second year, they rely on successive single-word utterances. Infants do not begin to put words together in phrases until late in their second year. However, this linguistic development represents a major accomplishment in a child's communicative power. The significance of two-word utterances is that these telegraphic phrases possess more meaning than either word uttered in isolation. That is, two-word phrases convey the meanings of word A and word B, plus the meaning of each word's relationship to the other. Examples of simple two-word phrases used include noun–verb: "baby eat"; verb–noun: "give ball"; noun–noun: "Daddy ball").

Sentence structure becomes complex in several ways in a child's third year. At about 27 months, children begin to ask questions, though initially only by intonation. Children may ask some "wh-questions" at this time, but initially with the verb and subject transposed (e.g., "Where car is going?"). Wh-questions emerge in correspondence with conceptual knowledge and receptive understanding of the same types of questions. "Who," "what," and "where," which have more concrete referents, precede "when," "how," and "why." Queries that require transposition of verbs occur when children have begun to use auxiliary verbs and copulas or linking words (e.g., "Is the bike outside?"). Tag questions are also complex interrogative forms added on after other question forms have appeared (e.g., "We are having ice cream, aren't we?").

Negative sentences also follow a pattern of increasing complexity as they gradually approximate accurate syntactic rules. To the frustration of adults, negative statements are among the highest frequency utterances made by toddlers. Children first make negative comments by placing a negative marker at the beginning of a sentence. This is followed by placing the negative marker inside the sentence next to the relevant verb, but without the use of copulas and auxiliary verbs. Finally, though not until about age 4, children begin to accurately use inflections and negative markers together.

Stage I	No want milk.
Stage II	Kitty no eat candy.
Stage III	I can't fix the bike.

Complex sentences contain at least one independent clause and at least one subordinate or dependent clause. Sentences with more than one independent clause are referred to as **compound sentences.** Both advanced types of sentences combine two or more ideas in a single sentence through the use of conjunctions, relative pronouns, or other linguistic linkages. "And" is the first conjunction to appear and is observed in children as young as 25 months of age, though initially the "and" joins nouns (e.g., "me and Mommy") rather than clauses. **Relative clauses** that modify subjects (e.g., "I like the doll that has the green hair") appear later. By 3 or 4, many children are using compound and complex sentences by adding elements to the beginning or end of kernel sentences. Still later (4 to 13 years of age), children add clauses internally to sentences in a process referred to as **embedding** (e.g., "I saw the girl who is in my class at the park").

CLOSE-UP

MEANINGFUL DIFFERENCES IN EVERYDAY EXPERIENCES OF YOUNG AMERICAN CHILDREN

Research is increasingly clear that a child's intellectual and social destiny is largely determined prior to entering school. In fact, for children who live in poverty, it may be impossible for educators to undo the effects of early childhood experiences with their parents. Hart and Risley (1995) found that when children of university faculty parents far outpaced their same-age peers from poor families when compared on the basis of language development. The implication of these findings is that, while all parents have the opportunity to provide rich intellectual experiences required for healthy cognitive development, the failure to do so may lead to deficiencies that are all but impossible to rehabilitate once children reach school age.

There were pronounced differences in the amount and quality of interactions between parents and their children as observed monthly across three years by Hart and Risley (1995). Across three income groups, it was found that the more educated the mother, the more she spoke to her children. Welfare, working-class, and professional parents addressed their children an average of 600, 1200, and 2000 words per hour, respectively. As a consequence, Hart and Risley estimated that by the time these children reached age 3, the welfare children would have heard 10,000,000 words, working-class children would have heard 20,000,000 words, and professional children would have heard 30,000,000 words.

In addition to the differences in number of words heard, parents of the different groups studied differed what they talked about to their children. For example, welfare parents made positive comments to their children an average of 6 times per hour, as compared to 15 times per hour for working-class parents and 30 times per hour for professional parents.

These linguistic differences led to significant differences in intellectual accomplishments when children were followed up in the third grade. While performance differences based upon SES tended to diminish across time, differences in parental behavior remained a strong predictor of their children's cognitive success.

Hart and Risley (1995) predicted that it would take 40 hours of supplemental care every week from birth on to compensate for the observed differences in parental behavior. While this option is unrealistic, there is clearly a need for better/more parent training, mentorship programs, parental aides, and access to quality child care.

Source: Meaningful Differences in Everyday Experiences in Young American Children, by B. Hart and T. R. Risley, 1995, Toronto: Paul H. Brookes Pub. Co.

MORPHOLOGICAL DEVELOPMENT

A **morpheme** is defined as the smallest part of a word that possesses meaning. Morphemes that can stand alone with meaning are referred to as free morphemes, while those that cannot stand alone are referred to as **bound morphemes**. While a language frequently adds new free morphemes, it rarely adds new bound morphemes. Of the two, free morphemes appear first in infants' language as their first words (e.g., bottle, Mommy, ball, cup, etc.). Not until much later (beginning at about 24 months) do bound morphemes (inflections) begin to appear (e.g., -ed, -ing, pre-, etc.). The latter, along with auxiliary verbs, are referred to as morphological inflections and emerge along a predictable pattern (see Table 4–5).

An index of the sophistication of a children's language is based upon the frequency of morphemes in their utterances. **Mean Length Utterance (MLU)** is calculated by dividing the number of morphemes in an utterance by the number of utterances (at least 50). An MLU of 1.0 is observed when infants are at the one-word-phrase stage. By the time children have MLUs of 3.0 or higher, they are usually incorporating at least some morphological inflections into their phrases. When a child's MLU is greater than 4.0, the score is no longer a valid index of language development.

Morphological development appears to be particularly difficult for children with language impairments and an index that distinguishes language problems from cognitive deficits. Even children with language delays, however, acquire morphemes in normal pattern. Although many children "catch-up" in later childhood, they often retain minor deficits in morpheme development, particularly those with verb use (Bedore & Leonard, 1998). Hence, these children, and those who are not "late bloomers," may benefit from early intervention in speech and language (Paul & Alforde, 1993).

Table 4–5   Sequence of Acquisition of Morphological Inflections

---

  1. Present progressive (eat<u>ing</u>)
2/3. Prepositions (in/on)
  4. Plural (boot<u>s</u>, Sho<u>es</u>)
  5. Irregular Past Tense (came, went)
  6. Possessive (daddy'<u>s</u> chair)
  7. Copula, Uncontractible of "to be" ("there <u>you are</u>")
  8. Articles (a, the)
  9. Regular Past Tense (jump<u>ed</u>)
10. Third Person singular, Present tense, Regular (jump<u>s</u>)
11. Third Person singular, Present tense, Irregular (does, has)
12. Auxiliary, Uncontractible (can, will)
13. Copula, Contractible ("It'<u>s</u> mine")
14. Auxiliary, Contractible ("I'<u>ll</u> take it.")

Source: From E. H. Wiig, E. M. Semel, *Language Assessment and Intervention for the Learning Disabled.* Published by Allyn & Bacon, Boston, MA. Copyright ©1980 by Pearson Education. Adapted by permission of the publisher.

Language Content

Content develops along two parameters: receptive and expressive language. The former typically progresses at a more rapid rate but is not necessarily a prerequisite for expressive development. In other words, children sometimes use words in their speech before they understand their meaning. The best example of this rate difference is the word spurt in comprehension that takes place between 15 and 16 months, which precedes an analogous production word spurt 3–4 months later. This is because the cognitive requirements for comprehension are fewer than those needed for production (Casasol & Cohen, 2000).

Receptive Language

Neonates are capable of learning speech in their first days of life. Bertoncini, Bijelac-Babic, Jusczyk, Kennedy, and Mahler (1988) discovered that infants would alter their pattern of sucking when a tape emitting phonetic sounds ("ba") suddenly changed to a new sound ("da"). This ability to discriminate sounds is a necessary prerequisite to speech production. Within the first few months, a mother might notice that her child will become quiet or pause at the sound of mom's voice but not at that of a stranger's voice. Later, when infants develop some head control, they will turn their heads toward sounds by sound localization. Although infants begin to recognize familiar words in speech by about 7.5 months, it is not until the end of children's first year that they begin to acknowledge specific

Tommy and his mother signing to each other.

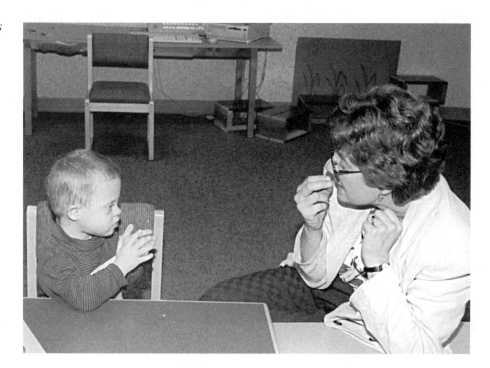

words. This is evident when children respond differentially to their names. Not surprisingly, one of the first words recognized by infants is the word "no."

By the end of their first year, infants recognize a few high-frequency words and can demonstrate this skill by looking directly at the named objects. One-year-olds are also learning to follow simple commands like "wave bye-bye," or "give me a kiss." However, these commands are often accompanied by gestures or signals.

The aforementioned gap between comprehension and production is exaggerated from 15 months of age until about the third year of development when the gap narrows again. Still, the next 6 months represent a turning point in children's receptive language, as infants learn to follow simple novel commands that do not have gestures, such as "put the toy on the table" or "give mommy a drink." By 13 months of age, infants begin to understand grammatical morphemes. At 16 months, infants point to body parts upon request. A child's understanding of speech is nearly perfect by the end of their second year, as they can discriminate accurate and inaccurate phonemes, morphemes, and syntax (Morgan, 1996).

Until their second year, an infant's word understanding is referent specific. During their second year, these same infants begin to categorize concepts by making gradually more sophisticated generalizations (Oviatt, 1982). For example, they learn that cats and dogs belong to a category of animals. Later, they learn that even though horses have some of the same characteristics as dogs, they do not belong to the same class. Still, 2-year-olds are bound by literal interpretation of adult language and are unable to solve the figurative meaning behind clichés, metaphors, or analogies. By age 3, young children can both interpret and use figurative speech. A child might be overheard saying, "Rover is a pig." Anaphoric terms, such as "this," "that," "it," and "there," are difficult terms to master, though three-year-olds are typically able to solve such directions as "put the spoon there." Four-year-olds can understand passive sentences (e.g., "I had wanted to take you to the park") but use them infrequently in conversation. A 6-year-old is quite good at solving subtle messages in language, such as sarcasm and humor that rely on irony (Winner, 1988). Since children's language is still literal, transparent metaphors, such as "hold your tongue," might be understood by these youth, though it is not until much later that children are able to decode opaque metaphors, such as "smell the roses" (MacArthur, 1990).

Expressive Language

Documenting the development of expressive language is easier since one does not have to make inferences about the invisible cognitive processes that underlie this form of communication. Though children represent meanings much earlier, their first real words do not generally appear much before a child's first birthday. However, intentional pointing emerges near the end of the first year. It has been found that emergence of pointing and speech may be related to speech expression and comprehension in later childhood (Butterworth & Morissette, 1996).

Universally, the first words that infants use represent salient features of children's immediate environments. Actions and objects dominate early words, though nouns appear to be more easily learned and more frequently used than verbs (Casasola & Cohen, 2000). This makes sense, since objects have a concrete referent, while actions are not permanent and their dimensions change with each event. For example, "jumping" can only be labeled when someone jumps, and then the action is gone. Additionally, jumping can be on one foot or two feet, executed by mom or dad, a few inches or over a high jump, and so on. Words that represent objects that move or are acted upon in a variety of different ways (e.g., baby doll) are more frequently used than objects that do not move (e.g., wall).

At 18 months, when infants typically possess a 50-word vocabulary of mostly nominals, their language content begins to change significantly. It is at this juncture in development that children begin naming many different objects that are less salient and less important. Some have referred to this transition as a "naming spurt," and it corresponds with a sudden sharp increase in children labeling everything they see (Gopnik & Meltzoff, 1992). This milestone also seems to be the threshold for combining words into successive single-word utterances and two-word utterances. Finally, at about this stage, a sharp rise in the use of both verbs and adjectives has been observed (Klink & Klink, 1990).

At 2 years, toddlers have acquired a vocabulary of about 300 words. With words paired together in telegraph-like sentences, children use only key words (e.g., "baby up" stands in for "the baby is standing up"). A rapid growth in novel **semantic relationships** takes place in children's second year. For example, Braine (1963) documented novel use of two-word utterances of a toddler. In successive months the child used 24, 54, 89, 250, 1400, and 2500 new phrases.

Perhaps because of their limited repertoire of words, toddlers commonly **overextend** the use of words. For example, these children might mistakenly refer to all men as "Daddy" since men have physical characteristics similar to their fathers. At the same time, these toddlers might alternately look at Dad and his friend Bob when they hear their names, reflecting a lag in production as compared to cognitive understanding. **Underextensions** occur when categories are defined too narrowly. For example, very young children might use the word "chair" to refer to their highchairs and the dining room chairs but do not include the rocking chair or kitchen stool in this category. It is also common for children to use known words idiosyncratically to fill in for concepts for which they have no words.

Preschool programs commonly spend much time teaching young children color terms, a behavior that maintains very little functional value when compared to the many other conceptual categories available. Little ones can typically supply a color of an object to the request, "What color is this?" by age 2, though not necessarily accurately. Colors closest to primary (e.g., red-reds) are learned most easily (Andrick & Tager-Flusberg, 1986). More complex content reflecting concepts that are not concrete typically do not appear much before a child's third birthday. For example, time and space are relative terms, and words used to reflect these concepts begin to appear at about age 4 when concepts such as "before," "after," "next to," "in front of," "first," and "last" are observed.

Though a child's vocabulary development is influenced, to some unknown but significant degree, by experiences, the normal rate of word acquisition has been described (Reed, 1994). By 2 years a child typically uses 300 words, 1000 by 3 years, 1500 by 4 years, over 2000 by 5 years, and nearly 3000 words by age 6. By contrast, a child's receptive vocabulary is approximately 20,000 to 24,000 words by age 6.

LANGUAGE USE

The final category of language function, language use, is more difficult to define, assess, and plan for instruction. This aspect of language refers to the effectiveness of the speaker in establishing and maintaining mutually rewarding interactions with others. Some children have very well-developed language form and content but are simply unable to engage others in conversations. Even as adults there are people who, for example, can talk and talk but are not desirable conversation partners because they are insensitive to the subtle rules of communication that make interactions mutually rewarding.

Three types of behavior comprise language use. **Speech acts** are the speakers' intentions or purposes for communicating. People communicate to give information, ask questions, make requests, tell a story or entertain, make protests, and show surprise, among other things. When communicating with others, people also make judgments about the listener that allow modifications to the content and style of the communication. These **presuppositions** include, but are not limited to, assessments of social status, educational or developmental level, and the intimacy of relationships. For example, one estimates the level of interest that the listener might have in a particular topic as well as the degree of background knowledge that the listener holds. If these judgments are inaccurate, one could talk over someone's head or, conversely, offend someone by appearing condescending. Finally, conversations have subtle rules, that may vary from culture to culture, that allow humans to converse in a reciprocal manner. **Conversational postulates**, as these rules are called, include skills in initiating conversations, balanced turn-taking, questioning, repairing a breakdown in conversations, maintaining interactions, and closing a conversation.

The earliest appearance of language use is in the form of conversational postulates. For example, neonates have been observed engaging in reciprocal

Four-year-olds exhibit a variety of conversational skills.

turn-taking with caregivers in the first days of life. Eye blinking and mouth and tongue movements can become routinized back-and-forth actions between a child and caregiver. However, it will be several more years before these skills become refined. A child of 9 months will play many reciprocal games, demonstrating conversation-like turn-taking (e.g., peek-a-boo). This turn-taking skill is used primitively in dialogues when a child is 18 to 24 months of age.

During the period when children first begin to use intentional communication, many of their language intentions are nonverbal. For example, a child may point to a favorite doll. Yet, the purposes of this intent could be several. The child might be making a request to acquire the toy, telling mom that the doll is nice, protesting the removal of the doll, or asking if the doll is hungry. In context, a parent can interpret these limited regulatory requests. Even at this age, these same 1-year-old speakers have been observed altering their communication for their listeners.

By the latter half of their second year, children begin to use language for a variety of new functions that integrate regulatory purposes with interactional skills. At 2 years of age, children have learned that a single utterance can serve more than one function. Because conversation has now taken on a social purpose, toddlers need to maintain conversational topics. However, many conversations break down as children appear to flit in and out of a conversation more often than they stay on topic. Limited skills, such as repeating or imitating words or parts of words used in the previous sentence, are used to maintain conversations. These children might fix a topic breakdown by attempting to articulate with greater clarity. By contrast, 4-year-olds are capable of carrying on a conversation for several minutes, discussing the same or related topics. Skills used to fix topic breakdowns include rephrasing sentences, shortening utterances, and expanding their sentences.

Three- and 4-year-old children will adapt their communication based on their perceived assessment of the listener's prior knowledge. They may give more or less information based on the extent of previous experiences their listeners are judged to possess. Furthermore, these preschoolers can be observed altering the length of sentences, affect (e.g., facial expression, voice intonation, body language), and language content when interacting with younger children or infants (Shatz & Gelman, 1973).

FACTORS AFFECTING LANGUAGE DEVELOPMENT

Multiple factors can affect the rate and pathology of linguistic acquisition. For example, many developmental disabilities can directly affect language form. Clefts of the lip and/or palate and oral-structural anomalies associated with Down syndrome influence phonological production. Cerebral palsy may result in reduced respiratory capacity that hampers speech production as well. Other developmental disabilities affect children's rate of learning and slow the acquisition of content and use. Autism, for example, is linked with aberrations in all areas of language development.

New evidence has been found that many children inherit their language deficits. In a small controlled study, Spitz and Tallal (1997) found that 50% of those infants with a positive family history of language impairments had a significant language delay themselves at 2 years, though development was normal in all other domains. Moreover, the children with no family history also had no delays in language development at 2 years. Bedore and Leonard (1998) reported that immediate family members of children with speech and language delays are two to seven times more likely than family members of children with normal language development to have language disorders themselves.

Though patterns of language development are universal (see Table 4–6), there are some cultural and sociocultural factors that influence the rate of acquisition of language (Wood, 1992). For example, Chaudhary and Suparna (1991) found that children differed across nuclear and extended families, with children from single units having more rapid language development. Lewis (1997) worried over the

Table 4–6   Milestones of Language Development

Birth	Responds to noises (activity stops)
	Frequent crying
	Vowel-like sounds "e" and "a"
1 month	Vocalizes
	Responds to voices
	Special cry for hunger
	Vocalizes pleasure
4 months	Imitates simple gestures
	Repeats syllables (da-da-da)
	Localizes sounds
	Uses vowel sounds "o" and "u"
	Expresses displeasure without crying
8–11 months	Produces consonant sounds in babbling
	Stops activity momentarily when told "no"
	Combines two syllables in vocal babbling "ba-da"
	Babbles using adult-like intonation
	Shows understanding of some words
	Waves "bye-bye"
	Plays "peek-a-boo" and "pat-a-cake"
12 months	Says 5–10 words
	Points to familiar objects when named
	Expresses wants
	Says "no" with authority
18 months	Points to 2–3 pictures named
	Names familiar objects upon request
	Intelligible speech 25% of time
	Imitates last word spoken
	Uses own name in conversation
24 months	"Sings" along with music
	Uses plurals
	2-word phrases
	Responds to choices
	Utterances have communicative intents
	Intelligible speech 65% of time
	Overextensions ("goed," "feets")

Table 4–6 *(continued)*

3 years	Knows a few songs—approximates correct pitch
	Can carry on a conversation
	4-word sentences
	Past tense and present tense (-ed)
	"wh-" questions
	Uses pronouns I, her/him, hers/his, she/he
	Intelligible speech 80% of time
4 years	Says "excuse me" to interrupt conversation
	Will retell story read by someone else
	Carries out instructions with prepositions
	Participates in group songs
	Defines words
	Can tell what simple things are made of
5 years	Knows birthday, phone number and parents' names
	5-word sentences
	Describes events in past/future with logical sequence
	Answers questions related to a spoken content or story
	Beginning to understand abstract concepts
	Compound sentences with 2 main clauses

loss of oral traditions in African American families and recent immigrant groups, whose story-telling practices are devalued by the Anglo American school system and obstructed by urban life. The loss of nuturance and social exchange through family lore is believed to signal the loss of critical language stimulation.

Idiosyncrasies in parenting also influence language development. Schacter and Straye (1982) described a specialized manner of interaction between mothers and infants called "motherese." Tactics of motherese were found to be correlated with the rate of language development and include use of extensions, shortened sentence length and simplified vocabulary, repetitions or rewording, and talking about events within a child's world. Though gender differences do exist in communication with infants, Klink and Klink (1990) concluded that fathers also engage in "motherese."

Not surprisingly, there are qualitative language differences between the way mothers and fathers relate to their infants (Kornhaber & Marcos, 2000). Fathers' language tends to be more regulating and contains action directives aimed at task completion. Mothers, on the other hand, tended to be more expressive and play oriented. In turn, infants' language tended to reflect the linguistic content of the respective parent.

Children with disabilities who have language delays may require specially structured opportunities to facilitate language development. For example, children with language delays benefit from opportunities to engage in structured play with children whose language is developing normally. These peer models provide their friends with more things to talk about, correct models of language structure, and appropriate ways for using language in a social situation (Roberston & Weismer, 1997).

COGNITION

The process by which human beings learn has been under inquiry and discovery for hundreds of years. The acquisition of knowledge, also known as **cognition**, is a complex phenomenon in which infants, children, and adults are constantly learning about their world. This development allows human beings to learn to reason (both concretely and abstractly), to think logically, and to organize information about their environment in a way that will bring order to their world. Cognitive development is closely tied to the other developmental domains. Failure to follow the normal developmental pathway can result in difficulties in social and emotional development and produce blocks to the development of communication skills.

The basis of cognitive development is linked to neurological growth and maturation. An explosion of biological brain research over the past decade has revolutionized the way fetal and infant cognition is viewed. For example, it is now held that even prior to birth, the human fetus is capable of behavioral learning. Between the 36th and 38th weeks of gestation, an infant's movement and heart rate respond to the sound of its mother's voice.

Early experiences are key to neurological development, as the brain goes through a process of "pruning" unnecessary neurons and neural connections based upon those experiences (Joseph, 2000). As the brain sheds these neurons, unique and environmentally specific neural pathways create individual cognition. Gradually, a child's perception, selective attention, learning, memory, language, personality, and cognition are sculpted. At the same time, the brain is capable of plasticity and can actually "sprout" and alter neural pathways to adjust to auditory and visual experiences. Repeated exposure to specific stimuli eventually mold the brain to selectively respond to those stimuli, while those pathways that might have responded to other stimuli drop out and die.

The study of cognitive development has resulted in the evolution of many theories about learning and the conceptual frameworks that correlate with those theories. Ensuing controversy over incompatible theories, as well as questions left unanswered, both frustrate and fascinate students. Most theories are based on observations of behaviors that can be related to age, maturity, and environment. Explanations typically hypothesize a link between observed behaviors and unobservable processes. For example, if an infant loses interest in a toy that has dropped off the highchair (the observed behavior—looks away or plays with something new), one can hypothesize that the child has not yet learned that objects still exist when out of sight of the observer (the process–object permanence). All models of cognitive development deal with how humans gather information, process it in both short-term and long-term memory, and relate it back in a relevant fashion to be used in determining and executing action.

Children appear to be born with the innate ability for learning, but this potential is developed only through interaction with the environment. Using their senses to gather and process information leads to the ability to understand relationships between themselves, objective reality, and the world at large. Furthermore, development of the intellect occurs jointly with physical growth, development of motor skills, language development, and learning social skills. Children progress serially through stages of cognitive development—learning skills and having insights in which ideas fit into their pictures of the world.

Case Study

ACCEPTANCE: INTERVIEW WITH MARSHA MOORE

When we were finally given a diagnosis for Michael, it was not good. The prognosis we were given was infantile autism with moderate to severe mental retardation. We were told that because we had a large family and much responsibility to our other children, we should consider applying for institutional placement for Michael in the state institution for the mentally handicapped. It would be several years before space would come available. Four or five years was a long time and by then we may be ready.

You know, to be honest, it was almost a relief to hear someone say that there was a place where "trained personnel" could take care of your child on an ongoing daily basis. After all, it was obvious that after a year of sleepless nights and frazzled emotions, we were not prepared to care for him! We thought about this possibility for less than a half hour. This was truly not an option for us. We never did put our name on the waiting list. I can't help sometimes wondering what our lives would be like if we had.

The time that we received Michael's diagnosis was the saddest time in our lives. Somehow, it seemed almost too painful to feel such deep sorrow for very long. It didn't hurt as much to be angry. Part of our anger focused on the medical establishment. What stupid, uncaring human beings they were! How could anyone even suggest institutionalizing this beautiful little boy of ours? How can they predict Michael's future? We'll show them. We will prove them wrong!

I also felt resentment and anger toward others who seemed to be enjoying their lives in ways I thought would never again be possible. Did they know how precious their "perfect" children were?

I put on a happy face for everyone outside the home, but often even a casual remark would hurt me deeply. Friends, who were trying to be upbeat, would tell me how lucky I was to "at

Michael Moore and his dad.

least" have five "other" beautiful healthy children, as if Michael was a puppy and the deformed runt of the litter or something, as if that should make me happy. To me, there was no consolation.

We worried about how our extended family would react, but they were all very supportive. I think my mom and dad knew how devastated we were, but I don't think my brother and sisters had a clue as to what our family was going through. We tried to keep a stiff upper lip when they'd call. We'd talk about other things and not really cry or complain or go into detail over the phone. I think everything was very gradual for them, seeing Michael over a period of time and realizing he wasn't changing.

After the diagnosis, I remember working for hours out in the yard and just crying and crying and crying. I felt sorry for myself, I felt sorry for Jim, I felt sorry that the kids would always have a retarded brother. I couldn't imagine how Mike

(continued)

would be when he was 10, just like I really can't imagine what he'll be like when he's 20. When you have a typical child, you imagine an adult and you assume he's going to be bright and handsome and charming. But with Michael, I was so fearful. What would he be like when he was 5 years old or 10 years old? The thought of having to bathe a 10-year-old child, having to change his diaper, and wipe his runny nose was almost scary. I thought, "I don't want this. This wasn't included in my grand scheme of life."

Michael is 10 now and I'm not horrified by his needs and he's not repulsive to me. It's just part of my routine in life. It doesn't mean that I don't ever feel discouraged and that I don't ever feel sad when I look at him and compare him to other little boys his age, but the sadness isn't as

intense now as it was in the beginning. I find so much more pleasure in just Mike and how he is right now. I just enjoy him for the dumb little things he does; like the smile that he gives me out of the corner of his eyes sometimes.

There is still the burden of taking care of a child with severe disabilities. Michael was up this morning at 4:30 A.M. and would not go back to sleep, so Jim brought him into bed with us. I can't sleep when the both of them are in bed with me. So I got up and I went to the grocery store this morning at 5:00 A.M. It's not what a typical family would be experiencing at this time in their life, but it's our life and I think you learn to just grow to enjoy and appreciate even the little things he does. I really can't imagine Mike any other way.

THEORIES OF COGNITION

Jean Piaget is the most well-known theorist associated with the **cognitive-developmental approach.** Piaget was originally trained as a biologist and applied many biological principles and methods to the study of human development. Many of the terms he introduced to psychology were drawn directly from biology (Slavin, 1994). He based his earliest theories on careful observation of his own three children. His theory is appreciated because of the ease in adapting constructs of the model to the descriptive observations of infants and their learning processes.

Piaget's model identified four distinct stages of cognitive development he referred to as sensorimotor, preoperational, concrete operational, and formal operational (see Table 4–7). Each stage is characterized by the emergence of new abilities and the reorganization of a child's thinking about the world. Piaget held that development precedes learning and that the developmental sequence for cognitive skills is largely fixed (Slavin, 1994).

The **sensorimotor stage** of development integrates gross and fine motor development with the senses of sight and hearing. This stage (birth to age 2) consists of simple learning governed by sensations. Primitive reflex activity progresses to repetitive activity and, later, to imitation. In the reflexive stage, repetitive action of the reflexes allows infants to eventually draw associations between their activity and a response. As an example, sucking (initially reflexive) on a nipple produces a milk flow and consequently leads to a feeling of fullness. Later, infants understand (have gained knowledge about) the relationship between the act of sucking and the outcome. Such experiences are used by the developing intellect as a foundation for advancing along a progressive course to the next stage.

Table 4-7   Piaget's Stages of Cognitive Development

Stage	Approximate Ages	Characteristics
Sensorimotor*	Birth to 2 years	**Reflex Activity** (0–1 mo.): Reflexive movement in sucking/swallowing, etc. **Primary Circular Reactions** (1–4 mo.): Repetition of movements becomes more coordinated toward end of period. **Secondary Circular Reactions** (4–8 mo.): Can focus on outside world; repetition of movements that produced interesting stimulation. **Coordination of Secondary Schemes** (8–12 mo.): Generalize use of acquired actions to solve new problems. **Tertiary Circular Reactions** (12–18 mo.): Exploration and experimentation of environment with previously learned schemes. **Invention of New Means Through Mental Combinations** (18–24 mo.): Ability to comprehend that one thing can represent another thing.
Preoperational	18 to 24 months – 7 years	**Stored Imagery or Representational Thought:** Characterized by deferred imitation. **Symbolic Ability:** Characterized by pretend play and language development. **Egocentrism:** unable to view the world from another's perspective.
Concrete Operations	6 to 8 years to 12 years	**Decentration:** Focus on several attributes of object simultaneously. **Reversability** of mental operations; Use of *logic* to solve problems; **Conservation:** Amount does not change with change in shape; **Relational thinking:** larger, shorter, etc.; Understands *hierarchical relationships* and that *objects can belong to more than one class.*
Formal Operations	12 years and up	**Versatile Flexible Thinking Process:** Reasoning about hypothetical problems; systematic searching for solutions to problems. Abstract thinking.

*Sensorimotor stage adapted from *Atypical Infant Development*, by M. J. Hanson, 1984, Austin, TX: PRO-ED. *Source:* From *Child Development and Personality*, by D. H. Mussen, J. J. Conger, J. Kagan, and A. C. Huston, 1990, New York: Harper Row.

This stage is the beginning of voluntary behavior. Deliberate activity begins when infants learn that certain behaviors can elicit specific responses. Accommodation begins with an infant incorporating and adapting actions with the recognition that certain activities produce a specific response. An infant may begin to cry upon hearing the voice of its mother, having learned from previous experience that the general response to crying is mother picking up and cuddling the infant. This is the beginning of the recognition of sequence and is an early experience with cause and effect.

It is later that both the quality and quantity of activity can be identified. Activities such as grasping progress to shaking (as with a rattle) that produces both movement and noise. An infant learns during this progression that degrees of shaking produce different qualities of sound. It is also during this time period that infants learn separateness from other objects in their environment and realize that their environment can be controlled by their own behavior. During this stage, infants demonstrate imitation, object permanence, and attachment, which are memory-related behaviors (Cohen & Gelber, 1975).

Imitation, the repetition of a sound or activity or both actions and sounds of another individual, implies there has been storage of information within an infant's brain. In fact, studies by Butterworth and Hopkins (1988) determined that infants probably have the capacity at birth for imitation; observations of even very young infants showed they can imitate the facial expressions of caregivers. This initially may be a reflexive activity, but through the progression of learning it is broadened and becomes more sustained to include not only expressions but also verbalization and motor activity.

Object permanence can be described as the demonstration of knowledge that an object exists even though it can no longer be seen. Infants between four months and 8 months will search for an object if it is at least partially exposed. Infants between 8 months and one year of age will seek out an object even if it cannot be visualized at all (Ault, 1977). For example, when a rattle is placed under a blanket, an 8- to 12-month-old infant recognizes that the rattle still exists and will actively attempt to remove the blanket and expose it. This implies that short-term memory functions and is being demonstrated on the basis that knowledge exists even without the reality of observation.

Attachment is also a strong indicator of memory in infants. Fear of strangers appears to develop between 6 and 8 months of age and involves recognition memory. This implies that infants draw from an experience base that recognizes the comfort in familiarity and a lack of trust in the unfamiliar. Whether this is based on sight, smell, or sound remains unclear, though it is obvious that long-term memory is being demonstrated (Seamon, 1980).

The last stage of Piaget's sensorimotor development precedes transition to the next level of learning. This stage occurs between 18 months and 2 years of age. Increased gross motor skills and past experience with achievements in behaviors increase an infant's ability to interact with the environment. An increased understanding of object permanence accompanies the initiation of intellectual reasoning. Infants can recognize that an object has singular properties that are separate from the individual possessing the object. An example of this ability is the recognition that a ball will roll even if not necessarily pushed by a person having possession of the ball. Infants at this stage begin to actively engage in manipulating their environment by attempting to remove barriers that detain them from reaching a desired goal. Toward the end of this period, expressive language skills are emerging that increase the ability of young children to successfully interact with their environment.

Piaget's **preoperational stage** in cognitive development (2–7 years) is characterized by rapid intellectual development. During this period of development, children view the world only in direct relationship to themselves. They seem to be unable to view a situation from a perspective other than their own, and their thinking processes are generally concrete. They are increasingly able to use language to express ideas and use toys symbolically to replace objects in play (e.g., using a broom as a "horse"). Finally, children in the preoperational stage begin to understand the relationships between size, time, and weight, and their thought processes are intuitive, based on just knowing without reasoning.

Though the final stages of Piaget's theory extend beyond early childhood, they are introduced here to show the longitudinal nature of his observations. **Concrete operations** (7–11 years) is the stage of logic. It is during this period that children can classify, sort, and organize facts about their world to use in problem solving. They continue to solve problems concretely based on perception since most have not yet developed abstract thinking. In looking at the development of memory in children at this stage, the processes of selective attention, strategies used for retention, and the duration of memory must be explored. There is no doubt that age makes a difference in the abilities of children to both attend to learning and remember what has been learned before. During this process, children also develop the ability to build on past memories and use their current environment for new learning.

Formal operations (11 years to adulthood) is the stage of adaptability, flexibility, and abstraction. During this stage, adolescents can make hypotheses and use them to think in theoretical and philosophical terms. These individuals are aware of the contradictions in life, can analyze them practically, and can act upon the conclusions.

Long-term memory ability in children is variable. Use of selective attention processes and strategies improves with age. For example, increasing evidence suggests that an infant's visual habituation, or the ability to focus without distraction, is a useful predictor of cognitive abilities in children (Hood & Murray, 1996). There is no comparison between the ability of children and adults to process information and recall the same information over time. Flavell (1971) and Flavell, Friedrichs, and Hoyt (1970) determined that maturation is necessary for the development of individual awareness about memory and the relationship of meaning to performance. However, Flavell et al. (1970) also determined that young children recognize their limitations. Through this determination, children learn how to use available resources to succeed in the learning process, which in turn allows them to become more adaptive to their environment (see Table 4–8).

As children age, their cognitive capabilities are typically referred to as intelligence. Though many myths surround intelligence as a construct, it is generally the collective ability to child's ability to reason, solve problems, and commit information to memory. The most misleading assumption about intelligence is that it is fixed at birth. In fact there are several factors that can greatly influence a child's ability. In fact, research indicates a steady rise in the IQ performance from generation to generation. This rise has been attributed to such factors as better nutrition, more schooling, better educated parents, and more complex environments including "smart" toys and computers (Ceci, 1996). While generational changes in IQ have significant implications for society, the changes themselves are unrelated to a biological change in human potential. Rather, it is clear that environmental manipulation can greatly enhance cognitive growth.

Table 4–8   Milestones of Cognitive Development

Age	Behavior
1 month	Responds to voices
	Inspects surroundings
4 months	Shows anticipatory excitement
	Plays with rattle
	Repeats new behaviors
	Plays with hands, feet
4–8 months	Repeats new behaviors
	Plays with hands, feet
	Finds partially hidden object
	Indicates continuation of play by repeating movement
	Touches adult to restart activity
	Reaches for second object
	Anticipates trajectory of object
	Imitates familiar action
	Finds hidden object
	Plays 2–3 minutes with single object
	Recognizes names of family
8–12 months	Imitates new action
	Responds to simple request with gestures (e.g. "point to _____")
	Uses "tool" to retrieve object
	Knows "no"
	Responds to simple verbal request
12–18 months	Enjoys looking at a book
	Shows understanding of category
	Places round, and later square, piece in puzzle
	Stacks toys
	Imitates "invisible" gesture
	Matches objects
	Points to named objects
	Brings objects from another room on request
	Identifies at least one body part
18–24 months	Points to pictures named
	Activates mechanical toys
	Plays with playdough and paints
	Matches object to pictures
	Sorts objects
	Understands personal pronouns and adjectives
	Matches sounds to photo of animals
24–36 months	Understands the concept of one
	Identifies clothing items for different occasions
	Engages in simple make believe play
	Matches shapes and colors
	Knows gender
	Identifies body parts with function
	Sorts shapes
	Completes 3–4 piece puzzle
	Begins to understand long and short

Table 4–8 *(continued)*

Age	Behavior
3 years	Completes 10% of a task with little supervision
	Counts to 3 orally
	Draws a circle in imitation
	Knows most prepositions
	Locates big and little
	Sorts by size
4 years	Remains on task for 10 minutes with distractions present
	Knows more and less, many and few
	Matches coins
	Draws a line between two parallel lines
	Places three simple pictures in a sequence
	Locates objects that don't belong
	Determines three ways that objects are similar or different
5 years	Completes 50–75% of task
	Determines when a task is done
	Names letters and alphabet sounds
	Counts orally to 10
	Names penny, nickel, and dime
	Reads and writes numerals to three
	Relates today, tomorrow, and yesterday to days of the week
	Copies letters and numbers
	Prints own name
	Colors within lines
	Makes judgments in time and speed
	Draws a picture to illustrate three pieces of information
	Reads simple three letter words paired with pictures
	Reads numerals on a clock face
	Names days of the week
	Counts orally to 100
	Draws a 3–6 part person

SOCIAL DEVELOPMENT

Social development governs the emergence of individual emotions and personality. Human beings are constantly involved in a dynamic relationship with other human beings and their environment. This involvement is essential for survival. People need social relationships in order to learn the rules for adapting to community norms that govern living within a society. Social rules, however, are not always constant across settings, culture or time. Part of social development is learning how to seek the information necessary to learn current rules and recognizing the steps that may be necessary when old rules change and new rules are adopted.

Such rules are learned through interactions with adults and other children. Among other factors, heredity, culture, economics, and the community differentially influence social development. Developmental delays can occur when infants and young children are seriously deprived of early social nurturance by caregivers. Through nurturance, caregivers provide reliable stimulation to the senses, establishing a mechanism for the development of a trust relationship. This reciprocal confidence in primary caregivers is the first step toward being able to expand and develop other attachment relationships. In more dramatic cases, infants who do not experience "mothering" with some sort of consistency fail to gain weight regardless of appropriate caloric intake, are lethargic, and do not show a normal developmental progression. Some of these infants may even die if the emotional isolation occurs over a long enough period of time.

Infants initially require an individual caregiver to provide a relationship in which learning the social rules occurs. Providing the cues for what will be the personality development of an infant, this nurturing person (or persons) represents a major influence in early infancy. This influence frequently remains as one of the most significant relationships throughout the life span of a person.

Social skills appear at an early age with the ability of an infant to recognize family members. These skills continue to mature throughout one's life span as different social skills are necessary at different ages. For example, it is acceptable for toddlers to hug family members and acquaintances lavishly, but in adolescence, such displays of affection are usually viewed as immature. Normal social development is achieved when an individual exercises the rules of social conduct acceptable for a given age, gender, economic status, and culture.

Human beings are accustomed to receiving "rewards" for appropriate social behaviors. This is a learned response from early infancy, when interactions between infants and significant caregivers include feedback of a physical nature that becomes associated with an activity generally perceived as pleasurable. As an example, an infant initially responds physically by body movement and then with vocalization upon hearing the caregiver approach, and this activity results in the infant being picked up and cuddled. Infants soon learn which of their behaviors initiate desired responses in caregivers and incorporate these activities into their interactions with other human beings.

A transition takes place at about 18 months, when toddlers become very mobile. Mothers' responses to infants change from primarily positive to more instructive and prohibitive ("no") (Lipari, 2000). In fact, these interactions are important to neurological development, when the sequence of the interaction does not end in "shame." Episodes where children go from excitement to sudden deflation (at "no") to recovery in a relatively brief interval stimulate the orbitofrontal portion of the brain (cognition) and the limbic system (emotional) and improve their connectivity to each other. Consequently, an emotional resiliency develops where young children develop the ability to regulate their emotions and their impulses.

Young children with disabilities are at risk for the development of distorted social skills. Because all developmental areas are interlinked, an impairment in one area can significantly alter the ability of an infant or child to initiate or respond to interactions in ways that build or maintain social relationships. Physical impairments, such as cerebral palsy, may prohibit postures or gestures that progress to social interactions. Oberservations of children with visual impairments indicate that their ability to see affects functional play (use of toys or objects as a representation of real objects) but not symbolic play (substituting a toy in form or function by attributing imaginary quality) (Lewis, Norgate, Collis, & Reynolds, 2000). The later is necessary for language acquisition, while both affect a child's ability to engage in social play. Caregivers need to learn to read the signals of infants or children with disabilities and use these signals in their interactions with the child. Teaching families relevant mechanisms to establish relationships with their disabled children is one of the initial responsibilities of an early childhood educator.

As in other areas of human development, research and understanding of social development are influenced by theory. For example, Erik Erikson (1968, 1980), posited that humans progress through eight discrete stages of psychosocial development. Each stage represents contrasting constructs that form a continuum. That is, at the beginning of each stage, a person's psychosocial behavior is negative or immature; by the end of each stage, desirable resolution has occurred. At each stage, individuals can be characterized as "working to resolve" the contrasting elements. For example, infants are working to resolve mistrust into trust of other humans.

SOCIAL PLAY

Play is the medium through which infants and toddlers acquire and execute social relationships. It is within play activities that people behave just to enjoy or amuse themselves. Yet play is a significant precursor for both physical and mental growth and for the acquisition of normal social maturation. Playing is a form of self-expression and is required in the normal dynamic of growth as a significant part of social development (see Table 4–9). McKimmey (1993) claimed that, in addition to facilitating language, social play helps children learn sympathy, empathy, the difference between feelings and actions, ability to focus, and other social skills.

Play is universal and crosses all the physical and social boundaries of the world (Piers, 1972). Activities that are both fantasy and real constitute play. Play can be individual or collective, can involve a small or large group, and can occur anywhere and at any time. Play activities can be divided into three general groups: motor (physical exercise, action toys, etc.), intellectual (mental activities such as card and board games), and sensory (spectator activities, such as track meets, ball games, etc.). Very young children, between 2 and 4 years of age, generally prefer to engage in motor play activities.

Though some claim that neonates have little personality, observations of newborns reveal that they begin to engage in simple play within hours of birth. As mentioned earlier, reciprocal interactions involving facial expressions, eye movements, and sounds begin very early and serve as reinforcers to caregivers, who are drawn to this "playful" little being. Infant interactions with their environment generally remain within the context of relationships with their primary caregivers. Social-affective play may involve stretching or turning an infant's arms or legs, patting or stroking, and presenting bright objects or introducing sounds to elicit responses, such as cooing (Hughes, 1975; Johnson & Medinnus, 1974; Neisworth & Bagnato, 1987). An infant's typical response to social play is pleasure that is derived from nurturing relationships with familiar people. Thus, play provides a context for learning that emotional responses from caregivers can be provoked by

Table 4–9   Milestones of Social-Play Development

Age	Behavior
1–6 months	Smiles
	Regards face
	Establishes eye contact
	Laughs
	Discriminates strangers
6–12 months	Enjoys frolic play
	Lifts arms to mother
	Shows separation anxiety
	Cooperates in social games
	Tests parental reactions during bedtime
	Likes to be in constant sight and hearing of an adult
12–18 months	Difficult to discipline independent behavior
	Displays frequent tantrums
	Needs and expects routines
	Shows a sense of humor
	Tends to be messy
	Enjoys being the center of attention
	Hugs and kisses parents
18–24 months	Shows jealousy at attention to others
	Desires control of others
	Enjoys solitary play
	Attempts to comfort others in distress
2 years	Distinguishes self as separate person
	Strongly possessive, dependent, clings, and whines
	Frustration tantrums peak
	Parallel play
	Values own property and uses the word "mine"
	Begins to obey and respect simple rules
	Takes pride in own achievements and resists help
3 years	Plays games with another person
	Takes turns in games 25–50% of the time
	Responds and makes verbal greetings
	Plays with one or two others
	Cooperates with others in group activities
4 years	Behaves according to the desires of others
	Volunteers
	Conforms to group decisions
	Takes turns in games 75% of the time
	Verbalizes feelings before physical aggression
5 years	Tries again after change or disappointment
	Leaves provoking situations
	Sacrifices immediate reward for delayed reward
	Accepts friendly teasing
	Comforts a playmate in distress
	Cooperates in group games with loose rules
	Protects other children and animals
	Offers help to others voluntarily

smiling, cooing, and other such behaviors. In fact, some refer to play as "the work" of young children (MacDonald, 1989).

Once infants have begun to develop voluntary motor skills, play progresses to acquiring new skills. Manipulating objects repetitively brings repeated pleasure that commonly accompanies success. On the other hand, play can produce frustration when attempts to learn new skills are not immediately successful (Brooks-Gunn & Lewis, 1982). By the time infants reach 1 year of age, they are able to participate in imitative games. These may include repetitive games, such as pat-a-cake, itsy-bitsy spider, and peek-a-boo. Such games generally involve an infant and an adult, but they are setting the stage for the later initiation of play with other children.

Though these initial social relationships are necessary to the development of social skills, children generally learn many of the rules of social conduct from other children. Peers are less tolerant of deviations from an established standard than are adults who can reason beyond what is obvious. Social play in the preschool years can be categorized into five sequential stages: solitary play, spectator play, parallel play, associative play, and cooperative play (Cass, 1971). The rate of progress at which an individual child transcends these stages is dependent upon both the opportunities a child has for interactions and the integrity of the social contacts that are available.

In some cases, children with greater economic stability may have the advantage because more social contacts are arranged to provide the opportunities for

Mother and child engage in social-affective play.

engaging play experiences and may allow for a more rapid progression. For example, in established supervised play groups, parents have the means to take the initiative in providing toys and games that promote peer interactions.

Solitary play involves both isolation and independence. This play experience can involve an individual child within the same physical area as a group of children. Children involved in solitary play are involved with their own activities and their own group of toys. They enjoy the physical presence of other children but do not speak to other children, nor do they attempt to decrease the physical distance between play areas. They also show no interest in the activities of other children that differ from their own activities. Young children will also engage in solitary play in their own homes while with a caregiver. Though engaging in independent play, a child may frequently move the activity to the vicinity of the caregiver.

Spectator play is also frequently referred to as onlooker play. This occurs when a young child observes the play activities of other children but makes no attempt to enter in the activity. This play may involve conversation about the nature of the activity between the observer and child involved.

Parallel play also involves independent play between children in a group. Children play with toys that are like those of the children around them but of their own choosing and in their own fashion. This play involves children playing be-

Toddlers frequently engage in parallel play.

side each other but not with each other. Toddlers frequently engage in parallel play, which is consistent with their world view that objects have properties independent of involvement. Additionally, toddlers' language development is just beginning to allow for verbal expression in social context.

Associative play occurs between the ages of 3 to 4 years. Individual children will play with other children, engaging in similar or even identical activities. Without adult facilitation, associative play generally lacks organization. Though toys may be shared, each member acts without regard for the group wishes, since no group goal has been established. When an individual child initiates an activity, the entire group typically will follow this lead. During this stage, there may be occasional attempts by individual children to control both group behavior and group membership. Four-year-olds begin to establish strong preferences for associates and may begin to have a "best friend." This "friend" may change frequently during the course of a play experience, depending upon the direction of the play. Hence, children have learned initial strategies to gain power over other children; yet these young children are incapable of wielding power wisely. For example, it is typical of children of this age to be bossy and selfish, to begin to taunt and name-call, and to boast and bend the truth a little.

Cooperative play occurs when activities are organized. Children involved in cooperative play are engaged in a goal-directed activity that has been planned by the group to accomplish some defined end. Formal games become important during this stage, and the end goal frequently involves some competition. Group members have designated roles that are generally both assigned and directed by one or two accepted "leaders" of the group. Even at this age, children develop a great sense of either belonging or not belonging to cooperative play groups. During this final stage of play development, there may be gender splits with children seeking membership in same-sex groups.

Play enhances skill development in both motor activities and emotional development. Active play develops muscle control, cognitive development, and socialization. Through play, children learn about their physical world and its relationship to themselves. Intellectual stimulation is provided through manipulation of shapes and work with texture, color, and size.

Perhaps most importantly, play is the most effective medium through which children develop language (McKimmey, 1993). As early as 18 months, toddlers begin to pretend, demonstrating an awareness of symbolic thought—a prerequisite of language. Children can experiment with abstract thought through fantasy and fabrication within the acceptable context of creativity without being diverted by conformity to a norm of the society. Play becomes less spontaneous and more structured with age.

Because children are not as tolerant of violations of codes within their own play group, externally initiated codes of behavior for the group facilitate learning of acceptable social behaviors. Hence, children who are culturally different adjust more easily to new social situations when dramatic play is a part of the curriculum (McKimmey, 1993). Truth, honesty, fair play, self-control, and leadership skills are learned within the group and provide an important mechanism for teaching the standards of the society and personal accountability for individual actions.

Case Study THE DIARY OF ESTHER ANNA BERKE: MONTH 5

March 16–30: No major changes occurred during this time. Esther continued to eat well and gain weight but had multiple seizures each day. Most seizures appeared to be painless, but one kind must hurt because it makes her cry. The doctor altered her medication again, now her daily dosage is 0.8 ml Depakine, 1 g Sabril, and 0.33 mg Rivotril. We have also started her on 250 mg of Vitamin B_6 (pyridoxine) each day. Some people have obtained dramatic relief from seizures with this vitamin. We haven't seen any effect yet, so we will increase the dose and see if that helps.

April 1–15: Esther weighed 6.5 kg on her 5-month birthday, for a total gain of 2 kg since she was born and 1.3 kg in the last month alone. She is now 66 cm long. This is at the 50th percentile for weight and the 80th percentile for length for her age, so she is getting bigger! We took her off Depakine, it made her very sleepy and didn't seem to help control the seizures. We also boosted her Vitamin B_6 to 275 mg each day.

SELF-HELP SKILLS

Self-help skills include independent feeding, dressing, toileting, and personal responsibility (see Table 4–10). The term **adaptive skills** also refers to the same set of behaviors and either term may be used by various assessment tools and curriculum packages. The acquisition of skills that enable children to interact independently with their environment is linked closely to both motor development and cognitive skill development. For example, children will not independently use the toilet until they:

1. Have gained sufficient muscle control to stay dry for an hour or two at a time
2. Can move themselves to the toilet
3. Are cognitively aware of the "signs" of urgency to void
4. Know what action to take to avoid an "accident"

Historically, planning for instruction of self-help skills has followed a strict developmental model, but more recent research illustrates that skills once thought to be prerequisites could be skipped for children with significant developmental disabilities. While recognizing this, the following description of self-help skills is based upon knowledge of typical developmental patterns.

Table 4–10 Milestone of Self-Help

1–4 months	Coordinates sucking, swallowing, and breathing
	Recognizes bottle
4–8 months	Swallows strained or pureed foods
	Feeds self a cracker
	Holds own bottle
8–12 months	Drinks from held cup
	Finger feeds
	Sleeps 10–12 hours
	Cooperates in dressing
12–18 months	Cooperates in washing and drying
	Undoes bows and snaps
	Has regular bowel movements
	Indicates when wet or soiled
	Cooperates in dressing
18–24 months	Sits on "Potty Chair"
	Unzips, zips, removes unlaced shoes
	Washes and dries hands partially
	Helps with simple household tasks
	Food preferences apparent
24–36 months	Delays sleeping by demanding things
	Understands and stays away from common dangers
	Undresses with assistance
	Washes hands and brushes teeth
	Uses toilet with assistance, daytime control
4 years old	Takes responsibility for toileting
	Serves self and helps set table
	Dresses with supervision
	Uses spoon and fork well
	Uses toilet regularly without asking
	Puts comb and brush in hair
	Puts shoes on correct feet
	Knows front from back
5 years old	Drinks from water fountain, serves self and carries tray
	Carries liquid in open container without spilling
	Wipes self after toileting
	Uses comb/brush, washes face and ears in bath and dries with towel
	Zips up front opening of clothing
	Dresses and undresses functionally without being told
6 years old	Cuts and spreads with knife, cuts with knife and fork
	Independently washes and dries hands after toileting
	Bathes, showers, and "cleans up" independently
	Washes own hair
	Selects and uses clean and protective clothing
	Ties shoes
	Turns clothing right side out
	Uses proper brushing strokes (toothbrush)

Source: Adapted from "Behavioral Competencies and Outcomes: The Effects of Disorders," by M. J. Hanson and M. F. Hanline, 1984, in M. J. Hanson (Ed.), *Atypical Infant Development* (pp. 109–142). Austin, TX: PRO-ED.

INDEPENDENT EATING AND DRINKING SKILLS

As in all other areas of development, a neonate eats and drinks reflexively only, though parents might swear there is some intent involved when a hungry infant wakes parents throughout the night and keeps them further vigilant during the day with demands to be fed. This aspect of child care can be exhausting for parents, as infants demand food five to eight times a day, requiring approximately 30 minutes for each feeding.

Though the sucking reflex is present at birth, it is not until infants are 4 months old that they suck voluntarily with enthusiasm and vigor. Young infants consume exclusively liquid diets of either breastmilk or formula for the first 4 to 6 months. At about this time, infants begin to take some responsibility for eating by holding their bottle. Simultaneously, solid pureed foods will be tolerated, though infants may remain very passive, not offering to close their lips around the spoon or to push food from the front of the tongue toward the back of their mouth.

A dramatic transition of independence takes place at about 8 months of age. Infants, who now have well-developed fine motor skills, will drink from cups with help, will feed themselves finger foods (crackers, etc.), and may refuse to drink from their bottles. Very "grown up" now, these infants should be on the same eating schedule as adults, though, like adults, enjoying between-meal snacks.

By age 2, toddlers are often independent eaters and drinkers. However, this does not mean that they can do so with grace. Using a spoon, toddlers can feed themselves. However, this level of independence is often paired with independent decision making. It is not uncommon for toddlers to maintain a narrow range of food preferences or to go through stages where they eat very little.

Child self-feeding.

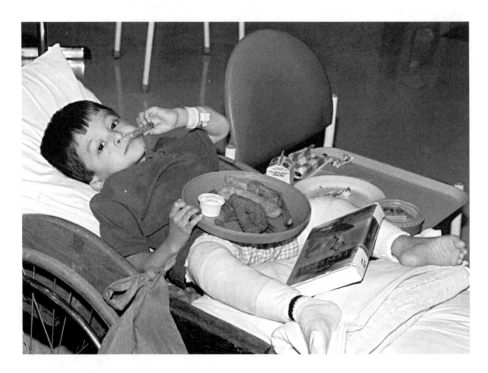

Three-year-olds eat well with a spoon and may be able to use a fork to stab foods. These youngsters now display some very sophisticated skills at the table, serving themselves drinks or portions of food. Additionally, vegetables become a food to avoid. Independence in the use of utensils is achieved by 4 years of age. Four-year-olds also enjoy helping prepare meals and are able independently to make simple meals, such as cereal and toast, by age 5.

DRESSING SKILLS

The first indication that infants are thinking about dressing skills is when they begin to tug at their feet and incidentally pull off socks or shoes. At about the same time, approximately 9 months, significant progress in dressing is made when infants assist with dressing by lifting their arms to remove or put on a shirt, stepping into a pair of suspended pants or shoes, and holding still during diapering. Since undressing is easier, toddlers take off jackets, shoes, socks, and unbuttoned pants at about 18 months. Though they will try earlier, children have little success in dressing even in articles of clothing that are easy to put on (pants, loose shoes) until they are about 2 years of age. A 2-year-old may learn to fasten large buttons and small front buttons by 3 years of age. Zippers and buckles are more difficult fine motor tasks that may be mastered at age 4 or 5. Usually by the time children are 4, they will be able to dress by themselves, though it is not until age 5 that most dressing errors (putting clothes on backwards or inside out) are recognized and self-corrected. Complex dressing tasks such as tying shoes and fixing stuck zippers emerge at 5 years of age but may not be mastered until age 6 or 7.

TOILETING SKILLS

Toilet training begins at birth, as muscle control is gradually gained. A very young infant is seldom dry, dribbling small quantities of urine almost constantly. Gradually, muscle control permits infants to sustain first brief, and then longer, periods of dryness. By 8 months, infants begin to stay dry for reasonable lengths of time and may communicate their recognition of "wetness" by pulling at their diapers. Parents should not, however, consider toilet training until at least 18 months or later if a child does not stay dry for an hour or more.

One index of sufficient bladder control is whether toddlers remain dry during their naps. Bowel control is more easily achieved than bladder control, as infants begin to have routine bowel movements one or two times a day by 8 months of age. Training for bowel control can begin at 12 months and may be accomplished as early as 18 months. This process is often not completed until age 3, though it is typically more easily accomplished by girls than boys. By 5 years of age, children can be expected to independently care for all toileting needs, including wiping and washing hands afterwards.

PERSONAL RESPONSIBILITY

Children can be expected from an early age to begin to take on responsibility for themselves. Toddlers, for example, can follow directions to pick up their toys, though this behavior might not become habitual until some years later.

Two-year-olds will put their coats away regularly when the routine is expected. By 3 years of age, children can take on a variety of responsibilities, such as wiping up spills, helping to clear the table, and placing dirty clothes in a hamper.

Parents should begin brushing an infant's teeth as soon as the primary teeth begin erupting. As infants gain sufficient fine motor control, parents can ask infants to attempt to imitate tooth brushing. Though cleanliness is not the goal, as caregivers follow after children and brush with precision, children learn valuable patterns of routine daily care. Bathing and washing are similar responsibilities that can be transferred to young children. By age 4, children should be able to bathe themselves and brush their teeth with acceptable proficiency. While 4-year-olds are unpredictable, 5-year-olds are generally happy to assist in the completion of jobs around the home. Given chores, children tend to be cooperative and reliable.

THE FUTURE OF HUMAN DEVELOPMENT

Knowledge and practice in the next few decades will be dramatically influenced by changes in technology in ways that we cannot begin to predict. Theories of human development will change more rapidly as technology enables researchers

A child involved in motor planning.

to investigate and solve riddles previously inaccessible to observation. In the past, cognitive, linguistic, and social behaviors have been largely explained by guesses about what goes on underneath one's skin, rather than by knowledge of actual neurological or endrocrinological processes. Now, we know that the brain, in particular, is at peak capacity for learning during the very period of interest in this text. In addition to nutrition, nurturance and secure relationships with an adult(s) stimulate brain growth, which is in turn related to children's social and cognitive development. With increased understanding of the importance of these early years, policymakers must be compelled to invest in bringing educational services to all families of very young children (Lewis, 1997). There is little doubt that comprehensive early childhood education will help to level the field for families across economic lines.

Based on this new knowledge, early childhood educators can help families to select and design programs that more reliably influence children's acquisition of desirable behaviors. Concomitantly, professionals will need to learn more about family systems, so that we are able to respond sensitively and effectively to diverse characteristics. This issue is infinitely more complex and intractable than the mind-boggling changes in technology that we are likely to encounter in the coming decades.

Technology is also likely to influence children's development in a more direct way. Increasingly, human activities are interwoven with computers. Computers have and will continue to take over traditional routines of daily life. It is possible that such basic activities as reading, teaching, and shopping will be replaced by computers. These changes will not only influence what children need to learn, but they can also influence if and how they will learn. That is, if children's early learning experiences vary significantly because of interactions with technology, their neural pathways will become hardwired differently than today's youth, who have had different kinds of experiences.

All of these changes will take place without our having gained an understanding of the importance of early experiences. For example, is it necessary for children to learn to read? Even if technology replaces this skill, will the loss of literacy affect future generations' chances of survival? Will the neural pathways used to read be formed in other ways, or will these pathways be replaced by other hardwiring more adaptive to the demands of the 21st century? The risk we have taken, without the consent of children, is that some types of early learning experiences will be critical for survival—but not sustained because of our fascination with technology.

STUDY GUIDE QUESTIONS

1. In what areas of development must educators have knowledge?
2. Briefly explain development during the embryonic stage.
3. Describe development of the fetus throughout the fetal stage.
4. What are the requirements for a viable fetus?
5. Why do different children grow at different rates?
6. Would you expect the same pattern of growth across all children? Explain.

7. List and explain the three universal developmental patterns of growth governing motor development.
8. Why is continual monitoring of physical growth important in the early years of life?
9. What is the function of the cardiovascular system and its relationship to the respiratory system?
10. Explain the function of the renal system.
11. Why is the gastrointestinal system important to physical growth?
12. Describe the relationship between myelinization and neurological development.
13. How is bone maturation related to growth?
14. How is physical growth measured?
15. Describe a "normal" newborn in the first days of life.
16. What would be a "normal" infancy growth pattern?
17. Devise your own theory of child development, and be sure to cite previous theorists when elements of your theory are aligned with those of prominent theorists described in this chapter.
18. According to MacDonald (1992), what does emotional warmth or affection provide for humans? What may result if a child does not experience such affection?
19. In what way is child development sequential and universal?
20. Explain the remarkable plasticity of the human brain.
21. What is the theory of peak periods of learning?
22. Briefly explain how the following influence a child's development: family configuration and lifestyle, and child care.
23. Several factors influence bonding. Name three of these.
24. There are several educational factors believed to influence a child's growth. List five of these factors.
25. Why is it important to evaluate a child's development according to relevant culture, rather than according to dominant culture?
26. Describe the sequence and age milestones of hip control.
27. Explain the progression of development from reflex to reaching to grasping.
28. What are the five principles of language development?
29. Explain the three aspects of language considered when discussing form.
30. Briefly outline the general development of phonological skills and sentence structure.
31. What is a morpheme? How do we measure the sophistication of language?
32. Describe the receptive language abilities of a child around the following ages: 1 year, 18 months, 2 years, 3 years, 6 years.
33. As children begin to develop expressive language, actions and objects dominate their early vocabulary. Explain why this may be so.
34. Describe a child's language use at the following ages: neonate, 12 months, 2 years, 3 years, and 6 years.
35. Define cognition.
36. Describe the four phases of Piaget's model of cognitive development.
37. Define accommodation.
38. What is the importance of imitation in cognitive development?

39. Define attachment.
40. Name three factors that may influence social development.
41. Identify and discuss the five stages of play.
42. How do children learn social behavior through play?
43. List the traditional skills that fall into the domain of self-help.
44. Describe a child's eating and drinking repertoire at the following ages: 4–6 months, 8 months, 2 years, 3 years, 4 years, 5 years.
45. Describe a child's dressing skills at the following ages: 9 months, 18 months, 2 years, 4 years, 5+ years.
46. When should training of bowel and bladder begin?

REFERENCES

Allen, E. A., & Marotz, L. (1989). *Developmental profiles: Birth to six.* Albany: Delmar.

Andrick, G. R., & Tager-Flusberg H. (1986). The acquisition of colour terms. *Journal of Child Language, 13,* 119–134.

Ault, R. (1977). *Children's cognitive development.* New York: Oxford University Press.

Bandura, A. (1971). *Social learning theory.* New York: General Learning Press.

Baecher, C. M. (1983). *Children's consumerism: Implications for education.* Paper presented at the Bush Center in Child Development and Social Policy, Yale University, New Haven, CT.

Beck, F., Moffatt, D., & Lloyd, J. (1973). *Human embryology and genetics.* Oxford: Blackwell Scientific Publications.

Bedore, L. M., & Leonard, L. B. (1998). Specific language impairment and grammatical morphology: A discriminant function analysis. *Journal of Speech, Language, and Hearing Research, 41,* 1185–1193.

Beentjes, J. W., & VanderVoort, T. H. (1988). Television's impact on children's reading skills. *Reading Research Quarterly, 23,* 389–413.

Bertoncini, J., Bijelac-Babic, B., Jusczyk., P. W., Kennedy, L. J., & Mahler, J. (1988). An investigation of young infants' perceptual representations of speech sounds. *Journal of Experimental Psychology, 117,* 21–33.

Bigge, J. (1991). *Teaching individuals with physical and multiple disabilities* (3rd ed.) Upper Saddle River, NJ: Merrill/Prentice Hall.

Bowlby, J. (1958). The nature of the child's tie to his mother. *International Journal of Psychoanalysis, 39,* 350–393.

Bowlby, J. (1960). Grief and mourning in infancy and early childhood. *Psychoanalytic Study of the Child, 15,* 9–52.

Bowlby, J. (1969). *Attachment and loss.* London: The Hogarth Press.

Braine, M. C. (1963). The ontogeny of English phrase structures: The first phrase. *Language, 39,* 1–13.

Bronfenbrenner, U. (1977). Toward an experimental ecology of human development. *American Psychologist, 32,* 513–531.

Bronfenbrenner, U. (1979). Contexts of child rearing: Prospects and problems. *American Psychologist, 34,* 844–850.

Brooks-Gunn, J., & Lewis, M. (1982). Affective exchanges between normal and handicapped infants and their mothers. In T. M. Field & A. Fogel (Eds.), *Emotion and early interaction* (pp. 161–188). Hillsdale, NJ: Earlbaum.

Buchholz, E. S. (Sept., 1997). Even infants need their solitude. *Brown University Child & Adolescent Behavior Letter, 13*(9), 1–3.

Burchinal, M. R., Roberts, J. E., Hoopers, S., & Zeisel, S. A. (2000). Cumulative risk and early cognitive development: A comparison of statistical risk models. *Developmental Psychology, 36,* 793–807.

Bussey, K., & Bandura, A. (1992). Self-regulatory mechanisms governing gender development. *Child Development, 63,* 1236–1250.

Butterworth, G., & Hopkins, B. (1988). Hand-mouth coordination in the newborn baby. *British Journal of Developmental Psychology, 6,* 303–314.

Butterworth, G., & Morissette, P. (1996). Onset of pointing and the acquisition of language in infancy. *Journal of Reproductive and Infant Psychology, 14,* 219–232.

Campbell, F. A., Pungello, E. P., Miller-Johnson, S., Burchinal, M. & Ramey, C. T. (2001). The development of cognitive and academic abilities: Growth curves from an early childhood education experiement. *Developmental Psychology, 37,* 231–242.

Casasola, M., & Cohen, L. B. (2000). Infants' association of linguistic labels with causal actions. *Developmental Psychology, 36,* 155–168.

Cass, J. (1971). *Helping children grow through play.* New York: Schocken Books.

Ceci, S. J. (1996). *On Intelligence: A bio-ecological treatise on intellectual development.* Boston: Harvard University Press.

Chaudhary, N., & Suparna, N. (1991). Early language learning in a multilingual environment. *Early Child Development and Care, 76,* 135–143.

Cohen, L., & Gelber, R. (1975). *Infant visual memory.* In L. Cohen & P. Salapatek (Eds.), *Infant perception: From sensation to cognition, Vol I.* New York: Academic Press.

Coll, C., G., Buckner, J. C., Brooks, M. G., & Wei, L. F. (1998). The developmental status and adaptive behavior of homeless and low-income housed infants and toddlers. *American Journal of Public Health, 88,* 1371–1373.

Dahn, L., & James, L. (1972). Newborn temperature and calculated heat loss in the delivery room. *Pediatrics, 49,* 504–506.

Davis, B. E., Moon, R. Y., Sachs, H. C., & Ottolini, M. C. (1998). Effects of sleep position on infant motor development. *Pediatrics, 102,* 1135–1141.

Erel, O., Oberman, Y., & Yirmiya, N. (2000). Maternal versus nonmaternal care and seven domains of children's development. *Psychological Bulletin, 126,* 727–747.

Erikson, E. H. (1963). *Childhood and society* (2nd ed.). New York: W. W. Norton.

Erikson, E. H. (1968). *Identity, youth and crisis.* New York: Norton.

Erikson, E. H. (1980). *Identity and the life cycle* (2nd ed.). New York: Norton.

Festschrift, C. (July, 1994). Primitive reflexes: Their contribution to the early detection of cerebral palsy. *Clinical Pediatrics, 33*(7), pp. 388–398.

Finn, M. (1977). *The politics of nutrition education.* Unpublished dissertation, Ohio State University, Columbus.

Flavell, J. (1971). First discussant's comments: What is memory development the development of? *Human Development, 14,* 272–278.

Flavell, J., Friedricks, A., & Hoyt, J. (1970). Developmental changes in memorization processes. *Cognitive Psychology, 1,* 324–340.

Gabbard, C., & Hart, S. (1995). A note on trichotomous classification of handedness and fine-motor performance in children. *Journal of Genetic Psychology, 156,* 97–105.

Gay, S. (1998). *Freud: A life for our times.* New York: W. W. Norton & Co.

Gesell, A., & Thompson, H. (1934). *Infant behavior: Its genesis and growth.* New York: McGraw-Hill.

Gopnik, A., & Meltzoff, A. N. (1992). Categorization and naming: Basic-level sorting in eighteen-month-olds and its relation to language. *Child Development, 63,* 1091–1103.

Guo, G. (1998). The time of the influences of cumulative poverty on children's cognitive abilty and achievement. *Social Forces, 77,* 257–282.

Hart, B., & Risley, T. R. (1995). *Meaningful differences in everyday experiences in young American children.* Toronto: Paul H. Brookes Pub.

Henggeler, S. W., Cohen, R., Edwards, J. J., Summerville, M. B., & Ray, G. E. (1991). Family stress as a link in the association between television viewing and achievement. *Child Study Journal, 21,* 1–10.

Hoffman, L. W. (1989). Effects of maternal employment in the two-parent family. *American Psychologist, 44,* 283–292.

Hood, B. M., & Murray, L. (1996). Habituation changes in early infancy: Longitudinal measures from birth to 6 months. *Journal of Reproductive & Infant Psychology, 14,* 177–186.

Huesmann, L. R., Moise-Titus, J., Podolski, C. L., & Eron, L. D. (2003). Longitudinal relations between children's exposure to TV violence and their aggressive and violent behavior in young adulthood: 1977–1992. *Developmental Psychology, 39,* 201–221.

Hughes, J. (1975). *Synopsis of pediatrics* (4th ed.). St. Louis: C. V. Mosby Co.

Johnson, R., & Medinnus, G. (1974). *Child psychology: Behavior and development* (3rd ed.). New York: Wiley & Sons, Inc.

Joseph, R. (2000) Fetal brain behavior and cognitive development. *Developmental Review, 20,* 81–98.

Kennedy, J. H. (1992). Relationship of maternal beliefs and childrearing strategies to social competence in preschool children. *Child Study Journal, 22,* 39–60.

Klink, M., & Klink, W. (1990). The influence of father caretaker speech on early language development: A case study. *Early Child Development and Care, 62,* 7–22.

Kornhaber, M., & Marcos, H. (2000). Young children's communication with mothers and fathers: Functions and content. *British Journal of Developmental Psychology, 18,* 187–210.

Landry, S. H., Swank, P. R., Assel, M. A., Smith, K. E., & Vellet, S. (2001). Does early responsive parenting have a special importance for children's development or is consistency across early childhood necessary? *Developmental Psychology, 37,* 387–483.

Lester, B. M., & Brazelton, T. B. (1982). Cross-cultural assessment of neonatal behavior. In D. A. Wagner & H. W. Stevenson (Eds.), *Cultural perspectives on child development.* San Francisco: Freeman.

Leventhal, T., & Brooks-Gunn, J. (2000). The neighborhoods they live in: The effects of neighborhood residence on child and adolescent outcomes. *Psychological Bulletin, 126*, 309–337.

Lewis, A. C. (1997). Learning our lessons about early learning. *Phi Delta Kappan, 78*, 591–593.

Lewis, V., Norgate, S., Collis, G., & Reynolds, R. (2000). The consequences of visual impairment for children's symbolic functional play. *British Journal of Developmental Psychology, 18*, 449–464.

Lipari, J. (2000, July/August). Four things you need to know about raising baby. *Psychology Today*, pp. 39–43.

MacArthur, F. (1990). Miscommunication, language development and enculturation in L. P. Hartley's "The Go Between." *Style, 24* (1), 103–112.

MacDonald, K. (1992). Warmth as a developmental construct: An evolutionary analysis. *Child Development, 63*, 753–773.

McDonald, J. D. (1989). *Becoming partners with children: From play to conversation*. San Antonio, TX: Special Press.

McCormick, S., & Schiefelbusch, R. L. (1990). *Early language development*. Upper Saddle River, NJ: Merrill/Prentice Hall.

McKimmey, M. A. (1993). Child's play is serious business. *Children Today, 22*(2), 14–15.

McLaughlin, T. F., & Vacha, E. F. (1992). The social, structural, family, school, and personal characteristics of at-risk students: Policy recommendations for school personnel. *The Journal of Education, 174*(3), 9–25.

Monahan, S. C., Buchanan, C. M., Maccoby, E. E., & Dornbusch, S. M. (1993). Sibling differences in divorced families. *Child Development, 64*, 152–168.

Morgan, J. L. (November, 1996). Knowing isn't saying: Early receptive language abilities. *Brown University Child & Adolescent Letter, 12*(11), pp. 1–4.

Nielson, A. C. (1988). *Nielson report on television*. Northbrook, IL: Author.

Neisworth, T., & Bagnato, S. (1987). *The young exceptional child: Early development and education*. New York: Macmillan Publishing Co.

Orlin, M. N., & Effgen, S. K. (1997). Effect of otitis media with effusion on gross motor ability in preschool-aged children: Preliminary findings. *Pediatrics, 99*, 334–338.

Oviatt, S. L. (1982). Inferring what words mean: Early development in infant's comprehension of common object names. *Child Development, 53*, 274–277.

Paul, R., & Alforde, S. (1993). Grammatical morpheme acquisition in 4-year-olds with normal, impaired, and late-developing language. *Journal of Speech and Hearing Research, 36*, 1271–1276.

Pearl, D., Bouthilet, L., & Lazar, S. J. (Eds.). (1982). *Report by the Surgeon General on television violence. Television and behavior: Ten years of scientific progress and implications for the eighties*. Washington, DC: Government Printing Office.

Piaget, J. (1963). *The origins of intelligence in children*. New York: W. W. Norton & Co. Inc.

Piers, M. W. (Ed.) (1972). *Play and development: A symposium*. New York: W. W. Norton.

Reed, V. A. (1994). *An introduction to children with language disorders*. New York: Macmillan.

Reis, H. T., Collins, W. A., & Berscheid, E. (2000). The relationship context of human behavior and development. *Psychological Bulletin, 126*, 844–872.

Rheingold, H. L., & Cook, K. V. (1975). The content of boys' and girls' rooms as an index of parents' behavior. *Child Development, 46*, 459–463.

Robertson, S. B., & Weismer, S. E. (1997). The influence of peer models on the play scripts of children with specific language impairments. *Journal of Speech, Language & Hearing Research, 40*, 49–62.

Schacter, F., & Straye, A. (1982). Adults talk and children's language development. In S. Moore & C. Cooper (Eds.), *The young child: Reviews of research*. Washington, DC: National Association for Young Children.

Schor, E. L. (2003). Family pediatrics: Report of the Task Force on the Family. *Pediatrics, 111*, 1541–1571.

Seamon, J. G. (1980). *Memory and cognition: An introduction*. New York: Oxford University Press.

Shatz, M., & Gelman, R. (1973). The development of communication skills: Modifications in the speech of young children as a function of the listener. *Monographs of the Society for Research in Child Development, 38* (Serial No. 152).

Siegel, E. (1982). A critical examination of studies of parent-infant bonding. In M. H. Klaus & M. O. Robertson (Eds.), *Birth, interaction, and attachment: A round table*. Skillman, NJ: Johnson & Johnson.

Skeels, H. M. (1942). A study of the differential stimulation on mentally retarded children: A follow-up report. *American Journal of Mental Deficiency, 46*, 340–350.

Skeels, H. M. (1966). Adult status of children with contrasting life experience: A follow-up study. *Monographs of the Society for Research in Child Development, 31* (3).

Skinner, B. F. (1953). *Science and human behavior*. New York: Macmillan.

Skinner, B. F. (1957). *Verbal behavior*. New York: Appleton-Century-Crofts.

Slavin, R. E. (1994). *Educational psychology theory and practice*. (4th ed.). Boston: Allyn & Bacon.

Spitz, R. V., & Tallal, P. (1997). Look who's talking: A prospective study of familial transmission of language impairments. *Journal of Speech, Language & Hearing Research, 40*, 990–1002.

Thomas, A., & Chess, S. (1981). The role of temperament in the contributions of individuals to their own development. In R. M. Lerner & N. A. Busch-Rossnagel (Eds.), *Individuals as producers of their development: A life-span perspective*. New York: Academic Press.

Vandell, D. L., & Ramanan, J. (1992). Effects of early and recent maternal employment on children from low income families. *Child Development, 63*, 938–949.

Villani, S. (2001). Impact of media on children and adolescents: a 10-year review of the research. *Journal of the American Academy of Child and Adolescent Psychiatry, 40*, 392–401.

Vygotsky, L. S. (1962). *Thought and language*. Cambridge, MA: MIT Press.

Vygotsky, L. S. (1978). *Mind in society*. Cambridge, MA: Harvard University Press.

Winner, E. (1988). *The point of words*. Cambridge, MA: Harvard University Press.

Wood, D. (1992). Culture, language, and child development. *Language and Education, 6*(2), 123–140.

Zigler, E. F., & Stevenson, M. F. (1993). *Children in a changing world: Developmental and social issues* (2nd ed.). Pacific Grove, CA: Brookes/Cole.

5 Development and Risk During Prenatal, Natal, and Postnatal Stages

The physical connections between mothers and their infants that exist before pregnancy, during pregnancy, during the labor and delivery process, and during the immediate period after birth can affect the later physical and developmental health of children. **Prenatal** refers to the period before conception through gestation. **Natal** conditions affect the mother or the infant during the labor and delivery process, and **postnatal** conditions affect the mother or the infant after delivery and during the first 30 days after birth. A fourth term, **perinatal**, is commonly used to designate a period that actually overlaps all of the preceding periods. Technically, the perinatal period begins at the 29th week of gestation and ends between the 1st and 4th weeks after birth. At any time during any of these periods, problems may arise that can compromise the physical or cognitive growth of the infant. While knowing the cause or timing of injury seldom guides early childhood professionals as they design intervention plans, this knowledge can be useful to families in understanding their children.

PRENATAL GROWTH AND DEVELOPMENT

Prematurity is when a developing fetus is born prior to the 37th week of gestation. It is important to distinguish between premature infants and those who are of low birth weight, small for gestational age, or have intrauterine growth retardation. Though babies from all these categories are at risk due to their size and other factors, premature infants have a unique set of risk factors associated with immature physical development corresponding to the gestational age of the baby.

Viability is the gestational age when a fetus can survive outside of the womb with or without medical or technological intervention. With current medical practice, a fetus is considered **viable** at a gestational age greater than 23 weeks beyond conception. In fact, the survival of premature infants is directly related to advances in neonatal medical technology. With the improved survival rates of premature infants, it has become possible to identify a normal progression of preterm growth and development. Consequently, researchers have also investigated interventions aimed at improving the quality of survival and assisting families in meeting the needs of their medically fragile infants.

While infants born between the 33rd and 36th week of gestation have increased risk compared to full-term infants, those born at less than 32 weeks are at extreme risk for significant developmental delays. The corresponding fragility of underdeveloped organ systems, particularly the brain, affects both physical growth and neurological development. Indexes used to project fetal physical growth are gestational age, birth weight, and medical conditions. Maternal and fetal conditions (e.g., maternal high blood pressure or physical anomalies such as a heart defect) can either independently or collectively influence fetal growth. In spite of preexisting conditions, appropriate interventions can alleviate or control high-risk medical conditions, while permitting infants to progress along a corrected growth curve established specifically for infants born prematurely. Furthermore, potential delays can be mediated by strong maternal language interactions, a positive home environment, and early intervention programs (Apgar, 1997).

EFFECTS OF PREMATURITY ON BODY SYSTEMS

Fetuses who will eventually be born prematurely proceed along the same predetermined pattern as that of full-term fetuses until birth itself interrupts this normal course of development. Though this interruption does not change the normal developmental sequence, it does have an impact on the schedule over which development occurs. That is, premature infants are born with underdeveloped organs, which are not sufficiently capable of meeting the demands of independent life without the support of the mother's womb. The following is an analysis of the particular organ systems that are compromised when infants are born prematurely. Note that all systems, while described in a discrete manner, are essentially linked, with insult to one or more systems affecting the development of other systems.

Respiratory System

Surfactant is a chemical agent needed for independent breathing that is not produced in sufficient quantity until the 32nd to 33rd week of pregnancy. This chemical prevents the lungs from sticking together during expiration. Without surfactant, the lung surfaces stick together, causing the small airsacs to collapse. The tiny airsacs, called **alveoli**, permit normal exchange of oxygen and carbon dioxide. Collapsed alveoli cause oxygen deficiency, leading to lung disease and, if serious enough, death. Respiratory function can be further compromised by an immature nervous system. Since breathing is governed by nerve impulses, weak or absent stimulation (as is the case in prematurity) results in inconsistent patterns of breathing. Consequently, it is common for preterm infants to experience **apnea**, in which an infant stops breathing for periods of seconds or minutes.

Cardiovascular System

Blood vessels in premature infants are unusually fragile and break easily. This fragility increases the risk of bleeding into the brain (**intracranial bleeding** or stroke) or other vital organs. A second condition associated with an immature cardiovascular system is **anemia**, since underdeveloped bone marrow is unprepared for the body's demand to produce red blood cells. These conditions place additional stress on the young heart, which is poorly equipped to meet the body's demands for oxygen and nutrients.

Neurological System

The younger the fetus, the greater will be the probable impact of delivery on a developing neurological system. In particular, the relationship between cardiovascular proficiency and neurological functioning is critical. That is, the more premature the infant, the more likely it is that the blood and oxygen supply to the brain will be compromised. Hence, the brain, which itself is immature and consequently vulnerable to any interruption in the vital oxygen and nutrient supply, can incur permanent damage to its cells. Furthermore, the immature neurological system is incapable of sending or receiving messages efficiently. Thus, other systems in the body, all of which are dependent upon the nerve network for adequate functioning, have decreased ability to respond to the body's demands.

Renal and Gastrointestinal Systems

In addition to being affected by their own immaturity, the kidneys and gastrointestinal systems are seriously affected by compromised cardiovascular and neurological systems. The kidneys are unable to maintain normal sodium and calcium levels or to sufficiently filter waste. The gastrointestinal tract is capable of absorbing nutrients, but the large bowel is too short, so the passage of food is too rapid to permit sufficient absorption, increasing the risk of malnutrition. Interestingly, when the cardiovascular system is weakened (as in prematurity) infants' bodies tend to protect the organs that are the most important to survival. Accordingly, the gastrointestinal system is not considered critical to an infant's preservation, so blood flow is detoured away from the intestine to provide increased blood to the brain, heart, and kidneys.

Muscular System

Studies have documented the developmental evolution of tone, deep tendon reflexes, pathologic reflexes, and primitive reflexes for infants born between 24- and 32-weeks gestation. Ironically, while motor development in full-term infants follows a pattern of upper extremities to lower extremities (cephalo-caudal) and from the center of the body to the extremities (proximal to distal), the preterm developmental progression of tone and reflexes emerges in the opposite directions (Allen & Capute, 1990). **Micropremature infants** (24–26 weeks of gestation) show generalized **flexion** of the lower extremities at birth. These parameters give providers the opportunity to determine whether these infants are following a progressive course typical of gestational age or whether they are experiencing delays.

Skeletal System

Poor nutrition contributes to bone growth deficiency, which is necessary for linear growth. Most importantly, calcium loss (rickets) in the newly forming bone structures will delay both growth and maturation. A premature infant's inability to adequately coordinate sucking and swallowing, along with gastrointestinal inefficiency, can cause nutrient deficiency. Height is one of the most critical measures in determining the progression of a normal growth curve in premature infants. In spite of adequate weight gain, infants who fail to grow in height (one should expect 0.5 cm to 1 cm of linear growth per week) deviate from the normal expectation.

Integumentary System

The skin in premature infants is extremely fragile due to ratio of body surface to weight, low storage of brown fats, and poor glycogen supply (Subramanian, Yoon, & Toral, 2001). For a very premature infant, the skin surface provides no protection from heat or water loss and no barrier against infection. These infants are also at risk for the development of yeast infections on the skin surface. Infection can then progress into the bloodstream through breaks in the fragile surface. External heat sources (i.e., isolettes), filtered air, and good hygiene practices are necessary to provide both warmth and protection for these infants.

Indexes of Growth in Premature Infants

As with term infants, weight is an unpredictable measure of both gestational age and maturity. Premature infants who have been under physiological stress during pregnancy will exhibit signs of lower birth weight, along with less-advanced organ function. Head circumference, as a measure of brain growth, is used to make growth predictions. **Corrected gestational age** (gestational age versus chronological age) is used to determine if appropriate growth and development are occurring. This measure is considered to be accurate at least through the first year of life. Prematurity affects growth and development, sometimes only during early life. But prematurity sometimes can produce effects that will alter the course of an individual's entire life. Recognition of the normal progression provides the opportunity for planning interventions and aligning resources that will promote development to the maximum potential of the affected infant.

MATERNAL CONDITIONS AFFECTING PREGNANCY OUTCOMES

PRECONCEPTUAL MATERNAL CONDITIONS

Conditions exist in some women that will affect their own health as well as the development and overall health of a fetus if pregnancy occurs. Actively educating women about these conditions and encouraging them to seek health care and counseling before becoming pregnant is a practice that early educators can adopt. Some of these conditions are diabetes, hypertension, heart disease, drug and alcohol addiction, obesity, age, and some genetic conditions (e.g., cystic fibrosis, PKU, etc.). Attention to risk factors and provision of necessary interventions significantly reduce the risks to both the mother and infant.

Socioeconomic and environmental factors play an important role in the prevention of prenatal and natal complications. Poverty influences both living conditions and physical conditions that increase the incidence of prematurity. For example, women who are physically or sexually abused are at greater risk for low birth weight and preterm delivery (Curry, 1998). Limited economic opportunities frequently lead to poor prenatal care, poor diet, and increased complications of pregnancy (e.g., pregnancy-induced hypertension), all of which may lead to premature delivery. Consideration of socioeconomic issues prior to becoming pregnant, with an exploration of available resources, decreases the incidence of complications of pregnancy.

PRENATAL MATERNAL CONDITIONS

A **term pregnancy** averages approximately 280 days (10 lunar months or 40 weeks) and terminates in the delivery of a viable fetus that is capable of independent life. Delivery prior to the 37th week of pregnancy is considered to be premature. Viability within the context of current technology exists at about 23 weeks gestation.

The number of times a woman has been pregnant (**gravida**) and the number of live infants that she has delivered at greater than 20-weeks gestation (**parity**) is important information in giving prenatal care. That is, the more times a woman has been pregnant, the greater the risk for problems associated with the pregnancy than for those who have been pregnant fewer times. These problems may include faster labors with quick and uncontrolled deliveries, failure of muscle contraction of the uterus with significant bleeding, and malpositioned placentas. Previous premature delivery is related to the increased probability of a subsequent pregnancy ending in premature delivery and earlier in the gestation than the previous delivery.

Age is an important factor that can be related to the increased incidence of both premature delivery and appearance of physical and genetic abnormalities in the infant. Women younger than 20 and women over 40 have an increased risk of spontaneous abortion, toxemia of pregnancy, premature delivery, and congenital abnormalities in the fetus. These mothers frequently have other risk factors present that increase the possibility of pregnancy complications, for example, socioeconomic factors in young women and health problems (preexisting hypertension, diabetes) in older women.

Socioeconomic standing is an important factor in the incidence of premature delivery. This includes race, culture, shelter, food, money, and social support structures. Studies show that young, single mothers with few support networks have both an increased incidence of unplanned pregnancy and a higher incidence of premature delivery and low-birth-weight infants (Report of Consensus Conferences, 1987).

Nutrition is one of the most significant factors associated with maternal/infant well-being. Poor nutritional habits, along with variations in such preexisting conditions as obesity or malnutrition, will severely affect a fetus both during gestation and following birth (Tiedje, Kingry, & Stommel, 1992). Prematurity and low birth weight are determined in the first trimester, suggesting that fetal growth may be dependent upon maternal nutrition before conception ("Pre-conception," 1999). Maternal behaviors that promote malnutrition (e.g., anorexia) result in decreased stores of nutrients for the developing fetus. These infants may be born with **growth retardation** (weight is lower than the 10th percentile and chest circumference is lower than the 3rd percentile for gestational age) and may have brain injury due to diminished oxygen and nutrition supply caused by a poorly functioning placenta (Peleg, Kennedy, & Hunter, 1998).

Maternal obesity (20% over the standard weight) can also produce both maternal and fetal problems. Infants born to obese mothers may be large, thereby increasing problems with delivery. Maternal obesity may also produce **hypoglycemia** (low blood sugar) in infants, leading to serious neonatal problems. Conversely, a large percentage of women fail to have adequate weight gain; those who gain less than 21 pounds during pregnancy increase the likelihood of fetal death by 1.5 times (Tiedje et al., 1992). On the other hand, it appears that women who engage in regular heavy exercise throughout pregnancy actually reduce the risk of pre-term delivery (Soares & Beard, 1998).

Maternal infections can play a significant role in fetal outcomes. Both bacterial and viral infections cause a multitude of disabilities for the fetus and neonate. Meningitis, cytomegalovirus, rubella, toxoplasmosis, and many other maternal infections, as well as their impact on newborns, are discussed elsewhere in this text. Many of these infections can be avoided by prenatal education and attention to behaviors that place a mother at risk for contracting an infection.

Chronic diseases in mothers may have an effect on a fetus. These conditions include kidney disease, cancer, thyroid disease, Rh sensitization, hypertension, cardiovascular disease, diabetes, genetic disorders (e. g., PKU), respiratory disease (e.g., cystic fibrosis), neurologic disorders (e.g., multiple sclerosis), infectious disease (e.g., hepatitis), psychiatric disorders, and mental retardation. Some of these conditions have a known effect on developing fetuses, and through appropriate prevention measures, risk to the fetus can be decreased.

Transmission of HIV virus from mother to child is the dominant form of acquisition of HIV in infants. Sixteen hundred infants are born daily infected with HIV, 1,500 of these in sub-Saharan Africa (Newell, 2003). Risk of maternal transmission can be greatly diminished by using antiretroviral drugs during pregnancy, delivery, and the neonatal period. Also, voluntary caesarean section reduces the risk of HIV transmission to a newborn, along with alternatives to breastfeeding. Unfortunately, in the areas of the world that pose the greatest risk to mother–child dyads, most of these preventive procedures are unavailable.

Utilization of prenatal care in which a woman's pregnancy is monitored by a health care professional is statistically the most important factor in decreasing problems associated with any of the maternal conditions. For example, early and consistent care decreases the incidence of prematurity associated with risk factors (Tiedje et al., 1992). At the same time, lack of prenatal care is one of the most reliable predictions that problems will occur. Many of the conditions discussed in this chapter could be identified through good prenatal care, thereby reducing risks to mother and infant.

COMMON CONDITIONS OF GESTATION

The following conditions are frequently seen during gestation. They lead to the need for advanced intervention for the pregnant woman and also account for the greatest majority of premature deliveries. Educating pregnant women, through prenatal care, to look for signs of complications can decrease the incidence of problems to the fetus. Table 5–1 summarizes these conditions.

Table 5–1 Conditions of Gestation

Condition	Characteristics
Placenta previa	The placenta implants in the bottom segment of the uterus instead of in the top segment. Requires bed rest until the fetal gestation is sufficient for independent breathing after birth.
Abruptio placenta	The placenta prematurely separates from the wall of the uterus. Causes decreased availability of oxygen and nutrition, decreased blood flow to the fetal brain with decreased tissue perfusion, and even fetal death.
Toxemia of pregnancy	Causes an elevation in maternal blood pressure, decrease in urine output, and decreased ability of the kidneys to conserve protein and salts, which contributes to swelling of the extremities that may advance to the liver and brain. Reduces blood flow to the uterus and the placenta then begins to shrink in size, causing fetal growth retardation.
Prolapsed or entangled cord	The length of time the flow is obstructed can be a critical factor in determining whether the fetus will asphyxiate in utero and die, or whether blood flow will be resumed at a point where neurological damage may occur but the fetus will survive the insult.
Hypoxic–ischemic brain injury	Hypoxia, decreased oxygen levels, and ischemia, death of the cells and tissue due to decreased blood flow, can occur together or separately. Such neurological damage generally includes severe mental retardation, intractable seizures, and spasticity.
Meconium aspiration syndrome	The fetus either gasps before delivery (usually from asphyxia) or meconium is aspirated into the trachea and airways with the first breath of the infant whose mouth and nose have not been cleared of the amniotic fluid that contains meconium particles. This initiates a state of pneumonia.

Placenta Previa

Placenta previa is a condition in which the placenta implants in the bottom segment of the uterus instead of in the top segment. A normal site of implantation of a fertilized egg is in the upper half of the uterus. When a placenta previa occurs, the placenta implants over the opening of the cervix. Many pregnant women who have a placenta previa will have several episodes of bleeding through the second and third trimesters of the pregnancy. Several factors may initiate the onset of sudden and excessive bleeding. These include contractions of the uterus, intercourse, and excessive fetal activity. This bleeding is generally not painful but can result in a large blood loss over a very short period of time and places an unborn infant at high risk for death.

Ultrasound is often conducted after the woman has had an episode of bleeding and then seeks care to determine the cause. The ultrasound will diagnose the condition. Women with known previa are placed in the hospital and on bed rest until the length of gestation is sufficient for the fetus to be capable of independent breathing after birth. This is to assure that immediate care is available for both the woman and the unborn infant should sudden, excessive bleeding occur from the placenta. The babies are then delivered by cesarean section, and those women who have received consistent care generally are able to carry their infants close to term before delivery is necessary.

Abruptio Placenta

Abruptio placenta is a condition in which the placenta prematurely separates from the uterine wall before delivery of the fetus. This can occur at any time during gestation and to varying degrees of separation. The impact on both the mother and the fetus can be significant. Partial separation of the placenta will result in vaginal bleeding, which may be small or large, and is generally associated with abdominal pain in the mother. The fetus may be affected by a decreased blood flow and may respond by either a drop or an increase of the heart rate. This change in blood flow can have a significant impact on the long-term outcome for the infant. Effects include decreased availability of oxygen and nutrition, decreased blood flow to the brain, and even death. Repeated abruptions will result in growth retardation along with any of the fetal factors of an acute abruption.

Acute and total abruptio placenta will result in fetal death. When the placenta fully separates from the uterine wall, the fetus loses the supply of oxygen and nutrients that are essential to sustain life. This condition also has significant maternal effects. Many women who have a total abruption have an increased risk of bleeding from many systems that may even result in the death of the mother.

Pregnancy-Induced Hypertension and HELLP

A major problem associated with delivery is referred to as pregnancy-induced hypertension (PIH). This condition presents a variety of symptoms that produce variable effects in individual pregnancies. The exact cause of the cluster of symptoms and why they occur during pregnancy remains unknown, though factors that increase an individual's vulnerability to PIH have been identified: diabetes, multiple gestation, and hypertension.

The incidence of PIH affects 7% of pregnancies in the United States. This ratio may increase to as high as 25% in mothers who are diabetic. Maternal death from this condition may be as high as 2%, with fetal death rates being approximately 20% (Besinger, Repke, & Ferguson, 1989).

For unknown reasons, blood vessel spasms occur—alternately expanding and contracting—with resulting damage to the lining of the vessels. Resulting damage to the veins and red blood cells passing through these vessels signals the body to release platelets. Platelet action in the bloodstream causes a clotting over the damaged tissue/cells, increasing the vessel volume and further clogging the flow of blood. Additional stress on the cardiovascular system results when a victim's kidneys react to the loss of red blood cells (hemolysis) by retaining water, further adding to the blood volume. As the volume increases, so does the blood pressure in order to push blood past this damage. This is the hypertension created in PIH. If the pressure continues unabated, the body will signal the kidneys to retain water to make up for the damaged red blood cells, and the vessels themselves "leak" fluid, causing swelling (edema). Decreased blood flow puts additional stress on multiple systems (heart, lungs, brain, kidneys and liver). These factors can lead to abruptio placenta and eclampsia.

When the liver becomes involved, the risk to mother and infant increases significantly. This condition is known as HELLP (hemolysis, elevated liver, low platelets). As mentioned, clotting reduces blood flow and oxygen supply to the body. Lacking oxygen, the liver begins to die. Both maternal and fetal vascular systems are affected. Mothers are at risk of liver rupture/damage, abruptio placenta, hypoglycemia, and pancreatitis, among other effects. Infants who survive are at very high risk of intrauterine growth retardation (IUGR) in addition to risk of kidney, cardiovascular, and neurological damage.

Maternal Diabetes

Diabetes in a pregnant woman can be present prior to the pregnancy or can come about during gestation. Infants of diabetic mothers, regardless of the onset, are at significantly higher risk for natal and postnatal complications.

Gestational diabetes is a condition of increased blood sugar that is initiated by the pregnancy. It is usually diagnosed during the second trimester through laboratory analysis. Generally controlled through diet, diabetes may occasionally require the use of insulin. Though the condition disappears after delivery, it does appear to be a predictive factor for the development of age-onset diabetes later in the mother's life and increases the risk of maternal diabetes during later pregnancies. Risk factors for congenital diabetes are the same as those that are predictive of later onset diabetes. These factors include advanced age, family history of diabetes, non-White ethnicity, obesity, and cigarette smoking (Hughes, Agarwal & Thomas, 1997; Solomon, 1997).

Preexisting diabetes in a woman who then becomes pregnant raises many issues for maternal care during gestation. The physiological changes that occur in the human body during gestation have a significant effect on the ability of a woman to maintain normal control of her diabetic condition. Nutritional factors and insulin needs are inconsistent during the course of the gestation and will, in turn, affect fetal well-being. Precise control of diabetes decreases the risk to a fetus, but this control requires a multidisciplinary approach to the pregnancy and a mother who is committed to providing every opportunity to her fetus for normal growth and development.

Infants of diabetic mothers have an increased risk for congenital abnormalities. The most frequently occurring anomalies are complex heart defects. Babies may also be born very large for their gestational age, which increases the possibility for birth trauma. Many of these infants also require a longer gestation for lung maturation to occur and, without this advantage, these infants have an increased rate of respiratory distress syndrome. These infants also will have significant problems with blood sugar control and tend to have a decreased ability in the first few days of life to coordinate their sucking, breathing, and swallowing mechanisms, which make feeding consistent.

Rh Sensitization

Each human being has a blood grouping that has been inherited from her or his parents. They, in turn, pass the genetic framework to their children. There are situations that arise in which the antigen of the mother and that of the unborn fetus are not compatible. When this occurs, the mother produces antibodies against the fetal blood.

Rh is a blood group or collection of molecules on the red blood cells. Blood groups used to identify persons blood compatibility include A, B, AB, and O, each of which can either be Rh factor positive or negative. Either the Rh factor is present (Rh+) or absent (Rh−) in an individual's blood system.

Rh sensitization occurs when a female who has a negative blood Rh is exposed to positive blood Rh. This may occur during a blood transfusion or as a result of a pregnancy when the partner has a positive Rh blood type. Sensitization may occur with any pregnancy, even those that end in miscarriage at a very early gestation. The positive Rh antigen crosses the placenta, and the maternal response to this foreign protein is to produce antibodies against the perceived invasion. This is a normal response of a healthy immune system.

The initial pregnancy in which Rh-positive and Rh-negative blood are involved is not affected, but subsequent pregnancies, in which the mother now has an activated antibody against Rh-positive, will be affected if the fetus has a positive blood Rh. The result of fetal exposure to the maternal antibody is profound fetal anemia. If not diagnosed and treated in utero, the fetus may die or have problems caused by the anemia.

Progress in medical technology and public awareness has significantly decreased both the occurrence of Rh sensitization and the effects of the process on the development of an affected infant. Treatment consists of giving blood transfusions in utero or exchanging the fetal blood to prevent the breakdown of the normal blood cells. Either of these interventions support the affected fetus until the gestation has progressed to viability or the ability of the fetus to breathe outside the uterus has been determined. Severely affected infants may also require exchange transfusions because of the high levels of bilirubin that build up in the bloodstream as a result of the breaking apart of the affected red blood cells. Transfusion is done to prevent the effects of high bilirubin concentrations on normal brain development. Severe mental retardation and/or cerebral palsy may occur with very high levels of bilirubin. Prevention of sensitization is now possible with RhoGAM. This vaccine destroys any positive cells that enter the maternal circulation, preventing the mother from producing antibodies that will eventually destroy the blood cells of the unborn fetus.

Premature Rupture of the Membranes

Premature rupture of the membranes is a common initiating factor in premature delivery. Normally, in premature rupture of the membranes, the bag of waters that surrounds the fetus breaks prior to the 37th week of pregnancy. This may either initiate the onset of uterine contractions and subsequent delivery or place the woman and fetus at risk for infection with the loss of the protective barrier around the infant.

The reasons for premature rupture may vary. Though most instances are not explained, an infant who has acquired an infection is thought to initiate the process in many cases. Even with a ruptured sack, the placenta and infant continue to produce fluid, and the woman continues to leak fluid throughout gestation until delivery occurs. Any bacteria (or virus) that may be present in the vaginal tract of the mother can find their way into the uterus and come into contact with the fetus. Careful observation of the mother and infant for signs of distress or infection can delay a potential delivery. Infants who experience a premature loss of the bag of waters are at risk of interruption of normal physical growth related to the alterations in the environment. Ironically, however, rupture of the membranes tends to speed up the process of maturation of the lungs in a fetus. An infant's self-protective mechanisms sense impending delivery and actually accelerate the maturation process.

Premature Labor

Regular uterine contractions that produce dilatation of the cervix signal the onset of labor. Contractions and dilatation occuring prior to the 37th week of gestation is defined as **premature labor**. While considerable variation exists across sources, it is estimated that as many as 10% of all births have episodes of premature labor. This rate increases when women are at risk due to socioeconomic factors and inadequate prenatal care. That is, women receiving care tend to be educated regarding warning symptoms of labor and are more likely to seek help before labor has progressed to the point of making premature delivery unavoidable. Many women will have regular uterine contractions prior to delivery. This may result from uterine weight, fetal movement, stress, diet, exercise, and many other factors. However, unless there is cervical change and movement of the cervix from a backward to a forward position, premature labor may not be occurring.

One cause of premature labor, an incompetent cervix, is defined as a premature thinning of the lining of the cervix. As a result, the cervix becomes too weak to withstand the pressure of the fetus. Pelvic pressure and spotting may be symptoms of an incompetent cervix, which can result in premature birth or miscarriage. Prior damage to the cervix, such as a biopsy or abortion, can be the cause of incompetency.

In many cases, premature labor can be controlled with medication and bed rest. Careful monitoring of maternal conditions and the status of the fetus are critical in any situation in which an attempt is being made to stop labor. If the labor is progressing and delivery is unavoidable, current technology allows for acceleration of fetal lung maturity with medication (within 36–48 hours), which allows a woman undergoing premature labor to deliver her infant with decreased risk.

Case Study   THE DIARY OF ESTHER ANNA BERKE: MONTH 6

April 16–30: The neurologist continues to tinker with Esther's medications, she is currently taking Rivotril, Vitamin B_6, Sabril, and Lamictal every day. Her seizures have decreased somewhat in frequency but increased somewhat in intensity.

May 1–15: No major changes during this time, we are busy planning Sarah's trip to the United States in June to have Esther examined by several specialists.

Esther Anna 6 months old.

MATERNAL/INFANT NATAL COMPLICATIONS

Labor is precarious for infants who are expected to pass from the dependent world of dark, warm liquid to a world that is bright, cold, and dry and that requires an independent ability to both breathe and excrete waste products. The physiological adaptations are easier when the labor and delivery process do not place additional stress upon infants.

Labor is the process in which a mother and fetus work together toward the goal of delivery of the infant. The uterus provides the contractions that produce pressure on the emerging part of the fetus to dilate the cervix. Dilatation is necessary to provide a passage for the infant from the protective environment of the uterus into the world. Labor requires that both the mother and infant participate to successfully complete the process.

Factors may occur that influence the ability of either the mother or the fetus to be effective during the labor and delivery process (see Table 5–2). Maternal factors may include an ineffective labor pattern that:

1. does not produce the uterine pressure necessary for dilatation to occur
2. has too few uterine contractions
3. is accompanied by high-risk maternal conditions, such as toxemia of pregnancy

All these factors place the mother at risk during the labor process. Fetal conditions may also influence the course of the labor and delivery. The normal position of the fetus for delivery is head down. It is possible for a fetus to present in an abnormal position. The fetus may be breech (bottom first), transverse (sideways),

Table 5–2   Maternal/Infant Natal Conditions

Condition	Characteristics
Dysfunction of labor and/or delivery	Ineffective labor pattern, too few uterine contractions, or maternal conditions that place the mother at risk for a normal labor process. These may be malposition of the fetus, large size for gestation, and congenital defects that prevent proper positioning.
Prolapsed or entangled cord	The length of time the flow is obstructed can be a critical factor in determining whether the fetus will asphyxiate in utero and die, or whether blood flow will be resumed at a point where neurological damage may occur but the fetus will survive the insult.
Hypoxic–ischemic brain injury	Hypoxia, decreased oxygen levels, and ischemia, death of the cells and tissue due to decreased blood flow, can occur together or separately. Such neurological damage generally includes severe mental retardation, intractable seizures, and spasticity.
Meconium aspiration syndrome	The fetus either gasps before delivery (usually from asphyxia) or meconium is aspirated into the trachea and airways with the first breath of the infant whose mouth and nose have not been cleared of the amniotic fluid that contains meconium particles. This initiates a state of pneumonia.

large for gestation, or have congenital defects that prevent proper positioning to occur. The health status of the fetus also influences its ability to withstand labor.

Dysfunctional labor may be improved with the use of medication to increase both the number and strength of uterine contractions. However, if medication is not effective, then delivery by caesarean section may be necessary. Medication must be closely monitored to make sure that the fetus can withstand the increased uterine pressure. In large-for-age infants, their shoulders may fail to pass below the mother's pubic bone, which can cause cord compression that, in turn, may lead to asphyxia. Assessment of the maternal pelvis (by examination) and the estimated fetal size (by ultrasound) prior to the onset of labor may prevent a shoulder dislocation. Anticipation of this occurrence may lead health care providers to surgically deliver the infant.

PROLAPSED CORD/ENTANGLED CORD

The umbilical cord is the lifeline by which a fetus is connected to the placenta, which is connected to the mother. This structure contains one large blood vessel and two smaller vessels that carry oxygenated blood and nutrients from the fetal side of the placenta to the fetus. The two small vessels return blood with fetal waste products to the fetal side of the placenta, where an exchange takes place across a membrane to the maternal side of the placenta. The cord vessels are protected by a thick membranous cover and a thick jelly-like substance on the inside.

The length of any umbilical cord varies. Length of the cord may be a factor in the likelihood of becoming entangled. In many normal vaginal deliveries, the umbilical cord is wrapped around the neck of an infant or, occasionally, around other areas of the body, such as the chest or abdomen. Monitoring equipment used during labor can give care providers information that an umbilical cord may be entangled with an infant's body parts.

If an infant is wrapped up in its own cord, there may be slight decreases in the fetal heart rate during a contraction. Occasionally a fetus may become entangled in the cord during gestation, decreasing blood flow through the cord. The length of time the flow is obstructed can be a critical factor in determining whether the fetus will asphyxiate in utero and die or whether blood flow will be resumed to permit the fetus to survive the insult. Even though neurologic damage is likely, infants are born without any indications of an in utero insult but display obvious and profound symptoms of neurological deficits after delivery. Symptoms of damage may include seizures, abnormalities in muscle tone, and the absence of primitive reflexes.

Abnormal positioning of a fetus may cause the umbilical cord to fall from the uterine cavity (prolapsed cord) after the mother's water has broken. Since the normal position of a fetus for a vaginal delivery should be head down, when the fetus is breech or transverse, space is available for a cord prolapse.

Prolapse of the umbilical cord places a fetus at risk for loss of blood flow due to cord obstruction. The presenting part of the fetus can come to rest on the cord and blood flow either significantly decreases or stops completely. The fetus then experiences asphyxia, and death occurs rapidly. If prolapse occurs, the emerging part of the fetus must be manually held off the cord, allowing for blood flow, and delivery by cesarean section is done immediately. Infants who are delivered rapidly can expect normal recovery, but if a prolapsed cord occurs outside of the health care setting, even if the infant survives, significant neurological damage is likely.

Neonatal Conditions

Hypoxic–Ischemic Perinatal Brain Injury

Hypoxia (decreased oxygen levels) and **ischemia** (death of the cells and tissue due to decreased blood flow) can occur together or separately. This condition accounts for the largest group of infants with severe nonprogressive neurological deficits that happen prior to and during delivery. Permanent changes in the neurological structure of the brain matter follow such injuries. Such neurological damage generally includes severe mental retardation, intractable seizures, and spasticity.

Hypoxic–ischemic brain injury can occur during gestation or during the labor and delivery process. Any situation that causes a decrease in blood flow or oxygen supply or an increased level of carbon dioxide can result in the condition.

The cycle is repetitive, unless intervention (change of position or supplemental oxygen) increases the blood flow again. Infants do not have the reserves of larger children and adults, and smaller decreases in central blood pressure may severely impact blood flow to the brain.

Infants who have experienced either prenatal or natal asphyxia syndrome may have problems with independent respiration and hyperactive responses to the environment. Seizures are often observed between 12 and 72 hours after birth. The earlier the onset of the seizures, the greater the insult on the neurological status of the infant. As many as 80% of these infants experience severe mental retardation, and 50% exhibit spastic quadriplegia (McCormick, 1989).

Brain damage from asphyxia can be determined by diagnostic imaging methods such as CT Scan or MRI (described in Chapter 6). Death of the brain neurons results in the transformation of brain matter into fibrous tissue. This injured brain matter is ultimately replaced in many areas by cysts, and these can be located by scanning methods. Other affected areas of the brain can be identified through the seizure patterns that emerge. Certain seizure patterns are known to evolve from specific brain areas.

MECONIUM ASPIRATION SYNDROME

Meconium is the accumulation of fetal waste products that collect in the bowel during gestation. The rectum should not relax until after the infant is delivered, but when a fetus experiences asphyxia or when an infant is overdue, the muscles of the rectum relax and meconium is passed by the infant into the amniotic fluid. This results in a green staining of the fluid, which is generally obvious with rupture of the bag of waters. Even mild asphyxia can initiate the passage of meconium and set the infant up for possible aspiration syndrome. This material contains fetal waste products as well as fetal sludge (skin, hair, cells, etc.), which can be swallowed or absorbed through the intestinal wall.

Meconium aspiration syndrome occurs when a fetus either gasps before delivery (usually from **asphyxia**) or when meconium is aspirated into the trachea and airways with the first breath of the infant whose mouth and nose have not been cleared of the amniotic fluid that contains meconium particles. This aspiration can lead to pneumonia, which may be mild to severe. Multiple physical problems can result from aspiration syndrome, affecting the respiratory system, the cardiovascular system, and the neurological system. Permanent neurological dysfunction is common.

A relatively new treatment for infants with severe respiratory distress involves diversion of blood from the infant and conducting it through a membrane oxygenator to artificially exchange oxygen and carbon dioxide, warming the blood and returning it to the infant's body. This method, referred to as extra-corporeal membrane oxygenation (ECMO), is a heart-lung bypass procedure which greatly increases the chances of survival. However, even with the use of this sophisticated technology, developmental problems occur in approximately 20% of survivors (Wildin, Landry, & Zwischenberger, 1994).

CLOSE-UP

PUBLIC POLICIES AND THE ORPHANS OF AIDS IN AFRICA

The AIDS epidemic is catastrophic in sub-Saharan Africa. Prevalence of persons who are HIV positive is 40% in some countries (and rising), and millions of children have lost their parents to the disease. In countries where poverty is a majority condition, the scope of this burden is unprecedented. The world has already missed the opportunity to prevent widespread death and a chaotic upheaval of culture. To stop the abysmal slide toward hopelessness, massive aid is needed.

For mothers, several urgent needs exist: improved maternal nutrition, antenatal care, and vaccinations of infants. However, the greatest need, and ultimately the only permanent solution, is prevention. Education on smaller family size, use of condoms (where women have some negotiating power), and use of other contraceptives is needed. Progress in these areas related to: (a) reducing the transmission of HIV; and (b) avoiding pregnancy in families where parents have contracted a fatal disease, can happen if there is a greater investment in existing health care infrastructures.

Orphans of parents who died of AIDS are generally best served in extended families. Yet, relatives are often financially unable to care for these orphans, so children are sent to orphanages. Institutional care in sub-Saharan Africa, in addition to being overwhelmed by large numbers of orphans, is both more expensive and less desirable from a sociocultural standpoint. Subsidizing families who would be willing to provide a home to orphans of the AIDS epidemic would cost as little as $100 per year per child. Still, even if these funds were immediately available (they are not), the task of distributing the money would be onerous. In Tanzania, an estimated 1.5 million orphans need homes. Finding willing foster families, distributing the resources, and monitoring the welfare of AIDS orphans is a formidable objective.

Educational needs of orphaned children are relative to a geographic area of the globe that currently educates only about half of its youth. Yet the cost of tuition, supplies, uniforms, and transportation is only about $40 per child each year. Again, assuming the funds became available, administration of resources to ensure that children received this educational benefit would be a great challenge. It is difficult for North Americans to conceive the totality with which the AIDS virus has injected itself into the fabric of African society. For example, one of the first steps recommended for shoring up the education infrastructure is to provide antiretroviral drugs to HIV-positive teachers so that teacher absentee rates may drop sufficiently to permit educational benefit to attending children.

Teens are among the most vulnerable to HIV transmission because young people experience severe peer pressure to have multiple sex partners and because girls are often pushed into prostitution for material benefit. Vocational training that would produce financial alternatives to prostitution could help alleviate the latter problem for as little as $100 to $500 per student. Moreover, successful training of youth in key vocational areas would help the struggling nations of Africa build a viable workforce while reducing the death rate of citizens in their potentially most-productive years.

While some progress has been made in jarring the world into action, the current effort is far too small to address the great suffering. In order to achieve the objectives identified: (a) national and international agencies must work in concert with each other; (b) funds must be channelled from debt-relief programs directly to schools and families; and (c) funds from the newly established Global Fund to Fight AIDS, Tuberculosis and Malaria must go to maternal and infant health care programs. Young children who have lost both parents should be given the highest priority—for their sake and for the sake of the nations of sub-Saharan Africa.

Source: From "Public Policies and the Orphans of AIDS in Africa," by A. Bhargava and B. Brgombe, 2000, *British Medical Journal, 326,* pp. 1387–1389.

POSTNATAL CONDITIONS

Many of the postnatal complications that infants encounter are a result of prematurity. In addition, infants affected with congenital abnormalities, congenital infections, acute infections, birth trauma, and many other factors will be found within the neonatal intensive care units in this country. The following discussion addresses only a select few of the conditions that affect these infants. Those discussed frequently result in outcomes that place these infants and young children in early intervention programs. Table 5–3 summarizes these postnatal complications.

PREMATURITY

Prematurity is the largest issue affecting pregnancy outcomes in our society. It is also the single most common cause of sickness and death worldwide. An estimated 8–10% of all births are premature, accounting for 75% of all neonatal deaths and 50% of all handicaps. As reported by the March of Dimes (2002), infants born within the normal birth weight range comprise 92.4% of the total population, those with low birth weight 7.6%; 57,967 or 1.4% of babies born in the United States weigh less than 1500 grams (very low–extremely low birth weight). African American infants comprise 37% of infants born at less than 1000 grams (Subramanian et al., 2001), more than twice the expected ratio, and certainly related to prenatal conditions. Infants delivered before the 37th week of gestation also account for a major portion of the health care dollars being spent within the United States. For example, the average hospital stay for infants at 24 weeks gestation is 4 months, with an average cost of $294,849 per survivor (Walling, 1998).

Gestational age is a critical factor in determining what problems a particular premature infant may encounter. Pregnancy dating is not a perfect science and lacks the ability to determine precisely in which week of gestation a particular infant may be. Technology currently makes it possible for survival of infants as young as 23 weeks gestation, but these infants have the potential of a multitude of problems that affect them at birth, within the first weeks of life, and that may follow them into their future. The risk of death or permanent disability increases

Table 5–3 Postnatal Conditions

Condition	Characteristics
Prematurity	Infants delivered before the 37th week of gestation. Those infants who are both premature and growth retarded (or small of gestational age) have two factors that impact their prognoses.
Intraventricular hemorrhages	Bleeding which may cause brain damage.
Apnea of prematurity	Pauses in breathing due to position or to neurological lapses.
Respiratory distress syndrome	Difficulty breathing caused by the absence of, or a deficiency in the amount of, surfactant present in the lungs of the infant.
Bronchopulmonary dysplasia	Chronic lung disease of infancy.
Patent ductus arteriosus	A cardiac defect that frequently occurs in the very low-birth-weight and extremely low-birth-weight infant. This condition can result in increased respiratory distress.
Hypothermia	Low body core temperature which places the infant at risk for other physical problems, such as increased respiratory distress, low blood sugar, and possibly for intraventricular hemorrhage.
Retinopathy of prematurity	Retinas of premature infants subjected to excess oxygen show an over-growth of connective tissue surrounding blood vessels. This overgrowth ultimately damages vision.
Anemia	A deficiency in the number of red blood cells available to the infant.
Poor nutrition	Difficulty with sucking, swallowing, and breathing coordination, and feeding apnea requires either continuous tube feeding of mild or inter-mittent tube feedings.
Periventricular leukomalacia	A condition of brain development and function that is related to cerebral blood flow both prior to delivery and during the neonatal period. Most frequently in premature infants; most often seen, and most profound symptom, is spastic diplegia.
Failure to thrive	Inability of the infant to maintain or gain weight sufficient for healthy growth and development.

significantly as birth weight declines. Follow-up of survivors who weigh less than 700 g indicates that the chances of severe neurological abnormalities is 100% (Stephens, Richardson, & Lewin, 1997).

Birth weight, along with gestation, is a more useful indicator of outcome than gestational age alone. Infants who are both premature and growth retarded (or small for gestational age) have two factors that threaten their prognoses. Infants born at less than 2800 g (6 lb 3 oz) at 38 weeks gestation are considered **low birth weight**. These infants may experience many of the problems commonly as-sociated with premature infants, to varying degrees. These problems may include respiratory distress, apnea (breathing pauses), poor temperature control, and

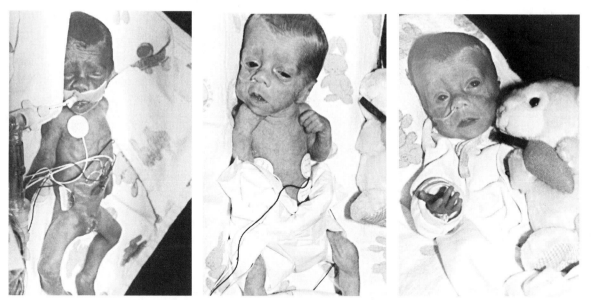

A. A 25-week preterm infant on day two of life weighing 800 g (1 lb 12 oz). B. Same infant at 4 weeks weighing 1200 g (2 lb 12 oz). C. Infant at 8 weeks weighing 1900 g (4 lb 3 oz) and ready to go home.

problems with nutrition. Though survival rates for this group are as high as 95%, developmental delays are a concern (Paz et al., 1995). Such delays may result in lowered cognitive ability and poor school achievement (Apgar, 1997).

Infants delivered at less than 1500 g (3 lb 5 oz) are considered **very low birth weight**. Such infants may be both premature and/or growth retarded. These infants are at risk for respiratory distress, bleeding within the brain and surrounding structures, infections, apnea, nutritional problems, and potential visual defects. Infants who are considered growth retarded, within this context, may be at risk for developmental delays due to a history of extended insufficiency of the placenta to supply adequate nutrition to the fetus during the pregnancy. As compared to infants born at the 50th percentile, those born weighing less than 1500 g are 70–100 times more likely to die in infancy (the rate is 5–30 times higher for infants who weigh less than 1500 g) (Peleg et al., 1998).

Infants delivered at less than 750 g (1 lb 10 oz) are considered **extremely low birth weight**. Survival rates for these very fragile infants have steadily increased over the last 10 years, and now, the expectation for survival is around 70%. In spite of technological advances which have increased the survival of premature infants with decreasing gestational ages, the same cannot be said of long-term sequelae. Of survivors, greater than 45% require some special services that includes special education (Hack et al., 1994). In one long-term, follow-up study, Grunau (2002) found that 48 of 74 extremely low-birth-weight survivors who were neurologically healthy with average broad intelligence had at least one area of learning disability. These infants have the highest risk factors for poor or delayed outcomes. Those infants who escape intraventricular bleeding, chronic lung disease, and environmental factors such as poverty and child abuse have a good chance of surviving with normal cognitive and motor development (Stephens et al., 1997).

Extremely low-birth-weight infants frequently have some degree of intraventricular bleeding, which may cause brain damage. The effects of the bleeding are variable, with deficits including a wide range of developmental delays. Visual and hearing deficits are common with these very immature infants. **Retinopathy of prematurity** (ROP) is a common occurrence caused by the need for long-term oxygen therapy (for apnea of prematurity) and capillary fragility, which may lead to bleeding in the capillaries that supply the retina of the eye. Hearing loss is common and is related to drug therapy necessary for survival and the neurological impact from bleeding or decreased oxygen.

Infection is a frequent complication for the extremely low-birth-weight infant. The immune system does not become functional for several months after birth, leaving the infant at significant risk for any environmental or human bacteria or virus. Many of the common care needs of the infant, such as intravenous feedings and airway support, place the infant at risk for the development of an infection.

Nutrition is a major complicating factor with extremely low-birth-weight infants. The gastrointestinal tract requires the initiation of oral feedings before maturation can occur. The ability of these infants to tolerate oral feedings is extremely variable. Because of chronic decreased blood flow and lower oxygen levels supplying the system, lung disease places the intestine at risk for perforation. Lung growth is necessary for healing, and this growth will be compromised in the presence of inadequate nutrition. The interventions to provide sufficient calories for growth impact other organs, such as the liver or kidneys. Long-term, intravenous therapy leads to poor liver function. Failure of the infant to be able to feed increases the potential for total system failure that can ultimately lead to death.

RESPIRATORY DISTRESS SYNDROME (RDS)

Respiratory distress syndrome (RDS) is a common condition found in premature infants; 50% of infants born between 28–32 weeks develop RDS (Pramanik, 2001). It is caused by an absence of, or a deficiency in, the amount of surfactant (a naturally occurring chemical sometimes referred to as lung soap) present in the lungs of the infant. Surfactant increases the surface tension of the lung, allowing the alveoli or tiny air sacs to open and stay open with the respiratory effort of the infant. Decreased amounts, or the absence, of surfactant cause the air sacs to collapse upon themselves with expiration. Without sufficient surfactant to lubricate the lung tissue, premature infants are then unable to generate enough pressure to reopen the collapsed segments of the lung. This creates the condition in which there is decreased lung surface tissue available for the work of exchanging oxygen for carbon dioxide between the lungs and the blood vessels. This low oxygen state can ultimately result in neurological damage along with the advent of stiff lungs that require very high pressures to re-expand the collapsed segments.

Infants suffering from respiratory distress syndrome display symptoms of respiratory failure. These symptoms include an increased respiratory rate, retraction of the space between the ribs, audible grunting noise when breathing, and a blue-tinged or pale color to the skin, in spite of supplemental oxygen. If the symptoms persist without appropriate intervention, infants will eventually tire from their effort and quit breathing. Mechanical ventilation such as a respirator or ventilator is used to treat this disease. Recently, an artificial surfactant has been developed that may decrease the likelihood of chronic lung disease (McNab & Blackman, 1998). However, animal-derived surfactant is thought to be more effective, since the latter contains essential proteins (Subramanian et al., 2001). Along with surfactant therapy, use of antenatal steroids has been found to accelerate lung maturity and allow the use of a gentler ventilation technique, all of which minimize lung damage and have reduced the mortality rate associated with RDS by more than 50% in the last decade (Pramanik, 2001).

Mechanical ventilation has certain risks that are inherent in its use. These include lung damage from increased artificial pressure, tearing of small airways resulting in air leaks between the external lung surface and the rib cage (pneumothorax), bleeding into the lungs from increased pressure, damage to the small capillaries that are part of the circulation pathway (pulmonary hemorrhage), and the development of cysts created in the airways from excessive pressure (pulmonary interstitial emphysema), all of which can ultimately lead to chronic lung disease of infancy (bronchopulmonary dysplasia). Gentler ventilation techniques, such as high frequency ventilation, continuous positive airway pressure (CPAP), and synchronous intermittent mandatory ventilation are three techniques under investigation that attempt to provide supplemental oxygen while reducing damage to infants' lungs (Pramanik, 2001). While oxygenation increases the survival rate of premature infants, those with extreme prematurity frequently acquire chronic lung disease and ROP as a side-effect of the treatment itself (Stephens et al., 1997).

BRONCHOPULMONARY DYSPLASIA (BPD)

Chronic lung disease of infancy is called **bronchopulmonary dysplasia (BPD)**. This is the condition in which lung injury has occurred during the treatment of premature lung disease. This can be from the effects of positive pressure from extensive oxygen use. Occasionally a full-term infant who has had meconium aspiration or acute pneumonia from infection may contract BPD. Health care providers who treat these infants are aware of the potential implication of the treatments but are committed to provide the necessary intervention for acute respiratory failure and then deal with the effects over the course of the first two to three years of life.

Most extremely low-birth-weight infants will develop BPD, with most requiring home oxygen therapy through the first year of life. Aggressive treatment of the accompanying health care problems allows for the possibility of recovery, and many infants show normal lung function over the course of early childhood.

Infants with BPD show symptoms of respiratory distress. These include an increased respiratory rate, increased effort for breathing that may be displayed by retraction of the space between the ribs, the use of abdominal and neck muscles to breathe, the need for supplemental oxygen, and pale or dusky skin color. Additional symptoms may be poor tolerance for activities of daily living and symptoms of cardiac failure, which result from the strain placed on the heart and liver by chronic low oxygen levels and the need to maintain circulation through the injured lungs.

Bronchopulmonary dysplasia can also show up as a cluster of health problems for affected infants. These include, but are not limited to, problems with both acute and chronic infections, cardiovascular problems (including high blood pressure), kidney stones, vitamin and mineral deficiencies (which may result in bone fragility), feeding problems, and poor growth. This combination of factors then places these infants at significant risk for developmental delays. Stephens et al. (1997) found that the longer infants required mechanical oxygenation, the greater the likelihood of cognitive delay. Emotional problems, such as failure to bond, are most likely related to repeated and prolonged hospitalizations and irritability that is frequently seen in infants with chronic air hunger from lung disease.

Infants experiencing the effects of BPD can recover. Aggressive attention to the nutritional needs (allows for new lung growth) and the respiratory needs (prevents further deterioration), as well as medication to control cardiovascular effects, provide the time for healing to occur. When incorporated into the efforts of professionals, there is the need for early intervention to allow the child to develop normally within the constraints of his or her physical limitations.

Another significant problem associated with this disease is the dramatic impact on family structure. Many of the care needs of the infant may require skilled nursing. This may mean the addition of strangers to the inner family. Family systems that are already stressed may not survive the additional burdens this chronic disease places on individuals.

PATENT DUCTUS ARTERIOSUS (PDA)

Patent ductus arteriosus (PDA) is a cardiac defect that frequently occurs in the very low-birth-weight and extremely low-birth-weight infant. Because fetal circulation bypasses the lungs via an opening between the pulmonary artery and aorta, it is critical that this opening spontaneously close upon birth. Yet premature birth may prevent the complete transition to independent functioning, resulting in decreased cardiac output. This condition can result in increased respiratory distress for these infants and may have to be treated with medication or, in some cases, surgically closed at one of the most vulnerable periods, within the first week or two of life.

HYPERBILIRUBINEMIA

Most infants born at very low birth weight develop an abnormally high bilirubin level (Subramanian et al., 2001). This high level of dead blood cells is the combinant result of unusually high rate of red blood cell destruction and the inability of the immature liver and kidney to filter these metabolic byproducts from the system. Dangerously high bilirubin counts can result in deafness, mental retardation, cerebral palsy, and death. In order to treat bilirubin levels, phototherapy using special blue lamps penetrates the skin and breaks down bilirubin into a more water soluble product. If phototherapy fails, a blood transfusion of up to 90% of a neonate's blood may be conducted.

NEUTRAL THERMOREGULATION

Low-birth-weight infants do not have the physical or physiological mechanisms to maintain body temperature. Heat loss occurs rapidly in these infants through **convection** (heat loss with the delivery of unwarmed gases such as oxygen), **conduction** (heat loss to unwarmed surfaces such as a mattress), evaporation (heat loss through fluid loss through the skin), and **radiation** (heat loss through dissipation from the body into the air). **Hypothermia** (low body core temperature) then places the infant at risk for other physical problems, such as increased respiratory distress, low blood sugar, and possibly, intraventricular hemorrhage. Efforts are taken to preserve body temperature during any interaction with the very premature infant.

Temperature regulation may continue to be a problem for infants with chronic diseases. Poor regulatory mechanisms in infants with neurological deficiencies places them at risk for cold stress in what may appear to be a normal environment. Other conditions that may produce temperature instability are those in which there is decreased blood flow to the skin. This may occur in children who have congenital heart defects or acute and chronic infections or in infants who have problems with lung disease.

INTRAVENTRICULAR HEMORRHAGE (IVH)

The neurological system is one of the most vulnerable in any infant. This is particularly true for the premature infant. Because the rich capillary beds that lie next to the ventricles of the brain are extremely fragile in premature infants, they are prone to bleeding or leakage when there is oxygen deprivation leading to rapid changes in blood pressure (McNab & Blackman, 1998). Many factors that can influence low-birth-weight infants may result in an **intraventricular hemorrhage**. Extremes of temperature with rapid fluctuation cause dilatation and constriction of blood vessels, which may cause leakage or rupture of the vessels. Changes in blood pressure affect blood flow in the fragile vessels, also resulting in breakage or leaking. One of the most critical factors leading to IVH is the acid balance of the blood. Infants who are **acidotic** (high levels of blood acid) are predisposed to fragility of the vessels, which increases the risk of bleeding (Dijxhoorn, Visser, Rouwen, & Huisjes, 1987). Acid buildup can occur with lung disease (high carbon dioxide levels and decreased oxygen), low blood sugar, infections, and temperature instability, among other factors.

An inverse relationship results between an infant's gestational age and the incidence and severity of IVH, with the majority of occurrences happening within the first 72 hours of birth (Subramanian et al., 2001). Moreover, the area of bleeding, the size of affected area, the age and weight of an infant, and many other physical factors determine the amount and potential damage to function that may occur as a result of IVH. Bleeding that is acute and rapid tends to have greater impact on the overall stability of an infant in the acute phase.

Intraventricular hemorrhages are categorized into four grades. The grade of the hemorrhages can be predictive of the long-term outcome for a child, though this predictive value is not always accurate. For example, a grade IV bleed frequently results in hydrocephalus, or swelling of the fluid-filled cavities in the brain, and the subsequent need for replacement of a ventricular peritoneal shunt. These infants require ongoing developmental follow-up after discharge from the hospital and are at significant risk for serious developmental delays. Injuries to infants who sustain grades I and II bleeding often resolve without permanent neurological abnormalities. On the other hand, approximately 40% of all children with grade III and 90% of those with grade IV bleeding develop significant cognitive and/or motor disabilities (Subramanian et al., 2001).

Related to IVH is a second neurological disorder that occurs in premature infants called **periventricular leukomalacia (PVL)** or damage to the white matter of the brain. Also believed to be caused by rupturing of the blood vessels in the brain, PVL is associated with the development of cysts or fluid-filled holes, generally on both sides of the brain. Extremely low-birth-weight infants with PVL are at a 10–15% risk for spastic cerebral palsy and other developmental disabilities such as cognitive, speech, and visual impairments (Subramanian et al., 2001).

APNEA OF PREMATURITY

Premature infants have a very high incidence of irregular breathing patterns. In fact, it has been found that 90% of infants born at less than 1000 grams will suffer apnea of prematurity (AOP) (Hack, Wilson-Costello, & Friedman, 2000). Pauses in breathing are called episodes of apnea. These may be apparent at birth for those infants that do not require ventilation or may develop over the first few days of life. This apnea results from central nervous system immaturity or may be a result of posture in the small infant. Many cases may actually be attributed to a combination of both factors. When pauses occur, the infant's response is generally a decrease in the baseline heart rate. This may be a small decrease or it may be substantial. Many infants will require stimulation by caregivers or, if the apnea is particularly severe, may require mechanical ventilation.

Initial apnea in the infant may not be severe. It is the case in which the infant does not self-stimulate (autoregulatory effect from the nervous system) and proceeds to more profound states of apnea that creates conditions requiring intervention to prevent decreased oxygen to the brain, heart, and kidneys. Failure to appropriately intervene can lead to secondary apnea (respiratory failure/arrest), which is more difficult to reverse. Apnea can lead to the buildup of acid in the blood, placing affected infants at risk for bleeding into the brain.

Several interventions are possible to decrease the incidence of apnea. These may include continuous external stimulation, such as an oscillating mattress and medications that stimulate the central nervous system to regulate respiration. These methods may be necessary for the first few months of life until the nervous system has matured sufficiently to have acquired more consistent regulatory control. Many premature infants may be discharged from the hospital with continuous cardiac/respiratory monitoring and medication, provided their caregivers have been educated to appropriately respond to apnea events.

Case Study   THE DIARY OF ESTHER ANNA BERKE: MONTH 7

May 16–30:   Esther weighs 7.15 kg and measures 67 cm long, still at the 50th percentile for weight and at the 70 percentile for length. She is current taking 0.125 mg Rivotril, 300 mg Vitamin B_6, 1 mg Sabril, and 2 mg Lamictal per day.

Her seizures have decreased somewhat in frequency but increased somewhat in intensity. Sarah took the kids to America on May 29. Esther traveled well, she slept most of the trip, only waking up to drink a bottle here and there. We were concerned that the trip would really disrupt her schedule, but she adjusted quite well.

June 1–15:   Esther was examined by an eye specialist on June 9. He said that her left eye never really developed inside. He couldn't even really see an optic nerve. But she does have vision in her right eye. There is a large coloboma, but it doesn't hinder her main vision. He said she probably won't have 20/20 vision, but she will be able to see. He also said that children that grow up with vision in one eye usually are able to compensate for it quite well. Sarah is in the 5th month of her pregnancy and doing well. Sarah and the kids went to a Berke family reunion on June 13, then flew to Spokane, Washington on June 14 to see her parents and another specialist.

INFECTIONS

Dangerous infections have several vectors of opportunity in premature infants. As mentioned, the first line of defense to infection—skin—is a target for yeast infection in premature infants. Moreover, stays in intensive care units present hazards in access to staphylococci and streptococci infections, among other agents of infection. Infants with intravenous tubes and/or catheters are at great risk of infection. Therefore antibiotic and antifungal treatment are commonly a part of a regimen for premature neonates. The continuing crisis in medicine related to drug-resistant bacterial and fungal strains has resulted in conservative administration of the most powerful antibiotics and antifungal treatments. Such caution is meant to preserve the effectiveness of these reliable treatments for the most dangerous infection situations (Subramanian et al., 2001).

RETINOPATHY OF PREMATURITY (ROP)

Because of their size and gestational age, low-birth-weight infants face the possibility of permanent damage to their vision. One third of infants born at 24 weeks develop ROP, with this rate decreasing by one half for each additional week of gestation (Walling, 1998). This factor is variable, depending on the ventilation needs of the infant and the necessity for the use of supplemental oxygen during visual maturation, which takes place between 40 and 44 weeks after conception.

Prolonged exposure of fragile blood vessels in the retina to excessive levels of oxygen constricts and disrupts normal growth of retinal blood vessels. Abnormal new vessels develop which are accompanied by fibroblasts that produce scar tissue. The new blood vessels are then prone to leakage or rupture and grow outward from the retina into the interior space of the eyeball. In many cases, this overgrowth spontaneously recedes, permitting the retina to develop normally. In other instances, scar tissue growths continue to spread around the eye. When this scar tissue contracts, it pulls on the retina, causing the retina to detach, eventually causing blindness.

At one time, ROP in low-birth-weight infants was controlled with the use of less oxygen; but decreased oxygen increased infant mortality rates and created a significantly higher incidence of cerebral palsy. Today, oxygen is administered liberally in an effort to save increasingly smaller premature infants. A mature retina is not affected by increased oxygen use. This is why few full-term infants have ROP. When given supplemental oxygen, premature infants must be closely monitored in order to keep arterial blood oxygen levels within a range to prevent **hypoxia**, while minimizing risk of eye damage from the oxygen. In cases where deterioration of the retina proceeds rapidly, surgery may be implied. Cryotherapy, freezing of the blood vessels, and laser surgery are used to encourage overgrown vessels to recede (Fleck, 1999). If these procedures fail, more invasive surgery of the eye may be conducted to reduce contraction on the scar tissue which causes retinal detachment. Unfortunately, to date, the success rate of such innovative surgical procedures is limited.

Retinopathy of prematurity is currently categorized into four stages. Stage One and Stage Two damage generally resolves completely without treatment. Some infants with mild ROP which resolves either spontaneously or by laser/cryotherapy surgery undergo regression later in life in the form of strabismus, myopia, ambliopia, glaucoma or retinal detachment. Stage Three damage may require laser treatment, while Stage Four damage will require surgery to attempt to reattach the retina. Most infants who proceed to Stage Four will have significant visual defects from this disease in spite of the surgical intervention.

ANEMIA

Anemia is the condition in which there is a deficiency in the number of red blood cells available to the infant. This can result either because of a failure in the production of cells or because cells are being used or destroyed faster than they can be replaced. Prematurity results in infants who are affected with anemia for both of these reasons.

Since premature infants have immature bone marrow, production of red blood cells, which takes place in the marrow, is inhibited until the marrow has matured. In addition to the inability to produce new cells, premature infants are nutritionally deficient, especially in iron, which also leads to decreased blood cell production. Even with supplemental iron in the diet, premature infants often are unable to take in sufficient amounts of oral feedings to meet requirements. Infants may become symptomatic with anemia as demonstrated through decreased activity, poor feeding, increased apnea, and slowed weight gain. Premature infants require multiple blood transfusions during their initial weeks of life. Parents now have the option of requesting a Directed Donor in many hospitals. This program allows parents and close family members to donate blood to be used by the individual infant, thus decreasing parent anxiety over multiple blood transfusions.

NUTRITION

Immediately after birth, there is a concern for maintaining glucose levels. Premature infants, lacking sufficient glycogen stores to make the transition from maternal supplies to self-regulation, often require a continuous intravenous supply of glycogen to prevent hypoglycemia and its symptoms of seizures, jitteriness, lethargy, and apnea (Subramanian et al., 2001).

The ability to eat and digest food is critical to life. Yet premature infants require a very high caloric intake due to body heat loss and rapid growth. Moreover, feeding is much more complex, because these infants have not developed an instinctive desire to eat. Alterations in either physical or physiological processes that affect eating or digestion place a child at risk for the development of delays. Eating problems also increase the impact of an existing disability on the course of the child's life. Adequate fluids and sufficient caloric intake of essential proteins, fats, carbohydrates, and vitamins and minerals are essential for growth and development.

Term infants are born with primitive reflexes that allow them to initiate a suck and to coordinate breathing and swallowing. These reflexes disappear as maturation occurs, and the act of eating becomes voluntary. Premature infants, dependent upon gestation, may not have matured to the point of a primitive reflex state. Oral feeding for these infants is not possible. As maturity occurs, these reflexes emerge and learning to eat becomes possible.

Chronic disease in premature infants has an impact on both the ability to learn to eat orally and the digestion of food for growth. Disease increases the need for caloric intake in order to maintain a minimal state of health and for growth to occur. The combination of events increases the risks that an infant will fail to grow.

Premature infants require a minimum of 120 Cal/kg of body weight each day for growth to occur. Chronic disease increases the daily caloric intake requirement to 150 Cal/kg of body weight for the same growth pattern to occur. The expectation is that the infant will gain approximately 15 g (1/2 oz) to 30 g (1 oz) of weight every day. This allows for the linear growth and brain growth that is critical to a normal developmental progression.

Maintaining electrolyte/fluid balance is also difficult, as fluid levels are likely to fluctuate dramatically due to treatments such as radiant warmers, because of a high proportion of water to other body mass and because of poorly developed kidney function. Prenatal steroids can be used to help maintain electrolyte balance and prevent neurological, cardiac, respiratory, and other collateral effects (Omar, DeCristofaro, Agarwal, & LaGamma, 2000).

Difficulty with sucking, swallowing, and breathing coordination may necessitate tube feedings. Nonnutritive sucking (as from a pacifier) catalyzes a learning drive and allows nutritive sucking to develop. At the same time, factors such as fatigue, illness, and congenital defects affect the rate and success of learning.

A feeding problem not limited to prematurely born infants is gastroesophageal reflux, or spitting up during or after eating. Infants with developmental delays are at greater risk of more severe and persistent symptoms related to poor coordination of gastrointestinal processes (Borowitz, 2002). While the vomiting is almost never a threat to nutrition, the occurrence can be lessened by appropriate positioning during and after feeding (i.e., infant lying down on stomach or with at least 30 degree trunk elevation in a supine position), thickening of food, increasing frequency of feedings, or adminstering medication. Usually when children begin to sit independently, gastroesophageal reflux diminishes.

Occupational therapy may be necessary within the neonatal period to assist in planning care for the premature or sick infant who is feeding poorly and not gaining weight. Many interventions may be tried to provide opportunities for the child to successfully feed. Infants who cannot take in a minimal amount of fluids and/or calories for normal growth may require further interventions to assist in the feeding process. This may involve the placement of a **gastrostomy tube** or a gastric button through which feedings can be given directly into the stomach, bypassing the esophagus. Even infants who are receiving primary nutrition through a feeding tube are continually orally stimulated to teach them oral feeding. Once oral feeding begins, mother's breastmilk, augmented with additional nutritional supplements, is the best choice to prevent necrotizing of the intestine—a common reaction to premature feeding (Subramanian et al., 2001).

FAILURE TO THRIVE

Failure to thrive can be described as the condition of growth failure in infancy and early childhood. Parameters for determining adequate growth are dependent upon placement in standard growth charts that are guidelines for a normal growth curve. Infants and young children who fall at least two standard deviations below the norm over a designated time period (generally 2 months) are suggestive of growth failure. This condition may be the result of a multitude of problems that affect the infant. These include, but are not limited to, inadequate economic means for adequate food, chronic disease (congenital heart defects, BPD, etc.), genetic disorders, emotional distress, and abuse. The signs of failure to thrive include decreased weight, decreased height, small head size, and any combination of these. Prolonged failure will ultimately affect brain growth, leading to more complex problems.

Failure to thrive may be termed as either **organic** (specific physical causation) or as **nonorganic** (without specific physical cause). Many physical conditions that result in poor growth can be treated with a resultant improvement in growth rates. These interventions may include increasing caloric intake through dietary changes, medications, and the treatment of other physical factors that may impact growth, such as chronic ear infections.

Nonorganic failure to thrive is the more commonly occurring condition. Nonorganic factors that influence the ability of an infant to grow normally include economics, ignorance, poor parenting skills, and ongoing family stresses. Feeding problems arise in these situations, resulting in prolonged malnutrition and, if not corrected, may lead to delayed mental development and, in the most severe cases, may even lead to death of the infant. Many of these infants appear to lose the will to live during periods of profound depression. This despondency can be significantly improved by a nurturing and consistent caregiver.

The ability to influence failure to thrive in infancy is dependent upon the age at onset, the cause, and the requirements for treatment. The earlier the infant is affected, the poorer the long-term outcome. However, Wright and her colleagues (1998) compared children identified as failing to thrive who received regular home visits by health professionals for 2 years to a control group which received no intervention. Though the primary intervention consisted of dietary management, families also received input from pediatricians and social workers. At 3 years of age, 76% of the treated children had recovered, compared to 55% of the control group.

In severe cases of failure to thrive, comprehensive interdisciplinary planning is necessary. Specialized dietary preparations and specialized feeding techniques may be necessary to counteract the behaviors of the infant and its aversion toward feeding. Prolonged nutritional deficits will place the child at risk for learning problems that may affect gross motor skills, expressive language, and social skills.

INTERVENTION FOR INFANTS AND CHILDREN BORN PREMATURELY

Though not all children who are premature will have the same needs, the following interventions are considered when planning hospital follow-up (McNab & Blackman, 1998). The most important factor in improving outcomes for infants who are born prematurely is to keep them healthy in early childhood. These interventions support health:

◆ speech therapy for children with chronic lung disease to promote feeding and language
◆ physical/occupational therapy for children with chronic lung disease who have poor exercise tolerance and tire easily
◆ home-based therapy to avoid exposure to infants with low/poor immunity to risk of infection
◆ emotional support to the family, including group meetings
◆ aggressive attention to the nutritional status of infants
◆ regular opthamological examination in children with prolonged oxygen treatment
◆ special adaptations for children with mild/severe ROP to promote sensory integration

Families with children born prematurely undergo tremendous emotional and financial hardship (Subramanian et al., 2001). Educators can expect this stress will be manifest in confusion, anxiety, frustration, guilt, and anger. Due to prolonged neonatal hospital care and the sequelae of medical and neurological trauma, premature infants often lack the spontaneity and responsiveness of term infants. These factors can interrupt maternal–infant bonding. Professionals can assist by being ready to answer questions, to encouraging quality interactions between infants and parents, to providing a sounding board and to help intervene for those who express a need to access resources that might directly or indirectly diffuse some of the stress such families experience. Later in infancy and early childhood, infants with unresolved medical and developmental difficulties are at risk for child abuse and failure to thrive (Pramanik & Pramanik, 2001). Therefore, ongoing home visits by social workers and health professionals is advised, especially in situations where professionals observe a disruption in parents' attachment during their infants' NICU stays.

SUBSTANCE ABUSE AND PREGNANCY OUTCOMES

Since substance abuse during pregnancy may be associated with many disabling newborn conditions and is entirely preventable, more detailed discussion is focused in this area. Alcohol, drugs, and cigarettes are all considered **teratogens**. A teratogen is an agent introduced into the mother's womb that causes either physical or neurological harm to an embryo or fetus. While a range of environmental substances are dangerous, the most common will be discussed here.

FETAL ALCOHOL SYNDROME

Though the in utero effects of alcohol have been acknowledged for centuries (Weiner & Morse, 1988), it was not until the 1970s that the term **Fetal Alcohol Syndrome (FAS)** was officially attached to the constellation of characteristics now considered criteria for this syndrome (Jones & Smith, 1973; Jones, Smith, Ulleland, & Streissguth, 1973). Though it is believed that FAS and Alcohol Related Birth Defects (ARBD) are grossly underrecognized and underreported, FAS reportedly occurs in 1–3 per 1000 live births (Gardner, 1997). These statistics make FAS the leading known cause of mental retardation.

Children born with FAS may not be identified at birth, and if suspected at some later point, must be medically diagnosed with the syndrome. The three primary characteristics of FAS described by Burgess and Streissguth (1992) are:

1. Growth deficiency
2. Abnormal facial features
3. Central nervous system dysfunction

Additionally, the physician must find strong evidence of maternal alcohol consumption during pregnancy (Burgess & Streissguth, 1992). If some, but not all, of the characteristics mentioned are present at birth, and if the mother is known to have been a heavy drinker during pregnancy, these infants will be labeled **Fetal Alcohol Effects (FAE).** Though the latter is not a medical diagnosis, both the cause and the effects may be as serious as in FAS. Fetal Alcohol Effects may also be referred to as Alcohol Related Neurodevelopmental Disorder (ARND).

Infants with FAS are short for their chronological age and tend to weigh less than average. As these children age, they do not tend to catch up to their peers, but they are more likely to be closer to expected weight than height (Streissguth,

LaDue, & Randels, 1988). Facial characteristics commonly attributed to FAS include a short, upturned nose, thin lips, wide-set eyes, flat midface, epicanthic folds, and ear anomalies (Streissguth et al., 1988).

The average IQ of individuals with FAS was found to be around 68 (borderline mental retardation), with a range of 20 to 105 (Streissguth et al., 1988). When academic content is concrete (in early elementary), children with FAS or FAE may do quite well. However, abstract content causes such children to experience increasing difficulties (Burgess & Streissguth, 1992). It is because of the transition in intermediate school years to more abstract content that children with FAS or FAE tend to plateau in terms of academic achievement (Streissguth et al., 1988).

The behavioral characteristics of FAS are the most distressing for caregivers. Typical behavior patterns may or may not be associated with neurological damage sustained by vulnerable fetuses. That is, for a majority of infants and preschoolers with FAS or FAE, postnatal environments are chaotic and sometimes transient. These conditions alone could cause the kinds of abnormal developmental behaviors seen in children with FAS or FAE. Behaviors seen within this population (not necessarily in all children with FAS or FAE) include hyperactivity and impulsivity, language and communication difficulties (especially in social conventions), noncompliance, immaturity, and difficulty in self-regulation, judgment, and decision making (Burgess & Streissguth, 1992). Children with FAS or FAE appear to be unresponsive to subtle kinds of consequences (e.g., praise, reprimands) that help other children regulate their behavior. For example, children who are hyperactive tend to get into situations in which they are frustrated and become aggressive. Yet, it is difficult to isolate consequences that are effective in changing this impulsive behavior. As these children reach adolescence, their behavior may become more serious, as lack of judgment leads them to steal and lie (Burgess & Streissguth, 1992). These behaviors cause significant concern in terms of adaptation to vocational and community settings.

Etiology

The cause of FAS and FAE is always alcohol consumption during pregnancy. Alcohol crosses the placenta and enters the fetal bloodstream. A fetus's immature liver and neurological systems are less capable of metabolizing the alcohol than a mother's systems. Consequently, the alcohol becomes toxic. There is no known safe level of alcohol intake below which point it can be said that a developing fetus would be safe from alcohol's danger. However, it is probable that such factors as the gestational timing, duration of alcohol use, and overall maternal health (e.g., age, nutrition, genetics, etc.) interact with the amount of alcohol consumed to influence fetal development (Stevens & Price, 1992). Musculoskeletal/organ anomalies, intellectual/behavioral deficits, and growth retardation are thought be linked to exposure during the first, second, and third trimesters respectively (Gardner, 1997).

It may also be that the pattern of drinking affects neurological outcome. That is, Thomas and Riley (1998) believe that the symptoms seen in newborns going through alcohol withdrawal (from maternal alcohol consumption immediately prior to birth) are also likely to occur during gestation. Seizures, delirium tremors, and violent agitation associated with subsequent withdrawal may compound the adverse affects of alcohol exposure when women "binge drink." Though the incidence of FAS and FAE is relatively high in some ethnic groups (i.e., American Indians and Native Alaskans), the toxic risk of alcohol to a fetus appears to be the same for all women (Burgess & Streissguth, 1992).

Treatment

FAS and FAE are disabilities that require the mobilization of multiple agency resources. For example, families may require drug rehabilitation before they can be expected to nurture a child with multiple needs. An early interventionist may be asked to mediate services by foster care, child protection, mental health, drug rehabilitation, public schools, public assistance, corrections, and public health. None of these agencies working in isolation is likely to be effective in meeting the many needs of families who have children with FAS. Three factors have been found to improve the prospect of these children: a stable and nurturing home of good quality, having few changes of households, and not being the victim of violence (Streissguth & O'Malley, 1997).

Early intervention for children should center around social language, learning weak-rule governed behavior, and sustained attention (Howard, Williams, & McLaughlin, 1994). Specific suggestions for helping parents of children with Fetal Alcohol Syndrome/Effects include (Tanner-Halverson, 1998):

1. Foster independence in self-help and play.
2. Give choices and encourage decision making.
3. Establish a limited number of simple rules, and use consistent language to remind children of the rules; for example, "this is your bed, this is where you are supposed to be."
4. Use established routines so children know what to expect—advise well in advance of changes in routines.
5. Teach new skills in small pieces.
6. Be concrete and teach by showing rather than just telling.
7. Set limits and be consistent in expecting children to follow them by having predetermined consequences for both following and not following rules.
8. Review rules for getting rewards and change rewards often.
9. Do not negotiate rules.
10. Redirect behavior rather than threatening.
11. Intervene before behavior escalates and avoid overstimulating situations.
12. When giving instructions, repeat and ask child to repeat instructions back.

PRENATAL EXPOSURE TO DRUGS

At the height of the "cocaine baby" media anxiety, it was suggested that the single most challenging educational problem of the 21st century would be the after effects of maternal use of recreational drugs during pregnancy (Chasnoff, 1989). Yet longitudinal research, which has been conducted with more care and across greater numbers of children, has failed to validate early dramatic claims (Covington & Templin, 1998; Gustavsson & MacEachron, 1997). Still, there is sufficient reason to be concerned about the effects of both prenatal and postnatal exposure to such drugs as tobacco, cocaine, and methamphetamine.

Cocaine/Crack and Methamphetamines.

The physiology of cocaine (crack) and methamphetamines on adults and fetuses is similar, though the drugs themselves vary considerably in price, availability, and addictiveness. Crack is the least expensive and is a crystallized form of cocaine (the powder form). Furthermore, crack provides a more powerful, though shorter lived, high, and is significantly more addictive than either powder cocaine or methamphetamines. Each of these drugs causes blood vessels to constrict, resulting in increased blood pressure. In a pregnant woman, the placenta itself constricts, reducing oxygen flow to the fetus.

Likewise, fetuses directly exposed to cocaine that has crossed the placenta experience "highs" along with associated side effects. Since a fetus is unable to metabolize or break down the drug as easily as her mother, cocaine can stay in the fetal system for up to four times as long as in an adult's system. Primary risks to a fetus include premature birth, placenta previa (Handler, Mason, Rosenberg, & Davis, 1994), abruptio placenta, spontaneous abortion or prematurity, and possible neurological damage (Chasnoff, 1998). In spite of the apparent risks, it now appears that for most infants the long-lasting neurological consequences of cocaine or methamphetamine use by themselves during pregnancy are either absent or so subtle that they cannot be detected by common diagnostic procedures (Susman, 1996).

A neonate born to a drug-using mother will not always show signs of prenatal exposure, just as some infants born to alcohol abusers do not. However, those neonates that do show signs of prenatal exposure have a recognizable constellation of behavioral characteristics. No abnormal attributes in appearance are associated with prenatal cocaine or methamphetamine effects. Neonates who are obviously affected appear to have poorer than normal motor performance and in their response to environment, they tend to be less cuddly, harder to console, and less alert to environmental stimuli (Delaney-Black & Covington, 1996). These withdrawal features may persist for a few days, weeks, or months. Perhaps the most enduring and disturbing behavior is hypersensitivity to stimuli, which in some children will remain a serious problem for years.

The long-term, permanent neurological damage to the brain from prenatal exposure to cocaine, once thought to be significant, is now considered to be associated more with polydrug use (Napiorkowski & Lester, 1996) and/or environmental conditions than with by crack/cocaine exposure alone (Hulse, 1997; Susman, 1996). Such characteristics include problem behaviors, such as difficulty with habituation, short attention span, and hyperactivity, and **attention deficit hyperactivity disorder (ADHD)** (Calhoun & Alforque, 1996; Covington & Templin, 1998; Weintraub, Bental, Olivan, & Rotschild, 1998). In well-controlled studies, where children with and without prenatal cocaine exposure were matched for such factors as income, age, ethnicity/race and gender, there appears to be no significant long-term effects of cocaine alone (Gustavsson & MacEachron, 1997; Susman, 1996). Yet, children who are raised in poverty and generally chaotic environments tend to do poorly in social, language, and cognitive development, whether or not they are exposed to cocaine. Regardless of the cause, children in both groups may require substantial resources in order to compensate for their environmental disadvantage. However, Susman (1996) did find that children who were prenatally exposed to cocaine and subsequently born prematurely fared well when they returned home to a stable and positive home environment. Thus, it appears that more important than the drug exposure itself is the environment in which children are raised.

Bellinghausen (2000), reported on the current drug scene as it related to childbearing women. While cocaine use by pregnant women has declined over the past decade, there has been an alarming increase in the use of methamphetamines for this same population. In fact, women who, for one reason or another, were unable to "get clean," intentionally switched to methamphetamines during pregnancy, believing its effect to be more benign, if not totally safe. Like cocaine, it appears that the most consequential factors related to long-term physical, neurological, and behavioral effects of methamphetamines are related to a "drug lifestyle." Specifically, women using drugs are less likely to eat well, leading to maternal/fetal malnutrition. Moreover, most methamphetamine users are polydrug users, often using alcohol, opiates, or other drugs to counter the effects of methamphetamine. Plessinger (1998) suggested that the metabolic threshold of vulnerability to the potential damaging effects of methamphetamine use during pregnancy was lowered by these other conditions (i.e., malnutrition, alcohol use, tobacco use). Therefore, researchers have not found compelling evidence that methamphetamine use by itself directly affects prentally exposed infants' long-term behavior significantly.

The sequelae described for cocaine applies to infants who have been prenatally exposed to methamphetamine: low birth weight, small for gestational age (SGA), abnormal behavioral patterns (i.e., excessive crying, jitteriness, etc.). Finally, it is clear that the mother's behavior is not the only important influence as fathers who use methamphetamine are more likely to be abusive, resulting in an unsafe postnatal environment for mother and child. Again, Bellinghausen (2000) concluded, the best course of action is to provide a nurturing responsive environment—particularly in the first year of life.

Fortunately, a recent longitudinal study of newborns (Buchi, Zone, Langheinric, & Varner, 2003), conducted in Utah between 1990 and 2001, found no significant increases in prenatal exposure to methamphetamine or marijuana and found a dramatic decline in cocaine prevalence. An interesting clue to understanding the unexpected low rate of infant exposure to methamphetamine at the same time use of the drug by women is increasing sharply may be revealed in a study conducted by Half et al. (1993). In following inner-city teens who self-reported lifelong substance abuse, it was found that during pregnancy the use of drugs declined (verified by urine assays) in the following manner: tobacco use fell from 54 to 26%, alcohol use dropped from 78 to 28%, marijuana use lessened from 44 to 8%, and methamphetamine use declined from 22 to 2%. For some reason, these girls made the judicious decision to refrain from drug use, knowing the health risks during pregnancy.

Case Study

A PARENT'S PERSPECTIVE ON FETAL ALCOHOL SYNDROME: INTERVIEW WITH JAMES HOLDEN

Part of the difficulty with the diagnosis of Fetal Alcohol Syndrome is there are so many variables we don't know. We don't know how much the parents were drinking, and we know these children often had absolutely no prenatal care. April's mother just showed up at the hospital, had the baby, checked herself out and left.

April was 2–3 months old when we got her. She was in a good home, but a court order had deemed the home was not a culturally appropriate home—they wanted her in a Native American home. But, here again, I think part of the trouble of the system is, that although they offer a wide variety of training for foster parents, those folks really didn't know what to look for. They really didn't know what the danger signs would be. We got this child and we knew instantly this was not the child we had been led to believe we would be receiving.

She slept all the time and wouldn't take any nourishment. Her little arms and legs were scrawny and she couldn't do anything that was developmentally appropriate for her age. At 3 months, you would expect to see her head moving, and she should be responding to light or sound, but she was lethargic; she'd just lie there and not do anything.

Within 3 or 4 weeks she started waking up and we knew immediately it was going to be a battle. She was so flighty even then. As soon as she started waking up, she would start quivering even when we were holding her. She didn't like to held, to be walked, to be rocked, to be touched, or to be cuddled. We couldn't do anything to comfort her, so she did a lot of screaming.

As we get closer to an educational experience for these children, we considered Head Start and ECAP, which are great programs, but they're already heavily weighted with children of color and children of poverty that we fear our Indian children won't have appropriate models. When we get children in kindergarten who have no social skills, who can't work with large groups or small groups, who are hyperactive, and a lot are on medications, our teachers are just totally overwhelmed.

Our children receive occupational and physical therapy and speech therapy at home. So with three of them, we have our own little group, but there's not much interaction with other children their age. And that really concerns us, because I know there's a lot of children like that out there.

As soon as the children turn 3, the therapists may want us to take them in to their offices. You can't blame them, they're getting overloaded too, there are so many of these children. So we have to find treatment for them somewhere, and we would prefer that they be in smaller sessions,

Holden children at the ocean.

(continued)

but with some other children on a consistent basis. I don't see anything like that. Most of the therapists want one-on-one. So, as far as working in small groups, these children aren't doing that yet.

These children won't get into the early childhood program in the schools until they're 4, unless they're identified as developmentally impaired. Our district has a propensity to identify only those children who have neurological or physical handicaps as eligible for preschool services.

Every time I go to a foster care meeting or see other foster care folks, we're all saying the same thing. We're talking about terribly chemically impacted children. These are children who desperately need some kind of intervention for social and behavioral issues, but until they're 4 we often can't get services unless they also have a pronounced physical disability.

Cigarette Smoking

Cigarette smoking in North America increased dramatically for females in the late 1960s when the tobacco industry began to market specifically to this gender, then decreased significantly from the 1970s to the 1980s, with men representing the largest group of quitters or abstainers (Fried, 1993). Since 1991, the incidence of adolescent cigarette smoking has risen every year, with one in five teenagers being a smoker (Blumenthal, 1998). Of these teenager smokers, approximately 76% are addicted and 70% continue to smoke into their adulthood. The relative proportion of heavy smokers favored women (57% to 31% for men) who were European American or Hispanic (40% and 33% respectively as compared to 12% African American) (Blumenthal, 1998; Fried, 1991). It is estimated that 18 to 20% of pregnant women continue smoking throughout their pregnancy (Blumenthal, 1998). Though cigarettes contain over 2000 active ingredients, nicotine is considered the most harmful (Zuckerman, 1991).

For unborn children, exposure to tobacco that crosses the placenta causes vasoconstriction of the blood vessels and subsequent hypoxia or reduction of oxygen-carrying capacity of the hemoglobin, due to an increase of carbon monoxide, which binds with the hemoglobin (Zuckerman, 1991). Beginning very early in pregnancy, this process can have a degenerative effect (i.e., necrosis and reduced thickness) on the integrity of the placenta (Jauniaux & Burton, 1992). Several outcomes that increase infant morbidity and mortality have been associated with maternal smoking before or after birth; these include placenta previa (Handler et al., 1994), stillbirth, premature abruption, and Sudden Infant Death Syndrome (Gustavsson & MacEachron, 1997). The immediate risks of smoking on newborns include preterm delivery, intrauterine growth retardation, and low birth weight (an average of 200 grams less than infants not exposed to tobacco) (Hakim & Tielsch, 1992; Hanrahan et al., 1992; Zuckerman, 1991).

There also appears to be a direct relationship between the amount of smoking and the reduction of birth weight (Floyd, Zahniser, Gunter, & Kendrick, 1991; Zuckerman, 1991). It has been estimated that for every additional five cigarettes smoked per day, a newborn's birth weight is lowered by 26% (Kleinman & Madans, 1985). However, when mothers stop smoking either before or during pregnancy, the risk of problems goes down (Floyd et al., 1991). The third trimester of pregnancy seems to be the period most vulnerable to the harmful effects of nicotine (Fried, 1993).

Prenatal exposure to tobacco is also correlated with a high incidence of lung disease (i.e., bronchitis, pneumonia, tracheitis, and laryngitis), respiratory illnesses, and middle-ear disease (Floyd et al., 1991; Hanrahan et al., 1992). Nicotine is a known carcinogen when metabolized during the prenatal period, and nicotine poses an increased risk of cancer to the baby (Wise, 1998). Moreover, smoking causes a reduction in breastmilk volume and is perhaps the reason why heavy smokers are less likely to breastfeed and tend to wean their children sooner (Fried, 1993). As with Down syndrome, the risk of smoke-related problems for neonates seems to increase as the age of mothers increases (Wen, Goldenberg, & Cutter, 1990).

There is also a relationship between the amount of smoking by mothers and the degree of developmental delay in their babies. In general, children born to heavy smokers tend to do worse on standardized tests of development than infants born to light smokers or nonsmokers (Fried, 1993). Long-term effects of smoking (again, dose dependent) indicate that when exposed, children do less well in cognitive and language domains (Zuckerman, 1991). Others have documented an increased incidence of hyperactivity, attention deficit disorders, and learning disabilities (Floyd et al., 1991; Fried, 1993).

For cigarette smoking, as with other drugs, we should caution that neurologically vulnerable infants may do just as well as uncompromised infants when exposed to a nurturing environment; ". . . responsive care taking appeared to be a protective factor for those preterm children with biologic vulnerability" (Zuckerman, 1991, p. 34). In fact, numerous intervening variables interact with prenatal smoking. For example, Jacobson, Jacobson, and Sokol (1994) argued that when controlled for alcohol consumption, childhood stature was not affected by smoking at all. Nevertheless, it has been impossible to separate the isolate effects from collateral effects of teratogens. In the meantime, it is most reasonable to assume the worst and recommend against nicotine use during and after pregnancy. Finally, it is important to note the harmful effects of cigarette smoking to persons of any age. This is particularly clear to your authors, who lost their dear friend and original co-author of this text, Patricia Port, to lung cancer.

IMPLICATIONS FOR INFANTS AND CHILDREN PRENATALLY EXPOSED TO DRUGS

It appears that the drug which is most harmful to a fetus, with known long-term and significant effects, is alcohol. There is also little question that cigarette smoking poses a substantial threat to the long-term development of children. Because these drugs cross the placenta—a direct link between mother and infant—women who have exposed their babies to drugs are blamed and often punished for their actions. Removal of children to foster care is common; a two-fold increase in the number of children in foster care between mid-1980 and mid-1990 was linked to cataloging children as neglected or abused because of maternal drug use. Some suggest that such removal of children from their biological families is a moral obligation of society, necessary to protect children from the risk of violence and neglect associated with drug using families (National Association for Families and Addiction Research and Education, 1998). On the other hand, Gustavsson and MacEachron (1997) suggested that this criminalization of maternal drug use tends to victimize poor minority women, with foster care becoming a major form of family life for too many minority children. While this alleged victimization is clearly a social-ethical concern, it is also of practical concern for early intervention specialists' work in very complex social systems, chaotic family lives, and possible adversarial situations between state and family. Managing the system requires knowledge of the social welfare and child protection systems, legal rights of families and children, as well as careful execution of mediation and professional cooperation skills.

Interestingly, children who have been exposed to a single drug or polydrug use (and poverty) have similar developmental implications. Deficits in social skills and mild to moderate cognitive delays are common to all groups. For early interventionists, these general intervention apply (Calhoun & Alforque, 1996; Gardner, 1997):

1. Involve multidisciplinary intervention, including educators, social workers, behavioral specialists, and health care providers
2. Provide positive, structured, and predictable environment
3. Avoid highly stimulating environments
4. Provide direct training of social skills
5. Adapt tasks to meet individual learning strengths
6. Carry out functional analysis of serious behavioral problems
7. Provide concrete, clear, and immediate consequences for both desired and undesired behaviors
8. Give careful attention to diet and health care

CLOSE UP

THE DIRECT COST OF LOW BIRTH WEIGHT

Medical and technological advances have significantly increased the survival rates of low-birth-rate infants, including a doubling of the survival rates of extremely low-birth-weight infants between 1978 and 1995 (those weighing less than 2 pounds). Because of this success, the overall number of low-birth-weight infants has increased, causing a dramatic impact on the cost of health care. As with other technological advances, changes in the treatment of these very tiny humans have been made in the absence of ethical debate and practical considerations. Yet, Lewit, Baker, Corman, and Sinono (1995) provide compelling evidence for a social debate over current practices.

Lewit and colleagues studied the immediate and long-term direct cost of low-birth-weight infants as compared to infants born of normal birth weight, all born in 1988. To establish a point of reference, low-birth-weight infants comprised about 7% of all infants born during 1988. Yet, the medical care of these small infants consumed 35% of all health care costs for 1-year-olds. Infants who were extremely premature and experienced respiratory distress syndrome incurred almost three times the medical expenses as other low-birth-weight babies.

During the preschool year, the medical costs, though significantly lower for all children, continued to be almost three times higher for those of low birth weight. However, even though children born at low birth weight delayed entry into kindergarten later than other children, the overall use of resources was not substantially greater than that of other children.

When these children reached school age, the medical costs were more than four times higher than that of other children. In addition, these children used substantially greater resources in school. Those born less than 2500 grams were 50% more likely to be enrolled in special education, with each child in special education costing approximately 50% more than children born of normal birth weight. In addition, more children born low birth weight repeated grades and were therefore more likely to drop out of school, have lower earnings, commit more crimes, and require more social services.

To put this dilemma into context, Lewit and colleagues indicated that the overall cost of low birth weight was about one-third the direct cost of smoking and two-thirds the direct cost of alcohol abuse; the cost in 1988 for low birth weight was several times the direct cost of AIDS amongst all persons. These figures should provide a context for discussion of ways to reduce the rate of premature birth and low birth weight. Moreover, in the face of economic limits, it may be time to consider the medical/ethical policy regarding the extraordinary measures taken to preserve the lives of micropremature infants. According to the authors, "the evidence suggests that residual problems experienced by adults who were born low birth weight may be large in term of increased morbidity, lost earnings, and increased demand for health and social services."

Source: From "The Direct Cost of Low Birth Weight" by E. Lewit, L. S. Baker, H. Corman, and P. H. Sinono, Spring 1995, *The Future of Children 5*(1), pp. 1–23.

In Conclusion

One of the greatest challenges for society over the next decade will be to identify and plan interventions for decreasing the impact of prematurity on infants, and their families, and to influence life choices that affect the health of future children. This plan should include education about prevention, assistance to families involved with children with special needs, and interdisciplinary discussion regarding approaches that promote optimal functioning for affected children. Alcohol and substance abuse are two factors that increase the likelihood of premature birth. Most of these highly preventable early births are the consequence of social neglect of women whose lives are challenged by health problems (including depression), poverty, abuse, and poor education. Early childhood professionals who work with children born prematurely or affected by drug abuse will also be working within the context of families who have significant needs. Moreover, medical services are likely to be an ongoing part of the lives of children who are born prematurely. Therefore, a broad understanding of social and health services will be necessary in order to serve these children and their families well.

STUDY GUIDE QUESTIONS

1. Discriminate between the terms prenatal, natal, perinatal, and postnatal.
2. Explain how prematurity influences the vulnerability of different body systems.
3. Describe the impact of maternal conditions (e.g., age, weight, socioeconomic status, etc.) on fetal growth.
4. Describe the following conditions of pregnancy in terms of mechanism and risk to fetuses: placenta previa, abruptio placenta, toxemia of pregnancy, maternal diabetes, premature rupture of membranes, and Rh sensitization.
5. During labor itself, there are several conditions that place neonates at risk. Identify and describe these.
6. Explain how hypoxia–ischemia places a newborn at risk for developmental delays.
7. What is meconium, and when does it pose a threat to infants?
8. Discriminate between low, very low, and extremely low birth weight.
9. What is the relationship between RDS and BPD?
10. Explain the heat regulation concerns of premature infants.
11. A major concern to early childhood professionals of premature infants is IVH. Explain why this is so.
12. Define apnea and describe its relationship to prematurity.
13. ROP is a common outcome of the treatment of prematurity. Explain why this is so and what is being done to prevent ROP.
14. What is the relationship between nutritional needs of premature infants and anemia?
15. Define "failure to thrive" and explain the difference between organic and nonorganic failure to thrive.
16. What are the defining characteristics of FAS?
17. Why are children with FAS such a challenge to families and professionals?
18. Explain the way in which cocaine and methamphetamines influence a mother and fetus physiologically.
19. What are the "withdrawal" symptoms of neonates affected by cocaine/methamphetamines?
20. Explain the relationship between possible long-term behaviors associated with cocaine/methamphetamines and their treatment.
21. Summarize the influence of tobacco on unborn infants.

REFERENCES

Allen, M., & Capute, A. (1990, Supplement). Tone and reflex development before term. *Pediatrics,* 393–399.

Apgar, B. (1997). Pregnancy outcome and intelligence at age five. *American Family Physician, 55,* 1928–1930.

Bellinghausen, P. (Sun., April 30, 2000). Meth use linked to birth woes. *The Billings Gazette.* Retrieved January 10, 2003 from *http://www.manpinc. org/drugnews/ v00.n578.a03.html*

Besinger, R. E., Repke, J. T., & Ferguson, J. E. (1989). Preterm labor and intrauterine growth retardation: Complex obstetrical problems with low birth weight infants. In D. K. Stevenson & P. Sunshine (Eds.), *Fetal and neonatal brain injury. Mechanisms, management and risks of practice* (pp. 11–33) Toronto: BC Decker Inc.

Blumenthal, S. J. (1998). *Young women and smoking.* Fact Sheet published by the Department of Health and

Human Services: U.S. Public Health Service's Office on Women's Health. Retrieved 15, 2003 from *http://www.inwat.org/young*

Borowitz, S. M. (2002). Gastroesophageal reflux in infants. Children's Medical Center of the University of Virginia. Retrieved April 10, 2003 from *http://med.virginia.edu/cmc/tutorials/reflux/symptoms.htm*

Buchi, K. F., Zone, S., Langheinrich, K., Varner, M. W. (2003). Changing prevalence of prenatal substance abuse in Utah. *Obstetrical Gynecology, 102*(1), 27–30.

Burgess, D. M., & Streissguth, A. P. (1992). Fetal Alcohol Syndrome and Fetal Alcohol Effects: Principles for educators. *Phi Delta Kappan, 1,* 24–30.

Calhoun, G., & Alforque, M. (Fall, 1996). Prenatal substance afflicted children: An overview and review of the literature. *Education, 117,* 30–39.

Chasnoff, I. J. (1989, July). *National epidemiology of perinatal drug use.* Paper presented at the conference on Drugs, Alcohol, Pregnancy and Parenting, Spokane, WA.

Chasnoff, I. J. (1998). Silent Violence: Is prevention a moral obligation? *Pediatrics, 102,* 145–149.

Covington, C., & Templin, T. (1998). Prenatal cocaine exposure and child behavior. *Pediatrics, 102,* 945–951.

Curry, M. A. (October, 1998). Abused women at higher risk for maternal infant complications. *Women's Health Weekly,* 6–7.

Delaney-Black, V., & Covington, C. (1996). Prenatal cocaine and neonatal outcome: Evaluation of dose-response relationship. *Pediatrics, 98,* 735–741.

Dijxhoorn, M. J., Visser, G. H. A., Rouwen, B.C.L., & Huisjes, H. J. (1987). Apgar score, meconium and acidemia at birth in small for gestational age infants born at term, and their relation to neonatal neurological morbidity. *British Journal of Obstetrics and Gynaecology, 94,* 873–879.

Fleck, B. W. (1999). Therapy for retinopathy of prematurity. *Lancet, 353*(9148), 166–167.

Floyd, R. L., Zhniser, M. P. H., Gunter, E. P., & Kendrick, J. S. (1991). Smoking during pregnancy: Prevalence, effects, and intervention strategies. *Birth, 18*(1), 48–53.

Fried, P. A. (1993). Prenatal exposure to tobacco and marijuana: Effects during pregnancy, infancy and early childhood. *Clinical Obstetrics and Gynecology, 36*(2), 319–337.

Gardner, J. (1997). Fetal alcohol syndrome—recognition and intervention. *Maternal and Child Nutrition, 22,* 318–322.

Grunau, R. E. (2002). Extremely low birth weight children often have complex learning disabilities. *Archives of Pediatric Adolescent Medicine, 156,* 615–620.

Gustavsson, N. S., & MacEachron, A. E. (1997). Criminalizing women's behavior. *Journal of Drug Issues, 27*(3), 673–688.

Hack, M., Taylor, G., Klein, N., Eiben, R., Schatschneider, C., & Mercuri-Minich, N. (1994). School-age outcomes in children with birth weights under 750 grams. *The New England Journal of Medicine, 331*(3), 753–759.

Hack, M, Wilson-Costello, D. & Friedman, H. (2000). Neurodevelopment and predictors of outcomes of children with birth weights of less than 1000g, 1992–1995. *Archives of Pediatric & Adolescent Medicine, 154,* 725–731.

Hakim, R. B., & Tielsch, J. M. (1992). Maternal cigarette smoking during pregnancy: A risk factor for childhood strabismus. *Archives of Ophthamology, 110,* 1459–1462.

Half, J. A., Henggeler, S. W., Felice, M. E., Reynoso, T., Williams, N. M. & Sheets, R. (1993). Adolescent substance use during pregnancy. *Journal of Pediatric Psychology, 18*(2), 265–271.

Handler, A. S., Mason, E. D., Rosenberg, D. L., & Davis, F. G. (1994). The relationship between exposure during pregnancy to cigarette smoking and cocaine use and placenta previa. *American Journal of Obstetrics and Gynecology, 170*(3), 884–889.

Hanrahan, J. P., Tager, I. B., Segal, M. R., Tosteson, T. D., Castile, R. G., Vunakis, H. V., Weiss, S. T., & Speizer, F. E. (1992). The effect of maternal smoking during pregnancy on early infant lung function. *American Review of Respiratory Disease, 145*(5), 1129–1135.

Howard, V. F., Williams, B. F., & McLaughlin, T. F. (1994). Children prenatally exposed to alcohol and cocaine: Behavioral solutions. In R. Gardner, D. M. Sainato, J. O. Cooper, T. E. Heron, W. L. Heward, J. Eshleman, & T. A. Grossi (Eds.), *Behavior analysis in education: Focus on measurably superior instruction* (pp. 131–146). Belmont, CA: Brooks/Cole.

Hughes, P. F., Agarwal, M., & Thomas, L. (1997). Gestational diabetes and fetal macrosomia in a multi-ethnic population. *Journal of Obstetrics & Gynaecology, 17,* 540–544.

Hulse, G. (1997). Assessing the relationship between maternal opiate use and neonatal mortality. *Addiction, 7,* 1033–1043.

Jacobson, J. L., Jacobson, S. W., & Sokol, R. J. (1994). Effects of prenatal exposure to alcohol, smoking, and illicit drugs on postpartum somatic growth. *Alcoholism: Clinical and Experimental Research, 18*(2), 317–323.

Jauniaux, E., & Burton, G. J. (1992). The effect of smoking in pregnancy on early placental morphology. *Obstetrics & Gynecology, 79*(5), 645–648.

Jones, K. L., & Smith, D. W. (1973). Recognition of the Fetal Alcohol Syndrome in early infancy. *The Lancet, 2,* 999–1001.

Jones, K. L., Smith, D. W., Ulleland, C. N., & Streissguth, A. P. (1973). Pattern of malformation in offspring of chronic alcoholic mothers. *The Lancet, 2,* 1267–1271.

Kleinman, J. C., & Madans, J. H. (1985). The effects of maternal smoking, physical stature, and educational attainment on the incidence of low birthweight. *American Journal of Epidemiology, 121,* 843–855.

Lazzaroni, F., Bonassi, S., Manniello, E., Morcaldi, L., Repetto, E., Ruocco, A., Calvi, A., & Cotellessa, G. (1990). Effect of passive smoking during pregnancy on selected perinatal parameters. *International Journal of Epidemiology, 19*(4), 960–966.

March of Dimes (2002). All birthweight categories: US, 2000. Peristats: An interactive perinatal data source. Retrieved October 10, 2002 from *http://peristats. modimes.org/dataviewus.cfm*

McCormick, M.C. (1989). Long-term follow-up of infants discharged from neonatal intensive care units. *Journal of the American Medical Association, 261,* 24–31.

McNab, T. C., & Blackman, J. A. (1998). Medical complication of the critically ill newborn: A review for early intervention professionals. *Topics in Early Childhood Special Education, 18,* 197–206.

Napiorkowski, B., & Lester, B. M. (1996). Effects of in utero substance exposure on infant neurobehavior. *Pediatrics, 98,* 71–76.

National Association for Families and Addiction Research and Education. (1998). Silent violence: Is prevention a moral obligation? *Pediatrics, 102,* 145–149.

Newell, M. L. (2003). Antenatal and perinatal strategies to prevent mother-to-child transmission of HIV infection. *Research Society of Tropical Medicine and Hygiene, 97*(1), 22–24.

Omar, S. A., DeCristofaro, J., Agarwal, B.I., & LaGamma, E. F. (2000). Effect of prenatal steroids on potassium balance in extremely low birth weight neonates. *Pediatrics, 106*(3), 561–567.

Paz, I., Gale, R., Laor, A., Danon, Y. L., Stevenson, D.K., & Seidman, D.S. (1995). The cognitive outcome of full-term small for gestational age infants at late adolescence. *Obstetrics & Gynecology, 85*(3), 452–456.

Peleg, D., Kennedy, C. M., & Hunter, S. K. (1998). Intrauterine growth retardation restriction: Identification and management. *American Family Physician, 58,* 453–461.

Plessinger, M. A. (1998). Prenatal exposure to amphetamines. Risks and adverse outcomes in pregnancy. *Obstetrical Gynecology Clinicians of North America, 25*(1), 119–138.

Pramanik, A. (2001). Respiratory distress syndrome. *eMedicine Journal. 2*(7). Retrieved August 2, 2003 from *http://www.emedicine.com/ped/topic1993.htm*

Pre-conception factors may contribute to early birth, poor fetal growth. (January, 1999). *Women's Health Weekly,* 13–15.

Report of Consensus Conferences. (1987). *American Nurses' Association: Access to Prenatal Care: Key to Preventing Low Birthweight,* Kansas City, MO: American Nurses' Association, 24–32.

Soares, J. A. C., & Beard, R. W. (1998). Maternal leisure-time exercise and timely delivery. *American Journal of Public Health, 315,* 737–740.

Solomon, C. G. (October, 1997). Risk factors identified for diabetes during pregnancy. *Women's Health Weekly,* 9–10.

Stephens, R. P., Richardson, A. C., & Lewin, J. S. (1997). Outcome of extremely low birth weight infants (500–999 grams) over a 12 year period. *Pediatrics, 99,* 619–622.

Stevens, L. J., & Price, M. (1992). Meeting the challenge of educating children at-risk. *Phi Delta Kappan, 1,* 18–23.

Streissguth, A. P., LaDue, R. A., & Randels, S. P. (1988). *A manual on adolescents and adults with Fetal Alcohol Syndrome with special reference to American Indians* (2nd ed.). Seattle, WA: University of Washington Press.

Streissguth, A. P., & O'Malley, K. D. (1997). Fetal Alcohol Syndrome/Fetal Alcohol Effects: Secondary disabilities and mental health approaches. *Treatment Today, 9*(2), 16–17.

Subramanian, K. N. S., Yoon, H., & Toral, J. C. (2001). Extremely low birth weight infant. *eMedicine Journal, 2,* 11–13. Retrieved October 10, 2002 from *http://www. emedicine.com/ped/topic2784.htm*

Susman, E. (Sept, 1996). Cocaine's role in drug-exposed babies problems questioned. *Brown University Child and Adolescent Behavior Letter, 12*(9), 1–3.

Tanner-Halverson, P. (1998). Strategies for parents and caregivers of FAS and FAE children. The National Organization on Fetal Alcohol Syndrome. Retrieved October 10, 2002 from *http://www.nofas.org/strategy*

Tiedje, L. B.., Kingry, M. J., & Stommel, M., (1992). Patient attitudes concerning health behaviors during pregnancy: Initial development of a questionnaire. *Health Education Quarterly, 19,* 481–494.

Thomas, J. D., & Riley, E. P. (1998). Fetal alcohol syndrome: Does alcohol withdrawal play a role? *Health & Research World, 22,* 47–54.

Walling, A. D. (1998). Outcomes of infants born at 24–26 weeks of gestation. *American Family Physician, 57*(9), 2220–2222.

Weiner, L., & Morse, B. A. (1988). FAS: Clinical perspectives and prevention. In I. J. Chasnoff (Ed.), *Drugs, alcohol, pregnancy and parenting* (pp.127–148). Lancaster, UK: Kluwer Academic Publishers.

Weintraub, Z., Bental, Y., Olivan, A., & Rotschild, A. (1998). Neonatal withdrawal syndrome and behavioral effects produced by maternal drug use. *Addiction Biology, 3,* 159–170.

Wen, S. W., Goldenberg, R. L., & Cutter, G. R. et al. (1990). Smoking, maternal age, fetal growth, and gestational age at delivery. *American Journal of Obstetric Gynecology, 162,* 53–58.

Wildin, S. R., Landry, S. H., & Zwischenberger, J. B. (1994). Prospective, controlled study in developmental outcome in survivors of extracorporeal membrane oxygenation: The first 24 months. *Pediatrics, 9,* 404–408.

Wise, J. (1998). Carcinogen in tobacco smoke may be passed to fetus. *British Medical Journal, 317,* 555.

Wright, C. M., House, D. C., Callum, J., Birks, E., Jarvis, S., Service, P., & Terrace, D. (1998). Effect of community based management in failure to thrive: Randomized controlled trial. *British Medical Journal, 317,* 7158–7162.

Zuckerman, B. (1991). Drug exposed infants: Understanding the medical risk. *The Future of Children, 1*(1), 26–35.

Zuckerman, B., & Bresnahan, K. (1991). Developmental and behavioral consequences of prenatal drug and alcohol exposure. *The Pediatric Clinics of North America, 38*(6), 1387–1406.

6

Conditions Affecting the Neurological Function

Early childhood special educators are often a family's first link to intervention services and, consequently, also a first bridge between medical treatment and other professional therapies. It is critical, therefore, to have both substantive knowledge and reference information regarding the most common conditions that are associated with neurological damage. Though educators cannot be as intensely trained as medical personnel, a basic understanding of medical procedures and conditions is necessary in order to be conversant with other professionals and with parents.

Early childhood special educators may also find themselves in the role of interpreter for parents and for others who need to understand the medical nature of a child's neurological condition in order to plan effective intervention. Educators can refer to this text to refresh their own understanding of a condition, as well as to help parents interpret information given by health professionals. Though health professionals are often very direct and thorough, a parent's own ability to "hear" such information can be limited by the normal, initial emotional responses to a child's trauma or poor prognosis. Later on, early childhood special educators may be called upon to fill in missing information when parents are better able to "hear" and to understand.

This chapter is devoted to conditions that may affect a child's neurological functioning, including: knowledge of diagnostic testing, etiological factors resulting in damage to the nervous system, and characteristics of specific medical conditions common to early childhood special education. The neurological system is comprised of the central nervous system (brain and spinal cord) and the peripheral nervous system (12 cranial nerves and motor/sensory nerves in the extremities). Neurological impairments can be so subtle that they cannot be detected by medical or educational diagnostic techniques. On the other hand, significant damage to the nervous system can affect functions in all developmental domains, including movement, communication, social interactions, and cognitive functioning. Specific permutations of brain damage can also vary. Four children with a similar medical history of prematurity might have any one or all of the following neurological conditions: seizures, cerebral palsy, mental retardation, or attentional deficits. Some forms of damage to the neurological system occur very early in fetal development; other children may be affected long after birth. Causes of neurological damage include prenatal exposure to toxins, birth trauma and infections, as well as other factors.

DIAGNOSTIC TOOLS

The first step in clarifying various medical or disabling conditions is medical testing. These tests can be expensive, time consuming, and frightening for families engaged in the process. A simple understanding of the diagnostic tools involved can help alleviate a parent's concern or lack of understanding. Diagnostic tools involve both invasive procedures, in which a body system must be penetrated, and noninvasive methods, in which the body is not penetrated.

X RAYS

One of the oldest noninvasive tools used to evaluate an individual's condition is the X ray. **X rays** are a form of invisible electromagnetic energy that have a short wavelength which bombards a specific area of the body. Because of their very short wavelength, X rays are able to penetrate most substances, some substances more easily than others. The density of the tissue and the voltage power used affect the degree to which various tissues are penetrated by the X rays. These rays make certain substances fluoresce so that the size, shape, and movement of organs can be observed. The X rays themselves are invisible to the human eye but can be captured as an image on a specially coated film.

X rays are useful in detecting foreign bodies and fractures or for illuminating radioactive substances that have been introduced to the body. For example, radioactive dye may be injected into a blood vessel, and X rays can trace the resultant pathway.

Excessive exposure to X rays, particularly over a short period of time, can pose a serious health hazard. X rays have the potential to damage living cells, especially those that are dividing rapidly. The risks include damage to bone marrow and other blood-forming organs, damage to genes resulting in genetic/chromosomal mutations (which can be passed to future generations), onset of fetal death or malformation, and the development of cataracts. Finally, exposure to X rays over a long period of time can be carcinogenic. Such damage is avoided by using the lowest possible radiation doses, by using a lead shield to protect tissue that is not of concern, and by avoiding X rays when there is any possibility of pregnancy.

COMPUTERIZED AXIAL TOMOGRAPHY

The **computerized axial tomography** (CAT scan, also commonly known as CT) was developed in 1972 and was proclaimed the most important diagnostic device to be invented since X rays were first introduced. While operating on similar physical principals as an X ray (radiology), a CAT scan is 100 times more powerful than its predecessor. To conduct this exam, individuals are placed in a circular chamber and are bombarded with focused X rays coming from several planes (e.g., cross-sectional, horizontal). A detector, positioned opposite the X-ray source (scanner), picks up the X rays, which have been absorbed at different rates, depending on the density of the tissue through which they have passed. These measurements are reconstructed using a computer to produce clear, three-dimensional images of body tissue and structure on an oscillating screen. CAT scans are used to distinguish interior body structures such as lesions, bleeding in the brain, hydrocephalus, and tumors. An advantage of CAT scans over X rays is their ability to detect structures not visible on conventional tests and their ability to evaluate the targeted body part from many different angles simultaneously. Though more expensive and more risky (increased radiation exposure) than ultrasonography, CAT scans are considerably more accurate in detecting such problems as tumors or abscesses (see Figure 6–1).

MAGNETIC RESONANCE IMAGING

Magnetic resonance imaging (MRI) is a relatively new technology that is now used widely in the diagnosis of abnormalities in cardiovascular, orthopedic, and neurological systems. Unlike CAT scans and X rays, magnetic resonance imaging does not rely on radiation, thereby reducing the risks of radiation exposure. Instead, a powerful magnetic force is used to attract ions within cells toward the edges of an organ. An image of those ions lined up on the edges of an organ reveals whether an anomaly has occurred, for example, the growth of a tumor, torn cartilage, or a fracture.

During imaging, a patient lies very still inside a massive, hollow, cylindrical magnet. Children may be given a powerful sedative or even general anesthetic for the average half-hour examination. Short bursts of magnetic power are emitted.

Figure 6–1 A CAT Scan
Slice

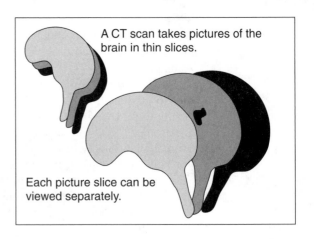

A CT scan takes pictures of the brain in thin slices.

Each picture slice can be viewed separately.

These cause the hydrogen atoms in the patient's tissues to line up parallel to each other like little magnets. The machine detects this alignment as an image and a computer processes the information in much the same way as a CAT scan but shows normal and abnormal tissues with greater contrast. The test is particularly valuable for studying the brain and spinal cord, identifying tumors, and examining the heart and major blood vessels.

FUNCTIONAL IMAGING

While X rays, CAT scans, and MRIs are useful in analyzing gross anatomical abnormalities, they are not useful in monitoring actual chemical activity. Two relatively new techniques, which have been used largely for research purposes until recently, are capable of measuring this function. Positron emission tomography (PET) and **single photon emission computer tomography (SPECT)** are noninvasive techniques that are particularly valuable for evaluating neurological disorders.

PET scanning detects positively charged particles that have been labeled with radioisotopes and injected into the blood. Because of their instability, these substances are taken up in greater concentration by areas of tissue that are more metabolically active, such as tumors. Detectors linked to a computer make a picture of how the radioisotopes are distributed within the body. PET scans can detect brain tumors, locate the origin of epileptic seizures, and examine brain function. Similar to the CAT scan in producing images of the brain in several planes, the PET scan makes a biochemical analysis of metabolism rather than anatomy. PET scanning equipment is expensive to buy and operate, so it is currently available in only a few urban centers, but its contributions are so valuable that its use is likely to become more widespread in the future.

PET and SPECT are safe procedures. They require only minute doses of radiation and carry virtually no risk of toxicity or allergy. Advances in radioisotopic scanning depend on the continuing development of radioactive particles specific to certain tissues.

ULTRASONOGRAPHY

In this noninvasive procedure, high-frequency sound waves (inaudible to the human ear) are passed through a patient's skin and focused onto an organ of interest. The sound waves travel at variable speeds depending on the density of the tissue through which they are passing. For example, the waves travel through bone much faster than they travel through muscle. These sound waves bounce back to the transducer as an echo and are then amplified. A computer processes these echoes into electrical energy and displays them on a screen for interpretation. The images are displayed in real time, producing motion on a television screen. The images can then be translated into photographs for permanent examination. A distinct advantage of ultrasound over other techniques is the absence of risk incurred by exposure to radiation as in some other diagnostic techniques (see Table 6–1).

Ultrasonography is frequently used during pregnancy to view the uterus and fetus. The technique helps in early pregnancy to establish fetal gestational age, determine if there is a multiple pregnancy, evaluate fetal viability, confirm fetal abnormalities, and guide amniocentesis. Later in pregnancy, an ultrasound may be carried out if the growth rate of the fetus seems slow, if fetal movements cease or are excessive, or if the mother experiences vaginal bleeding.

In a newborn child, ultrasound can be used to scan the brain to diagnose hydrocephalus, brain tumors, or brain hemorrhage and to determine if other organs, such as the kidneys, appear normal. A type of ultrasound is also used in echocardiography to investigate disorders of the heart valves. Doppler ultrasound is a modified version of ordinary ultrasound that can look at moving objects, such as blood flowing through blood vessels and the fetal heartbeat in pregnancy.

ELECTROENCEPHALOGRAPHY

Electroencephalography (EEG) is a conventional, noninvasive procedure used to detect normal and abnormal electrical activity within the brain. EEGs detect, amplify, and measure electrical activity on the scalp produced by the brain's neurons. The analysis is typically conducted in a small room designed to eliminate electrical interference and distractions. Small electrodes are placed in a definitive pattern on the scalp but do not produce shock or otherwise aversive stimuli.

Table 6–1 Comparison of Diagnostic Tools

Tool	Risk of Radiation	Powerful Tool	Multiple Analyses	Expensive
X Ray	X	limited	NA	low
CAT Scan	X	X	X	X
Ultrasound	none	limited	X	low
MRI	none	X	X	X
PET/SPECT	low	X	X	X
EEG	none	X	X	X

While the results directly measure only surface activity, changes in electrical patterns effectively represent the activity of deeper structures. These impulses are recorded as brain waves on moving strips of paper.

This diagnostic technique is commonly used to detect the presence of abnormal brain activity that might be related to seizures. Different types of seizures emit differential brain waves. During testing, after an initial baseline is completed, various forms of stress, such as deep breathing or bright lights, may be introduced in order to elicit brain wave patterns typical of seizure disorders.

While EEGs are useful diagnostic tools, they are also more unreliable than many techniques and should be interpreted with caution. For example, approximately 20% of individuals who do not have brain damage will have abnormal readings on electroencephalography. On the other hand, a significant portion of individuals with seizures or other kinds of brain damage will have unaffected EEGs.

An EEG can also be used to evaluate hearing loss. Sounds are introduced through earphones, and the subsequently evoked electrical potentials are amplified via EEG and can then be separated from other electrical activity by computers. The resulting record reveals whether sound has been perceived by the brain.

NEUROLOGICAL DISABILITIES

The diagnostic tools described previously are widely used to attempt to verify the presence or absence of unusual patterns of neurological functioning in children who have physical, cognitive, behavioral, or language development concerns. As you will see, these tools are very often too primitive to provide definitive answers, though in many cases are helpful in identifying problems. The remainder of the chapter will isolate a variety of relatively high-incidence neurological disabilities that early childhood professionals are likely to encounter.

CEREBRAL PALSY

Cerebral palsy is one of the most common disabilities in our society. It encompasses a broad category of nonprogressive neuromuscular conditions affecting muscle tone, movement, reflexes, and posture. Cerebral palsy results from brain injury sustained during the early stages of development, and though the damage to the brain itself gets no worse during an individual's life, children may develop deformities across time. The original injury to the brain must occur before 16 years of age for the condition to be classified as cerebral palsy.

The incidence of cerebral palsy (approximately 1.5–2.7 per 1000 live births in developed countries and much higher in developing countries) has not changed significantly since the 1960s, even though modern medicine has improved the prognosis of premature infants below 2500 g (5 lbs, 8oz.) (Rosen & Dickinson, 1992). In fact, since 1960, there has been a 20% increase in the incidence of cerebral palsy as a result of life saving treatment of very low birth weight infants (Bhushan, Paneth, & Kiely, 1993). The rate continues to be high because of the concomitant success in decreasing the mortality of even smaller babies, who do not respond as well as more mature infants to intensive, lifesaving medical treatment. For example, from the early 1970s to the mid 1980s, the survival rate of infants with birth weights below 1500 g

Case Study JENNIFER WARITZ, SEARCHING FOR A DIAGNOSIS

Jennifer was born in Montana, in a small rural railroad town. I was very sick throughtout my pregnancy, and I can remember saying, "It's just not right, something's wrong." We couldn't get a heartbeat until about 6 months into the pregnancy, although we had done an ultrasound so we knew she was there. Everybody thought that she was going to be a big baby and that everything was going to be okay and that I was just being paranoid.

Jennifer's delivery was a repeat cesarean section, but when she was born she was blue and immediately began having seizures. Of course being in a rural area, nobody really knew what was going on and they just whisked her away before we had an opportunity to hold her. She was placed in the incubator with IVs everywhere and a heart monitor, because she frequently stopped breathing and had to be resuscitated. The doctor, a longtime family friend, was almost in tears when he said, "I don't know what's wrong with Jennifer, but I don't think she's going to make it through the night." I received this message alone in my hospital room.

Jennifer remained in the hospital for another 2 weeks. The hardest part was to leave her there, and to go home without the baby that we had been anticipating for 9 months. I returned to the hospital every day for feedings but it just got to the point that we decided we needed to take her home, regardless.

Jennifer was so fragile, she only weighed 5 pounds 2 ounces and had absolutely no sucking reflex at all. She dropped almost 1 pound within the first 24 hours; she was so frail, had very low muscle tone (like a limp rag doll), and was almost lifeless. At one point, we were asked to use an alarm blanket that would go off if Jennifer quit breathing. It was really a hard decision to make, but we knew that we would lie awake every night waiting for that buzzer to go off. We

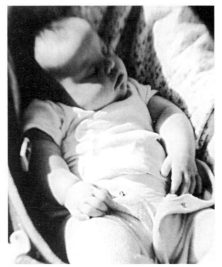

Jennifer Waritz asleep as an infant.

felt that if it was her time to go, it was her time to go, so we declined to use the alarm.

We didn't know of anybody else who had a child with these concerns so there was a period of time when we carried a lot of guilt. We used to think, "What did we do, what did we do? Why did this happen to us? Why is she like this? Why, why, why, why, why?" All these "why" questions and there were no answers. Not once did we ever get a name and a number of another family who had already experienced all this grief. It would have been most beneficial for us to have been able to talk to someone who really could say, "I understand, and know what you're feeling and going through."

It took us a good 3 months just to settle in with Jennifer and to feel comfortable and accepting of her. Then, the search was on. We needed to know what Jennifer's condition was; what her diagnosis was. We got connected with a genetics specialist, who told us that Jennifer had a rare condition where the surface of the

(continued)

brain is smooth and she would probably die before the age of 2. We were told that if she lived, she would be so severely involved that it would be an extreme burden on the family and that we should consider placing her in an institution. I cried all the way home that day. My husband had an even harder time, and he began to withdraw from Jennifer, because he was afraid that he would get too attached and then lose her.

Several months later, I asked the specialist to retest. They found that she did have the ripples on the surface of the brain, but that she had microcephaly; her brain was smaller, but there was definitely a clear cranial pattern. I was told she would be severely disabled; Jennifer is moderately to severely involved, both mentally and physically.

Jennifer has very little speech; she can feed herself now, but requires assistance in order to do that. She has to have total assistance to get dressed and bathed and she's completely incontinent so she requires diapering. She's mobile in her chair and she can crawl around and pull herself up onto furniture. Her tests indicate functions somewhere between 12 and 18 months of age. Socially, she is very much aware and very connected to her environment and probably at a 24-month or above level. That's been our saving grace; she has been such a pleasant child.

Jennifer's condition was just labeled as cerebral palsy, though we were told, "We really don't think that this is what it is, but this is the best term that we can use for her right now." We went through 5 years of thinking that she had cerebral palsy, but every doctor we saw said, "This is the funniest looking case of cerebral palsy that I have ever seen." Finally we were told that Jennifer's features looked very similar to children who have Kabuki Makeup Syndrome, so we went to another genetics specialist.

As soon as we walked into the room, the geneticist became very excited. I mean if this man could have done backflips he probably would have. He was thrilled, "Oh my! Oh my! This is it! This is it!" He started shouting down the hall, "Bring me those papers my colleague in Germany sent me." The research was all on children

with Kabuki Makeup Syndrome and this colleague of his in Germany was following one of the first Caucasian children to be diagnosed with it and had just sent him this information.

The geneticist looked for all the distinguishing features of Kabuki Makeup Syndrome; the little lines and the loops in the fingers, the S-shaped eyebrows, the way the corners of her lips turn down, the way her eyes appear to be bigger than her eye sockets, and the retardation in her bone growth. Jennifer demonstrated the syndrome, and they consider her to be one of the most involved cases of the children they know. At that time of her diagnosis, there were only 69 other children who had actually been diagnosed and most of those were in Japan.

We were pleased to have an answer, to have this diagnosis, but we didn't know anybody else with the same syndrome. There are a whole group of people who have cerebral palsy, and we had been really connected with them. We thought, "Oh, no, now what do we do?" But it was such a relief just to have someone say, we're almost 100% sure that this is what she has, that these are the features that match this disorder and we feel comfortable diagnosing her with this. In the meantime, the research is still continuing. The specialists think there is a large number of undiagnosed cases out there and that as the information gets out, Kabuki Makeup Syndrome will become a common diagnosis, like Down syndrome, and will also have an identified genetic link.

I have met only one other child with Kabuki Makeup Syndrome. It was such a relief to get that diagnosis and to have a clearer picture of what Jennifer's possible outcomes could be, instead of just guessing all of the time. It was probably even good that I had heard all the worst predictions possible, because I have accepted those things and I know that's as bad as it could ever be for Jennifer. So every improvement that Jennifer makes, even the smallest improvement, is like a huge milestone for us because we're just one step beyond the possibility of her needing institutionalization; we've been successful at keeping her with us at home, just as we would either of our other children.

(3 lbs 5 oz) improved in developed countries from 15%–40% to 75% (Rosen & Dickinson, 1992). Infants born at very low birth weight comprise 25% of the 5,000 infants diagnosed with CP in the United States each year (Adler, 1995). However, it is not just premature birth that causes cerebral palsy. Brain damage causing cerebral palsy may occur before, during, or after birth. The physical traits and etiological conditions of persons with cerebral palsy are diverse.

Cerebral palsy is categorized according to the site of cerebral damage, the extent of brain damage, and the parts of the body affected by that damage. Whatever the origin, cerebral palsy causes a functional miscommunication between a person's movement intentions and subsequent motor responses.

Reflexes

One way to describe cerebral palsy is as an interruption of normal reflex development. As an infant's neurological system develops, motor reflexes move from "primitive" to "voluntary." Whereas all infants differ slightly in their rate of development, a significant injury to the brain, either prenatally or postnatally, may impair the normally smooth transition to such a degree as to cause cerebral palsy. It is this poor transition that is now known to be highly predictive of cerebral palsy when observed both prenatally and postnatally. When observed via ultrasound from the about the 10th week of gestation, cramped synchronized general movement, chaotic movement, absent fidgetiness, or abnormal fidgetiness marked infants who would later develop mild to severe cerebral palsy with nearly 100% accuracy (Barclay, 2002).

Primitive reflexes are developed in utero and are present in the early months of life. They are responsible for involuntary motor responses to specific stimuli. For infants with intact neurological systems, the presentation of a given stimulus, such as a touch to the cheek, is predictably followed by a motor response; in this case, the head turns toward the touch and is known as the rooting reflex. Primitive reflexes may be a kind of natural "hardwiring" that equips the child with basic motor patterns and established neurological pathways. While thought to be useful prenatally (Fetters, 1984), primitive reflexes have limited utility to infants after birth. As infants mature, most primitive reflexes are neurologically integrated, giving the child control over them. Primitive reflexes gradually disappear and are replaced by postural, or adaptive, reflexes. When this does not happen, persistent primitive reflexes can interfere with a child's development of voluntary movement.

It is generally agreed that reflexes are key to normal motor development. The presence (or absence) of primitive and adaptive reflexes provides a prediction of developmental potential. Predictable reflex patterns are considered "neurodevelopmental markers" and the best index of brain dysfunction, particularly cerebral palsy. For an optimistic motor outcome, primitive reflexes should appear before 3 months and disappear by 6 months; if primitive reflexes do not disappear by 12 months of age, there is a pessimistic prediction for walking (Festschrift, 1994). Therefore, early childhood educators should be aware of reflex patterns so that noticeable deviations in development can be spotted. Since the objective of subsequent neuromotor intervention is to limit the influence of atypical reflexive development, early identification provides the greatest promise of mediating motor problems.

Figure 6–2
Typical Moro
Reflex

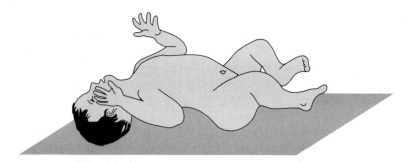

Figure 6–2
Typical Moro
Reflex

The **moro reflex** is the most commonly used index of reflexive maturity and is present at birth (see Figure 6–2). When a child's head is suddenly dropped backwards, the child's arms fly back and out in a symmetrical **abduction** (away from body) and **extension** (straightening of the joints); then the child's arms flex and return to the body in **adduction** (toward body), as if to embrace someone. Abnormal neurological maturation is indicated when the moro response:

1. Is absent in the neonatal period
2. Is asymmetrical
3. Persists beyond three to four months of age

The **asymmetrical tonic neck reflex** (ATNR), also commonly assessed, is sometimes referred to as the "fencer's reflex." When a child's head is turned to one side, the extremities of the same side are extended, while the extremities on the opposite side of the body are **flexed** (bent at the joints) (see Figure 6–3). In normally developing infants, the response is usually partial or incomplete. On the other hand, when the response is well-defined and easily provoked, this is usually a sign of some negative neurological involvement. The ATNR reflex begins to disappear in the first few months. It has been speculated that the ATNR reflex can persist even into early childhood and may be the cause of mild motor problems in children who are "clumsy" or awkward in motor play (Henderson, French, & McCarty, 1993).

Other primitive reflexes seen at birth include the rooting, grasp, startle, and stepping reflexes. The **rooting reflex** occurs when an infant's cheek is lightly stroked. In response, a child will turn its head toward the touch. Stimulating the palm of an infant's hand will elicit the grasp reflex, or flexion of the hand. A **startle reflex** occurs when a sudden noise or movement causes children to thrust their arms outward and then pull them back. It is apparent that if these involuntary responses were to persist, they would interfere with normal motor routines. For example, if the grasp reflex persisted, individuals would never be able to voluntarily release objects once placed in the hand's palm. The disappearance of these reflexes, mostly within the first four to six months of life, is a necessary transition referred to as **reflex integration**.

Several reflexes could interfere with walking and are typically integrated within the first 6 months. By holding a child in a vertical position so that the feet touch the surface, one can elicit the **stepping reflex** (see Figure 6–4). This step-like response encourages many parents to inaccurately conclude that their children are

Figure 6–3
Typical
Asymmetrical
Reflex

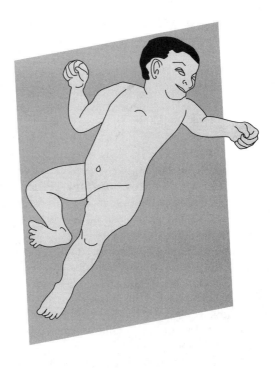

Figure 6–4
Typical
Stepping Reflex

precociously ready to begin walking. The **Babinski reflex** is stimulated by stroking the sole of an infant's foot. If the Babinski reflex is present, infants will respond by spreading their toes. A third commonly assessed reflex of the lower extremities is the plantar reflex. The latter is observed when pressure applied to the ball of an infant's foot is followed by flexion of the toes around the stimulus, as if to grasp the object.

Primitive reflexes are replaced by adaptive and postural reflexes. If these reflexes do not develop appropriately, then a child's motor skills will not progress. The sucking and swallowing reflexes are **adaptive reflexes** that are present at birth, though still immature. These reflexes work in harmony when mature and are usually well-developed by six months of age. When they are fully developed, a child has good tongue control and lip closure when sucking. These reflexes are paired with the ability to move food from the front to the back of the mouth; to control the path of food to the esophagus (rather than trachea); and to move food down the esophagus to the stomach.

While much of human movement is voluntary, a significant part of balance is reflexive. Appearance of **postural reflexes** requires the brain to integrate several modalities (sight, hearing, motor movement etc.) simultaneously. Unlike primitive reflexes, which interfere with movement if persistent, postural reflexes actually supplement movement and help to prevent injury. A **parachute reflex** (see Figure 6–5) results when an infant is held horizontal and prone, and then lowered toward the floor. As if to break the fall, infants will extend their arms and legs toward the surface. Several reflexes evolve that permit children to maintain an upright position, as infants learn to sit and stand. Lateral head righting at 2–3 months is generally the first postural reflex to appear. An **equilibrium reflex** is stimulated whenever a child moves or is pushed out of a midline (vertical) position. Resisting gravity, the equilibrium reflex involuntarily causes the body to realign its trunk vertically. Similarly, when an infant's trunk is pushed out of an upright position either to the side, front, or back, the head righting reflex will attempt to hold the head in an upright position. A final and complementary reflex is referred to as **protective extension**. In this case, an infant, pushed out of midline from either a sitting or standing position, will reach out (extension) and attempt to protect itself from falling. Children will first learn to protect themselves from falls to the front, then from falls to the sides, and finally from falls to the rear.

Muscle Tone

Posture, consistency of muscles, and joint range of motion are all affected by dimensions of muscle tone. Three categories are generally used to define a child's muscle tone: normal, hypertonic, and hypotonic. Infants with abnormally high or

Figure 6–5
Typical
Parachute Reflex

tight muscle tone (**hypertonia**) show restricted ranges of motion. By contrast, **hypotonia,** or very loose tone, is seen in children who show little strength to resist gravity or joint movement. While the former have very tense muscle consistency, the latter tend to have flaccid muscle tone. Both hypertonicity and hypotonicity are indexes of neurological insult and are also likely to result in delayed if not abnormal motor development.

Assessment of muscle tone can be accomplished by comparative analysis of **range of motion**. One test of muscle tone is head rotation, in which the head is passively turned when flexed and when extended. The Scarf sign is a second test of muscle tone. In this test a child's arm is extended across the chest toward the opposite shoulder. In both cases, the degree to which movement is permitted or prohibited gives an index of the neurological maturity: in normally developing children, the range of motion must be neither too loose nor too tight for the chronological age of a child.

Affected Site

Cerebral palsy can be described by the extent of involvement (neurologically affected) if one imagines the body dissected vertically and horizontally (see Figure 6–6). **Hemiplegia** occurs when one side of the body is affected (double hemiplegia involves both sides, with one side more severely impaired, and the arms more affected than the legs) and is caused by traumatic brain injury in the opposite side of the brain. In paraplegia, the lower extremities are affected, and in **quadriplegia** (or tetraplegia), all four extremities are involved. Similarly, all four extremities are affected in **diplegia**, with greater involvement of the legs than the trunk and arms. Finally, **monoplegia** and **triplegia** have involvement of one and three extremities, respectively. It is generally believed that diplegia is associated with injury that occurs to the brain before birth, while quadraplegia and hemiplegia occur as a result of complications in the neonatal period (Cooke, 1990).

Characteristics of Cerebral Palsy

Though definitions vary, the type of cerebral palsy can generally be classified according to the type of muscle movement or muscle tone abnormality manifested. The most common descriptions of the types of CP indicate the state of muscle tone, the area of injury within the central nervous system, and the quality of muscle control.

Figure 6–6
Breakdown of Cerebral Palsy by Body Part

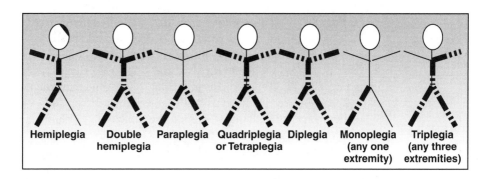

Hemiplegia | Double hemiplegia | Paraplegia | Quadriplegia or Tetraplegia | Diplegia | Monoplegia (any one extremity) | Triplegia (any three extremities)

Hypertonia, occurs when the **pyramidal tract** (the motor cortex and spinal cord) is damaged. Eventually, hypertonia limits joint movement because of shortened muscles and ligaments. If this muscle tightness is severe, it contributes to the development of deformities of the spine, joint dislocation, and contractures (Bigge, 1991).

Infants born with cerebral palsy are initially hypotonic, but if their floppiness persists through the first year without the development of other tone problems, generalized hypotonia is diagnosed. Hypotonia is often correlated with cognitive deficit. Hypotonic infants tend to rely on external support and are delayed in the development of motor skills. They also have poor posture and hypermobile joints.

The pyramidal nerve fibers originate in the brain and pass through the spinal cord to attach to motor cells in the body. When cerebral damage occurs outside the pyramidal nerve group, it is said to be **extrapyramidal**, and the resulting condition is called **athetosis**, or **dyskinesia**. Rather than being responsible for initiation of movement, extrapyramidal nerves are responsible for controlling and coordinating posture, tone, and locomotion. Dyskinesia affects approximately 20% of all children with cerebral palsy. Athetosis, or variable muscle tone, ranges from rigid to flaccid. Injury, often due to jaundice, is responsible for athetosis, which affects all four extremities. Slow worm-like or writhing movements, more pronounced in a child's head and hands, are accentuated when children attempt to move and when they become emotional. Children with athetosis may have difficulty sitting, walking, eating, and speaking. Typically, the excessive movement associated with athetosis is not observed until the second year of life, even though abnormalities in tone, reflexes, and posture can be diagnosed earlier.

With **ataxic cerebral palsy**, which is very rare, children have difficulty balancing well while walking. The cerebellum is the site of injury in this type of cerebral palsy (Bigge, 1991). Ataxia interferes with coordination in balancing and hand use. The individual bobbles while standing and walking and tends to overshoot a target. Children with ataxia tend to exaggerate movement in an effort to balance, and the constant effort to stabilize can cause rigid movement.

Spastic cerebral palsy, in which the muscle tightens and resists efforts to move, is the most common type and results from injury to the pyramidal tract of the brain, usually due to hemorrhaging after premature birth or severe brain damage (perhaps caused by prolonged oxygen deprivation). Spastic movement has been characterized as a "jackknife" response, in which joints express hyperresistance to extension or flexion up to a certain threshold, and then resistance is suddenly released. The status of a child's tone may change over time; many children have hypotonia in infancy, and this progresses to spasticity.

Naturally, all movement, including that of both large and small muscle groups, can be affected by cerebral palsy. The diagnosis of just one type of cerebral palsy is rare (Bigge, 1991), and it is typical to encounter a diagnosis such as "mixed spastic/athetoid quadriplegia with underlying ataxia." Early in development, signs of neuromuscular damage include the absence of primitive reflexes or the later failure to integrate these reflexes. Hence, development of head control, crawling, sitting, and walking tends to be delayed.

Severity of Involvement

A diagnosis of cerebral palsy is almost meaningless unless it is also paired with a description of the degree of involvement or the degree to which a child is affected motorically. Variations of motor involvement range from mild to severe, based on the degree to which a child's impairment interferes with independent motor and functional behaviors. Descriptions of the general characteristics of children with mild, moderate, and severe motor involvement are presented in Table 6–2.

Associated Characteristics of Children with Cerebral Palsy

Because cerebral palsy results from damage to the central nervous system, interference with normal movement is almost always accompanied by collateral damage to other biological functions such as hearing and cognition. Furthermore, the motor involvement itself affects functioning in a number of skill areas. For example, self-help skills, such as feeding and dressing, are limited by the degree of motor dysfunction.

Difficulty in feeding children with cerebral palsy, especially those with dystonia, is common (Dahl & Gebre-Medhin, 1993). Approximately 50% of children with cerebral palsy experience feeding problems and 48% have growth retardation (Thommessen, Kase, Riis, & Heiberg, 1991). The most common feeding problems include poor self-feeding, poor swallowing and chewing from oral-motor dysfunction, and inordinately long feeding sessions. Frequent vomiting, dental problems that cause pain and infection, rumination, reflux, and poor appetite are also not uncommon (Dahl & Gebre-Medhin, 1993; Fee, Charney, & Robertson, 1988).

Table 6–2 Diagnostic Criteria for Severity of Cerebral Palsy

Degree of Involvement	Characteristics
Severe Handicap	1. Total dependence in meeting physical needs 2. Poor head control 3. Deformities, present or potential, which limit function or produce pain 4. Perceptual and/or sensory integrative deficits which prevent the achievement of academic and age-appropriate motor skills
Moderate Handicap	1. Some independence in meeting physical needs 2. Functional head control 3. Deformities, present or potential, which limit independent function or produce pain 4. Perceptual and/or sensory integrative deficits that interfere with achievement of academic and age-appropriate motor skills
Mild Handicap	1. Independence in meeting physical needs 2. Potential to improve quality of motor and/or perceptual skills with therapy intervention 3. Potential for regression in quality of motor and perceptual skills without intervention

Source: Teaching Individuals with Physical, Health, or Multiple Disabilities 4/E by Bigge/Best/Heller, ©2001. Adapted by permission of Pearson Education, Inc., Upper Saddle River, NJ.

Diets tend to be restricted in texture and taste, as many children are given pureed or powdered foods, which are easy to prepare and feed (Reilly & Skuse, 1992). Subsequently, children's energy intake and nutritional status are frequently compromised; two-thirds of the children studied by Dahl and Gebre-Medhin (1993) were below the 10th percentile for energy intake. To assist in monitoring a child's diet, Fee et al. (1988) identified several physical characteristics that can indicate to a caretaker a child might be malnourished (see Table 6–3). Feeding difficulties apparently begin at birth when a large percentage of infants have difficulty sucking during nursing (Reilly & Skuse, 1992). From direct observations of mealtime, Reilly and Skuse (1992) described typical mothers' behavior as mechanical and lacking in verbalization. They concluded that the stress associated with difficult feeding reduced mothers' typical nurturing. Although maternal behavior returned to normal levels as soon as mealtimes were completed, the loss of this valuable opportunity may be significant in terms of social and linguistic development.

The overall growth patterns of children with cerebral palsy are substantially depressed when compared to standardized measurements. While measurements are within the normal range by 12 months of age (when corrected for gestational age), many infants have fallen well behind their nondisabled peers in both height and weight (Reilly & Skuse, 1992). A distinct growth chart based upon the cumulative

Table 6–3   Signs of Malnutrition

Body Part Affected	Observable Physical Symptoms of Malnutrition	Possible Nutritional Inadequacy
Overall body	Low body weight, short stature, edema (swelling)	Calories Protein
Hair	Looseness, sparseness, dullness	Protein
Skin	Xerosis (dryness), follicular keratosis (growth, e.g., wart, lesion)	Vitamin A
	Solar dermatitis (inflammation)	Niacin
	Petichiae, pupura (easy bruising, and tiny red patches)	Ascorbic Acid
Subcutaneous tissue	Decreased subcutaneous tissue	Calories
Nails	Spoon-shaped appearance	Iron
Eyes	Dry conjunctiva, keratomalacia (cell death of the cornea)	Vitamin A
Lips	Cheilosis (fissures and dry scaling of the lips)	Iron B-complex vitamins Riboflavin
Gums	Swelling, bleeding	Vitamin C
Tongue	Glossitis	Niacin, folate, riboflavin Vitamin B_{12}
Skeletal system	Bone tenderness	Vitamins C and D
Muscles	Decreased muscle mass	Protein, calories

Source: From "Nutritional Assessment of the Young Child with Cerebral Palsy," by M. A. Fee, E. B. Charney, and W. W. Robertson, 1988, *Infants and Young Children, 1*(1), pp. 33–40. Copyright ©1988 by Lippincott Williams & Wilkins. Reprinted with permission.

collection of growth in height and weight has been proposed by Krick, Murphy-Miller, Zeger and Wright (1996). These researchers suggested that standard growth charts fail to provide useful information for children with quadraplegic cerebral palsy who tend to be lighter and shorter than the norm, a difference that cannot be accounted for by nutritional limitations alone.

Seizure Disorders

Approximately one-third of children with cerebral palsy also have some form of epilepsy. Children with spasticity are most likely to experience seizures, while children with athetosis are least likely. The most common types of epilepsy observed are **tonic-clonic** and **partial complex** seizures.

Mental Retardation

The average incidence of severe mental retardation in accompaniment with cerebral palsy is 25%. By contrast, the majority of children with cerebral palsy have IQs above 50, in spite of the inherent bias built into intelligence tests when used for children with motor impairment. Taken as a group, however, children with cerebral palsy are more likely to have delayed development in sensorimotor behaviors (Cioni, Paolicelli, Sordi, & Vinter, 1993). This makes sense, since these infants and preschoolers are prevented from exploring and interacting with their environments to the same extent as children who have no motor involvement. Figure 6–7 illustrates the comparative results of children with cerebral palsy and nondisabled, same-age peers on measures of cognitive development.

Some types of cerebral palsy are more likely than others to be associated with intellectual deficits. For example, hemiplegia is rarely associated with cognitive deficits when it is not paired with seizures (Vargha-Khadem, Isaacs, Ver Der Werf, Robb, & Wilson, 1992).

Etiology of Cerebral Palsy

It has been held that premature birth and birth complications, such as asphyxia, constitute major causes of cerebral palsy. On the other hand, this assumption has been debated on the grounds that many children who experience birth-related problems do not show signs of motor involvement later in childhood (Grant, Joy, O'Brien, Hennessy, & McDonald, 1989). Additionally, approximately half of all children with cerebral palsy are born full-term to apparently healthy mothers (Seppa, 1998). Further, it does not appear that cesarean delivery reduces the risk of cerebral palsy (Scheller & Nelson, 1994). Even Freud speculated that **central nervous system (CNS)** abnormalities preceded both birth complications and the asphyxia commonly associated with cerebral palsy. This stand was supported by a major study conducted by the National Collaborative Parental Project (Eicher & Batshaw, 1993) that found that less than 10% of all cases of cerebral palsy were the result of asphyxia alone. Recent research has focused on prenatal infections as a major potential contributor to cerebral palsy (Seppa, 1998).

Two opposing characteristics of the brain are associated with the long-term prognosis of children who have received neurological insult during the fetal or neonatal period. The developing brain is especially vulnerable to trauma or

Figure 6–7
A. Results Obtained by Infants with CP in Scale 1, Compared with Mean Step Scores (Continuous Line) and Standard Deviations (Broken Lines) of Unaffected Subjects of Cioni et al., 1993. B. Results Obtained by Infants With CP in Scale 1, Compared With Mean Step Scores (Continuous Line) and Standard Deviations (Broken Lines) of Unaffected Subject of Cioni et al., 1993

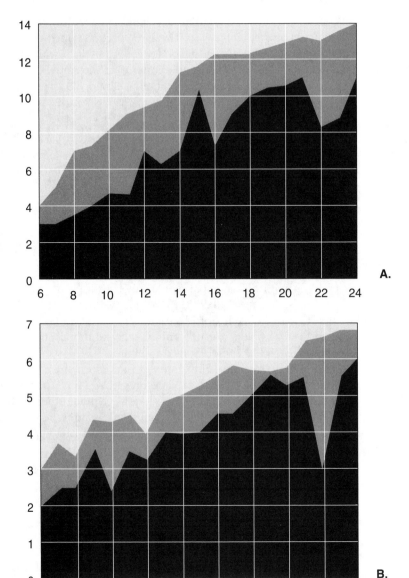

physiological disruptions. On the other hand, very young nervous systems are more plastic and may repair or compensate for damage at a rate and effectiveness that cannot be matched by older children and adults (Farmer, Harrison, Ingram, & Stephens, 1991). As a consequence, abnormal CAT scans at birth can appear normal 12 months later, with no apparent residual motor or cognitive damage (Eaton, Ahmed, & Dubowitz, 1991). Still, 36% of all cases of cerebral palsy are associated with a birth weight below 2500 g (5 lbs, 8 oz.), and 30% of all cases were attributed to brain damage before or during birth (Rosen & Dickinson, 1992). Furthermore, low APGAR scores appear to be highly predictive of cerebral palsy (Moster, Lie , & Markestad, 2002). For example, infants with 5-minute APGAR scores between 0–3 were found to have an 81-fold increased incidence of cerebral palsy over infants with APGAR scores between 7–10. Among very low-birth-weight children, several factors have been found to correlate with positive outcomes versus eventual development of cerebral palsy. Neonates who spend long periods of time on a ventilator, develop widespread infection, have a severe neurological abnormality, or have residual signs of prenatal infection are at greater risk of developing cerebral palsy than infants who do not experience these risk factors (Wilson-Costello et al., 1998).

To illustrate the diversity of circumstances associated with cerebral palsy, Veelken, Schopf, Dammann, and Schulte (1993) delineated the known and probable causes of 53 children with cerebral palsy who had very low birth weight. Table 6–4 provides a sample of these causes, which range from rupture of the umbilical cord to obstruction of the tracheal tube. The resultant motor impairments range from spastic hemiplegia to severe spastic triplegia.

In addition to birth-related injury, congenital causes are cited as a second large category responsible for cerebral palsy, though causation in many cases is based on speculation. Naeye, Peters, Bartholomew, and Landis (1989) studied over 40,000 live births, of which 150 (0.37%) were diagnosed with cerebral palsy between birth and age 7. Of those with quadriplegia, 53% had a probable congenital cause, while 35% of the nonquadriplegic cases had a verifiable congenital origin. Hence, birth asphyxia accounted for just 14% of the cases of cerebral palsy in the quadriplegic group and a negligible percentage of cases (0.01%) in the nonquadriplegic group.

Cerebral palsy can result from neurological damage after birth as well. Infections such as bacterial meningitis and encephalitis can cause severe neurological damage. Anoxia caused by submersion syndrome (water accidents) or near-suffocation is another cause of cerebral palsy. Prenatal abnormalities such as a reduced blood supply to the placenta, cysts, and abnormal brain development are also associated with cerebral palsy. To a small degree, genetic and metabolic disorders contribute to the incidence of cerebral palsy. Finally, environmental toxins such as prenatal exposure to radiation, industrial waste, and alcohol exposure have been associated with cerebral palsy (Eicher & Batshaw, 1993).

However, it is still apparent that a large percentage of cases of cerebral palsy have no known etiology. It is these cases that sometimes result in unfortunate speculation and self-blaming by families. Professionals may inadvertently add to parents' guilt by asking probing questions about prenatal and perinatal history. In most cases, while such information might be interesting, it is of no functional use and may be better left unprobed.

Treatment of Cerebral Palsy

Though many infants and preschoolers with cerebral palsy receive center-based treatment in the form of physical and occupational therapy or special education, these are also usually paired with expectations that parents complete

Table 6–4 Type of Cerebral Palsy, Timing of Brain Injury, and the Event Which Was Related to Cerebral Palsy in Very Low-Birth-Weight Infants

Type of CP	Timing	Event Related to Injury
spastic diplegia, moderate	prenatal	maternal epilepsy, placental bleeding
dystonia	prenatal/delivery	gross cephalic deformity, lifeless at birth
spastic diplegia, moderate	delivery	cord rupture during cesarean section, hypovolemic shock
spastic diplegia, moderate	delivery	marginal placenta, hypovolemic shock
spastic tetraplegia	delivery	cord prolapse, lifeless at birth
spastic diplegia, severe	delivery	severe and prolonged fetal bradycardia, refusal of cesarean section
spastic hemiplegia	delivery/immediate postnatal	stained amniotic fluid; no resuscitation efforts within 30 minutes after birth
spastic diplegia, moderate	neonatal	intraventricular hemorrhaging; cerebral depression
dystonia	neonatal	repeated resuscitations on day 6 following artificial airway obstruction
spastic diplegia, moderate	neonatal	heart arrest on day 3, resuscitation
spastic tetraplegia	neonatal	severe hypoxia; artificial airway tube obstruction on day 3
spastic tetraplegia	later	encephalopathy of unknown origin in infancy, neurological deterioration
spastic diplegia, mild	later	bacterial meningitis on day 42, neurological and sonographic deterioration
spastic tetraplegia	later	skull fracture, subdural hematoma, neurological deterioration
spastic diplegia, moderate	prenatal	severe placental bleeding, severe decelerations on cardiotocography
spastic diplegia, moderate	delivery/neonatal	vaginal delivery despite breech presentation, infection with strep B
spastic diplegia, moderate	delivery/immediate postnatal	severe cardiac depression after birth
spastic diplegia, moderate	immediate postnatal	cardiac depression after birth, delayed airway management despite severe signs of RDS
severe diplegia, moderate	immediate postnatal	defect of incubator heating and respirator during transportation, resulting in hypothermia and ineffective ventilation
spastic diplegia, moderate	neonatal	hyperkaliemia on day 2, fall of hematocrit, IVH IV on ultrasound
spastic diplegia, moderate	neonatal	severe apnea and bradycardia on day 2 after extubation
spastic diplegia, moderate	neonatal	dramatic clinical deterioration with seizures day 8
spastic diplegia, severe	neonatal	septicemia with thrombocytopenia on day 2 cardiac arrest, resuscitation on day 4

Source: From N. Velkenn, M. Schopf, O. Dammann, and F. Schulte, "Etiological Classification of Cerebral Palsy in Very Low Birthweight Infants," 1993, *Neuropediatrics, 24,* 74–76.

home programs. Much research has been conducted on the efficacy of home programs; yet there continues to be a general lack of follow-through on the part of parents that is not reflective of parents' overall interest in their children's welfare (Hinjosa & Anderson, 1991). Instead, this lack of participation may be due to expectations set by therapists that were perceived by parents to be unrealistic. The following are excerpts from interviews of parents taken by Hinjosa and Anderson (1991):

> I would do it but then, as a mother, I would get frustrated. . . I was feeling like, "Wow, what is wrong with me?" It was like I was just tired, and it's like they said, "Don't try to take an hour and do it. Do it, like, when you are changing his Pampers, or when you are doing this." But, with me, when I finish his Pampers, I have to move on to something else. 'Cause I have the other child here, I can't, you know, do that (Irene, p. 275).

> The other therapist told me, "Don't let her walk." I mean, that's like saying, "Don't let her eat." because I can't watch her all the time, and she wants to walk, you know. If it is going to make her become independent and this is what she wants to do, I'm going to let her do it! (Carol, p. 276).

In general, Hinjosa and Anderson (1991) made the following recommendations to therapists regarding expectations for family home intervention:

♦ Explore the needs of parents and assist them in developing their own interventions, which should foster their own creativity and reinforce their efficacy as the primary caregiver.
♦ Provide follow-up positive support and feedback related to family solutions and implementation of their own plans.
♦ Assist parents in developing activities that are consistent with the total family needs and that are realistic.
♦ Implement collaborative goal selection and treatment plans that are sensitive to a family's daily schedules, and recognize that parents may be unable to follow through as consistently as is recommended.

Research efforts conducted to determine the overall effectiveness of early intervention for infants and preschoolers with cerebral palsy yield mixed findings. Turnbull (1993) concluded that, while some children do no better than could be expected given natural maturation, overall those with and at risk of cerebral palsy who receive physical therapy experience substantially greater motoric development than those without physical therapy. Other researchers found that young children who received physical therapy alone progressed at least as well in all domains as those who received short-term infant stimulation and physical therapy (Palmer et al., 1990).

For children with cerebral palsy, management of physical development is a primary focus in early intervention, as well as later education. Physical therapists may be the primary or only specialists working with families. Their role is to monitor physical development, detect changes in orthopedic status, and to plan and implement specific motor development strategies (Dormans, 1993). It may be necessary for children to wear day and/or night braces, to undergo corrective surgery, or to be fit for orthopedic equipment such as crutches, a walker, or a wheelchair. The goal of physical development however, is to facilitate the greatest amount of movement while concurrently working to diminish interfering abnormal movement or reflexes.

The primary focus of physical management is often **positioning** and **handling**. Positioning refers to the treatment of postural and reflex abnormalities by careful, symmetrical placement and support of the child's body. Efforts are made to adapt seating and standing equipment so that a child's skeleton can be aligned in a posture that is as normal as possible and to inhibit the interference of primitive reflexes. Parents and teachers can be trained in proper positioning techniques, but an occupational or physical therapist should be consulted for the specific needs of an individual child.

For example, a child with cerebral palsy who still has a dominant asymmetrical tonic neck reflex (ATNR) would extend the limbs on the side of the body toward which the head is turned and flex the limbs on the side of the body that is opposite. If the child is allowed to fall into this position much of the time, some muscles of the body would shorten and might cause contractures that would eventually deform the affected bones and joints. Furthermore, the child's face might be in an awkward position for speech, eating would be difficult, and the child would not be able to bring objects to the midline for functional use with both hands.

This child would best be seated in a device adapted to prevent looking to one side, thus inhibiting the ATNR. This might be done by placing blinders to the side of the child's head so that the child looks straight ahead. Any person feeding or talking with the child would approach from directly in front of the child. Now, the limbs could be used at midline in a symmetrical fashion.

A child with low muscle tone might be positioned in a standing device that provides a slight forward incline and straps to support the child's weak muscles and to encourage flexion of the head and arms. This postioning would allow stimulation of the child's weight bearing joints and limbs and keep the child upright to interact with other children and adults.

Handling involves preparation of a child for movement and positioning. A child who is hypertonic and very stiff may be difficult to dress, for example. If a parent or therapist provides gentle shaking or stroking of the child's arms before putting on a shirt, it will be much easier to bend the child's elbow and pull the shirt over as needed. Even soft lighting and music may relax the child's muscle tone in preparation for such an activity. Accurate assessment of an individual child's need for handling is best carried out by an occupational or physical therapist.

In addition to physical therapy, a nutritionist should be involved with families whose children have compromised nutritional intake. However, some general considerations for all children with oral-motor involvement were advised by Fee et al. (1988): frequent short feedings, development of a structured feeding program by a physical and occupational therapist, and increased caloric concentration of food, including nutritional formula supplements.

SEIZURES

As many as 1 in 10 persons has a **seizure** at least once in a lifetime. In childhood, approximately 2 million Americans experience recurring seizures, defining a condition known as epilepsy (Hingley, 1999). Seizures are the result of abnormal electrical discharges in cerebral neurons. Different types of seizures result from corti-cal involvement of different regions of the brain. The physiology of seizures, re-gardless of type, is an imbalance between the usual coordinated efforts of neurons that are excited (activated to perform a function) and those that are inhibited (pre-vented from activating when not needed). During a seizure, the normal commu-nication between neurons is interrupted by millions of electrical impulses occurring at the same time and and that are more intense than usual, resulting in abnormal brain activity which can usually be detected on an EEG.

While a person who has a seizure may have epilepsy, this is not always nec-essarily the case. **Epilepsy** is a condition in which seizures are recurrent. Though epilepsy is not provoked by external sources (e.g., metabolic disturbances, ex-posure to poison, or severe insult to the central nervous system) seizures may be caused by such events. According to Brunquell (1994), all humans have a thresh-old for seizures, beyond which a clinical seizure will occur. Most person's thresh-olds are so high that normal life challenges will not push them past these limits. On the other hand, those with multiple daily seizures have very low thresholds as compared to persons who have less frequent seizures. Individual threshold lev-els are presumed to be both genetically determined and interactive with environ-mental events (Brunquell, 1994).

Though there are 30 different types of seizures, they have been grouped into three categories of epileptic seizures as recognized in the International Classifica-tion of Epileptic Seizures: **partial** (those that result from activation of one area of the brain), **generalized** (those that involve activation of the entire brain and af-fect the whole body), and unclassified seizures. In simple partial seizures, indi-viduals may be conscious, while consciousness is impaired with complex partial seizures. Either of these two conditions may progress to a partial seizure with sec-ondary generalization, in which an individual totally loses consciousness.

Of the seizures described above, generalized seizures are the most commonly discussed in educational literature, and these include the following: **absence** (pe-tit mal), tonic, **clonic, tonic-clonic** (grand mal), **myoclonic**, and **atonic seizures** (see Table 6–5). In each of these seizures loss of consciousness is a clas-sification criteria.

Over 150 known causes of seizures have been identified, though in 70% of in-dividual cases it is not possible to pinpoint the cause (Hingley, 1999). Most diag-noses are related to factors also associated with other forms of neurological damage. Factors associated with the risk of seizures include perinatal trauma, fe-tal distress, congenital and postnatal infections (e.g., cytomegalovirus, meningitis, and influenza), teratogens, malformations or tumors, head injuries, and chromo-somal abnormalities (e.g., juvenile myoclonic epilepsy resulting from an anomaly of the short arm of chromosome 6).

The relationship between seizures and mental retardation seems to be related to the presence of associated neurological disabilities, or severe cognitive delay (Goulden, Shinnar, Koller, Katz, & Richardson, 1991; Shepherd & Hosking, 1989). It seems that the risk of seizures is low in persons with mild mental retardation who do not have cerebral palsy or other types of disabilities (Goulden et al., 1991). Laybourn and Hill (1994) referred to the relationship between seizures and other risk factors as "epilepsy-only" and "epilepsy-plus." Children in the latter group tend to have a poorer overall prognosis, including greater intellectual impairment, resistance to drug treatment of seizures, and other physical disabilities.

On the other hand, the effects of seizures themselves on cognitive functioning are associated with the type, age of onset, and frequency of seizures. Overall, children with seizures tend to have diminished concentration and mental processing (Dam, 1990). Generally speaking, the earlier the onset of seizures, the poorer the prognosis. Furthermore, each seizure has the potential for causing further brain injury due to a depletion of neurological metabolites. Children are most at-risk of further brain injury when seizures are prolonged for 15 minutes or more, in a condition referred to as **status epilepticus**.

There is some indication that children with seizures are more likely to have behavior problems than children without epilepsy. In general, Austin, Risinger, and Beckett (1992) found five factors that increased the likelihood of behavior problems:

1. Female gender
2. Families that had high levels of stress
3. Families that perceived themselves as having low levels of mastery over family events or outcomes
4. Families with little extended family support
5. High frequency of seizures

Approximately 4% of children experience breath-holding spells (Morelle, 1993). While these are not seizures, they are involuntary. Usually appearing before 18 months of age, breath-holding tends to disappear by age 5. Typically, breath-holding proceeds from a stressful event (e.g., crying or anger) to a change in color, and then to a forceful inspiration. At other times, the breath-holding may

Table 6–5 Types of Seizures

Type of Seizures	Description
Absence	Sudden interruption of ongoing activity and the assumption of a blank stare for 1 to 15 seconds. Usually normal intelligence. Good response to therapy, though many have poor social adaptation and difficulty sustaining attention
Tonic	Rigid muscular contraction, often fixing the limbs in some strained posture
Clonic	Alternate contraction and relaxation of muscles, occurring in rapid succession
Tonic clonic	Rigid muscular contraction followed by the appearance of clonic activity
Myoclonic	Sudden, brief, shock-like muscle contractions. Usually normal intelligence, but may experience delays in social development
Temporal lobe (Psychomotor)	Repetitive movements such as chewing, lip smacking, rocking: may have bizarre sensory/emotional changes
Atonic	Sudden reduction in muscle tone. In more severe cases, persons may slump to the ground
Infantile Seizures	Long-term prognosis is very poor, mental and neurological damage affect over 80% of cases
Febrile Seizures	Tonic clonic seizures result from high temperatures. Usually do not require medication and terminate when fevers are gone

be prolonged enough to lead to loss of consciousness, slow pulse, and incontinence. The cause of breath-holding episodes is unclear, though the incidence overlaps with some tonic-clonic seizures (Morelle, 1993). Procopis (1992) reported a family history in about a third of cases. Medication, though sometimes prescribed, is generally neither necessary nor effective (Procopis, 1992). To assist parents, professionals should provide reassurance and information. For some children, whose temper tantrums precipitate episodes, behavioral intervention may be necessary, though the aim is to change the precipitating behavior and not the breath-holding, which is involuntary.

Treatment

Medical treatment of epilepsy primarily includes the use of several drugs (see Table 6–6). Drugs affect children differently than they do adults. For example, Phenobarbital may cause some children to become hyperactive, whereas this drug is generally a sedative in adults (Dichter, 1994). Because of this effect, and the tendency of Phenobarbital to adversely affect cognitive functioning and memory, its use is not recommended for younger children (Dichter, 1994). Sometimes with prescribed medication, a child's seizures will be resistant to a first attempt. Adding a second drug may be successful in eliminating or reducing seizures. The goal of drug treatment is to select the medication which will have the greatest control while causing the fewest side effects while maintaining a good quality of life.

Table 6–6   Drugs Prescribed for the Treatment of Epilepsy

Category A: Prescribed to compensate for depressed inhibitory neuron functioning

Generic Drug Name	Common Product Name	Use
Barbiturates	Phenobarbital	Sedation, generalized seizures
Valproic Acid	Depakene	Multiple seizure types
Diazepam	Valium	Adjunct for generalized seizure control with other medications
Ethosuximide	Zarontin	Petit mal seizures
Vigabatrin	Sabril	Experimental drug, decreases seizures by 50% when resistant to other therapy

Category B: Drugs used to counter hyperactive excitatory processes

Generic Drug Name	Common Product Name	Use
Carbamazepine	Tegratol	Partial and generalized tonic-clonic seizures
Phenytoin	Dilantin	Partial and generalized tonic-clonic seizures experimental for individuals who are therapy resistant
Gabapentin	Neurontin	Individuals who are therapy resistant
Lamotrigine	Lamictal	Experimental for individuals who are therapy resistant
Paraldehyde	Paral/Paraldehyde	Used rectally to stop threatening prolonged seizures

This is why, initially, many children go through a period of "experimentation" in order to find the right combination of drugs for a particular child (Hingley, 1999). In the past decade, eight new antiepileptic medicines have been introduced (Table 6–7). Though most are useful primarily with adults or with children with very intractable seizure disorders (i.e., Lennox-Gastaut syndrome), experimental applications are in progress for very young children (Nguyen & Spencer, 2003).

However, in 30% of cases, seizures cannot be controlled through medication (Brunquell, 1994). Recent medical advances have made surgery (see Table 6–8) a more viable option for persons with intractable seizures (Fish, Smith, Quesney, Andermann, & Rasmussen, 1993; Nguyen & Spencer, 2003). Procedures (i.e., video EEG, CAT scans, MRI, and PET) that have helped evaluate those who are and those who are not candidates for surgery, concomitant with improved surgical techniques, make the procedure safer than in the past. Advanced imagery

Table 6–7 New Medications for Controlling Seizures

Drug	Ages Approved by FDA	Seizure Type	Use	Concerns
Felbamate	Adults & 2–14 w/Lennox Gestaut	partial seizures w/out generalization	monotherapy	very restricted use; associated w/anemia and kidney failure
Gabapentin	> 12 yrs	partial seizures	adjunctive	
Lamotrigine	a: Adults b: children	a: partial/generalized b: generalized	a: adjunctive b: add-on	
Topiramate	2 years and older	partial and generalized; Infantile spasms; Lennox Gastaut	adjunctive	
Tiagabine	Adults and adolescents	partial seizures	adjunctive	may exacerbate generalized seizures
Vigabatrin	Not approved in U.S.	refractory partial seizures; considered by some the drug of choice for infantile spasms	add-on	reports of irreversible visual field defects
Oxcarbazepine	a: Adults b: children > 4	partial seizures w/ and w/out secondary generalization	a: monotherapy or adjunctive b: adjunctive only	
Levetiracetam	Adults	partial seizures w/ and w/out secondary generalization	adjunctive	
Zonisamide	Adults	partial seizures	adjunctive	small percentage of patients developed kidney defects

Source: From "Recent Advances in the Treatment of Epilepsy," by D. K. Nguyen and S. S. Spencer, 2003, *Archives of Neurology, 60,* pp. 929–935. Reprinted with permission of the American Medical Association.

Table 6–8 New Surgical Treatment Options for Persons with Seizures

Treatment	Description	Effectiveness
Resective Surgery	Surgical removal of abnormal tissue; may lead to unacceptable deficits if lying in functional cortex	Significantly decreases both frequency and duration of seizures in large percentage of patients
Multiple Subpial Transections	Series of parallel cortical slices made perpendicular to long axis of gyrus in patients with seizures arising from language, motor or sensory zones of cortex	Small sample sizes to date preclude statistical conclusions; preliminary results suggest good effectiveness with minimal neurological damage
Gamma-Knife Surgery	Focused radiation applied to a single point within the brain	After a long delay (12–36 mo) may free > 50% of patients of seizures with significant improvement in a large percentage of remaining patients

Source: From "Recent Advances in the Treatment of Epilepsy," by D. K. Nguyen and S. S. Spencer, 2003, *Archives of Neurology, 60,* pp. 929–935. Reprinted with permission of the American Medical Association.

techniques are also useful in locating previously undetectable lesions (Nguyen & Spencer, 2003). In general, surgery is more effective in improving one's quality of life if done in childhood than if delayed until adulthood (Brunquell, 1994).

New developments include a NeuroCybernetic Prosthesis (NCP) which is a surgically implanted device that stimulates the vagus nerve in the side of the neck with an electrical burst lasting about 30 seconds and occurring every 5 minutes throughout the day (Hingley, 1999). However, this treatment is currently used only for older children and adults and has not yet been applied to very young children with difficult-to-control seizures. A related treatment involving deep brain stimulation has been attempted, though findings to date fail to support the efficacy of such an approach (Nguyen & Spencer, 2003).

Families of children with seizures can be assisted in several ways. As with other children with disabilities, there may be a tendency of parents to treat children with seizures differentially. For example, the potential hazard of having a seizure in traffic, near water, or in other dangerous situations may cause parents to become over-cautious. Furthermore, when a seizure happens to occur concurrently with some action, such as enforcement of a family rule, parents may experience guilt and anxiety over future compliance requirements. The social and emotional effect of these family responses may affect sibling and peer relationships. Professionals can offer advice on the importance of consistency in childrearing practices and normalcy of daily routines. Research indicates that children's overall developmental prognoses are best when they receive high-quality medical treatment and minimal use of drugs (Laybourn & Hill, 1994). Yet, professional educators themselves appear to lack sufficient information on seizures and the needs of specific children with seizures (Laybourn & Hill, 1994). Since seizures are so common in the early childhood special education population, this lack of knowledge can prevent professionals from serving children and families well. Minimally, professionals should be

Table 6–9   Treatment Protocol for Generalized Tonic-Clonic Seizures

The typical seizure is not a medical emergency, but knowledgeable handing of the situation is important. When a child experiences a generalized tonic-clonic seizure, caregivers should follow these procedures.

- Remain calm. Take time to reassure others that the child will be fine in a few minutes; if appropriate, remind other children of the correct conduct under these circumstances.
- Carefully lower the child to the floor and clear the area of anything that could hurt her.
- Put something flat and soft (like a folded blanket) under her head so it will not bang on the floor as the body jerks.
- Since you cannot stop the seizure, let it run its course. Do not try to revive the child and do not interfere with the child's movements.
- Turn the child gently onto one side. This keeps the airway clear and allows saliva to drain away:
    Do not try to force the mouth open
    Do not try to hold onto the tongue
    Do not put anything in the mouth
- When the jerking movements stop, let the child rest until she regains consciousness.
- Breathing may be shallow during the seizure and may even stop briefly. In the unlikely event that breathing does not begin again, check the child's airway for an obstruction and give artificial respiration (remember—no objects in the child's mouth).
- Some children recover quickly after this type of seizure and others require more time. A short period of rest is usually advised. If seizures are routine, caregivers should encourage children and families to maintain daily activities with as little disruption as possible.

Source: Adapted from *Epilepsy School Alert*, Epilepsy Foundation of America, 1987, Washington, DC.

well-versed on the protocol for treating children with generalized clonic-tonic seizures and aware of the symptoms of common types of seizures (see Table 6–9).

Multidisciplinary services indicated for children and families of children with seizures include medical, counseling, social skills programming, family support, education, and advocacy. According to Laybourn and Hill (1994), recent literature on family dynamics has paralleled early childhood philosophy. That is, historically, families were often viewed as needing the assistance of "experts" to help them overcome the emotional and psychological trauma and fear of public attitudes regarding their child's disability. Current efforts contrast this perspective, and focus on the positive aspect of services, which concentrate on the practical, financial, and medical needs of families. The latter perspective is based on actual data gathered from families who seemed to react sensibly to their children's disabilities and found friends, relatives, and professionals to be sympathetic and helpful.

In contrast, group programs designed to help parents cope with children with epilepsy are perhaps less successful. Hoare and Kerley (1992) established group counseling programs for a large number of parents whose children had recently received a diagnosis of epilepsy. Only 35% of parents expressed interest in the therapy, and only 12% actually attended, with a high rate of attrition in the latter group. A majority of the parents indicated they were not concerned with public attitudes but desired more information about epilepsy and its management. In summary, professionals may be overly concerned with parental coping and not sufficiently concerned with becoming an information resource for parents.

ATTENTION DEFICIT HYPERACTIVITY DISORDER (ADHD)

The term attention deficit has been recognized for at least the last half century. In a 1902 address to the Royal College of Physicians, G. F. Still described 20 children in his clinical practice who were aggressive, defiant, and resistant to discipline; these children were excessively emotional or passionate and showed little self-control (Barkley, 1997). Furthermore, these children were described as impaired in attention and quite overactive. Because ADHD is a hidden disorder, children are often blamed for their misbehavior and adults expect that they could behave appropriately if they would "just try."

The primary symptoms of ADHD have changed very little since 1902, as was evident in the DSM-III-R Diagnostic Criteria for Attention Deficit Disorder, with and without hyperactivity, published by the American Psychiatric Association in 1987. However, in 1994, the terminology relating to ADHD changed with the APA's publication of the *Diagnostic and Statistical Manual of Mental Disorders* (1994). There is much controversy and disagreement among professionals as to the utility and meaning of this term (Bender & McLaughlin, 1995). In spite of this disagreement, descriptions of behaviors associated with the condition have remained remarkably consistent. Though the definition has remained stable, the number of children identified with this disorder has not; the overall incidence of ADHD has increased markedly in the past decade. Furthermore, increasing numbers of very young children with ADHD are being identified. However, less is known about the characteristics and functioning of preschool age children than of school age children with ADHD. Wilens et al. (2002) compared the psychopathology of preschool versus school age children identified with ADHD and found the younger children's behavior matched that of the older youth. Both preschoolers and school age children were found to have substantial impairment of social, cognitive, and overall functioning along with clinically significant psychopathology. Finally, preschoolers' manifestation of ADHD symptoms were qualitatively the same as those of school age children. It is no surprise, then, that many preschoolers are now medicated daily with drugs intended to reduce activity levels and improve concentration.

Characteristics

Interviews with parents of children with ADHD reveal that, even in infancy, symptoms of the disorder are manifest (Friedman & Doyal, 1992; Quinn, 1997). Early signs include squirminess, inability to adjust to change, frequent high-intensity negative moods, irregular sleep patterns (often requiring less sleep), and difficulty in feeding. These symptoms evolve into the behavioral triad defining ADHD. The primary symptoms of ADHD include inattention, impulsivity, and hyperactivity. Barkley (1993) postulated another primary symptom—poor delay of response. Inattention manifests itself when children fail to attend and concentrate on the task at hand. Preschool children often move from activity to activity, rapidly shifting their attention from one thing to another. If you ask them what they are supposed to be doing, many times they cannot tell you. These children also appear to be distracted by their own thoughts as well as the behaviors of other children and adults. What can be somewhat frustrating and promising is that these children will concentrate for longer periods of time in highly enjoyable activities such as going skiing for the first time.

Impulsivity has been viewed as another primary symptom. This can be seen when these children behave in ways that appear to others as though they do not understand the consequences of their actions. These children get into difficulty because they respond too soon and come to decisions too rapidly. They interrupt conversations at meals, cannot take turns at preschool, and interrupt the play of others a great deal of the time. As a consequence, secondary problems develop in self-esteem, interpersonal relationships, and learning (Fouse & Morrison, 1997).

The third primary symptom of ADHD is hyperactivity. This characteristic is the most widely known and easiest to recognize. Most parents and caregivers term this characteristic as "always on the go," " in constant motion," "never sitting still," or "always fidgeting, talking, or making noise." Children identified as ADHD with hyperactivity have a much poorer prognosis than children without hyperactivity. The former are more likely to have conduct problems, to be more impulsive, and to be rejected by their peers.

The newest diagnostic criteria suggested by Barkley (1993) replaces inattention with disinhibition or poor delay of response. Barkley feels that children with ADHD cannot delay their actions sufficiently and have little tolerance for delay intervals between tasks. Barkley's contribution is based on the earlier work of Bronowski (1967, 1977), who postulated that as our language evolved, humans developed the skill to delay their response to a signal, message, or event. This ability is said to be part of the evolutionary changes of the frontal lobes. Frontal lobe differences can be seen in preschool children who cannot delay between tasks or activities or who respond too quickly to stimuli. There have been several secondary characteristics associated with ADHD, including poor school performance, learning disabilities, delays in speech and language development, poor problem solving abilities, and slightly more difficulties in sensory and motor skills.

Etiology

Since the first edition of Barkley (1981) as well as early classic texts in the field (e.g., Ross & Ross, 1976; Safer & Allen, 1976), considerable research as to the etiology of ADHD has been carried out. This research has been somewhat inconsistent and conflicting in findings. Most of the senior researchers in the field view the cause of ADHD as having multiple etiologies (Barkley, 1997; Lerner, Lowenthal, & Lerner, 1995). Various data-based correlates of ADHD have included prenatal exposure to nicotine (Linnet et al., 2003) and heroin (Ornoy, 2003), exposure to toxins in the environment (Marlowe, 1986), gender favoring males 5 to 1 (Barkley, 1997; Farley, 1997), differences in the brain's ability to use glucose fast enough to maintain normal thought (Zametkin et al., 1991), and inheritability (Anastoploulos & Barkley, 1991). In addition, several theories that have no empirical support, ranging from diet (Conners, 1980) to sugar sensitivity (Milich, Wolraich, & Lindgren, 1986), have been with us for some time and continue to appear in the popular press at this writing.

Conduct disorders, the most severe form of ADHD, appear to be related to the quality of a child's home environment. Specifically, marital harmony/discord may be the best predictor of this chronic antisocial behavior (Murray & Myers, 1998). Although children born into low-income families are at higher risk of ADHD, an enriched in-home environment (usually associated with higher income and parental education levels) can significantly improve behavioral outcomes (Orney, 2003). This finding reflects that general opinion of scientists that what is now categorized as a single ailment will eventually prove to be several discrete but related disorders that have different causes and subsequent treatments (Friedman & Doyal, 1992). For example, it has been suggested that ADHD follows a genetic continuum that includes Tourette syndrome and learning disabilities (Whitman, 1991). While these disabilities can appear independently, they also overlap in symptoms and outcomes (see Table 6–10). What is certain is that this disorder starts early in childhood and will follow an individual for the rest of his or her life (Barkley, 1997; Lerner et al., 1995).

Treatment

There is a wealth of data regarding the effective treatment of infants and children with ADHD. The information available today is clearly more empirically sound and is more accessible to both parents and professionals. The primary treatment of preference has been and continues to be stimulant medication therapy. In 1995, nearly half a million prescriptions for Ritalin or similar drugs were written

Table 6–10   Infant and Preschool Stages of ADHD

Age	Needs	Difficulties	Treatment Program
Atypical infants and toddlers	Self-regulation including: Arousal Deviant attentiveness Crying Irritability Sleep disorders Structure Limit setting Control issues Dependency Parental–child interactions that are clearly affected	Neurologic dysfunction Overaggressive/ oppositional behavior Short attention span Hyperactivity Low threshold of frustration Temper tantrums Sleep disorders Accident proneness	Parent education and counseling Behavior modification Environmental manipulation Educational intervention nursery school/Head Start Occupational/physical therapy Play therapy Medication Diet
Preschool	Proper nursery school placement Increasing attention span for learning Increasing social awareness and interaction	Hyperactivity Aggression Poor socialization Learning delays Developmental issues when ADHD is not the only problem	Parent and teacher education Behavior management Environmental Proper diet Medication Other therapies as needed (OT/PT/speech)

Source: Adapted from *Attention Deficit Disorder: Diagnosis and Treatment from Infancy to Adulthood* (pp. 205–206), by P. O. Quinn, 1997, New York: Brunner/Mazel.

for children between the ages of 3 and 6 (Gibbs, 1998). Medication has been highly effective for young children with ADHD (Barkley, 1997). The two most common medications employed have been Cylert (Pemoline) and Ritalin (Methylphenidate). Even with such positive outcomes, the use of medication therapy is not without side-effects that caregivers need to monitor (e.g., tics, weight loss, insomnia, stomach aches, headaches, dizziness, nail biting, reduced speech, irritability, nightmares, sadness, and staring). Recent research indicated that over half of children tested displayed the most common side-effects during medication therapy as well as under placebo conditions (Barkley, DuPaul, & Mc-Murray, 1991). When two doses of Ritalin were compared (3 mg/kg versus 5 mg/kg), the most common side-effects under either dosage level were decreased appetite, insomnia, anxiousness, irritability, and proneness to crying. However, many of these side-effects were also found during the placebo phase of the research. Moreover, medical treatment of ADHD and other behavioral problems appears to be much more conservatively prescribed for younger children than for older children. DeBar, Lynch, Powell, and Gale (2003) found that most children receiving psychopharmacotherapy were those whose behavioral symptoms were accompanied by substantial other risk factors such as parental substance abuse, history of child abuse, and out-of-home placement.

Another common intervention with young children with ADHD has been to employ behavioral parent training in the home (Barkley, 1997; Tutty, Gephart, & Wurzbacher, 2003). As students become older, behavioral interventions, such as token economies, behavioral contracting, and self-management procedures, alone or in combination with stimulant medication, have been effective at school (Abramowitz, Eckstrand, O'Leary, & Dulcan, 1992; O'Leary, Pelham, Rosenbaum, & Price, 1976; Williams, Williams, & McLaughlin, 1991). As the home environment is the best predictor of severe social maladaptation, chaotic and fractured families may require intensive support while their children need positive integrated educational experiences where they can play and work alongside appropriate peer role models (Murray & Myers, 1998). Tutty et al. (2003) found that a combined treatment program of stimulant medication and parent training on behavioral and social skills (as compared to stimulant medication only) improved parents' perception of consistency in disciplinary practices and consequent effectiveness in reducing overall rate of ADHD-related behavior in their children.

A child with ADHD can have a devastating effect on families (Friedman & Doyal, 1992). Not only are there the predictable daily management problems that require extraordinary supervision, but parents often must deal with marital stress and guilt caused by accusatory suggestions by family, friends, and professionals that the behavior problems are a consequence of misguided parenting. The following quote exemplifies the frustration felt by parents of children with ADHD (Colin, 1997).

> I decide to mention Willie's behavior in school to the pediatrician. 'Does every child yell like this?' I ask embarrassed.
>
> The pediatrician tells me not to worry. 'Oppositional behavior,' he calls it, is common among three-year-olds and should go away on its own. He laughs when I tell him how Willie substituted 'old wallpaper' for the offending 'stupid idiot.'

'He's obviously very creative.' the pediatrician says, still smiling.

I stare at him blankly. They never call Willie creative in school. In fact, his teacher rarely says anything positive about him. Why is it so hard for her to appreciate the good things about my son—his sense of humor, his vocabulary, his wonderful singing? (pp. 24–25)

Several excellent texts are available for parents who have children with ADHD. In addition, there is a wealth of information for teachers and other care providers to assist children with attention deficit hyperactivity disorder. For example, many Internet sites, including parent-specific websites and support networks, are established. The following practical suggestions will prove useful in helping families of children with ADHD (Friedman & Doyal, 1992):

◆ Provide constant nurturance through love, support, and kindness.
◆ Keep undesirable activities (e.g., car travel, shopping) brief.
◆ Provide immediate (nonviolent) consequences for acting out to limit repetition of behavior.
◆ Limit physical punishment and verbal violence since these are imitated by children with ADHD.
◆ Limit access to violence on TV since children with ADHD are more likely than other children to be influenced by this violence.
◆ Set behavioral rules and establish clear rewards for rule following.
◆ Do not try to force children with ADHD to go to sleep, but set routine bedtime, where child must play quietly and independently until they are ready for sleep.
◆ Use daily schedules to help young children predict their day and learn self-control.

TRAUMATIC BRAIN INJURY

Head injuries, accounting for 40% of fatalities in children ages 1 to 4, are caused by physical assault (abuse) over 50% of the time; assault is the cause of 90% of cases of **traumatic brain injury** (TBI) (Ewing-Cobbs et al., 1998; Keenan, et al., 2003). Each year approximately 180 of 100,000 children experience a traumatic head injury (Wade, Taylor, Drotar, Stancin & Yeates, 1998). Traumatic brain injury (TBI) may also be the result of accidental trauma to the head such as a car accident or a fall. In children, some common causes of TBI are falls from shopping carts, walkers, and from windows (Waaland, 1990). Keenan et al. (2003) found that the greatest risk of inflicted TBI was posed to: infants under 12 months, males, those born to young mothers, those whose mothers were non-European American, and infants who were the product of multiple births.

The outcomes and prognoses differ for the two types of head injury, with a better overall health picture for children who suffer non-inflicted (caused by other than child abuse) TBI. In 1992, Congress added TBI as a separate disability category under IDEA, defining it as:

. . . an acquired injury to the brain caused by an external physical force, resulting in total or partial functional disability or psychosocial impairment, or both, that adversely affects a child's educational performance. The term applies to open and closed head injuries resulting in impairments in one or more areas, such as cognition; language; memory; attention; reasoning; abstract thinking; judgment; problem-solving; sensory, perceptual, and motor abilities; psychosocial behavior; physical functions; information processing; and speech. The term does not apply to brain injuries that are congenital or degenerative, or brain injuries induced by birth trauma. (U.S. Federal Register, 1992)

Children whose head injury is the result of a blow to the head have a specific type of brain injury that includes lacerations, contusions, and external **hematomas** to the skull, scalp, and brain. However, when a head injury is the result of inertia that involves rapid acceleration followed by rapid deceleration, the type of injury is more generalized as in a concussion and internal hematomas. These children often make rapid physical recovery and may show no evidence of cognitive processing deficits until several months later. Like seizures, brain injury that results in temporary or permanent disability may not appear on typical diagnostic tests such as MRIs or EEGs. While long-term effects include deficits in personal independence, behavioral/emotional skills, social functioning, cognitive processing skills, and motor functioning, there is no typical profile of a child who is head injured (Wade et al., 1998; Yim-Chiplis, 1998).

The symptoms of TBI generally fall into one of three categories:

◆ Physical symptoms: nausea, vomiting, dizziness, headache, blurred vision, sleep disturbance, fatigue, lethargy, and other sensory loss.
◆ Cognitive deficits: attention, concentration, perception, memory, speech/language, or executive functions.
◆ Behavioral changes or alterations in degree of emotional responsivity (irritability, anger, disinhibition, or emotional lability (Mild Traumatic Brain Injury Committee, 1993).

The severity and manifestation of brain injury is dependent upon the extent and location of damage and may range from mild to severe. With early and ongoing intervention, symptoms of brain damage may decrease, though there is considerable variability in improvement across children. This is particularly true of infants and preschoolers whose brains are still maturing at a rapid rate.

Children whose head injury is the result of physical abuse generally have patterns of trauma that include massive retinal hemorrhages, broken bones (especially ribs), and major head trauma such as cerebral hematomas, hemorrhages, edema, and stroke (Ewing-Cobb et al., 1998). Generally speaking, children with inflicted TBI are more likely to suffer long-term mental deficiency than children who suffer accidental TBI, possibly as a result of concomitant environmental factors which are associated with child abuse (Ewing-Cobb et al., 1998).

The term "shaken baby syndrome" is used to describe TBI that results from repeated severe shaking of an infant. It is hypothesized that the movement of the brain within the skull can cause serious brain injury in infants (Smith, 2003). However, some question whether the movement, without rapid deceleration or impact, such as shaking a baby's head against a pillow is sufficient to cause brain hemorrhage associated with long-term injury. Whatever the mechanism, it is clear that a child can sustain long-term brain damage even when there is no external evidence of harm.

There are a few general guidelines for educators who work with children with TBI, though these suggestions will not be appropriate for all variations of the disability:

◆ Provide repetition and consistency.
◆ Demonstrate new tasks, state instructions, and provide examples to illustrate ideas and concepts.
◆ Avoid figurative language.
◆ Arrange materials and tasks to promote as much independence as possible.
◆ Reinforce lengthening periods of attention to appropriate tasks; provide extra time for task completion.
◆ Probe skill acquisition frequently and provided repeated practice.
◆ Build in prompts and teach strategies for memory (picture cues, verbal prompts, etc.).
◆ Provide breaks to avoid fatigue.
◆ Reduce unnecessary distractions.

Families of children with TBI are often adversely affected by the stress of chronic behavioral and cognitive changes in their child, with parental adjustment and parent–child interactions growing worse over time (Wade et al., 1998). Unlike children whose brain injury is lifelong, those with TBI and their parents remember how they were before the trauma and as a result have a different set of emotional and psychological needs than other children and parents. The following suggestions are for working with families of children with TBI:

◆ Build a team of professionals, including family, child, educators, and rehabilitation specialists.
◆ Provide behavioral intervention for social/emotional problems.
◆ Acquire a full assessment of the child across developmental areas.
◆ Plan intervention that includes a variety of learning methods and materials.
◆ Conduct frequent assessments (every 30–60 days in the first year post-injury).
◆ Ensure, if injury was inflicted, that all appropriate safety net services to child and family are in place.
◆ Provide substantial support in terms of counseling, instruction, and respite to families.

CLOSE-UP

THE CONSEQUENCES OF CHILD ABUSE OF GIRLS

It is estimated that 1.6 new cases of child abuse occur in the United States each year. Of these, 52% are cases of neglect, 25% are from physical abuse, and 13% are comprised of sexual abuse. This number is even more astounding when considering that the number of serious injuries resulting from child abuse quadrupled from 1986–1993.

A longitudinal study of girls who were abused and a cohort group who had not been abused showed abused girls were significantly more likely to manifest physical and behavioral abnormalities. Specifically, girls who were sexually abused were more likely to have oppositional disorders, depression, suicidal tendencies, ADHD, and conduct disorders. These girls scored low on measures of frustration tolerance, appropriate social skills, attention to task, and sociability.

In addition to behavioral problems, these girls exhibited an alarming rate of physical/medical problems. As compared to nonabused cohorts, there was a five-fold increase in physical problems included vomiting, headache, eating disorders, postraumatic stress disorder (PTSD), self-injury, asthma, uninary tract infections, and skin problems.

While the emotional fallout of child abuse is great, there is also a direct fiscal cost to society. Fifty-six billion dollars per year is spent dealing with the consequences of child abuse. These costs include long-term problems of substance abuse, violence, HIV and other sexually transmitted diseases, health care utilization, teen pregnancy, diminished academic achievement, and subsequently lowered occupational status. In comparison, the total cost associated with cancer is approximately $104 billion per year. As great as these costs are, the United States is clearly not invested in solving the problems of child abuse. That is, the U.S. government spends approximately $28 per victim of child abuse on research compared to $1,735 per cancer victim. Put another way, the research investment for child abuse is approximately 5 cents/$100 of cost while we spend $2/$100 of cost for cancer research.

Source: Adapted from *Childhood Maltreatment and Adverse Outcomes: A Prospective Developmental Approach,* by F. Putnam, American Psychiatric Association Annual Meeting, May 1999, Washington, DC.

Congenital Physical Malformations

Neural Tube Defects

The most critical time for development of the nervous system is between the 3rd and 4th week of gestation (Hauser, 2003). It is during this time that the neural groove closes and forms the vertebral column, which houses the spinal cord and is joined to the other soft tissue structures surrounding the nerves. Any disturbance in the developmental sequence will result in **neural tube defects** and incomplete closure. The resulting abnormality can be severe (anencephaly), moderately severe (myelomeningocele), or less severe (meningocele and **spina bifida occulta**).

Spina bifida is the term used to describe an incomplete spinal column and the relationship of the spinal cord and contents to the defect. The term is frequently used interchangeably with any of the neural tube defects. These include spina bifida occulta (see Figure 6–8), meningocele, and myelomeningocele. Spina bifida affects about 1 out of every 1000 live births in the United States (Public Health

Figure 6–8
Internal Schema
of Spina Bifida
Occulta

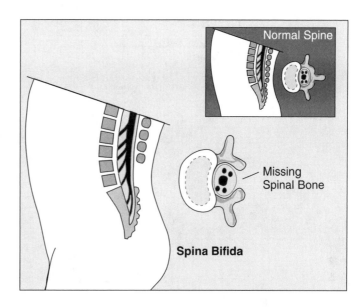

Reports, 1998a). Treatment is dependent on the level along the spine at which the defect is located, as well as on the existence of other complications (e.g., hydrocephalus or urinary tract involvement).

Anencephaly

Anencephaly is a congenital malformation in which the brain does not develop and the skull, which would normally cover the brain, is absent. A membrane occasionally covers blood vessels that do develop within the cavity where the brain should be contained. This defect is one of the most commonly occurring neural tube defects and frequently occurs in conjunction with other midline defects of the spinal cord and the spine, which covers the cord.

Anencephalic infants will either be stillborn or die shortly after delivery. Though anencephaly and other neural tube disorders can be spotted via ultrasound, the most accurate diagnosis is made by a laboratory test for maternal or amniotic fluid alpha-fetoprotein (AFP) (Public Health Reports, 1998b). This protein increases in both the mother's blood stream and in the amniotic fluid when a neural tube defect is present. Genetic counseling is available for families who experience this condition and can be especially valuable when planning future pregnancies. Development of anencephaly occurs between the 16th and 26th day after conception (Shapiro, 1990). No single factor seems to be responsible for the malformation, though genetic influence may be associated. There is a 5% recurrence rate within families (Shapiro, 1990). Environmental factors have also been linked correlationally to this malformation.

Meningocele.

The normal spinal cord is fully protected by bony structures called vertebrae. **Meningocele** is a neural tube defect that generally appears in the lumbar area of

Figure 6–9
Internal Schema
of Meningocele

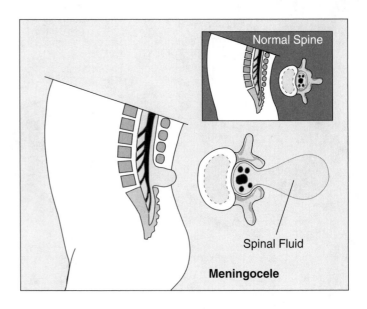

the vertebrae where the spinal cord is exposed (near the base of the spine). It is a soft tissue mass that is covered by skin and does not contain nerves or nerve roots. The **cerebrospinal fluid** (CSF) and meninges are affected in this defect (see Figure 6–9). Meningoceles are sometimes associated with genetic syndromes (Kousseff, 1984).

A meningocele is surgically repaired during the first few days of life. There is generally no paralysis or sensory loss and hydrocephalus rarely occurs. Occasionally there will be breakdown of the skin covering the defect, which increases the risk of infection of the spinal tract. There are sometimes nerve roots trapped within the sac, and this may cause weakness of the legs, but full recovery generally accompanies repair of the defect.

Myelomeningocele

Of all the defects that occur under the heading of spina bifida, myelomeningocele occurs the most frequently and has the most significant long-term effects. In **myelomeningocele**, both the spinal cord and its covering, the **meninges**, push through the skeletal defect to the surface (see Figure 6–10). As with the other forms of spina bifida, this can occur at any level along the spine. The higher the defect occurs in relationship to the head, the more severe the complications for an infant. Associated problems may include paraplegia, hydrocephalus, incontinence, sexual dysfunction, skeletal deformities, and mental impairment.

There is no known cause for myelomeningocele. Researchers suspect that a combination of factors that include heredity, environmental factors (women who bear one child with a neural tube disorder are at a significantly higher risk during subsequent pregnancies of a similar outcome), such as occupational exposure, socioeconomic status and geographic area (independent of race), and possibly vitamin deficiency may be responsible for the occurrence of neural tube defects

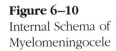

Figure 6–10

Internal Schema of
Myelomeningocele

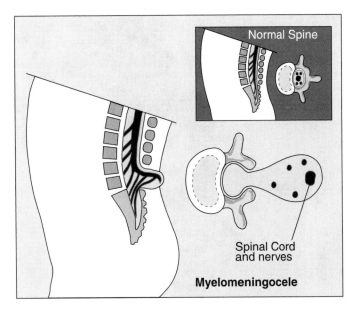

(Hauser, 2003; Mill, 1989; Mulinare, 1988). The intake of greater than 400 micrograms of folic acid during pregnancy via prenatal vitamins is known to reduce the incidence of neural tube defects (Public Health Reports, 1998a). Furthermore, the incidence of neural tube disorder is higher in women of Indian or Pakistani origin, who tend to have significantly lower concentrations of red-cell folate (Michie, Chambers, Abramsky, & Skooner, 1998).

Myelomeningoceles differ in size as well as location. They may be as small as a dime or as large as an apple. The size of the defect is not always the key to the complications that may arise. Severe neurological involvement may accompany a small defect as well as one that is large.

At birth, the defect may be covered with a thin membrane. This is frequently broken during the birth process, and cerebral spinal fluid leaks from the open area, placing the infant at significant risk for meningitis. A broken membrane also increases the need for surgery within the first few days of life.

Surgical repair of a myelomeningocele replaces the contents of the exposed sac into the spinal column and closes the defect. Occasionally the defect may be so large that it requires a skin graft to cover the open area of the back. Within the next 1- to 2-week period, at least 90% of these infants will require a shunt in order to treat hydrocephalus, which appears as part of the abnormality (National Institute of Neurological and Communicative Disorders and Stroke, 1986).

Prior to 1960, most infants affected with myelomeningocele were sent home and managed without the benefit of surgery. Fewer than 20% survived the first 2 years of life, with the majority dying within the first month (Laurence, 1964). In 1959, the University of Sheffield in Sheffield, England, developed a comprehensive plan for the treatment of affected infants. This plan included repairing the spinal defect within the first few days of life, placing a shunt for hydrocephalus, and establishing a home program, using the services of a team of surgeons,

Myelomeningocele before and after surgery.

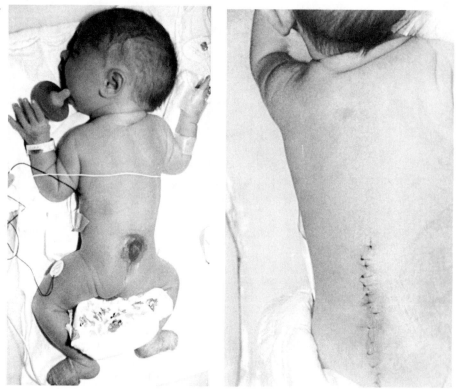

physicians, physical therapists, and social workers (Sharrard, Zachary, Lorber, & Bruce, 1963). The two-year survival rate increased to over 70% but presented the community with a whole new set of problems. These included providing services for surviving children who had severe disabilities, degrees of bladder and bowel dysfunction, and lower extremity paralysis. These are the problems that continue to affect children with myelomeningocele.

Most recently, medical advances in prenatal surgery of the open lesion have improved the prognosis even further. Because the unprotected neural tissue in a fetus is progressively traumatized in utero by chronic exposure to chemicals in the amniotic fluid, prenatal repair of the opening can rescue the spinal cord from damage that would occur throughout the remainder of pregnancy. In 1998, in the first reported case of in utero surgical repair of an open spina bifida and concomitant placement of a cerebrospinal shunt, the male infant failed to develop hydrocephalus and had met all developmental milestones (including motor) at 6 months; he developed full use of both legs (Adzick, Sutton, Crombleholme, & Flake, 1998). While this procedure has since proven to be quite successful in reversing the damage to the spinal cord and improving leg function beyond what would be expected, a majority of children still require a ventriculoperitoneal shunt (Fetal Surgery, 2002). However, this elective surgery has to date been limited to highly selective candidates and poses a significant risk of fetal death and maternal death. A less risky surgery that is currently experimentally promising with animals is robotic endoscopic surgery.

Common problems experienced by infants and children with a repaired myelomeningocele include genitourinary and orthopedic abnormalities. These problems are anticipated within the neonatal period and realized during infancy and early childhood. Defects in the upper lumbar spine area will affect hip flexion and may require children to use a wheelchair, whereas defects in the lower lumbar spine area may allow the child to walk with the aid of braces and crutches. Regardless of the level of the defect, many of these children also have club feet that often require casting.

Many affected children have significant problems with the genitourinary system. Because of the nerve involvement in the lumbar spine, the bladder frequently is atonic (without muscle tone). The bladder becomes distended with urine and lacks the nerve impulses required to empty itself. This buildup of urine provides the perfect setting for bacteria to grow, and chronic urinary tract infections place the child at risk for kidney disease. In addition, many of these children lack the nerve impulses for normal bowel control. Rectal muscles lack tone, allowing stool to leak, increasing the opportunity for contamination of the urinary tract with bacteria from feces. These children are also at risk for problems with skin breakdown, both from decreased circulation and decreased sensation below the level of the defect. Consequently there is a higher rate of chronic infections. Caregivers must be educated regarding the best method of promoting adequate bladder and bowel function to decrease the risks of chronic problems. Methods of prevention may include insertion of a bladder catheter, learning to place downward pressure on the lower abdomen to empty the bladder, administration of antibiotics, or in severe situations, the creation of an **ostomy**.

An ostomy is an opening made from an internal tube to an external source to allow for passage of urine or stool from the body. The formation of an ostomy is a surgical procedure. A stoma is the external opening that is on the abdomen at the site of the ostomy. The site is dependent on the reason for creation of the ostomy. Ostomies are created in the presence of many of the gastrointestinal and genitourinary defects. They may be temporary or permanent depending on the condition requiring their creation. Ostomies placed for urine diversion are generally permanent, whereas ostomies created for stool diversion may frequently be temporary until staged repairs of abnormalities can be successfully accomplished. A pouch is worn over the external stoma for the collection of urine or stool. This pouch requires careful monitoring to prevent skin irritation from urine or stool. In the absence of other disabilities, a child can be taught to monitor and maintain the external pouch. In situations in which children are neither physically nor mentally able, caregivers or even educators must be adept at both monitoring and maintaining the stoma and pouch. Careful monitoring of an ostomy can prevent foul odors, leakage, and skin irritation. This is essential to promoting self-esteem in the child and allowing a normal lifestyle.

Many children with myelomeningocele have average to above-average intelligence. This is dependent upon the presence of malformations within the brain that correlate with the defect (e.g., Arnold-Chiari malformations). Opportunities must be provided to allow for these children to reach their full potential in the presence of extensive physical disabilities.

Cases of infants born with myelomeningocele, as well as those with Down syndrome and duodenal atresia, stimulated what is known as the "Baby Doe" legislation. These laws were enacted by the federal government to protect the rights of infants with birth defects to receive definitive care for correctable defects and supportive care for problems related to defects that are not correctable but are compatible with life. Health care providers and educational systems are mandated by law to serve the needs of these children. In spite of the multiple problems experienced by infants and families affected with myelomeningocele, the expectation of parents for their children can generally be a happy and independent life.

MICROCEPHALY

Microcephaly means very small head and brain. This condition can be either primary or secondary, depending on the reasons for the limited brain growth. Primary microcephaly generally occurs during the first or second trimester of pregnancy and can result from genetic malformations, chromosomal abnormalities, or exposure to toxic agents (e. g., radiation, chemicals such as drugs or alcohol, and infections). Secondary microcephaly usually occurs during the last trimester of pregnancy, during the labor and delivery process, or during the period of early infancy. Some of the factors responsible for secondary microcephaly are infections, birth trauma, inborn errors of metabolism as in Hurler syndrome, and decreased oxygen supply related to many different causes (Morris & Rodger, 1998; Tam, 1997). Either primary or secondary microcephaly may result in only minor developmental delays or may range to profound disabilities and mental retardation.

Small head size in infants is usually identified with a head circumference that falls at least two standard deviations below the mean on a standard growth chart for age. Microcephalic head size also tends to be disproportionate to both the weight and the linear growth of a child. In spite of the significant difference, many of the chromosomal abnormalities that cause small head size have varying degrees of disability. Still, many of these conditions are also associated with other physical and developmental disabilities, such as cataracts and skeletal abnormalities.

The most common development of microcephaly after the second trimester of pregnancy is related to hypoxic–ischemic cerebral injury. This generally occurs during the birth process or during the neonatal period and is caused by decreased blood flow to the brain, which in turn, decreases oxygen levels (hypoxia) and causes cellular death (ischemia) from lack of oxygen and glucose. Many affected infants are full term and initially have a head circumference that is within normal parameters for height and weight. Conditions that cause hypoxic–ischemic brain dysfunction may be trauma or infection. Development of microcephaly following such events has a major impact on the long-term neurological outcome of an infant. The neurological impairment that occurs generally includes cognitive impairment, cerebral palsy, seizures, and cerebral atrophy (Hill, 1991; Volpe, 1987).

There is no medical treatment for microcephalus. Many of the children with minor impairment show some degree of autism and many are hyperactive. Both conditions increase the need for carefully planned educational opportunities that address the individual needs of a child and also assist parents with the difficult job of raising a child with special needs.

HYDROCEPHALUS

Hydrocephalus is a condition where there is an excessive accumulation of cerebrospinal fluid in the ventricles of the brain. These four ventricles are fluid-filled sacs that occupy space within and around the brain mass. The cerebrospinal fluid bathes the brain and spinal cord, providing both protection and nutrition. Though capillary circulation throughout the brain is the main source of nutrition and the elimination of waste products, there is additional diffusion of nutrients from the cerebrospinal fluid to the brain tissue.

Hippocrates was one of the first physicians to describe hydrocephalus. He felt that chronic seizures caused the condition and that treatment should be laxatives, vegetable ingestion, and sneezing (Rocco, 1985). Failure of these treatments would then require surgical intervention that consisted of opening the skull extending to the brain material itself. Additional treatment involved the frequently used approach to any disease process—"bloodletting" (Rocco, 1985).

Untreated hydrocephalus causes the head to increase in size beyond two standard deviations above the mean on the standard growth chart. Swelling of the ventricles can be caused by an obstruction in the drainage system, an overproduction of spinal fluid, or a failure in reabsorption of cerebrospinal fluid into the general circulation. As an example, meningitis may either cause swelling that results in blockage of the ventricles (a cause of hydrocephalus) or a blockage of the ventricles and subsequent build-up of fluid may lead to bacterial build-up and meningitis itself (an effect of hydrocephalus) (Mactier, Galea, & McWilliam, 1998). When the ventricles fill with excess fluid, they become massively dilated, placing pressure on the brain matter. If left unchecked, the brain structures may become permanently damaged, and mental retardation will occur.

Hydrocephalus may also be caused by the presence of a tumor or head trauma. Long-term outcomes for infants who are either born with or develop hydrocephalus after birth are dependent on the cause of the problem, presence of any other neurological problems, and the time frame from onset until a diagnosis is made and treatment is initiated (Jansen, 1988). Early diagnosis and treatment significantly improves the possibilities for normal development and the prevention

Hydrocephalus before and after surgery.

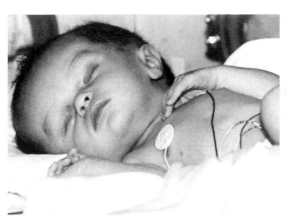
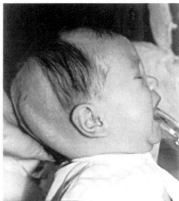

of mental retardation. Head ultrasounds, computerized tomography, and magnetic resonance imaging are the methods used for definitive diagnosis. The medication Diamox can sometimes aid in controlling the condition without surgical intervention by pulling excess fluid into the circulatory system, where it can be excreted by the kidneys.

Failure to control hydrocephalus medically may ultimately result in the need for surgical intervention in which a temporary or permanent shunt is placed between the ventricles and the abdominal space. Shunting procedures require the surgical placement of a soft pliable plastic tube between the ventricle and either the heart or the peritoneum (a closed sac lining the abdomen). Generally, the peritoneal cavity is used in children because it provides the opportunity to loop extra catheter tubing into the abdominal space, allowing a child to grow without needing replacement of the system. Most shunts have a small bubble reservoir that is seeded under the skin, usually behind the ear. This reservoir contains a one-way valve that controls the amount of cerebrospinal fluid that can be drained from the ventricle at any one time, depending on the pressure within the ventricle. This reservoir also provides a method of checking on the flow of the system; this is especially useful when a shunt failure is suspected. The ease with which the valve can be pumped (gently pushed) is an aid to evaluating the shunt for free flow of fluid. Symptoms of shunt failure are similar to those of increased pressure from obstruction. This tube must be watched carefully for blockage. Symptoms of tube obstruction may include a decreased level of consciousness, vomiting, temperature instability, seizures, and if the pressure gets high enough, loss of brain mass and even death.

Hydrocephalus may be evident on prenatal ultrasound, or it may be completely without evidence at birth. However, infants affected with significant blockage prior to birth, which has been identified by prenatal testing, may require delivery by cesarean section to attempt to preserve functional brain material and also decrease the risk of injury to a mother attempting to deliver an infant with a very large head by the vaginal route. Many cases of significant prenatal hydrocephalus will result in brain wasting from pressure during the developmental process. Surgical intervention in these cases is done not to protect the brain, but for comfort to an infant and to assist families in providing adequate physical and emotional care.

Hydrocephalus frequently occurs with other neural tube defects, such as myelomeningocele. In the latter, initial repair of the spinal defect is the first stage of surgical care, and placement of a ventricular/peritoneal shunt is the second stage. Closure of the primary defect (myelomeningocele) causes obstruction of cerebrospinal fluid that results in the need for a shunt.

Hydrocephalus is a lifelong disorder that requires consistent follow-up (Buxton & Punt, 1998). Management of the shunt, observations for function, and awareness of the symptoms of possible infections are requirements of not only the family and care providers but also of educators who may be working with these children. Awareness of symptoms that may be displayed by an individual child is part of the educational plan.

The cognitive and psychosocial development of children varies significantly, depending on the underlying cause of the hydrocephalus. Many children with hydrocephalus have normal intellectual development (Amacher & Wellington,

Case Study

THE DIARY OF ESTHER ANNA BERKE: MONTH 9

This month features Esther's diary from July 16-Aug. 15. These are the same notes that we show her doctor so you can see what her progress is like. In my opinion, her physical therapy program and specialized diet don't seem to help control her seizures very much. We did phase out one of her medications (Lamictal) without seeing much change in seizures, so that was good. She isn't very "stable"—her eating, sleeping, and seizure patterns change frequently. We will continue with both her customized program and her diet and see what happens. She was 75 cm long (95th percentile) and weighed 7.3 kg (20th percentile) on her 9-month birthday.

Excerpts:

July 16–31: Theravite and # 16 are both vitamin supplements.

July 16, Friday Diet: 24 oz. formula, 16 with electrolyte solution for seizure control, 2 oz. apple juice, 2 T. mixed cereal and apple juice with # 16 added twice (forgot theravite), and 1 T. beef with about 1 t. mixed cereal. **Seizures:** 4 during the night: infantile spasms, lasting 10–15 min., 6 during the day: infantile spasms, some pretty hard, lasting 10–15 min. Some were just 2–3 min. long. Once they stopped before Sarah could get the solution mixed up and given to her. Sarah forgot her medications in the A.M.

July 18, Sun. Seizures: 5 A.M., short hard infantile spasm, 10 min., 7 A.M., infantile spasm, milder, 10 min., 12:45, infantile spasms, each spasm long, 10 min. 1:15 mild infantile spasms, 2–3 min., (both of these were in a noisy restaurant, while she was trying to fall asleep), 5 P.M., infantile spasm, hard at first, 15 min., 9 P.M., mild infantile spasms, about 5 min. while falling asleep.

She's sleeping much better at night now. Hooray! She doesn't always have the cold hands and feet phenomenon with each seizure

episode. She's also not as stiff as before, just likes to keep the head twisted to the right side.

July 19, Mon. Seizures: 6 all about 10 minutes, all pretty mild. The last one lasted 5 minutes and ended in a black, tarry stool.

July 21, Wed. Seizures: During the night,. . . a LOT. 6 or 7, one every hour for a while. One or two were very short and mild (2–3 min). Most were intense and weird patterns. During the day, 4 seizures, hard 15–20 min. By weird patterns, I mean: her infantile spasms usually are flexor spasms with head turned right and tongue stuck out. These new ones extend her arms and head turns hard left and she squeals with each one. Sometimes these two alternate, sometimes there are mild flexor spasms, sometimes a longer flexor is thrown in. Things may be quiet and then all of a sudden, she does one of these extensor ones. Her arms and legs aren't always cold, but usually. (Almost) ALWAYS in the past (except for the partials she had for 2 months), the infantile spasms (flexor) would start hard and taper off gradually. She's not as stiff and arched as before, but it seems the days after a night full of seizures, she's much more passive, not sleepy really. She's still irregular in sleeping/eating habits. Sleeps like charm for the first few hours at night and then starts seizures.

July 27, Tues. Diet: We quit feeding her solids because no stool for 7 days, she is quite constipated. at least 16 oz. formula with elect., No # 16, 3 oz. prune juice **Seizures:** Night, about 4–5, varying. Day, at least 2 hard spasms.

July 28, Wed. Diet: 16 oz. formula with elect., 3 oz. prune juice, no supplements.

Seizures: Night, only 2, 1 mild spasms, 1 hard, A.M.—1 hard spasm, 10 min., 5 P.M.—1 med. 10 min., 7 P.M.—1 hard seizure, and finally a stool!! Very black and thick, but not hard. Not much it seems for 9 days backlog. She seemed quite re-lieved, however, and promptly fell asleep. Her last dose of Lamictal was on 7/27, Tues. It was reduced from 2x to 1x a day earlier in July. Sarah gave it to her in the evening, thinking we could deal with possible withdrawal seizures during the day. But the seizures have been much worse at night. Go figure. We'll see what happens now that she's off it completely. She's only taking Riv-otril and Sabril now. A chemist friend of ours wondered why we were giving her a base (am-monium chloride) after I said that the alkalinity in her muscles was causing all the contractions. Her eyes are tracking together much better but her face and lips looked really asymmetrical to-day. She uses her left side MUCH more than her right, except it's the left side of her face that is asymmetrical. She's not arching any more except in between the hard spasms.

July 31, Sat. Seizures: 12:30 A.M.–7:30 A.M. 9 infantile spasms, first one was hard, the rest were medium to mild, 10:15 A.M. infantile spasm "com-plex" (long individual spasms), but duration was only 5 min., 11:15 A.M.—small myoclonic jerks while falling asleep (these are becoming more common), 2:00 P.M.—infantile spasm, medium, 10 min., 6 P.M.—infantile spasm hard, 10 min.

Excerpts from Aug. 1–15:

August 1, Sunday (not a good record keeping day) Seizures: During night, 5, one with mild spasms, lasting an hour, the rest were shorter, 10:15 A.M.—infantile spasm, hard, 15 min (loud singing at church maybe set them off?), After-noon—3 mild infantile spasms, 7:15 P.M.—infantile spasm, med/hard, 15 min.

August 4, Wed. Seizures: 12:30 A.M.—infantile spasm, hard, 2:30—infantile spasm, mild, 4:30—the same, 6:30—the same, 11:30 A.M.—infantile spasm, hard to mild, 20 min. then twitching for a while when sleeping, 1:30 P.M.—infantile spasm, mild, 15 min. upon waking, 6:30 P.M.—infantile spasm, med, 10 min, sleep.

Notes:

Subdued all day. Didn't try to lift her head like before. The seizures seem to be changing from the hard, short kind to the mild, long ones.

Some are very mild with only her tongue stick-ing out and her feet lifting and thumping on the bed. Silent, otherwise. When she began the Lamictal, the end of April, suddenly the seizures became more intense and shorter. So maybe she's going back to the more "simpler" infantile spasms, but they sure last a lot longer. Hands and feet still get cold, but not every time. One series of spasms had a frequency of only every 15–20 seconds. She tried to drink a bottle in be-tween the spasms.

Her face seems asymmetrical like before, and the flaky-type skin that was always around her eyebrows has returned. Congestion is becoming a problem. It used to happen during some seizures (we were told it was a side effect of the Rivotril). Now it's very prevalent whenever I give her drops, to the point she seems to be gasping for breath until she finally coughs . . . usually af-ter the spasms have ended. During one seizure today, I just quit the drops. Sometimes it's hap-pening when she drinks a bottle, too. As soon as she coughs/clears her throat, it's gone.

August 6, Friday Seizures: All night, from 12:30 to 6:30 this was a VERY bad night. She was "twitchy" in between the spasm episodes, some were hard, some mild. The mild one lasted longer. Sometimes Sarah fell asleep while giving her the drops. Wed. night she fell asleep before getting her meds, and Thurs. night, the same, only she fi-nally got them at 4 A.M.. Morning: Seizures and twitching in between leisurely drinking a bottle. Afternoon: no seizures until 5:45 P.M.—infantile spasm, hard to mild, 25 min., then slept, 7 P.M.—infantile spasm, hard to mild, 15 min., 8 P.M.—the same, Now she's asleep, whew!

August 7, Saturday Seizures: During night, NONE! Hurrah! 8:30 A.M.—infantile spasm, mild, 10 min., 1–2 P.M.—infantile spasm, hard—10 min. mild for the rest of the hour, finally slept at 3:30, 5:15 P.M.—infantile spasm, woke up, 7 P.M.—infantile spasm, very hard, 5 min, mild, 5 min, 8 P.M.—infantile spasm, mild, short.

Congestion is still a problem during bottles and seizures. She fell asleep without a seizure preceding.

August 9, Monday Seizures: During night, NONE. 4:30 P.M.—2 myoclonic jerks as she fell asleep, Evening—at one point she stiffened with her eyes really wide. The left eye was not tracking with the right, crossing sometime. Lasted about 5 min. while falling asleep.

August 10, No seizures: Very sleepy. Arched back and fussy when awake. Hard to do NACD program, or feed. Only seems happy when drinking something. Her tongue moves a lot and she tried to get one hand in mouth. Right arm is stiff by her side, doesn't use it much at all, although kicks her right leg. (Looks like a stroke victim). Her kness stay stiff a lot of the time, feet are pointed out. Drools and spits up a lot. Head turned hard to the right. Eyes not tracking together as well as before, but better than last night. A few times this P.M., she pulled her knees up 2 or 3 times, a little like the rhythmic infantile spasms, but there were no other signs of a seizure. Deja vu. It is so similar to week of July 2–7 or 8. The long episodes of seizing and then nothing, but the arched back in exchange.

August 14, Sat. Seizures: 12–6 A.M.—Another bad night, 6 hours of infantile spasms, off and on. Last few hours cycle: sleep 15 min, seize 10 min. The rest of the day is a blur. If she wasn't sleeping or seizing, she was arched way back whimpering and fussing. She wouldn't take bottles or solids. Somewhere in here, her left arm started hanging by her side like her right arm used to be earlier this week, but she's waving around the right arm now. Also during the week, she tries to raise her eyebrows, but only the left one goes up (like Spock).

Esther Anna and her mother, Sarah.

August 15, Sun. Seizures: Basically a repeat of Saturday. During the night, though, when seizing, it seemed to help to hold her while giving her the drops. The seizures seemed to stop sooner. She did sleep longer/better when propped on a pillow.

1984). Frequent shunt infections, plugged shunts, and other malfunctions may affect development of an otherwise normal brain. Early evaluation of possible developmental delays is necessary, and many of these children benefit from early childhood developmental stimulation programs. Shunt tubing is versatile and can withstand normal childhood activities. It is essential that children participate as fully as possible in age-appropriate activities so that the illness not be an unnecessary deterrent to full enjoyment of life.

In Conclusion

Children affected with a neurological disability, regardless of the cause, have idiosyncratic responses to their conditions. Continuing research into causes of neurological disabilities, both physical and functional, will provide educators with the knowledge base to devise new and innovative approaches to interactions with each child and family. Prevention is the goal, but providing optimal care for affected families is a more realistic short-term objective.

One area in which early childhood professionals must become more knowledgeable is that of ADHD and related behavioral disorders. With the present rise in incidence, which is recognized at younger ages, children with significant management needs cause havoc in preschool programs for children with special needs. In fact, this young population of children, who tends to be so disruptive, is more difficult to manage than older children because their language and cognitive skills are less well developed, and therefore, they are less able to understand rules and their consequences. On the other hand, because the time it takes to remediate behavioral problems is longer than the length of time that the behavior has been in a child's repertoire, very early intervention is optimal. One approach that holds much promise as a method of assessing and identifying effective strategies for preschool children is functional analysis. Using this method, the factors that motivate and sustain undesirable behavior are carefully observed and measured. When these factors are identified, systematic attempts are made to alter the conditions that maintain such behaviors. More research, however, is clearly needed. Therefore, future efforts in early childhood special education should be devoted to research in behavioral management of significant behavior problems, training of professionals to use such strategies, and, if warranted by the findings, widespread application in early childhood settings.

Study Guide Questions

1. Why should early childhood special educators know the etiologies and courses of disabling conditions?
2. Differentiate between invasive and noninvasive procedures. Give an example of each.
3. What are the medical uses of X rays? What precautions should be taken when X rays are used?
4. In what ways do CAT scans provide more information than X rays?
5. What are the advantages of the MRI over CAT scans and X rays?
6. Describe how PET scans are carried out. What special information do PET scans provide?
7. What are the primary medical uses of ultrasound?
8. What kind of information does an EEG provide?
9. What is cerebral palsy?
10. How has modern medicine maintained the incidence of cerebral palsy?
11. Describe the relationship between primitive reflexes and normal motor development.
12. Name and describe the primitive reflexes seen at birth.

13. What is the main difference between primitive reflexes and postural reflexes? How do primitive reflexes interfere with postural reflex development in children with cerebral palsy?
14. Name and describe three general terms used to describe muscle tone. How do the terms apply to abnormal muscle tone in children with cerebral palsy?
15. Differentiate each of the following: hemiplegia, paraplegia, quadriplegia, and diplegia.
16. Differentiate hypertonia and hypotonia.
17. Briefly describe the characteristics of athetosis, ataxia, and spasticity.
18. Compare and describe cerebral palsy that is severe, moderate, or mild.
19. What nutritional and feeding problems often accompany cerebral palsy?
20. In addition to feeding problems, what other conditions are often presented with cerebral palsy?
21. How should therapists work with parents of children with cerebral palsy?
22. What is meant by positioning and handling?
23. How are seizures activated?
24. Define epilepsy.
25. Differentiate each of the following types of seizures: absence, tonic-clonic, and myoclonic.
26. How do seizures affect cognitive functioning?
27. Summarize this chapter's advice about assisting families of children with seizure disorders.
28. What should one do if a child experiences a tonic-clonic seizure?
29. What are the characteristics of ADHD?
30. What are the recommended treatments for ADHD?
31. Why is it difficult to describe a child with traumatic brain injury? What are some common symptoms?
32. Identify five general recommendations that might be made to those who work with children with traumatic brain injury.
33. What is anencephaly?
34. What are the effects of spina bifida occulta?
35. How is meningocele treated? What are the long-term effects?
36. What is myelomeningocele?
37. How is myelomeningocele treated?
38. What physical problems are common for children with repaired myelomeningocele?
39. What is the Baby Doe legislation?
40. What is microcephaly, and what causes it?
41. What is hydrocephalus?
42. How is hydrocephalus controlled?

REFERENCES

Abramowitz, A. J., Eckstrand, D., O'Leary, S. G., & Dulcan, M. K. (1992). ADHD children's responses to stimulant medication in two intensities of a behavioral intervention program. *Behavior Modification, 16,* 193–203.

Adler, T. (1995). Infant CP protection. *Science News, 147*(8), 119.

Adzick, N. S., Sutton, L. N., Crombleholme, T. M., & Flake, A. W. (1998). Successful fetal surgery for spina bifida. *Lancet, 352*(9141), 1675–1677.

Amacher, A., & Wellington, J. (1984). Infantile hydrocephalus: Long-term results of surgical therapy. *Child's Brain, 11,* 217–229

American Psychiatric Association. (1987). *Diagnostic and statistical manual of mental disorders* (3rd ed., revised). Washington, DC: Author.

American Psychiatric Association. (1994). *Diagnostic and statistical manual of mental disorders* (4th ed., revised). Washington, DC: Author.

Anastopoulos, A. D., & Barkley, R. A. (1991). Biological factors in attention deficit disorder. *Children and Adults with Attention Deficit Disorder Educational Research, 5,* 1.

Austin, J. K., Risinger, M. W., & Beckett, L. A. (1992). Correlates of behavior problems in children with epilepsy. *Epilepsia, 33*(6), 1115–1122.

Barclay, L. (2002). General movements in preterm infants predict cerebral palsy. *Archives of Pediatric & Adolescent Medicine, 156*(5), 460–467.

Barkley, R. A. (1981). *Hyperactive children: A handbook for diagnosis and treatment.* New York: Guilford.

Barkley, R. A. (1993). A new theory of ADHD. *The ADHD Report, 1*(5), 1–4.

Barkley, R. A. (1997). *ADHD and the nature of self-control.* New York: Guilford.

Barkley, R. A., DuPaul, G., & McMurray, M. (1991). Attention deficit disorder with and without hyperactivity: Clinical response to three dose levels of methylphenidate. *Pediatrics, 87,* 519–531.

Bender, W. N., & McLaughlin, P. J. (1995). The ADHD conundrum: Introduction to a special series on attention deficit/hyperactivity disorder. *Intervention in School and Clinic, 30,* 196–197.

Bhushan, V., Paneth, N., & Kiely, J. L. (1993). Impact of improved survival of very low birth weight infants on recent secular trends in the prevalence of cerebral palsy. *Pediatrics, 91*(6), 1094–1100.

Bigge, J. L. (1991). *Teaching individuals with physical and multiple disabilities* (3rd ed.). Columbus, OH: Macmillan.

Bronowski, J. (1967). *Human and animal languages. In honor of Roman Jakobson* (Vol. 1). The Hague, Netherlands, Mouton.

Bronowski, J. (1977). *Human and animal languages. A sense of the future* (pp. 103–131). Cambridge, MA: MIT Press.

Brunquell, P. J. (1994). Listening to epilepsy. *Infants and Young Children, 7*(1), 24–33.

Buxton, N., & Punt, J. (1998). Failure to follow patients with hydrocephalus shunts can lead to death. *British Journal of Neurosurgery, 12*(5), 399–402.

Cioni, G., Paolicelli, P. B., Sordi, C., & Vinter, A. (1993). Sensorimotor development in cerebral palsied infants assessed with the Uzgiris-Hunt scales. *Developmental Medicine and Child Neurology, 35,* 1055–1066.

Colin, A. (1997). *Willie: Raising and loving a child with attention deficit disorder.* New York: Viking.

Conners, C. (1980). *Food additives and hyperactive children.* New York: Plenum.

Cooke, R. W. (1990). Cerebral palsy in very low birthweight infants. *Archives of Disabled Children, 65,* 201–206.

Dahl, M., & Gebre-Medhin, M. (1993). Feeding and nutritional problems in children with cerebral palsy and myelomeningocoele. *Acta Pediatrica, 82,* 816–20.

Dam, M. (1990). Children with epilepsy: The effect of seizures, syndromes, and etiological factors on cognitive functioning. *Epilepsia, 31*(4), 26–29.

DeBar, L.L., Lynch, F., Powell, J., & Gale, J. (2003). Use of psychotropic agents in preschool children: Associated symptoms, diagnoses, and health care service in a health maintenance organization. *Archives of Pediatric & Adolescent Medicine, 157*(2), 150–157.

Dichter, M. (1994). The epilepsies and convulsive disorders. In K. J. Isselbacher, E. Braunwald, J. D. Wilson, J. B. Martin, A. S. Fauci, & D. L. Kasper (Eds.), *Harrison's principle of internal medicine* (13th ed., pp. 2223–2333). New York: McGraw-Hill.

Dormans, J. P. (1993). Orthopedic management of children with cerebral palsy. *Pediatric Clinics of North America, 40*(3), 645–657.

Eaton, D. G. M., Ahmed, Y., & Dubowitz, L. M. S. (1991). Maternal trauma and cerebral lesions in preterm infants. Case reports. *British Journal of Obstetrics and Gynecology, 98,* 1292–1294.

Eicher, P. S., & Batshaw, M. L. (1993). Cerebral palsy. *Pediatric Clinics of North America, 40*(3), 537–551.

Ewing-Cobbs, L., Kramer, L., Prasad, M., Canales, D. N., Louis, P. T., Fletcher, J. M., Vollero, H., Landry, S. H., & Cheung, K. (1998). Neuroimaging, physical and developmental findings after inflicted and noninflicted traumatic brain injury in young children. *Pediatrics, 102,* 300–307.

Farley, D. (1997). On the teen scene: Attention disorder overcoming the deficit. *FDA Consumer, 31*(5), 32–36.

Farmer, S. F., Harrison, L. M., Ingram, D. A., & Stephens, J. A. (1991). Plasticity of central motor pathways in children with hemiplegic cerebral palsy. *Neurology, 41,* 1505–1510.

Fee, M. A., Charney, E. B., & Robertson, W. W. (1988). Nutritional assessment of the young child with cerebral palsy. *Infants and Young Children, 1*(1), 33–40.

Festschrift, C. (1994). Primitive reflexes: Their contribution to the early detection of cerebral palsy. *Clinical Pediatrics, 33,* 388–398.

Fetal Surgery. (2002). Update in obstetrics from SMFM Annual Meeting 2002. Retrieved December 2, 2002 from *http://www.medscape.com/viewarticle/424571_3*

Fetters, L. (1984). Motor development. In M. J. Hanson (Ed.), *Atypical infant development* (pp. 313–358). Austin, TX: PRO-ED.

Fish, D. R., Smith, S. J., Quesney, L. F., Andermann, F., & Rasmussen, T. (1993). Surgical treatment of children with medically intractable frontal and temporal lobe epilepsy: Results and highlights of 40 years' experience. *Epilepsia, 34*(2), 244–247.

Fouse, B., & Morrison, J. A. (1997). Using children's books as an intervention for attention-deficit disorder. *Reading Teacher, 50,* 442–446.

Friedman, R. J. & Doyal, G. T. (1992). *Management of children and adolescents with attention deficit-hyperactivity disorder* (3rd ed.). Austin, TX: Pro-Ed.

Gibbs, N. (November, 1998). The age of Ritalin. *Time, 152*(22), 86–94.

Goulden, K. J., Shinnar, S., Koller, H., Katz, M., & Richardson, S. A. (1991). Epilepsy in children with mental retardation: A cohort study. *Epilepsia, 32*(5), 690–697.

Grant, A., Joy, M. T., O'Brien, N. O., Hennessy, E., & MacDonald, D. (November, 1989). Cerebral palsy among children born during the Dublin randomized trial of intrapartum monitoring. *The Lancet,* 1233–1235.

Hauser, W.A. (2003). Epidemiology of neural tube defects.*Epilepsia, 44* (Suppl 3), 4–13.

Henderson, H. S., French, R., & McCarty, P. (1993). ATNR: Its possible impact on motor efficiency in children. *Physical Educator, 50*(1), 20–23.

Hill, A. (1991). Current concepts of hypoxic-ischemic cerebral injury in the newborn. *Pediatric Neurology, 7,* 317–325.

Hinjosa, J., & Anderson, J. (1991). Mother's perceptions of home treatment programs for their preschool children with cerebral palsy. *The American Journal of Occupational Therapy, 45*(3), 273–279.

Hingley, A. T. (1999). Epilepsy: Taming the seizures, dispelling the myths. *FDA Consumer, 33*(1), 28–33.

Hoare, P., & Kerley, S. (1992). Helping parents and children with epilepsy cope successfully: The outcome of a group programme for parents. *Journal of Psychosomatic Research, 36*(8), 759–767.

Jansen, J. (1988). Etiology and prognosis in hydrocephalus. *Child's Nervous System, 4,* 263–267.

Keenan, H.T., Runyan, D. K., Marshall, S. W., Nocera, M.A., Merten, D. F., & Sinal, S. H. (2003). A population-based study of inflicted traumatic brain injury in young children. *JAMA, 290*(5), 621–626.

Kousseff, B. (1984). Sacral meningocele with conotruncal heart defects: A possible autosomal recessive trait. *Pediatrics, 74,* 395–398.

Krick, J., Murphy-Miller, P., Zeger, S., & Wright, E. (1996). Pattern of growth in children with cerebral palsy. *Journal of the American Dietetic Association, 96*(7), 680–685.

Laurence, K. (1964). The natural history of spina bifida cystica. *Archives of Diseases of Childhood, 39,* 41–50.

Laybourn, A., & Hill, M. (1994). Children with epilepsy and their families: Needs and services. *Child Care Health and Development, 20,* 1–14.

Lerner, J. W., Lowenthal, B., & Lerner, S. R. (1995). *Attention deficit disorders: Assessment and teaching.* Pacific Grove, CA: Brooks/Cole Publishing Co.

Linnet, K.M., Dalsgaard, S., Obel, C., Wisborg, K., Henriksen, T.B., Rodriguez, A., Kotimaa, A., Moilanen, I., Thomsen, P.H., Olsen, J., & Jarvelin, M.R. (2003). Maternal lifestyle factors in pregnancy risk of attention deficit hyperactivity disorder and associated behaviors: Review of the current evidence. *American Journal of Psychiatry, 160,* 1028–1040.

Mactier, H., Galea, P., & McWilliam, R. (1998). Acute obstructive hydrocephalus complicating bacterial meningitis in childhood. *British Medical Journal, 316*(7148), 1887–1890.

Marlowe, M. (1986). Metal pollutant exposure and behavior disorders: Implications for school practices. *Journal of Special Education, 2*(2), 251–262.

Michie, C. A., Chambers, J., Abramsky, L., & Skooner, J. (1998). Folate deficiency, neural tube defects, and cardiac disease in UK Indians and Pakistanis. *Lancet, 351*(9109), 1105.

Mild Traumatic Brain Injury Committee. (1993). Definition of mild traumatic brain injury. *Journal of Head Trauma Rehabilitation, 8*(3), 86–87.

Milich, R., Wolraich, M., & Lindgren, S. (1986). Sugar and hyperactivity: A critical review of the findings. *Clinical Psychology Review, 6,* 493–513.

Mill, J. (1989). The absence of a relationship between the periconceptional use of vitamins and neural-tube defects. *New England Journal of Medicine, 321,* 430–435.

Morelle, M. J. (1993). Differential diagnosis of seizures. *Neurologic Clinics, 11*(4), 737–754.

Morris, A. A. M., & Rodger, I. W. (1998). Leukotrienes and the brain. *Lancet, 352*(9139), 1487–1488.

Moster D., Lie R.T., & Markestad T. (2002). Joint association of Apgar scores and early neonatal symptoms with minor disabilities at school age. *Archives of Disabled Child, Fetal, & Neonatal Education, 86*(1), 16–21.

Mulinare, J. (1988). Periconceptional use of multivitamins and the occurrence of neural tube defects. *Journal of the American Medical Association, 260,* 3141–3145.

Murray, B. A., & Myers, M. A. (1998). Conduct disorders and the special-education trap. *Education Digest, 63*(8), 48–54.

Naeye, R. L., Peters, E. C., Bartholomew, M., & Landis, J. R. (1989). Origins of cerebral palsy. *American Journal of Diseases of Children, 143,* 1154–1161.

National Institute of Neurological and Communicative Disorders and Stroke. (1986). *Spina bifida: Hope through research.* Bethesda, MD: National Institute of Health.

Nguyen, D. K., & Spencer, S. S. (2003). Recent advances in the treatment of epilepsy. *Archives of Neurology, 60,* 929–935.

O'Leary, K. D., Pelham, W. E., Rosenbaum, A., & Price, G. H. (1976). Behavioral treatment of hyperkinetic children: An experimental evaluation of its usefulness. *Clinical Pediatrics, 15,* 510–515.

Ornoy, A. (2003). The impact of intrauterine exposure versus postnatal environment in neurodevelopmental toxicity: Long-term neurobehavioral studies in children at risk for developmental disorders. *Toxicology Letters, 140–141,* 171–181.

Palmer, F. B., Shapiro, B. K., Allen, M. C., Mosher, B. S., Bilker, S. A., Harryman, S. E., Meinert, C. L., & Capute, A. J. (1990). Infant stimulation curriculum for infants with cerebral palsy: Effects on infant temperament, parent-infant interaction, and home environment. *Pediatrics Supplement, 85*(3), 411–415.

Procopis, P. G. (March, 1992). Breath-holding attacks in children. *Modern Medicine of Australia,* pp. 36–37.

Public Health Reports (1998a). Please, more folate. *Public Health Reports, 113*(4), 293.

Public Health Reports (1998b). FDA study finds test kits effective in spotting birth defects. *Public Health Reports, 113*(5), 382.

Putnam, F. (May, 1999). *Childhood maltreatment and adverse outcomes: A prospective developmental approach.* American Pychiatric Association Annual Meeting. Washington, DC.

Quinn, P. O. (1997). *Attention Deficit Disorder: Diagnosis and Treatment from Infancy to Adulthood.* New York: Brunner/Mazel.

Reilly, S., & Skuse, D. (1992). Characteristics and management of feeding problems of young children with cerebral palsy. *Developmental Medicine and Child Neurology, 34,* 379–388.

Rocco, C. (1985). *Historical background: The treatment of infantile hydrocephalus.* Boca Raton: CRC Press.

Rosen, M. G., & Dickinson, J. C. (1992). The incidence of cerebral palsy. *American Journal of Obstetrics and Gynecology, 167,* 417–423.

Ross, D. M., & Ross, S. A. (1976). *Hyperactivity: Research, theory and action.* New York: John Wiley & Sons.

Safer, D. J., & Allen, R. P. (1976). *Hyperactive children: Diagnosis and management.* Baltimore: University Park Press.

Scheller, J. M., & Nelson, K. B. (1994). Does cesarean delivery prevent cerebral palsy or other neurologic problems of childhood? *Obstetrics & Gynecology, 83*(4), 624–630.

Seppa, N. (1998). Infections may underlie cerebral palsy. *Science News, 154*(16), 244–245.

Shapiro, K. (1990). Anencephaly. In Buyse, M. (Ed.), *Birth defects encyclopedia* (pp.139–140). Dover, MA.

Sharrard, W., Zachary, R., Lorber, J., & Bruce, A. (1963). A controller trial of immediate and delayed closure of spina bifida cystica. *Archives of Diseases of Childhood, 38,* 18–25.

Shepherd, C., & Hosking, G. (1989). Epilepsy in school children with intellectual impairments in Sheffield: The size and nature of the problem and implications for service provision. *Journal of Mental Deficiency Research, 33,* 511–514.

Smith, J. (2003). Shaken baby syndrome. *Orthopedic Nurse, 22*(3), 204–205.

Tam, D. A. (1997). Microcephaly in Hurler syndrome. *Clinical Pediatrics, 36,* 51–52.

Thommessen, M., Kase, B. F., Riis, G., & Heiberg, A. (1991). The impact of feeding problems on growth and energy intake in children with cerebral palsy. *European Journal of Clinical Health, 45,* 479–487.

Turnbull, J. D. (1993). Early intervention for children with or at risk of cerebral palsy. *American Journal of Diseases of Children, 147*(1), 54–59.

Tutty, S., Gephart, H., & Wurzbacher, K. (2003). Enhancing behavioral and social skill functioning in children newly diagnosed with attention-deficit hyperactivity disorder in a pediatric setting. *Journal of Developmental and Behavioral Pediatrics, 24*(1), 51–57.

U.S. Federal Register, 57(189), September 29, 1992, p. 44802.

Vargha-Khadem, F., Isaacs, E., Ver der Werf, S., Robb, S., & Wilson, J. (1992). Development of intelligence and memory in children with hemiplegic cerebral palsy. *Brain, 115,* 315–329.

Veelken, N., Schopf, M., Dammann, O., & Schulte, F. J. (1993). Etiological classification of cerebral palsy in very low birthweight infants. *Neuropediatrics, 24,* 74–76.

Volpe, J. (1987). *Neurology of the Newborn.* Philadelphia: W.B. Saunders.

Wade, S. L., Taylor, H. G., Drotar, D., Stancin, T., & Yeates, O. (1998). Family burden and adaptation during the initial year after traumatic brain injury in children. *Pediatrics, 102,* 110–116.

Waaland, P. K. (1990). *Pediatric traumatic brain injury.* Rehabilitation Research and Training Center on Severe Traumatic Brain Injury, Virginia Commonwealth University, Richmond, VA.

Whitman, B. (1991). The roots of organicity: Genetics and genograms. In P. J. Accardo, T. A. Blondis, & B. Y. Whitman (Eds.), *Attention deficit disorders and hyperactivity in children* (pp. 37–56), New York: Marcel Dekker, Inc.

Wilens, T.E., Biederman, J., Brown, S., Tanguay, S., Monuteaux, M.C., Blake, C., & Spencer, T.J. (2002). Psychiatric comorbidity and functioning in clinically referred preschool children and school-age youths with ADHD. *Journal of the American Acadamy of Child & Adolescent Psychiatry, 41*(3), 262–268.

Williams, B. F., Williams, R. L., & McLaughlin, T. F. (1991). Treatment of behavior disorders by parents and in the home. *Journal of Developmental and Physical Disabilities, 3,* 385–407.

Wilson-Costello, D. Borawski, E., Friedman, H., Redline, R., Fanaroff, A. A., & Hack, M. (1998). Perinatal correlates of cerebral palsy and other neurologic impairment among very low birth weight children. *Pediatrics, 102,* 315–323.

Yim-Chiplis, P. K. (1998). The child with traumatic brain injury returns to school. *Pediatric Nursing, 24,* 245–248.

Zametkin, A. J., Nordahl, T. E. Gross, M., King, A. C., Temple, W. E., Rumsey, J., Hamburger, S., & Cohen, R. M. (1990). Cerebral glucose metabolism in adults with hyperactivity of childhood onset. *New England Journal of Medicine, 323,* 1361–1367.

7 Inborn Variations of Development

My child will never be considered a poster child. She does not give professionals the satisfaction of making great progress, nor is she terribly social. But I need the same type of investment by professionals as any other parents of children with disabilities. The most important thing any educator can do for me is to love my Mary.

(Carol Maloney, mother of daughter with Rett Syndrome)

When one considers all the ways in which human development, from embryology to birth, might vary, the fact that so many children are born without apparent disabilities is miraculous. This chapter is devoted to the description of variations in development that originate before a child's birth. These variations do not insinuate devaluation, inferiority, or undesirability of persons born with differences. Rather, the variations in development result in patterns of physical and/or behavioral characteristics that enable professionals to reliably group children according to similarities. Sometimes specific treatments are implicated when a child has membership in a certain group. For example, children with cystic fibrosis usually receive postural drainage treatments because respiratory congestion is always a symptom of the disease. *Usually, however, membership in itself tells us very little about the specific treatments to be used for a child because individual differences are so great.* Furthermore, most treatments are not universally effective for all children with the same characteristics. Anyone who has worked with children with autism can verify that determining what reinforcers, activities, and instructions work for one child will not necessarily provide guidance for another child with the same label. This chapter includes an introduction to basic genetics, which helps in understanding the causes of genetic deviations in development. The third section of this chapter is devoted to common disabilities that have no known etiology. It is probable that most of these disorders will eventually be linked to genetics. This chapter intentionally includes more information than will seem necessary for a foundations text, because this text is intended as a reference for later use by early childhood professionals. It is clear from working with parents that the more they can learn about their child's disability, the more capable they feel. Thus, it is the responsibility of professionals to become as knowledgable as possible and to be able to help parents seek further information and resources.

Still, it should be noted that the following descriptions are generalizations based on current understanding of groups of children with categorical disabilities. It would be a mistake to assume that one could make specific educational or programmatic recommendations for individual children based on the characteristics and types of treatments described in this chapter. This general information provides a broad beginning point. Beyond that, families and early childhood professionals must define programs based on the unique characteristics of children and their families.

GENETICS

Genetics is the study of heredity and variations in the characteristics of organisms, both plant and animal. In humans, genetic research provides information about development and diseases. To understand how individual variability occurs, understanding gene physiology and function in relation to human growth and development is necessary. Treatment and sometimes prevention of disabilities and diseases are made possible by recognizing the role that both genes and the environment play in human development.

Chromosomes are the basic genetic units and stay constant in number within a species and across generations. The first link between genes and chromosomes was made in 1911 by T. H. Morgan, using saliva from a fruit fly (Risley, 1986). An entire set of DNA within organisms is referred to as a species' genome. Each human DNA sequence has two parallel strands (one acquired from each of the parents). The human genome is comprised of over 3 billion of these DNA base pairs. **Genes** are regions of a chromosome made up of molecules that collectively define a particular trait. Genetic mapping is a process of connecting specific genes to individual chromosomes and chromosomal regions (Guyer & Collins, 1993). For example, the gene for muscular dystrophy is located on the "p21" region of the X chromosome. The gene is labeled Xp21. By contrast, Prader-Willi syndrome occurs when a region of the 15th chromosome is missing or deleted. The deleted region is called 15q11-13. Only about 2% of the human genome is made up of genes, with the remainder comprised of noncoded areas with an as yet undetermined function. Structural support and/or regulatory function of where, when, and how many proteins are produced are the hypothesized functions of the uncoded genome, some of it actually referred to as "junk" DNA.

Genes themselves do not perform moment-to-moment life functions; proteins actually perform at the cellular level to cause the dynamic changes in human cells in reaction to tens of thousands of environmental signals both from within and outside the cells. Large, complex sequences of amino acids make up protein molecules, the constellation of which is referred as a cell's proteome. Future research certainly will focus on the exploration of proteome structure and function as they relate to health and disease.

Recently, the study of genetics has been facilitated by new technologies. As a result, the genes responsible for many inherited traits such as Huntington's disease, fragile X syndrome, Duchenne muscular dystrophy, and cystic fibrosis have been isolated. Isolating and identifying genes, understanding their mutations, and learning about their protein products have increased knowledge about disabilities and diseases. This molecular approach is unlike past approaches to genetics, thus the term "new genetics" has been applied (Thompson, McInnes, & Willard, 1991).

The Human Genome Project is an example of new genetics. This is an international project whose goal was to map and sequence the entire genetic code of human chromosomes by the year 2003 (Human Genome, 2002). It was believed that mapping the human genome would lead to prediction, understanding, and, eventually, to the prevention or curing of many human disabilities and diseases (NIH, 1990).The purposes of this project are several-fold and range from such esoteric interests as pure scientific curiosity to the discovery of biological bases for environmental, health, climate, and energy solutions to human problems. Relevant to early childhood are intentional research to discover cures for genetic and genetic/environmental disabilities through drug therapy, gene replacement, inactivation of anomalous genes, or other yet-to-be-discovered methods. As close as the Human Genome Project is to completion, this product of tens of thousands of scientists is both fertile ground for generations of future research and application and, at the same time, is yielding important information on a daily basis. One interesting insight is that the human genome consists of less than one-third the quantity predicted, and contains only twice as many genes as a tiny transparent worm. This discovery led to the conclusion that our human complexity is more than the sum of our genetic base. In fact, 99.9% of nucleotide bases are identical in all people. A major outcome of the Human Genome Project is the understanding that protein production is the key to human functioning and that it is the study of protein expression that will lead to specific treatments of genetic mutations. This exciting area of research, proteomics, should lead to new drug design and gene repair.

While holding great promise, this knowledge nevertheless brings with it numerous ethical questions about how such information should be used. Public dialogue, education, and policies are needed to address the social, legal, and ethical implications of the Human Genome Project. To date, however, participation by society at large in directing this project has been limited.

Behavioral genetics represents another emerging area of genetics. This subdiscipline is so named because researchers seek the identification of genes associated with behaviors such as violence, mental illness, and alcoholism. A majority of studies, however, refute the notion that genes, by themselves, cause behavior. Many geneticists warn that research in behavioral genetics should be reviewed critically. It is agreed that scientific and popular media should emphasize that rarely do genes alone determine behavior; rather, genes interact with the environment to cause variations in behavior. "Genes act in environments, and as a result, changing the environment can often change the effect of the gene" (Billings, Beckwith, & Alper, 1992, p. 236).

CELLULAR ACTIVITY OF GENETICS

The human body contains more than a billion miles of **deoxyribonucleic acid (DNA),** with an average cell possessing more than a meter of this substance. DNA is a nucleic acid compound that carries the chemical coding needed to transmit genetic information from generation to generation. A chromosome is a chain of DNA. Human cells possess a total of 46 chromosomes, or 23 pairs of chromosomes (see Figure 7–1). That is, each member of a chromosome pair has matching genes at the same location and in the same sequence. Of the 23 chromosomal pairs, 22 are called autosomes. The 23rd pair is comprised of two **sex chromosomes**: X and Y. The X and the Y chromosome combination determines the gender of an individual—XX in females and XY in males.

Alleles are one of two alternative versions of a gene, with complimentary alleles residing on each of the two chromosomes in a pair. A **homozygote pair** will inherit identical alleles for a certain trait, such as two genes for cystic fibrosis. A **heterozygote pair** has two different alleles for a particular trait, such as one normal gene and one gene for cystic fibrosis. **Genotype** refers to the combination of alleles inherited for a particular trait within an individual; **phenotype** refers to the observable expression, or appearance, of the genotype in an individual. When speaking of whole chromosomes, the term **karyotype** is used to describe the number and configuration of the chromosomes. Some genetic testing is done to examine the whole chromosome for variations that may indicate problems. For example, when a child is suspected of having Down syndrome, an analysis of the child's karyotype will be conducted to determine if there is an extra chromosome or extra chromosomal material causing this genetic difference.

Figure 7–1
Drawing of the
Individual
Chromosomes

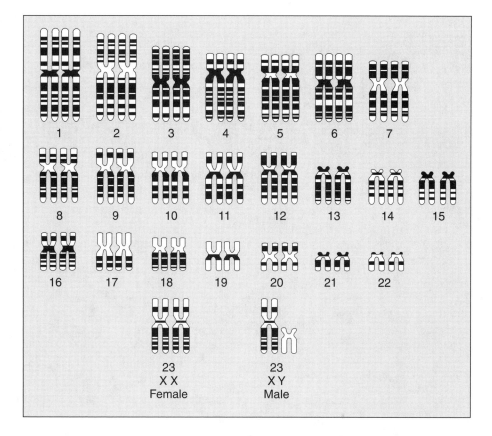

The purpose of cell division is to ensure growth, development, and repair of an organism. The two types of cell division are **mitosis** and **meiosis** (see Figure 7–2). Mitosis produces two identical daughter cells each containing the full set of 46 chromosomes. This occurs in all body cell reproduction. Chromosomes replicate and the cell divides once to create two identical cells, as in the regeneration of skin cells. Meiosis produces sex cells, called germ cells, or **gametes,** each with only one half the full complement of chromosomes (one from each chromosome pair). These cells are involved in reproduction. A sperm is a male gamete, and an ovum is a female gamete. When these cells join during conception, the resultant cell(s) will have a full set of chromosomes—one of each chromosome pair from each parent. Abnormalities in chromosome number or structure can arise during either of these processes of cell division. An example is Down syndrome, in which the 21st chromosome, usually in maternal meiosis, does not divide, resulting in three 21st chromosomes, or trisomy 21.

SINGLE GENE DISORDERS

Single gene inheritance is the type of inheritance described by Mendel's principles. Such variations are mutations of genes. This may involve one or both genes

Figure 7–2
Comparison of
Mitosis and
Meiosis Cells

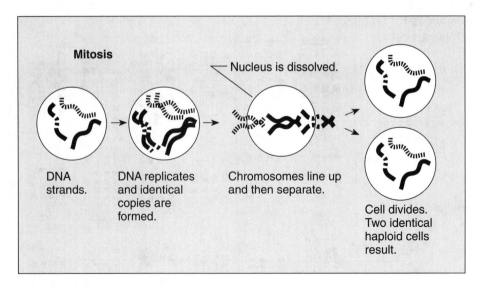

Mitosis

Nucleus is dissolved.

DNA strands.

DNA replicates and identical copies are formed.

Chromosomes line up and then separate.

Cell divides. Two identical haploid cells result.

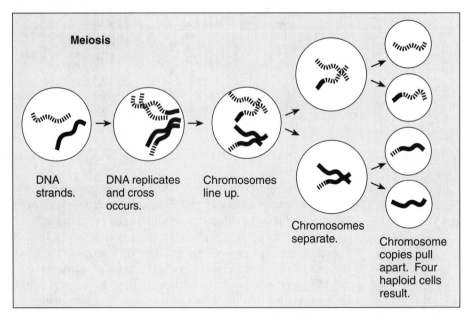

Meiosis

DNA strands.

DNA replicates and cross occurs.

Chromosomes line up.

Chromosomes separate.

Chromosome copies pull apart. Four haploid cells result.

of a chromosome pair. Examples of single gene disorders are cystic fibrosis, hemophilia, and sickle cell anemia. The occurrence of abnormalities varies. For example, for hemophilia, the occurrence rate is 1 in 10,000 live births. By contrast, sickle cell disease occurs once in every 400 live births among African Americans (Thompson et al., 1991).

There are about 4,000 observable single gene characteristics, 3,000 of which are considered genetic disorders. In several hundred of these diseases, the biochemical defect has been identified, and in many, as mentioned previously, the responsible gene has been isolated (Thompson et al., 1991). Single gene disorders are transmitted from one generation to another in three ways: recessive, dominant, and sex linked. A **recessive gene** is one whose genetic information is typically overruled by genetic information of a more dominant gene. Usually, it takes two recessive genes, one from each chromosome of a pair, in order for the trait to be expressed. On the other hand, only one **dominant gene** is typically needed for that gene's trait to be expressed. The terms recessive and dominant describe only the phenotypic expression, or observable trait; they do not describe what is happening at a molecular or biochemical level. For example, in the case of inheritance of a single recessive gene, the characteristic trait(s) of the disorder is usually not expressed. Nevertheless, at the biochemical level, both the dominant and recessive genes are being expressed. The phenotype may also be a combination of recessive and dominant genes acting together (Thompson et al., 1991). **Sex-linked disorders** are transmitted on either the X or Y chromosomes. However, most sex-linked disorders are inherited on the X chromosome. Hemophilia and color blindness are examples of sex-linked genetic differences.

Recessive Gene Inheritance

Tay Sachs, phenylketonuria (PKU), cystic fibrosis, and sickle cell anemia are a few of the many recessive single gene disorders (see Figure 7–3). As mentioned, usually a recessive gene is expressed only if it is inherited from both parents. For example, if the recessive gene for sickle cell anemia is inherited from both parents, the person will show signs of the disease. In this case, the offspring have a 25%

Figure 7–3
Pattern of
Inheritance of
Autosomal
Recessive Genes

Autosomal Recessive Inheritance Pattern

Disorders are caused by a pair of altered genes on the autosomes.

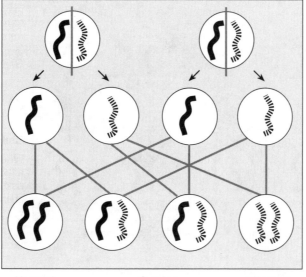

Parents

Both parents are carriers of the altered gene (though they are clinically normal).

Gametes

Children

When both parents are carriers, there is a 25% risk of having an affected child (male or female) with each pregnancy.

Normal (25%) **Carrier** (50%) **Affected** (25%)

chance of receiving two recessive genes and, consequently, of having the disorder. If just one affected gene is inherited, the person will not show signs of the disease except at the biochemical level. This is because the gene is paired with a dominant gene, and the dominant gene is the one phenotypically expressed. This person is a **carrier,** and although carriers have no signs or symptoms of the disease, they may transmit the gene to their offspring. There is a 50% chance of inheriting one gene and becoming a carrier and a 25% chance of not inheriting the gene from either parent.

Dominant Gene Inheritance

Huntington's disease, familial hypercholesteremia, and some forms of muscular dystrophy are examples of dominant single gene disorders (see Figure 7–4). Dominant genes are phenotypically expressed whenever they appear. Persons having just one of the genes will show signs of the disorder. Therefore, if one parent has the dominant gene and the other parent does not, the offspring have a 50% chance of receiving the dominant gene. Early identification of the possession of dominant gene disorders can help parents decide whether or not to prevent the inheritance. At this time, prevention of transmission can only occur when parents decide not to reproduce or, once conception has taken place, to abort a fetus with a genetic disease.

Figure 7–4
Pattern of
Inheritance for
Autosomal
Dominant
Genes

Autosomal Dominant Inheritance Pattern

Disorders are caused by a single altered gene on one of the autosomes.

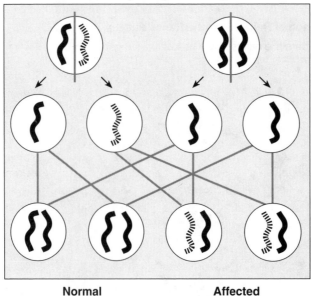

Parents

Either parent may have the gene, or the disorder may be due to a new gene alteration (mutation).

Gametes

Children

When one parent is affected, there is a 50% risk of having an affected child (male or female) with each pregnancy.

Normal
(50%)

Affected
(50%)

{ Normal Gene   Affected Gene

Recessive and dominant traits are not strictly determined by the presence or absence of a normal/abnormal gene. As with most things in nature, heredity is not so simple. If one normal and one mutant gene are present, then the result of their combined production of genetic material is what determines the dominant or recessive nature of the trait (Thompson et al., 1991). For example, if there is enough gene product between the two genes to provide for normal functioning, then the mutant gene and its related disorder are overruled and therefore recessive. For example, a hypothetical "syndrome Q" needs 56 units of normal gene product in order for the syndrome to be expressed. From the mother, who is a carrier of the mutant gene, the fertilized cell receives 10 units of normal gene product and 40 units of mutant Q gene product. From the father, who is not a carrier, the fertilized cell receives 50 units of normal gene product. Since there are 60 units of normal gene product, the offspring of this union will yield sufficient gene product for the gene trait to function normally. In this child, the gene for syndrome Q is recessive.

If there is not enough genetic product between the two chromosomes to function normally, then the gene and the disorder are said to be dominant. For example, in sickle cell anemia, a recessive gene produces abnormal hemoglobin. If that gene is inherited from each parent, then the blood will make abnormal hemoglobin. In this case, the person has sickle cell anemia. On the other hand, if one abnormal gene and one normal gene are inherited, the blood will contain some normal and some abnormal hemoglobin. Although both genes are functioning, the person will show no symptoms of the disorder, because there is enough normal hemoglobin produced to outweigh the effects of the abnormal gene. These individuals do not have sickle cell anemia, but they are carriers of the recessive gene and can therefore transmit the gene to their children.

Sex-Linked Inheritance

Sex-linked disorders have the affected gene on either the X or Y chromosome. Most sex-linked disorders are related to the X chromosome. Hemophilia and Duchenne muscular dystrophy are examples. The incidence of these types of disorders is highest in male offspring. Males inherit X-linked diseases from their mothers, the source of their X chromosome. In males, such diseases are usually more significant since there is no complementary X chromosome. Females with two X chromosomes are usually not affected, because the second X chromosome compensates for the recessive gene on the affected X chromosome. Only a few genetic disorders are X-linked dominant. In this case, an affected male parent passes the disorder on to all daughters but to none of the sons. This is because the son receives his X chromosome from the mother and the Y from the father. The daughter, on the other hand, receives one of her two X chromosomes from the father and, because it is dominant, will have the disorder. However, such diseases are usually of a less severe nature in females because they possess two X chromosomes. The normal X chromosome helps counteract the abnormal member of the pair (see Figure 7–5). Fragile X and Duchenne muscular dystrophy are similar in that females are usually carriers but may show mild symptoms of the disorders. In these cases, the unaffected/normal X chromosome may not completely compensate for the affected X chromosome, and some form of the disorder is manifest.

Figure 7–5
Sex-Linked
Chromosomal
Disorders

X-linked Recessive

Either parent may have the gene present on the **X** chromosome.

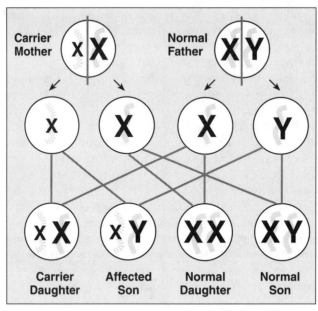

Parents

Since females have two **X** chromosomes, in order to be **affected** they must have an altered pair of genes. (Only one **X** chromosome is altered here.)

Gametes

Children

When a woman has an altered gene on only one **X** chromosome, she is a carrier (usually not affected) and with a normal father, they have a 25% risk of having an altered son.

Key: **X** Normal X chromosome.   **Y** Normal Y chromosome.

      X   Affected X chromosome.

CHROMOSOME DISORDERS

In **chromosome disorders,** whole chromosomes or chromosome segments are responsible for a problem rather than a single gene or combination of genes (see Figure 7–6). These variations can include an extra chromosome, extra chromosome material, structural abnormality, or absence/deletion of a chromosome. Turner syndrome, (discussed later in this chapter), is an example of a chromosome disorder in which there is a whole or partial absence of one of the two X chromosomes. Chromosome disorders of this nature are common, occurring in 7 out of every 1,000 births. It is estimated that 50% of all spontaneous abortions in the first trimester are due to these chromosomal abnormalities.

MULTIFACTORIAL DISORDERS

Multifactorial disorders account for two types of genetic problems: congenital disorders and the predisposition to a disease, usually with onset in adulthood. Congenital disorders account for malformations such as cleft palate, spina bifida, and various heart anomalies. Prenatal environmental factors may also be involved

Figure 7–6
Chromosomal
Disorders

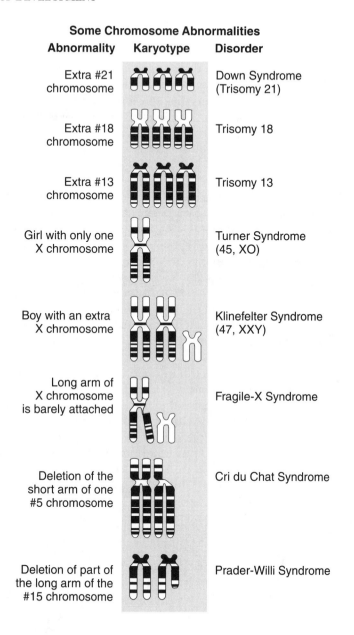

Some Chromosome Abnormalities

Abnormality	Karyotype	Disorder
Extra #21 chromosome		Down Syndrome (Trisomy 21)
Extra #18 chromosome		Trisomy 18
Extra #13 chromosome		Trisomy 13
Girl with only one X chromosome		Turner Syndrome (45, XO)
Boy with an extra X chromosome		Klinefelter Syndrome (47, XXY)
Long arm of X chromosome is barely attached		Fragile-X Syndrome
Deletion of the short arm of one #5 chromosome		Cri du Chat Syndrome
Deletion of part of the long arm of the #15 chromosome		Prader-Willi Syndrome

in these disorders. Many diseases do not appear until adulthood. These are exacerbated by a probable genetic predisposition to acquire the disease. A few examples currently believed to be affected by genetic predisposition include heart disease, obesity, arthritis, some forms of cancer, and metabolic problems, such as diabetes mellitus. It is also believed that lifestyle moderation, such as diet and exercise, can affect the course of some of these diseases.

Genetic Testing

One American in 100 is born with a serious genetic disorder, which may be chromosomal, sex-linked, or multifactorial (March of Dimes [MOD], 1992). Genetic testing and counseling are conducted for people who have questions and concerns about problems that may affect their offspring. There are several reasons to consider genetic testing: family history of genetic disorders, a child with a genetic disorder, two or more miscarriages or a baby that died in infancy, ethnic origin (e.g., sickle cell anemia is more prevalent among African Americans), first cousins planning to have a child together, and pregnancy of a woman over age 35.

Analysis of blood samples can detect genetic disorders. Hemophilia, Tay Sachs disease, cystic fibrosis, sickle cell anemia, and Duchenne muscular dystrophy are detected in this way. Blood samples also show if a person is the carrier of a recessive gene that could be passed on to offspring. Amniocentesis, chorionic villus sampling, and, more recently, fetal blood sampling from the umbilical cord are prenatal tests that can be used for early detection of abnormalities (Sach & Korf, 1993). **Amniocentesis** is a painful and risky procedure that removes fluid from the sac surrounding the fetus. A long, thin needle is inserted through the abdomen to withdraw approximately four teaspoons of amniotic fluid. Of every 400 amniocentesis tests performed by a qualified physician, one spontaneous abortion is likely to occur. Amniocentesis can reveal chromosomal, metabolic, and biochemical disorders. For example, DNA tests can be conducted to detect such problems as cystic fibrosis or sickle cell anemia. Down syndrome is the most common chromosomal problem detected with this procedure. **Chorionic villus sampling** (CVS) is conducted vaginally or abdominally and requires a small tissue sample from the chorion or outer sac that surrounds the fetus. Chorionic villus sampling can be conducted earlier in fetal development than amniocentesis, but the risk to a fetus is higher. **Fetal blood sampling** (also called percutaneous umbilical blood sampling) can be conducted even earlier than CVS and detects the same problems. A needle is guided into the abdomen and through the uterus to the umbilical cord, from which a blood sample is withdrawn.

Other prenatal tests include ultrasound and **alpha-fetoprotein** screening (AFP). **Ultrasound** is used to visualize the fetus and its developing organs. Congenital malformations, such as spina bifida, can be detected using this procedure. AFP screening is a blood test conducted to detect neural tube disorders, such as malformations of the spinal cord, the spinal column, and the brain. This test, however, produces many false positives, since the level of AFP fluctuates during pregnancy. For this reason, AFP testing is usually used as a screening tool leading to further diagnostic tests, such as those mentioned above.

A new and controversial technology has recently been developed, through which the embryos bound for *in vitro* implantation can be analyzed for genetic defects prior to implantation (Dolan, 2002). Referred to as Preimplantation Genetic Diagnosis (PGD), this groundbreaking technique will certainly test ethical benchmarks in the future.

GENE THERAPY

Though gene therapy is presently experimental, discoveries of the next century may provide treatments for various genetic disorders. One type of gene therapy introduces a normal gene into a cell nucleus to replace an abnormal gene. The cell can then function normally. For example, in diabetes mellitus, in which the body is unable to produce insulin, a gene that provides the genetic information needed to initiate insulin production might be introduced. However, the inserted genes are not passed on to the next generation because normal genetic material is not placed in the germ cells. For now, because such therapy is so exploratory, education and caution are necessary to facilitate judgment regarding the relative benefits and risks of therapy compared to the prognosis for the disease (Haan, 1990).

Germ line therapy introduces genes into the germ or sex cells, as well as into the somatic cells. The consequences of this therapy may be profound. Future generations would be influenced if such therapy is successful, and stability of the entire gene pool could be compromised by eliminating certain genes while potentially creating other new abnormalities. For this reason, and because it is believed there is a risk of serious ethical abuse, most geneticists agree this type of therapy should not be undertaken (Hann, 1990; Sach & Korf, 1993), even if it could be successful in reversing the effects of a serious genetic defect in some children.

GENETIC VARIATIONS IN DEVELOPMENT

CYSTIC FIBROSIS

Cystic fibrosis (CF) is the most common fatal genetic disease in the United States. Approximately 1 in 23 persons in the United States is a carrier of the CF gene (Cystic Fibrosis Foundation, 1999a). Cystic fibrosis affects the exocrine glands, which secrete body fluids. In children with cystic fibrosis, the **exocrine glands** overproduce a thick, sticky mucus that eventually clogs the lungs and blocks functioning of the pancreas. The sweat glands are also affected and produce perspiration containing two to five times the normal amount of sodium (Anfenson, 1980).

Characteristics

Individuals with cystic fibrosis produce an excessive amount of thick, sticky mucus (Cystic Fibrosis Foundation, 1999b). In the lungs and respiratory tract, this mucus blocks airways and interferes with breathing, eventually resulting in respiratory failure. This mucus further inhibits the pancreas from releasing enzymes to the digestive tract necessary for breaking down foods (Cystic Fibrosis Foundation, 1999b). Consequently, children with cystic fibrosis are unable to sufficiently metabolize fats and proteins. The sweat glands' tendency to excrete abnormally high amounts of sodium provides the basis for the "sweat test," the primary diagnostic measurement for cystic fibrosis. Because of an excessive release of salt, exposure to fevers and extreme heat are two conditions that can be especially harmful. Heat can cause serious depletion of sodium and may result in confusion, seizures, and other electrolyte imbalance problems.

As a consequence of these physiological disturbances, children with cystic fibrosis have chronic symptoms of persistent coughing, recurrent wheezing, repeated respiratory infection, excessive appetite, poor weight gain or even weight loss (Cystic Fibrosis Foundation, 1999c). The progression of cystic fibrosis symptoms varies across individuals with the disease. Some children may be affected primarily in the respiratory system; in others, the pancreas and digestive systems might be more significantly affected. No diagnostic tests have yet been devised to predict the course that will be taken in specific patients with cystic fibrosis. In the past, it was very unusual for those affected by cystic fibrosis to live long enough to go to school; most died in infancy (Cystic Fibrosis Foundation, 1999c). However, with recent treatment advances, there has been a substantial improvement in life expectancy, doubling in the last two decades of the 20th century (Gaylor & Reilly, 2002).

Dibble and Savedra (1988) described numerous secondary physical complications that have emerged concomitant with improved survival of patients with cystic fibrosis. For example, there is an increased incidence of respiratory dysfunctions: lung infections, bloody mucus, and pneumothorax (rupture in the lung, releasing air into the chest cavity). As the life expectancy of patients with cystic fibrosis increases, so does the probability of their developing diabetes; as many as 40% to 60% of persons with cystic fibrosis may acquire hyperglycemia.

Etiology

Cystic fibrosis is an autosomal recessive gene, transmitted genetically to offspring when both parents are carriers. Carriers inherit a single cystic fibrosis gene located on one of the two number 7 chromosomes. For these individuals, the second chromosome 7 remains unaffected and blocks the expression of the harmful gene. A child afflicted with cystic fibrosis has two cystic fibrosis genes, one present on each chromosome 7. The defective gene disrupts chloride-sodium regulation, leading to multisystem failure including lungs, digestive and endocrine systems and kidneys (Gaylor & Reilly, 2002).

Treatment

Diagnosis of cystic fibrosis is usually made by the second or third birthday, though for some children, symptoms may go undiagnosed for months or years. Treatment of cystic fibrosis involves a multidisciplinary approach to address the numerous issues likely to arise for both child and family. Professionals likely to be included on the team are a medical director, nurse, physical therapist, clinical pharmacist, respiratory therapist, nutritionist, social service worker, geneticist, and possibly others, all of whom will work together with a patient with cystic fibrosis on long- and short-term treatment goals. Typical family routines in daily treatment of children with cystic fibrosis include:

1. Adequate nutrition with a high carbohydrate and protein diet, adequate salt intake, pancreatic enzyme preparations, supplemental doses of fat soluble vita-

mins, and adequate fluid intake. Chronic malnutrition is prevalent in children with cystic fibrosis. Most can compensate for the nutritonal deficiency through the consumption of energy-dense foods and pancreatic enzyme supplements. Others require a surgically implanted gastrostomy which permits night-time or day-time food infusions. The latter can aid in normal growth and overall health status (Rosenfeld, Casey, Pepe, & Ramsey, 1999).

2. Prevention of infection through frequent bronchial drainage treatments, aerosol inhalation therapy, use of antibiotics, and a mist tent while sleeping or resting are key aspects of treatment. Ninety percent of children/adults with cystic fibrosis die of lung disease or gradual decline of lung function caused by repeated bacterial infection (McCarthy, 1999). Young children may need to be taught to cough expectorant into a tissue, but should not be encouraged to suppress coughing either physically or by using cough suppressants (Cystic Fibrosis Foundation, 1999c). Some children may take as many as 25 pills per day, requiring adult supervision during the preschool years. In recent years, due to the spread of pan-resistant bacteria, respiratory tract infections have become increasingly difficult to treat with antibiotics. Therefore, double-lung transplantation has emerged as an increasingly possible and effective choice for persons with cystic fibrosis (White-Williams, 2002).

3. Promoting healthy development by encouraging normal social relationships, reinforcing self-image, continued contact with supporting agencies, continuous support when children are hospitalized, and emphasis on a child's identity as a "typical child" whenever appropriate. Even though children with CF may have limited stamina, they should be encouraged to engage in regular exercise, which helps loosen mucus.

Although treatment practices are limited and a cure still undiscovered, many advances in treating cystic fibrosis were made in the 1980s and 1990s. Advances that have improved life quality and expectancy include drug developments such as *Pulmozyme*, approved in 1993, as a mucous thinner, and new antibiotics, such as INS365, which stimulates cells to secrete chloride, which in turn makes mucous less thick and sticky (Cystic Fibrosis Foundation, 1999b). Still, widespread, pan-resistant bacteria make drug therapy increasingly difficult (White-Williams, 2002).

Since the 1989 identification of the abnormal protein causing cystic fibrosis, many new treatment methods have been researched. Experimental methods, such as genetically bypassing the problems caused by the abnormal protein or therapeutically altering the defective protein in the bloodstream, are being investigated ("Scientists Forecast," 1989). One other experimental approach is gene therapy, considered "the ultimate 'correction' strategy." This potential cure for CF has yet to be perfected, but important steps were taken throughout the 1990s. To accomplish the cure, scientists manufacture normal genes in a laboratory and deliver the genes through a variety of methods such as nose drops or a tube entering the lungs. The normal genes would correct the damage done by the defective CF cells. However, much work remains to be done before gene therapy cures CF (Cystic Fibrosis Foundation, 1999a). Individuals with cystic fibrosis are primary candidates for lung transplants, usually performed after age 18. Although lung transplants have improved mortality rates, White-Williams (2002) reported only a

1-year survival in 30% of recipients. Moreover, progress in lung transplants has been hampered by lung availability, which declined significantly in the late 1990s (White-Williams, 2002).

In the preschool years, children with CF may or may not display symptoms that affect their daily lives. Some children may have frequent and serious lung infections that could interfere with typical social and cognitive opportunities. Monitoring developmental progress and providing enriching educational programs should be a priority for educators of young children with CF. Other than constraints that might be placed on children by their medical condition, intervention should be developmentally and socially relevant.

Though cost varies from one family to another, depending on the severity and stage of the disease, family economics are almost always strained by this disease (Stullenbarger, Norris, Edgil, & Prosser, 1987). The cost of hospitalization is so high that families without medical insurance usually suffer financial crisis (Cystic Fibrosis Foundation, 1999c). The social effects of cystic fibrosis on the entire family can also be difficult. Parents, siblings, and the children themselves are emotionally affected. Though families of children with disabilities are as resilient to life's challenges as other families, and though new technology offers unprecedented hope for a cure to cystic fibrosis, adjusting to the possible loss of a child or sibling with cystic fibrosis can begin as early as preschool. Finally, genetic counseling has also proven to be an effective means to alleviating fears and guilt in parents of children with cystic fibrosis (MOD, 1987).

CLOSE-UP

GENETIC SCREENING

While some genetically caused disabilities are largely impervious to the demographic characteristics of their victims, others are quite selective. For example, many genetic disabilities are gender specific, choosing either male or female victims almost exclusively (e.g., muscular dystrophy and fragile X syndrome). Some genetic diseases are more prevalent in specific racial groups. Cystic fibrosis is more common in persons of European descent. Two other diseases that are ethnically specific are Tay Sachs Disease and sickle cell anemia, commonly found in persons of Jewish and African descent respectively.

O'Sullivan (1998), in studying the history of these diseases, found evidence that preference had been given to the research and resultant screening and treatment of some of these culturally based diseases over others. She concluded that genetic study should be governed more carefully by ethical considerations than it has in the past. This is especially true given the genetic breakthroughs in the last decade (e.g., gene cloning, gene therapy, and the Human Genome Project) that have the potential for extreme ethical abuse and catastrophic consequences.

As evidence of a lack of ethical guidance, O'Sullivan compared Tay Sachs disease to sickle cell disease. Tay Sachs causes progressive degeneration of the nervous system, leading to blindness, deafness, hydrocephaly, and eventual death in the preschool years. Sickle cell disease affects the circulatory system of its victims, where misshapen red blood cells cause infection, ulcers, blood clotting, painful "sickle cell crises," and eventual death in adolescence or early adulthood.

While both diseases are autosomal, recessive, single-gene disorders, the prevalence within their high-risk groups is very different. In Ashkenazi Jews, the rate of sickle cell disease live births is about 1 in 4,100, while sickle cell disease is found in about 1 in 500 African American infants. Although the natural incidence indicates that sickle cell disease occurs at a much higher rate, screening methods applied to the diseases have resulted in almost complete eradication of Tay Sachs disease since the 1970s, when screening methods were begun, while there has been a very small drop in the incidence of sickle cell disease. The latter is due to a natural decline rather than because of screening efforts.

In the case of Tay Sachs, the voluntary screening program was conducted in a very sensitive manner and often within the context of cultural practices, that is, using community matchmakers to ensure that carriers did not marry. By contrast, a national compulsory screening program for sickle cell disease begun in the 1970s was abandoned by 1980 because of poor implementation. While couples who were carriers received inadequate education and genetic counseling, the test results were frequently used to turn down insurance, employment, and Air Force applicants. Possibly due to such mismanagement, this screening tool was also perceived as a racist attempt to limit the African American population in the United States.

While she does not accuse anyone of racism or unethical practice, O'Sullivan implies that the differential approaches and subsequent effectiveness were related to some degree of cultural bias. O'Sullivan suggests that by presenting undergraduate students with this ethical paradigm and others, they will become more active and ethical professionals once they become a part of the researchers, practitioners, and socially active citizens who will decide what we do with the genetic breakthroughs of the coming decades.

Source: From "Use and Design of Genetic Screening Programmes: A Study," by H. O'Sullivan, 1998, *Journal of Biological Education, 32*, pp. 97–103.

Down
Syndrome

DOWN SYNDROME

Down syndrome was one of the first causes of mental retardation to be categorized as a syndrome. Identified in 1866 by Langdon Down, the syndrome has variously been termed cretinism, unfinished or ill-finished child, and mongolism. Down referred to the syndrome as a retrogression to the Mongoloid race, since children and adults resembled persons of this ethnic group in several phenotypic ways. This name remained common in educational and medical communities until the 1960s, when it was replaced with the more dignified label Down syndrome. The prevalence of Down syndrome ranges from 1 in 600 to 1 in 1,000 live births. This incidence makes Down syndrome the second largest genetic cause of mental retardation after fragile X syndrome.

Characteristics

Though more than 50 traits have been associated with Down syndrome, individuals with this disability may have a few or many of the known characteristics (Fishler & Koch, 1991). Mental retardation ranging from mild to severe is present in almost all individuals with Down syndrome. However, with changing educational practices over the last century, children's educational opportunities combined with innovative teaching methods have greatly improved the cognitive expectations and achievements of children with Down syndrome. Phenotypic characteristics include short stature and clubbed short fingers, epicanthal folds (skin at inner corner of eye forms a fold, making eye appear to be slanted), sloping forehead, flat **occipital lobe,** ruddy cheeks, speckled iris, malformed ears, flat nose bridge, upward tilt to nostrils, simian line in palm (a single deep wrinkle running across the width of the palm), third toe longer than second, and a gap between big toe and next one. A high palate and small oral cavity often lead to tongue protrusion.

Medical conditions also commonly accompany this disability. Neonates often have life-threatening conditions, such as duodenal atresia, where the small bowel is partially or fully blocked, and patent ductus arteriosis, in which the duct con-

A child with Down syndrome.

necting a fetus's blood system to the maternal blood supply does not close automatically after birth. Because of these and other medical conditions, the life expectancy of children with Down syndrome was only 9–12 years in the early part of this century. Chronic heart problems and depressed immune response, resulting in frequent upper respiratory infections, often led to premature death. In a more recent analysis, Eyman, Call, and White (1991) concluded that while medical problems do affect the overall life expectancy of persons with Down syndrome, restricted mobility and poor eating patterns of infants are more significant risk factors. Most individuals who do not have significant associated disabilities have an overall life expectancy of greater than 50 years.

One of the most dominant physiological characteristics is hypotonia, or low muscle tone. Consequently, infants with Down syndrome typically have delayed motor and speech development. Children also have a high incidence of hearing impairments with a tendency toward high-frequency hearing losses (Marcell & Cohen, 1992). Because the hearing losses tend to be conductive, the susceptibility of these children to middle ear disease may be a related factor. Visual impairments are also more common in children with Down syndrome than in typically developing children.

As the life expectancy of individuals with Down syndrome improves, researchers have identified specific areas of premature aging. These differences range from the innocuous, such as accelerated aging and turnover of red blood cells (Wachtel & Pueschel, 1991), to the dangerous, as with premature deterioration of the thyroid function, leading to hypothyroidism in a large percentage of adults with Down syndrome (Pueschel, Jackson, Giesswein, Dean, & Pezzullo, 1991) and a 15–20 fold increased risk of developing leukemia (Solomon, 2002). Of greatest concern is the tendency toward premature dementia in middle age, leading to behavioral deterioration (Evenhuis, 1990).

Etiology

The discovery of chromosomes quickly led to the identification of genetic anomalies causing Down syndrome. Instead of the normal complement of 23 pairs of chromosomes in each cell (46 total), most individuals with Down syndrome have an extra 21st chromosome and 47 total chromosomes. The three 21st chromosomes, referred to as **trisomy 21,** are always associated with at least a few of the physical or behavioral characteristics described earlier. In addition, two other chromosomal defects can cause Down syndrome:

1. A **translocation** trisomy is the existence of extra chromosomal material that has become attached to another chromosome. The size of the misguided genetic material may vary from a piece of one arm to an entire chromosome.
2. In **mosaicism,** a portion of cells have 46 chromosomes and another percentage (usually 10% to 12%) of the cells have the extra 21st chromosome (47).

The genetic history of each of these types of Down syndrome also varies. In typical trisomies, the extra 21st chromosome is associated with **nondisjunction during meiosis** (Figure 7–7). In other words, when cell division takes place to

Figure 7–7
Diagram of Cell
Division
Leading to
Down
Syndrome

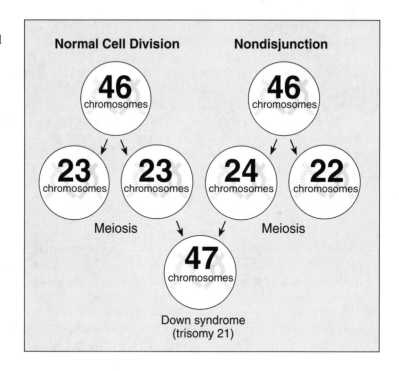

create either an ovum or sperm, there is an incomplete detachment of the 21st pair, with one cell receiving 22 chromosomes and the other 24. In Down syndrome, the cell with 24 chromosomes (including the extra 21st) combines with a normal complement of 23 chromosomes.

Translocation trisomies are typically genetically transmitted from a carrier parent to an affected child and occur in approximately 5% to 10% of cases of Down syndrome. Research indicates that the different causes of just Down syndrome described are associated with differences in developmental and physical characteristics (Fishler & Koch, 1991; Johnson & Abelson, 1969). Specifically, Fishler and Koch (1991) observed that, on the average, children with mosaicism and translocations had fewer physical traits associated with Down syndrome and greater intellectual potential. This finding conflicts, however, with Johnson and Abelson (1969), who found that individuals with mosaicism had the lowest average intellectual functioning of the three types of Down syndrome.

Why some gametes have aberrant cell division, resulting in extra chromosomes, is still unknown. However, for some time, researchers have recognized the contribution of maternal age to the incidence of Down syndrome. Generally speaking, as women grow older, the chances of conceiving a child with Down syndrome grow progressively more likely (Chan, McCaul, Keane, & Haan, 1998). Women older than 35 years of age are considered high risk and may generally be advised to undergo prenatal testing, such as amniocentesis, when pregnant. A second factor associated with the incidence of Down syndrome is maternal exposure to low level radiation over a long period of time. Smoking and use of oral contraceptives have also been linked to Down syndrome incidence (Solomon, 2002). None of these correlations, however, provide an explanation for nondisjunction, but knowing their relationship to Down syndrome is useful in genetic counseling for women considering pregnancy.

Very recently, the entire 21st chromsome was mapped. In fact, it was the second chromosome to be mapped because it is the smallest and contains the fewest number of genes. This small size explains why trisomy 21 is one of the only viable human trisomies, affecting the fewest genes. It is hoped that this genetic map will help explain which genes are responsible for the Down syndrome (Solomon, 2002).

OTHER TRISOMY DISORDERS

While Down syndrome is the most common live birth trisomy, other trisomy conceptions are common, and some occur even more frequently than trisomy 21. However, most of these chromosomal anomalies are spontaneously aborted because their characteristics are incompatible with life. Other fetuses may survive the pregnancy but may be stillborn or will likely die within a few days or weeks of birth. Trisomies 13, 16, and 18 are the most common of these chromosomal anomalies.

Treatment

Early intervention for children and their families should focus on several dimensions. For parents, education regarding the etiology and long-term outcomes is needed. Parents may want to read literature or be put on mailing lists for magazines or newsletters, join support groups, or join the National Down Syndrome Society, a powerful advocacy group.

Intervention goals for children will likely be comprehensive, with early emphasis on motor and language development. Physical and occupational therapists and communication specialists should be involved. Speech development is often impeded by both cognitive delays and oral structural problems. However, Steffens, Oiler, Lynch, and Urbano (1992) found that the patterns of vocal development in children with Down syndrome paralleled those of normally developing children, even though the average rates of development in the former were slightly slower. **Augmentative communication** (sign language, communication boards, and other devices) can reduce frustration and enhance language development. Feeding may also be an issue, since children tend to be underweight in infancy. Later, as toddlers and preschoolers, hypotonicity and slow metabolic rates sometimes contribute to an excessive weight gain (Chad, Jobling, & Frail, 1990). Regular exercise should be scheduled both to reduce body fat and to correspondingly increase energy levels.

There is increasing evidence that, with certain instruction (i.e., early intervention, use of behavior analytic methods, and integration), many preschool and elementary students are able to stay at or above grade/age expectancies in some academic areas, notably in reading (Rynders & Horrobin, 1990). As children with Down syndrome grow older, their relative intellectual abilities diminish compared to the rate of progress made by typical children (Rynders & Horrobin, 1990). Even so, children with Down syndrome now being served in public schools are accomplishing feats once believed impossible. The potential of such children (indeed all children) is undoubtedly limited by our own boundaries in educational technology.

Fragile X
Syndrome

FRAGILE X SYNDROME

Until recently, the prevalence of mental retardation in males had been explained by social and behavioral gender differences (De La Cruz, 1985). The identification of fragile X syndrome challenged that assumption. This syndrome was first identified in 1969 when Lubs discovered the genetic abnormality in the X chromosomes of a mother and her son. Now, fragile X syndrome is considered the leading genetic cause of mental retardation (Crawford, 2001). Fragile X is believed to account for 40% of the X-related forms of mental retardation and 10% of all cases of mental retardation (Rogers & Simensen, 1987). Additionally, fragile X may be even more prevalent than these statistics indicate, since many carriers who have the anomalous chromosome but do not have mental retardation go undiagnosed (Santos, 1992; Sudhalter, Cohen, Silverman, & Wolf-Schein, 1990). Yet, many early childhood professionals do not have a good understanding of this disability. Wilson and Mazzocco (1993) found that only 36% of professional educators responding to a survey had knowledge of fragile X, while 64% were knowledgable about Down syndrome, which appears to be less prevalent.

Characteristics

Prior to its identification, and even now, children with fragile X syndrome were misdiagnosed with ADHD, autism, nonspecific mental retardation, pervasive developmental disorder, learning disability, and emotional impairment (Schmidt, 1997). These "misreads" suggest the variability and severity of characteristics for this syndrome. The fragile X mutation ranges from partial to full, with the full mutation obviously corresponding to more apparent and severe syndrome-related characteristics. Females who are affected by fragile X generally express either mild to moderate forms of mental retardation. Only half of those females with a full mutation are recognized as having a disability, though most have some form of learning disability (Turner, Robinson, Wake, Laing, & Partington, 1997). Males, on the other hand, tend to range from borderline to profoundly mentally retarded (De La Cruz, 1985; Sudhalter et al., 1990; Wolff, Gardner, Paccia, & Lappen, 1989). Of males with the fragile X chromosome, 80% express mental impairment, whereas only 30% of females with the fragile X chromosome are mentally retarded (Keenan, et al., 1992). Furthermore, longitudinal documentation indicates a steady deterioration in mental functioning as these children age (Keenan et al., 1992; Santos, 1992; Simensen & Rogers, 1989). Unvalidated theories regarding this alleged decline include progressive neurological deterioration (Santos, 1992), increased emphasis on cognitive/reasoning skills as children age (Santos, 1992), and failure of the rate of intellectual growth to keep pace with expectations of standardized IQ tests (McClennen, 1992). Fragile X has a specific pattern of learning characteristics. Strengths include relatively strong language and visual skills, while weaknesses include difficulty with grammar and math (De La Cruz, 1985; Keenan et al., 1992). Males in particular have difficulty in processing novel sequential information, short-term memory, and problem solving that requires complex generalization (Reiss & Freund, 1990).

Even though the most predominant characteristic of fragile X syndrome is mental retardation, all body systems are affected, including the hormonal, neurological, and cardiac functions. Most children with fragile X have a normal appearance at birth (Keenan et al., 1992). Prominent physical features are most apparent in postpubertal males. Characteristic features in adults include a long face, large ears, prominent forehead, underdevelopment of the midface region, prominent jaw, and enlarged testicles (De La Cruz, 1985; Meryash, 1985; Santos, 1992; Simensen & Rogers, 1989). Meryash (1985) also noted that a majority of individuals with fragile X tend to be short in stature. The variability in facial features of females with fragile X makes it difficult to use physical features as an index in diagnosis (Rogers & Simensen, 1987).

As with intelligence, researchers have recorded a progressive degeneration of adaptive behavior in males with fragile X syndrome (Dykens, Hodapp, Ort, & Leckman, 1993). After making steady gains in adaptive behavior until early adolescence, skills then begin to decline. Several behavioral phenomena are associated with the syndrome, though considerable variability exists among individuals with fragile X. Many express distinctly autistic-like characteristics, such as unusual hand mannerisms (hand flapping and hand biting), stereotypic behaviors (rocking), and speech and language disorders (perseveration, echolalia, dysrhythmia, and inappropriate speech) (Keenan et al., 1992; Meryash, 1985; Sudhalter et al., 1990). Other traits include hyperactivity, attentional deficits, bizarre responses to surrounding environments, hypersensitivity to environmental stimuli, emotional problems, motor delays, poor eye contact, and social avoidance (Hagerman, 1992; Keenan et al., 1992; Meryash, 1985; Santos, 1992; Simensen & Rogers, 1989; Wolff et al., 1989).

Females may also have social difficulties, including problems with peer relationships, shyness, depression and mood disorder, loneliness, and a tendency to withdraw and act uncomfortable around others (Mazzocco, Baumgardner, Freund & Reiss, 1998). While social skills tend to be most affected by the fragile X chromosome, other adaptive behaviors appear to be especially well developed relative to mental impairment (Dykens et al., 1993). Whether institutionalized or not, males have strong daily living skills in areas such as toileting, personal grooming, and domestic responsibilities.

Etiology

Fragile X syndrome derives its name from the form of its mutation on the X chromosome. The "fragile" site on the X chromosome is located on the long arm at the Xq27 gene (FMR1) (Keenan et al., 1992; Meryash, 1985; Rogers & Simensen, 1987; Simensen & Rogers, 1989). This long arm may be separated or connected by only a thin strand (Meryash, 1985). This defective gene cannot produce the fragile X protein (FMRP) which is necessary for brain cells to cleanly communicate with each other. Though most prevalent in males, fragile X, more so than any of the other X-related chromosomes, also affects females (Meryash, 1985; Simensen & Rogers, 1989). Sudhalter et al. (1990) noted that 1 in 1,350 males and 1 in 2,033 females have the hereditary abnormality. However, since females possess two X chromosomes, the one intact X chromosome tends to overrule the effects of the fragile X chromosome. Santos (1992) explained the incidence of fragile X characteristics in females as a selective inactivation of the normal X chromosome, which then allows expression by the other X chromosome at the fragile site. By contrast, males have only one X chromosome and are therefore always vulnerable to the defective genetic anomaly.

Fragile X is of a familial nature, transmitted from generation to generation in a unique fashion (Santos, 1992; Wolff et al., 1989). The defective chromosome is most commonly transmitted by the mother who may be affected or unaffected; however, it has been noted that unaffected males may transmit the fragile X chromosome to their daughters (Santos, 1992). Furthermore, genetic studies of families with the fragile X chromosome revealed that as the affected chromosome is transmitted from generation to generation, the incidence of fragile X syndrome increases in frequency and severity (Turner et al., 1997).

The site of the X chromosome responsible for its fragility is normally comprised of a region of repeated proteins of 20–40 repeats in length. Across generations, this region can slowly increase in length, gradually becoming less stable. When duplicates lengthen past 50 or so, each subsequent generation can suddenly expand rapidly to 200. Two hundred repeats appears to be the threshhold for manifestation of symptoms of fragile X and represents a full mutation. Fragile X catergorization is separated by the number of protein repeats in the following way (Crawford, 2001):

- ◆ Common: 6–40 repeats
- ◆ Intermediate: 41–60 repeats
- ◆ Permutation: 61–200 repeats
- ◆ Full: >200–230 repeats

The full mutation is considered the disease-causing population where the symptoms of fragile X are manifest, while the permutation mutation range represents the carrier population. The permutation incidence ranges between 1 in 246–468 for females to 1 in 1,000–2,000 for males.

The fragile X chromosome travels through families in an unusual manner. A typical family pedigree is one in which all children of female carriers of the syndrome have a 50% chance of inheriting the gene from their mothers. Males who are carriers will pass the gene to their daughters, but obviously may not pass the gene to their sons. When a male carrier passes the abnormal gene to his daughter, the likelihood of mental retardation is low. On the other hand, mental retardation is common (55%) in the daughters of females who inherited the abnormal fragile X gene from their carrier fathers (Meryash, 1985; Santos, 1992). Therefore, mental retardation is more likely to occur when the female transmits the mutated X chromosome.

Treatment

Fragile X syndrome is rarely detected at birth and may not be identified until school age in affected children with mild disabilities. Among the various professionals that should be involved in treatment are health professionals, child study teams, therapists, and educators (Keenan et al., 1992). Medical treatment of the syndrome itself is limited, though stimulant medication, such as Ritalin, has been somewhat effective in controlling behaviors associated with hyperactivity and attentional deficits (Santos, 1992). The primary treatment for fragile X syndrome is educational, with early childhood special education providing the greatest promise for long-term adaptive and intellectual benefits. Because there is considerable variability within the population of individuals with fragile X syndrome, components of educational programs should be designed to fit children's behavioral needs and not the disability itself. It is likely that components would include functional skills training, physical therapy, and speech therapy (McClennan, 1992; Meryash, 1985).

Genetic research into a biological cure has three main foci (FRAXA Research Foundation, 2002). One is gene therapy, where normal genes are injected into brain cells, a technique that has been successful on mice and has great promise for humans. A second is gene repair, which may be possible with fragile X, since the entire normal DNA sequence is present, but ill-attached. Though the cell's normal machinery has been "turned off" in fragile X, there may be ways to restore function without introducing new genetic material. A third focus is psychopharmacology research to discover effective and safe medication to treat the symptoms of fragile X (in their infancy), may also prove to be a viable remedy for the defective gene.

Genetic counseling of families with the mutant X chromosome is very important. Because of the unique pattern of transmission and the tendency of the syndrome to be underdiagnosed and silently carried by females, it is important to educate both nuclear and extended families when the sydrome is positively diagnosed. In instances where extensive genetic counseling, follow-up family education, and prenatal screening were implemented, there has been a dramatic reduction in the incidence of fragile X syndrome (Turner et al., 1997).

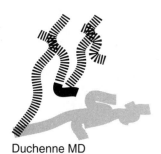

Duchenne MD

MUSCULAR DYSTROPHY

Several hereditary muscle-wasting diseases fall under the category of muscular dystrophy. The factors that unify these disorders is the progressive loss of muscle tissue which is concurrent with increases in fat and connective tissue and subsequent muscle weakness (Emery, 1998). The most common form of progressive muscular disease is Duchenne muscular dystrophy (DMD). Approximately 1 in every 3,500 males is born with DMD (Shapiro & Specht, 1993). A milder but similar disorder, Becker muscular dystrophy, affects 1 in 30,000 male children. Though the severity of DMD is most prominent during the school-age years, its onset is generally early childhood.

Characteristics

The course of DMD follows a fairly predictable pattern (Lynn, Woda, & Mendell, 1994; Shapiro & Specht, 1993). Usually in early childhood (ages 3 to 6), children begin to have weakness in gross motor activities like running and jumping, and they fall often. The disability is positively identified when children rise from the floor using the Gower's maneuver or are unable to get up without using their arms for support. Children tend to waddle when walking and gradually develop scoliosis (spine curvature of the lower back). This misalignment of the body is a primary cause of respiratory disease, as the bellows of the lungs are compromised by the child's posture. As the muscles weaken, **contractures** form in the lower extremities. Between the ages of 8 and 12, children physically deteriorate rapidly and usually are unable to walk by the age of 12. Many children with DMD develop some degree of mental retardation, ranging from mild to moderate, due to

THE DIAGNOSIS: INTERVIEW WITH TOM AND ANN SIMPSON

Tommy Simpson was born with Down syndrome. I was only 34 when he was born and since we did not anticipate any problems, I hadn't had any extra tests or anything like that. When I was 7 months pregnant, the doctor thought the baby might be breech so he suggested I have an ultrasound to determine his position. The medical technician took a long time doing the ultrasound; he checked and rechecked his figures two or three times, then told us the doctor would need to talk to us. Later, we were told the doctors suspected the baby was a dwarf.

By the time the baby was born, we knew there might be something wrong, but I had decided it really didn't matter. I was just worried about having the baby and making sure we loved him. The rest didn't seem to matter so much, and I remember my labor coach thought that was wrong. She said, "If there are any problems you should have the information, know about it. You should be investigating." I just felt that I wanted to wait until the baby was born and then deal with it.

No heart problems had been found, so we expected no problems with the birth itself. My mom came out a week and a half before the baby was born so she and I ran all over town and had a lot of fun. I taught class the evening he was born, came home, and by about eleven o'clock, I knew the baby was coming. We went to the hospital and my labor was pretty easy. I don't think the nurses expected anything unusual; I don't think there was anything on my chart.

The birth came quickly. Smack! and not even the resident was there. I was just so happy and the nurses were really proud they had delivered him. He had come easily, but he was very blue and almost inert. The nurses worked on him and even when he was picked up, he was still very inactive. I remember by the time the doctor and my labor coach rushed in, it was all over. The doctor looked at the baby, and checked me over, but he didn't say anything. Still, I think he suspected. He said he was going to call the genetics counseling expert.

The baby came, but he wouldn't nurse and he opened one eye just a little bit. The nurses had to put him under special lights because he had jaundice. The genetics counselor and his assistant wanted to talk to my husband and me together. Now, I knew there was something wrong. When I called Tom he literally ran out of the house and left the door wide open, even in the cold. I held the baby and tried to get him to nurse, as they were talking to us. I was sharing the room with another woman, my labor coach was there, and the nurses were there. It was a difficult moment and I didn't have any privacy.

The doctor said they thought the baby had Down syndrome, and we'd heard of it, but we really didn't know what it meant. I remember we all started bawling, even with my roommate on the other side of the room, and it seemed so weird. I would have done things differently, but at the time when it's happening to you, you just take what's coming no matter how uncomfortable it is.

After the nurses knew, they switched us to a private room, but I wished they'd put a no visitors order in. I still had too many visitors and calls. We'd all waited for this baby for a long time, and not that many people expected anything to be wrong, so people kept calling and coming. I didn't deal with that very well. We all cried; everybody was so sad. The worst thing was the baby wasn't doing very well.

His breathing was high and shallow and he never nursed. The nurses had to keep sticking him for blood samples, because his skin was so thick, and he had a heart murmur so they thought he might have a heart problem. He went into the Intensive Care Unit that evening. I cried, and cried, and cried, and cried. It was ten o'clock at night and I didn't want to call my husband and mother because I knew they were both tired. I went down to see Tommy in the nursery about two in the morning, but it was so hard having him taken away.

People would visit me and I would try to be sociable and that was difficult too. Most people were understanding when I told them the baby had Down syndrome but I didn't really talk too much about it. You know it's funny, because now it's not upsetting to me, but those first few months I was terribly upset. I could cope, but I was really upset about it, and had a hard time talking about it. Now it seems like he's a neat little kid and we love him for just who he is, but it was so hard at first.

After Tommy was born with Down syndrome, and we went home from the hospital, my mom acted as my gatekeeper. She was great. She hardly let anyone talk to me by phone, and I really appreciated that because I didn't feel like talking to too many people.

One of my sisters called and said, "Well it's not like it's a tragedy or anything."

But I thought, "Oh, honey, it is; this is."

She reminded me she'd volunteered for Special Olympics, and she had a friend with a child who had Down syndrome and I said, "Did you know them when the baby was born?"

No, she'd met them when the child was five years old. I said, "Ask them what it was like when their child was born."

Tommy Simpson and his dad.

But my sister went on, "Oh, it's no big deal, it's not a tragedy, it's great."

I told her, "You need to understand that you've invalidated all of my feelings. Ask your friend."

Later she talked to her friend who confided that she had felt much of the same thing. I learned you do work through it, but you also have to recognize that sadness and disappointment are valid. It is a tragedy. Tommy is not going to go to college, he's not going to do a lot of things. He is a neat kid. But he's not going to do those things that you don't realize you expect for your child in your life.

the course of the disease. By middle to late adolescence, muscle tissue is almost completely replaced by fat or fibrous tissue. Children usually die before the age of 20, due to respiratory and heart failure. However, some individuals live into their 20s and are able to go to college or seek other occupations.

Those children with muscular dystrophy who are able to walk after the age of 15 are categorized with Becker muscular dystrophy (Lynn et al., 1994). Such individuals tend to have a much slower disease progression and may live to be 40 or 50 years of age.

Etiology

Duchenne muscular dystrophy and Becker muscular dystrophy are both X-linked recessive inheritance patterns. Males who receive the affected genes (p21 region of X chromosome) are severely affected, whereas females who carry the gene are either normal or only mildly affected (Shapiro & Specht, 1993). Though females who carry the genetic mutation pass it on to 50% of their offspring, the gene responsible for DMD is randomly inactivated in half of the males who receive it. Approximately one-third of all cases of DMD are the result of a new mutation of the Xp21 gene and not the result of family history (Emery, 1998). For these reasons, genetic counseling for Duchenne-type dystrophy is very difficult.

Treatment

Treatments are available to assist families and children to cope with the disease. Often, surgery for scoliosis is conducted to improve children's comfort and appearance, though this is not believed to return muscle strength nor prolong walking. Sometimes the aggressive use of tendon-transfer operations and bracing can prolong children's ability to walk for 1 to 3 years (Shapiro & Specht, 1993). While seemingly a modest goal, this accomplishment can be very meaningful to children and their families.

Treatment priorites for families are related to maintenance of function and comfort of the children and emotional support for the families.

1. Provision of a well-balanced diet with adequate fiber to avoid constipation.
2. Discouragement of long periods of bed rest, which can accelerate weakening of the muscles.
3. Encouragement of everyday activities within child's limits, avoiding strenuous exercise (e.g., supervised swimming). Children may be encouraged to walk as long as they can to slow muscle weakening, and even when no longer ambulatory spending as much time as possible standing with the aid of a standing board. Later, when using a wheelchair, long periods of sitting in the same position should be avoided for the same reason.
4. Passive range of motion exercises by parents or caretakers to prevent contractures (fixation of joints in a certain position due to lack of movement), with exercises demonstrated by a physical therapist.
5. Anticipation of respiratory problems should be vigilant. Regular pulmonary evaluations should be made even before problems occur to prevent lung damage or serious respiratory disease. Immediate treatment of respiratory infection is recommended, including antibiotics. Later, when respiratory

complications occur, children will benefit from postural drainage therapy and eventually assisted ventilation.

6. Use of lightweight splints or orthoses can prolong walking.
7. Implementation of an intervention program that addresses all areas of development, including language, social, and cognitive domains.

Several types of experimental research are investigating complex treatments for children with muscular dystrophy (Emery, 1998). Gene therapy involves implanting normal muscle cells into the muscles of boys with DMD. So far, there is insufficient evidence to determine if such attempts will assist in the recovery of muscle function. Another, perhaps more promising, research line includes "gene insertion," where a person's cells are programmed to "read" DNA in such a way as to produce the protein deficiency of DMD. Still other research is investigating the effectiveness of a protein substitute for dystrophin using a protein already produced in the body, *utrophin.* Each of these procedures bear the promise of finally solving the problem of this devastating disease. Steroid treatments, specifically *Prednisone,* have enjoyed some success in prolonging ambulation, delaying surgery, and even increasing muscle strength in some cases. However, severe symptoms of muscular dystrophy and related myopathies may begin in early childhood.

For early educators, the goals of intervention are very different than for children with cognitive disabilities. Yet, Emery (1998) reported that up to one-third of boys with Duchenne type dystrophy have some degree of cognitive disability. Therefore, an intervention plan should be global. Management of muscular function and alignment requires the ongoing participation of a physical therapist. Early interventionists should seek family input in determining educational priorities. Family support and interagency coordination will assist families to make short- and long-term decisions regarding the education and care of their child.

PHENYLKETONURIA

Phenylketonuria (PKU) is an inherited autosomal, recessive, inborn error of metabolism. Though many other metabolic disorders exist, PKU serves to illustrate issues surrounding metabolic errors (see Table 7–1). This error results in the inability of individuals to use the essential amino acid phenylalanine. Buildup of phenylalanine results in mental retardation from defective **myelinization** in the brain and degeneration of both gray and white matter (Hayes, Rarback, Berry, & Clancy, 1987).

Many infants born with PKU are blond with blue eyes and have a fair complexion. Symptoms of untreated cases are vomiting, failure to thrive, short stature, a distinct odor to urine and sweat, seizures, and a rapid progression of mental retardation (Hayes et al., 1987). This disorder may occur as frequently as 1 in every 15,000 live births in the United States (Nyhan, 1990).

Though previous family history is a marker for diagnosis, this defect cannot be detected by prenatal amniocentesis. Therefore, PKU cannot be diagnosed prior to the delivery of an infant. All newborns between 48 and 72 hours of age are initially screened for phenylalanine levels through a simple blood test obtained by sticking the infant's heel. All specimens are sent to a state-sponsored laboratory in order to increase the standardization of results. Results are available within 2 to 3 weeks of birth.

Table 7–1 Metabolic Disturbances

Disability	Characteristics	Cause	Treatment
Hypoglycemia	Decreased glucose for cells: If untreated can cause cerebral palsy, mental retardation, failure to thrive. Symptoms of glucose depletion: sweating, poor color, decreased attention, jitteriness, sleepiness/lethargy, seizures.	Metabolic error, other disease processes, genetic defect, stress, nutritional deficiency, infection	High-protein diet, education of all caregivers, including educators, on symptoms and treatment of hypoglycemia
Galactocemia	Inability to metabolize galactose found in milk produced by mammals. If ingested, galactose builds up and becomes toxic. Toxic levels cause MR, failure to thrive, liver disease, cataracts, and if untreated—death.	Genetic disorder	Lifelong elimination of galactose completely from diet. Casein hydrolysate and soybean formulas are used as milk substitute. Must educate child and other adults on safe foods. If not treated early, child will need comprehensive early intervention (cognitive, nutritional, visual, etc.)
Hypothyroidism	Inadequate production of thyroid hormone. Cause deficiencies in skeletal formations and height, lethargy, abnormal facial features (broad, flat nose, wide-set eyes, coarse features), developmental retardation, and motor, language, visual delays.	Unknown; possibly genetic	Thyroid replacement therapy; with treatment, children score within normal limits. Early intervention for children not treated early. PT/OT, nutritionist, visual specialist, and speech/ language therapy needed
Thalassemia	Insufficient production of amino acid compounds decreases the production of hemoglobin. Mild to severe anemia is the result. Failure to thrive, poor appetite; can lead to mild-moderate developmental delay, cardiac conditions.	Genetic; can occur in conjunction with sickle cell disease	Diet control to reduce the amount of iron; health maintenance in nutrition and feeding, in severe cases, routine blood transfusions

Phenylketonuria was the first inherited disease that could be successfully treated with diet. The goal of diet therapy is to restrict the oral intake of phenyl-alanine, thereby preventing excess buildup in the blood that will cause mental re-tardation, while still providing an adequate diet for normal growth and development (Hayes et al., 1987). Any solid foods that are high in protein (cow's milk, meats, dairy products, etc.) are excluded from the diet of children with PKU (Hayes et al., 1987). Most states within the United States offer assistance to families affected with PKU by providing the dietary supplements essential for normal growth and development. The most commonly used products for infants and children are Lofenalac, a low-phenylalanine formula that is used with infants, and Phenyl-Free, a food source that is used with older children.

Current screening programs and available treatment have significantly decreased the incidence of retardation caused by PKU. However, failure to detect the disorder in a newborn (an example may be when there is a home delivery) will result in retardation. Initially, the only symptom may be irritability. This may rapidly evolve to severe vomiting with the sudden onset of seizures. Once neurological symptoms appear, normal recovery without retardation is rare. Affected children also have a decreased life span (Nyhan, 1990).

Families with children affected by PKU require counseling and education, as well as positive, ongoing reinforcement of dietary goals to be successful with control of the disease. Success of children and families is dependent on understanding the diet and the reasons for restrictions, making sure that the diet is age-appropriate through the developmental years, and decreasing exposure to infections for an affected child (Hayes et al., 1987). As children get older, it may become increasingly difficult to adequately monitor the diet. Therefore, the entire family must have a commitment to success. Some research has suggested that for PKU (unlike galactosemia) dietary restrictions can be lifted later in life.

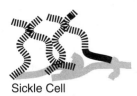

Sickle Cell

SICKLE CELL DISEASE

Sickle cell disease causes its victims to experience chronic and often painful episodes for which there is currently no cure and only limited treatment. Sickle cell disease affects 70,000 Americans and disproportionately afflicts persons with African ancestry (Marlowe & Chicella, 2002). Furthermore, because most of the largest cities in the United States have a high ratio of African American residents, the incidence of sickle cell disease is likely to be higher in urban than in rural areas (Brown, Armstrong, & Eckman, 1993).

Characteristics

The name of the disorder is derived from its principal characteristic. Abnormal, sickle-shaped red blood cells proliferate and eventually clog the blood vessels (see Figure 7–8) causing unpredictable acute and chronic tissue death (necrosis) in all major organs of the body (Thompson et al., 1992). The most prominent feature of sickle cell disease is pain (Marlowe & Chicella, 2002). Though usually not constant, the episodic periods of pain are acute and typically last 3–14 days. Approximately 20% of individuals with sickle cell disease have frequent and severe painful episodes referred to as **sickle cell crisis** (Shapiro, 1989). This pain is most likely to occur in one's abdomen, back, extremities, and chest. Several other complications can accompany sickle cell disease: infections, meningitis, spleen dysfunction, enuresis, delayed physical growth, and bone inflammation and decay (Hurtig & Viera, 1986). Blood vessel blockages in the brain eventually result in seizure activity and stroke even during childhood (Adams, McKie, & Hsu, 1998).

Because research is so limited, few conclusions are made regarding cognitive and behavioral associates of sickle cell disease (Brown et al., 1993). Four

Figure 7–8 The Sickle Cell Process

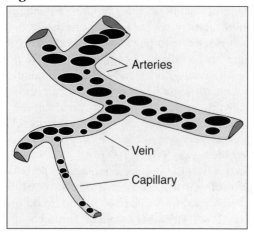

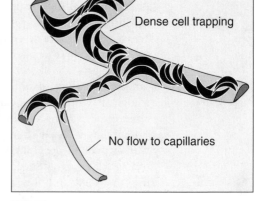

 Typical round-shaped red blood cells. Blood flows easily to all levels of the circulatory system

Abnormal sickle-shaped red blood cell. Blood clogs easily and results in pain.

physiological aspects of sickle cell disease have been documented, which Brown and colleagues believe can eventually compromise an individual's cognitive functioning:

1. Numerous tiny strokes in the central nervous system, specifically the brain
2. Anemia
3. Malnutrition
4. A compromised blood supply to the brain

In spite of these potentially harmful conditions, research to date indicates that children with sickle cell disease appear to suffer no loss of intelligence and no reliably measured deficit in academic performance as compared to peers without sickle cell disease (Brown et al., 1993). Furthermore, it seems that, psychologically, children with sickle cell disease may be no more likely to experience coping problems than children who are healthy (Armstrong, Lemanek, Pegelow, Gonzalez, & Martinez, 1993). On the other hand, extensive testing of preschoolers with sickle cell disease revealed significant deficiencies in both motor and cognitive readiness skills on the *Pediatric Examination of Educational Readiness* (Chua-Lim, Moore, McCleary, Shah, & Mankad, 1993). In this same study, measurements using the *McCarthy Scales of Children's Abilities* confirmed that intellectual abilities were within normal range. Brown et al. (1993) noted that such research is complicated by variables that, in themselves, could account for academic and social problems, namely, poverty or social class, absenteeism caused by frequent hospitalizations, family structure, and absence of support networks. All these characteristics are associated with cognitive and social difficulties; they also happen to be disproportionately characteristic of minority populations.

Etiology

Sickle cell disease is genetically transferred to the child. The disease is caused by a mutation of genes on the 11th chromosome (Nagel, 1993). According to Pollack (1993), 8% of the African American population carries the sickle cell gene. Three types of sickle cell disease exist (Brown et al., 1993; Pollack, 1993). Sickle cell anemia, the most severe, is homozygous (both 11th chromosomes affected) and is caused by two abnormal genes on the 11th chromosome. Two other heterozygous (only one 11th chromosome contains sickle cell anomaly) genotypes (HbSC and HBS-thalassemia) also result in some form of sickle cell disease. Nagel (1993) explained that the latter result from a multigene interaction, with different gene combinations producing a gradient in severity of the disease across affected individuals. Therefore, the course of the disease is unpredictable, ranging from mild to severe symptoms (Chua-Lim et al., 1993).

Treatment

The highest mortality rates from sickle cell disease are in the first 5 years of life, because of susceptibility to infections, and again near adulthood because of multiple system failure (Serjeant, 1985). Newborn screening and aggressive medical care have increased the life expectancy and quality of life of patients with sickle cell disease. However, very little is known about sickle cell disease, in spite of the fact that it is two times more prevalent than cystic fibrosis and nine times more common than PKU (Brown et al., 1990). Brown and colleagues noted that research on sickle cell disease lags far behind that of other congenital illnesses, implying that there is a link between the oversight of researchers and the ethnicity of its victims (see Table 7–2).

Diet is a concern in children with sickle cell disease who tend to expend energy more quickly and to possess less body fat than other children (Koop-Hoolihan, Van Loan, Mentzer, & Heyman, 1999). An overexpenditure of energy compared to nutrient intake is thought to be responsible for growth retardation. Consequently, children are often encouraged to take vitamin supplements, though with limited success. Therefore, support and planning from a nutritionist should be a part of the intervention plan for children with sickle cell disease.

Pain-coping methods, as with other types of chronic pain, often involve positive thinking/self-statements (Thompson et al., 1992). However, for preschoolers, the degree to which such an intervention might work is limited by their cognitive development. Marlowe and Chicella (2002) reported that treatment of pain in those with sickle cell disease is grossly undermedicated, often failing to adequately control the pain. Because medical providers fear an addiction to opiates, they are reluctant to prescribe sufficient pain medication. In fact, the addiction rate is 1–3% for persons with sickle cell disease, whereas the potential for attenuating the excruciating pain of a pain episode is high. Distrust of medical providers and hoarding of drugs to thwart future episodes are common reactions to improper pain management.

Treatments aimed at prevention of pain are also being explored (Marlowe & Chicella, 2002). For example, fetal hemoglobin which is resistant to sickling can prevent the sickle cell sequelae leading to painful episodes. The effectiveness of

Table 7–2 Comparative Table of Screening Paradigm for Tay Sachs Disease and Sickle Cell Disease

	Tay Sachs Disease	Sickle Cell Disease
Ethnicity	Ashkenazi Jews	African American
Screening	Voluntary	Compulsory in several states
Effectiveness	65% reduction in births from 1970–1980	No effect; abandoned in 1980
Education	In all cases thorough education emphasizing lack of blame to carriers	No accompanying education
Screening organization	Community-based plan to conduct screening	National screening funded by federal government; state controlled

this treatment is dependent upon successful regulation of dosage and the degree to which a child adheres to his or her treatment regimen.

Parents of children with sickle cell disease may cope with medical and disciplinary problems differently than parents of healthy children. Armstrong et al. (1993) found that in families in which there was significant lifestyle disruption, parents tended to cope by focusing on their child's medical, rather than emotional, needs. However, parents of children with sickle cell disease also tended to be more aware of effective and less-punitive disciplinary practices than parents of healthy children. These parents endorse the use of praise and mild punishment, perhaps because of their reluctance to inflict any more pain than necessary on children who already suffer from random and unavoidable pain caused by the disease itself.

TURNER SYNDROME

Turner Syndrome

Henry Turner first described Turner syndrome in 1938 (Williams, Richman, & Yarbrough, 1992). Found only in women, this disorder results when one of the two X chromosomes is absent (50%–55%), partially absent (12%–20%), mosaic where only a portion of the cells have a missing X chromosome (30%), or in rare instances, translocated. In most cases, there is a single X chromosome, and the characteristics of Turner syndrome are more severe than in partial or mosaic cases. The incidence of Turner syndrome is relatively rare, occurring in 1 to 4 cases per 10,000 live births (Hall & Gilchrist, 1990).

Characteristics

Girls and women with Turner syndrome are short in stature and fail to develop ovaries. One of the diagnostic characteristics of Turner syndrome is immature development of reproductive organs, with most women being infertile. Additionally, webbing of fingers, toes, and/or neck is not uncommon. Some individuals with Turner syndrome have kidney (Williams et al., 1992) or heart abnormalities (Downey et al., 1991).

The reported IQs average 90 to 95 (range 50–140), which are well within the normal intellectual range, though slightly lower than average (Rovet, 1990, 1993).

Moreover, a distinctive pattern of cognitive functioning has been observed in girls with Turner syndrome (Downey et al., 1991; Rovet, 1993; Williams, et al., 1992). Visual memory and visual-constructional reading and arithmetic abilities tend to be significantly lower than that of typical children. In school, children with Turner syndrome tend to have lower academic achievement than their peers (though not significantly lower than siblings), and as adults, they generally attain significantly lower occupational status.

Individuals with Turner syndrome tend to have delayed social maturity, possibly stemming from peer interactions that are disrupted by the odd appearance and unusually short stature of these girls. Furthermore, girls with Turner syndrome tend to lack subtle social awareness skills, such as being able to "read" facial affect (Mazzocco et al., 1998). In spite of these findings, Rovet (1993) noted that adolescent girls with Turner syndrome tended to view themselves as intelligent, well behaved, and having normal appearance. Nevertheless, girls with Turner syndrome do seem to have a higher incidence of significant behavior problems than their peers as well as hyeractivity, depression, and loneliness (Mazzocco et al., 1998).

Etiology

Turner syndrome is not considered to be familial. Therefore, after one child is born with Turner syndrome, subsequent pregnancies do not carry an increased risk of the disorder (Hall & Gilchrist, 1990). Unlike Down syndrome, absence of the X chromosome is not thought to be associated with maternal age. This may be because the absent X chromosome is paternally (father) initiated approximately two-thirds of the time (Mathur et al., 1991) and has been associated with advanced paternal age (Hall & Gilchrist, 1990).

Interestingly, most fetuses (98% to 99%) with a missing sex chromosome spontaneously abort, as compared to a spontaneous abortion ratio of 15% of all conceptions (Hall & Gilchrist, 1990). Hence, Turner syndrome has been estimated to represent as many as 1% of all conceptions. This disability can often be identified prenatally by ultrasound and confirmed through either amniocentesis or chorionic villus sampling.

Temple and Carney (1993) hypothesized that the absence or reduction of sex hormones, normally stimulated by both X chromosomes, adversely affects brain development during fetal growth. The impact of hormone deficiency is thought to be quite specific, resulting in the unique cognitive profile described above. That is, Turner syndrome is thought to be the result of absence of a "Turner" gene(s) rather than the absence of the X chromosome per se (Zinn, Page, & Fisher, 1993). In cases where two normally functioning chromosomes are present, these genes "turn on" growth production hormones necessary for healthy fetal development.

Treatment

Early intervention and family support may contravene some of the expected social and cognitive problems associated with Turner syndrome. Preschool intervention might focus on readiness for mathematics and reading skills and opportunities to model and reinforce appropriate social skills. However, because of the type of intellectual deficits described previously, it is very likely that cognitive problems will not surface until children begin academic tasks in school.

When girls with Turner syndrome reach puberty, hormonal replacement is usually recommended. The replacement therapy may continue into adulthood. In rare cases, spontaneous menstruation begins, and these girls are more likely to be fertile than others.

SYNDROMES WITH UNKNOWN CAUSES

Though the syndromes just described have a known etiology, there are a host of other disabling conditions whose origin continues to baffle researchers. In fact, a large majority of children have no known cause for their mental retardation. Environmental deprivations, such as nutrition, affection, and stimulation, may be the primary cause of most cases of mild to moderate mental retardation. On the other hand, it is likely that those syndromes that are distinctly articulated (e.g., autism) from others have some type of genetic or multifactorial origin. For example, genetic research has recently led to the identification of very common disabilities such as fragile X syndrome as well as more rare anomalies such as Prader-Willi syndrome (see Table 7–3).

AUTISM

Although autism is relatively rare (5–60/10,000 depending upon the definition used in identification), it is a highly visible disability. In fact, the characteristics of autism are neither discrete nor unchallenged (Wing, 1997). Some children who are identified with autism in infancy or early childhood are later identified with other disabilities. Other children who have not been labeled autistic possess behaviors termed "autistic-like." According to the American Psychiatric Association (APA, 1997), autism is classified as a pervasive developmental disorder (PDD). Historically, however, such terms as childhood schizophrenia, childhood psychosis, atypical personality disorder, and symbiotic psychosis were used to identify persons who are now labeled autistic.

Though autism has been categorized by others in various ways, Wing (1997) described this disability as a spectrum of disorders which have a triad of common characteristics: impaired social interactions, deficits in communication, and negligible imagination and extreme behavior. In an attempt to avoid the pitfalls of labeling children across the spectrum when current criteria and identification practices appear to be arbitrary, difficult to apply and will change as children age and move in to different environments, Wing provided a subgrouping based upon the aspect of social impairment alone.

1. *Aloof group:* children appear indifferent to others though they may tolerate physical affection from others. The more severely disabled children in this subgroup tend to have little or no speech and few functional skills apart from ambulation and often engage in repetitive body movements including self-injury. More mildly aloof children with autism tend to have mild learning disabilities, and though they typically have language, it is generally delayed in onset with abnormalities such as

Table 7–3   Incidence Inborn Variations in Development

Disability	Characteristics	Cause	Treatment
Cornelia de Lange Syndrome	Facial anomalies (long eyelashes, thin lips, confluent eyebrows, upturned nose, small face), microcephaly, mental retardation, hearing loss, severe language delays (superior language in rare cases), stereotypy sometimes evolving into self-mutilation	Unknown	Family support; speech/language focus, behavioral intervention for stereotypy (self-mutilation usually does not occur until after early childhood), comprehensive early intervention
Prader-Willi Syndrome	Stage I: Neonatal-hypotonia, weak/absent cry, large head, feeding problems, failure to thrive Stage II: Childhood—overeating is dominant trait, pear-shaped body, short stature, almond-shaped eyes Stage III: Adolescent—significant behavior problems, mild/moderate MR, good self-help, weak social skills	Missing portion of long arm of 15th chromosome (15q11–13). Paternal in origin. Father is carrier.	Family respite care/support groups, early management of insatiable appetite (nutritionist, environmental controls, behavioral self-management), social skills training, exercise programs in early childhood (swim, dance, soccer, etc.)
Rett Syndrome	Normal development (infancy) Stage I: Onset of developmental deterioration (6–18 months). Very intrusive stereotypy begins (i.e., hand wringing) Stage II: Rapid deterioration for a few weeks to months Stage III: Relative stability with some developmental growth for up to 10 years Stage IV: Regression—sometimes to primitive language and motor state	Unknown; possibly metabolic	Medication for seizures; PT/OT, nutritional monitoring for failure to thrive, music therapy to increase movement and social relatedness, family support and collaboration
Williams Syndrome	Failure to thrive, cardiac problems, elfin-like appearance (small chin, large ears, blue iris, wide mouth, wide-set eyes, broad forehead); mild–moderate MR, remarkable verbal proficiency, deficit in nonverbal ability; hypersocial, friendly, talkative, affectionate; later behavior problems; impulsive, hyperactive, self-destructive	Deletion of genes on chromosome 7	Nutritionist; focus on strengthening talents in language and social affability; PT/OT, later behavioral self-control instruction to manage activity level; parent counseling to avoid guilt when behavior problems arise—reassure parents that this behavior is a predictable sequelae of the syndrome

Case Study JOSH'S DIAGNOSIS: INTERVIEW WITH AMY FINKEL

Getting the diagnosis of autism was really difficult. We started recognizing that there was a problem when Josh was about 18 months old, because there was no speech, no words, nothing. We'd go to the physicians and they'd tell us, "Don't worry, he has two older siblings who do the talking for him. Don't worry, he'll talk. It's really common when kids have an older brother or sister to have a speech delay." So we'd go home thinking, okay, nothing's wrong, everything's fine. Then, as Josh got to be 2, we went again to the doctor's. "Are you sure nothing is wrong? He's still not talking. He's mute. What's going on here?"

"Well," they said, "He's had a lot of ear infections, maybe he has a hearing impairment or maybe there's a lot of fluid built up in his ears." So the first thing we did was to go to the ear, nose, and throat doctor. We had a special hearing test done. Because Josh was totally nonverbal, we couldn't rely on the standard hearing test with the head phones. They actually gave him some anesthetic, knocked him out, attached electrodes to his brain, and then introduced a sound into the ear canal and his brainwaves were monitored to show whether or not he was hearing properly. The results of that test came back normal. So we thought, okay, Josh has an older brother and an older sister, his hearing is fine, we won't worry about it.

But, at about 2½, there was still no speech and there were some odd behaviors that were emerging. Josh was very much a loner. He didn't like to play with the other kids, he quit responding to his name. He would over-selectively attend to toys, but he wouldn't play with them appropriately. He would line up his toys, in a certain way. He'd line them up perfectly so that one end of a toy had to be touching each wall. If you walked through the room and accidentally kicked a toy out of the way with your foot, Josh would come unglued and obsess on starting all the way from the beginning and putting everything back in that special order. That was really a big problem.

Josh was also enthralled with certain things in the environment, like dirt. Inside, he'd play in the dirt around all my house plants and I couldn't get him away from it. Outside, he'd sit in the pea gravel and swim in it, and we couldn't get him out of it. He wouldn't swing on the swing or go down the slide. He wouldn't interact at all with other children, including his brother.

There was no communication, not even pointing. Josh wouldn't take me by the arm and pull me over to show me something like other kids would do. For me, it was scary. If he was crying, I had no idea what was wrong. I didn't know if he had a really bad stomach ache, or had hurt himself, so I was constantly inspecting his body, looking for some sign of something being wrong. I became paranoid and I would take him into the doctor all of the time until it got to the point that the doctor would think, "Oh no! There's that Mrs. Finkel again, thinking there's something wrong with her son!"

echolalia being common. Behaviorally, these children often experience sleep disturbances, limited food tolerance, and motor stereotypies such as hand-flapping and rocking. For these children, daily activities must be highly routinized or they become agitated and act out.

2. **Passive group:** Children in this subgroup do not initiate interactions but do not reject approaches by others. The diagnosis may be missed entirely in the pri-

So we went back to the doctor, begging, "Look there *is* something wrong with our son. There's something wrong!" They said, "Don't worry, he's got an older sister and an older brother. Einstein didn't start talking until he was 5. He's had lots of ear infections. Don't worry, it's just a speech delay. Go home and leave us alone!"

Then finally, when Josh was almost 3, I could no longer be in denial. There were just too many bizarre things going on in addition to no speech. Basically, we went to the doctor again and threw a temper tantrum right there in the doctor's office. We refused to leave until they told us what was wrong with our son or referred us on until someone could tell us what was wrong. Otherwise Josh probably would have been 4 years old before we knew what was wrong. We got the actual diagnosis just before his 3rd birthday. It took us well over a year and a half to get that diagnosis, and we only got it as the result of throwing a tantrum in the office and refusing to leave.

The doctor had very little bedside manner when he told us Josh's diagnosis, and I think in retrospect, I'm glad he was as brutally honest as he was, because it got me busy. He said, "Your son is autistic and probably retarded. He'll never go to college. You'll have to take care of him the rest of your life. He'll never get married, he'll never have his own children. He'll probably never have a job."

At the time I thought the doctor was cruel and heartless and maybe he could have said things a little more gently. He stripped us of all the hopes and dreams that we had, that any parent has for his child. The next day, what was most devastating with the diagnosis of autism, was that nobody could tell us what to do about it.

We asked our physician. We asked different people in our community, "What is autism? What can we do?" No one had a definite answer for us; no protocol. So we were left devastated by the diagnosis and then very much alone in the community in terms of where do we go for resources. Where do we find out what the treatment is? What do we do for our son? It was devastating.

Josh Finkel.

mary years, though eventually they are identified because of learning and social interaction problems.

3. ***Active but odd:*** While children in this subgroup often have fluent speech with good grammar, their communication is typically repetitive and lacks reciprocity. The play and interests of these children is similarly narrow, perseverating on topics such as train timetables, mathematical calculations, or dinosaurs. These

children also exhibit difficult behavior such as frequent and severe temper tantrums, aggression, and egocentricity.

4. *Loners:* This high functioning subgroup of children tend to have fluent speech but prefer to be alone, lack empathy, and are socially egocentric. Many individuals in this group achieve successful careers as adults and can learn to apply the rules of social interaction by direct instruction.

About two thirds of children with autism are identified in infancy when caregivers note such behaviors as disinterest in toys, indifference to caregivers or physical contact, aberrant sleep patterns, excessive crying, irritability and stiffness, and an avoidance of eye contact (Mauk, 1993). Development may appear normal in the other third of children with autism until 12 to 18 months of age, at which point language and social skills may regress or fail to progress (Wing, 1997). Like many other disabilities, boys are three to four times more likely to be affected with autism than girls. Early childhood, from ages 2–5, tends to be a period of intense behavioral disturbance, with relative improvement between ages 6–10 and the sometimes reappearance of behavioral problems in adolescence and early adulthood (Wing, 1997).

Finally, most persons with autism have some degree of mental retardation. Andolsek (1998) reported that 75% of children with autism have mental retardation, while 40% of individuals with autism have IQs below 50. Though the range is very broad, the combination of mental retardation and other behavioral and language disabilities often results in profound developmental needs. According to Eaves (1992), autistic development is not consistent with developmental patterns in other forms of mental retardation, but can be "described as strange, distorted, even bizarre" (p. 70). **Savant** behavior, in which an individual shows extreme aptitude in one area (e.g., music or mathematics) along with autism, is very rare.

Etiology

There is no known cause of autism, though historically parents, mothers in particular, were blamed for their child's autistic behaviors. It was believed that women who failed to show love and nurturance psychologically impaired their child to such a degree as to cause autism. Thankfully, today, few women are accused of this misguided and harmful assumption.

Autism is often associated with chromosomal anomalies, such as Cri du chat, fragile X syndrome, Williams syndrome, Down syndrome, XXY, congenital rubella, and PKU (Wing, 1997). In fact, there is evidence that genetic factors contribute to many cases of autism. For example, the risk of reoccurrence in families with autism is 200 times higher than in the general population (Piven, Palmer, Jacobi, & Childress, 1997). Some researchers found that relatives of children with autism often exhibit characteristics that are milder and nonpathological, but qualitatively consistent with those of children with autism (i.e., lack of emotional responsiveness, oversensitivity, special interest patterns and oddities in social communication), though other researchers have failed to replicate such findings (Piven et al., 1997). Providing further evidence to the gene theory, Holden (1997) reported the preliminary identification of a gene linked to autism; one that regulates seratonin (a chemical neurotransmitter) in the brain. Gene mapping found that children with autism are more likely to have a shortened form of the seratonin transporter gene. Evidence that this is the culprit gene has been supported by studies that show that certain antidepressant drugs such as Prozac, which increase the availability of seratonin, also suppress the symptoms of autism. However, even if this gene is associated with autism, it is likely to be one which acts in concert with others, since 16% of the general population also has the shortened gene version.

Nongenetic disorders also resemble autism, if only for a period of time; these include Rett syndrome, fetal alcohol syndrome, severe mental retardation, severe deafness and blindness, and deaf-blindness (Mauk, 1993). One theory is that excessive testosterone in the fetus causes brain anomalies and subsequent cognitive dysfunction consistent with autism (Tordjman, Ferrari, Sulmont, Duyme, & Roubertoux, 1997). Epilepsy has been associated with a large percentage of children with "setback" autism (Wing, 1997). Most theories, however, have either been discredited (as in maternal neglect) or remain unvalidated. Mauk (1993) concluded that current evidence leads to a hypothesis that autism is the expression of multiple etiologies. In other words, there may be no such thing as "autism," but many different brain disorders may be expressed similarly enough to fall under the autism umbrella (see Table 7–4).

Treatment

One of the first steps to treatment is the exclusion of other potential causes of autistic behavior. For example, Eaves (1992) noted that the self-abuse in autism may mimic the tongue, finger, and lip biting of those with Lesch-Nyhan syndrome or otitis media, which commonly leads to head banging. Given the present limitations in behavioral and medical technology, autism is a lifelong condition, usually requiring very substantial resources. Treatment is likely to be complex, and no single intervention strategy will work with all children. In fact, even for a single child, a strategy that seems to be effective at one point may lose its potency over time or overnight.

Generally, intervention should be directed at development of present skills (e.g., converting speech fluency into reciprocal social interactions) while minimizing limiting behavior such as self-stimulation and self-injury. Behavioral intervention, involving systematic training, has been most effective in teaching new sets of skills

Table 7–4 Frequency of Secondary Disabilities Associated with Autism

Deafness	20%
IQ above 100	5%
IQ between 70–100	20–30%
Severe MR	30–35%
Mild MR	30–35%
Seizure disorder	25%
Affect isolation	88%
Perceptual inconsistencies (visual/hearing/touch)	80%
Stereotypy/twiddling	82%
Self-injury	65%
Nonverbal	50%
Echolalia	75%

while reducing intrusive behavior. However, even those methods are rigorous, slow to show improvement, and difficult to maintain over long periods. With the intense behavioral characteristics and limitations of technology, autism is considered one of the most demanding of developmental disabilities for families (Brown, 1999). The availability of multidisciplinary personnel, including a communications specialist, early childhood educator, social worker, counselor, respite care worker, and behavioral specialist, is desirable. Though one should not presume that a family will need emotional help, some may benefit from ongoing counselling and will benefit from ongoing support. In addition, parents should be cautioned when investigating costly but questionable dietary, medical or other unconventional methods that promise a "cure" for their children (Andolsek, 1998). Rhythmic entrainment (Orr, Myles, & Carlson, 1998) is such a method, where externally produced music is thought to re-entrain the body to its natural rhythmic patterns (50–65 beats per minute) of the heartbeat and aid in relaxation. While this method seemed to be effective in reducing self-injurious behavior in a small number of experimental subjects (e.g., Orr et al., 1998), further empirical evidence should be required of this and all intervention methods before being widely accepted by educators or recommended to parents.

Because one of the most common deficits of autism is social adaptation, many educators are aware of the research that the optimal educational environment is an integrated one with peers trained to act as social models. In such cases, educators need to provide specific instruction for peers on both social interaction skills and attitude (Clark and Smith, 1999). Parents are a necessary part of planning, since they can educate both teachers and peers on their child's social and communication repertoire and strategies. Specific target skills between model peers and children with autism are turn-taking, sharing, initiating and maintaining play, asking for help, using conversation skills, and being appropriately affectionate (see Table 7–5). To facilitate these interactions, language boards and other augmentative communication systems such as sign language can be used to mediate conversations (Cafiero, 1998). When taught to use visual cues early, children with autism have the possibility of generalizing this skill to picture-reading systems, self-management systems using visual reminders, and language boards in social interactions.

According to Dawson and Osterling (1997), there are six elements common to effective programs that educate children with autism.

1. Curriculum content that addresses children's ability to attend to critical environmental stimuli, imitate others, and to produce and understand language;
2. Highly structured and supportive teaching environment that plans for skill generalization (i.e., uses natural daily routines);
3. Predictable and routine classroom environment;
4. A functional approach to behavior problems teaching relevant skills;
5. A planned transition from preschool to elementary school; and
6. Family involvement.

In a study designed to test the validity of these elements, Schwartz and Sandall (1998), followed three children with autism from preschool through early elementary school. Each of the children displayed very different symptoms and func-

Table 7–5 Communication Deficits in Autism

Aspect of Speech	Communication Deficits
Speech Phonology (speech sounds)	Impaired receptive and expression in children with the mixed receptive-expressive syndrome and, especially, with severe verbal word deafness in which phonological decoding may be so compromised as to preclude speech comprehension and verbal expression
Prosody (rhythm and melody to speech)	In children with speech: singsong or rising intonation, high-pitched voice or monotonous, "robotic" voice
Syntax (grammar and word order)	Impaired reception and expression in children with the mixed receptive–expressive syndrome and with less severe verbal auditory word deafness
Semantics (vocabulary and meaning of language)	Impaired expression and reception in all children with autism—e.g., impaired comprehension of questions, open-ended questions and nonliteral language such as irony, sarcasm, and jokes; word-retrieval problems and unusual, pedantic word choices; echolalia; difficulty formulating coherent discourse; narrow range of topics
Pragmatics (communicative and conversational use of language)	Impaired receptive and expressive communication in all persons with autism—e.g., impaired interpretation of tone of voice, body posture, and facial expression; gaze avoidance; failure to answer; speaking to no one in particular; failure to initiate, pursue, or terminate conversations; difficulty with taking turns; poor maintenance of topic; perseveration and ceaseless questioning

Source: Adapted from I. Rapin, "Autism," 1997, *New England Journal of Medicine, 337,* 97–104.

tional levels, though all were initially noncompliant or combative. The preschool program used a blend of applied behavioral analysis and family focused developmental approach as well as instructional methods that were effective and systematic. Embedding these procedures into a natural integrated preschool classroom, the classes focused on social, communication, and play skills. When followed several years later in elementary school, all three children were thriving in inclusive classrooms with minimal to no special education support. It was concluded that the key to their sustained social and cognitive progress was in controlling noncompliant/violent behavior in the preschool years.

TOURETTE SYNDROME

Like autism, Tourette syndrome is a bewildering and sometimes devastating disability. Until 1972, the syndrome, also referred to as Gilles de la Tourette Syndrome after the French researcher who identified the disorder in 1885, was thought to be quite rare (50 known recorded cases). At that time, the Tourette Syndrome Association was initiated by a distraught father of a child with Tourette syndrome. Now, the syndrome is identified in as many as 1 in 200 children (Leckman et al., 1998). The most obvious characteristic of individuals with this disorder is the expression of tics. While 4% to 23% of all children experience tics (Torup, 1972), Tourette syndrome represents the most severe expression. The average age of tic onset is 5, though tics can appear between ages 2 and 7 and are three times as likely to affect boys as girls. The period of most severe tic behavior is about age 10, with nearly half of children becoming tic-free by 18 years of age (Leckman et al., 1998). Manifest in the form of motor movement or vocalizations, tics have a sudden, unpredictable onset and are purposeless and irregular. Factors such as stress tend to increase the frequency, while sleep thwarts their appearance (Lerer, 1987).

Characteristics

As children age, the intensity and form of symptoms also change. Because Tourette syndrome is so misunderstood by educators, children often go undiagnosed for years or suffer the misdiagnosis of learning disability or ADD (Rosen, 1996). The most common early symptoms involve eye movement, as in eye blinking (Murray, 1997). Eventually, children may have whole body involvement including jumping, kicking, spitting, smelling, squatting, and licking. Between the ages of 8 and 15, vocal tics may also appear and include barking, whistling, echolalia, grunting, coughing, snorting, and humming. Examples were provided by Santos and Massey (1990, p. 71) "'shut up,' 'stop that,' 'oh, okay,' and 'I've got to.'" The frequency of tics can vary from a few times when children are tired or tense to 100 times per minute in those most severely affected (Murray, 1997).

One of the more disturbing tendencies of Tourette syndrome is a disinhibition of aggression, where children may be unable to avoid destructiveness such as crushing an egg or a lightbulb when placed in their hand (Rosen, 1996). Throughout one's lifetime, tic patterns may vary, and in the early stages of the disorder, remissions may occur in which children are symptom free (Bronheim, 1991; Lerer, 1987).

Until recently, researchers had not acknowledged an "aura" experienced by many individuals with Tourette syndrome that sends them a message to perform a tic or ritual behavior (Murray, 1997). Their inability to ignore or defy these messages causes individuals another form of anxiety. In instances where persons are able to temporarily avoid performing a tic, the self-control is exerted at great expense. That is, the urge, resisted at one point, must be eventually performed, usually in a more severe form.

In addition to tics, approximately 50% of all children with Tourette syndrome have learning disabilities (Burd, Kauffman, & Kerbeshian, 1992). Burd et al. found a mean IQ of 94 in a sample of 42 children with Tourette syndrome. These findings suggest that the intelligence profiles of individuals with Tourette syndrome spans the normal range. Difficulty in basic writing skills, including handwriting, may lead to placement of children in special education programs (Rosen, 1996).

Either as a direct or indirect consequence of the syndrome, attentional deficits and impulse control are also common in children with Tourette syndrome. Knell and Comings (1993) provided some evidence that Attention Deficit Hyperactivity Disorder and Tourette syndrome are genetically linked. Unfortunately, medical treatment for attentional difficulties may produce the onset or exacerbate the symptoms of Tourette syndrome.

Obsessive compulsive behavior is a third associated disorder in 55% to 74% of cases of Tourette syndrome (Walkup et al., 1988). The impulse to complete tasks to perfection or to complete certain rituals, such as "evening up," in which actions or materials must be symmetrical, is a unique form of obsessive behavior found in persons with Tourette syndrome (Walkup et al., 1988). Understandably, individuals may experience excessive fear of expressing their tics or compulsive behaviors in public (Walkup et al., 1988). In addition to the movement characteristics of Tourette syndrome, these children are particularly vulnerable to psychological distress, including frustration, low self-esteem, anger, and hyperactivity (Rosen, 1996). Often ridiculed by their peers and misunderstood by teachers, children experience serious anxiety related to social encounters (Bronheim, 1991; Burd et al., 1992; Lerer, 1987; Levi, 1991).

Etiology

Approximately one third of all children with Tourette syndrome also have coprolalia, the involuntary use of vulgar or obscene gestures or language (Levi, 1991). Yet, with concentration, children may be able to suppress tics, though compromising their ability to attend to other tasks (Bronheim, 1991). Because of these characteristics, some claimed that the disorder is psychological and that the behaviors are purposeful rather than physical. However, it is now widely accepted that the actual cause is an autosomal dominant genetic disorder (Rosen, 1996). Kurlan (1992) hypothesized that the defective gene thought to cause Tourette syndrome results in developmental damage to the area of the brain responsible for primitive motor, vocal, and emotional processes (basal ganglia). He further hypothesized that male sex hormones adversely affect this abnormal brain development, while female sex hormones beneficially influence this development, explaining the differential incidence of Tourette syndrome across genders.

While the precise cause of this disorder is unknown, it is possible that a combination of factors contribute (Cohen, Detlor, Shaywitz, & Leckman, 1992). For example, Bower (1990) concluded that the basic cause of Tourette syndrome is a genetically caused deficiency of seratonin (chemical) in the brain (neurological), which controls emotions and initiates responses to external stimuli (environmental). According to this theory, individuals with Tourette syndrome inherit two defective genes (one from each parent). It was postulated that approximately 15% of the general population carries at least one of these genes, and that half of the carriers have addictive, compulsive, emotional, or learning problems.

Treatment

This disorder can cause heartache for parents as well as children with the disorder. To know that one's child will be ridiculed or mistreated is a lifelong frustration for parents. Children and parents can be comforted by knowing that tics are out of the control of an individual with Tourette syndrome. Informing teachers and parents of other children may also reduce the stigma of tics. Santos and Massey (1990) recommended consideration of the following factors in planning intervention for a child with Tourette syndrome:

1. Family's ability to cope and provide support
2. School responsiveness
3. Peer group response
4. Choice of vocation and acceptance in the workforce
5. Need for intimacy and long-term relationships
6. Family planning
7. Access to legal or advocate services

Case Study   THE DIARY OF ESTHER ANNA BERKE: MONTHS 11 AND 12

Sept. 16–Oct. 15: Esther continues to be unstable, rarely showing the same patterns more than 2 days in a row. She only gained 100 g for the month, weighing 8.6 kg on Oct. 12 (only the 35th percentile for her age) and measuring 76 cm (the 85th percentile for her age). If she gets much longer she won't fit in the stroller (it is a twin stroller!). She started a new drug, prednisone, an anabolic steroid, on Oct. 14, it makes her cranky and arch her back/neck a lot, but it seems to reduce the frequency of her seizures (too early to tell for sure). At times her right arm and leg become very stiff and she doesn't move them, almost like a person with a stroke, we're not sure why. Sarah's mother has agreed to come for 3 weeks to help when the new baby is born, she will arrive Oct. 28. Otherwise, her diet continues, her latest blood test showed almost everything

was "normal," which was good, except her white blood cell count was high (sign of an infection?). Her diet seems to be helping "normalize" her blood, especially her sodium/potassium levels. The dietitian wants to run an amino acid profile on her blood as well.

Happy birthday, Esther Anna! She was one year old on Nov. 15. She measured 76 cm long and weighed 8.3 kg. Pictures of her birthday party will be available soon. We want to move to America, but have decided to wait until next year after Joel gets a little bigger. We need some stability in our lives right now. We want to gain better access to the latest information and experimental treatments for Aicardi Syndrome (there will be a big conference on Aicardi Syndrome in July 2000).

Generally, stress, anxiety, tiredness, and excitement exacerbate the symptoms of Tourette syndrome. Helping families to manage their children's activities to moderate situations that might cause overexcitement, tiredness, and anxiety should be an intervention goal. On the other hand, relaxation tends to reduce the symptoms. Teaching families and children techniques for motor and emotional relaxation will provide children with a mechanism for preventing or minimizing symptoms.

In the most severe cases, medication is the treatment of choice, either for the tics or the associated attentional deficits. For example, *Haloperidol*, the drug of choice for over three decades, initially diminishes symptoms in 70% of individuals but concurrently introduces the risk of side effects, such as lethargy, weight gain, poor school performance, and depression, as well as a variety of neurological symptoms (Murray, 1997; Santos & Massey, 1990). The most serious side effect of Haloperidol is a neuromotor disorder called tardive dyskinesia. Recently, drug alternatives which may be both more effective and reduce side effects have been explored with some success (Sallee, Nesbitt, Jackson, Sine, & Sethuraman, 1997).

Though relief may be gained from medication, the symptoms rarely subside entirely (Bronheim, 1991). Because of the dangerous side effects, Santos and Massey (1990) recommended that medication only be used when the symptoms of Tourette syndrome are so serious that they compromise a child's development.

Oct. 16–Nov. 15: Esther lost weight this month, she weighed 8.6 kg on Oct. 12 and only weighed 8.2 kg on Nov. 15 (only the 25th percentile for her age). She still measures 76 cm. She is tapering off prednisone now, she is much happier, let me tell you! I think it helped her, she seems to have fewer seizures and to sleep longer at night. Sarah's mother came Oct. 28 for 3 1/2 weeks to help, that was a real blessing. We had some cupcakes with candles to celebrate her birthday. At one year old, she still doesn't respond to many stimuli, and she can't hold up her head or move her arms or legs in a coordinated manner.

Esther Anna (top) and her baby brother.

As an alternative, behavioral self-management interventions have been effectively used to limit the onset of some of the associated disorders (obsessive-compulsive and attentional), though these treatments may be too sophisticated for preschool age children.

PHYSICAL ANOMALIES

CONGENITAL HEART DEFECTS

Congenital heart defects are a problem for a significant number of infants and young children. It is estimated that approximately one out of six infants are born with congenital heart disease, and approximately 3% of newborns have a major heart anomaly (Copel, 1999). Furthermore, many genetic disorders and other physical abnormalities are accompanied by heart defects. Most of these infants are ill enough within the neonatal period to require intervention. Consequently, it is estimated one-third of all deaths due to congenital anomalies between 5 months gestation and 1 year after birth are the result of cardiovascular abnormalities (Copel, 1999).

Congenital defects are generally categorized into either cyanotic or noncyanotic abnormalities. Categorization is dependent on the heart's ability to direct

Figure 7–9
Fetal Circulatory
Patterns

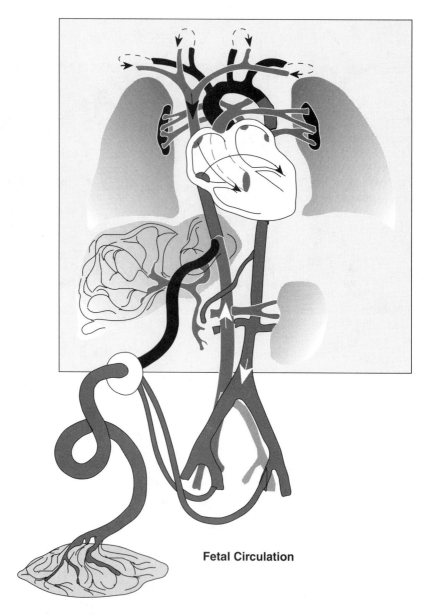

Fetal Circulation

blood flow to and from the lungs and then to the general circulation. Situations in which blood bypasses the lungs result in decreased oxygen available to cells and produce a blue-tinged color to the skin, known as **cyanosis**. Diagnosis followed by appropriate treatment is the key to decreasing the general adverse effects of congenital heart defects.

Understanding the differences between fetal circulatory patterns and those required of an infant after birth provides a means for understanding how an affected fetus can survive a significant defect through the period of gestation. Fetal circulation consists of parallel circuits. When fetal blood bypasses the lungs, either the

Figure 7–10
Establishment of Independent Heart and Lung Function in Infants Changes the Direction of Blood Flow

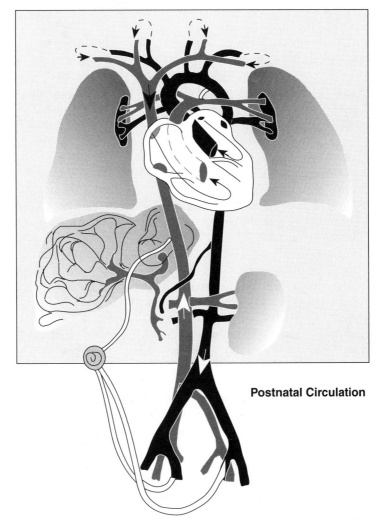

Postnatal Circulation

right or left ventricle will pump blood directly to the general circulation (see Figure 7–9). The pressure in either ventricle during this period is similar. This parallel structure allows for fetal survival in spite of a variety of significant cardiac defects. Even if one of the ventricles is completely obstructed, the other ventricle can maintain sufficient blood flow with little effort.

The birth process results in a remarkable change in the blood flow pattern of the infant. With the infant's first breath, blood flows into the lungs and the blood flow from the placenta ceases (see Figure 7–10). At the same time, an increase in the independent breathing of newborns results in oxygenation of the blood from the infant's own lungs, which, in turn, causes closure of the ductus venosus and the narrowing of the ductus arteriosus. Finally, changes in intracardiac pressures result in the functional closure of the foramen ovale. These changes dramatically increase the work of the heart, especially the left ventricle. It is with this demand that many congenital defects will produce symptoms that lead to recognition of an existing cardiac defect.

Most congenital cardiac defects produce symptoms that are diagnosed within the first week of life. Symptoms may include respiratory distress, a heart rate over 200 beats per minute, a heart murmur, difficulty with feeding, and failure to gain weight. Many of these may persist into childhood (depending on the defect) with the addition of exercise intolerance, poor physical growth, delayed development, recurrent infections, squatting, clubbing of the fingers and toes, and increased blood pressure. Many of these children also have chronic behavior problems, possibly related to repeated hospitalizations.

Certain cardiac defects are known to be associated with specific genetic malformations and maternal conditions. For example, there is an association between Down syndrome and endocardial cushion defects. Males have an increased risk for coarctation of the aorta, aortic stenosis, and transposition of the great vessels; whereas, females have an increased incidence of atrial septal defects. When a mother is diabetic, there is a high risk for significant multiple cardiac defects in the fetus. Congenital rubella is associated with narrowing of the pulmonary arteries and patent ductus arteriosus. Lesions associated with prematurity or low birth weight are also found with an increased incidence of both patent ductus arteriosus and ventricular septal defects.

Endocardial cushion defects occur when there is abnormal development of the septa between the atria and the ventricles, which includes a malformed, deficient, or abnormally attached mitral valve. This abnormality results in mixing of oxygenated and nonoxygenated blood between the right and left atria and the right and left ventricles with incompetent valves. This defect may appear as an isolated cardiac defect but more commonly is associated with other malformations and very frequently with Down syndrome.

CLEFT LIP AND CLEFT PALATE

Cleft lip and cleft palate (roof of mouth) are commonly occurring defects that may be present as often as 1 out of every 700 live births (Eliason, 1991). Cleft lip and/or palate may occur as an isolated defect (lip or palate), in conjunction with each other, or associated with other congenital abnormalities. It appears that approximately 20% of children with cleft lip/palate have additional congenital malformations, such as skeletal malformations, mental retardation, cardiovascular problems, gastrointestinal malformations, or facial anomalies (Milerad, Larson, Hagberg, & Ideberg, 1997). A cleft is a division or split that occurs between two tissue planes. Many recognized congenital syndromes present have this associated defect (e.g., trisomy 13, 15, or 21). The clefts that appear in either the lip or palate are separate defects but there may be a relationship due to the fact that the disruption in normal development occurs during a relative time period in gestational development, between the 5th and 13th week of gestation.

Formation of the lip and palate occurs in stages from about the 5th to 12th weeks of gestation. It is during this time that the normal fusion process fails, with a cleft occurring. The specific cause for a lip/palate defect is not generally known but may be related to prenatal exposure to teratogens (i.e., maternal alcohol consumption), other anomalies, or possibly to genetic factors (since an increased incidence has been noted in families) (McInerney, 1985). Teratogens have also been connected to the incidence of clefts. For example, benzodiazepines, drugs prescribed to reduce anxiety, insomnia, or epilepsy in women, are sometimes taken in the first trimester of pregnancy before women realize they are pregnant (Dolovich et al., 1998).

The cause of isolated defects is different than those appearing with multiple congenital anomaly syndromes, of which more than 300 have been identified (Cohen & Bankier, 1991). Ethnic origins also appear to have some relationship to the occurrence of isolated defects. That is, Native Americans have the highest incidence, while African Americans have the lowest (Vanderas, 1987).

Cleft lips and palates are classified as unilateral (affecting one side) or bilateral (affecting both sides) and as either complete or incomplete. Approximately 25% of all reported cases involve an isolated cleft lip with another 25% involving an isolated cleft palate (Hardy, 1988). The occurrence of a cleft lip without a cleft palate decreases the potential difficulties that face affected infants.

Clefting of the lip involves a split that affects the lip and gum and may extend upward into the nose. In cases involving bilateral lip clefts, the defect may be extensive enough to join together at a point behind the gum. In these cases a section of the lip and gum appears to hang freely from the septum of the nose. The majority of infants with a bilateral cleft lip also have a cleft palate. The impact of such extensive abnormalities on appearance presents significant problems for families. In many cases, the disfigurement is initially so overwhelming that parents experience difficulties in looking past the defect to the infant, and initiation of parent/child bonding is interrupted.

Facial disfigurement (with resulting parental rejection) and feeding difficulties are the two most significant problems that face an infant affected with an isolated cleft lip. Society places a great deal of importance on external appearance, and the face is central to this view. It is vital that health care providers, extended family members, and other individuals involved in providing service give support during the initial bonding experience of new parents of an infant with a cleft lip. This will allow for every opportunity to get past negative feelings and to promote bonding.

Infants with a cleft lip may have difficulty establishing a normal feeding pattern. Interruption in the integrity of the lip produces the challenge of providing optimum nutrition to foster the necessary growth required before surgical repair can be attempted. Feeding devices are available that can use either breastmilk or prepared formulas to promote a feeding pattern that is as close to normal as possible. Many infants with an isolated cleft lip can successfully breastfeed. These infants feed using structures within the mouth to express milk from a nipple. Tongue movements assist with this process and, though helpful, the lip is not essential to establish a successful suck. Referral to appropriate experts within the community can provide support for a successful feeding experience for an infant with an isolated defect.

A cleft palate involves a split in the hard or soft palate or, in some cases, both. Infants who are born with a cleft palate experience a wider variety of problems than do those infants born with an isolated cleft lip. These include facial deformities, speech impairment, hearing loss, infections, feeding problems, and learning disabilities that may or may not be related to either speech or hearing problems.

The potential for failure to thrive because of a decreased ability to eat is a significant problem for infants born with a cleft palate. Feeding problems are generally a result of the physical defect but may also be related to other disabilities. Normal sucking requires the tongue and/or the palate to stabilize the nipple and then to suck milk. This is dependent on the method chosen to feed an infant—breast or bottle. Cleft palates prevent nipple stabilization and create an abnormal suck. Devices such as extended nipples placed on squeeze bottles, flexible tubing placed next to a breast and connected to a bottle of pumped milk, and standard nipples with enlarged holes are available to assist with feeding. Each defect may require adaptation of feeding devices and techniques. Evaluation by an occupational therapist should be made prior to initial discharge from the hospital after birth, and a method of feeding devised. This plan includes parental instruction and referral to appropriate resources within the community for ongoing follow-up.

Another significant problem associated with cleft palate is acute and chronic middle ear infection. Acute infection may be a single episode in a susceptible infant that can be cleared with antibiotic treatment. Chronic infection results from a defective opening between the bacteria-laden oral cavity, up the eustachean tubes, to the middle ear space. Surgical repair of the cleft does not significantly decrease the incidence of infection (Yetter, 1992). Therefore, conductive hearing loss from repeated infections is a common occurrence. Though the procedure is controversial, many infants will be placed on preventive antibiotic therapy and may even have drain tubes surgically placed through the eardrum, in an effort to reduce infection and subsequent hearing loss.

Speech delay also frequently accompanies a cleft palate. Sucking is necessary to develop muscles used to make speech physically possible. Alterations in the normal sucking process delay the muscle development. Moreover, the presence of a single cavity (nose and mouth) alters the normal sound production. Both the medical condition and the possibility of social isolation decrease the opportunities these infants have for verbal interaction with the adult world, a vital link to the development of speech.

Another problem faced by children with a cleft palate is related to the normal progression of tooth eruption. Dentition is not only delayed, but in many cases, normal tooth formation may be absent. Early evaluation by a dentist with appropriate referral for orthodontics is part of the teaming approach necessary to meet the total needs of an infant and family.

Hearing loss and speech delay lead to speech-related learning disabilities. These may be influenced by the social isolation that frequently results from the facial disfigurement that is part of this defect. In addition, educators sometimes make erroneous assumptions about intelligence in children with facial defects. Richman (1978) found that teachers both underestimated ability and had lower expectations for performance from students with moderate or severe facial disfigurement.

Families of infants who have a cleft palate require a multidisciplinary approach to meet their needs. This teaming should include the primary care physician, plastic surgeon, public health nurse, speech pathologist, audiologist, dentist, social worker, occupational therapist, and educator. Team collaboration provides for long-term planning to assure that both actual and potential needs of infants and families can be met.

Children whose defects have been successfully repaired may continue to experience alterations in social interactions and with learning. Persistent problems with articulation and with hypernasality of the voice may lead to ongoing anxiety in group interaction and to low self-esteem. Stereotyping must be avoided and identification of personal biases toward the importance of physical attractiveness are important topics in discussion within the team when planning the approach to services for each infant and family affected by this defect.

In Conclusion

Scientific discoveries such as gene therapy, gene cloning, and genetic selection in fertility are likely to alter the "natural" genetic course of the human species. Many disabilities could go the way of Tay-Sachs, selectively becoming eliminated from the gene pool. Others could be treated by replacing defective genes with normal genes to prevent a disease such as sickle cell anemia. Whether these imminent changes will eventually be healthy for our species or harmful is a question seldom asked. When we get to the point of asking, "Do we want 'this variation' or, 'that variation'?" will we be active participants or spectators in a dialogue regarding the ever-expanding knowledge or technology of genetic manipulation?

For example, Pueschel (1991) argued against the practice of using prenatal diagnosis to detect Down syndrome, on the grounds that the overriding purpose is to determine whether or not an abortion is needed. The arguments for prenatal screening and selective abortions of affected fetuses include:

1. It benefits the individual woman and her family.
2. It also benefits society because such procedures have a eugenic effect in eliminating defective genes from the gene pool.
3. It reduces the financial burden to society.
4. It is preventive medicine.
5. It increases the quality of life for the family.
6. The fetus has a right to be born healthy. (Pueschel, 1991, p. 186)

Pueschel pointed out various unforeseen and ultimately questionable outcomes of prenatal diagnosis. For example, many physicians have been found liable for "negligent genetic counseling" when there was a "wrongful birth" of a child with Down syndrome. Other medical personnel have lost court battles because a specific diagnostic test that might have detected Down syndrome was not conducted. In the latter, parents claimed that they were deprived of the opportunity to make a decision to terminate the affected fetus.

A second issue surrounds the practice in our society of deeming genetic difference as a negative. Many of the arguments previously mentioned, for example, are a part of the mythology surrounding persons with Down syndrome. The thoughts of Pearl S. Buck (1973) regarding her daughter illustrate the belief that lives can be richer, not necessarily worsened, by the membership of persons with disabilities:

> In this world, where cruelty prevails in so many aspects of our lives, I would not add the weight of choice to kill rather than to let live. A retarded child, a

handicapped person, brings his own gift to life, even to the life of normal human beings. That gift is comprehended in the lessons of patience, understanding, and mercy, lessons which we all need to relive and to practice with one another, whatever we are.

A study conducted by Meryash (1992) may shed the most light on this issue. When women were asked what factors would influence their decision to abort a child with fragile X syndrome, the most salient answer was a fear that the parents' social lives might be disrupted. It is worth noting that women who were more likely to select abortion were (1) more highly educated, (2) had a greater knowledge of fragile X, and (3) had other children with disabilities. Furthermore, the women identified the advice of their physician as an important factor in making a decision to abort. The latter is of concern to Pueschel, who fears that professionals who do not know or work with children with disabilities will be unfairly negative. "Genetic research has the potential for misunderstanding and misapplication; there may be a time when we are tempted to cross the line from curing or preventing a medically burdensome disease to enhancing genetic traits. Society must be able to place wedges in this potential slippery slope."

STUDY GUIDE QUESTIONS

1. How is individual variability related to treatment and prevention?
2. What is genetics?
3. Describe the basic mechanisms of inheritance. Define the following terms in the course of your answer: (1) chromosomes, (2) genes, (3) traits, (4) genetic mapping, (5) chromosomal region, (6) deletion, (7) mutation, (8) protein product, (9) "new genetics," and (10) the human genome.
4. What is the interplay of genetic codes and environmental factors on the cause and treatment of genetic diseases?
5. Describe cellular activity. Define the following terms in the course of your answer: (1) DNA, (2) nucleic acid compound, (3) alleles, (4) homozygote, (5) heterozygotes, (6) genotypes, (7) phenotypes, (8) mitosis, (9) meiosis, (10) gametes, and (11) errors in cell division.
6. How many chromosomes are there within a cell structure? How many of these are autosomes? What is the 23rd pair?
7. Describe single gene disorders.
8. Discuss the relationship among the following: dominant and recessive traits; male and female sex-linked traits.
9. Define chromosome disorder.
10. Define multifactorial disorders and congenital disorders.
11. What are the major types of genetic testing, and which genetic diseases can be most readily diagnosed?
12. What is the purpose of gene therapy? What are the social and ethical implications of gene therapy and advanced genetic testing?
13. What roles do the exocrine glands and the pancreas play in the development of the symptoms of cystic fibrosis?
14. What is meant by "secondary physical complications" in cystic fibrosis?
15. Briefly describe the etiology and treatment of cystic fibrosis.

16. Describe the most common characteristics of Down syndrome and the possible degree of variation from child to child.
17. What are the primary medical and educational issues facing persons with Down syndrome?
18. Differentiate between translocation and mosaicism.
19. Describe the chief characteristics of fragile X syndrome.
20. Briefly describe the etiology and treatment needs of children with fragile X syndrome.
21. Describe the primary characteristics, etiology, and treatment of Duchenne muscular dystrophy.
22. How does the buildup of phenylalanine cause mental retardation?
23. What preventive and treatment procedures are used to reduce rates of mental retardation from PKU?
24. What are the characteristics of sickle cell disease?
25. The treatment of sickle cell disease has developed slower than other "lower incident disorders." Why might this be?
26. Describe Turner syndrome: (a) etiology, (b) chief characteristics, and (c) treatment.
27. What are the characteristics of autism?
28. What is it about autism that makes this disability especially challenging for parents? For educators?
29. What general recommendations can be made in the treatment of children with autism?
30. What are the most common manifestations of Tourette syndrome?
31. What percentage of children with Tourette syndrome also experience learning disabilities? What implications does this have for instruction or treatment?
32. How does fetal heart circulation differ from heart function after birth? How does this protect the unborn child?
33. What are the symptoms of congenital cardiac defects?
34. At what point in development is a cleft lip and/or palate formed? What can cause this to happen?
35. Why is counseling especially important for families of very young children with cleft lips and/or palates?
36. What significant problems are associated with cleft lips and/or palates?

REFERENCES

Adams, R. J., McKie, V. C., & Hsu, B. F. (1998). Prevention of a first stroke by transfusions in children with sickle cell anemia and abnormal results on transcranial Doppler ultrasonography. *The New England Journal of Medicine, 339*, 5–11.

American Psychiatric Association. (1997). *Diagnostic and statistical manual of mental disorders* (3rd ed.). Washington, DC: Author.

Andolsek, K. M. (1998). Characteristics and symptoms in patients with autism. *American Family Physician, 57*, 809–811. (Reprinted from Rapin, I. [1997]. Autism. *New England Journal of Medicine, 337*, 97–104.)

Anfenson, M. (January, 1980). The school-age child with cystic fibrosis. *The Journal of School Health*, 26–28.

Armstrong, F. D., Lemanek, K. L., Pegelow, C. H., Gonzalez, J. C., & Martinez, A. (1993). Impact of lifestyle disruptions on parent and child coping, knowledge, and parental discipline in children with sickle cell anemia. *Children's Health Care, 22*(3), 189–203.

Billings, P. R., Beckwith, J., & Alper, J. S. (1992). The genetic analysis of human behavior: A new era? *Social Science and Medicine, 35*(3), 227–238.

Bower, B. (July, 1990). The ticcing link. *Science News, 138,* 42–44.

Bronheim, S. (1991). An educator's guide to Tourette syndrome. *Journal of Learning Disabilities, 24,* 17–22.

Brown, G. (Jan/Feb,1999). The sometimes son. *Humanist, 59*(1), 46–47.

Brown, R. T., Armstrong, F. D., & Eckman, J. R. (1993). Neurocognitive aspects of pediatric sickle cell disease. *Journal of Learning Disabilities, 26*(1), 33–45.

Buck, P. S. (1973). *The child who never grew.* New York: Day.

Burd, L., Kauffman, D. W., & Kerbeshian, J. (1992). Tourette syndrome and learning disabilities. *Journal of Learning Disabilities, 25,* 598–604.

Cafiero, J. (1998). Communication power for individuals with autism. *Focus on Autism & Other Developmental Disabilities, 13,* 113–122.

Chad, K., Jobling, A., & Frail, H. (1990). Metabolic rate: A factor in developing obesity in children with Down syndrome. *American Journal on Mental Retardation, 95*(2), 228–235.

Chan, A., McCaul, K. A., Keane, R. J., & Haan, E. A. (1998). Effect of parity, gravidity, previous miscarriage, and age on risk of Down's syndrome: Population based study. *British Medical Journal, 317*(7163), 923–924.

Chua-Lim, C., Moore, R. B., McCleary, G., Shah, A., & Mankad, V. N. (1993). Deficiencies in school readiness skills of children with sickle cell anemia. *Southern Medical Journal, 86*(4), 397–401.

Clark, D. M., & Smith, S. W. (1999). Facilitating friendships: Including students with autism in the early elementary classroom. *Intervention in School and Clinic, 34,* 248–251.

Cohen, D. J., Detlor, J., Shaywitz, B. A., & Leckman, J. F. (1992). Interaction of biological and psychological factors in the natural history of Tourette syndrome: A paradigm for childhood neuropsychiatric disorders. In A. J. Friedhoff & T. N. Chase (Eds.), *Gilles de la Tourette syndrome* (Vol. 35, pp. 31–40). New York: Raven.

Cohen, M. M., & Bankier, A. (1991). Syndrome delineation involving orofacial clefting. *Cleft Palate Journal, 28,* 119–120.

Copel, J. A. (October, 1999). *Congenital heart disease* (Vol. 1., No. 6). Retrieved October 2, 2002 from *http://hygeia.org/poems6.htm*

Crawford, D. C. (2001). *FMR1 and the fragile X syndrome.* Human Genome Epidemiology Network: CDC. Retrieved October 2, 2002 from *http://cdc.gov/genomics/hugenet/factsheets/FS_FragileX.htm*

Cystic Fibrosis Foundation. (September, 1999a). *Gene therapy and cystic fibrosis.* Cystic Fibrosis Foundation, Bethesda, MD.

Cystic Fibrosis Foundation. (September, 1999b). *Facts about cystic fibrosis.* Cystic Fibrosis Foundation, Bethesda, MD.

Cystic Fibrosis Foundation. (September, 1999c). *Teachers guide to cystic fibrosis.* Cystic Fibrosis Foundation, Bethesda, MD.

Dawson, G., & Osterling, J. (1997). Early intervention in autism. In M. J. Guralnick (Ed.), *The Effectiveness of Early Intervention* (pp. 307–326). Baltimore: Brookes.

De La Cruz, F. F. (1985). Fragile X syndrome. *American Journal of Mental Deficiency, 90,* 119–123.

Dibble, S. L., & Savedra, M. C. (1988). Cystic fibrosis in adolescence: A new challenge. *Pediatric Nursing, 14,* 299–303.

Dolan, S. (2002). Preimplantation genetic diagnosis (PGD): Success and controversy. *Report from the Annual Clinical Genetics meeting.* Retrieved October 10, 2002 from *http://www.medscape.com/ viewarticle/432290_2*

Dolovich, L., Addis, A., Vaillancourt, J. M. R., Power, J. D. B., Koren, G., & Einarson, T. R. (1998). Benzodiazepine use in pregnancy and major malformations or oral cleft: Meta-analysis of cohort and case-control studies. *British Medical Journal, 317,* 839–843.

Downey, J., Elkin, E. J., Ehrhardt, A. A., Meyer-Bahlburg, H. F. L., Bell, J. J., & Morishima, A. (1991). Cognitive ability and everyday functioning in women with Turner syndrome. *Journal of Learning Disabilities, 24*(1), 32–39.

Dykens, E. M., Hodapp, R. M., Ort, S. I., & Leckman, J. F. (1993). Trajectory of adaptive behavior in males with fragile X syndrome. *Journal of Autism and Developmental Disorders, 23,* 135–145.

Eaves, R. C. (1992). Autism. In P. J. McLaughlin & P. Wehman (Eds.), *Developmental disabilities: A handbook for best practices* (pp. 68–81). Stoneham, MA: Butterworth-Heinemann.

Eliason, M. J. (1991). Cleft lip and palate: Developmental effects. *Journal of Pediatric Nursing, 6*(2), 107–113.

Emery, A. E. H. (1998). The muscular dystrophies. *British Medical Journal, 317,* 991–996.

Evenhuis, H. M. (1990). The natural history of dementia in Down's syndrome. *Archives of Neurology, 47,* 263–277.

Eyman, R. K., Call, T. L., & White, J. F. (1991). Life expectancy of persons with Down syndrome. *American Journal on Mental Retardation, 95*(6), 603–612.

Fishler, K., & Koch, R. (1991). Mental development in Down syndrome mosaicism. *American Journal of Mental Deficiency, 96,* 345–351.

FRAXA Research Foundation. (July, 2002). Are there any treatments available? Retrieved December 2, 2003 from *http://fraxa.org/html/about_treatment.htm*

Gaylor, A. S. & Reilly, J. C. (2002). Therapy with macrolides in patients with cystic fibrosis. *Pharmacotherapy, 22*(2), 227–239.

Guyer, M. S., & Collins, F. S. (1993). The Human Genome Project and the future of medicine. *American Journal of Diseases of Children, 147,* 1145–1151.

Haan, E. A. (1990). Ethics and the new genetics. *Journal of Paediatric and Child Health, 26,* 177–179.

Hagerman, R. (1992). Medical aspects of the fragile X syndrome. In B. B. Shopmeyer & F. Lowe (Eds.), *The fragile X child* (pp. 19–29). San Diego: Singular Publishing Group.

Hall, J. G., & Gilchrist, D. M. (1990). Turner syndrome and its variants. *Current Issues in Pediatric and Adolescent Endocrinology, 17*(1), 1421–1440.

Hardy, J. D. (1988). *Hardy's textbook of surgery,* 2nd ed. Philadelphia: J. B. Lippincott.

Hayes, C., Rarback, S., Berry, B., & Clancy, M. (1987). Managing PKU: An update. *Maternal/Child Nursing, 12,* 119–123.

Holden, C. (1997). A gene is linked to autism. *Science, 276,* 905.

Human Genome Project Information. (2002). Human Genome Project Progress. Retrieved October 2, 2002 from *http://www.ornl.gov/hgmis/ project/progress.html*

Hurtig, A., & Viera, A. (1986). *Sickle cell disease: Psychological and psychosocial issues.* Urbana, IL: University of Illinois Press.

Johnson, R. C., & Abelson, R. B. (1969). Intellectual, behavioral, and physical characteristics associated with trisomy, translocation, and mosaic types of Down syndrome. *American Journal of Mental Deficiency, 73*(6), 852–855.

Keenan, J., Kastner, T., Nathanson, R., Richardson, N., Hinton, J., & Cress, D. (1992). A statewide public and professional education program on fragile X syndrome. *Mental Retardation, 30,* 355–361.

Knell, E. R., & Comings, D. E. (1993). Tourette's syndrome and attention-deficit-hyperactivity disorder: Evidence for a genetic relationship. *Journal of Clinical Psychiatry, 54*(9), 331–337.

Koop-Hoolihan, L. E., Van Loan, M. D., Mentzer, W. C., Heyman, M. B. (1999). Elevated resting energy expenditure in adolescents with sickle cell anemia. *Journal of the American Dietetic Association, 99,* 195–199.

Kurlan, R. (1992). The pathogenesis of Tourette's syndrome: A possible role for hormonal and excitatory neurotransmitter influences in brain development. *Archives of Neurology, 49,* 874–876.

Leckman, J. F., Zhang, H., Vitale, A., Lahnin, F., Lynch, K., Bondi, C., Kim, Y., Peterson, B. S. Course of tic severity in Tourette syndrome: The first two decades. *Pediatrics, 102,* 14–20.

Lerer, R. J. (1987). Motor tics, Tourette syndrome, and learning disabilities. *Journal of Learning Disabilities, 20,* 266–267.

Levi, S. L. (1991). *The Tourette Syndrome Association, Inc. Journal of Learning Disabilities, 24*(1), 16–22.

Lynn, D. J., Woda, R. P., & Mendell, J. R. (1994). Respiratory dysfunction in muscular dystrophy and other myopathies. *Clinics in Chest Medicine, 15*(4), 661–674.

Marcell, M. M., & Cohen, S. (1992). Hearing abilities of Down syndrome and other mentally handicapped adolescents. *Research in Developmental Disabilities, 13,* 533–551.

March of Dimes. (1987). *Genetic counseling.* Spokane, WA: March of Dimes Birth Defects Foundation.

March of Dimes. (1992). *Genetic testing and gene therapy* (No. 09-576-00). White Plains, NY: Author.

Marlowe, K. F., & Chicella, M. F. (2002). Treatment of sickle cell pain. *Pharmacotherapy, 22*(4), 484–491.

Mathur, A., Stekol, L., Schatz, D., Maclaren, N. K., Scott, M. L., & Lippe, B. (1991). The parental origin of the single X chromosome in Turner syndrome: Lack of correlation with parental age or clinical phenotype. *American Journal of Human Genetics, 48,* 682–686.

Mauk, J. E. (1993). Autism and pervasive developmental disorders. *Pediatric Clinics of North America, 40*(3), 567–578.

Mazzocco, M. M. M., Baumgardner, T., Freund, I. S., Reiss, A. L. (1998). Social functioning among girls with fragile X or Turner syndrome and their sisters. *Journal of Autism and Developmental Disabilities, 28,* 509–516.

McCarthy, M. (1999). Inhaled antibiotics effective for cystic fibrosis. *The Lancet,* (9148), 215.

McClennen, S. (1992). Cognitive characteristics, assessment, and intervention in fragile X syndrome. In B. B. Shopmeyer & F. Lowe (Eds.), *The fragile X child* (pp. 33–58). San Diego: Singular Publishing Group, Inc.

McInerny, T. G. (1985). Cleft palate repair—surgical procedure and nursing care. *AORN Journal, 42,* 516–527.

Meryash, D. L. (1985). *The fragile X syndrome.* (Report No. MF01/PC05). Silver Spring, MD: American Association of University Affiliated Programs for Persons with Developmental Disabilities. (ERIC Document Reproduction Service No. ED 276 194)

Meryash, D. L. (1992). Characteristics of fragile X relatives with different attitudes toward terminating an affected pregnancy. *American Journal of Mental Retardation, 96,* 528–535.

Milerad, J., Larson, O., Hagberg, C., & Ideberg, M. (1997). Associated malformations in infants with cleft lip and palate: A prospective, population-based study. *Pediatrics, 100,* 180–187.

Murray, J. B. (1997). Psychophysiological aspects of Tourette's syndrome. *The Journal of Psychology, 131,* 615–621.

Nagel, R. L. (1993). Sickle cell anemia is a multigene disease: Sickle painful crises, a case in point. *American Journal of Hematology, 42,* 96–101.

National Institute of Health. (1990). Ethical, legal and social implications of the human genome initiative. *NIH Guide for Grants and Contracts, 19*(4), 12–14.

Nyhan, W. (1990). Phenylketonuria. In M. Buyse (Ed.), *Birth defects encyclopedia* (pp. 1382–1383). Dover, MA: Center for Birth Defects Information Services, Inc.

Orr, T. J., Myles, B. S., & Carlson, J. K. (1998). The impact of rhythmic entrainment on a person with autism. *Focus on Autism and Other Developmental Disabilities, 13,* 163–167.

O'Sullivan, H. (1998). Use and design of genetic screening programmes: A study. *Journal of Biological Education, 32,* 97–103.

Piven, J., Palmer, P., Jacobi, D., & Childress, D. (1997). Broader autism phenotype: Evidence from a family history study of multiple-incidence autism families. *The American Journal of Psychiatry, 154,* 185–190.

Pollack, C. V. (1993). Emergencies in sickle cell disease. *Emergency Medicine Clinics of North America, 11*(2), 365–378.

Pueschel, S. M. (1991). Ethical considerations relating to prenatal disagnosis of fetuses with Down syndrome. *Mental Retardation, 29*(4), 185–190.

Pueschel, S. M., Jackson, M. D., Giesswein, P., Dean, M. K., & Pezzullo, J. C. (1991). Thyroid function in Down syndrome. *Research in Developmental Disabilities, 12,* 287–296.

Reiss, A. L., & Freund, L. (1990). Fragile X syndrome. *Biological Psychiatry, 27,* 223–240.

Richman, L. (1978). The effect of facial disfigurement on teachers' perception of ability in cleft palate children. *Cleft Palate Journal, 15,* 155–157.

Risley, M. S. (1986). *Chromosome structure and function.* New York: Van Nostrand Reinhold.

Rogers, R. C., & Simensen, R. J. (1987). Fragile X syndrome: A common etiology of mental retardation. *American Journal of Mental Deficiency, 91,* 445–449.

Rosen, A. R. (1996). Tourette's syndrome: The school experience. *Clinical Pediatrics, 35,* 467–470.

Rosenfeld, M., Casey, S., Pepe, M., & Ramsey, B. W. (1999). Nutritional effects of long-term gastrostomy feedings in children with cystic fibrosis. *Journal of the American Dietetic Association, 99,* 191–196.

Rovet, J. F. (1990). *The cognitive and neuropsychological characteristics of females with Turner syndrome.* In D. B. Berch & B. G. Berger (Eds.), *Sex chromosome abnormalities and human behavior* (pp. 38–77). Boulder, CO: Westview.

Rovet, J. F. (1993). The psychoeducational characteristics of children with Turner syndrome. *Journal of Learning Disabilities, 26*(5), 333–341.

Rynders, J. E., & Horrobin, J. M. (1990). Always trainable? Never educable? Updating educational expectations concerning children with Down syndrome. *American Journal on Mental Retardation, 95*(1), 77–83.

Sach, B. P., & Korf, B. (1993). The human genome project: Implications for the practicing obstetrician. *Obstetrics and Gynecology, 81*(3), 458–462.

Sallee, F. R., Nesbitt, L., Jackson, C., Sine, L., & Sethuraman, G. (1997). Relative efficacy of haloperidol and pimozide in children and adolescents with Tourette's disorder. *The American Journal of Psychiatry, 154,* 1057–1062.

Santos, C. C., & Massey, E. W. (1990). Tourette's syndrome: Tics, jerks and quirks. *Postgraduate Medicine, 87*(1), 71–74.

Santos, K. E. (1992). Fragile X syndrome: An educator's role in identification prevention, and intervention. *Remedial and Special Education, 13,* 32–39.

Scientists forecast new approaches for developing treatments. (1989, September). *Cystic Fibrosis Foundation Commitment,* p. 2.

Schmidt, M. (1997). Fragile X syndrome: Diagnosis, treatment and research. *Journal of the American Medical Association, 277,* 1169.

Schwartz, I. S., & Sandall, S. R. (1998). Outcomes for children with autism: Three case studies. *Topics in Early Childhood Special Education, 18,* 132–144.

Serjeant, G. R. (1985). *Sickle cell disease.* New York: Oxford University Press.

Shapiro, B. S. (1989). The management of pain in sickle cell disease. *Pediatric Clinics of North America, 36,* 1029–1045.

Shapiro, E., & Shapiro, A. K. (1981). Tic disorders. *Journal of the American Medical Association, 245,* 1583–1585.

Shapiro, F., & Specht, L. (1993). The diagnosis and orthopaedic treatment of inherited muscular diseases of childhood. *The Journal of Bone and Joint Surgery, 75*(3), 430–454.

Simensen, R. J., & Rogers, R. C. (1989). School psychology and medical diagnosis: The fragile X syndrome. *Psychology in the Schools, 26,* 380–389.

Solomon, L. (July, 2002). Researchers seek answers to Down syndrome. *WebMD Medical News.* Retrieved December 2, 2003 from *http://content.health.msn.com/content/article/3608.1134*

Steffens, M. L., Oiler, D. K., Lynch, M., & Urbano, R. C. (1992). Vocal development in infants with Down syndrome and infants who are developing normally.

American Journal on Mental Retardation, 97(2), 235–246.

Stullenbarger, B., Norris, J., Edgil, A. E., & Prosser, M. J. (1987). Family adaptation to cystic fibrosis. *Pediatric Nursing, 13,* 29–31.

Sudhalter, V., Cohen, I., Silverman, W., & Wolf-Schein, E. G. (1990). Conversational analyses of males with fragile X, Down syndrome and autism: Comparison of the emergence of deviant language. *American Journal of Mental Retardation, 94,* 431–441.

Temple, C. M., & Carney, R. A. (1993). Intellectual functioning of children with Turner syndrome: A comparison of behavioural phenotypes. *Developmental Medicine and Child Neurology, 35,* 691–698.

Thompson, M. W., McInnes, R. R., & Willard, H. F. (1991). *Genetics in medicine* (5th ed.). Philadelphia: Saunders.

Thompson, R. J., Gil, K. M., Abrams, M. R., & Phillips, G. (1992). Stress, coping, and psychological adjustment of adults with sickle cell disease. *Journal of Consulting and Clinical Psychology, 60,* 433–440.

Tordjman, S., Ferrari, P., Sulmont, V., Duyme, M., & Roubertoux, P. (1997). Androgenic activity in autism. *The American Journal of Psychiatry, 154,* 1626–1627.

Torup, E. (1972). A follow-up study of children with tics. *Acta Paediatricia Scandinavica, 51,* 261–268.

Turner, G., Robinson, H., Wake, S., Laing, S., & Partington, M. (1997). Case finding for the fragile X syndrome and its consequences. *British Medical Journal, 315*(7117), 1223–1226.

Vanderas, A. P. (1987). Incidence to cleft lip and palate among races: A review. *Cleft Palate Journal, 24,* 216–225.

Wachtel, T. J., & Pueschel, S. M. (1991). Macrocytosis in Down syndrome. *American Journal on Mental Retardation, 95*(4), 417–420.

Walkup, J. T., Leckman, J. F., Price, A., Hardin, M., Ort, S. L., & Cohen, D. J. (1988). The relationship between obsessive-compulsive disorder and Tourette syndrome: A twin study. *Psychopharmacology Bulletin, 24*(3), 375–379.d.

White-Williams, C. (2002). Lung transplantation. *Medscape,* Retrieved December 2, 2003 from *http://www. medscape.com/viewarticle/436545*

Williams, J. K., Richman, L. C., & Yarbrough, D. B. (1992). Comparison of visual-spatial performance strategy training in children with Turner syndrome and learning disabilities. *Journal of Learning Disabilities, 25,* 658–664.

Wilson, P. G., & Mazzocco, M. M. (1993). Awareness and knowledge of fragile X syndrome among special educators. *Mental Retardation, 97*(4), 221–227.

Wing, L. (1997). The autistic spectrum. *The Lancet, 350,* 1761–1766.

Wolff, P., Gardner, J., Paccia, J., & Lappen, J. (1989). The greeting behavior of fragile X males. *American Journal of Mental Retardation, 93,* 406–411.

Yetter, J. F. (1992). Cleft lip and cleft palate. *American Family Physician, 46*(4), 1211–1219.

Zinn, A. R., Page, D. C., & Fisher, E. M. C. (1993). Turner syndrome: The case of the missing sex chromosome. *Trends in Genetics, 9*(3), 90–93.

8   *Sensory Impairments and Infections*

This chapter is devoted to the effects of bacterial and viral infections on developing fetuses, neonates, and infants. While some of the diseases resulting from these invasive organisms are negligible, other infections can cause severe and multiple disabilities or even death. Though there are many other causes of vision and hearing losses, sensory impairments, especially in vision and hearing, are often the result of a significant infection in a neonate or young child.

HEARING IMPAIRMENTS

Hearing is the act of receiving and processing sound vibrations. The auditory mechanisms within the ear permit humans to discriminate differential sound waves within their environment. Yet, a large number of children have degraded or impoverished hearing which affects their ability to remember, requires more time and effort to process incoming auditory information, and consequently interrupts their ability to communicate effectively (Jerger & Martin, 1995). Approximately 1 child in 22 experiences some type of hearing loss at birth or soon after (National Institute of Health Consensus Statement [NIHCS], 1999). Of those, 65% are born with a hearing loss, and another 12% develop this disability within their first 3 years of life.

HEARING PROCESS

The auditory mechanism is functionally separated into three components: external, middle, and inner ear (see Figure 8–1). The **external ear**, consisting of the auricle, auditory canal, and tympanic membrane, is responsible for collecting sound waves. Physical energy is channeled down the auditory canal, where it vibrates the tympanic membrane (eardrum).

The **middle ear** cavity lies beyond the tympanic membrane. Sound vibrations are mechanically transmitted from the tympanic membrane to stimulate, in sequence, three tiny bones: the malleus (hammer), incus (anvil), and stapes (stirrup). The latter is attached to a small opening that leads to the inner ear, referred to as the oval window. The **eustachian tube** intersects the middle ear to form a continuous passage to the throat. The purpose of the eustachian tube is to equalize internal and external air pressure on the tympanic membrane. Excessive

Figure 8–1
Anatomy of the Ear

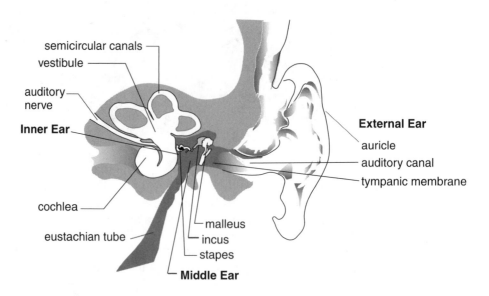

semicircular canals

vestibule

auditory nerve

Inner Ear

cochlea

eustachian tube

malleus
incus
stapes

Middle Ear

External Ear
auricle
auditory canal
tympanic membrane

Figure 8–2
Pathway of
Sound Through
Outer, Middle,
and Inner Ear

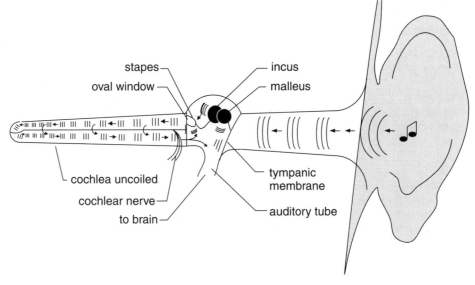

buildup of pressure within the middle ear can cause the sensitive tympanic membrane to rupture.

Sound waves traveling to the **inner ear** from the vibration of the eardrum and bones of the middle ear are transmitted through the oval window to the **cochlea** (see Figure 8–2). Tiny nerve endings within the cochlea, referred to as hair cells, are stimulated by the movement of cochlear fluid. The resulting energy (now electrical) is transferred to the temporal area of the brain by way of the eighth cranial nerve, or **auditory nerve**. Contained within the inner ear are the **vestibule** and the three **semicircular canals**; these structures also contain neural hair cells. Movement of these cells, caused by forces of gravity and motion, provides information through the eighth cranial nerve to the brain regarding the body's equilibrium status.

HEARING LOSS

Sounds are heard along two dimensions: loudness and pitch. Pitch is determined by the frequency of sound waves. Normally, speech sounds range between frequencies of 500 and 2,000 cycles per second. Loudness, or sound intensity, is measured in decibels (dB), and hearing is considered normal when sound is audible at 10 dB. Hearing losses, which range from slight (sound audible at 15–25 dB) to profound (sound audible at more than 90 dB), are the result of a variety of insults to the auditory system.

Approximately 50% of hearing losses have an unknown cause. The etiology, location, and severity of damage to the ear are variables used in determining immediate and long-range treatment for children with hearing loss (see Table 8–1). A **conductive hearing loss** is one that disrupts mechanical conduction of sound as it is transferred from the outer ear through the middle ear. Though several factors can contribute to a conductive hearing loss, most causes can be treated effectively

Table 8–1   Factors That Place Children At Risk of Hearing Loss

Prenatal/Natal Period	After Neonatal Period	Treatments
TORCH Diseases Cytomegalovirus*	Head Trauma†	Cochlear Implants
Rubella* Herpes*	Neurodegenerative Diseases	Assistive Devices (Hearing Aides)

Toxoplasmosis*
  Syphilis*
	Childhood Diseases
	  Mumps*
	  Measles*
	Bacterial Meningitis*
	Noise-Induced Hearing Loss	

Otitis Media*		Vibrotactile Aids
Craniofacial Anomalies Cleft Palate†		
Tinnitus (ringing in the ears)		
Otosclerosis		

Genetic
  Waardenburg Syndrome
  Usher Syndrome
  Treacher-Collins Syndrome
  Albinism
  Down Syndrome†
  Family History		

Low Birth Weight (<1,500)†		
Hyperbilirubinemia†		
Severe Depression at Birth		
Ototoxic Drugs		

*Covered in this chapter and covered elsewhere in this text.
†Covered elsewhere in this text.
Source: From *Hearing in Children* (3rd ed.), by J. Northern and M. Downs, 1984, Baltimore: Lippincott Williams & Wilkins. Reprinted with permission.

and efficiently through medical intervention. Furthermore, the degree of hearing loss for most conductive etiologies ranges from mild to moderate. The most common cause of hearing loss is **otitis media**, or middle ear disease.

Otitis media is the most common cause of conductive hearing loss in children. Either viral or bacterial infections cause a buildup of fluid in the middle ear and eustachian tube, which reduces mobility of the membranes and bones necessary to adequately transfer sound intensity to the inner ear. Symptoms of otitis media are a red, bulging tympanic membrane, frequent ear pulling, and irritability. A single infection usually will result in only temporary and mild hearing loss. However, chronic middle ear disease (serous otitis media) can result in a more persistent and significant hearing loss that might substantially interrupt normal acquisition of language. Treatment of otitis media includes myringotomy (tubes placed through the eardrum to drain fluid), antihistimines (to reduce swelling of the eustachian tube), and antibiotics, which will generally work with bacterial infections, even though most middle ear infections are viral.

Conductive hearing losses are common in children with a variety of disabilities. For example, children with Down syndrome are at increased risk of middle ear infection for two reasons:

◆ A depressed immune response system
◆ An anomaly resulting in a more horizontal than normal eustachian tube, which prevents adequate drainage of the middle ear

Similarly, serous otitis media is quite common in children with cleft palates, whose eustachian tube drainage is hindered by the palate malformation.

Sensorineural hearing losses result from damage to the cochlea or auditory nerve hindering the brain from receiving sound messages. Genetic inheritance accounts for well over half of known abnormalities that result in serious sensorineural hearing loss. There are several hundred known genetic syndromes, with recent research showing that many of these are the consequence of multiple gene involvement (Current progress, 1995). Noise, such as jet engine, rifle fire, and loud music can cause sensorineural hearing loss or "noise induced deafness." Unlike conductive hearing losses, sensorineural hearing losses require amplification or surgery to improve hearing.

Intrauterine infections also account for a large percentage of serious sensorineural hearing impairments. Toxoplasmosis, maternal rubella contracted during the first trimester, herpes, mumps, syphilis, and cytomegalovirus are all associated with malformations that result in hearing loss. Meningitis, a bacterial infection, is the leading postnatal cause of hearing loss, accounting for 10% of acquired deafness in the United States (Kaplan, 1997). Bacterial meningitis affects the structure of the delicate snail-shaped cochlea.

Neonates and premature infants also are at risk of acquiring hearing losses. For example, asphyxia of infants during delivery may damage the cochlea, resulting in sensorineural hearing loss. High bilirubin levels resulting in severe jaundice may also cause permanent damage to the central nervous system. Other neonatal factors include cerebral hemorrhage, apnea, and, in some cases, antibiotic drugs, which can become toxic.

An uncategorized, but very real, hearing loss is referred to as a central auditory processing disorder (CAPD). A child who experiences CAPD has difficulty filtering speech messages, even though hearing tests reveal normal acoustical sensitivity (Atlantic Coast, 2002). Perceived as sensory overload, messages which lack redundancy (e.g., minimal repetition of content), are particularly difficult for children with CAPD to decode. Like children with other types of hearing losses, those with CAPD benefit from interventions which focus on heightened attentiveness and minimized interference to communication.

IDENTIFICATION OF HEARING LOSS

Though the critical period of language development is during the first 3 years of life, the average age at which children are diagnosed with a hearing loss is close to age 3 (NIHCS, 1993). The National Institute of Health concluded that one factor contributing to delayed identification is the practice of screening only

Case Study   MADDY'S MENINGITIS AND ITS EFFECTS: INTERVIEW WITH KIM SHAFER

When Maddy was only two months old, she woke one day, listless and not herself. Just to be safe, I took her into the doctor's office and he didn't seem that concerned until he touched the top of her head. Within 30 seconds he was back in the room telling me that we were going to the hospital by ambulance and that she possibly had meningitis.

It was then I learned what that soft spot was on the top of her head and how important that was. It's where the two pieces of the brain haven't merged yet. And that soft spot actually tells you if there is any swelling in the brain. Usually, it should be soft and dipped, but this time it was swollen which meant the fluid and swelling from Maddy's spine had already built up around her brain.

So, we spent 12 scary days in the hospital and Maddy seemed to come back pretty fast. We knew another baby was in the hospital at the same time fighting for her life, so we thought we were pretty lucky. Lots of prayers were answered.

Two days after she was released from the hospital, we went to her doctor for a check-up. We were thinking that we'd have to take Maddy to physical therapy or occupational therapy because the meningitis caused her to lose all her muscle control so she was like a newborn again. She couldn't lift her head or roll over, so we expected that challenge, but it was something we were okay with. I remembered there had been a test done in the hospital, and I asked the doctor if he'd gotten the results back. Oh, Gosh! It was like he'd forgotten, so I figured it must not be a big deal. I had just sent my husband and my other daughter to the restroom.

But when the doctor came back into the room, he said the two sentences that I will never forget in all my life. "It looks like she's going to be deaf. The other doctor is concerned with the results of the test." I was just standing there thinking, what did he just tell me? I was thinking that my husband was not there, and my kids wouldn't understand this. I was alone and terrified and confused, and

high-risk children—thereby eliminating up to half of those infants with hearing impairments. Even after parents suspect a hearing loss, the delay is normally one year before the child receives formal testing. Early identification of hearing loss would enable families and practitioners to plan and implement a remedial program to enhance cognitive and social development. Management of hearing loss within 1 year of birth appears to alleviate most of the adverse affects on communication, psychological problems, and functional capabilities (Kennedy, Kim, Dees, Campbell, & Thornton, 1998).

Two tools are considered the most efficient in screening newborns for hearing loss because they measure brain activity rather than physical responses to sound (NIHCS, 1993). The first, auditory brain stem response (ABS), can be conducted without sedating an infant and is highly accurate. Sounds are presented through earphones while an infant sleeps and brain responses are measured through electrodes taped to the infant's head. Evoked otoacoustic emissions (EOAE) is a relatively new screening procedure that is less costly and less complex while still being highly sensitive. In this case, a tiny microscope is placed in the ear canal to

I'd have to repeat this to my husband when he came back to the room. I felt so all alone and not sure what this was all about.

I had never known a deaf person in my life. I'd never had that exposure; neither had my husband. We went out to the parking lot, cried our eyes out and said, "Okay, where do we go from here?"

Then, in the mail we got this letter that told us that the Deaf Service Center had sign language classes and they would make home visits where they came out to your house and actually sat down with you. We started sign language classes there once a week. Maddy and I would go and she'd play in the other room and I'd sit down with a couple of other parents. The other parents were a great resource for me because they had already gone through the things I was now going through. We became really close friends and learned sign language together.

Maddy started the sign language program when she was about 4½ months old and by 7 months old she was starting to sign. "Wow! She's communicating! This is really cool!" Her first words were "more," because she could get more, and "candy." At that time, Maddy also got hearing aids.

Mark, Kim, Amanda, Cassie, and Maddy Shafer.

We used the hearing aids, but at 18 months, the ear, nose, and throat specialist said, "You know, they have a great device called a cochlear implant that you should think about because the hearing aids don't seem to be working." I was thinking, Gosh! She's only 18 months old, have we really given this a good try? I mean she couldn't yet communicate back to us. So we asked the sign language therapist if she could really tell us whether Maddy was hearing or not. I just wasn't ready for an implant yet, so I put it off.

detect sounds "sent-out" by the movement of cochlear hair cells in the inner ear. Even though a patient being screened must remain still for 2 to 5 minutes, this test is particularly useful for infants and young children who will not or cannot cooperate with more rigorous procedures. After children are 6 months old, it is possible to conduct behavioral testing in which they are trained to consistently respond to the emission of a noise. However, this procedure requires well-trained professionals and is less reliable when used with infants who have developmental delays.

DEVELOPMENTAL IMPLICATIONS AND RESOLUTIONS

Children with hearing losses are identified early when they fail to startle, do not localize sounds, and have delayed acquisition of language milestones. In some cases, hearing losses are misdiagnosed as cognitive delays. The developmental domain most directly affected by hearing loss in infancy is language. However, children with hearing losses generally score within the normal intelligence range when tested on nonverbal measures. Social skills may also be affected since interpersonal communication is considered an essential component of social interactions.

Two factors are related to the interaction between hearing loss and developmental progress. First, since it is estimated that the ability to learn language peaks between age 2 and 4, it is critical to identify hearing loss early and to provide adaptive intervention at the earliest possible age. Second, the age of onset and degree of hearing loss influence the degree to which children's language and cognitive skills will be affected. Because of this relationship, it is believed that a large percentage of preschoolers with hearing impairment could be dually diagnosed with learning disabilities (Mauk & Mauk, 1992).

There are several augmentative communication systems that should be considered early. Sign language systems, which use hand gestures to communicate, include American Sign Language (ASL), Signing Exact English (SEE-II), and cued speech. American Sign Language is considered a unique language with its own sentence and word structure (syntax and morphology) and is widely used by adults with deafness. This language is the most efficient manual communication system. By contrast, SEE-II resembles spoken and written English in sentence/ word structure and usage and may therefore facilitate the acquisition of written language skills and academic skills.

It is important that children with hearing losses not only learn manual sign, but also be taught to make use of residual hearing, speech (lip) reading, and oral speech to communicate. Since most individuals in our society communicate through speech and do not know manual sign, children will be most able to communicate with hearing persons if they also learn to supplement sign with conventional language modalities. Yet even the most observant and well-trained deaf children will not catch a majority of speech messages when relying only on residual hearing and speech reading. **Total communication** combines manual sign with oral methods of communication and is the most frequently adopted approach.

Assistive devices for children with hearing losses include hearing aids, which amplify the sound. These devices should be fitted at an early age to encourage hearing perception and listening skills necessary for language development. Hearing aids assist but do not replace natural hearing abilities. However, significant progress has been made in eliminating irrelevant background noise. "Completely-in-the-ear-canal" (CIC) aids and the invention of directional microphones allow for more natural amplification. Yet, young children do not automatically link the sounds heard through amplification to the sounds' sources. They must be taught to pay attention to sounds, to orient toward sound sources, and to discriminate between relevant and irrelevant noises. Various amplification devices are available and must be matched specifically to each child's characteristics: age, degree of hearing loss, family environment, and cognitive abilities.

Assisted listening devices (ALDs) are an alternative to the hearing aids in certain situations where the speaker can be separated from the amplifier. When possible, this separation eliminates much of the background noise that makes it difficult for wearers of hearing aids to filter relevant incoming information. Although ALDs cannot replace hearing aids, they can improve the performance of hearing aids and are especially useful if hearing loss is limited to specific environments. Four types of ALD devices are available (Atlantic Coast, 2002):

◆ Hardwire: In one-to-one situation, the hearing person wears the microphone which has a thin wire running to receiver on the person with the hearing loss.
◆ FM: Radio signal, often used in classrooms with children with hearing losses.
◆ Infrared: An infrared signal is emitted from TV or at movies to the person wearing the receiver. This requires a direct line-of-sight from an infrared source to the receiver.
◆ Loop: A loop of wire is placed around the perimeter of a room to serve as a transmitter by generating an electromagnetic field which can be picked up by a receiver.

Some children with deafness are candidates for cochlear implants. Cochlear implants are electronic devices that can be implanted by surgery to transform sound vibrations into nerve impulses for transmission to the brain. Such transmission stimulates nerve cells for children with bilateral sensorineural hearing loss. Children as young as 2 years of age can have a cochlear implant surgically placed. The devices do not restore normal hearing, but when used with speech reading, cochlear implants allow a greater understanding of speech. Each generation of cochlear implants improves the degree of satisfying acoustical information available to patients. To date, however, cochlear implants have not been a panacea. For example, these devices might be of limited use to children with multiple disabilities and those whose hearing loss preceded language acquisition.

Preschool programs serving children with hearing impairments require some unique considerations. Harrington and Meyers (1992) made the following recommendations:

1. Access services by personnel with certification competencies for teachers of preschool children with hearing impairments as delineated by the Council of Education for the Deaf.
2. Use transdisciplinary teaming, including an occupational therapist, physical therapist, psychologist, social worker, counselor, audiologist, speech-language pathologist, educator of the deaf, and a parent, to collaborate in assessment and planning.
3. Obtain oral interpreters and/or sign interpreters as needed for children with profound deafness in mainstream settings.
4. Adapt classrooms so that ceilings and walls use acoustical tiles, floors are carpeted, and visible fire alarm systems are installed.
5. Furnish classes with amplification systems (e.g., FM auditory training system), captioning equipment, computer software designed for children with hearing impairments, and telecommunication devices (TDD) to interact with parents who are deaf and members of the deaf community.

As noted by Harrington and Meyers (1992), accommodation of classrooms for children with hearing impairments is expensive and will challenge service providers who are already uncertain of financial resources. Moreover, controversial findings on the relative benefits of integrated versus self-contained programs for children with hearing impairments fail to provide overwhelming support for such costly modifications in regular classrooms. While some argue that integrated programs will lead to greater social and emotional competency as well as improved communication skills in a mainstream setting (Ryalls & Larouche, 1992), others argue that the effect is just the opposite. Opponents of integration believe that children with hearing losses will be isolated from their peers who lack the skills to communicate effectively, and that children with hearing losses will suffer socially and emotionally. In one study, self-reporting children who were hearing impaired and educated in integrated settings rated their self-confidence and social competence higher than their peers in residential programs (Cartledge & Cochran, 1996). While more study is needed, it does at least appear that placing students in integrated settings does not harm children socially as many educators and parents have feared.

People with deafness differ from people with other disabilities in that they have developed their own social communities of peers and deaf culture. Segregation of this culture, largely self-selected, has led to controversy that directly affects parents of very young children with deafness. Even among those who are deaf, persons who acquire deafness adventitiously may be excluded (Darrow, 1993). In fact, Janesick (1990) argued for recognition of the Deaf community (big "D" for congenital deafness) as a distinct cultural and linguistic minority. Contending that inclusion in this community is something to be proud of, proponents of the movement shun attempts to bridge the communication gap.

Educating children with multiple disabilities poses more complex educational considerations. For example, children who are hearing impaired with learning disabilities may fail to thrive in highly structured environments which do not give them the opportunity to learn to adapt to natural changes in their environments (Mauk & Mauk, 1992). These children also tend to experience a greater degree of failure, whether integrated or segregated, and therefore require opportunities that enhance their level of success and self-esteem.

INFORMING AND WORKING WITH PARENTS

Unless the cause of hearing loss is known, parents of children with hearing losses should receive genetic counseling, since a large percentage of these children have inherited their disability. Very early in a child's life, parents of children with deafness must make a decision regarding linguistic instruction that will influence their child's entire life. Those parents who prefer their children be given every chance to become a part of the hearing world are likely to choose an educational program that emphasizes oral communication or total communication. Other parents might feel that an inclusive setting would result in social and communicative isolation, particularly since communities of deaf individuals are often very active socially and rely on sign language for communication. While a self-contained manual language does not necessarily preclude integration, this approach is usually paired with a philosophy of isolation and specialized educational programs. Still other parents, due to an absence of community resources or their economic circumstances, feel that they have little choice other than to accept the only services that are offered. Parents must be provided with objective information on the implications of educational choices—and the advocacy skills to negotiate alternative services in areas of restricted options. The National Institute on Deafness and other Communication Disorders (NIDCD, 1999) is one of the most comprehensive resources for parents and educators of children with hearing losses.

Through a variety of coordinated programs, NIDCD is engaged in continuing education, research, and dissemination of research and information. Linking parents to this and other helpful resources is made easier through emerging technology such as the Internet.

VISUAL IMPAIRMENTS

Visual acuity is measured by comparing the distance at which a person is able to see an object with clarity to the distance at which a person with average visual acuity (20/20) clearly sees the same object (see Figure 8–3). For example, what a person with 20/70 vision sees clearly only to 20 feet, a person with average visual acuity would be able to see accurately as far away as 70 feet. A visual impairment is legally defined as a visual acuity of 20/200 or less in the best eye with correction. Additionally, those whose peripheral field of vision is 20 degrees or less are considered legally blind, even though visual acuity might be normal (see Figure 8–4). **Low vision** is assessed when visual acuity is 20/70 or worse in the better eye with correction.

Figure 8–3
Visual Acuity:
20/20 Vision
Compared to
20/70 Vision

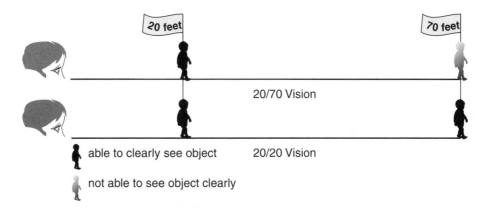

Figure 8–4
Peripheral
Vision

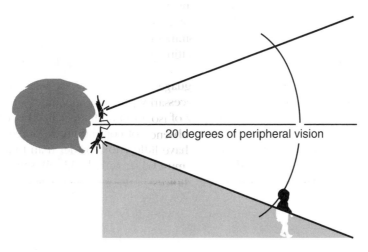

While legal blindness is a relatively low incidence disability (1 in 1,000), approximately 30% to 70% of children with severe visual loss experience one or more other disabilities (Kirchner, 1988). Unfortunately, the incidence of visual impairments has not declined, and may be rising in the United States. For example, recent advances in medical technology, which allow very premature and low-birth-weight infants to survive, has radically increased the incidence of children with retinopathy of prematurity (Uslan, 1983). Also, research has demonstrated a relationship between poverty and the incidence of visual impairments, and poverty rates for young children continue to increase (Chalifoux & Fagan, 1997). Thus, it can be projected that the incidence of visual impairments will also increase. On the other hand, many causes of visual impairments might be considered preventable. Goldstein (1980) estimated that two out of three of the cases of blindness worldwide might be prevented through control of infection and malnutrition.

It is believed that newborns have a visual acuity of 20/200 and that children do not develop normal visual acuity until about age 5 (Allen & Marotz, 1989). This "developmental visual impairment" combined with infants' cognitive immaturity make assessment of mild to moderate visual impairment unreliable before 6 months of age. More important to children and their families than the clinical determination of visual disability is the retention of functional visual abilities. According to Hoon (1991), professionals should emphasize to parents the importance of maximizing a child's residual vision for use in everyday activities rather than focusing on visual deficiencies.

VISUAL PROCESS

Entering light initially strikes the **cornea** of the eye, which serves both a protective and refractive function. The cornea bends the angle of light and channels that light through the fluid-filled anterior chamber. Once the light strikes the **lens**, accommodation takes place, in which the lens changes shape, becoming more or less spherical depending on the nearness of an object or the intensity of light. The elastic properties of the lens permit it to cause a constriction of the iris, which widens the pupil (opening in the eye) to regulate the amount of light entering the vitreous humor (**accommodation**). The **vitreous humor** is a second fluid-filled space lying behind the eye's lens, which maintains the internal pressure of the eye and shape of the eyeball. The rays passing through this chamber intersect at a focal point on or near the **retina**. The retina is a complex neurological network directly linked to the central nervous system; neural fibers from the retina gather to form the **optic nerve**, which transmits an electrical image to the occipital portion of the brain (see Figure 8–5). Here the visual cortex of the brain perceives and interprets the images.

Refractive Errors

Defects in the curvature of cornea and lens or abnormal eyeball shape change the focal point of light rays and are referred to as refractive errors. **Myopia**, or nearsightedness, results when the shape of the eyeball is abnormally long (or less frequently due to corneal or lens curvature), causing the image of a distant object to converge in front of the retina. Infants who are nearsighted see near objects nor-

Figure 8–5
Visual Process
and Eye
Anatomy

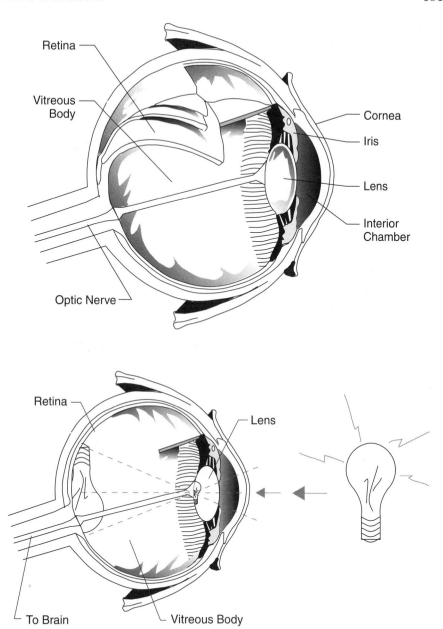

mally, while images of distant objects are distorted. The opposite is the case of **hyperopia**, or farsightedness, in which far objects are seen with greater acuity than near objects. In this case, the eyeball shape is abnormally short, and the image converges behind the retina. To remediate hyperopia and myopia, eyeglasses or contacts with an appropriately adjusted spherical (section) lens are placed before the eye. **Astigmatism** is caused when the cornea is abnormally shaped. An oval-shaped cornea will cause the light to be refracted unevenly. The fuzzy distortion that results from astigmatism can be corrected by using eyeglasses or contacts with parabolic- or toric-shaped lenses.

Errors in Binocular Vision

Six sets of muscles permit the eyes to act in concert to follow a moving object and to focus images correspondingly on both retinas. A disruption in this coordination will upset the correspondence and result in a double image being perceived by the cortex. In a chronic situation, referred to as **amblyopia**, the brain will suppress one of the images and the affected eye will begin to deteriorate in performance. **Strabismus**, also resulting from muscle dysfunction, is when the two eyes do not focus on the same image. One eye may be focused directly at an object and the other eye is turned elsewhere. Strabismus can usually be corrected through lenses, surgery, or muscle exercise programs. Untreated strabismus may progress into amblyopia.

Central Nervous System Dysfunctions

In instances where the eye physiology is not impaired, yet a child experiences loss of visual ability, there may be damage to the central nervous system. Damage to the optic nerve or the cerebral tissue within the occipital portion of the brain may cause **cortical visual impairments**. These visual losses may be complete or partial, though researchers have not been able to link the amount or type of loss to specific type of central nervous system damage (Hoon, 1991). Cortical visual loss may be paired with intrauterine and postnatal infection (e.g., syphilis, meningitis), traumatic brain injury (e.g., drowning), perinatal injury (e.g., anoxia), and seizures. Often, this type of visual impairment involves damage to the brain. Mental retardation may accompany cortical visual impairments.

Rhythmic eye twitching or tremors are referred to as **nystagmus**. The etiology of nystagmus may be either neurological or muscular, with the former generally associated with more serious visual impairments.

Just as with other areas of development, visual ability undergoes a normal progression from infancy through the preschool years. Lags in visual skills or deviations in the appearance of a child's eyes (e.g., redness, tearing, crusted, droopiness) can be assessed according to a developmental reference and indicate that intervention is needed (Optometric Extension, 1995). A visual specialist will be able to recommend methods of training visual skills.

CAUSES OF VISUAL IMPAIRMENT

Perhaps half of all cases of blindness may be genetic in origin (Bateman, 1983). Two common genetic causes of visual impairments are associated with genetic syndromes: albinism and Down syndrome. Down syndrome is a chromosomal aberration that is commonly associated with such visual disorders as severe myopia, cataracts, amblyopia, strabismus, glaucoma, and nystagmus (Shapiro & France, 1985). All children with Down syndrome should have regular ophthalmological examinations. Visual impairments accompanying **albinism** are related to a lack of melanin or pigmentosa. The eyes of a child with albinism lack color and are extremely sensitive to light, requiring tinted lenses. Nystagmus is also frequently associated with albinism.

The most common cause of congenital visual impairment is exposure to infections. Rubella may lead to retinopathy, cataracts, glaucoma, and structural malformations. Cytomegalovirus, toxoplasmosis, herpes simplex, and congenital syphilis are associated with visual impairments ranging from lesions to central nervous system malformations. Researchers are also just beginning to understand the relationship between HIV infection and visual impairments in children. Visual impairments can also be the result of exposure to dangerous chemicals prenatally (e.g., alcohol) or postnatally (e.g., lead).

A **cataract** is a clouding or opacity of the lens. The location and degree of deviation from transparency caused by the cataract(s) will determine the amount of distortion and obstruction of vision. The treatment of cataracts involves surgery to remove the portion of the lens affected. Corrective lenses are necessary to compensate for the lens removed in surgery.

Glaucoma is caused by a buildup of pressure in the anterior chamber of the eye. In most cases, the onset of glaucoma is unrecognized until much damage has already been done to peripheral vision. Untreated, glaucoma will cause continued serious visual loss or blindness. However, medical treatment (usually medication) can arrest the otherwise progressive degeneration of vision. Since children with other visual losses often have secondary visual problems, they should be observed throughout childhood for signs of glaucoma (i.e., excessive tiredness, severe headaches, dizziness, loss of field vision, and tearing).

Late visual bloomers include those children who, like children with motor, language, and social developmental delays, experience maturational delays in visual ability (Harel, Holtzman, & Feinsod, 1985). These children appear to be blind at birth and during their first months of life, but they typically develop normal visual ability by 18 months to 3 years. Research on delayed visual development is sparse, though it seems that the syndrome is associated with delays in development of specific processes of the central nervous system (e.g., myelination).

CLOSE-UP

CYBERSENSES AND THE FUTURE OF SEEING AND HEARING

Intervention for children who are born with or acquire hearing and visual losses may become less dependent on education and more reliant on medicine as the future unfolds. Technology is at the brink of bridging sensory input and direct neural input through the use of neural implants. Cochlear implants were the first generation of a rapidly evolving field of bionics that holds great promise for millions of persons worldwide with visual, hearing, and motoric limitations. Artificial sensing devices take advantage of both commercially available technology (e.g., microprocessors, TV cameras, mikes, advanced programming skills, imbedded technology) as well as newly emerging applications of cybernetics, cybermedicine, and nanotechnology.

More modest, though not yet perfected, technologies that may soon provide groundbreaking benefit for persons with visual impairments are eye transplants, retinal implants, and artificial visual eyes. An artificial "eye," in development by William Dobelle, uses a microvideocamera and utrasonic range finder mounted on a pair of sunglasses. The two stimuli communicate with a waist-mounted microcomputer that enhances the edges of visual images and sends these data to a second adjacent computer, which then sends signals to an array of implanted electrodes in the brain. Though still rudimentary in the processing of information, where vision is as if seeing shadows through foggy glass, the expected advancement of nanotechnology and research of brain functioning itself may render artificial vision viable in the near future. On a more spectacular scale, Kevin Warwick of England became his own experiment, when he implanted an electrode pin into a nerve in his arm and subsequently linked his nervous system to an external computer. His wife (also injected with an electrode) and he were able to send basic signals to each other through their respective nervous systems *vis a vis* a computer. Warwick was able to control an electronic hand by his thoughts and to "sense" the surface tension experienced by the electronic hand. Relevent to persons with visual impairment, a blindfolded Warwick was able to judge how near or far objects were from him when hooked up to a device that transmitted electronic pulses.

Persons who are deaf and those with hearing loss have been at the forefront of bionics with the constant improvement and application of cochlear implants. Additionally, bone-anchored hearing aids and auditory brain stem implants offer possible solutions for some who are not candidates for cochlear implants. Bionic ears use a microphone to detect sounds that are sent to a speech processor (outside the body) where the sounds are analyzed, processed, and converted to electronic signals. The signals are sent to a miniature array of electrodes in nerve cells of a listener's cochlea. From there, the stimuli are transmitted to the brain for interpretation. It is the role of a bionic ear's microprocessor software (constantly being refined) to filter background noise, attenuate loud noise, and enhance soft sounds.

Worth mentioning is that along with optimism related to bionic application for persons with sensory deficits should be a measure of understanding, if not caution, regarding parallel applications. Development of such fantastic possibilities carries with it certain questions regarding the probable evolution of humanity toward an almost certain merging of humans and computers. Before the end of this century, Cyborgs (cybernetic organisms) who posses such futuristic capacities as superhuman intellect, telepathic capabilities, communal thinking, and hypersensibilities may replace the hapless and heterogenous human beings that currently populate the earth. Like almost every revolution in science in the past century, this technology will be upon us before society has an opportunity to weigh in on a change that will have such broad consequences.

Source: Kevin Warwick's website at *http://www.kevinwarwick.org*.

DEVELOPMENTAL IMPLICATIONS AND RESOLUTIONS

Children with visual impairments, particularly those with other disabilities, display unusual patterns of eye contact. Yet, one of the first intentional acts of infants is eye gaze. Normal language, cognition, and social skill development, are dependent on eye gaze which sets the occasion for social and language interactions and provides visual memory that enables infants to feel "safe" in exploring their world (Morse, 1991). To mediate the visual attentional differences in children with visual impairments, Morse made the following recommendations to caregivers: develop a trusting interpersonal relationship; establish routine play and social interactions; use clear, colorful (if relevant), and closely spaced cues to attend; reduce irrelevant sensory information.

Children who are visually impaired will usually experience delays in other areas as well, even when they possess normal intelligence. Muscle tone is likely to be hypotonic since normal mobility is generally impeded (Teplin, 1983). Because language development depends on imitation of mouth movements as well as nonverbal language cues, children who are visually impaired often experience delays in speech development as well as in conversational abilities. This inability to see nonverbal cues and subtle forms of language may result in self-orientation or social isolation (Hoon, 1991). Finally, children with blindness frequently present stereotypical behaviors such as rocking or postural abnormalities (Batshaw & Perret, 1988).

One factor affecting the interaction between visual impairments and later functioning is the timing of onset. **Congenital** (born with) blindness and **adventitious** blindness (developed later) differentially affect the type of intervention a child might need. Because adventitious blindness occurs after a child has had visual experiences, such children are able to "picture" images of their world conceptually, if not visually, after sight is lost.

The primary goal of early intervention is to have children make the best use of their residual vision. According to Morse (1991), special training is needed to teach infants with blindness to "pay attention." Paying attention requires that infants learn to screen out irrelevant sensory stimuli while vigilantly seeking new information. Additionally, infants must learn to use previously gained information in new situations to make decisions. Very young children can be motivated to use their residual vision if caregivers limit the amount of assistance provided to that which is necessary to ensure safety and success. Beyond that, infants and toddlers should be encouraged to explore, to move independently about their environments, and to risk an occasional bump or bruise to increase mobility.

Prevention of secondary disabilities requires an interdisciplinary approach to give attention to physical development, language acquisition, and social skills. Caregivers can assist in facilitating normal development in other areas by providing enriching experiences with activities, materials, and interactions that make use of residual vision as well as tactile, auditory, kinesthetic, and olfactory senses.

INFORMING AND WORKING WITH PARENTS

As with any disability, team members who interact with parents should be considerate enough to present more than once any new information related to the visual impairment. It is almost certain that parents who receive a large amount of technical information, especially if this information leads to emotional reactions, will be unable to focus on the details of the conversation. Using the concept of anticipatory guidance, team members can time the delivery of information to intersect with parents' ability to "hear" and a child's need for services. This practice, of course, assumes the need to tailor timing to suit individual children and their families (Hoon, 1991).

Furthermore, information givers should be knowledgeable enough to be able to answer most questions that parents might ask. However, it is worse to give misinformation than to give no information, especially regarding developmental predictions of children's future visual abilities or related developmental prognoses. Whenever possible, vision specialists should assist in informing parents. It may also be appropriate and necessary to explain the nature of the visual loss to children themselves. For example, children with congenital blindness may not recognize a deficiency until they are told and realize how they are different from their peers.

The absence of visual referents that are gained from cumulative visual experiences prevents children with visual impairments from developing conceptual, perceptual, sensory, and body awareness of space and environment. Hence, a primary objective of early intervention should be to train **orientation** skills, which will enable young children with visual impairments to achieve **mobility**. Orientation training is necessary to enable young children with visual impairments to gain a sense of position in space. Children are taught to take advantage of other senses, such as touch, smell, and hearing, to replace sight. Mobility training should be coupled with orientation; that is, teaching children their location in the room as well as how to move around their environment. According to Clarke (1988), orientation and mobility technology underwent an exciting evolution during the 1980s (see Table 8–2).

Curriculum specifically designed for infants and toddlers includes precane skills, sensory awareness, trailing, using a sighted guide, and environmental familiarization. Advances in mobility devices for very young children generally consist of modified adult devices, such as shortened long canes, or devices specially designed for children, such as a push toy that provides both support and protection for a toddler who is blind. Selection of appropriate orientation and mobility adaptations should be based on several factors identified by Clarke (1988): a child's motor skills, degree of visual loss, concern for safety of the child and others, adaptability of the child to change required for continuous accommodation, need for formal training, degree of independence in travel required, cost (which can range from several thousand to just a few dollars), the need for maintenance, and the availability of technology. Orientation and mobility (O & M) specialists are available and should be regularly consulted for selection, adaptation, and evaluation of mobility devices for specific children (Clarke, 1988). Guide dogs are not an option for infants and toddlers, since canines cannot be assigned until children reach age 16. However, preparation in orientation and mobility, even in early childhood, helps prepare children for independent movement and eventual guide dog ownership if needed.

Table 8–2   Mobility Devices for Infants and Preschoolers

Vendors	Product	Advantages
Electronic Travel Aids (ETAs): Electronic devices that detect obstacles and provide users with auditory and/or tactual signals.	Laser Cane: Nurion; Sonicguide: Wormaid International	May be used to teach concepts and stimulate reaching prior to locomotion.
Suspended Movement Devices: Devices suspended from an overhead support that allow freedom of movement within a limited space.	Baby Swings: "Jolly Jumpers"	Provide upright movement experiences in space.
Infant Walkers: Wheeled devices with seats that allow infants to propel themselves with their feet.	Commercial Walkers	May stimulate child due to change in environment.
Scooterboards: Small wooden, foam, or plastic platforms on wheels	Cookie Monster Crawl-Along: Educational Teaching Aids; Midline Positioning Scooter: Achievement Products	Allow for independent mobility in prone, supine, and seated positions. Provide trunk support for creeping; allow hands to be free to manipulate objects.
Wheelchair Devices: Manual or battery-powered devices that transport nonambulatory children.	Manual Devices: Toddler Cart: Achievement Products Powered Devices: Amigo Mini: Amigo Playpen; Cribs	May allow greater independence and exploration.
Cruising Surfaces: Surfaces used to pull to standing position and maintain balance while stepping.		Provide comfort and stability while moving about the environment. Help child to learn about the arrangement of space. Provide a training ground for learning to trail.
Push Toys (supported / stooped): Low, weighted toys or objects used for support while walking in a stooped posture.	Large wooden trucks; Large beach balls	Allow child to practice balancing in semi-upright posture. Serve as bumpers to protect child from obstacles in path.
Orthopedic Walkers: Therapeutic support devices, without seats, used to assist in walking.	Children's Full Body Suspension Walker: Achievement Products	Serve as bumpers to protect child from obstacles in path.
Walking Hoops and Guiding Sticks: Hoops and sticks used to encourage walking without direct physical contact with another person.	Hula hoops; PVC pipes	Offer security and support while learning to walk without physical contact with another person.
Riding Roll Toys: Wheeled children's riding toys that are propelled by pushing with the feet.	Tyke Bikes: Environments, Inc.	Are "normal" devices used by nondisabled children. Serve as bumpers to protect child from obstacles in path.

Table 8–2 *(continued)*

Vendors	Product	Advantages
Push Toys (Supported/Upright): Wheeled children's push toys that offer support while walking upright.	"Tuff Stuff" Shopping Cart: Kaplan	Serve as bumpers to protect child from obstacles in path. Are "normal" devices used by nondisabled children.
Walking Ropes: One or two ropes, running horizontally, that serve as tactual guides while walking or running.	Rope Clothesline	Provide practice in trailing. Guide child in a straight line while walking or running.
Cane Instruments: Nonrolling devices that may be used in the environment as a bumper and a probe much as along cane is used.	Hockey sticks Plastic baseball bats	Are "normal" devices used by nondisabled children. May be arced side to side to clear a complete path in front of child.
Canes: Standard canes modified for young children.	Collapsible or rigid canes: White Cane Instruments for the Blind (WCIB)	May encourage confidence while walking independently. May help child to avoid the development of inappropriate gait patterns. May eliminate the need to remediate skills later on.

Source: From "Barriers or Enablers: Mobility Devices for Visually Impaired and Multiply Handicapped Infants and Preschoolers," by K. L. Clarke, 1988, *Education of the Visually Handicapped, 20,* pp. 115–133. Reprinted with permission of the Helen Dwight Reid Educational Foundation. Published by Heldref Publications, 1319 Eighteenth St., NW, Washington, DC 20036-1802. Copyright ©1988.

A parent's role in facilitating language in infants who are visually impaired may be particularly difficult. As mentioned, vision is important to nonverbal communication (e.g., gestures, smiling, facial expressions) and to help parent-child dyads in communication regarding a mutual focus of attention. In the absence of these important communication tools, it appears that children who are visually impaired tend to have delayed language development, particularly in the area of pragmatics (Kekelis & Prinz, 1996). Communication of young children with visual impairments tends to be egocentric. Furthermore, parents, teachers, and other adults tend to limit the opportunities for meaningful conversation by visually impaired children by taking many more conversational turns and by using more directives and labeling, and less commenting and questioning than are provided for sighted children. Because infants and children who are visually impaired do not spontaneously give the same feedback in conversation as sighted children, it is important to teach parents (and teachers) to share conversational turns equitably, to ask meaningful questions and wait for the answers, and to make relevant comments and expect relevant comments about mutual experiences.

As compared to children who are sighted, those with visual impairments may face a lifetime of "disadvantage." Chalifoux and Fagan (1997) described a paradigm of poverty associated with children who are blind that conspires to limit the

Table 8–3 Factors Leading to Disadvantage in Children Who Are Visually Impaired

Risk Factors	Cause(s)	Outcome
Limited Financial Resources	As child: greater likelihood of only one employed parent As adult: unemployment, underemployment	Lack of assets and material possessions; dispossession of hopes and dreams
Substandard Housing	Limited financial resources; negative attitudes of landlords	Run down, overcrowded houses—especially detrimental to children who are visually impaired, who benefit from quiet areas to study; more likely to live in high-crime areas, further limiting mobility
Educational Deficits	Disability-specific areas of education are usually neglected; often fail to learn appropriate social mannerisms	Limited self-confidence; poor social adaptation; leads to sedentary, isolated lifestyles
Poor Health, Physical or Mental	Isolation; disease process that lead to visual impairment	Negative feelings of emotional well-being
Family Difficulties	Parental: stress of adjusting to child with disability Child: Overprotection	Parental marital discord Limited independent living skills—causing further familial hardship

Source: From "Labeling Children Who Are Visually Impaired 'Disadvantaged,'" by L. M. Chalifoux and B. Fagan, 1997, *Journal of Visual Impairment and Blindness, 91*, pp. 531–539.

potential of these children (Table 8–3). Knowledge of such disadvantage can help educators anticipate and act to prevent such factors from adding further handicaps to children who are visually impaired.

Chalifoux and Fagan (1997) made several recommendations for actions that can be taken to mitigate the factors that lead to the developmental and economic deprivation of children who are visually impaired.

1. Early education should be organized around hands-on experiences in all important environments, where sighted persons engage in running commentaries about the world these children are experiencing.
2. Planning for adulthood should take place in early childhood, where parents learn to become active in planning transitions that will lead to independent, confident children.
3. Involvement in recreational activities that involve risk taking, fitness, and social integration.
4. Families require social support, respite, and sufficient financial security, which often requires the involvement of extended family members and community agencies.
5. Children require early and ongoing social skills training to emphasize social awareness, pragmatic interaction skills, and avoidance of stereotypic behavior.

Case Study   EARLY DIAGNOSIS: INTERVIEW WITH MARSHA MOORE

Almost from the very beginning, before he was 3 weeks old, I had the sinking suspicion that there was something really wrong with Michael. He did not respond to me. He did not quiet to my voice or touch. He would not, maybe could not, make eye contact. He cried day and night, even during bath time or while nursing. He did not nurse well. He was stiff and would not cuddle, but rather would arch his back and flail his arms and hands. He was our sixth child and we were experienced parents, but Michael was not like the rest. We took him several times to our new hometown general practitioner. The doctor believed that Michael was "just colicky," and prescribed a medicine to relieve him (and I suppose the entire family) of the discomfort we all felt.

When Michael was almost 4 months old, we returned to Denver to visit our previous pediatrician. At first, the appointment was relaxed and friendly. We exchanged small talk about our new home in Wyoming and our other children. Once the examination began, it was apparent that our doctor had that same sinking notion that something was just not right. He examined Michael for several minutes, and then called in his physician's assistant and one of his nurses. All three continued to examine Michael, coaxing him to track their pen lights and a squeak toy; pulling him to sit and checking out his fat, pink perfect little body. I continued to jabber on ner-vously about all my motherly concerns. In my heart I hoped that I had been foolish to feel so anxious. They said little to each other and absolutely nothing to Jim or me. Perhaps we were expected to read minds! Finally our doctor turned to us and said, "I think Michael is blind."

We had seen Michael reach for toys. We had seen him stare into the lights over the kitchen countertop. We had seen him focus on his mobile over his crib. And although both eyes often crossed and at times seemed disconnected, I still could not believe the diagnosis of "blind." Later we would find that his vision problems were just the "tip of the iceberg."

Before we left to return home, our pediatrician arranged for us to see a pediatric ophthalmologist, and a neurologist and to get a CT scan at a nearby hospital. We had driven almost five hundred miles for medical information and did not want to go home without some answers. It was almost 9 p.m. by the time we left the neurologist's office. Michael had been poked and prodded for almost 12 hours and was tired, overstimulated and literally "strung out." Jim and I were numb. How could all of this be happening to us?

The results of the CT scan and both examinations were inconclusive. Michael's eyes were healthy. He had strabismus, but there seemed to be no physical reason why he would not be able to see. There was a question, however, as to whether his brain could "see" and whether a label of cortical blindness would be appropriate. The neurologist was guarded in his prognosis. The CT scan showed irregularities in Michael's brain. He acknowledged that Michael's development was a little slow, but we were assured that there was little reason to worry. We were instructed to contact a therapist who worked in the outskirts of Denver. Mike's condition was not "that" delayed and would probably improve as he matured with added infant stimulation. Somehow, neither Jim nor I was convinced.

We drove all night and arrived home early the next morning. We said little to each other during the trip back. I cried, and he sighed! We both recognized that this was only the beginning.

Michael was 5 months old when he began with his first therapy session in Denver. The therapist was a true godsend. Because we lived so far away, she scheduled the entire afternoon for

Michael. We brought the whole family to his first appointment. Therapy was definitely going to be a group effort! All winter long, we worked with Michael on a daily basis, going through the routines that the therapist had taught us and improvising along the way, but we saw little change. Michael had learned to independently roll over, but still was unable to sit up by himself. He could not yet position himself on hands and knees. He was not even belly crawling. His mode of transportation was either to roll from place to place or to arch and push himself on his back. I spent many hours on the floor with him, trying in every way I knew possible to encourage him to explore his world. I would leave little trails of marshmallows and graham crackers all over the carpet in hope that he would be motivated to creep to get them. We sang to him, read to him, stacked blocks with him. We bought bags of lentils and rice for him to play in. We made pudding finger paints. We purchased vibrating pillows and hot and cold water bottles. At 10 months, he was still crying through the night, and although I was still nursing him, he had never made eye contact with me.

He had earlier made somewhat of a small "breakthrough" with Jim. When he was almost 8 months old, Jim was playing on the sofa with him; talking, growling, tickling him, when suddenly, Jim whispered "Look, look." I looked over to see that Michael was staring intently at Jim's face. Jim was beaming and did not move for fear that Mike would lose contact. It took only a few seconds before Michael began to cry big alligator tears. Why was this connection so frightening to Michael? Why did he pull away from us so? What was wrong with *us*? We both felt so helpless!

Our first Wyoming winter seemed very long and very bleak for a multitude of reasons. I stayed in telephone contact with our Denver pediatrician and with the therapist, but was not able to get back to Denver until April, when the snow finally melted and the roads cleared. At that time,

Michael Moore plays the piano at home.

Michael saw a battery of specialists at Denver Children's Hospital. He would be a year old in May and there was still no conclusive diagnosis.

We scheduled a week-long hospital assessment again in July and saw several different "developmental" authorities who worked out of other clinics. These trips were so difficult for Mike. He was in strange places, with strange people, strange routine, strange food. He seemed so disoriented and fussed or cried constantly. Yet, this time we received a diagnosis. Finally, after 14 months, we had a name to give to what was happening with Mike: infantile autism with severe mental retardation. We were relieved and very sad. How could Michael ever enjoy this type of existence? How could his life be worth anything? We felt so angry. This wasn't fair! What did Michael ever do to deserve something like this? What did any of us do to deserve this? Where do we go from here?

INFECTIONS IN EARLY CHILDHOOD

Human beings have been afflicted with both common and complex ailments since the beginning of recorded history. Sore throats, earaches, coughing, and fevers commonly interfere with the normal activities of daily living, and those are symptoms that cause the most concern for parents of young children (Kai, 1996). These are generally symptoms indicating an invasion by biological agents. The interaction is complex between humans and the microorganisms that cause infection. These **biological agents** cause damage to human cells by either living on cells or by causing inflammation of the cells. **Inflammation** is caused by the **toxin** given off by the particular **organism** causing a specific infection. This toxin acts like a poison to human cells. Biological agents may travel throughout the body in the bloodstream or by way of the lymph system. The effect of an infection on a particular individual is dependent on the agent involved, the overall health of the individual when exposed, and the age of the person affected.

For some infecting agents, premature babies, term newborns, infants, and young children are affected differently than older children and mature adults. Reactions among very young children may include lowered rather than elevated body temperatures, a decrease instead of increase in the total white blood cell count, and a more rapid progression of an infecting agent producing more significant symptoms. In addition, very young children have immature immune systems and are less capable of dealing with an infection than an individual with a mature and healthy system. Individuals with compromised immune systems, such as infants with chronic diseases, are also at a much higher risk of developing infection. As a result of these factors, neonates, infants, and young children may have more frequent episodes of significant infections that require more extensive interventions. Biological agents that may cause infections in humans include bacteria, viruses, mycoplasmas, fungi, protozoa, rickettsias, and nematodes. Two of the most common infectious agents are bacteria and viruses.

Due to complications associated with meningitis, this child lost part of both legs in early childhood.

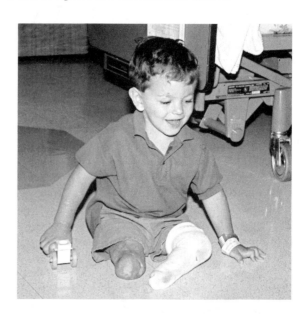

BACTERIAL INFECTIONS

By adulthood, everyone has experienced an infection. In spite of this, few have actually seen what causes the illness. **Microbes**, or germs, are so small that they can only be seen through a microscope, and **bacteria** are microbes that are found abundantly in nature. Many bacteria are incapable of causing disease and live in harmony with humans. Yet even bacteria that generally are beneficial can cause significant infections in humans under the right circumstances by becoming **pathogenic** (disease causing).

Pathogenic bacteria create infections that continue to be a significant cause of infant **morbidity** and **mortality** in the United States, constituting approximately 20% of neonatal deaths each year (Magid, 1995). Such infections can occur either prior to delivery from an infected mother or shortly after delivery from exposure to infected persons or objects in the environment. An infant's condition can be profoundly affected, depending on the particular organism responsible for a specific infection and the time between exposure to infection and initiation of appropriate treatment. For example, infants infected by **group B streptococcus** may show subtle objective symptoms such as mild respiratory distress, but the infants deteriorate quickly if not treated, to the point that death may occur. Medical care providers need to use observable signs along with a maternal history and a review of risk factors when deciding whether to start early and aggressive treatment. Pneumococcal disease is of particular danger to infants and young children with HIV/AIDS, and sickle cell disease and has become the leading cause of bacterial meningitis (Van Beneden, Whitney, Levine, & Schwartz, 2000). Children in nonfamily daycare, particularly those who begin day care at a young age, are at increased risk of acquiring pneumococcal disease. Moreover, treatment of this disease in early childhood is complicated by increasingly penicillin-resistant strains of the bacteria (Van Beneden et al., 2000).

A history of poverty places children at risk for the development of infections. For example, childhood vaccination is significantly lower for children who are poor and live in inner cities, and for minorities (i.e., African American and Hispanic) (Kenyon, Matuck, & Stroh, 1998; "Vaccination Coverage," 1998). A direct relationship exists between socioeconomic status and low birth weight, as well as the development of both prenatal and postnatal infections (Hughes & Simpson, 1995). The greater the degree of poverty, the lower an infant's birth weight, and consequently the greater the vulnerability to infection. Poverty is also linked to many of the maternal conditions that lead to infection, such as low birth weight, poor nutrition, environmental injustice (e.g., toxic waste dumps, pollution, crime), lack of prenatal care, drugs, alcohol, smoking, and inadequate attention to chronic disease states, such as hypertension. Appropriate assessment of the physical condition of an infant at delivery provides health care workers with the information necessary to determine risk factors that may indicate the presence of a bacterial agent. Keys to effective treatment of an infected infant are awareness of the possibility of infection, assessment of presenting signs and symptoms, and aggressive treatment of any suspected infection in an at-risk infant.

Infants born through infected amniotic fluid or those who acquire a bacterial infection shortly after birth are at high risk for disability or death from the infection. Initial symptoms of an infection include temperature instability, poor feeding, respiratory distress, low blood sugar, and lethargy. Symptoms may also be as subtle as a lack of appropriate response to environmental stimulation. Multiple physical system failure can occur very rapidly in an affected newborn. In those infants with multiple system involvement for whom death does not occur, there can be significant long-term developmental effects. Those disabilities occurring most frequently include visual impairment, hearing loss, and mental retardation. Such secondary disabilities may be the result of the infectious process or a result of the treatment used to save an infant's life. Infants experiencing infections at birth, or shortly afterwards, warrant early screening for developmental progress, identification of potential problems, and possible initiation of early intervention programs to provide the opportunity for full development.

Though neither bacterial nor viral, hookworm is a parasitic invasion that affects 1 billion individuals worldwide according to the March of Dimes (2001). Considered a disease of the tropics, and limited mostly to immigrating children and southeastern and Gulf states, hookworm has recently been identified a major world health concern. The vector for hookworm is soil contaminated with human feces and is transmitted through exposure to the skin. Anemia and malnutrition are the most common effects of chronic hookworm infection. Parasitic hookworms attach to intestinal lining and feed on the intestinal wall, resulting in significant blood loss. Pregnant women suffering from anemia due to hookworm show a compromised fetal environment, iron deficiency, and malnutrition. Intrauterine growth retardation, low birth weight and prematurity, transplancental transmission of the hookworm, and even fetal death can result. In addition to the potential perinatal risk factors mentioned, infected infants who are not treated suffer anemia and malnutrition and associated physical and mental developmental problems. Work is being conducted to develop a vaccination for hookworm. In the meantime, this social/health issue is one that belongs to the entire world community.

CLOSE-UP

APPROPRIATE PRINCIPLES IN THE USE OF ANTIBIOTICS IN CHILDREN

HIV/AIDS emerged as the most deadly epidemic of the second half of the 20th century, even though its devastation trails far behind viral and bacterial epidemics in human history. However, the discovery of antibiotics in this same century yielded astounding progress in controlling diseases that once presented ominous health threats. Now, as we enter a new millennium, overuse of the very antibiotics that saved countless lives threatens to place humans at even greater health risk. Antibiotics like penicillin have been effective in destroying bacterial infections such as otitis media, pneumonia, and sinusitis in their human hosts. However, bacteria are incredibly adaptive, and in less than 50 years, almost all common microbes have managed to mutate into antibiotic-resistant strains.

Three factors have led to the overuse of antibiotics. First, there are two types of antibiotics, wide spectrum and narrow spectrum. The former are useful in treating a wide variety of bacteria, while the latter are useful in treating very specific bacteria. While wide spectrum antibiotics are often prescribed for the sake of expedience, their overuse hastens the resistance of bacteria. Secondly, American families have become overdependent on antibiotics in order to keep children in school/day care so that parents (both of whom usually work full time) can avoid taking time off work to care for sick children. Parents have increasingly put pressure on health care providers to prescribe antibiotics for children, even when the infections are minor or when antibiotic prescriptions are inappropriate (i.e., for viral infections which are unaffected by antibiotics). Third, congregation of children in day-care centers has hastened the spread of antibiotic-resistant bacteria. Similarly, the American work culture, which places a premium on work productivity, has created "toxic environments," where people go to work when they are ill rather than take time off to get well or return to work before they are well, thereby spreading the disease-resistant bacteria. This practice may be further compounded with the possibility that this return to work is abetted by wide spectrum antibiotics.

Some specialists warn that we may be evolving, health wise, into a "postantibiotic era," where few effective treatments are available to patients with microbial infections. In order to prevent this from happening, several steps need to be taken: (1) prescription of narrow spectrum antibiotics; (2) educate parents (and physicians) that viral infections will not respond to antibiotics; (3) encourage parents to resist repeated dependence upon antibiotic prescriptions for mild bacterial infections, even if it means the illness would last longer and possibly delay return to work/school.

Source: From "Appropriate Principles in the Use of Antibiotics in Children," by M. Green, 1997, *Clinical Pediatrics, 36*, pp. 207–209.

VIRAL INFECTIONS

Viruses are the smallest infectious agents and are more difficult to identify and control because of their unique properties. Like bacteria, viruses are biological agents but differ from true microorganisms. A virus consists of genetic material, either DNA or RNA, and an enclosing shell of protein. Genetic materials contained in a virus's DNA or RNA make the virus capable of reproducing and attaching itself to susceptible cells. Most viruses have specific cell preferences where they will attach and reproduce. Examples of cell preferences may be nerve, muscle, or blood cells. Once in a host individual, viruses can survive in an inactive state for extended time periods with activation and occasional reactivation periods that produce the disease itself. Other viral infections do not produce recognizable diseases in the infected individual but create a carrier state enabling an individual to transfer viruses to others.

Prevention of many dangerous viral diseases has been accomplished largely through the development of **vaccines**. These consist of either active viral replications that have a decreased capability of causing infection and disease or an inactive virus introduced into the human being to activate the immune system to produce **antibodies**. Once established, antibodies prevent an acute infection if the individual is exposed to an active virus of normal virulence. Through a series of childhood immunizations, many common viral diseases such as polio and smallpox have been nearly eliminated or greatly reduced in early childhood (see Figure 8–6). Still, progress is not without setbacks. For example, shortages of vaccination in 2002 were the result of reduction in manufacturing and insufficient stockpiles. Although this is likely to be a temporary shortage in the United States, shortages and postponements resulted in altered the Center for Disease Control recommendations for vaccine use (CDC, 2002).

Potent drugs are continuously being developed to counteract specific viral agents. The success of these drugs in preventing or controlling viral infections has been variable. When prevention is not possible, antiviral drugs specific to a given virus itself can shorten the duration of some viral diseases (Margo & Shaughnessy, 1998). Many serious viral infections such as hepatitis B and HIV, with neither vaccination or cure, fall into this category.

Viral infections and many of the common congenital disabilities related to specific agents are frequently discussed under the umbrella of the TORCH infections (see Table 8–4). Many professionals add syphilis to this group as a separate entity and refer to them as the STORCH infections. In this text, syphilis will be included under other infections (O). The letters TORCH represent toxoplasmosis (T), other infections (O), rubella (R), cytomegalic inclusion virus (C), and herpes

Figure 8–6
Recommended Immunization Schedule

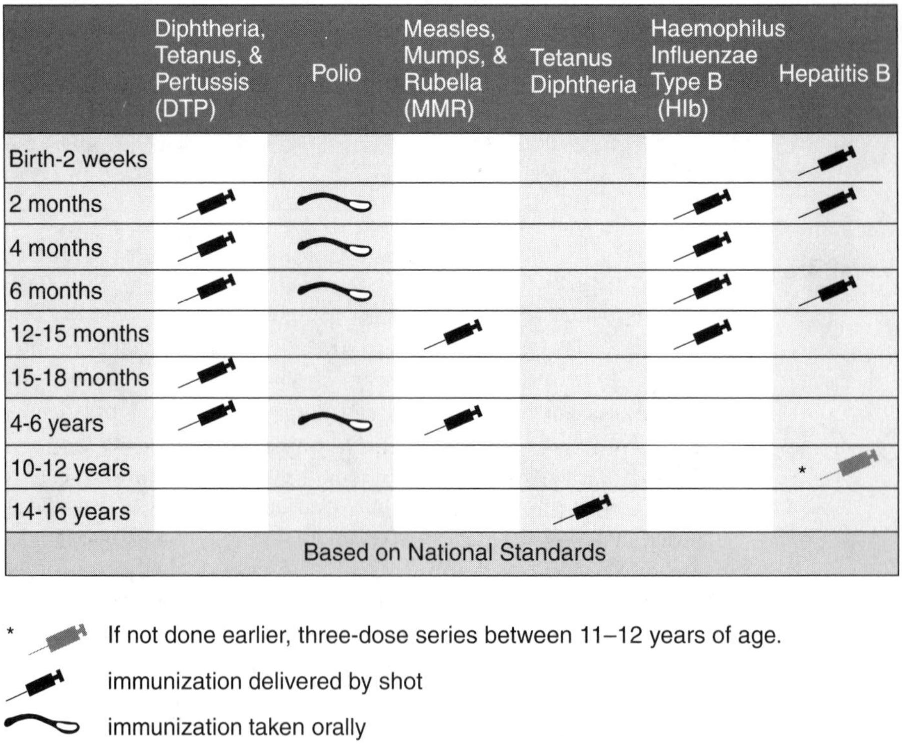

Based on National Standards

*   If not done earlier, three-dose series between 11–12 years of age.

    immunization delivered by shot

    immunization taken orally

Table 8–4   TORCH Infections

T	Toxoplasmosis
O	Other (Varicella-Zoster, Mumps, Rubeola, Syphilis, Hepatitis, HIV/AIDS)
R	Rubella
C	Cytomegalic Inclusion Virus (CMV)
H	Herpes simplex

Table 8–5   Characteristics/Outcomes of Congenital Infections

	Toxoplasmosis	Chicken Pox	Hepatitis B	Syphilis	HIV/AIDS	Rubella	CMV	Herpes
Blindness	X	X		X		X	X	X
Deafness	X	X		X		X	X	X
Retardation	X	X		X		X	X	X
Seizures	X	X		X		X	X	X
Liver affect			X	X	X	X		
Spleen affect			X	X	X	X		
Hydrocephalus	X	X		X			X	X
Microcephaly	X	X		X		X	X	X
Jaundice			X		X	X		
Brain atrophy	X	X		X		X	X	X
Transmitted at birth		X	X	X	X	X		X
Transplacental	X	X	X	X	X	X	X	?
"Shed" virus			X	X	X	X	X	X
Hydrops				X				

(H). Because of the variability in pathology and outcome of these infections, they are usually discussed as independent entities (see Table 8–5).

Toxoplasmosis

Pregnant women must be especially careful to avoid infection by **toxoplasmosis** (*Toxoplasma gondii*), a **protozoan**, acquired by humans from contact with the feces of infected cats or birds and from the ingestion of raw or partially cooked meat. This infection is discussed as part of the TORCH viral infections, since the protozoan acts upon the RNA and DNA of the cell in the same manner as viruses. Likewise, antibodies are developed following acute infections.

This infection can be acquired by a pregnant woman during any stage of pregnancy and subsequently transmitted to an unborn fetus. Maternal infections during either the first or second trimester appear to be most commonly associated with infections that cross the placenta **(transplacental)**. This occurs when the protozoa cross from the maternal side of the placenta to the fetal side, infecting the developing fetus. Congenital toxoplasmosis infections (acquired before birth) can cause significant abnormalities. Fetal conditions resulting from an acute infection are dependent on the gestation of the fetus at the time of infection.

Prevention of toxoplasmosis can be accomplished by educating women of childbearing age to avoid the ingestion of raw or undercooked meat, changing a cat's litter box, or gardening without gloves. It is also important to recognize that, in rare instances, untreated maternal infections can affect subsequent pregnancies with fetal infections and an increased incidence of in utero fetal death.

Fetal effects of congenitally acquired toxoplasmosis often include a classical triad of hydrocephaly, cerebral calcification, and **chorioretinitis** (inflammation of the retina and blood vessels that supply the retina with nutrition) with resulting visual impairment. Other features commonly associated with congenital toxoplasmosis include microcephaly, deafness, seizures, **encephalitis**, enlargement of the spleen and liver, anemia, jaundice, and mental retardation. The infection itself may not always be apparent at birth and frequently the onset of symptoms is delayed for several months. Treatment of an infected mother may include drug therapy, but most drugs are not effective at treating an infected infant. Though these agents are useful in destroying the harmful protozoa, damage already done to the infected infant cannot be reversed.

The prognosis for infants born with congenital toxoplasmosis infection is poor. As many as 15% of infected infants who are born alive will die within the neonatal period, and 85% of the survivors have severe developmental delays and vision problems (Leclair, 1980). Long-term care includes ongoing assessment for detection of developmental problems and initiation of early intervention programs.

Rubella

Rubella, also known as German measles, generally causes minor illness in children but is much more of a problem for a pregnant woman. This viral infection has been preventable by immunization since 1969. A woman may be susceptible if she has not had rubella in the past or has failed to develop sufficient antibodies due to inadequate immunization. An exposed, pregnant woman may pass the infection to her fetus through the placenta. Fetal effects are thought to be the most devastating during the first trimester when the virus attacks the developing organs and tissues of the embryo; however, evidence suggests that rubella transmitted during the 4th and 5th month of pregnancy also results in fetal infections and significant fetal effects.

Stillbirth is a common outcome of congenital rubella infection. Other common fetal effects include microcephaly, cataract formation, significant cardiac anomalies, and deafness. Many infants born with congenital infection also demonstrate intrauterine growth retardation. Infants born with congenital rubella syndrome who suffer from severe intrauterine growth retardation, microcephaly, and other symptoms of central nervous system disease have an 80% mortality rate within the first year of life (Bolognese, Aldinger, & Roberts, 1981). This risk is especially true if these infants also suffer from associated defects such as cardiac malformations. Such abnormalities may be particularly difficult to manage because of the constellation of life-threatening problems associated with rubella syndrome.

Some infants born with congenital rubella have no apparent symptoms at birth. Yet, 70% of these infants will show effects of the disease before reaching 5 years of age. The effects most frequently seen include hearing loss, cataracts, autism, abnormal behavior patterns, impulsivity, hyperactivity, and learning disabilities (Mauk & Mauk, 1992). The long-term outlook for children with congenital rubella often involves multiple disabilities and requires intensive intervention.

Of concern is the finding that infants with no obvious effects at birth can shed large amounts of active virus for up to 18 months, infecting others, without caregivers being aware of the condition. Shedding occurs through the infant's urine, stool, and saliva. Individuals coming into contact with shedding infants need to be aware of the infection in order to take appropriate personal precautions to prevent the spread of active virus. Health care professionals and caregivers who are not adequately immunized or who have not had a previous rubella infection should refrain from contact with an infant with rubella syndrome. Even though rubella has been almost entirely eradicated through early childhood vaccinations, publicity on the possible effects of the MMR (measles, mumps, and rubella) immunization has led to a decline in MMR immunizations since 1997 (Thomas, Salmon, & King, 1998). This decline will almost certainly lead to an increase in the number of cases of congenital rubella. Individuals placed within situations in which exposure may occur (e.g., day-care settings or classrooms) should establish whether they have adequate immunity. This can be done through laboratory testing prior to involvement.

Treatment recommendations:

1. A neonate born with rubella needs to be isolated from contact with other infants and nonimmunized children and adults for up to a year.
2. Assessment of the physical and developmental needs of the affected infant is necessary so appropriate early intervention can be planned.
3. Special attention must be paid to any associated defects, especially cardiac, that place infected infants at a higher risk for secondary infections.
4. Attention to nutrition should be vigilant, as poor feeding can lead to failure to thrive.
5. Early eye and ear examinations to determine visual and hearing needs.
6. Referrals to community agencies that provide services for infants with significant disabilities are almost always necessary.

Cytomegalic Inclusion Virus

Cytomegalic inclusion virus is the most common congenital viral infection. Approximately 80% of adults have antibodies in their blood for human **cytomegalic inclusion viral infection (CMV)** though the causative infection may have produced no noticeable symptoms. Between 10 and 15% of infants infected with CMV at birth will be affected, while the remaining 85–90% of infected infants are asymptomatic (Mauk & Mauk, 1992). Moreover, a large segment of the general population tests positively by the end of adolescence, indicating a past primary infection. This medium-sized virus is one of the four herpes viruses seen in humans; the three others are herpes simplex, varicella-zoster (chicken pox), and Epstein-Barr virus. A pregnant woman who becomes infected with CMV through exposure to body fluids, or who experiences a reactivation of a past CMV infection, can transmit the virus to her unborn child. Such transmission can cause serious consequences, including brain damage. Prevention of CMV infections is a prime goal of research, though, to date, no effective prevention or treatment has been established. Research on a vaccination for women to protect fetal exposure is promising (March of Dimes, 2001). Those previously uninfected pregnant women who work in child-care settings are at highest risk and should practice hygienic hand washing and other precautions related to exposure to body fluids.

Live CMV can be transmitted throughout pregnancy, producing congenital neonatal infections at any point prior to delivery. Reported rates of transplacental transmission to a developing fetus differ significantly, from 20% to 45% (Preece et al., 1983). Studies have not indicated that primary infection during the first trimester produces more serious complications for the fetus than infection later in the pregnancy (Preece et al., 1983). This finding does not change the fact that in known infections, fetal effects may be predicted based on the gestational age of the pregnancy when the infection occurred. There is no question, however, that cytomegalovirus can cause a significant interruption in the normal developmental progress of a fetus.

Specific congenital anomalies that have been noted in neonates born with congenital CMV infections include microcephaly, deafness, chorioretinitis, optic atrophy, enlarged liver and spleen, platelet destruction, calcifications in solid organs (such as the liver) and the brain, seizures, Dandy-Walker malformations (cystic formations that replace solid structure of the brain), intrauterine growth retardation, congenital heart defects, and abdominal wall defects. Even infants who show no apparent infection at delivery have shown delays in speech and language development on follow-up.

Current medical treatment for a symptomatic infant is limited. Generally, care is supportive, aimed toward treatment of the symptoms presented by an individual infant. **Antiviral** drugs may be used, especially in infants with life-threatening infection, who display central nervous system symptoms. However, the adverse effects of these drugs must be carefully considered to determine whether the benefits outweigh the risks. Infants born with microcephaly as a result of congenital CMV infection frequently display significant developmental impairment. This finding supports the suggestion that the microcephaly is the result of intrauterine viral encephalitis. Encephalitis frequently results in brain-cell death, which causes a halt in brain growth or shrinking of brain tissue.

Infants born with congenital CMV infection shed live virus through urine, stool, and other body fluids, including saliva, throughout their lifetime. Nursing mothers with current infections will also shed live virus through their breastmilk, though this resolves once the active infection state is over. The definitive diagnosis of a suspected neonatal infection is made through isolation of the virus from a urine or saliva sample. No specific isolation of infected infants or children is required; however, pregnant women should not care for infected children. Caregivers who are pregnant can also acquire an infection through the handling of infected breastmilk. Awareness of an infection or of those infants and children affected with congenital disease is critical in preventing the infection of a pregnant caregiver. The suggestion that a relationship exists between recurrent CMV infections and the development of acquired immune deficiency syndrome (AIDS) in at-risk individuals is also being explored.

Extensive resources may be necessary to meet the developmental needs of infants born with congenital CMV. Assessment of an infant to determine risk for developmental delay and to identify interventions is essential before initial discharge from the hospital. Reassessment of an infected infant must be done at intervals to determine if appropriate programs are in place to meet individual and family needs. Visual screening to identify impairments is a high priority. If problems are detected, neurological assessment determines if visual disturbances are a result of physical or cortical damage and can determine appropriate methods for early intervention.

Developmental impairments related to hearing loss also require monitoring. Current research attempts to identify the best method of early diagnosis of sensorineural hearing loss resulting from congenital CMV, especially in infants who present with **asymptomatic** congenital infection. These infants appear to be at significantly increased risk for late onset hearing loss (Hicks et al., 1993).

Initiation of physical and occupational therapy programs to improve outcomes need to be established and undertaken within the parameters of providing service to the entire family unit. Support services should be provided to parents or caregivers with realistic information based on individual evaluation regarding an infant's long-term outcome.

Herpes

Genital **herpes** infections are among the most common venereal diseases in the United States. Approximately 40 million people have herpes. In adults, the virus produces itching, burning, soreness, and small blisters in the genital area. The blisters burst to leave small, painful ulcers, which heal within 10 to 21 days. Subsequent attacks tend to occur after sexual intercourse, after sunbathing, or when the affected person is run down. There is no cure for herpes, and sexual activity should be avoided until the symptoms have disappeared.

Herpes simplex virus types 1 and 2 are closely related and share 50% of their basic genetic code (Grossman, 1980). Herpes simplex type 1 is generally associated with oral lesions but can also be present with infection at other body sites. Herpes simplex type 2 is typically associated with genital infection and, as with type 1, can also occur at other body sites. Herpes belongs to a larger group of viruses that have common features; included in this category are CMV, varicella-zoster (chicken pox), and Epstein-Barr virus (mononucleosis).

Both primary infections and reactivation of the dormant virus result in shedding of live virus. This shedding is of critical importance to a pregnant woman since acquisition of the virus during pregnancy may have adverse effects on a fetus. Although transmission is rare, congenital herpes usually occurs when a woman has her first herpes episode early in pregnancy (Planned Parenthood, 1998).

Neonatal infections are usually acquired during passage through an infected birth canal in a normal vaginal delivery. This makes it vital that pregnant women with a history of genital herpes and their health care providers be certain that no lesions are visible (indicating an active infection) in the birth canal. The presence of lesions or a herpes-positive culture is an indication for delivery by cesarean section.

Women who have a primary herpes type 2 infection during pregnancy may experience more spontaneous abortions and more premature deliveries than those with reactivation of the dormant virus during pregnancy. There have been reports of this virus crossing the placenta, but such cases are rare. In most cases, affected newborns are exposed to the shedded virus in the birth canal. Approximately

33–50% of infants who undergo vaginal birth when the mother is experiencing her first episode of genital herpes will acquire the disease.

Neonates exposed to herpes infection generally are without any identifiable symptoms at birth. Symptoms include infection of the central nervous system. These symptoms may include irritability, vomiting, and the onset of seizures (Gast, 1983). It is difficult to diagnose very young children, who may also show symptoms of other disorders and then progress rapidly to herpes encephalitis or meningitis though this is not the generally recognized course of the disease (Margo & Shaughnessy, 1998). Usually encephalitis does not develop until later in the pattern of herpes infection (Whitley, Yeager, & Kartus, 1983). A rapid progression of the disease decreases the likelihood of success of the treatment.

It is estimated that 50% of neonates who acquire a herpes infection will die. Of those who survive, approximately 30% will have major neurological deficits as a result of the infection (Gast, 1983). Structural damage in the brain results from viral destruction of the gray and white matter. Hence, normal brain growth will be retarded, producing conditions such as hydrocephalus with frequent seizures, reduction in cortical growth with concurrent visual and hearing impairment, and mental retardation.

Specific focal areas of brain infection may frequently be determined in the presence of seizures by EEG (Whitley, Soong, & Linneman, 1982). This finding was the result of research showing that certain types of abnormal electrical activity are associated with herpetic lesions within the brain (Kohl & James, 1985; Whitley et al., 1983). Measurement of seizure activity utilizing electroencephalography may be useful in tracking herpetic lesions and determining if there is any extension, especially during episodes of reactivation. Antiviral agents have been developed to treat herpes simplex infections in neonates, infants, children, and adults.

Infants who survive systemic herpes infections require developmental assessment and appropriate referrals for services prior to discharge from the hospital. Early intervention planning includes provisions for vision, hearing, physical, and occupational therapy. Caregivers need to be aware that these infants and children can shed active virus from lesions during reactivation phases and should take the appropriate steps to avoid infection. Protection includes covering the lesions and preventing direct contact of the affected area by other children and adults. Since many of these children also have frequent episodes of seizure activity, protective measures (e.g., head gear, removal of dangerous items) may be indicated.

Other Viral Infections

Under the "O" or "Other" category of TORCH are a variety of diseases, many of which are common childhood illnesses, such as chicken pox and mumps. Usually, though not always, these illnesses cause only temporary problems for an infant. Even when exposed in utero, there may be no long-term effects to an infant. However, HIV/AIDS, syphilis, and hepatitis are also among the "Other" diseases, and in almost all cases, these illnesses cause severe disabilities and/or death.

Chicken pox, Mumps, and Measles

Chicken pox is typically a childhood disease but when a pregnant woman becomes infected, her unborn child is at serious risk because of the infection. **Varicella-zoster** (Herpes virus varicella or V-Z virus) is a member of the DNA herpes viruses. Primary infections of varicella virus (chicken pox) produce immunity, though late reactivation of dormant virus residing in nerve cells can result in shingles (zoster) in an older child or adult. However, there is no documentation of adverse effects of reactivated virus with the presentation of shingles in a pregnant woman, fetus, or neonate. Susceptible individuals who experience prolonged contact with infected persons are at a very high risk for developing infection. Vaccinations are available for all three of these diseases.

Pregnant nonimmune women should avoid contact with people known to be infected with chicken pox. Because the virus is so capable of invading and causing infection, most individuals have acquired immunity through past infection before reaching the childbearing years. Therefore, chicken pox (V-Z virus) rarely occurs during pregnancy. Its incidence is as low as 1 to 7 cases in 10,000 pregnancies (Herrmann, 1982). Yet maternal infections can occur at any point during the pregnancy of a nonimmune mother and will have a significant effect on the neonate. Though rare, older children who develop infection can experience the same complications from the disease. Developmental disabilities in older children are generally related to the effects of encephalitis.

The more serious neonatal effects of V-Z infections result from a maternal infection early in the pregnancy and lead to congenital effects. Congenital varicella-zoster syndrome can result in a condition in which the brain stops growing and shrinks; the remaining space is taken by fluid-filled cysts. Microcephaly, chorioretinitis, cataracts, auditory nerve paralysis, and mental retardation with concurrent seizures can be the consequence. Other frequently occurring effects include limb deformities (most commonly involving one extremity), absence of fingers/toes, and eye abnormalities. In some cases, congenital infection is followed by skin scarring that frequently occurs on the limb that is deformed (Herrmann, 1982).

Another childhood disease that presents risks for pregnant women is mumps, a communicable virus causing swelling of one or both of the parotid glands that are located at the junction of the lower jaw and the neck. Currently, mumps are preventable through immunization with the live attenuated mumps virus vaccine that induces antibody production and protects an individual against acute infection. Acute mumps infections are generally self-limiting, lasting 9 to 14 days, with few complications. The most common residual effect of a mumps infection is deafness (Korones, 1988). There do not appear to be any specific congenital malformations associated with maternal mumps. However, infants exposed to mumps infections require early hearing screening with consistent follow-up. Identification of hearing impairments necessitates inclusion in early intervention programs to prevent secondary delays in other areas of development.

Measles virus, also called hard measles, is a communicable virus, like the mumps virus, that also produces a highly contagious infection. The virus is generally spread by droplets carried through the air, thus infecting susceptible individuals through the respiratory tract. The measles vaccine, introduced in 1963, has greatly reduced the incidence of epidemic outbreaks of measles in the United States. Underdeveloped countries have not enjoyed the same progress. Without the availability of vaccine or the advances in technology, these countries experience high infection rates with a significantly increased incidence of related morbidity and mortality.

The incidence of measles infections among pregnant women has decreased as in the general population. Fetal effects from maternal measles appear to be few. There is an increased incidence of preterm delivery during acute maternal infections, but there is no reported evidence of fetal malformations.

Measles infections in infants and young children are consistent with the infection rate of the general population. Those infants and children who do become infected are predisposed to otitis media as a complication of the infection. Pneumonia and encephalitis also occur and are potentially lethal in combination with the measles. A long-term effect of infection includes hearing impairment from ear infections. Viral encephalitis associated with measles can also cause visual impairment and interruption in normal brain growth.

Syphilis

Syphilis is a disease that can produce serious illness when contracted by either adults or children. It is generally considered a sexually transmitted disease but can be acquired by contact with infectious lesions that may be present on the mouth, skin, or other mucous membranes. The virus can also be transmitted to a fetus through transplacental passage. Syphilis can also be contracted by an infant through contact with a lesion during the birth process. The disease is caused by a very mobile bacterium, which was identified in 1905 by Schaudinn and Hoffmann, two German scientists. As far back as the late 1400s, the disease represented a widespread health problem throughout the world (Pusey, 1933).

After the discovery of penicillin in the late 1940s, primary and secondary syphilis infections decreased in the United States until 1977, when the incidence began a steady increase until 1990. Since that time, the incidence has declined by approximately 50%, even though the rate is still high with an overall incidence of 0.05% of live births (Division of STD/HIV, 1995). A primary infection consists of the development of a lesion, also called a **chancre,** at the site of the contact with an infected person. This chancre is generally painless but highly infectious. There may be the development of multiple chancres with a primary infection. If a primary infection is not detected and appropriately treated with penicillin, it will progress to a secondary, or disseminated, infection. The latter is a **systemic** response to the infection that can have serious effects on many organ systems, especially the kidney and brain. Individuals treated during the secondary stage may continue to have effects from damage to organ systems that occurred during the active infection. In untreated individuals, syphilis will progress to **tertiary** disease, late syphilis, which is clinically evident with severe degeneration of organ systems and leads to significant disabilities.

Pregnancy has no effect on the normal course of syphilis. Pregnant women who acquire an infection require the same diagnosis and treatment course as those individuals who are not pregnant. Furthermore, untreated infection will profoundly affect the outcome of pregnancy, since the syphilis bacterium is able to cross the placenta at any time. Asymptomatic infections can occur, making it more important that laboratory testing of all pregnant women takes place.

Although a high percentage of fetuses affected with syphilis do not survive pregnancy, those infants who do are frequently affected with intrauterine growth retardation, and 20% are born prematurely (Issacs & Moxon, 1991). Congenital effects from maternal syphilis generally produce significant disabilities. Central nervous system development is altered, resulting in severe mental retardation, visual and hearing impairments, and frequently seizures. Normal bone growth is also altered, resulting in orthopedic malformations and aberrant tooth formation.

It has been determined that congenital syphilis results in 40% of term deliveries to women with untreated syphilis; perinatal death occurs in 20% of these pregnancies (Issacs & Moxon, 1991). Neonatal effects of congenital infection generally consist of enlargement of the liver and spleen, jaundice, and swelling and destruction to the head of the femur, resulting in major orthopedic deformities. Another common finding is moist skin lesions, particularly located over the palms of the hands and on the soles of the feet. These lesions are highly infectious and caution is vital to prevent spread of the infection in a nursery population.

The degree of developmental disabilities of survivors of congenital syphilis infections is dependent on the gestational age of the fetus when the infection first occurred. Those infants who acquired infection during the first or second trimester of the pregnancy are at highest risk for significant neurological delays and for visual and hearing impairments. Inadequate treatment allows a congenital infection to progress toward tertiary infection as it does in the adult. The profound developmental delays caused by this progression leave these infants in need of multidisciplinary services for the infant and family.

The goal of treatment is prevention of both primary infections and further progression of the existing disease state. Comprehensive prenatal care allows for diagnostic testing to determine infection and aggressive treatment to prevent fetal involvement and the subsequent significant affects of congenital syphilis infections.

Hepatitis

Hepatitis is a viral infection that produces systemic damage to the liver. It is a complex disease involving several subtype categories that produce similar symptoms but leave different long-term effects. Many children are without symptoms; some may proceed to severe, overwhelming, and fatal acute infections; and others suffer progressive, chronic liver failure with **cirrhosis.** There is a significant connection between hepatitis B in infancy and later development of liver cancer; in developing countries where hepatitis B is endemic, liver cancer is one of the most common forms of cancer (American Liver Foundation, 2001).

Hepatitis A virus (HAV) is generally a mild disease and has been referred to as infectious hepatitis. This virus is transmitted through personal contact with food handled by an infected individual. Mainly conveyed by bowel movement, poor personal hygiene, poor sanitation, and overcrowding greatly increase the potential for spreading HAV infection. Even though 125,000–200,000 new cases occur each year, HAV infection in children is rarely fatal. Chronic liver disease may result, but less than a 0.1% overall mortality rate has been reported (Klein, 1988). As with any vaccination, there is a risk to children who have an allergic reaction to the vaccination or those who present with serious illness when vaccinated.

Hepatitis B virus (HBV) is a major health problem throughout the entire world. In the United States, about 140,000 new cases occur each year (American Liver Foundation, 2001). Though the virus does not cross the placenta in all cases of carrier mothers, it does cross 6% of the time. However, as many as 90% of exposed infants acquire the disease as they pass through the birth canal when the newborn is exposed to the virus from the carrier mother's blood or vaginal fluids. Although potentially fatal in infancy, newborns who are immediately administered hepatitis B immune globulin and vaccine are effectively protected. Most chronic HBV carriers eventually die from chronic active hepatitis, cirrhosis, or primary liver cancer. The surviving affected infants can potentially transmit hepatitis virus to family members, personal contacts, and health care providers. This includes day-care providers, teachers, and other children involved in the daycare setting.

Hepatitis B virus is a DNA virus that replicates in the liver. It can infect all body fluids, including tears, gastric juices, urine, saliva, and semen. Transmission can occur through puncture wounds, blood transfusions, small cuts, and abrasions and also by absorption through mucous membranes, such as in the mouth or vagina (Boehme, 1985). Screening of pregnant women to determine both acute infection and antibody status is critical. Many of those mothers infected with HBV will not have any symptoms. The Centers for Disease Control suggest that all pregnant women have prenatal screening and absolutely recommend that women who are in risk categories be screened and followed. Women at high risk include:

1. Those of Asian, Pacific Island, or Alaskan Eskimo descent
2. Woman who are Haitian or sub-Saharan African by birth
3. Women with acute or chronic liver disease or a history of undiagnosed jaundice
4. IV drug users
5. Those with personal contacts with HBV carriers
6. Those with multiple episodes of venereal disease or those who are prostitutes
7. Women who are sexual partners of hemophiliacs
8. Individuals who work in dialysis or renal transplant units
9. Individuals who work or live in an institution for persons with mental retardation
10. Health care professionals

Laboratory testing identifies women who are in an acute phase of infection through a positive hepatitis B surface antigen. This antigen is present on the surface of the virus and can be detected in the patient's blood serum. The presence of surface antigen indicates acute infection or a carrier state. Those individuals with a positive antigen will be tested for hepatitis B antigen. This is found only in individuals with a positive serum, and its presence is associated with active viral replication indicating the most highly infective state. It is during this time that a pregnant mother is at the highest risk to transmit infection to her fetus. Transmission may occur in as many as 90% of cases (CDC, 1988; Edwards, 1988).

The hepatitis B vaccine provides active immunity against the virus and is administered at birth, 1 month, and 6 months of age. Vaccinations can dramatically reduce the incidence of vertical transmission (mother to fetus) but can also reduce the incidence of transmission by other care providers who may contact the infection through provision of services. Teachers, day-care providers, health care workers, social service agency workers, and any other individuals who may have reason to provide service to individuals or families with HBV infections need to strongly consider seeking immunization against the virus. The potential for acquiring HBV virus is significant. Though not as widely publicized, the potential loss of productive individuals and resources is as high as the loss encountered with acquired immune deficiency syndrome.

Human Immunodeficiency Virus/Acquired Immune Deficiency Syndrome

The disease known in our society by the familiar term AIDS is the outcome or clinical manifestation of infection by a virus called the human immunodeficiency virus (HIV). Persons infected with HIV are said to be HIV positive, and in the early stages of the disease infants are usually nonsymptomatic or the symptoms are mild. As the disease progresses, the symptoms worsen. The most severe manifestation of the disease is referred to as Acquired Immune Deficiency Syndrome or AIDS. Children have a shorter incubation period (12 months) between acquisition of HIV and a transition to AIDS than do adults (8–10 years) (Simonds & Rogers, 1992). In spite of evidence of significant underreporting, there were 7,472 cases of pediatric AIDS in the United States in 1996 (Centers for Disease Control and Prevention, 1996). There were no known cases reported before 1982. Now, HIV ranks as the 7th leading cause of pediatric death (Porter, 2002). The disease is one that has disproportionately affected poor young minority women (Women and HIV, 1998). It is the third leading cause of death in women 24–44, but the number one cause of death in African American women, who accounted for 56% of female cases in 1996; Hispanic women accounted for 20% of all female cases.

Almost 93% of childhood AIDS cases occur by transfer of the virus from an HIV positive mother (1) through the placenta, (2) during childbirth, or (3) through breastfeeding (Landry & Smith, 1998). Though the role of the placenta in transmission of the AIDS virus is unknown, it is believed that the transfer of the virus occurs either late in pregnancy or during labor (Women and HIV, 1998). However, only about one fourth of HIV positive mothers transmit the virus to their unborn children. The remaining cases are accounted for by infection through blood products, such as blood transfusions in hemophiliacs or child sexual abuse. It has also been found that 14% of infants who are breastfed by HIV positive women contract the disease in this manner. Yet, in a sad acknowledgement of the desperate conditions elsewhere in the world, women in developing countries are advised that the benefits of breastfeeding outweigh the risk of infection (Women and HIV, 1998).

Currently, the HIV infection cannot be identified in the nursery population, even though infected children typically display behavioral characteristics such as irritability, inconsolability, poor feeding, and disrupted sleeping patterns that are similar to neonates who are drug exposed. Yet, it has been determined that all infants born to HIV-infected mothers have antibodies to HIV. Even so, there are no known cases of casual transmission of the HIV virus to caregivers in nursery, day-care settings, or schools (Wolters, Brouwers, Civitello, & Moss, 1995). While precaution in handling bodily fluids is the same as with children with hepatitis B, child-care workers need not be afraid to hug or engage in the human contact needed by children.

Because of the relationship between poverty, drug use, and HIV infection, infants and children infected with HIV represent a population already removed from mainstream health care. Furthermore, social and economic factors influencing families increases the likelihood that these children will not receive optimal treatment. Many times, maternal risk behaviors continue following childbirth, reducing the probability for either monitoring or intervening in the physical and developmental progression of childhood. Many of these children are abandoned in health care facilities or exposed to poor sanitation and overcrowding that speed up the progression of the infection. On the other hand, the life expectancy for infants and children with HIV infection continues to improve, with 50–60% surviving past age 6 (Meyers, 1994).

HIV infection in children is classified according to the rate at which the disease is progressing. In the best case, the disease is **static**, and infants and children gain developmental milestones, even though they tend to start behind and their rate of gain is slower than expected (Brouwers, Belman, & Epstein, 1994; Gay & Armstrong, 1995). When the disease is not static, it is either plateaued or subacute. In both cases, children tend to lose previously gained milestones, with the loss being more rapid in the subacute form. In 20% of the cases, infants begin to display symptoms in their first year of life. The life expectancy for these infants is much shorter (4 years) than for the remaining 80% of infected children who do not begin to have symptoms until school age or adolescence (Porter, 2002). Eventually, children experience severe deficits in cognitive, motor, social, and expressive language skills. Some children also experience autistic-like behaviors such as flat affect, loss of speech, and lack of interest in others (Wolters et al., 1995). Developmental function, both cognitively and behaviorally, is affected by slowed or interrupted brain development (myelinopathy) and later abnormalities that include brain atrophy and calcification (Gay & Armstrong, 1995).

In addition to behavioral declines, children's health progressively worsens. Symptoms include failure to thrive, enlarged lymph nodes, enlarged liver and spleen, enlarged heart, chronic bacterial infections, respiratory infections, diarrhea, and fevers. For unknown reasons, survival times are shorter for children infected prenatally or during the first year of life, compared to those who contract infection during later childhood and adulthood. *Pneumocystis carinii* pneumonia is the most common complication of the syndrome that affects survival in very young children. Although this very common bacteria is of little danger to those with intact immune systems, it can be very serious and even fatal to infants and children with HIV or AIDS.

Failure to thrive is a major problem affecting infants and young children with AIDS. Lactose intolerance and subsequent diarrhea are common findings among the affected pediatric population. Oral lesions due to yeast infections often result from prolonged antibiotic therapy. These lesions are very painful and may cause oral aversion and reduce the child's ability to maintain adequate food intake to support continued health. Consistency in caregivers is important to develop positive relationships that allow for optimum feeding practices.

Current practice for the care of infants of mothers who are either HIV positive or have AIDS is that of support and observation. These infants are usually not treated with antiviral medications unless symptoms develop. Once conversion to HIV positive occurs, medications are initiated to attempt to slow the progression of the disease. The decision about when to begin treatment is significant, as the HIV virus mutates so often that all currently used drugs eventually lose potency to drug-resistant strains of the virus, which significantly limits treatment options (Steele, 2001). On the other hand, treatment is most effective when begun early in the symptom progression.

Many medical centers are experiencing an increasing number of infants being abandoned after delivery by HIV positive mothers who are drug abusers and who are unable to care for their children. Many of these infants experience conditions related to premature birth or other conditions, including drug addiction, that place them at increased risk for developmental disabilities along with their HIV status. Placement in foster-care settings can provide the opportunity to deal with problems that arise as a result of the progression of the HIV status to AIDS.

Advocacy for infants and children affected with both HIV and AIDS is the prime role for those involved with planning care for these children. As economic disadvantage is closely associated with the prevalence of pediatric HIV, families are likely to benefit from an array of services. Often parents themselves are dealing with the grief, anxiety, and depression associated with AIDS and may have diminished energy to give to their child (Porter, 2002). Prevention of the progression of HIV and AIDS is the goal, but providing a quality of life to those currently affected is the issue. A multidisciplinary approach to the many problems encountered by this population is essential for establishing a systematic plan for meeting all the physical, developmental, and emotional needs of these children. An early first step is assessment of family resources and priorities. Family-centered intervention that is coordinated across many agencies should be based upon a respect for family expectations and goals. "Family" might include nonnuclear members, because of the illness or death of one or both parents.

Treatment suggestions:

1. Physical therapy for progressive hypertonicity and eventual loss of ambulation.
2. Language intervention for loss of ability, especially expressive and attentional problems.
3. Psychological intervention to deal with stress of living with a terminal illness which possesses strong social stigmatization.
4. Social worker to help child deal with the probable loss of one or both parents.
5. Continuous communication with health care providers as to the physical condition of child.

MENINGITIS/ENCEPHALITIS

Meningitis and **encephalitis** are both infections that involve the central nervous system with particular concentration in the brain. Though the factors causing these infections may occasionally appear to be the same, the implications for treatment differ depending on the infecting agent. The brain is protected by a fluid-filled sac that surrounds it and the spinal cord. Moreover, the brain matter is intertwined with blood vessels that provide blood flow for the transport of food and oxygen. In the absence of infection involving the central nervous system, pressure is maintained at a steady state, permitting normal blood flow (see Figure 8–7).

Figure 8–7
Brain with
Uninfected
Meninges

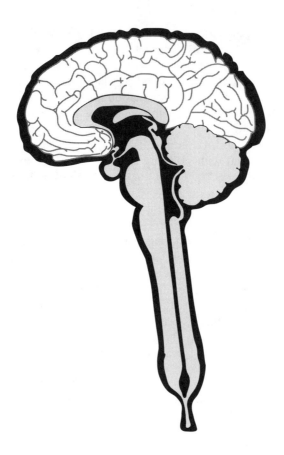

Meningitis

Meningitis is a condition in which infection occurs as the result of the entry of bacteria around the surface of the brain, producing inflammation of the **meninges**, the coverings that surround the brain and spinal cord (see Figure 8–8). The meninges are three membranes (i.e., dura mater, pia mater, arachnoid) that are between the skull and brain and also between the vertebral column and the spinal cord. It is in this area that the cerebrospinal fluid flows over the surface of the nervous system. *Cerebrospinal fluid* is a clear, colorless, odorless fluid that resembles water and contains glucose, proteins, salts, and white blood cells. Its function is to protect the nervous system from injury by acting as a shock absorber. It also carries oxygen and nutrition to the nerve cells and takes waste products away to be reabsorbed in the circulatory system. Small blood vessels that are part of the skull's lining act as the mechanism for exchange.

Meningitis does not refer to the guilty organism, rather to the condition that results from a bacterial or viral infection. For example, in 10–20% of the cases of bacterial meningitis, *streptococcal pneumoniae* is the infecting agent (Mactier, Galea, & McWilliam, 1998). With meningitis, swelling occurs and there also is degeneration of some of the surrounding nerve cells. It is this swelling and nerve destruction that cause the neurological disabilities that follow in 20–30% of acute

Figure 8–8
Brain Showing
Swollen and
Infected
Meninges

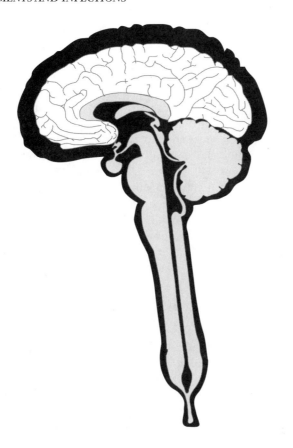

cases of meningitis (Arditi & Mason, 1998). On occasion there may also be an invasion of the infection into the brain matter itself through tears in the meninges. This increases the potential of permanent brain and nerve injury. Acute meningitis may produce significant symptoms in children; in 10% of cases, meningitis leads to death within a very short period of time (Arditi & Mason, 1998).

Acute bacterial meningitis is generally a disease of the young or the chronically ill (Sadovsky, 1998). Immaturity of the immune system in the very young and the compromised immune system in children with such disabilities as head trauma, spina bifida, and sickle cell anemia, places these individuals at greater risk for developing meningitis. Recurrent otitis media is also a condition related to a higher rate of meningitis (Arditi & Mason, 1998). Other factors that are risks for children but not adults include maternal education level, poverty, and lack of a primary care physician. However, the strongest risk factor for meningitis in children under 18 years of age is maternal smoking, with the risk increasing proportionately with the number of cigarettes smoked each day (Sadovsky, 1998). As many as 37% of cases of meningitis in children can be linked to maternal smoking.

About 45–145 cases of bacterial meningitis occur for every 100,000 people per year, and approximately 90% of these individuals survive the infection (Arditi &

Mason, 1998). Of those affected, approximately one fourth will have some degree of residual effect (Arditi & Mason, 1998). Residual damage ranges from very minor dysfunctions to significant multiple disabilities.

The initial symptoms include fever, vomiting, severe headache, anorexia, and drowsiness (Mactier et al., 1998). The actual diagnosis of meningitis is made through laboratory testing along with a physical examination. A **spinal tap** may reveal cloudy cerebrospinal fluid due to the increased number of white blood cells present in the fluid. Occasionally, the fluid may appear bloody because the tiny blood vessels in the skull's lining break from the increased pressure. Blood and spinal fluid cultures will determine which bacterium is responsible for the current infection. Powerful antibiotics that would be effective against any of the possible organisms are used until a specific organism is identified.

Survivors of acute bacterial meningitis may have long-term effects generally associated with the central nervous system. Seizures are common and may be resistant to normal anticonvulsant therapy. The intractable nature of the seizures may be the result of specific focal areas of the brain that have been attacked by the disease. Bilateral deafness may occur as a result of pressure placed on the auditory nerve by inflammation of the meninges. Deafness may also be caused by antibiotic therapy needed to eradicate the bacteria. Hydrocephalus frequently occurs because of scar tissue formation in the subarachnoid space that permanently affects the normal fluid pathways for cerebral spinal fluid. Occasionally, brain abscesses may develop that produce symptoms much like those of a brain tumor.

Children with disabilities from meningitis will require extensive services. In addition to the described effects of the infection, many of these children suffer from hyperactivity (along with their seizures), motor involvement (particularly cerebral palsy), and mental retardation.

Treatment considerations:

1. Environmental safety measures are necessary to protect these children from injury during seizures and during periods of erratic behavior.
2. Programs to deal with hearing impairments and visual problems may be part of the general plan when determining services.
3. Physical therapy for children with spasticity, ataxia.
4. Consideration of shunt in infants and children who experience hydrocephalus.

Encephalitis

Encephalitis is generally an inflammation of the brain and spinal cord (see Figure 8–9), which may occur as a result of viral or bacterial infection spread by the circulatory system or from movement of infection up neural **axons** to the brain. The infecting agent disperses throughout the brain and to the meninges causing inflammation. A majority of cases of encephalitis are associated with the childhood viral diseases mentioned earlier in this chapter.

Most cases of encephalitis in the United States occur during the summer since the major transmitting source is the mosquito (Whaley & Wong, 1989). Some kinds of viruses that eventually lead to encephalitis selectively attack specific types of neurons (as in polio), while others, such as the herpes virus, establish focal areas of in-

Figure 8–9
Brain Affected
by Encephalitis

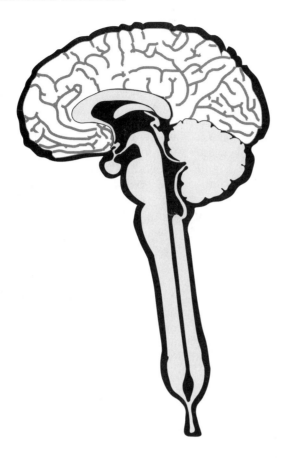

fection dispersed throughout the brain. The manner in which dispersion occurs determines the outcome of the nervous system function following an infection.

Encephalitis can be diagnosed when an individual has symptoms of early onset meningitis, but a spinal tap cannot confirm the presence of bacteria. In other words, ruling out meningitis is one part of the diagnosis of encephalitis because symptoms of the two diseases appear to be so similar. Additional diagnostic findings may be a normal white blood cell count and an elevated protein level in the spinal fluid. In this disease, early symptoms include an unsteady gait and seizures, with the later onset of a decreased level of consciousness. Medical measures are initiated to prevent further deterioration of the physical condition. Viral cultures will identify agents responsible for acute encephalitis, or occasionally a brain biopsy itself may be necessary to identify the virus producing the illness. Most cases of viral encephalitis will recover without significant long-term effects. This is not the case with herpes encephalitis; all virally induced encephalitis can potentially lead to permanent and significant damage. Furthermore, infants born to virally infected mothers and have experienced in utero viral encephalitis with subsequent interruption in brain growth will be born with severe neurological damage.

Effects of encephalitis on central nervous system function may include severe language disorders and muscle weakness or paralysis on one side of the

Case Study   MADDY'S COCHLEAR IMPLANT: INTERVIEW WITH KIM SHAFER

I just wasn't ready for the cochlear implant at first. My husband was ready though. He said, "I've read about these things, and I've seen the results." But we went on with hearing aids and sign language until just before Maddy's 3rd birthday. Then I was ready. I had seen enough. One of my friends had a daughter just about a year older than Maddy and I'd seen her have the implant and be successful with it.

It wasn't the device that scared me, it was the surgery. I would be taking a beautiful child who is perfect in every other way and letting the doctors cut her head open and take out a piece of her skull. What if something happened on that surgical table? I was scared to death. Maddy is my baby, and I don't have a replacement for her. I think I needed that extra year to think about the cochlear implant, because when Maddy was almost 3 years old I was ready.

We went in for the surgery and I didn't cry when I saw her the night before. They took her into surgery and it just seemed like all of a sudden the doctor was back saying, "It went great!" They actually tested the electrodes in the surgical room so they could tell whether they were going to work or not. After the surgery, we had to wait for the incision to heal. It was about a 5-inch cut that went from the bottom of her ear all the way to the top of her head.

The internal unit of the cochlear implant is a magnet and on the end of that is a group of electrodes that lead down into the cochlea in the middle ear. The cochlea has the hair cells that make it possible for most of us to hear normally. The sound bounces off those hair cells and goes into the brain. But Maddy's hair cells were damaged. They think it was probably not the medication she got for the meningitis, but from the swelling the meningitis caused. So, in the cochlear implant, that group of electrodes in the cochlea takes the place of those hair cells.

On the left side of Maddy's head, she also has an external unit. After the incision healed, they actually attached the external unit—it was held in place by the magnet inside her skull. We think that is so cool! The hole on the side of it is the microphone. All the environmental sounds go in through that microphone, down the wire—to a speech processor she wears in a little fanny pack. I'm trying to work with Advanced Bionics Corporation who makes Maddy's implant to produce a pouch that is more efficient. We need something that doesn't stick out when Maddy wears a tight-fitting shirt. She always looks like she's pregnant, you know? But that's a small price for what she's gained from this.

The speech processor has an on/off switch, a volume control, and a sensitivity dial, which at her age, she doesn't use because I don't know that she can really gauge that. An older person

body. Frequently, focal seizures occur, and EEG findings are sometimes abnormal, indicating the presence of a seizure disorder. Infants and children may experience impairments in vision and hearing, especially with herpes encephalitis. Reactivation of the virus, after the initial recovery from the illness, may further damage the nervous system. Affected children also have an increased incidence of behavior problems and hyperactivity, requiring environmental precautions to assure their safety. Depending upon the severity of the

will be able to tell whether environmental sounds are too much external noise. If they want to focus on communication, they will turn the processor's sensitivity down. Then the background noise will be diffused so that they can focus on a conversation.

So all the sound goes in the microphone, down to the processor, and within seconds comes back out, goes through the skull to energize the hairs on the cochlea and then she hears. Maddy has been working on understanding all that sound. That's what a new baby does when we repeat words to them and pretty soon they start to imitate. That's what Maddy's been doing for the last 2 years—repeating sounds back to us. Her language has gained in leaps and bounds.

I'm very proud of Maddy,

Maddy Shafer and the family pet.

she's doing a great job. When we were getting ready for the cochlear implant, we saw a great video that had some awesome examples of a little girl who had the implant and her success. It showed a teenager in sports wearing only a headband to keep the headpiece on. The message was that anything that is your goal in life and you want to accomplish you can still do it with the cochlear implant. Well I know it's true.

I really believe that the cochlear implant will help deaf kids to accomplish their goals and dreams even more so because they won't have that communication gap. Sign language is wonderful and I don't want Maddy to stop that. She has wonderful friends still using sign language, but to be able to communicate by voice and having people understand you and you understanding them is such a huge leap.

infection, children may experience mental retardation with all the adverse affects of developmental delay.

IN CONCLUSION

As children reach preschool and school age, parents will be faced with placement decisions. In the past, most children with blindness and deafness were sent to residential schools for the blind/deaf. However, with recent inclusion practices, it seems likely that most children with sensory impairments will be served in general classroom settings, even if these children also have other disabilities. Parents need to be aware of placement options, the implications of these options, and strategies to advocate for the choices made for children with visual impairments. Beginning early with low vision tools (e.g., Braille, large print text, electronic systems, etc.), social skills training, and mobility and orientation training can increase the degree of independence and social competence experienced in these settings by children with visual impairments. Likewise, techniques that enhance linguistic and social development for infants and preschoolers with deafness, such as auditory amplification, cochlear implants, use of sign language, and alternative communication methods, should begin as early as possible.

Rapid advancements in electronic/computerized capacities will likely continue to open new doors to academic, domestic, and vocational opportunities for persons with visual impairments. Very young children with visual impairments should be introduced to computer systems. Likewise, team members will be pressed to keep pace with developments in technology that might increase independent functioning while being practical and cost effective for families.

Procedures for treating many once untreatable causes of visual and hearing impairment will continue to evolve. Like other forms of early intervention, the cost of remediating loss of vision may be far less than the costs of long-term specialized intervention for children and families.

Each of the infections described in this chapter may have effects ranging from mild to devastating. The most effective way of decreasing the incidence of infections and their effects on children is through education. Many, though not all, infections can be prevented through a more cautious approach to living within our environment and within our society. Both a recognition of cause and an understanding of the nature of the action of bacteria and viruses can make a difference in the approach to prevention and treatment. Important advances have already nearly eradicated diseases such as rubella that place unborn children at risk of disabilities. Even AIDS, the most frightening epidemic of the late 20th century, could be wiped out with adequate education and preventative intervention.

STUDY GUIDE QUESTIONS

1. Into what three components is the auditory mechanism functionally separated? Describe the three practical functions of these components.
2. Along what two dimensions is sound heard?
3. What is the difference between a conductive hearing loss and a sensorineural hearing loss? What are common causes of a conductive hearing loss? Of a sensorineural hearing loss?
4. List the symptoms of otitis media and describe treatment for the infection.
5. What developmental domains are most affected by loss of hearing?
6. Name some sign language systems. Which is the most commonly used approach? Explain the debate in favor of and opposed to manual sign.

7. What are some disadvantages to using hearing aids?

8. List some considerations that should be made when serving preschool children with hearing impairments.

9. Discriminate between blindness and low vision.

10. Describe the visual process.

11. Describe three refractive errors in vision.

12. Name and explain two visual errors caused by a disruption in muscle coordination of the eyes.

13. What are cortical visual impairments?

14. What are common causes of visual impairments?

15. Define and give a brief description of each: glaucoma and cataracts.

16. What recommendations should be given to caregivers in working with children with visual impairments?

17. What is the difference between congenital and adventitious blindness?

18. What might be included in programs specifically designed for infants and toddlers with visual impairments? What factors should be considered in selection of appropriate orientation and mobility adaptations?

19. In what ways are children who are visually impaired disproportionately faced with a lifetime of "disadvantage?" How can educators intervene to limit this disadvantage?

20. Define biological agents. How do these agents cause damage to human cells? How do they travel throughout the human body?

21. When do pathogenic bacterial infections occur? What circumstances may affect an infant's outcome?

22. Explain the relationship between socioeconomic status, low birth weight, and infection.

23. Why is appropriate assessment of the physiological status of an infant at delivery important? What are the keys to effective treatment of an infected infant?

24. List the initial symptoms of an infection. What interventions are warranted for infants experiencing infections at, or shortly after, birth to provide opportunity for full development?

25. What are viruses and how do they differ from bacteria? How has prevention of viral diseases been accomplished?

26. What are the TORCH diseases? Briefly describe the cause, course, symptoms, and outcomes of each.

27. Explain what is meant by "shedding" of a live virus. How does shedding occur?

28. List characteristics of women who may be at high risk for contracting hepatitis B virus. What individuals should most strongly consider immunization against this virus?

29. How do social and economic factors contribute to placing children with HIV at high risk for disease progression?

30. Explain the differential causes, courses, and outcomes of meningitis and encephalitis. What is the difference between viral meningitis and bacterial meningitis?

References

Allen, K. E., & Marotz, L. (1989). *Developmental profiles: Birth-to-six.* Albany, NY: Delmar.

Allen, T. (1986). Patterns of academic achievement among hearing impaired students: 1974 and 1983. In A. Schildroth & M. Karchmer (Eds.), *Deaf children in America* (pp. 161–206).

American Liver Foundation. (2001). *Hepatitis B: Breaking the cycle of infection from mother to newborn.* Retrieved June 10, 2002 from *http://www.liverfoundation. org/db/articles/1036*

Arditi, M., & Mason, E. O. (1998). Three-year multicenter surveillance of *pneumococcal* meningitis in children. *Pediatrics, 102,* 1087–1098.

Atlantic Coast Ear Specialists. (July, 2002). *Central auditory processing disorders.* Retrieved July 30, 2002 from *http://www.earaces.com/ CAPD.htm.*

Bateman, J. B. (1983). Genetics in pediatric ophthalmology. *Pediatric Clinics of North America, 30*(6), 1015–1031.

Batshaw, M. L., & Perret, Y. M. (1988). *Children with handicaps: A medical primer.* Baltimore: Paul H. Brookes.

Boehme, T. (1985). Hepatitis B: The nurse-midwife's role in management and prevention. *Journal of Nurse-Midwifery, 30*(2), 79–87.

Bolognese, R., Aldinger, R., & Roberts, N. (1981). Prenatal care in the prevention of infection. *Clinics in Perinatology, 8*(3), 605–615.

Brouwers, P., Belman, A., & Epstein, L. (1994). Organ-specific complications: Central nervous system involvement: Manifestations, evaluation and pathogenesis. In P. A. Pizzo & C. M. Wilfert (Eds.), *Pediatric AIDS: The challenge of HIV infection in infants, children, and adolescents* (pp. 433–455). Baltimore: Williams & Wilkins.

Cartledge, G., & Cochran, L. (1996). Social skill self-assessments by adolescents with hearing impairment in residential and public schools. *Remedial & Special Education, 17,* 30–37.

Centers for Disease Control and Prevention (1996). *The Florida AIDS, STD, and TB monthly surveillance Report,* 139. Atlanta: U.S. Department of Health and Human Services.

Centers for Disease Control. (1988). Prevention of perinatal transmission of hepatitis B virus: Prenatal screening of all pregnant women for hepatitis B surface antigen, recommendations of the Immunization Practices Advisory Committee. *Morbidity and Mortality Weekly Report, 37*(2), 341–351.

Centers for Disease Control. (June, 2002). *Current vaccine shortages.* CDC: National Immunization Program. Retrieved June 10, 2002 from *http://www.cdc.gov/nip/ news/shortages/default.htm*

Chalifoux, L. M., & Fagan, B. (1997). Labeling children who are visually impaired "disadvantaged." *Journal of Visual Impairment and Blindness, 91,* 531–539.

Clarke, K. L. (1988). Barriers or enablers: Mobility devices for visually impaired and multiply handicapped infants and preschoolers. *Education of the Visually Handicapped, 20,* 115–133.

Current progress in finding genes involved in hearing impairment. (1995). *http://www.boystown.org/deafgene. registry*

Darrow, A. (1993). The role of music in Deaf culture: Implications for music teachers. *Journal of Research in Music Education, 41*(2), 93–110.

Diienstaf, J., Wands, J., & Koff, R. (1986). Acute viral hepatitis. In Isselbacher, K. (Ed.), *Harrison's principles of internal medicine* (11th ed.). New York: McGraw-Hill.

Division of STD/HIV Prevention. (1995). *Sexually transmitted disease surveillance.* U.S. Department of Health and Human Services, Public Health Service. Atlanta: CDC.

Edwards, M. (1988). Hepatitis B serology: Help in interpretation. *Pediatric Clinics of North America, 35*(3), 503–515.

Emmer, C. L., & Besser, R. E. (2002). Combating antimicrobial resistence: Intervention programs to promote appropriate antibiotic use. *Infectious Medicine, 19*(4), 160–173.

Gast, M. (1983). Herpes update 1983. *Missouri Perinatal Progress, 5*(4), 1–4.

Gay, C. L., & Armstrong, F. D. (1995). The effects of HIV on cognitive and motor development in children born to HIV-seropositive women. *Pediatrics, 96,* 1075–1080.

Goldstein, H. (1980). The reported demography and causes of blindness throughout the world. *Advances in Ophthalmology, 40,* 1–99.

Green, M. (1997). Appropriate principles in the use of antibiotics in children. *Clinical Pediatrics, 36,* 207–209.

Grossman, J. (1980). Perinatal viral infections. *Clinics in Perinatology, 7*(1), 257–271.

Harel, S., Holtzman, M., & Feinsod, M. (1985). The late visual bloomer. In S. Harel & N. Anastasiow (Eds.), *The at-risk infant: Psychosocial medical aspects* (pp. 359–362). Baltimore: Paul H. Brookes.

Harrington, M., & Meyers, H. W. (1992). Preschool programs for the hearing impaired: Young children with hearing disabilities deserve special attention. *Principal, 34*–36.

Herrmann, K. (1982). Congenital and perinatal varicella. *Clinical Obstetrics and Gynecology, 25*(3), 605–609.

Hicks, R., Fowler, K., Richardson, M., Dahle, A., Adams, L., & Pass, R. (1993). Congenital cytomegalovirus infection and neonatal auditory screening. *The Journal of Pediatrics, 123*(5), 779–782.

Hoon, A. H. (1991). Visual impairments in children with developmental disabilities. In A. J. Capute & P. J. Accardo (Eds.), *Developmental disabilities in infancy and early childhood* (pp. 395–411). Baltimore: Paul H. Brookes.

Hughes, D., & Simpson, L. (1995). The role of social change in preventing low birth weight. *The Future of Children, 5*, 50–63.

Issacs, D., & Moxon, R. (1991). *Neonatal infections.* Oxford: Butterworth-Heinmann.

Janesick, V. J. (1990). Bilingual multicultural education and the deaf: Issues and possibilities. *Journal of Educational Issues of Language Minority Students, 7*, 99–109.

Jerger, S., & Martin. R. (1995). Childhood hearing impairment: Auditory and linguistic interactions during multidimensional speech processing. *Journal of Speech and Hearing Research, 38*(4), 930–949.

Kai, J. (1996). What worries parents when their preschool children are acutely ill, and why: A qualitative study. *British Medical Journal, 313*, 983–987.

Kaplan, S. L. (1997). Prevention of hearing loss in meningitis. *Lancet, 350*(9072), 158–160.

Kekelis, L. S., & Prinz, P. M. (1996). Blind and sighted children with their mothers: The development of discourse skills. *Journal of Visual Impairment & Blindness, 90*(5), 423–437.

Kennedy, C. R., Kim, L., Dees, D. C., Campbell, M. J., & Thornton, A. R. D. (1998). Controlled trial of universal neonatal screening for early identification of permanent childhood hearing impairment. *Lancet, 352*(9145), 1957–1965.

Kenyon, T. A., Matuck, M. A., & Stroh, G. (1998). Persistent low immunization coverage among inner-city preschool children despite access to free vaccine. *Pediatrics, 101*, 612–617.

Kirchner, C. (1988). National estimates of prevalence and demographics of children with visual impairments. In M. D. Wang, M. D. Reynolds, & H. J. Walberg (Eds.), *Handbook of special education: Research and practice* (Vol. 3, pp. 135–153). Elmsford, NY: Pergamon.

Klein, M. (1988). Hepatitis B virus: Perinatal management. *Perinatal/Neonatal Nursing, 1*(4), 12–23.

Kohl, S., & James, A. (1985). Herpes simplex virus encephalitis during childhood. Importance of brain biopsy diagnosis. *Journal of Pediatrics, 107*(2), 212–215.

Korones, S. (1988). Uncommon virus infections of the mother, fetus and newborn: Influenza, mumps and measles. *Clinics of Perinatology, 15*(2), 259–272.

Landry, K., & Smith, T. (1998). Neurocognitive effects of HIV infection on young children: Implications for assessment. *Topics in Early Childhood Special Education, 18*, 160–169.

Leclair, J. (1980). Control of nosocomial neonatal viral infections. *Critical Care Quarterly, 3*(3), 71–77.

Mactier, H., Galea, P., & McWilliam, R. (1998). Acute obstructive hydrocephalus complicating bacterial meningitis in childhood. *British Medical Journal, 316*(7146), 1887–1890.

Magid, M. S. (1995). *Pediatric pathology.* Retrieved September 9, 1999 from *http://edcenter. med.cornell.edu/ CUMC_Pathnotes/Pediatric.html*

March of Dimes. (2001). Infections that threaten a healthy birth. 2001 *March of Dimes Research Report.* Retrieved September 10, 2002 from *http://www.marchofdimes.com*

Margo, K. L., & Shaughnessy, A. F. (1998). Antiviral drugs in healthy children. *American Family Physician, 57*, 1073–1078.

Mauk, G. W., & Mauk, P. P. (1992). Somewhere out there: Preschool children with hearing impairment and learning disabilities. *Topics in Early Childhood Special Education, 12*, 174–196.

Meyers, A. (1994). Natural history of congenital HIV infection. *Journal of School Health, 64*, 9–10.

Morse, M. (1991). Visual gaze behaviors: Considerations in working with visually impaired and multiply handicapped children. *RE:view, 23*(1), 5–15.

Naeye, R., & Blanec, W. (1970). Relation of poverty and race to antenatal infection. *New England Journal of Medicine, 283*(11), 555–560.

National Institute on Deafness and Other Communication Disorders (March, 1999). Retrieved August 29, 1999 from *http://www.nidcd.A\/articles/ article4.html*

National Institute of Health Consensus Statement. (March, 1993). *Early identification of hearing impairment in infants and young children. 11*(1), 1–25. Bethesda, MD: NIH.

National Institute of Health Consensus Statement. (March, 1999). *Facts about deafness.* Retrieved August 29, 1999 from *http://www.nih.org.A\/ articles/article5.html*

Optometric Extension Program (1995). Parent's guide to children's visual development. Retrieved August 29, 1999 from *http://www.children-special-needs.org/ parenting/preschool/visual_child_development.html*

Planned Parenthood Federation of America. (1998). *Herpes: Questions and answers.* Retrieved August 29, 1999 from *http://plannedparenthood. org/sti-safesex/ herpes.htm*

Porter, V. (2002). Angels on the web: Helping children and their families cope with AIDS. *Medscape Infectious Diseases, 4*(1). Retrieved July 9, 2003 from *http://www.medscape.com/viewarticle/ 433150*

Preece, P., Blount, J., Glover, J., Fletcher, G., Peckham, C., & Griffiths, P. (1983). The consequences of primary cytomegalovirus infection in pregnancy. *Archives of Disease in Childhood, 58*, 970–975.

Pusey, W. (1933). *The history of syphilis.* Springfield, IL: Charles C. Thomas Publishers.

Ryalls, J., & Larouche, A. (1992). Acoustic integrity of speech production in children with moderate and severe hearing impairment. *Journal of Speech and Hearing Research, 35,* 88–96.

Sadovsky, R. (1998). Tobacco smoke exposure and meningococcal disease risk. *American Family Physician, 57,* 2848–2849.

Shapiro, M. B., & France, T. D. (1985). The ocular features of Down's syndrome. *American Journal of Ophthalmology, 99,* 659–663.

Simonds, R. J., & Rogers, M. F. (1992). Epidemiology of HIV in children and other populations. In A. C. Crocker, H. J. Cohen, & T. A. Kastner (Eds.), *HIV infection and developmental disabilities: A resource for service providers* (pp. 3–4). Baltimore: Paul H. Brookes.

Steele, R. W. (2001). 2001 American Academy of Pediatrics National Conference and Exhibition: Pediatric infectious disease highlights. Retrieved June 10, 2002 at *Medscape Pediatrics, 3*(2). *http://www.medscape.com/viewarticle/415038*

Stewart, D. A., Gentry, C. G., & McLeod, R. (1991). Using instructional design principles to produce an IVD to enhance the linguistic environment of deaf children. *Journal of Special Education Technology, 11*(3), 121–135.

Sykanda, A. M., & Levitt, S. (1982). The physiotherapist in the developmental management of the visually impaired child. *Child: Care, Health and Development, 8,* 261–270.

Teplin, S. W. (1983). Development of blind infants and children with retrolental fibroplasia: Implications for physicians. *Pediatrics, 71,* 6–12.

Thomas, D., Salmon, R. L., & King, J. (1998). Rates of first measles-mumps-rubella immunization in Wales. *Lancet, 351*(9120), 1927.

Uslan, M. (1983). Provision of orientation and mobility services in 1990. *Journal of Visual Impairment and Blindness, 77,* 213–215.

Vaccination coverage by race/ethnicity and poverty levels among children 19–35 months—United States, 1997. (November 1998). *Morbidity and Mortality Weekly Report, 47*(44), 956–960.

Van Beneden, C. A., Whitney, C. G., Levine, O. S., & Schwartz, B. (October, 2000). Preventing pneumococcal disease among infants and young children: Recommendations of the Advisory Committee on Immunization Practices. *Morbidity and Mortality Weekly Report, 49,* 1–29.

Whaley, L. F., & Wong, D. L. (1989). *Essentials of pediatric nursing* (3rd ed.). St. Louis: C. V. Mosby.

Whitley, R., Soong, S., & Linneman, C. (1982). Herpes simplex encephalitis-clinical assessment. *Journal of the American Medical Association, 247*(3), 317–320.

Whitley, R., Yeager, A., & Kartus, P. (1983). Neonatal herpes simplex virus infection: Follow-up evaluation of vidarabine therapy. *Pediatrics, 72*(6), 778–785.

Wolters, P. L., Brouwers, P., Civitello., L., & Moss, H. A. (1995). Receptive and expressive language function of children with symptomatic HIV infection and relationship with disease parameters: A longitudinal 24-month follow-up study, *AIDS, 11,* 1135–1144.

Women and HIV. (1998). *Online Psych.* Retrieved September 10, 1999 from *http://www. onlinepsych.com*

9

Discretionary Programs for Infants and Toddlers with Special Needs

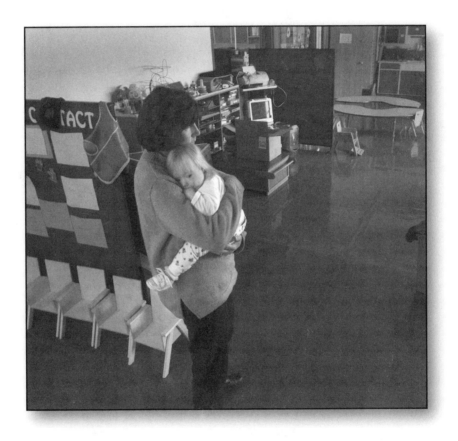

Shortly after her first birthday, Dawn was diagnosed with cerebral palsy. Her parents are confused, overwhelmed, and at a loss to know where to turn for information and help. Louis and Jeffrey are twins. At 6 months, Jeff is holding up his head, sitting unsupported, reaching for mom and dad, and chubby from many happy mealtimes. Lou has met none of these milestones. He is generally irritable and fussy, has problems sucking his bottle, and difficulty raising his head, arms, or legs. His

> *parents cannot figure out the difference in their boys. Both [Dawn and Lou] of these children are candidates for early intervention. Dawn has a definite diagnosis: a brain abnormality. Although Lou's pediatrician says it is too early to know for sure, he has symptoms that show he is at risk even without a diagnosis. That makes him eligible for early intervention, too.*
>
> (D'Amato & Lynn, 1999, 52)

Early intervention is often used to describe special services to very young children, particularly from birth through age 2. However, this simple definition does not do enough to convey the many implications of legally defined services to infants and toddlers. Early intervention also means professionals working in partnership with parents of children with special needs to help their children develop knowledge and skills (North Carolina, 1998). It is not unusual for parents to act as teachers or therapists, carrying out intervention programs at home that have been planned with specialists. Early intervention involves a comprehensive cluster of services that incorporates goals in education, health care, and social service for young children and their families (Hanson & Lynch, 1995). Sometimes an early intervention program actually provides wrap-around services that might mean family counseling, health care, therapy, and parent classes are all provided in the same building. Early intervention has as its center the life of families (Sontag & Schact, 1994) and is designed and delivered within the framework of informing and empowering family members (Berry & Hardman, 1998). Parents learn how to access resources and advocate for their children.

The intent of early intervention is multifaceted, but all these efforts work toward moderating or minimizing the effects of a disabling condition on a child's growth and development and preventing or reducing an at-risk condition (Hardman, Drew, & Egan, 1999). A directed, purposeful process aims at developing, improving, or changing conditions within an individual, in the environment, or with interactions with others (Umansky & Hooper, 1998). For early childhood professionals, early intervention is the heart and soul of what they do (Umansky & Hooper, 1998).

Early intervention is recognized as effective for (1) ameliorating and even preventing developmental disabilities, (2) reducing later grade retention of children, (3) reducing educational costs to school programs, and (4) improving the quality of family relationships (Salisbury & Smith, 1993). The most effective programs share these characteristics: they occur early in a child's life; they operate from a structured and systematic instructional base; they prescriptively address each child's assessed needs, and they include normally developing children as models (Salisbury & Smith, 1993). Significantly, children in early intervention programs show the most progress when their parents are involved in reinforcing new skills.

Early intervention for infants and toddlers differs from traditional educational services in several ways that are important for understanding current practice. First, it is sometimes difficult to diagnose a disability in a very young child. Since children don't mature at the same rates, some developmental lags may naturally or spontaneously disappear by the time a child is school age (Lerner, Lowenthal, & Egan, 1998). For example, many children are saying their first words by 18 months, but some may be 3 years old before they speak words. Assessment of cognitive abilities and language sometimes does not accurately predict a child's later performance. Even physical problems may not show up before 6 months of age because some time must pass before primitive reflexes are expected to disappear. Though a specific diagnosis is not possible, a very young child may be identified as developmentally delayed, communicating a need for special services without applying what may be an incorrect label or category. Children with developmental delays made up 64% of those served in early intervention programs and were most likely to enter early intervention after 21 months of age (U.S. Department of Education, 2000).

On the other hand, those children who were diagnosed before 12 months of age tended to have complicated and sometimes more severe physical and health issues. The latter made up almost 40% of the children served in early intervention (U.S. Department of Education, 2000) and needed services for reasons related to prenatal/perinatal abnormalities. One in six children in early intervention presented very low birth weight (Ventura, Martin, Curtin, & Matthews, 1999). A sizable number, 37%, had a history of care in the neonatal intensive care unit after birth, with half of those staying for more than a month (Hebbeler et al., 2001). Twenty-six percent of children in early intervention took prescription medication for a chronic condition and 16% used a medical device such as a respirator, breathing monitor, or nebulizer. Behavioral challenges, such as failing to pay attention, being easily startled, being very excitable, having sleep problems, and being aggressive with other children, were found in 10% to 40% of children in early intervention (Hebbeler et al., 2001).

A second aspect of early intervention that differs significantly is that the primary responsibility for the care of infants and toddlers usually falls to parents or to a consistent caregiver selected by parents. Often parents will take off several weeks of work to be with a newborn or grandparents become caregivers, before infants are turned over to a nonfamily member. A child younger than 3 years is most often cared for in her home. Even a child in commercial day care usually has contact with only a small number of people who interact with an infant or toddler every day and who do so in a familiar and secure environment. It is only reasonable to expect special interventions to be carried out by these same people and to be incorporated into the **natural routines** of daily life. Parents and caregivers may find themselves the mediators of treatment or instruction designed by others. It is essential that parents are provided an array of supports including information about the disability, information about services and resources, strategies for intervention, financial assistance, and social and emotional supports (McWilliam & Scott, 2001).

In addition, since so many basic skills are established in the earliest stages of development, intervention may have to address a multitude of domains. Movement, language, self-care, and cognition may be affected in different ways by the same disability, and certainly in different ways across different disabilities, requiring assistance from a number of specialists. A child with cerebral palsy, for example, may not learn to sit up, to hold a spoon, to form words, or to put together a simple puzzle without specific accommodations, instruction, or treatment. In many cases, when children with disabilities are identified before age 3, there are extensive medical needs involved as well. Consequently, a team of professionals may be required to consult or provide treatment to one child. Often these individuals represent different disciplines, and even different agencies, and the coordination of their services becomes complex. Among the support services that may be provided are speech pathology, audiology, psychological services, physical and occupational therapy, recreation, social work, counseling, and medical services (Committee on Children with Disabilities, 1999).

Finally, very young children are vulnerable to the influence of their surrounding environment. For example, an impoverished home may mean that a child's nutrition is put at risk; a lack of transportation may mean that appointments with a therapist will be missed; exhausted parents may mean an increased likelihood of abuse or neglect; and overly protective parents may keep children from necessary experiences or from reasonable expectations. A child's prognosis is greatly dependent on the parent's ability to provide for and cope with the child's special needs. It becomes critical to assess each family's health and resources and to provide support for their needs in order to benefit their child.

These attributes mean that early intervention must be designed to be family-centered, must attend closely to service coordination, and must encourage family empowerment in all aspects of decision making and delivery of services. A child's disability may be defined noncategorically, or a child's disabilities may be more severe and complex and require intensive therapy from a variety of professionals. Moreover, a family's needs may be just as important as the child's. These multiple factors play a large part in how IDEA legislation governing **discretionary programs** for infants and toddlers differs from the laws dealing with preschoolers from age 3 to 5. The specific mechanisms included in IDEA which foster successful early intervention include the possibility of noncategorical eligibility, team development of an **Individualized Family Service Plan (IFSP),** and designation of a **service coordinator.**

The goal of IDEA, Part C, early intervention for infants and toddlers with disabilities, is to:

- ◆ Enhance the development of infants and toddlers with disabilities and to minimize their potential for developmental delay.
- ◆ Reduce the educational costs to our society, including our Nation's schools, by minimizing the need for special education and related services after infants and toddlers with disabilities reach school age.
- ◆ Minimize the likelihood of institutionalization of individuals with disabilities and maximize the potential for their independent living in society.
- ◆ Enhance the capacity of families to meet the special needs of their infants and toddlers with disabilities.
- ◆ Enhance the capacity of state and local agencies and service providers to identify, evaluate, and meet the needs of historically underrepresented populations, particularly minority, low-income, inner-city, and rural populations.

Specific regulations for implementing IDEA, Part C, formally describe the appropriate delivery of services for all infants and toddlers who are disabled or at risk for disability and assure the rights of these children and their families. Table 9–1 summarizes family rights in early intervention.

Table 9–1   Family Rights in Early Intervention (North Carolina, 1998)

1. Receive a free, multidisciplinary assessment of the child to determine eligibility for special services.
2. Participate with the team of people who determines whether the child (and family) is eligible for special services.
3. If the child is eligible, participate in the planning and delivery of services and have an IFSP developed at no cost.
4. Receive early intervention services.
5. Have family needs assessed and addressed.
6. Receive help in the form of service coordination for child and family needs.
7. Receive help for transportation if that is necessary to benefit from services prescribed.
8. Have rights protected within the process of referral, assessment, and developing the IFSP.
9. Have qualified professionals working with the child and the family.
10. Have services provided (as much as is appropriate) in places that are typical for children of the same age without disabilities.
11. Resolve disputes with other team members or agencies through mediation, due process, or legal action if necessary.
12. Have plans developed for the child to transition to preschool services at age 3.

IDEA, PART C REGULATIONS

The federal Program for Infants and Toddlers with Disabilities (Part C of IDEA) assists states in providing comprehensive programs of early intervention for infants and toddlers with disabilities, ages birth through 2 years, and for their families (National Early Childhood Technical Assistance System [NECTAS], 1999). Each participating state must assure that early intervention will be available to every eligible child and his or her family. The governor of each state designates a lead agency to operate the program and appoints an **Interagency Coordinating Council (ICC)** to advise and assist. Currently all states participate, receiving annual funding based on the census figures of the number of children, birth through age 2 years, in their general populations (NECTAS, 1999). Lead agencies vary by state, as do specific definitions of who is eligible for services. As of August 30, 2001, about 230,400 infants and toddlers (almost 2% of children birth through age 2 in the United States) were directly served (Trohanis, 2002).

The purpose of Part C of IDEA is to develop a "system that provides early intervention services" and to "encourage States to expand opportunities for children under 3 years of age who would be at risk of having substantial developmental delay if they did not receive early intervention services." Eligible infants and toddlers are those under 3 years of age who need early intervention for one of two reasons: they display delay in one or more areas of development or there is a diagnosis of a physical or mental condition that has a high probability of resulting in developmental delay. Services must be family-directed, and special services such as evaluation, assessment, and planning take place only if a family approves and only with a family's participation.

Several factors may influence the extent to which families will agree to participate in the special services available to their very young children (Baird & Peterson, 1997). These factors include the nature of a family's concerns about their child, their level of stress and degree of support, their beliefs and values, their education level,

Case Study   TREATING JOSH'S AUTISM: INTERVIEW WITH AMY FINKEL

We probably spent 6 months of 60 hours a week in intensive research, after Josh's diagnosis. We talked to everybody on the phone; we made trips to Seattle to talk to a specialist, Dr. Alan Unis at the C.H.D.D.; we went to the Mayo Clinic to talk to their top people; we talked to parents across the country. We devoured books on the subject. Finally what we came across was something known as Applied Behavior Analysis (ABA), or the Lovaas Method. Applied Behavior Analysis/Lovaas Method/Discrete Trial Teaching Methodologies was really the only thing we found that had any kind of reputable data to back it up whatsoever.

We did try some peripheral therapies, such as Secretin I.V. infusions and mega-vitamin therapies. Anytime something came up, a prospective cure or treatment, we did a cost-benefit analysis to figure out the potential risks or side-effects and the potential benefits. We looked at each treatment individually and decided the ones we wanted to try.

But the major treatment we selected was ABA, which involved starting a home-therapy program, hiring therapists, and engaging in intensive one-on-one instruction for our son about 40–45 hours a week. The hardest part was envisioning in my head how we were going to do this. Just the physical arrangement of it: the people coming to my house; what they would be doing with my son; where they would do it. I remember distinctly the day I finally decided that we didn't have a choice, we had to do it, and I took the spare room apart.

It was a nice little guest room and I dismantled it to turn it into the therapy room. I remember it was as if we were doing everything in slow motion; carrying the bed out, taking the pictures off the wall. It was very surreal. We were told, in the beginning, to start out really bare, nothing on the walls. Anything that Josh might want to play with or that might be used as reinforcers for him were put up high on a shelf so that if he wanted them, he would be forced to communicate for them in some way.

Once the therapy room was set up, we hired a professional from outside the area to come in and hold a workshop so that my husband and I could be trained in the Lovaas methodology. We were lucky with the first therapist that we hired. She was a young intern at the University Programs in Communication Disorders where she worked 3 days a week with Josh in speech therapy.

Josh, back at that time, was pretty much an animal. He had no communication skills at all. If he didn't want to do something, he threw major temper tantrums. But we noticed that Robin, the speech intern, kept her cool, kept calm, kept working with him and by the end of the session, she'd get some results from him, after she wore him down. We decided, right then and there, that Robin would be the first person we'd hire.

We had no idea what Robin was going to do or what we were going to tell her to do, but we were just looking for someone we trusted with our son and that we thought had some basic skills. We were primarily tuned in to the speech therapy end of things at that time. Robin couldn't work for us while she was still working at the clinic, but we kept bugging her until she was done with her internship, and she agreed to come work for us in our home.

Robin really was a godsend because in the beginning we were just scared to death. The idea of someone being alone with my child in a room was frightening. What would they do to Josh? What would Josh do to them? We really had no clue. But Robin knew that we had to start with imitation skills. She gave us homework assignments. My husband taught block imitation and I taught gross motor imitation. We each did 5 or 6 hours a week; that's all we could handle in the beginning. Then Robin would come and help us through it—we helped each other, really, to learn the techniques. Giving us those little homework assignments in the beginning gave us something constructive to do, because we really hadn't known what to do to help our son.

That's how we got started with the home program. Then we all got training and learned more until Robin found someone she knew so we hired our second therapist. Over a period of 6 months, we went from about 10 hours of therapy a week up to 40–45 hours and we had a team of five therapists working in our home, 7 days a week.

Josh Finkel reading at school.

This was really tough to finance and we covered it out of our private funds. We had a small savings we had planned to use to buy a little lake place and a boat. We used that for that first year. The Department of Developmental Disabilities helped cover about 20% of the staffing just by providing respite care worker hours. The first thing we did was to cancel out cable, cancel our newspaper, cut back on all discretionary expenditures; we didn't go out to dinner, we had no more vacations, we ate a lot of chicken and potatoes that year.

But everything we read pointed to the need for early intervention. We were scared to death. We didn't know exactly what to do, but we knew we needed to do it fast. We knew we couldn't wait. We felt really fortunate that we had a savings account that we could draw on that first year because a lot of families don't.

We started the program with an animal. Josh had no communication skills whatsoever, he ate with his hands, he was tantruming all the time,

he was swimming in dirt, he was not potty trained at all, and he urinated on himself and smeared feces on the wall. He was an animal. Now, after 3 years, he has a vocabulary of over 300 words.

Josh has a number of questions he can answer and a number of phrases and words that he can say. He can tell me what he wants, he can say "I want muffin please." You can ask him if he wants something and he can say "Yes, please," or "No thank you."

He now eats with a spoon and a fork. Josh is in a regular kindergarten classroom with typically developing peers. He can swing on the swing sets, and he can slide down the slides. On the playground, now, you can't tell that he is disabled. He plays appropriately with his brother. He gives me hugs and kisses. He is 90% potty trained. He knows math, he knows his ABCs, and he knows prepositions and pronouns. The difference is just night and day.

their prior experience with children, and their rapport with those who provide services. For example, a family may be too emotionally involved in dealing with their child's diagnosis to make long-term plans. Other families may be so overwhelmed by immediate day-to-day survival that they cannot attend to other issues. On the other hand, some families will be eager to become involved. It is incumbent upon the service provider to respect the central, active role the family plays in the care of their child with special needs.

FAMILY-CENTERED EARLY INTERVENTION

Family-centered services have evolved from the original concept of parent involvement, when parents were encouraged to participate in activities that professionals felt were important (McWilliam, Tocci, & Harbin, 1998). Traditional approaches to early intervention were "expert driven, deficit oriented, and child-centered" without considering the important impact families had on their children (Wehman, 1998). Legislation in the 1960s and 1970s first mandated an educational role for parents as teachers of their own children (Wehman, 1998). In the 1970s, the law provided parents of school-aged children with disabilities with the right to participate in the educational planning process. In the 1980s and 1990s, legal policies established the family unit, rather than the child, as the focus of services (Wehman, 1998). Consequently, early intervention specialists sought to build partnerships with and to empower families (McWilliam et al., 1998). Today, families themselves are considered the recipients of early intervention services.

There are several benchmarks of best practice in family-centered early intervention (Baird & Peterson, 1997). For example, quality programs recognize and respect family members as experts on their child, as the ultimate decision makers, and as the constant in a child's life. Early interventionists must also honor a family's choices regarding their level of participation and understand the need for a collaborative, trusting relationship. Professionals need to respect differences in families' cultural identity, beliefs, values, and coping styles.

Family-centered services are constantly being redefined by practice. Today, to be family-centered means to be willing to orient services to the whole family, rather than just to the child (McWilliam et al., 1998). Being sensitive and establishing enough trust and good rapport with parents reduce distance between professionals and clients, and permit friendships, not just relationships as therapists or teachers. Several characteristics of effective family-centered service providers have been identified (McWilliam et al., 1998):

> **Positiveness:** thinking well of families. The philosophy of positiveness includes a belief in parents' abilities, a nonjudgmental mindset, an optimistic view of children's development, and an enthusiasm for working with parents.
>
> **Sensitivity:** walking in parents' shoes. Service providers must understand families' concerns, needs, and priorities. They must expand their own sensitivity, understand cultural differences, work through interpersonal challenges, and recognize parents' aspirations.

Responsiveness: doing whatever needs to be done. Responsiveness requires flexibility, not pushing an agenda, attending to parents' concerns, and taking action when parents express needs.

Friendliness: treating parents as friends. This entails developing a reciprocal relationship, building trust, taking time to talk and listen, encouraging parents, offering practical help, and conveying caring for both parents and child.

Child and community skills: being practical. This skill requires an awareness of how the economy influences the cultural climate, a familiarity with people and agencies in the community, and a desire to collaborate with other professionals for the mutual benefit of serving families.

One service provider summarized her understanding of her role this way:

> I let them know that my role is not only to work with their child, but to help their family be a family that feels better about itself—be a family that feels like it's more knowledgeable about how to care for this child and to work on whatever goals or whatever challenges it's facing at this point, or things that they've always wanted to do and just couldn't figure out how to make it all work together. (McWilliam et al., 1998, p. 213)

Several elements of IDEA, Part C, support a family-centered approach, but perhaps the most integral of these structures are service coordination and the IFSP (Thompson et al., 1997).

SERVICE COORDINATION

Imagine a family of a child with significant disabilities receiving early intervention services from three different agencies. There is likely to be confusion and frustration regarding scheduling of appointments, payment for services, and overlap of information and recommendations for home intervention. The first attempt by Congress to create an early intervention model that was comprehensive also created the need for a new method of managing the various agencies involved in service delivery for infants and toddlers with special needs. Thus a "*case manager*" role was designated in IDEA to assume the responsibility of overseeing the delivery of services to which children and their families are entitled. Specifically, "One person, together with the family, actively advocates for services in response to changing needs, and is responsible for implementation of an integrated program of services, in consultation with colleague specialists" (Division of Early Childhood, 1987). The law further stated that the professional most relevant to the needs of a child and family should serve as that family's case manager. For example, a physical therapist would be most appropriate for a child with muscular dystrophy, while a speech therapist would serve as the case manager for a child with a cleft lip and palate.

Several questions arose simultaneously with the requirement to provide case management. Educators and families asked: Who selects the case manager, the family or the agency? Can families serve as their own case manager? How many children should a case manager serve? What are the qualifications of a case manager? Partly as a result of the ensuing debate to resolve such questions, terminology in the law was changed from case manager to **service coordinator,** which reflects a less clinical and more pragmatic approach to delivery of services. Principles of service coordination generated by parents through a research survey lend understanding to family preferences regarding their relationship with a service coordinator (Early & Poertner, 1993). Parents indicated the following:

1. Parents should have a major role in determining the extent and degree of their participation as service coordinators.
2. Service coordinators should have frequent contact with children, families, and other key participants.
3. A single service coordinator should be responsible for helping families gain access to needed resources.
4. Parents and child should be involved in decision making.
5. Service coordinator roles and functions should support and strengthen family functioning.

Legally, service coordinators have responsibility for ensuring that seven major components of program delivery are completed according to federal and state laws:

1. Performing child evaluations and assessments
2. Developing, reviewing, and evaluating individual family service plans
3. Identifying of available service providers
4. Coordinating and monitoring the delivery of available services
5. Informing families on the availability of advocacy services
6. Coordinating with medical and health providers
7. Developing a **transition plan** to preschool services when appropriate

It is not necessarily a service coordinator's responsibility to directly provide these services, rather that person makes sure families have access to these services. In fact, the primary goal of service coordinators is to foster family empowerment. Strengthening a family's abilities to coordinate their own services promotes human development and helps build the overall capacity of individuals, families, and communities.

Service coordinators can empower families by improving a family's capacity to master a broad range of skills, by providing information to increase knowledge of their child's disability, giving choices and encouraging families to make their own decisions regarding types of services, and by showing parents how to access information or perform certain intervention strategies independently. Service coordinators can also improve liaisons and linkages to mobilize social supports within a family's community. Both **primary social supports** (i.e., close family, friends, and neighbors) and **secondary social supports** (e.g., health care providers, educators, and therapists) can provide families with a network capable of enabling them as caregivers of a child with special needs (Dunst, Trivette, & Deal, 1988). Just as service coordinators themselves must be careful to honor the privacy of families, they can work to protect families from other sources of unwarranted intrusion. Being careful to avoid paternalism, service coordinators can serve as advocates for family rights. Finally, service coordinators may be able to minimize stress by making essential resources available in a manner that eliminates or reduces unnecessary work or anxiety.

Early on, Berzon and Lowenstein (1984) described the personal characteristics of a case manager. These traits seem equally appropriate for today's service coordinator:

> To be effective, the case manager . . . must possess a high threshold for frustration, a high tolerance for ambiguity, an ability to measure barely perceptible increments, a sense of humor and an ability to turn to others for support. Personal flexibility, creativity, and persistence are also important. (p. 54)

Such recommendations reflect the importance of engaging in positive, proactive behavior. However, maintaining this attitude has not always been easy for public service professionals. Maroney (1986) described four perspectives held by many professionals toward parents; some of these views would interfere with the effectiveness of service coordinators:

1. Viewing families as problem-causing and interfering
2. Viewing families as resources to children (with no needs of their own)
3. Viewing families as team participants
4. Viewing families as needing resources (for themselves, independent of child)

The point is, professionals can be most effective when each family is viewed individually, rather than trying to fit all families into a "systems box." Any prior expectations of families are likely to limit relationships with at least some families.

Reading "case manager" as "service coordinator," Donner and colleagues (1993) made sense when they pointed out, "It is not enough for case managers to have the skills to do the tasks of their job, they also need attitudes that support families." These attitudes include: being positive; assigning no blame, no matter what; acknowledging that parents are trying; treating families as the experts on their needs; looking at the world from the parents' perspective; setting priorities based on family desires; and being sensitive to cultural, environmental, racial, religious, and sexual orientation differences.

INTERAGENCY SERVICES

When agencies need to coordinate their services to meet the needs of a particular child, it is the lead agency's responsibility to initiate the formal agreement regarding who delivers and pays for early intervention services. Part C funds were not intended to supplant services and funding already provided by public agencies, even though the latter might be contracted to provide services to children identified under Part C. For example, if an interagency agreement is formed with the Public Health Department, which already provides audiological assessment and treatment to the community, then Public Health, and not the lead agency for early intervention, is responsible for the cost of such services.

Ideally, depending on the services provided and the individual situations of families served, various financial arrangements can be made to ensure that no family is denied services for which they are eligible. Sources of funding include local, state, or federal funding through agencies providing services, a family cost-sharing using a sliding scale, private insurance, and Medicaid. The way in which state and local agencies choose to use these and other state and local services varies according to availability and the priorities of ICCs. Unfortunately, finding agencies that are sufficiently funded to serve all eligible families is becoming increasingly difficult because of economic recession, reduced charitable giving, and restrictive government budgets.

ELIGIBLE CHILDREN

Unlike IDEA regulations for older children, each state was given the responsibility of determining specific eligibility guidelines for early intervention services. In addition to serving children with developmental delays, states have been permitted and encouraged by Congress to serve children who are at risk of developing a delay later in childhood, defined by IDEA as "an individual under 3 years of age who would be at risk of experiencing a substantial developmental delay if early intervention services were not provided" (Section 632[1]). Infants and toddlers with developmental delays and those with **established risk** must be served by those states receiving Part C funding. Two other risk categories are discretionary and served at the will of each state: **biological/medical risk** and **environmental risk.**

Developmental delay. Infants and toddlers who experience delayed progress or who have fallen significantly below (usually 25%) the age-related norms in one or more areas have a developmental delay, which may be in communication, physical development, adaptive behavior (feeding, dressing, toileting, etc.), cognition, and social/emotional development. Because few reliable and valid instruments measure such delay, informed clinical opinion is important for determining a child's eligibility (Shackelford, 2002). Approximately 4% of all infants and toddlers fall into this category.

Established risk. Children who have a diagnosed physical or mental condition that gives them a high probability of later delays in development have an established risk. Conditions such as Down syndrome, PKU, muscular dystrophy, and sickle cell anemia are examples. Approximately 1% of all infants and toddlers have an established risk condition.

Biological/medical risk. Medical conditions that threaten to compromise a child's health, particularly perinatally, are predictive of later delays. For example, children born at low birth weight, with intraventricular hemorrhage, chronic lung disease, or failure to thrive are at risk for disabilities and developmental delays but may not have an identified disability or delay (approximately 2% to 3% of all infants and toddlers).

Environmental risk. An increasing proportion of children in our society grow up in conditions that place them at greater risk for developmental delays. Children who live in poverty, whose parents abuse drugs or alcohol, whose primary language is not English, or who are abused are examples of children who are environmentally at risk. It was predicted that by 2000, 38% of children under age 18 in the United States would be from ethnically and linguistically diverse groups where poverty is especially prevalent (Bosch, 1998).

Those who are environmentally at risk represent at least 25% of the United States' infants and toddlers. Most states are reluctant, for financial reasons, to serve so many at-risk children and have elected not to offer services to this population (Bosch, 1998). This situation is unfortunate since experts agree that children at risk are more vulnerable to the progressive effects of environmental factors and may have greater problems later on in life. At the same time, it is these same at-risk children who are most amenable to intervention and such intervention should lead to long-term cost savings.

In addition to the categories of services that might be provided under Part C, wisdom prevailed in the labeling of children served. Rather than giving children categorical labels, such as "seriously emotionally disturbed" or "mentally retarded," children and their families are simply identified as "eligible," with services determined and resources allocated according to assessed need. A simple designation of "eligible" avoids the issues of discrimination, testing error, and lowered expectations that are associated with categorical labeling.

PROCEDURAL SAFEGUARDS

States are required to establish a system that protects the fundamental rights of families and children who are eligible for services under Part C. The intent of **procedural safeguards** is to ensure both that the intended services are not denied to families with eligible children and that an impartial hearing can be requested when families believe their rights are violated. These safeguards are very much like those found under Part B of IDEA. Federal law and regulations stipulate the following due process rights (MHLP, 1990):

1. *Access to Records:* Upon the request of parents, all documentation regarding screening, evaluation or assessment data, eligibility determination, development and implementation of an Individualized Family Service Plan (IFSP), or other written, audiotaped, or videotaped communication regarding their child and family must be made available for examination.

2. *Notice:* Before initiation or refusal of services (i.e., identification, eligibility, service provision, or placement), parents must receive prior written notification.

3. *Confidentiality:* All personally identifiable information regarding a child or family member must be kept confidential. Only after parents have given written consent can information be released, and then it can be released only for the specific purpose for which the permission was given.

4. *Written Parental Consent:* Parents must give written consent before an agency can conduct an assessment or provide services to infants and toddlers. Additionally, agencies must ensure that parents are informed of their right to withdraw consent at any time. This right would be of little value to families who do not understand what "consent" means. Therefore, service providers need to explain information in a family's native language or mode of communication and then ask questions to make sure that family members have understood. As in Part

Case
Study   **MADDY'S PROGRESS: INTERVIEW WITH KIM SHAFER**

We enrolled Maddy in a special early intervention program, the Spokane Guilds' School, at 2 years old because she had a lot of frustration. She had this huge vocabulary of sign language and she babbled. Her mouth moved like yours and mine, but she couldn't hear it, and she thought she was saying the same things I was. So when she was playing with other kids and she'd say "yababbadabbadabba" and when they didn't answer, she'd bonk them on the side of the head like, "why aren't you paying attention to me?" Whoa, this wasn't socially acceptable, so we got her into the special program. I thought that maybe by having her in a preschool program early, she'd understand that there's a routine to things and there are certain things that are okay and not okay.

Maddy did very, very well there. The Guilds' School is just an amazing school, it's just awesome. But, when your child is 3 years old they have to go into a different setting and the families are scared because they've had all their services provided in one place. It's kind of a scary thing when you go into some of the school districts and they don't have a program for 3- to 5-year-olds.

Maddy started in public school when she was 3 years old. Linwood Elementary had a deaf/hard-of-hearing preschool and her preschool teacher had been there for years and she was just a wonderful teacher. Her teacher used to be a sign language interpreter, so she incorporated the sign language with the verbal language. Maddy went there from 3 years old and she still goes there, but this last year I saw such a huge leap with her language—her verbal language, her auditory language; her skills just kept increasing.

But, I thought that making a leap from the preschool, where she's getting mainly sign language, to going into a mainstream kindergarten would be a real struggle. I wanted something kind of in the middle. My next door neighbor is one of the directors of Head Start, which includes a great program called CAPE—Cooperative Approach to Preschool Education. The program serves kids from 3 to 5 or 6 years old. So we're there now with 6 other CAPE kids, kids with disabilities, and 12 kids who are low-income Head Start students, 18 kids in all. There are two lead teachers, a special education teacher, a speech/language thera-

B, states have the right to contest a parent's refusal of an evaluation by filing for a due process hearing. However, most professionals feel that only in extreme cases (e.g., suspected child abuse or neglect) should a parent's decision to refuse evaluation be challenged.

5. *Surrogate Parents:* Just as with school-age children with disabilities, the state has the responsibility to appoint surrogate parents for any eligible child whose parents cannot be found or are not known or if the child is a ward of the state. This surrogate is responsible for representing absent parents in duties related to evaluation, eligibility, placement, IFSP development, and so on. The state may not appoint a surrogate simply because parents are considered to be irresponsible.

6. *Continuity of Services:* Analogous to the "stay put" principle, the continuity-of-services right assures that children and their families will continue to receive services throughout any legal proceedings. However, given joint agreement of

pist, occupational therapist, physical therapist, and an aide. There are usually 6 hands-on adults to 18 kids which is a great ratio.

Maddy's language is getting clearer and clearer as she echoes the kids around her because there isn't sign language there. For the most part, she has to depend on her voice and her implant to hear. So it's been a really great resource for her.

Our other excitement is being selected winners by *Ladies' Home Journal* for an essay contest titled "My Daughter and What I Hope for Her in the Next Century." Your daughter had to be turning 1, 5, or 10 years old in the year 2000. My Mom suggested that I enter, so of course I put it aside until the night before it was due, then I whipped out this two page essay, showed it to my mom and she started bawling. I said, "Perfect!" sent it in and we won! We got this call saying that out of a thousand entries, we were one of six winners. The magazine is going to do a story on Maddy's life, each year for the next 10 years.

Maddy, Cassie, and Amanda Shafer (left to right).

Every year, someone from the magazine back in New York will come out and do a photo session and update as they follow Maddy's life. The one thing I was asked that I really hadn't given any thought to was "Are you nervous at all about if you have any problems that come up in your life? It's going to be in a magazine!" But I thought, you know, you can't predict the future, you just need to live your life the best you can.

parents and service provider, services may be withdrawn or changed. If a child has received services, and access to services is the issue under consideration, all services not in dispute should be provided.

7. ***Prompt and Unbiased Dispute Resolution:*** The latest revision of IDEA features mediation as an initial process to resolve disputes. Mediation allows both parties to discuss issues and to attempt compromise. Mediation is free and each state can supply names of mediators.

8. ***Impartial Hearing:*** Both agencies and families may file for an impartial administrative hearing if the rights of either are perceived to have been violated. Each state determines if the regulations for a fair hearing under Part B are to be used or if new regulations will be devised for infants and toddlers. Parents must receive written notification of the resolution within 30 days of filing a request for hearing.

9. ***Right to Appeal:*** Parents or schools may file a civil action in state or federal courts to appeal a resolution made during the administrative hearing.

10. ***Procedures for Resolving Systemic Problems:*** Parents and others have the right to file a complaint if it is believed that the state has failed to implement any Part C regulation(s). The state must arrange an independent investigation, with results (and resolution if necessary) completed within 60 days of the complaint.

It is the obligation of each service provider to ensure that due process rights are made clear to parents. These regulations are complicated and can be intimidating for early childhood professionals and must, therefore, be doubly obscure for many parents new to this field. The fact that professionals have the privilege of working more closely with parents in early intervention than with parents of older children provides greater opportunity to enhance families' self-advocacy by clarifying the law as much as possible.

ASSESSMENT

Although IDEA previously permitted the delivery of services to infants, toddlers, and their families before an IFSP was completed, amendments since then require that an IFSP be developed and have the written consent of parents before services can be delivered. In fact, the entire process of determining eligibility, planning a child's program, implementing the plan, and reviewing progress is similar to that of older children with disabilities (see Figure 9–1).

What does differ from assessment of older children is the evaluation process in early intervention that has two distinct but interrelated aspects: child assessment and family assessment. The primary purposes of assessment are to determine if infants are eligible for services and to provide sufficient information to plan intervention for a child and family (Lerner et al., 1998). Once a child is determined eligible for services and the IFSP is developed, assessment is necessary to measure progress and evaluate the effectiveness of the services provided. Federal regulations also require evaluation and assessment to be conducted in a nondiscriminatory manner.

IDEA GUIDELINES FOR ASSESSMENT

Each lead agency is to adopt nondiscriminatory evaluation and assessment procedures. The public agencies responsible for the evaluation of children and families are to ensure, at a minimum, that:

1. Tests and other evaluation procedures and materials are administered in the native language of the parents or other modes of communication, unless it is clearly not feasible to do so.
2. Any assessment and evaluation procedures and materials that are used are selected and administered so as not to be racially or culturally discriminatory.
3. No single procedure is used as the sole criterion for determining a child's eligibility.
4. Evaluation and assessments are conducted by qualified personnel.

Figure 9–1
Diagram of
Identification,
Eligibility,
Programming,
and Review for
Early
Intervention
Services

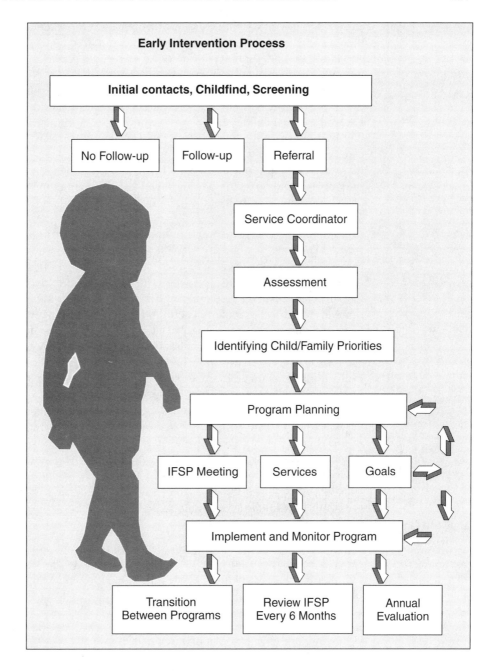

Simeonsson (1986) described three methods of assessment. A **psychometric approach** is used to compare a child to normal standards of development, intelligence, or achievement in order to determine performance discrepancies. That is, does a child's developmental rate keep pace with the usual expectations for typical children of the same age. In a **behavioral assessment,** practitioners examine factors that govern children's behavior under given conditions. In this approach, the goal of assessment is to determine the controlling impact of setting conditions and consequences on behavior. In other words, the goal is to determine what motivates a child's behavior so appropriate intervention can be planned. An important step in behavioral assessment is to carry out a **functional assessment,** which involves manipulation of those conditions in order to alter the observed behavior. For example, if a child is 18 months old and not attempting to make sounds, it may be observed that the child is placed in a playpen for much of the day at a child-care center and that when she does attempt to communicate, caregivers often overlook her verbalizations. It would be recommended, therefore, that caregivers provide multiple opportunities for interaction throughout the day and that they begin to consequate verbalizations by imitating or expanding on her communication attempts.

A child's age is irrelevant in the **qualitative–developmental assessment** approach. Early interventionists examine a child's skills, as well as a child's approach to people and tasks. These data provide information about where a child is on a developmental road map and where a child can be expected to go next. This global perspective on assessment provides rich information for program development, which is particularly useful in family-centered intervention.

In addition to these three approaches, a fourth, the **ecological approach,** is used by many early interventionists (Carta, Sainato, & Greenwood, 1988; Sexton, Thompson, Perez, & Rheams, 1990; Thurman & Widerstrom, 1990). Ecological evaluations focus on children, their environment, and the interaction between the two, providing information that is especially useful in program planning. Since a child's behavior and development are influenced by multiple factors, all these variables need to be considered in evaluation. Therefore, the key to ecological evaluations is to comprehensively analyze a child's real environment, taking into account a wide range of variables, including resources and materials, child behaviors, social relationships, and family/adult behaviors in order to develop a very specific profile and program.

ELIGIBILITY DETERMINATION

Two stages may be involved in eligibility determination. **Screening** is a relatively quick preliminary evaluation used to determine if a child should be referred for more in-depth assessment. Because full evaluations are costly in terms of time and money, screening helps to identify those children who are most likely to need services. There is, however, a drawback to this efficiency. By definition, screening tools are less accurate than follow-up assessment and, therefore, overlook many children who might actually benefit from special services.

Positive screening results lead to a **multifactored diagnostic evaluation** involving professionals from all relevant disciplines. This evaluation must be completed within 45 days of referral. In early intervention, this **multidisciplinary** team almost always includes parents, an educator, and a communication specialist. The purpose of a team approach to assessment is to have adequate expertise represented in all program areas.

State regulations guide practitioners in determining what data are needed in order to make an eligibility decision. Formal assessments use standardized tools, which compare a child's behaviors to those of a standard norm. For example, a 10-month-old child's language behaviors are compared to the average language behaviors of children at 10 months of age. With average being the "standard," a significant deviance from the standard indicates that a child may be either delayed or precocious. Standardized tools are also administered in a precise manner and scored according to a set of standard procedures. That is, any variation made in giving the test that is not provided for in the testing manual, such as timing, use of materials, or instructions, renders the results unusable for comparison purposes.

Informal assessments may include the use of commercially available or curriculum-referenced tools. Also used are interviews with parents, narrative descriptions of behavior, checklists, and rating scales. These latter data should be combined with more formal assessment data to make an eligibility determination. If a child is found to be eligible, programs have 45 days from the initial referral to plan and hold an initial IFSP meeting. Services would begin immediately following parental approval of the IFSP.

CLOSE-UP

RANDOMIZED TRIAL OF INTENSIVE EARLY INTERVENTION FOR CHILDREN WITH PERVASIVE DEVELOPMENTAL DISORDER

After years of debating whether or not early intervention can make significant differences in the later lives of young children with severe developmental delays, several studies based on approaches using intensive applied behavior analysis methods revealed important improvements could be achieved. The present study was designed to compare the effectiveness of intensive applied behavior analysis (ABA) procedures developed through the UCLA Young Autism Project (Lovaas, 1987) for treating children with pervasive developmental disorders and with autism to similar treatment implemented by parents trained by UCLA staff.

Children were assigned to either of two treatment groups. The intensive treatment group involved 30 hours per week of ABA intervention for each child for 2 to 3 years. Intensive treatment was carried out by teams of four to six therapists and the primary caregiver, who all worked one-to-one, in the child's home, using discrete trial formats that were highly individualized to maximize language, toy play, and self-care. Later in treatment, the children moved into school group settings.

Half of the children were assigned to a condition where parents were trained to use the same treatment approaches and were given a manual to assist them. Families were given two training sessions per week, totaling 5 hours per week, in their homes for 3 to 9 months. Parents collaborated with the trainers to select goals for their children, and parent trainers demonstrated ways to work toward these goals. The parent trainers observed parents working with their children and gave them feedback. Throughout the training, children in this group were also enrolled in special education classes in public schools for 10–15 hours per week.

The children who received intensive 30-hour-a-week discrete trial training benefited significantly more than the children whose parents had carried out treatment. The children with intensive treatment scored higher on IQ, visual spatial skills, and language development, though they did not score higher on adaptive behavior in everyday settings. The intensively treated group were assigned to less restrictive school placements, and a number of them performed in the average range on academic tests after treatment, though only one parent-trained child scored as well. Children with pervasive developmental delay in the intensive treatment may have gained even more than children with autism.

The authors concluded that intensive early intervention can be a powerful treatment. Intensive treatment is clearly needed to help preschool children with autism or pervasive developmental delay achieve average functioning. One-to-one training focused on skill building appears to be a necessary prerequisite for generalizing to appropriate school behaviors.

Reference: From "Behavioral Treatment and Normal Educational and Intellectual Functioning in Young Autistic Children," by O. I. Lovaas, 1987, *Journal of Consulting and Clinical Psychology, 55*, pp. 3–9.

Source: From "Randomized Trial of Intensive Early Intervention for Children with Pervasive Developmental Disorder," by T. Smith, A. D. Groen, and J. W. Wynn, 2000, *American Journal on Mental Retardation, 105*(4), pp. 269–285.

PROGRAM PLANNING

The most efficient assessment process combines eligibility determination with programming evaluation. Due to the developmental nature of both assessment and curriculum design, it is relatively easy in early intervention to use a curriculum-referenced tool to accomplish both purposes. A curriculum-referenced tool is linked to intervention objectives so that the assessment itself is sensitive to relevant behaviors. In early intervention, these tools are generally very practical and measure behaviors in all developmental areas. Some tools are specifically designed to measure very small steps in learning for children with significant disabilities. Others are closely linked to broad developmental milestones and their associated learning objectives for children with mild disabilities.

Day-to-day assessment provides input for dynamic decision making regarding the appropriateness of a child's objectives, intervention strategies, and programming alternatives. Research consistently indicates that continuous measurement (daily or several times a week) is the most effective schedule for assessing child progress on learning objectives. Furthermore, direct observation methods are most useful for daily data collection. Counting the frequency or rate of behaviors (e.g., number of times in a day that child wets), measuring the length of time that a behavior occurs (e.g., duration of independent sitting before falling sideways), and assessing the magnitude of behaviors (e.g., how far will a child reach across midline to grasp a toy) are examples of direct data collection.

Curriculum-based tools are also useful for measuring child progress on outcome objectives specified on IFSPs. Review of each IFSP must take place at least every 6 months since children can progress so rapidly through developmental stages at this early age. The comprehensive reevaluation must be completed at least annually. While it is possible for children to become ineligible for services through rapid development, the at-risk clause of Part C permits agencies to continue services should families so desire.

FAMILY ASSESSMENT

Development of IFSPs must include statements about family priorities, which necessitates the assessment of families. However, family assessment is the most sensitive and least well evolved component of early intervention programs (Hanson & Lynch, 1989). Yet, families are especially vulnerable during initial diagnostic stages because they are entering a new arena in which they must rely on the integrity and proficiency of strangers. Therefore, parents should only be evaluated voluntarily; assessment for the purpose of defining a family as it relates to care of a child with disabilities is an intrusion to which families of young children without disabilities are not subjected. For these reasons, educators are cautioned to fulfill this legal requirement with wisdom and empathy.

Any family assessment that is conducted must be voluntary on the part of the family. If an assessment of the family is carried out, the assessment must be conducted by personnel trained to utilize appropriate methods and procedures, be based on information provided by a family through a personal interview, and incorporate the family's description of its strengths and needs related to enhancing their child's development.

All aspects of a family's conduct that might influence their ability to meet the needs of their child with disabilities may be considered in the assessment. IDEA directed professionals to include a statement of family strengths and weaknesses on the IFSP (see Figure 9–2). Traditionally, a deficiency model focused attention on family needs rather than on their strengths. A more proactive way of looking at families is to concentrate on their relative strengths in formulating plans. Toward that end, the 1991 amendments to IDEA redirected educators to include a family-directed assessment of their respective resources, priorities for services, and concerns. Areas of family assessment may include domestic, child–parent interactions, educational, vocational, health, financial, and social domains. Again, while it may not be the responsibility of educational service agencies to provide for all the needs of a family, it is our responsibility to help establish linkages between families and corresponding services that will enable them to meet the needs of their child with special needs more effectively.

One approach to family assessment is a traditional format in which professionals survey parents through a standard protocol. In other words, all parents are asked a set of questions regarding specific skills, interests, and needs. Families might be interviewed or asked to fill out a written survey. Either way, professionals take the risk of offending parents who, while seeking help for their children, find the intrusion into their personal and family circumstances unwarranted. The following real account of a parent whose child was enrolled in a public program for low-income families illustrates the point.

Figure 9–2
Comparing
Family Strengths
and Weaknesses

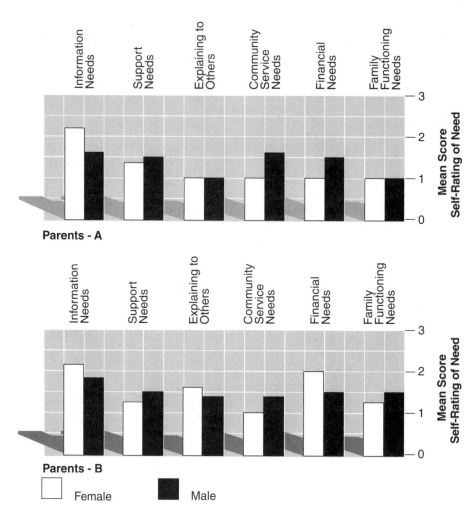

I wanted my son in an integrated preschool program but was unprepared for
the ordeal. The application process included an assessment of my very personal circumstances. I was asked questions related to the adequacy of our
housing and food, whether or not I am on welfare or on legal probation, how
I discipline my family, and if we use drugs, alcohol, or birth control.

This parent was from a middle-class family and therefore was not accustomed
to being treated as if her privacy was less important than the organization's right
to ask such questions. It was also apparent that the questions were viewed as perfectly legitimate for families who lived in poverty. While persons who have low
incomes are often subjected to intrusive questioning in order to receive other public services, the very implication that a family is deficient could place a barrier between professionals and that family.

Beckman and Bristol (1991), warned that assessment of families for the purpose of identifying needs of families as opposed to their children's needs could

Figure 9–3
Relationship
Between
Outcome of
Needs
Assessment and
Level of
Intrusiveness

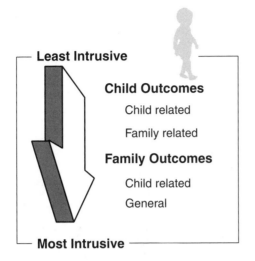

be unintentionally intrusive (see Figure 9–3). Take for example, a child who has cerebral palsy. Traditionally, professionals would concentrate on child-centered needs as they pertain to a variety of developmental areas but, particularly, motor development. Motor assessment, conducted by a physical therapist, can be viewed as minimally intrusive. When the physical therapist attempts to determine if family members have the time, resources, or skills to conduct necessary motor development activities at home, then the presumption on family privacy becomes more substantial, though perhaps not unreasonable.

Using the same child with cerebral palsy as our example, if the physical therapist concludes that the child requires a wheelchair, the family might be asked about their financial capacity to purchase this child-oriented equipment. Obviously, financial questions can become quite sensitive but, under the circumstances, relevant. The most obvious intrusion and least justifiable questions surround general family needs. For example, the physical therapist, in recognizing that this child is underweight and tends to have chronic upper respiratory infections, might question family resources to provide adequate nutrition or health care.

Asking questions regarding employment status, health care insurance, and mealtime habits represents a very delicate assessment issue that should only be approached with the greatest sensitivity. It is recommended that professionals conduct this assessment informally and only after establishing good rapport with family members (Beckman & Bristol, 1991). Winton and Bailey (1988) suggested an informal, four-stage process that should be initiated only after professionals and parents have built rapport with each other.

> **Phase I: Put family at ease:** Describe the purpose, structure, and confidentiality of interview.
> **Phase II: Interview:** Family members should do most of the talking after being asked open-ended questions and encouraged to discuss issues that are of importance to them.

> **Phase III: Summary, priority, and goal setting:** Thoughts and feelings of family members are summarized and needs listed in order of priority. Though professionals may help to articulate family goals, the family itself is given the responsibility for achieving the goals.
>
> **Phase IV: Ending interview:** After summary and articulation of goals, family contributions are acknowledged, and they are encouraged to provide continuous input to the plan.

Even this amount of structure may be both unnecessary and too overbearing for some families. It is possible that professionals who provide a continuous sounding board and use an IFSP in a dynamic manner will be as effective as those who use a more structured approach.

IFSP DEVELOPMENT

The IFSP is a form of documentation that reflects the emphasis on family-centered intervention highlighted throughout this text. IFSPs are created for infants and toddlers and their families when eligibility for early intervention is established. This legal document is the early intervention analog to an Individualized Educational Program (IEP) used with older students, but is more holistically conceived than the latter. Reflecting the rate of change in infants and toddlers, IFSPs are reviewed at least every 6 months or more often if needed.

The required components of an IFSP include the following:

1. A statement of child's developmental status in the areas of communication, physical, social/emotional, cognitive, and adaptive behavior, based upon the completion of a multidisciplinary assessment.
2. If a family agrees to its inclusion, a statement of family priorities, concerns, and resources, as they relate to enhancement of their child's development.
3. A statement of the major outcomes (goals) that a child is expected to achieve, with the criteria for mastery, timelines for implementation and expected completion, and procedures for measuring progress included.
4. A statement of the specific early intervention services that must be provided to meet the aforementioned child and family goals. Included are the frequency, duration, location, and method of delivering these services; the payment arrangements, if necessary; and when deemed necessary, a specification of "other" services that may be needed by a family, but that are not explicitly provided under Part C, and the steps that will be taken to secure those services. While these services may be written into the document, this does not mean that the services must be provided at public expense. Such services might include helping families to identify an agency to provide financial assistance, arranging for the child to access medical–health care services, or helping to prepare insurance papers.
5. A statement of the dates when services will be initiated and the anticipated duration of services.
6. The name of the service coordinator responsible for assuring that assessment, program planning, and program implementation are provided according to the law.

7. A statement of the steps that will be taken to ensure that a child makes a smooth transition from early intervention services to preschool education once a child reaches age 3. This includes training parents for the legal and programmatic changes expected.

While IFSPs are intended to serve as a blueprint for services and as a legal agreement with families, there was a conscious effort in developing IDEA to avoid some of the pitfalls of legislation regulating the adoption of IEPs in this country. The emphasis is rightly placed on the substance of intervention rather than on paperwork compliance.

Selecting IFSP Objectives

As in all areas of education, there is an increasing emphasis on planning children's programs to focus on real life. Notari-Syverson and Shuster (1995) recommended guidelines for the development of objectives that will be most relevant for very young children:

1. **Functionality:** skills needed to operate as independently as possible in daily routines
2. **Generality:** general rather than specific skills that can be adapted to meet individual needs and used in many situations
3. **Ease of integration:** skills that will be used naturally in activities and social interactions
4. **Measurability:** skills that can be seen/heard and counted or measured
5. **Hierarchical relationship:** increasingly complex skills that are logistically sequenced—each new skill building upon a previously learned skill

To provide a sounding board for determining whether or not goals and objectives selected for very young children adhere to the above criteria, Notari-Syverson and Shuster developed a checklist (see Table 9–2). The answer to each question should be "yes" if the goals and objectives meet real life needs.

Naturally occurring routines are well suited for the integration of skill domains. For example, bathing can be a context for language, social interaction, motor (fine and gross) execution, and cognitive growth, as well as an obvious avenue for self-help skill development. The point of having objectives written so that they can fit into daily caregiver routines is to increase both their relevancy for children and the likelihood that parents will have a reasonable chance of working instruction of objectives into their already demanding lives.

The best way to determine family routines is to simply ask parents to describe activities that occur during their typical day; what they do and where they go (Tisot & Thurman, 2002). Families may keep a week-long log of their activities: looking at books, caring for a pet, eating out, or attending church might be typical activities. Interviews with families can also reveal what behaviors would be important for an infant or toddler in these settings. And families may want to take their young child into new environments where they currently don't feel they can be successful.

Family comfort also should be evaluated. Some families may have an open-door policy and welcome service delivery in their homes; others may be more private and

Table 9–2 Checklist for Writing IFSP Goals and Objectives for Infants and Young Children

FUNCTIONALITY

1. Will the skill increase the child's ability to interact with people and objects within the daily environment?
   The child needs to perform the skill in all or most of the environments in which he or she interacts.
   Skill: Places object in container.
   Opportunities: Home: Places sweater in drawer, cookie in paper bag.
                                        School: Places backpack in cubby hole, trash in trash bin.
                                        Community: Places milk carton in grocery cart, soil in flower pot.
2. Will the skill have to be performed by someone else if the child cannot do it?
   The skill is a behavior or event that is critical for completion of daily routines.
   Skill: Looks for object in usual location.
   Opportunities: Finds coat on coat rack, gets food from cupboard.

GENERALITY

3. Does the skill represent a general concept or class of responses?
   The skill emphasizes a generic process, rather than a particular instance.
   Skill: Fits objects into defined spaces.
   Opportunities: Puts mail in mailbox, places crayon in box, puts cutlery into sorter.
4. Can the skill be adapted or modified for a variety of disabling conditions?
   A child's sensory impairment should interfere as little as possible with the performance.
   Skill: Correctly activates simple toy.
   Opportunities: Motor impairments—Activates light, easy-to-move toys (e.g., balls, rocking
                                        horse, toys on wheels, roly-poly toys).
                                        Visual Impairment—Activates large, bright, noise-making toys (e.g., bells,
                                        drums, large rattles).
5. Can the skill be generalized across a variety of settings, materials, and/or people?
   The child can perform the skill with interesting materials and in meaningful situations.
   Skill: Manipulates two small objects simultaneously.
   Opportunities: Home—Builds with small interlocking blocks, threads lace on shoes.
                                        School—Sharpens pencil with pencil sharpener.
                                        Community—Takes coin out of small wallet.

INSTRUCTIONAL CONTEXT

6. Can the skill be taught in a way that reflects the manner in which the skill will be used in daily
   environments?
   The skill occurs in a naturalistic manner.
   Skill: Uses object to obtain another object.
   Opportunities: Uses fork to obtain food, broom to rake toy; steps on stool to reach toy shelf.
7. Can the skill be elicited easily by the teacher/parent within classroom/home activities?
   The skill can be initiated easily by the child as part of daily routines.
   Skill: Stacks objects.
   Opportunities: Stacks books, cups/plates, wooden logs.

MEASURABILITY

8. Can the skill be seen or heard?
   Different observers must be able to identify the same behavior.
   Measurable skill: Gains attention and refers to object, person and/or event.
   Nonmeasurable skill: Experiences a sense of self-importance.
9. Can the skill be directly counted (e.g., by frequency, duration, distance measures)?
   The skill represents a well-defined behavior or activity.
   Measurable skill: Grasps pea-sized object.
   Nonmeasurable skill: Has mobility in all fingers.

Table 9–2 *(continued)*

10. Does the skill contain or lend itself to determination of performance criteria?
   The extent and/or degree of accuracy of the skill can be evaluated.
   Measurable skill: Follows one-step directions with contextual cues.
   Nonmeasurable skill: Will increase receptive language skills.

HIERARCHICAL RELATION BETWEEN LONG-RANGE GOAL AND SHORT-TERM OBJECTIVE

11. Is the short term objective a developmental subskill or step thought to be critical to the achievement of the long-range goal?
   Appropriate: Short-term objective—Releases object with each hand.
                          Long-range goal—Places and releases object balanced on top of another object.
   Inappropriate: The short-term objective is a restatement of the same skill as the long-range goal with the addition of an instructional prompt (e.g., Short-Term Objective—Activates mechanical toy with physical prompt. Long-Term Goal—Independently activates mechanical toy) or a quantitative limitation to the extent of the skill (e.g., Short-Term Objective—Stacks 5 1-inch blocks; Long-Range Goal—Stacks 10 1-inch blocks).
                          The short-term objective is not functionally or conceptually related to the long-range goal (e.g., Short-Term Objective—Releases object voluntarily. Long-Range Goal—Pokes with index finger).

Source: From "Putting Real Life Skills into IEP/IFSPs for Infants and Young Children," by A. R. Notari-Syverson and S. L. Shuster, *Teaching Exceptional Children*, Winter 1995, pp. 29–32. Copyright 1995 by The Council for Exceptional Children. Reprinted with permission.

find their routines disrupted by home services. Service providers should not be locked into well-meaning assumptions that mistakenly assume that home or the local child care center is the most natural environment for a particular family (Tisot & Thurman, 2002). The dynamics of a particular family also need to be considered. Financial or emotional stress may be increased (lessening the chance for successful teaching and learning) if a family is not allowed choice from a variety of options that define their best setting for services.

Bricker (2001) warned that setting is less important than what transpires in a location. No matter what the setting may be, the activities must be authentic, functional, and meaningful. The first guiding principle of early intervention must be, "the delivery of specialized and individualized services that enhance eligible children's development and learning." These children need services that go above and beyond those offered to typical children. The second guiding principle must be respect for the family's values, priorities, and needs. Specialized settings for some children are necessary and appropriate for a child to receive quality services that promote progress and expand future placement options (Bricker, 2001).

SERVICES DELIVERED

Several of the components of IFSPs mimic those of Individualized Education Plans (IEPs) (which will be described in Chapter 10). However, there are three distinct differences in these documents. First, the identification of a service coordinator described earlier in this chapter is different. Second, the services for which children and their families are eligible include some services unique to infants and

Case Study   **ISOLATION: INTERVIEW WITH MARSHA MOORE**

The most difficult thing for me after Michael's diagnosis was the deep sense of guilt I felt. Somehow, I must not be doing all the things that I had done with the other kids. Somehow I had lost my touch. What was wrong with me? Why couldn't I bond with this little boy? Why didn't he know me as his mother? Even though I understood that there was a physical and neurological justification for Michael's delayed development, I felt that somehow the environment I had provided for him just wasn't adequate. I felt responsible for his slow progress, and I think some of the frustrations that I experienced came from the fact that I assumed others looked at me and thought that I must not be doing enough.

After his diagnosis, I made the decision that no one would ever be able to say, "she didn't try!" So I set up a family schedule to work with him. Intervention was a day and night process for the entire family. Mike hated it. His brothers and sisters hated it. His dad hated it. I hated it. I think back now and realize that we were really overstimulating him. The specialists had told us to bring the world to Michael and that's what we did. Lucky that Michael was a tough little guy. He survived in spite of us all! During this time, we were living in a very small mining town in north-

eastern Wyoming. We felt physically isolated from medical facilities, shopping, entertainment, civilization in general. We often awakened to find antelope in the backyard! We were socially isolated as well. Because we had been transferred to the area shortly after Michael's birth, we had only a few acquaintances and no close friends. Our life seemed to be such a struggle, and although we lived there for almost 3 years, I can only remember bits and pieces about anything during that time. It sounds strange, but when the kids reminisce about neighbors, teachers, and schoolmates I have a difficult time placing names and faces. For 3 years, I missed a precious part of life with my husband and my five other children. I guess I didn't have the energy. I suppose my fear and sadness nearly consumed me. All I could think about was helping Michael to "get well."

Perhaps other things really weren't of any importance at that point in time. I think all parents want their circumstances to be the story of a miracle. I wanted Michael's story to have a happy ending. You know, the wonderful stories you see on TV or read about in the newspaper. You think, "My story will be the one that they print, and it will be the miracle."

toddlers. Finally, IFSPs must include a plan for a child's transition into other programs once they reach age 3. While transition plans are also used for school-age students, it is only when students reach age 14 and are preparing for transition to adulthood that such a plan is required in the IEP.

When children are found eligible for early intervention, assessment of services includes both those that will directly benefit that child and those that will support a child's family. The latter services are intended to indirectly benefit an eligible child by enhancing a family's capability of meeting the child's needs. In other words, if a family or family member has a need that is so great it prevents nurturance of the child with special needs, that family need is as important to address as the developmental needs of the child. While this practice makes sense, provision of **tertiary services** to families is both costly and complicated, as described earlier in this chapter.

Services to infants and toddlers and their families can be provided through a myriad of models and agencies. Though traditionally, public and private agencies have been centralized educational facilities, the law permits considerable flexibility in delivery models. It is clear, however, that those who crafted Part C envisioned the coordination of multiple resources; both public and private agencies may be involved when indicated by the needs of families.

Children who are eligible for early intervention may receive the following types of services if appropriate.

1. Assistive technology devices and services
2. Audiology
3. Family training, counseling, and home visits
4. Health services deemed necessary to enable infants and toddlers to benefit from the other early intervention services. (This may include clean intermittent catheterization or consultation by health care providers concerning the special medical needs of children eligible for services that will influence the delivery of those services. Specifically, services that are purely medical in nature and surgical services are excluded, as are devices that are used to control or treat a medical condition, as well as medical–health services such as immunizations.)
5. Medical services only for diagnostic and evaluation purposes
6. Nursing services
7. Nutrition services
8. Occupational therapy
9. Physical therapy
10. Psychological services
11. Service coordination
12. Social work services
13. Special instruction
14. Speech–language pathology
15. Transportation and related costs
16. Vision services

This list of services to children is not exhaustive. Other services such as respite care and other family support services should be provided when they are appropriate. In contrast to the services articulated for children, the law is vague about the kind of services that must be made available to families or family members in order to enable the families. In theory, families should receive those services that will permit them to adequately meet the needs of their children with disabilities. The law is so broadly stated that professionals worry about the fiscal and logistical nightmare of serving some families who might be very needy. Theoretically, families could receive counseling, drug and alcohol treatment, public assistance, and so forth. The list of family services could become so long and so expensive it could not realistically be provided.

Unlike service providers for school-age children under special education law, service providers may charge a fee to families of eligible infants and toddlers

(Tucker & Goldstein, 1991). However, services that cannot be charged for under any circumstances are evaluation/assessment and service coordination. Moreover, guidelines that are established to determine payment may not be used to deny services to children or families because of their inability to pay for those services.

A Sample IFSP

A family-centered IFSP should be positive, written with understandable language, and balanced in scope with specifics (McWilliam & Ferguson, 1998). There should be no professional jargon or doubletalk. What the family wants must be reflected on the IFSP, and what is written on the IFSP should show up in practice. Figure 9–4 is an example of an IFSP that should be examined part by part.

At first, identifying information must be included in order to ensure continued contact and monitoring of progress. This section would not only include the child's name, but also the parent's or guardian's. It is sometimes the case that a foster parent or surrogate parent should also be identified, since many at-risk children do not reside with their biological parents. Notes describing a parent or guardian's primary language, work and home phone numbers, and best time to call may improve later follow-up. It is also important to note significant extended family or non-related kin who may be a significant part of a child's family. Grandparents, live-in partners, step-siblings, and so forth may play an important role in children's lives.

The name of the legally specified service coordinator also must be included. It is helpful to the family to also include on the IFSP the coordinator's contact information, such as agency address and phone number. It may be wise to spell out the coordinator's responsibilities on the IFSP so that roles and expectations are clear to all involved.

A section is devoted to describing a child's present level of performance. This should include the results of any evaluations, assessments, and observations made on a child. The family's input regarding a child's strengths and needs also would be recorded in this section. Results from formal evaluations should be indicated as scores, percentiles, age equivalents, and so on, but they also should be summarized in everyday terms that are meaningful to the family and other professionals involved. Areas to describe include communication, cognition, social/emotional, motor skills, and adaptive skills. Physical development, including vision, hearing, and health are also included. Relevant medical information including a birth history should be reported.

A family assessment is important, but as noted earlier, it can be completed only with a parent or guardian's consent. Items to consider for this section might be a description of who makes up the immediate family and what is the neighborhood or community like? What friends or relatives are important in supporting the family? What activities does the family enjoy doing together? How is the child cared for during the day? What are the child's typical environments? Checklists might be used to indicate needs for transportation, housing, information on the disability or delay, training, help with insurance, Medicaid or SSI, recreation, child care, and so on. Parents or caretakers should be given the opportunity to raise their own concerns about a child or their family's needs.

Figure 9–4 Individualized Family Service Plan

Identifying Information

Child's Name: *Karmen Lynn Burch*   Nickname: *Bitsy*
Date: *10–1–03*

Gender: Male ___ Female *X*   Date of Birth *4–2–01*

Social Security Number: *371–16–5499*

Insurance type: __ private (company and policy #) _____
X Medicaid   __ Champus   __ none   __ other

Child's Primary Language/: *American Sign Language/English*
Mode of Communication

Initial Referral Date: *10–2–02*
Initial Referral Source: *Jackson County Health Department*

Does the child have a medical diagnosis? *X* Yes   __ No

If yes, what is diagnosis?   *Bilateral, severe hearing loss as a result of prenatal rubella infection*

Child's Primary Care Physician: *Glenn Stream, Jackson Clinic South*
Phone: *(517) 499–5228*

Is the child eligible for IDEA Part C services? *X* Yes   __ No

Parent/Guardian/Surrogate/Caregiver Information

Name: *Barbara Benson, Guardian*   Relationship to the child: *grandmother*
          and
Name: *Laura Burch, Parent*   Relationship to the child: *mother*

Address: *S. 8167 5th St., Apt. #40*   County: *Jackson*
City: *Jackson*   State: *MI*   Zip: *49200*
Telephone: Day: *(517) 554–9191*   (Night) *(517) 554–4252*
Best time to call: *7–9 a.m. and 6–9 p.m.*
Primary language/mode of communication: *English*

Service Coordinator Name: *Cheryl Tully*   Telephone: *(517) 768–2367*
Agency Name: *Michigan Deaf Services*
Address: *8237 Miller Ave.*   City: *Jackson*   State: *MI*   Zip: *49200*

Child's present level of performance

Child strengths:
Bitsy is a happy baby who seldom fusses. Her motor skills are good, she is running, climbing furniture, sleeping in a youth bed, putting together preschool puzzles. She feeds herself and is toilet trained during the daytime (sleeps in diapers). Her inoculations are up to date, vision is average, and though her height and weight are at about the 20th percentile, she appears healthy. Using the Brigance Inventory for Early Development, Bitsy scored at her age level in fine and gross motor and cognition. Bitsy is learning to communicate through American Sign Language and uses about one dozen signs.

Child concerns:
Bitsy was born 4 weeks prematurely, affected by maternal rubella. Her mother was 15 at the time of the birth and had received almost no prenatal care until the 7th month of gestation; father was not identified. Bitsy was treated in the NICU for almost 2 weeks before she was sent home. She has severe, bilateral hearing loss and does not make any speech sounds. She has very high activity levels and a very short attention span. She scored below the age 1 year level on the Brigance in the areas of receptive and expressive language. She has been fitted for hearing aids but refuses to wear them. Her grandmother and mother have decided against the use of a cochlear implant.

Figure 9–4 *(continued)*

Family Assessment:

Family strengths:
Bitsy's mother, Laura is attending an alternative high school program that will allow her to complete her degree by next year. She also works full-time as a waitress at the Highland Club, on the 6 p.m. to 2 a.m. shift and helps support Bitsy and Barbara, Bitsy's grandmother. Laura has relinquished Bitsy's guardianship to her mother Barbara. Barbara is on disability because of crippling arthritis. She stays home with Bitsy in the two-bedroom double-wide mobile home they share with Laura. Barbara transports Bitsy to doctor's appointments and to twice-weekly speech and language therapy. Bitsy's maternal uncle, Benjamin, often visits on weekends and brings his 4-year-old daughter and 5-year-old son along as playmates for Bitsy.

Family concerns:
Because of Bitsy's high activity levels and her lack of receptive language she is challenging for her grandmother Barbara to control. In addition, Barbara's arthritis periodically flares up, making it physically difficult to care for Bitsy. The family would also like to have Bitsy in an environment where she would have other children to play with and could receive daily instruction in sign language and speech. A priority for the family would be at least a half-time preschool program and afternoon daycare for Bitsy while Laura is attending school. There are also concerns about continuing Medicaid services and the paperwork that accompanies it. Barbara and Laura feel they do not know enough sign language to use with Bitsy as she continues to add to what she knows.

Major Outcomes:

We would like to see Bitsy use American Sign Language fluently enough that her expressive and receptive language will be improved to a level expected for her age.

We would like to see Bitsy's attention span increased to age-appropriate levels, so that she can sit and work on an interesting, developmentally appropriate project with an adult or small group of children for up to 10 minutes at a time. This might mean listening to a story, cutting out play dough, or using finger paints.

We would like to obtain preschool and day-care services appropriate to Bitsy's needs that would provide grandmother with respite during the day while Bitsy's mother is attending high school.

We would like to increase Bitsy's use of her hearing aids so that she wears them on a daily basis.

We would like to enroll Barbara and Laura in weekend sign language instruction so they can add more signs to what they use at home with Bitsy.

Intervention Services Needed:

Continued speech therapy and sign language instruction for Bitsy.

Behavioral intervention planning and consultation to Bitsy's grandmother and mother, as well as to any new caregivers, to motivate increased attending and appropriate behavior.

Instruction in sign language for Bitsy's grandmother, mother, and new caregivers.

Special educational instruction in a group setting.

Strategies Activities, and Services:

Cheryl Tully and Barbara Benson will begin the enrollment process for Bitsy to attend the Jackson Early Start Center, which provides early intervention services in an integrated preschool program. Speech and language therapy will be provided on-site and the Center's behavioral interventionist will work with the teacher and at home on Bitsy's ability to stay with a task for appropriate lengths of time, to follow simple instructions, and to wear her hearing aids.

Service Initiation and Duration:

Early Start Services will begin 10–5–03 and continue until 4–2–04 at which time Bitsy may begin transition to Head Start or Lynwood Deaf Preschool.

Barbara Benson and Laura Burch will attend parent sessions at the Southern Michigan Deaf Education Association Center in Chelsea, held every Saturday morning. Sign language instruction is provided and child care for Bitsy is also available at the center.

472

Figure 9–4   *(continued)*

The meetings also provide a parent network for families with deaf children. A deaf adult will act as a mentor and will meet with the family at their home one evening a week to provide additional sign language training and to advise the family on Bitsy's care and education.

Service Initiation and Duration:

Southern Michigan Deaf Education Association Center meetings will begin 10–3–03 and continue until 1–8–04 at which time the family and service coordinator will discuss the need to continue.

Transition Services:

The service coordinator will arrange for Barbara and Laura to visit two possible preschool programs for Bitsy to attend when she turns 3. One is an integrated Head Start program which provides speech therapy and employs staff who sign. The other is a self-contained preschool program at near by Lynwood Elementary School which serves only deaf children. Total communication and language instruction is emphasized and all teachers are certified as teachers of the deaf.
Transportation for Bitsy will be provided by the local school district.
The service coordinator will be responsible for providing complete records to the receiving program and will identify the main contact person who will follow-through with the family.

Evaluation:

The IFSP team will meet again in March, 2004 to discuss progress made on the outcomes identified. We will determine at that time if continued behavioral intervention is needed in the home and if sign language instruction for the family should continue. We will also be prepared to make a final decision on which program Bitsy will transition to.

Service providers:

Type of Service	Person Responsible	Funding Source
Center-based early childhood education	*Margaret Devon*	*Early Start*
Family support and sign language instruction	*Matthew Liese and Barbara Benson*	*Michigan Deaf Services*
Service coordination	*Cheryl Tully*	*Michigan Deaf Services*
Audiology and speech and language assessment	*Mary Manix, Jackson Clinic South*	*Medicare*
Medical records and billing to Medicare	*Nora Fishback, Jackson Clinic South and Barbara Benson*	*Jackson Clinic South*
Transition services	*Cheryl Tully and Laura Burch*	*Michigan Deaf Services*
Medical treatment	*Glenn Stream, Jackson Clinic South*	*Medicare*

This plan was developed by the following IFSP team members:

Name	**Title**
Barbara Benson	*Grandmother/Guardian*
Laura Burch	*Mother*
Cheryl Tully	*Service Coordinator*
Mary Manix	*Speech and Language Specialist*
Matthew Liese	*Michigan Deaf Services Coordinator*
Pamela Kruse	*Deaf Education Teacher*
Margaret Devon	*Early Start Coordinator*

An IFSP must clearly state the major outcomes that express what a child's team wants to see happen in the next 6 months. Also addressed are outcomes for the child's family. These outcomes must be related to the assessment information on a child's strengths and weaknesses and should reflect a family's concerns and priorities. The goals must be *functional* and *age appropriate* (Umansky & Hooper,

1998). It is important to consider the context in which the child lives and what skills are needed for that child to be more successful in those settings. For example, perhaps a family priority for a child is to become toilet trained because that accomplishment will allow greater access to a regular daycare program. If a young child needs to develop fine motor skills, it makes more sense to work on dressing skills like fastening Velcro than to have her sorting nuts and bolts. Functional goals make caring for a children easier by fostering more independence.

Outcomes should also be realistic (Umansky & Hooper, 1998). Goals that are achievable give families a greater sense of self-efficacy. One way to assure success is to think of 6-month outcomes as steps needed to reach long-term goals. For example, a family may want a child who is currently nonverbal to speak. The first step toward that goal may be to teach the child to communicate through a picture exchange system in which a picture card is selected to indicate a desire for a snack or a toy. The next time new 6-month outcomes are set, the child may be ready to use a communication board or signs to indicate wants. Later, these pictures or signs may be paired with vocalizations, and gradually those vocalizations are shaped to be meaningful words. But the first achievable 6-month step may be using the picture exchange. This task analysis (breaking an ultimate skill into its manageable subskills) should be done with a team so that all members can identify where the outcomes are leading, and all will recognize achievement of intermediate goals as substantive progress.

The IFSP must next indicate the intervention that is required to reach these outcomes. A series of questions should be considered. (1) What type of service will be devoted to each outcome targeted? (For example, speech and language therapy, social work, medical services, transportation.) (2) Who will provide this service and when and where will these take place? A child might be served at home, in family day care, in an outpatient facility, in an early intervention class, or in a hospital, depending on the child's level of need and the intensity of services required. (3) What type of assistive technology or specialized equipment or curriculum are needed to support the intervention? (4) How often each week and for how long during each session will specific therapies or experiences be provided? (5) How will these services be funded? Will private insurance, Medicaid, or family savings be needed? (6) Who will make arrangements for this funding?

An IFSP team must also discuss the settings in which intervention might be provided. When possible and appropriate, services should be delivered in a child's natural environment, but exceptions may be necessary under certain conditions. Services could be offered in a child's home or care setting. Delivery of services in a community program such as Head Start or in an early intervention classroom or even in a hospital setting may also be appropriate if a child's needs can only best be served in a more structured setting. It may be the case that a child's needs will be such that a center-based program that can provide intensive therapies is most appropriate. The service delivery model decision must be based on what children need. A team will indicate the options discussed to determine the most appropriate and natural setting and why other sites were rejected. It is also helpful to indicate any special adaptations, transportation, materials, equipment, curriculum, and so on that would be necessary to allow children to function in the setting selected.

As mentioned, a section of each IFSP must be devoted to plans for eventually transitioning toddlers to school services provided for children from age 3. Transitions might include changes in a child's teacher and other personnel, scheduling, transportation, expectations of children and their families, service delivery models, and philosophy of education. To make the movement from early intervention programs to preschool programs smooth, Part C requires that a specific transition plan be developed and included in all IFSPs as children approach age 3. Planning is to take place at least 90 days before a child's 3rd birthday; family members, a representative from the child's early intervention program, and a representative of the school district are to meet to plan transitional activities (Rosenkoetter, Hains, & Fowler, 1994).

Transition plans need to consider a number of factors. Procedures should be identified to help a child adjust to, and function in, a new setting. A smooth transmission of information about a child (including evaluation and assessment information and copies of IFSPs that have been developed and implemented earlier) to the local educational agency ensures continuity of services. Planning for these transitions should begin as early as possible to identify a setting that is most appropriate (Donegan, Fink, Fowler, & Wischnowski, 1995). Early childhood educators should work closely with parents to develop a plan that will facilitate adaptation to each child's new environment. The goal of transition planning is to enable children to be as successful as possible in their future environments. This means anticipating the skills needed of children and families in future preschool settings. Coordination between early intervention programs and preschool programs is also required to ensure that schools receiving young children understand a particular child's and family's needs and subsequently develop appropriate individualized programs.

The transition plan itself should answer the following questions (Destafano, Howe, Horn, & Smith, 1991, p. 69):

1. What services are available?
2. Which services are appropriate?
3. What steps must be taken before a child can enter the next program?
4. What skills does the next program require?
5. What additional skills does a child need?
6. What can the current program do to help a child succeed in her next program?
7. What is the next program not able to do to make sure a child succeeds?

An often-overlooked section of the IFSP that should be included is evaluation (Umansky & Hooper, 1998). The team should discuss how the actions planned accomplished the desired outcomes and make any modification that seems necessary to make IFSPs more effective. Questions to ask include: Was intervention carried out as planned in the IFSP? What changes in the child's skills occurred and were they the result of the intervention? Were unexpected or undesired outcomes observed? Did we actually achieve intended outcomes? Was the family satisfied with intervention? Were family priorities addressed? In fact, the crux of evaluation is "whether families think their child received the services they felt were needed and whether they perceive those services as having a positive impact on development and behavior" (Bailey et al., 1998).

Finally, IFSPs provide a space for all those who were involved in its making to indicate their participation. Team members must include the parents or guardians and early interventionists. The planning might also involve other family members (such as grandparents), individuals invited by the family, specialists knowledgeable in the child's area of disability, medical personnel, and a parent advocate.

EFFECTIVE FAMILY-CENTERED EARLY INTERVENTION

If early intervention has served its purpose well, then both child and family outcomes should be positive. Though child outcomes are more clearly measurable, it has been challenging to determine if families have been well served. Bailey and his colleagues (1998) recommended that several questions be answered in assessing family outcomes:

1. Does the family see early intervention as appropriate in making a difference in their child's life? Do families think their child received the services they felt were needed and did those services have a positive impact on their child's development and behavior? Dimensions that might be measured would include the type and amount of services provided, the quality of services, the extent to which these services affected a child, and whether the goals on the IFSP were attained.

2. Does the family see early intervention as appropriate in making a difference in their family life, beyond the impact on their child? To evaluate, one would have to ask if needs for information, social support, finances, childcare, and so on were met. Were the services provided culturally and personally appropriate or acceptable to the family? Were family goals on the IFSP attained?

3. Does the family have a positive view of professionals and the special service system? Ideally, families should report that encounters with service providers were supportive, responsive, and respectful, and that the system was accessible and helpful.

4. Did early intervention help enhance an optimistic view of the future? Turnbull and Turnbull (1997) defined hope as the "belief that you will get what you want and need" (p. 41). In order to assess this, one must ask, "What expectations do families have for their children and how strongly do they believe they will reach them?"

5. Did early intervention enhance the family's perceived quality of life? What is the family's perception in regard to their independence, standard of living, productivity, relationships, health, safety, leisure, and life satisfaction?

In general, despite the trauma and disappointment associated with the early diagnosis of a child's disability, early intervention may be one of the most positive experiences that parents of children with disabilities ever encounter (Bailey et al., 1998). Unfortunately, this initially positive view seldom endures as a child ages. Because early intervention is so different philosophically and practically from "the system" operating in public schools, early intervention has the potential to greatly influence the way children (especially those with disabilities) learn and how their families are treated. It is incumbent upon all early interventionists to find ways to support positive relationships between families and their children's service providers. The support provided can have enormous impact on the home environment for a child. One parent put it eloquently:

> Provide me with some ray of hope. Robbing me of hope is the worst thing you can do to me. Remember that after I leave your office, I will create an atmosphere at home of hope or despair, and surely one of hope is better for my child. You can give me hope through your attitude and what you say. Your belief that my child could defy the statistics will soften the facts that you must tell me. (Alexander & Tompkins-McGill, 1987, p. 362)

EVIDENCE-BASED PRACTICE

The involvement of many different professional disciplines in the treatment of very young children with disabilities and delays has contributed to the adoption of evidence-based practice to ensure effective intervention. Evidence-based practice is widely used in medicine and has grown rapidly in use among allied disciplines such as occupational therapy, physical therapy, speech and language pathology, and early intervention (Dunst, Trivette & Cutspec, 2002). Evidence-based practice involves using research-based evidence in making decisions about a treatment most likely to be beneficial in any individual's circumstances. Early intervention practices should be informed by research in order to help practitioners and parents achieve the best outcomes for children in their care.

Evidence-based practice provides a systematic approach for transferring research information into practice (Law, 2000). Goode, Lovett, Hayes, & Butcher (1987) recommended specific steps in this process.

1. First, professionals have to clearly define a child's area of need. For example, perhaps a child fails to develop speech, despite having no obvious physical disability or cognitive delay.

2. Next, the therapist or teacher gathers information from research studies about other children with the same problem and compares the effects of interventions that have been studied. Information can be found in professional journals, review articles, and from the Internet, though caution must be taken when using sources that have not been peer reviewed.

3. The therapist or teacher must be prepared to read and critically analyze related research articles. This may require training in judging the quality of research designs, the value of outcomes data, and the generality of effects.

4. Next the practitioner decides if the research is relevant to the child's problem. Is the setting similar? Are those carrying out the intervention the same kinds of support people available in this child's situation?

5. A summary of these research findings help the intervention team, including the family, make a decision about the intervention most likely to be effective for this child.

6. Next, the professional defines the outcomes of the intervention that can be expected, both for the child and the family.

7. The professional must make sure the family and others can carry out the intervention correctly. This may require some special training or assistance.

8. The team should continuously monitor the child's progress to determine if the recommended approach is effective. This means collecting baseline data, taking frequent measures of outcomes, and adjusting procedures as needed. If an intervention fails to achieve the outcomes desired, then the process would start again and another intervention might be recommended.

Efforts to integrate early childhood research and practices can be found in traditional research reviews, in recommended practice guidelines, and in books devoted to research-based intervention (Dunst et al., 2002). There are also a number of abstraction services available through Internet subscriptions that can assist in the process of gathering and reviewing research. Among these are:

> The Cochrane Library
> PubMed
> MEDLINE
> CINAHL
> HEALTHSTAR
> Psychlit
> PsychInfo
> ERIC

In addition, the Office of Special Education and Rehabilitation funds Centers for Evidence-Based Practices that develop reviews of research in many areas. The Orlena Hawks Puckett Institute is one of these Research to Practice centers that focuses on early intervention.

Evidence, research, and data are becoming a part of the common language for service delivery and an important factor in the decision making that goes into prescribing services. However, it is still critical that any review of research findings balances the strengths and limitations of the evidence with the practical realities of our care settings. Parents and practitioners have to be able to understand new material and use it in the right way. This can be undermined when resources are limited or when an individual child's circumstances are so unique they don't match those settings in which the research took place. Also, the family's values, preferences, and rights must always be respected, and new, promising innovations should not be disregarded because evidence supporting them are still being gathered. Despite these complications, evidence-based practice promises continuing progress in developing effective early intervention for all children in need.

IN CONCLUSION

Early intervention is complex and challenging, even after several decades of implementation (Hanson & Bruder, 2001). Early intervention is still a relatively new field, involves a variety of service delivery systems, serves a wide range of families and children, requires interagency and interdisciplinary teaming, and varies in implementation from state to state. In addition, children served in early intervention systems must transition into very different models when they become preschoolers. Despite its challenges, early intervention continues to grow. The key responsibilities that grow with early intervention include providing appropriate family-centered services, in a variety of environments, through collaborative teams of well-trained professionals to meet the full spectrum of child and family needs (Hanson & Bruder, 2001).

STUDY GUIDE QUESTIONS

1. What is meant by early intervention?
2. What rationales were provided as the basis for Part C in IDEA?
3. What are the five general principles which guided the IDEA regulations in regard to early intervention?
4. What are the ideals of good family-centered practices?
5. What kinds of tasks are accomplished by a skilled service coordinator?
6. Define and give an example of each of the four categories of eligibility under Part C of IDEA.
7. If a child is identified with a hearing impairment, what type of professional would be most appropriate for service coordinator?
8. How would you deliver service coordination to families if you wanted to comply with family preferences identified by Early and Poertner (1993)?
9. Memorize the procedural safeguards and be able to explain the meaning of each in terms of preserving the rights of families.
10. Know the regulations regarding assessment procedures under IDEA.
11. What are the legal timelines from referral of a child to delivery of services?
12. How is ongoing assessment useful in working with infants and toddlers?
13. Why is it advised that family assessment be family-directed?
14. What are the principal steps taken by Winton and Bailey to put parents at ease in conducting assessment?
15. Identify the required components of IFSPs.
16. Develop five goals/objectives, keeping in mind the five principles developed by Notari-Syverson and Shuster.
17. Explain the rationale for using natural routines in planning IFSP objectives.
18. Explain the purpose and legal requirements of transition planning.
19. What is meant by evidence-based practice?
20. What would be the advantages of the evidence-based approach?

REFERENCES

Alexander, R., & Tompkins-McGill, P. (1987). Notes to the experts from the parent of a handicapped child. *Social Work, 32,* 352–361.

Bailey, D. B., McWilliam, R. A., Darkes, L. A., Simeonsson, R. J., Hebbeler, K., Spiker, D., & Wagner, M. (1998). Family outcomes in early intervention: A framework for program evaluation and efficacy research. *Exceptional Children, 64*(3), 313–328.

Baird, S., & Peterson, J. (1997). Seeking a comfortable fit between family-centered philosophy and infant-parent interaction in early intervention: Time for a paradigm shift? *Topics in Early Childhood Special Education, 17*(2), 139–165.

Beckman, P. J., & Bristol, M. M. (1991). Issues in developing the IFSP: A framework for establishing family outcomes. *Topics in Early Childhood Special Education, 11*(3), 19–31.

Berry, J., & Hardman, M. L. (1998). *Lifespan perspectives on family and disability.* Boston, MA: Allyn & Bacon.

Berzon, P., & Lowenstein, B. (1984). A flexible model of case management. In B. Pepper & H. Ryglewicz (Eds.), Advances in treating the young adult chronic patient.

New Directions for Mental Health Services, no. 21 (pp. 49–57). San Francisco: Jossey-Bass.

Bosch, L. A. (1998). Early intervention in the new millennium: the critical role of school social workers. *Social Work in Education, 29*(2), 139–144.

Bricker, D. (2001). The natural environment: A useful construct? *Infants and Young Children, 13*(4), 21–31.

Carta, J. J., Sainato, D. M., & Greenwood, C. R. (1988). Advances in the ecological assessment of childhood instruction for young children with handicaps. In S. L. Odom & M. B. Karnes (Eds.), *Early Intervention for infants and children with handicaps* (pp. 217–239). Baltimore, MD: Paul H. Brookes.

Committee on Children with Disabilities. (1999). The pediatrician's role in development and implementation of an Individual Education Plan (IEP) and/or an Individual Family Service Plan (IFSP). *Pediatrics, 104*(1), 124–127.

D'Amato, E., & Lynn, V. (1999). Early intervention: What's it all about? *The Exceptional Parent, 29*(7), 52–54.

Destafano, D. M., Howe, A. G., Horn, E. M., & Smith, B. A. (1991). *Best practices: Evaluating early childhood special education programs.* Tucson, AZ: Communication Skill Builders.

Division of Early Childhood (DEC). (1987, March). Position statement and recommendations relating to P.L. 99–457 and other federal and state early childhood policies.

Donegan, M. M., Fink, D. B., Fowler, S. A., & Wischnowski, M. W. (February 1995). Making the transition to group care. *Exceptional Parent,* 29–31.

Donner, R., Huff, B., Gentry, M., McKinney, D., Duncan, J., Thompson, S., & Silver, P. (Winter/Spring, 1993). Expectations of case management for children with emotional problems: Parent perspectives. *Focal Point,* 5–6.

Dunst, C. J., Trivette, C. M., & Cutspec, P. A. (2002). Toward an operational definition of evidence-based practices. *Centerscope, 1*(1), 1–10.

Dunst, C. J., Trivette, C. M., & Deal, A. (1988). *Enabling and empowering families: Principles and guidelines for practice.* Cambridge, MA: Brookline.

Early, T. J., & Poertner, J. (Winter/Spring 1993). Case management for families and children. *Focal Point,* 1–4.

Goode, C. J., Lovett, M. K., Hayes, J. E., & Butcher, L. A. (1987). Use of research based knowledge in clinical practice. *Journal of Nursing Administration, 17*(2), 11–18.

Hanson, M. J., & Bruder M. B. (2001). Early intervention: Promises to keep. *Infants and Young Children, 13*(3), 47–58.

Hanson, M. J., & Lynch, E. W. (1989). *Early intervention.* Austin, TX: PRO-ED.

Hanson, M. J., & Lynch, E. W. (1995). *Early intervention: Implementing child and family services for infants and toddlers who are at risk or disabled* (2nd ed.). Austin, TX: PRO-ED.

Hardman, M. L., Drew, D. J., & Egan, M. W. (1999). *Human exceptionality: society, school, and family* (6th ed.). Boston, MA: Allyn & Bacon.

Hebbeler, K., Wagner, M., Spiker, D., Scarborough, A., Simmeonson, R., & Collier, M. (2001). *National Early Intervention Longitudinal Study: A first look at the characteristics of children and families entering early intervention services.* SRI International. Retrieved September 9, 2002 from *http://www.sri. com/neils/reports/html*

Law, M. (2000). Strategies for implementing evidence-based practice in early intervention. *Infants and Young Children, 13*(2), 32–40.

Lerner, J. W., Lowenthal, B., & Egan, R. (1998). *Preschool children with special needs: Children at-risk, children with disabilities.* Boston: Allyn & Bacon.

Lovaas, O. I. (1987). Behavioral treatment and normal educational and intellectual functioning in young autistic children. *Journal of Consulting and Clinical Psychology, 55,* 3–9.

Maroney, R. M. (1986). *Shared responsibility: Families and social policy.* New York: Aldine.

McWilliam, R. A., & Ferguson, A. (1998). The family-centeredness of individualized family service plans. *Topics in Early Childhood Special Education, 18*(2), 69–83.

McWilliam, R. A., & Scott, S. (2001). A support approach to early intervention: A three-part framework. *Infants and Young Children, 13*(4), 55–66.

McWilliam, R. A., Tocci, L., & Harbin, G. L. (1998). Family-centered services: Service providers' discourse and behavior. *Topics in Early Childhood Special Education, 18*(4), 206–232.

MHLP: Early Intervention Advocacy Network Notebook. (January, 1990). *Guide to Part H Law and Regulations.* 2021 L Street N.W., Washington, DC 20036.

National Early Childhood Technical Assistance System. (1999). *Overview of the Part C program under IDEA.* Retrieved July 10, 1999 from *http://www.nectas.unc.edu/partc/ptcoverview.html*

North Carolina. (1998). *Early intervention in North Carolina.* Retrieved July 10, 1999 from *http://www.dhhs.state.nc.us/dcd/icc_par. htm#FREI*

Notari-Syverson, A. R., & Shuster, S. L. (Winter 1995). Putting real life skills into IEP/IFSPs for infants and young children. *Teaching Exceptional Children,* 29–32.

Rosenkoetter, S. E., Hains, A. H., & Fowler, S. A. (1994). *Bridging early services for children with special needs and their families: A practical guide for transition planning.* Baltimore: Paul H. Brookes.

Salisbury, C. L., & Smith, B. J. (1993). *Effective practices for preparing young children with disabilities for school.* (ERIC Document Reproduction Service No. ED 358675).

Sexton, D., Thompson, B., Perez, J., & Rheams, T. (1990). Maternal versus professional estimates of developmental status for young children with handicaps: An ecological approach. *Topics in Early Childhood Special Education, 10*(3), 80–95.

Shackelford, J. (June, 2002). State and jurisdictional eligibility definitions for infants and toddlers with disabilities under IDEA. *NECTAC Notes #5* (Revised). National Early Childhood Technical Assistance Center.

Simeonsson, R. J. (1986). *Psychological and developmental assessment of special children.* Boston: Allyn & Bacon.

Smith, T., Groen, A. D., & Wynn, J. W. (2000). *American Journal on Mental Retardation, 105*(4) 269–285.

Sontag, J., & Schact, R. (1994). An ethnic comparison of parent participation and information needs in early intervention. *Exceptional Children, 16*(5), 422–431.

Thompson, L., Lobb, C., Elling, R., Herman, S., Jurkiewicz, & Hulleza, C. (1997). Pathways to family empowerment: Effects of family-centered delivery early intervention services. *Exceptional Children, 64*(1), 99–113.

Thurman, S. K., & Widerstrom, A. H. (1990). *Infants and young children with special needs.* Baltimore: Paul H. Brookes.

Tisot, C. M. & Thurman, K. S. (2002). Using behavior setting theory to define natural settings: A family-centered approach. *Infants and Young Children, 14*(3), 65–71.

Trohanis, P. L. (August, 2002). Progress in providing services to young children with special needs and their families: An overview to and update on the implementation of the Individuals with Disabilities Education Act (IDEA). *NECTAC Notes, 12,* 1–18.

Tucker, B. P., & Goldstein, B. A. (1991). *The educational rights of children with disabilities: A guide to federal law.* Horsham, PA: LRP Publications.

Turnbull, A. P., & Turnbull, H. R. (1997). *Families, professionals, and exceptionality: A special partnership* (3rd ed.). Upper Saddle River, NJ: Merrill/Prentice Hall.

Umansky, W., & Hooper, S. R. (1998). *Young children with special needs* (3rd ed.). Upper Saddle River, NJ: Merrill/Prentice Hall.

U.S. Department of Education. (2000). *Twenty-second annual report to Congress on the implementation of the Individuals with Disabilities Education Act.* Washington, DC: Author.

Ventura, S. J., Martin, J. A., Curtin, S. C., & Matthews, T. J. (1999). *Report of final natality statistics, 1996. Monthly vital statistics report, 47*(18), supp. Hyattsville, MD: National Center for Health Statistics.

Wehman, T. (1998). Family-centered early intervention services: Factors contributing to increased parent involvement. *Focus on Autism & Other Developmental Disabilities, 98*(13), 80–87.

Winton, P., & Bailey, D. (1988). The family-focused interview: A collaborative mechanism for family assessment and goal setting. *Journal of the Division of Early Childhood, 12,* 195–207.

10 Mandated Services for Young Children

Most IEPs are useless or slightly worse, and too many teachers experience the IEP process as always time consuming, sometimes threatening, and too often, a pointless bureaucratic requirement. The result is a quasi-legal document to be filed away with the expectation it won't be seen again except, heaven forbid, by a monitor or compliance officer. The point of the IEP exercise seems to be to complete the given form in a way

that commits the district to as little as possible, and which precludes, as much as possible, any meaningful discussion or evaluation of the student's real progress.

(Bateman, 1995, p. 1)

Many families become frustrated as they move from the Individualized Family Service Plan (IFSP) process, used when their children were infants and toddlers, to the **Individualized Education Program** (IEP) process, in place when their children turn 3 years of age. Transition from those services provided through infant and toddler programs to **mandated** preschool special education for children ages 3–5 years, means transition to the public school system, which can too often be a rocky road (Turnbull & Turnbull, 1997). While early intervention has adopted a family-centered approach in which services are assured for both the family and the child, special education services to children from 3 years to age 21 are focused primarily on the student. This shift takes place as planning moves from the IFSP to the IEP. Moving away from intensive family ownership and involvement creates an unwelcome challenge for many parents. Families who have become accustomed to high-quality early intervention services may quickly become disenchanted with special education programs where students are the central focus and family-centered planning is not a priority (Pruitt, Wandry, & Hollums, 1998).

Is the contrast an appropriate one? Certainly such a dramatic paradigm shift is not by intention. In the larger sense, the Individuals with Disabilities Education Act (IDEA) has done more to validate the role of parents as educational decision makers for their children and to encourage collaboration between parents and professionals than any other legislative mandate, court ruling, or public policy. IDEA explicitly calls for the active involvement of parents in all aspects of educational programming for their children with disabilities. In fact, the 1997 revision of IDEA (PL 105-17) demanded even greater parent involvement than in the past in terms of assessment and planning. As Turnbull and Turnbull (1997) contended, parents accustomed to family-centered early intervention programs are beginning to demand that such collaborative practices continue throughout their children's education.

It may be the case that millions of families of children with disabilities feel "disenfranchised and alienated from educational systems designed to help their children" (Kroth & Edge, 1997, p. 14). If professionals dominate the decision-making process and student-centered practices act to exclude family input, then the potential for profitable family interactions in educational planning and implementation is lost and the principles of IDEA are not well served. Active parental involvement in the educational process benefits children both academically and socially, but too many educators fail to understand the need to encourage parental participation (Pruitt et al., 1998). This lack of understanding may foster unsatisfactory levels of communication and collaboration.

CLOSE-UP

THE STATE OF CHILDREN IN AMERICA'S UNION: A 2002 ACTION GUIDE TO LEAVE NO CHILD BEHIND™ CHILDREN'S DEFENSE FUND

The trademarked Leave No Child Behind™ mission of the Children's Defense Fund was adopted by the Bush administration as the focus of its campaign, "No Child Left Behind" (H.R. 1). But the political reality is that the government's efforts have not been comprehensive enough nor well-funded enough to truly give all of America's children the help they need for a successful passage into adulthood. The recession that began in 2001 has left more children with unemployed parents and increased hardship. Tax cuts have caused reductions in services available to strapped children and families. One in every five children under age 3 in America is poor.

Imagine this fifth child as the member of a very wealthy family. Four of its siblings have plenty to eat and a comfortable house. The fifth child goes hungry and sometimes sleeps on the street. Four of its siblings receive stimulating preschool experiences, but the fifth is sent to unsafe or poor-quality child care with untrained caregivers. Every night, four children are read to while the fifth is not, and may even sit propped before a television screen that feeds her violence. As the children grow, four are sent to good schools but the fifth is sent to a crumbling school with old books and poorly trained teachers. Four of the children love learning and look forward to college, but the fifth comes to school not ready to learn, falls further behind with each grade, and thinks about dropping out.

America's "fifth" child is:

◆ twice as likely to be born without adequate prenatal care, at low birth weight, and at risk of death before her first birthday
◆ more than twice as likely to be abused or neglected
◆ twice as likely to repeat a grade or drop out of school and more likely to need special education
◆ more likely to begin school with thousands fewer words in her vocabulary
◆ more likely to suffer from asthma and respiratory ailments without treatment
◆ less likely to have a father at home or a steady family income
◆ twice as likely to be poor as an adult

America's fifth child is poor, hungry, homeless, unstimulated, abused, and neglected during the most important years of development.

What can you do to advocate for America's children? Support the comprehensive Act to Leave No Child Behind (S. 940/H.R. 1990) introduced by Senator Christopher

Dodd (D-CT). In contrast to the No Child Left Behind Act, this act calls for an estimated $75 billion annual investment for comprehensive child services including:

◆ fully funding quality child care and Head Start
◆ lifting every child from poverty—half by 2004; all by 2010
◆ providing health insurance to every child and parent
◆ expanding food programs so no child goes hungry
◆ providing safe, quality after-school and summer programs
◆ ensuring decent, affordable housing
◆ protecting children from neglect, abuse, and other violence
◆ ensuring families leaving welfare the supports needed to be successful

You can participate in Wednesdays in Washington and At Home™. This is an effort to mobilize a critical mass of women, youth, and concerned citizens from all walks of life to bear witness for children's needs. It means contacting local, state and national leaders to request support for children and families. Along these lines, you can vote for children's issues and practice asking the hard questions of our political leaders.

Finally, you can support efforts to make your city or county a Leave No Child Behind™ city or county. Help your local leaders issue a proclamation or resolution endorsing the Movement to Leave No Child Behind, Proclaim a Stand for Children Day, and urge your community members to stand up for quality child care and lifting families out of poverty. Sponsor public education about children's issues in your area.

Source: The State of Children in America's Union: A 2002 Action Guide to Leave No Child Behind™, 2002, by Author, 2002, Washington, D.C., Children's Defense Fund. Retrieved July 31, 2003 from http://www.childrensdefense.org/data.php.

A CHANGE OF PERSPECTIVE

Schools that are making positive strides do so by responding to the qualities, needs, and characteristics of families (D'Angelo & Adler, 1991). Special educators who wish to strengthen their partnerships with parents can take specific steps to do so. Epstein (1992) suggested six types of parent involvement that should be encouraged:

1. Parenting: establishing supportive home environments
2. Communicating: designing effective forms of interactive communications
3. Volunteering: organizing parent help in the school environment
4. Learning at home: assisting families with homework and other related activities
5. Decision making: including parents in school decisions
6. Collaborating with the community: integrating community resources to strengthen school programs

Professionals need to increase communication with families, use parent networks, and learn to understand family views and strengths in shared decision making (Pruitt et al., 1998).

When Pruitt and her colleagues interviewed 78 families with children in special education, they found almost 27% of respondents said they just wanted educators to listen to them. When asked, "What can educators do to be more sensitive to the needs of your family?" one mother responded:

> Taking input from the parents on what works. There are a lot of parents in special ed that don't keep it together. It is an overwhelming experience to have a handicapped child. Sometimes I think parents get written off as being out of line with things. Teachers must remember that there is a lot of value to what the parents say—even though they are hysterical or not rational—because they really do know that child. They may not be coping well right now, but they do know best. (p.165)

Another 23% of the parents interviewed indicated that the quality and quantity of communication between parents and professionals should be improved. The respondents felt professionals should use a more humane demeanor with parents, interact in an honest manner, and treat parents with dignity and respect. A father stated:

> Please don't talk to me like I'm an idiot or assume that I know what you are talking about. Another thing is sometimes I get the feeling that the professionals are talking to each other and not me. It's discouraging. Another thing I might say is that instead of telling me what you are going to do with my daughter, ask my opinion, give me some say in her education and placement. I don't know what all my options are and it's tough. (p. 166)

Other parents' recommendations to professionals included increasing knowledge about various disabilities, treating children with respect, and improving the IEP process. A parent suggested:

> Read the IEP. I took my daughter to school before school started, so she would know who her teachers were and could identify them. They hadn't even gotten her IEP, so they really didn't know her. I'm asking, who would be responsible for adapting her curriculum and keeping track of that. And they're asking me, How much adaptation do you think she'll need? I'm thinking, I don't know; I'm not the teacher! (p. 167)

Though equity is difficult to achieve, parents and professionals must be equal partners in a team striving for the same goals. The family-centered focus found in early intervention may change as the child enters special education in the school system, but the advantages of family–professional partnerships do not change. Early childhood professionals must "acknowledge that parents have equitable, collaborative roles because they possess critical information about their child, without which the educational process cannot be complete" (Pruitt et al., 1998). Collaboration with families is also an essential requirement of IDEA.

PARENT RIGHTS AND RESPONSIBILITIES

Parent involvement is so essential to the process of planning and providing services to a child in special education that IDEA is quite explicit about those rights to participation in the decision making (ERIC Clearinghouse on Disabilities and Gifted Education, 1999). Parents have the right to:

1. Have a free, appropriate public education for their child, at no cost to the family and designed to meet the unique education needs of the child

2. Request an evaluation if they suspect a child needs special education or related services
3. Be notified whenever the school wants to evaluate a child, change a child's placement, or refuse parents' request for an evaluation or change in placement
4. Give informed consent that is voluntary and may be withdrawn at any time
5. Obtain an independent evaluation if in disagreement with a school's assessment
6. Request a reevaluation if a child's present education program is no longer appropriate or if 3 years have passed and current information is not sufficient for new decision making
7. Have a child tested in the language she knows best, including sign language if appropriate
8. Review all of a child's school records, including teachers' classroom notes
9. Be fully informed of legal rights and due process provided by law
10. Participate in the development of an IEP and in making placement decisions
11. Request an IEP meeting at any time parents feel it is needed
12. Be informed of a child's progress at least as often as parents of children who do not have disabilities
13. Have children educated in the least restrictive environment possible that provides all the supports needed for children to participate with children who do not have disabilities
14. Participate in voluntary mediation or a due process hearing if needed to resolve differences with the school

Just as parents have certain rights, parents also have responsibilities in regard to their involvement in educational decision making (ERIC Clearinghouse on Disabilities and Gifted Education, 1999).

1. Parents should work to develop a partnership with their school, to share relevant information and observations that can be helpful in planning their child's program.
2. Parents need to ask for an explanation of any aspects of the program they don't understand, especially educational or medical jargon.
3. Parents need to monitor the IEP goals and objectives to be sure they are specific and agreeable.
4. Parents should examine and think about the IEP carefully before signing it.
5. Parents should request periodic reports on their child's progress, or suggest changes in the program if their child is not progressing.
6. Parents need to work directly with school personnel to resolve conflicts over assessment, placement, or educational program.
7. Parents have to keep good records so important information is not lost or forgotten.
8. Finally, parents who are interested can join a parent organization where they can share their knowledge, experiences, and support. The organized efforts of families has often the force that brings about needed changes to strengthen services to children.

When the provisions of IDEA are fully implemented, both letter of the law and the spirit of the law are protected. A supportive and mutually respectful relationship between families and professionals is the place where success starts (Beach Center on Families and Disabilities, 1999); the process of decision making will be collaborative and information about current best practices will be shared among the team members. Decision making is ongoing, dynamic, and individualized, with family-initiated goals and objectives given priority. Meetings and documents are jargon-free and technical information is explained when necessary. Professionals and families discuss all the options for a range of service settings, considering the advantages and disadvantages. In short, a true team implements IDEA as it applies specifically to each child.

THE INDIVIDUALIZED EDUCATION PROGRAM

Barbara Bateman and Mary Anne Linden, in their book, *Better IEPs* (1998), suggested that all professionals obey their humorously written but seriously conceived "IDEA Commandments":

I.   Thou shalt base all eligibility decisions on professional judgment, not on quantitative formulae.
II. Thou shalt open wide the door unto very needed service and placement for each eligible child.
III. Remember thou that categorical delivery of services is an abomination.
IV. Each IEP shall be based solely upon the child's needs. He or she who looks instead to availability of services shall know the inferno.
V.   Maketh every IEP in the image of its child. An IEP like unto another is a graven image. Despised by all who know IDEA.
VI. Place not all children in the same setting, but make available the entire continuum of alternative placements.
VII. Thou shalt not exclude parents from decisions that affect their children.
VIII. Thou shalt not burden parents with the cost of their children's special education and services. (Ask the Expert, 1999)

The IEP details a specific plan used by preschool education team members on a daily basis. IDEA regulations governing the required elements of an IEP specify that each contains the following components:

1. A statement of the child's **present levels of performance**
2. A statement of annual goals
3. A statement of short-term instructional objectives
4. A statement of educational services and related services to be provided
5. The date when services will begin and their duration
6. A description of the extent to which the child will be included in regular education settings
7. A statement of evaluation procedures

In addition to these components, the IDEA requires IEP teams to consider the following and address needs that are apparent for each child (Pacer Center, 1999):

1. Behavior strategies and supports for a child whose behavior impedes the learning of others

2. Language needs if the child has limited English proficiency
3. Communication needs of a child, with specific factors to consider if the child is deaf or hard of hearing
4. Provision of Braille for a child who is blind (unless the team determines it is not appropriate)
5. Needs for assistive technology devices or service

An IEP team includes people in several different roles (Pacer Center, 1999). In addition to the parents who are to be included in placement decisions for their child, teams must include at least one special education teacher and, at least one regular education teacher if the child participates in regular education. A local school district representative who can commit special education services is to be involved, and that person must also know about the general curriculum and local resources. One of the IEP team members must be able to interpret evaluation results; others must have knowledge or special expertise on the child's needs, including persons who provide related services. A family may invite additional persons, and older children should be involved when deemed appropriate by the family and team. In all cases, a child's parent or guardian must consent to the IEP, by officially signing it, before a service plan is implemented. Formats for IEPs vary widely and may exceed the basic requirements of the law. (A sample IEP is shown in Figure 10–1.)

Ideally, an IEP spells out where a child is developmentally, where a child should be going, how she will get there, when the child will reach specific goals, and how to tell if she has arrived (Heward & Orlansky, 1992). To ensure that an IEP is continuously relevant, it must be reviewed at least once a year by a child's team. In addition, parents may request a review prior to the annual review date.

Several factors are key to writing a functional IEP. These include:

1. A complete description of the child's current skills and behaviors on which to base future instruction
2. The writing of clear instructional objectives
3. The designation of specially designed instruction and related services
4. The identification of the appropriate and least restrictive setting for educational inclusion

PRESENT LEVELS OF PERFORMANCE

The first step in IEP development is to translate student evaluation results into practical planning information. IEP teams must use current information, state performance in concise and clear language, and identify specific skills. Teams draw from standardized test scores, medical records, observations, specialist's reports, and parent input. Crucial questions to be addressed are the following:

1. What is a student's current level of mastery in each specified skill area?
2. What is the nature of the specifically designed instruction that should be provided in each skill area? (Strickland & Turnbull, 1990)

Figure 10–1 Individualized Education Program

Child's Name: *Jennifer Lovinger* **Birthdate:** *6–19–01* **Age:** *38 mos* **School:** *Pine Valley, Preschool (3–5)*
Parents/Guardians: *Lyle & Julia Lovinger* **Address:** *W. 1125 Post, Pine Valley* **Telephone:** *328-3520*
Reason for referral: Jennifer is an adopted child whose mother was addicted to alcohol and cocaine. Jennifer showed evidence of both in her bloodstream at birth. She was premature and seizured at delivery. She continued to have tremors for several days as well as increased extension. Jennifer was slow to develop physical skills and lacks age-appropriate self-help skills. She is very active, difficult for the parents to control, and has frequent temper tantrums.
Present levels of performance:
Strengths: Jennifer's performance on the test of intelligence fell within the average range expected at this age. She was able to follow directions, imitate line drawings, and complete fine motor tasks. Jennifer is able to place shapes in a box, turn pages of a book, and use a peg board and use a spoon. Her mother reports that Jennifer can turn doorknobs and television and radio dials, and She can manipulate blocks. Jennifer's gross motor skills appear to be at developmentally-appropriate levels; she walks, jumps on two feet and runs with ease. She likes to throw objects and follows them visually. Jennifer sings preschool songs she learned from the television. She has good receptive and expressive language skills. Jennifer has normal hearing and vision.
Areas of concern: Jennifer's self-help skills are delayed and she is not cooperative in tasks such as washing hands unless it is done very quickly. Jennifer's toilet training is delayed and she does not indicate wet or soiled pants. Jennifer still does not hold her own glass when drinking and must be fed with a spoon. She also does not assist in undressing herself. Jennifer has a low frustration tolerance and does not adapt to new situations well. She tantrums frequently, banging her head and biting herself when upset. Her activity level is high, and it is difficult to maintain sustained attention to a task. Jennifer does not tolerate sensory stimulation well. She appeared to be tactilely defensive when touched and overreacted to different textures.

Statement of Major Annual Goals	Specific Education of Related Support Services Needed to Meet Annual Goals	Person(s) Responsible for Providing Services—Beginning and Ending Dates
1. Establish self-help skills, including self-feeding, toileting, and hygiene.	A detailed task analysis for each skill area will be used and Jennifer's entry level to each task identified. A system of graduated guidance will be used within self-help routines in the classroom and at home. Completion of each task and independent completion of any step in a task will be consequated with praise and access to a reinforcing activity.	Occupational therapist, special education teacher, and parent. Initiation of service: 9-6-03 Ending date: 8-15-04
2. Reduce temper tantrums in intensity and frequency (to a rate of no more than once a month).	Jennifer will be differentially reinforced for co-operative behavior and for using appropriate ways to say, "no." Each time a temper tantrum occurs, Jennifer will be placed in a chair away from other children and entertaining activities for one minute.	Any classroom staff who are present when these behaviors occur and parents at home. Initiation of service: 9-6-03 Ending date: 8-15-04
3. Increase sustained attention to tasks up to a duration of 15 minutes.	Provide structured one-on-one tutoring for short periods each day, initially with the teacher or paraprofessional, later using peer tutors. Use child-selected, high-interest materials and allow Jennifer to switch to various objects or toys, gradually requiring longer contact before switching is possible.	Special education teacher and aide. Initiation of service: 9-6-03 Ending date: 8-15-04

(continued)

Figure 10–1 *(continued)*

Related Annual Goal	Observable Behavior	Conditions	Criterion	Evaluation & Measurement Procedures—Review Dates
1. (a) Establish self-help skills	Jennifer will unbutton and remove her coat, take off her hat, and hang both in her cubby	With no teacher assistance other than verbal direction at the beginning of class each day and after outdoor play	Within 3 minutes of entering the classroom at least twice each day	The parent will record completion of the task and time required at entry each morning and the aide after outdoor play on a record sheet kept in Jennifer's cubby. Reassess procedure in 1 month.
1. (b) Establish self-help skills	Jennifer will remove her underpants and urinate in the toilet	When taken to the bathroom after snack, after lunch, after nap, and at any time she requests to use the toilet	Within 5 minutes of arrival at the bathroom each time she is taken	The aide will record time and success using a data sheet kept in the bathroom. Review progress in 2 months.
1. (c) Establish self-help skills	Jennifer will turn on water, use soap, scrub, and dry her hands	With verbal reminders and physical prompting when needed, after toileting and before eating snack and lunch	Requiring no more than one physical prompt and two verbal reminders	The aide will record number of verbal and physical prompts required. Review in 2 months.
2. (a) Reduce temper tantrums	Jennifer will say "No"	When she does not wish to participate in an activity	Without crying, hitting, or running away	Teacher will observe circle time each day and record number of invitations to participate given to Jennifer, times "No" is used and number of times crying, hitting, or running away occurs. Reassess in 1 month.
2. (b) Reduce temper tantrums	Jennifer will participate	In circle activities when invited to by the teacher	With appropriate singing, talking, or hand movements requested	Teacher records number of invitations to participate given to Jennifer, and if she complied appropriately or not. Review in 1 month, expand to table activities when possible.

3. (a) Increase sustained attention	Jennifer will manipulate, watch, or listen to a toy	Which she has selected while working one-on-one with the teacher, aide, or peer for a 15-minute session	For 3 minutes before switching to another toy	The teacher or aide will use 10-second interval recording to note engagement. Review in 1 month.
3. (b) Increase sustained attention	Jennifer will sit quietly	During story time	Without leaving her seat for 3 minutes	Aide will use 10-second interval recording to note quiet sitting.

Recommendations and justification for placement:
Jennifer will be integrated into a combination Head Start/School District preschool which serves primarily typical 3- to 5-year-old children from low-income families. This will allow Jennifer to observe appropriate peer models, to have opportunities to learn social and academic skills in preparation for kindergarten, and to engage in age-appropriate activities. A special education teacher is available to work directly with Jennifer and to advise on behavioral and self-help skills. The combination program also offers parent training and support for Jennifer's family.

Date of IEP meeting: August 20, 2003
Persons present—Name/position
Cheryl Howard, Special Education Teacher
Corrine Fry, Occupational Therapist
Betty Port, School Psychologist
Pat Lepper, School District Representative
Parent Signature
Lyle Lovinger   *Julia Lovinger*

Areas to be evaluated include speech and language, motor, sensory, cognitive, social, self-help, and play skills, as well as other skills particular to a child's disabling condition. Performance levels should be stated in the positive, so that a child's strengths and resources are examined. If there are delays in any area, the kind of intervention recommended for improving that specific skill area should be noted. For example, rather than stating that fine motor skills are not age appropriate, the present levels of performance should identify concretely what a child can do: "Amos can manipulate large puzzle shapes, use a spoon for eating, and stack blocks. He has not yet acquired the skills to fasten buttons and zippers, use a pencil to draw shapes, or lace his shoes, but these skills could be taught directly by his parents with the assistance of an occupational therapist."

INSTRUCTIONAL OBJECTIVES

Goals and objectives should be developed collaboratively by a child's IEP team and should consider the assessment information gathered to document a child's present level of performance and the parents' needs and preferences. In general, goals and objectives should address the following areas identified by Noonan and McCormick (1993):

1. Skills that are partially acquired or skills that are demonstrated in some contexts but not others (and can be improved upon or extended)
2. Skills that will permit a child to participate in routine daily activities with nondisabled peers (thus allowing inclusion in a least restrictive setting)
3. Skills that would be instrumental in accomplishing the greatest number of other skills or functional tasks (for example, basic fine motor skills like grasping can lead to self-feeding, dressing, playing with toys)
4. Skills a child is highly motivated to learn (activities that are self-reinforcing)
5. Skills that will increase opportunities for interactions with nondisabled peers (such as language and play)
6. Skills that will increase participation in future environments (such as handraising and taking turns needed in a kindergarten setting)

An IEP must include specifically developed, short-term instructional objectives. These statements describe the expected outcomes of educational intervention within a short-term timeframe of 1 to 3 months and assist in planning daily activities (Bailey & Wolery, 1992). Any good objective contains three main components: the observable behavior that a child is expected to perform, the conditions or situation under which the behavior is expected, and the criterion or how well the child must perform the behavior (Mager, 1962).

An observable behavior is one that can be seen or heard and, therefore, can be measured. "Being kind to others" is a description, not a behavior on which several people could agree. "*Handing a toy* to another child" is a behavior that could be observed and counted and that most people would accept as a demonstration of kindness. Usually objectives should contain action words that indicate a distinct movement, such as naming, reaching, or stacking. For example, the goal of "joining" in circle activities should be restated as the following behaviors: "*sits in* small group, *answers questions, sings songs, moves fingers and hands* with the music." By observing these behaviors, it would be clear that a child is joining in circle activities.

The second key component of a good objective is a description of the conditions under which the behavior is expected. Conditions are the situation in which learning is to be demonstrated and might include the materials used, the setting in which a behavior is to occur, or the people who would be present when the behavior is performed. Compare these two conditions under which a child is expected to count objects: "Charles will touch and count out loud the number of blocks up to three blocks *that appear one at a time on the computer screen.*" "Charles will *stand at the calendar in front of the circle group* and count off each date of the month in order, stopping with today's date." Both are good descriptions of conditions, and in both cases, Charles is expected to count, but the task of counting under the first set of conditions is probably much easier than performance under the second set of conditions. The second set of conditions implies a much more sophisticated knowledge level and would be influenced by more variables, including the changing number of days in a month, the size of the audience, and the use of numerals rather than semi-concrete images.

Conditions may describe the level of assistance or cueing that will be provided, the kind of audience that will be present, the mode in which the response will take place, and the kind of environmental contingencies present. An example of level of assistance might be: "*Using his crutches,* Tommy will walk with a friend from the school door to the swings," or at a later time, "Tommy *will use a cane* to walk alone from the school door to the swings." The kind of audience that will be present makes a difference as well. It is one thing for Darette to sing "Itsy Bitsy Spider" to her mother *during bath time,* and another for Darette to sing "Itsy Bitsy Spider" *on stage* for all the parents during the spring festival. The mode of performance can also vary; for example, it is important to indicate if a child will be *drawing, using a computer* keyboard, or *orally telling* a simple story. Finally, the kind of contingencies needed to ensure a particular performance may vary a great deal as well. For example, Arnold may eat all his soup when he is *given a bite of ice cream* after each bite of soup, or when he is *simply praised* after each bite. All these factors can have a substantial impact on the quality and strength of a child's overall performance and also inform instruction and evaluation.

The criterion for an instructional objective expresses how well a behavior is to be performed to be considered sufficiently learned. Criteria in some cases may be stated as percentage correct, duration of performance, level of proficiency, topography, intensity, or latency. The following examples illustrate each type of criteria respectively. "Katie will turn and make eye contact when her name is called by the teacher, *90% of the time.*" "Breanna will stay at the art table *for 10 minutes.*" "Jacob will walk, using only his wheeled walker for assistance, a distance of *20 feet across the classroom.*" "Juan will hold the crayon pinched *between his thumb and first two fingers.*" "Ming will speak in a voice *loud enough to be heard 3 feet away.*" "Amy Jo will remove her coat, with assistance unbuttoning, and hang it in her cubby *within 5 minutes* of entering the classroom."

Performance criteria should be stated in such ways as to identify consistent behavioral levels that are likely to be used and naturally reinforced (Bailey & Wolery, 1992). A child who touches a toy but does not shake it, lift it, listen to it, or in some way have fun with it is not really likely to play with the toy because of its own reinforcing properties. A better criterion for interacting with a toy might be to make it react in some way (rattle, roll, ring, etc.) because it is the toy's properties that will eventually maintain playful behavior.

Criteria should also reach for a high level of proficiency or automaticity that encourages **generalization** and independent functioning. For example, if the criterion for using "please" is "for 20% of the times a spoonful of food is offered during feeding," then a child is not likely to use the word "please" very often or under new circumstances. On the other hand, if a child is expected to use "please" 90% of the times any adult or child offers toys, food, activities, music, or television, then that child is likely to maintain use of the word "please" long past training and in new environments. "Please" will become automatic when choices are given and may generalize to become a word to request items or activities before they have been offered.

GUIDELINES FOR DEVELOPING GOOD OBJECTIVES

In summary, any time specific instructional objectives are developed, they should be worthwhile. It is perhaps because so many IEPs are written without thought to individual needs or attention to detail that many teachers see IEPs as a waste of time. The initial investment of thought and time in developing a truly individualized IEP pays off in long-term achievements for the teacher, parent, and child. Bailey and Wolery (1992) suggested the following guidelines for good objectives:

1. They should be developmentally appropriate; that is, they should address skills typical for a child's age (what other children of the same age might do) and skills matched to a child's development (within an individual's ability). For example, 4 year-olds like to put together puzzles, but Sheburra's puzzle may have only two pieces because that is the level of fine motor skill she needs to practice.

2. Objectives should be functional. Skills that help a child be more independent, help a child learn a more complex skill, help a child move to a less-restrictive environment, or help the family care for the child, are functional. For example, feeding herself with a spoon allows a child to be more independent and makes dinner less complicated for her mother.

3. Objectives should include skills valued by the parents and significant others. Toilet training, for example, is a a skill parents of preschoolers and child-care settings both appreciate.

4. Objectives should be realistic and achievable. For example, a child who can pull on socks is probably ready to learn to pull up pants with elastic waists.

5. Objectives should vary according to a child's stage of learning, including acquisition, mastery, and generalization. A child who has just learned to count to three may need practice counting many different toys, pictures, blocks, and so forth in order to generalize these counting skills to other situations.

SPECIAL EDUCATION AND RELATED SERVICES

The next step in IEP development is to decide what strategies, procedures, and materials will help a child achieve the instructional objectives that have been identified and how progress will be monitored (Noonan & McCormick, 1993). That is, an intervention team decides what to teach in order to attain the stated objectives; how to modify or adapt curriculum content, materials, and procedures; and how to arrange the environment to facilitate skill acquisition and generalization.

Special education is, by definition, specially designed instruction that includes adaptations that are significantly different from modifications normally made for typical students and are necessary to offset or reduce the adverse effect of a child's disability (Strickland & Turnbull, 1990). For example, specially designed instruction might include the use of a communication board to help a child initiate interactions and respond to peers in the classroom, the use of peers to model and reinforce offers to play or share toys, or the use of switch-activated toys as reinforcing consequences for verbalizations. Instruction can be modified according to:

1. Levels of assistance provided
2. The kinds of extrinsic motivation used
3. The arrangement of the environment and materials
4. The programming of opportunities for generalization

It is essential that specially designed instruction be both systematic and naturalistic (Noonan & McCormick, 1993). Students should be exposed to routine schedules, methods of instruction, and management strategies. Systematic instruction emphasizes consistency but does not require unnatural and mechanistic instruction. Educational plans should not be so rigid as to rule out regard for the interests and spontaneity of young children.

For example, specially designed instruction often will include providing assistance through prompting. Prompts may be verbal, gestural, auditory, movement, or picture cues that help a child respond without making errors. Prompts also include models and physical manipulation when necessary. Carefully programmed materials insert and then fade out prompts in such a way that a child can move errorlessly through each lesson.

Specially designed instruction almost always involves "reinforcement-rich" environments in which a child's appropriate responses may be positively **consequated,** making it more likely that the behavior will be repeated. Many natural reinforcers are available, including smiles, hugs, a favorite toy, or a special game. Sometimes the environment must be arranged to make it easier for children to obtain reinforcement for their efforts. For example, teaching during natural routines such as lunch, using age-appropriate and interesting materials, and presenting tasks through fun games and activities all make it more likely that a child's responses can earn reinforcement (Noonan & McCormick, 1993).

Finally, specially designed instruction must address the transfer of skills to other settings, other caregivers, and other appropriate situations. This generalization of newly mastered skills is ensured only through systematic and naturalistic procedures. Special education approaches should include the following generalization procedures (Stokes & Baer, 1977):

1. Common materials should be used both in training and in nontraining situations. For example, if a child is learning to use a straw to drink at school, her family should use straws to drink at home, too.

2. Naturally occurring contingencies should be emphasized. For example, a child learning to climb steps should be encouraged to climb the steps of a slide and enjoy the quick trip down the slide as a natural reward for her work.

3. Contrived contingencies should be designed to be subtle or not too obvious, so that they can be gradually reduced or eliminated. For example, a child might get a big handshake for speaking in front of the group but, later, receive a brief squeeze on the hand and, still later, a pat on the hand for the same behavior. Finally, just a wave or salute would be sufficient to maintain the behavior.

4. Generalization should be mediated by providing strategies that assist a child in new situations. Singing the "Clean-up" song may remind a child of where and how to put toys away, in her preschool, at home, and at her babysitter's house.

5. One should use variety in the kinds of prompts, reinforcements, and corrections used from time to time. For example, when giving directions to move from circle to table work, a teacher might sometimes say, "Please sit in your chair at the table," and other times, "Walk to the table quietly."

Related services are those supplemental support services that allow children to benefit from their educational experience. For example, a child who uses an electric wheelchair may require special lift-van transportation in order to attend school; a child who requires catheterization may need a nurse or paraprofessional to assist in the mechanics of emptying the bladder; and a mobility specialist may train a child who is visually impaired to use a cane to find her way around the school building so she can move independently from the bus to her classroom.

The provision of services to a wide range of eligible children and their families involves the coordinated efforts of many related personnel, including but not limited to, audiologists, nutritionists, nurses, occupational therapists, physicians, psychologists, physical therapists, social workers, speech–language pathologists, and vision specialists (Brown & Rule, 1993). Table 10–1 identifies examples of the related services each professional might provide. All of these personnel concentrate on working with families, addressing child development needs, and coordinating services. In addition, paraprofessionals contribute significantly to preschool education in both home and center settings by providing support to teachers and parents or by directly aiding children in daily activities (Brown & Rule, 1993).

LEAST RESTRICTIVE ENVIRONMENT

Another key feature of an IEP is the designation of an appropriate and least restrictive educational setting. IDEA makes it clear that children with disabilities should be placed, to the greatest extent appropriate, with peers who are not disabled. Each IEP must include an explanation of the extent to which the child will *not* participate in a regular class. This means more detail must be provided than in the past in regard to any limits placed on regular classroom participation (this would apply, for example if a preschooler had the opportunity to be in a regular Head Start or Kindergarten program; NASDSE, 1997). Children are also entitled to

Table 10–1   Personnel and Related Services

Professional	Examples of Services Provided
Audiologist	auditory training, speech-reading, and listening-device orientation and training
Nutritionist	assess food intake, eating behavior, and feeding skills; provide nutrition information and early intervention
Nurse	advise parents and caregivers on basic health needs; develop medical plans to treat developmental problems
Occupational therapist	enhance sensory function and motor skill; select, design, and build assistive seating and orthotic devices
Physician	provide a "medical home," comprehensive medical care, diagnosis, and treatment; instruct parents and caregivers in health care
Psychologist	assess psychological and behavioral needs and resources; plan and provide psychological and developmental interventions
Physical therapist	recommend or build adaptive equipment and mobility devices; recommend and implement environmental modification; teach handling, positioning, and movement techniques to facilitate motor functioning and posture
Social worker	make home visits to evaluate living conditions and parent-child interaction patterns; provide counseling; mobilize community resources
Speech–language pathologist	assess and diagnose communication and oral-motor abilities; provide appropriate therapy for oral-motor and communication skills
Vision specialist	assess visual functioning; provide communication-skills training, orientation and mobility training, and independent living skills training

participate in extracurricular activities, so modifications should be made to allow a child to take part in a class field trip or after-school program, for example.

Children should be served in a setting as close as possible to those which students would be assigned if they had no disabilities (LD OnLine, 1999). The IEP team should try to arrange placements in neighborhood schools, or at least consider and try to limit the time and distance students must be transported. As much as possible, a child would be removed from the normal school setting (such as school-sponsored child care) only if the nature and severity of the disability were such that education with normal peers couldn't be achieved even with supplementary aids and services (LD OnLine, 1999).

IDEA does not consider placement just a place. It is important that the student participate in a typical preschool curriculum as much as possible (Etscheidt & Bartlett, 1999). Several sections of IDEA relate to enabling a child to participate and progress in a general curriculum. An IEP must contain a statement of the supplementary aids and services that should be provided on a child's behalf to allow for integration in regular activities such as kindergarten. The law also calls for identifying strategies to deal with special factors such as behavior problems that would otherwise prevent a child from participating in the general curriculum with nondisabled peers. Finally, an IEP team must include a regular education teacher if a child is already participating in regular education. Transition planning and supportive services assist a child moving into less-restrictive settings.

Case Study

TRANSITIONING TO PUBLIC SCHOOL: INTERVIEW WITH TOM AND ANN SIMPSON:

Tommy just turned 3 and he learned to walk this summer. He used to really hate physical therapy and he's always had low muscle tone, even for a Down syndrome child. We've started taking gymnastics classes and he really likes all that. His fine motor skills are pretty good; he learned to eat right away, but he's real motivated to eat. He's always the best eater in his group. He was the last child in his group to learn to walk, but he was the first child to be able to eat.

Tommy's very social. He likes other children and he behaves appropriately. He goes to music class and we're in gym class and he really acts out a lot less than some of the other normal children. He follows directions to some extent. We have a lot of fun with him because we do all of the preschool things. We go to the library. We go shopping. We go to music class. He does all of that and likes all of it.

I don't think we've really had to readjust our routine for him, except that he's sick an awful lot. He's been in the hospital a couple of times. We did have to adjust to take him to therapy which he started when he was just a week or two old. There have been several really kind people along the way, who helped us, and his therapist was one of those. He started in a private school intervention program when he was about five months old.

Now, Tommy will be starting with the school district preschool program and I'm nervous about it. There have already been several miscommunications between me and the school about where he's supposed to go for testing and everything. I thought, "Oh my God, what's this going on?" So I just called the teacher and said my son's coming into your program, can I see your classroom? I could tell that most parents don't do that, but I felt I needed to do it.

The emphasis on preschool integration into natural child settings and regular education programs has presented a considerable challenge to many public school preschool programs. Not all public schools offer programs to nondisabled preschoolers, so innovative administrators must work to develop partnerships with community programs that might serve children with disabilities in integrated settings. At the same time, a continuum of services must be available so that a child who needs more intensive therapies and special education can also be appropriately served. In many cases, public schools have partnered with Head Start; in other instances, schools have enrolled normal peers to be a part of a special education preschool offered at the school.

There is good reason for the law to require placement in the least restrictive setting as long as appropriate services can be provided. Placing a child with a disability in an environment populated only by other children with disabilities may result in a limited educational experience (Thurman & Widerstrom, 1990). Such a setting does not provide typical role models who facilitate learning language, peer

So Tommy and I were introduced to the teachers and the children and it made me feel more comfortable.

Tommy's new school is in our neighborhood, and they will bus him from our house or from my babysitter's house. I felt good about his school; the kids in his special preschool class were verbal and at Tommy's level. I feel he needs to be with the normal kids in his neighborhood school.

I've been to a workshop on transitioning to the public school and I guess I know as much as anyone else does about what's going to happen. But I decided that I wasn't going to sit passively and wait. I've talked to other parents who live in this area. It's funny, even before Tom was born, we'd see the bus come and the neighbor's wheelchair come out and I remember thinking, "I wonder who that is." We didn't know our neighbors yet, and they are quiet people. But I talked to the father once about where his daughter went and he had been happy with the local school program.

The school system is a big bureaucracy and you've got to interface through all these people, but what you need is a manual to know who to talk to. I don't have much blind faith that it's all going to work out okay. I guess I watch each step a lot more and talk to people more, and am a lot more proactive. But yet I don't want to just beat those guys up, because I know what it's like. I work in a big bureaucracy too. I know how those things happen, but I also know I have a duty to my child and to myself, to be on top of these things too.

Getting Tommy into school reminded me of when Tommy was born. If you put yourself in the hands of the system you need to know it's designed for its own expediency rather than for your experience and comfort. One thing I have learned is be proactive about getting my needs and my child's needs met, but always try to be polite about it. I've talked to a lot of parents who just will take whatever comes, and I guess I'm not willing to do that.

interaction, and other functional skills. Segregation also does not encourage acceptance by typical peers and adults.

Still, it would be unwise to place children in settings that do not meet their most pressing needs and the preferences of their parents. A preschool setting is not "least restrictive" if it fails to provide appropriate services and support. Therefore, the concept of least restrictive should *not* be considered equivalent to providing one program for all children. Legislation and litigation uphold the need to provide a variety of possible placement opportunities. Hence, least restrictive environments are best facilitated through a continuum of program options which allow a child to enter at any point needed and move on to more- or less-segregated settings when it is deemed appropriate.

For example, a child who is born with a serious medical problem or physical disability may require a longer than normal hospitalization with the extensive involvement of a team of medical personnel. The hospital or residential setting would be considered the most restrictive on a continuum of placement options but, at this point in that child's life, would be the only appropriate setting for providing the care needed. When this child's health status reaches a satisfactory level, the hospital is likely to discharge the child to home care, sometimes accompanied by medical equipment, such as a respirator or heart monitor. Often, visiting nurses will be assigned to work with the parents and child in the home, and if the child's health continues to be fragile, other early childhood professionals may also provide in-home services.

As the child's strength and stamina increase, placement in a center-based program where the parents and child can work with therapists and special equipment becomes a reasonable option. Perhaps, at first, the child attends only three mornings a week and a physical therapist provides therapy and parent training in a setting where several other families are also present. When the child becomes stronger and her health is stable, placement in a full-time integrated preschool might allow more normal peer interaction. Typical peers would model and motivate speech and language development and mobility. Eventually, this preschooler enrolls in the neighborhood kindergarten program, with consultation from relevant specialists (Table 10–1).

As long as an integrated preschool program is properly structured and children are provided training and reinforcement for interaction, this option is clearly an ethical and developmental preference (Thurman & Widerstrom, 1990). However, preschool settings and their curricula should be scrutinized along several dimensions to determine their appropriateness for a particular child and family. Factors that warrant careful consideration are the following: the instructional methods used, experiences and activities provided, how generalization of skills is promoted, the physical environment, curricular adaptations, data collection and evaluation, and the use of technology (Sandall, 1993).

To ensure that schools have an entire range of placements available, IDEA requires school districts to provide a continuum of alternative programs (Yell, 1998). This continuum allows parents and professionals to choose from a number of options that come closest to meeting a child's need for services and the right to be educated with normal peers. As a child reaches school age, a variety of options might include (LD OnLine, 1999):

1. Direct instruction or consultative services within general education classrooms (such as a regular kindergarten)
2. Regular classroom instruction and specialized instruction within a resource room
3. Part-time specialized instruction in a special education classroom with some time in the regular classroom
4. Primary instruction in special education with some integration with normal peers at nonacademic times
5. Full-time special education and related services
6. Separate public or private day school in a special education facility
7. Public or private residential facilities
8. Homebound services
9. Hospital services

Even with the emphasis on a least restrictive environment, a child's team needs to remember that the regular setting is not always appropriate and should not be chosen if (Yell, 1998):

1. A child with disabilities will not receive educational benefits in the regular setting
2. Any marginal benefit would be significantly outweighed by the more significant benefits possible in a more specialized instructional setting
3. The child would be such a disruptive force in the general education setting that services could not be adequately provided

The least restrictive and most appropriate setting is one where critical goals for a child can be achieved. When a decision of the Sixth Circuit Court used the analogy that a child with a disability is not entitled to a "Cadillac education," but only to a "serviceable Chevrolet," it may have given some school personnel the impression that it was alright to provide less than an individual child needed as long as it was in keeping with what nondisabled children were receiving (Hurder, 1997). This is not the case, and any child whose disability is so severe that he or she can not learn in the regular curriculum must be given whatever specialized services will support that child's educational potential (Hurder, 1997).

INSTRUCTIONAL METHODS

Early interventionists need to be proficient with a variety of instructional methods in order to meet the needs of children with different disabilities, age levels, cultural beliefs, and family values (Sandall, 1993). Yet sometimes, educational philosophy dictates which instructional approach is used (Sandall, 1993). A **developmental** perspective is associated with enrichment activities that emphasize a stimulus-rich environment with age-appropriate activities and toys. Play and self-expression are encouraged. The behavioral perspective is associated with direct instructional methods that include a systematic analysis of objectives, sequencing of learning steps, and systematic reinforcement of desired behaviors. Activities and learning tasks are generally **teacher directed.** The interactional and ecological perspectives place more emphasis on how children and their environments influence each other. These latter perspectives are more often associated with responsive and active-learning techniques, such as milieu teaching, in which the environment is arranged to stimulate a child's interest and behavior on which a teacher can elaborate. The latter programs would also be described as **child directed** and emphasize natural events and routines. Still other programs focus on parents as teachers and emphasize parent–child interactions with support systems for families.

An appropriate program for preschool children with disabilities provides a balance of both highly structured (teacher-directed) activities and less structured (child-directed or developmental) activities. Such scheduling allows direct instruction on specific skills that provide multiple opportunities for skill acquisition, proficiency, and generalization within natural situations. For example, a specific language curriculum could be used during circle time, and a child with a language

Case Study

JENNIFER WARITZ, THE EDUCATION EXPERIENCE: INTERVIEW WITH TAMMY WARITZ

Jennifer began her early education at a private school for children under the age of 3 who have disabilities. She attended twice a week for a couple of hours at a time, and I was deeply involved in her therapy program. It was the most nurturing place we could ever have been. Sometimes it was difficult for us to see other children who weren't as involved as Jennifer, but it was also hard to see children who were more involved. We knew the pain those families were feeling.

The private school was such a supportive and caring environment, a loving and warm place to be. Everyone was very accepting and they not only worked with Jennifer, they worked with the family. We learned so much from being there. I guess that's why I do the parent advocacy work that I do today. I want to see the system change for families so they don't have to struggle for the services they need. Jennifer had physical therapy, occupational therapy, and speech therapy twice a week. Her team of professionals taught me so much, helped me learn the system, and helped me gain the knowledge that I needed. They recognized that I was going to be Jennifer's real "case manager," her advocate for the rest of her life, because she doesn't have a voice for herself.

When Jennifer turned 3, she was transitioned into a public school self-contained program. That was a scary time for us, because we were leaving the private school where we had been very much involved. (I'm not sure that it's natural for families to separate when the child is only 2 or 3 years old.) That fall, the big yellow school bus pulled up in front of the house, and we were expected to put her on the bus and wave goodbye. The first day I followed the bus to school to make sure that she got off at the right stop; it was still a huge transition for the family.

Jennifer spent 2 years in a self-contained program, and then the school district initiated a cooperative venture with Head Start to provide an integrated preschool program. The integrated program was originally set up for children who were much less involved than Jennifer, but I asked for Jennifer to be included, even though I was nervous about the change and wanted to make sure that Jennifer could still go back to the self-contained program if the integrated preschool didn't work for her.

I was afraid of how the other children would treat Jennifer and I was also worried about how the other parents would react to her. I was afraid there would be so much going on in the regular classroom that she wouldn't be able to learn. For the first 3 years of her life, all her teaching had been one-on-one, and even in the self-contained program, there had been only six to eight students at one time. The Head Start classroom served 12 children, was a regular preschool, and was very energetic, so I was really afraid that Jennifer's needs weren't going to be met.

In fact, Jennifer made more gains in the integrated program in the first year than she had made during her 2 years in the self-contained program. The social interaction was so important for her. Even though she wasn't on the same

disability would be systematically prompted to respond appropriately. During free play, the same child might be encouraged to verbalize about an object or activity that is self-selected.

In addition, generalization is best facilitated if instruction is carried over between both center and home. A center-based program provides opportunities for

level and couldn't do some of the same things, she was always right there with her peers. Jennifer developed a vocabulary of 5 to 10 words and was introduced to a communication board to help her express her needs and wants. We asked that Jennifer stay in the program an additional year where she continued to develop and make gains that allowed her to be moved right into a regular kindergarten classroom the next year.

Moving into kindergarten was even more difficult, because now there was only one teacher and maybe an aide if the teacher was lucky. We requested a full-time aide to assist Jennifer in that environment, because we couldn't expect the teacher to meet her needs. Jennifer spent half her day in the regular kindergarten and the other half of her day in a self-contained program for children with developmental impairments. I wanted both programs because of Jennifer's involvement; there are things that she needed to learn in order to be as independent as possible. She deserved the dignity to learn these self-help skills without her peers looking on. The self-contained program provided her with the occupational, physical, and speech therapy she still needed.

Currently, Jennifer is spending about 2 hours a day and lunch time with her first-grade class. Her aide is still there with her, but we made it clear that we didn't want that person attached to her side, that Jennifer needed to be free to interact naturally in her environment. That's what we've really focused on trying to do. When I went to the first-grade open house, I really didn't know quite how it was going for Jennifer, but there was her own little desk with her name tag and the same little books that everybody else had. When I

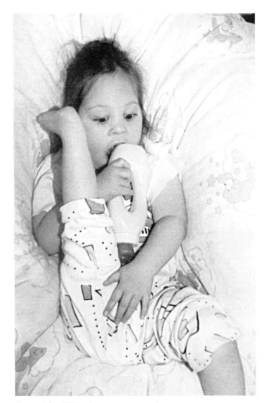

Jennifer Waritz.

looked on the other desks in the classroom, I saw they were all doing journals and Jennifer had one too. Sometimes an adult had helped Jennifer do her journal, but I could see there were children who'd also helped her. In almost every journal on the other students' desks was at least one page with a sentence written about Jennifer in the book. I realized, "She really does belong. She is a member of this classroom."

special instruction and socialization, while well-informed parents can intervene by continuing contingencies for specific behaviors during daily routines in a home setting. For example, a child who is learning to fasten clothing may be highly motivated to button a jacket when the whole class is going outside to the playground. The child's teacher uses this opportunity to instruct by providing partial prompts of physical assistance, as needed during coat buttoning. At home, the parents may use the same system of partial prompts to help the child learn to button clothing in the morning and then, as a reinforcer, allow the child to play outside for a while before boarding the bus for school.

EXPERIENCES AND ACTIVITIES

Early development occurs primarily within social contexts (Sandall, 1993). It makes sense then that intervention programs promote social behaviors between infants and their parents/caregivers and between preschoolers and their peers. Activities should also promote engagement or active involvement with the environment (Sandall, 1993). A range of experiences should be provided to accommodate different capability levels and varied interests.

Consider, for example, a 4-year-old child, Jonathan, with autism who is included in a preschool program for other 4- and 5-year-old children. This child is mobile only with the use of a walker, has no expressive or receptive language skills, and engages in **self-stimulation.** Most of the children are able to sit quietly in circle time and listen to the teacher read a story. Jonathan will turn away from the teacher and flap his hands and fingers in this situation. Adjusting for this individual child's interests will help Jonathan participate with the group. For example, using concrete objects or a flannel board increases Jonathan's attentiveness, allowing him to hold something in his hands during the story decreases self-stimulation, and letting Jonathan push the appropriate computer key as the story is told allows him to respond. The other children may even prompt Jonathan to keep his hands quiet as they listen to the story. None of these adaptations makes the story less appropriate or less interesting for Jonathan's peers and may, in fact, improve their attention and participation as well.

GENERALIZATION

A consistent finding in the research literature is the poor generalization of newly acquired behaviors to functional, less-structured settings by individuals with disabilities (Sandall, 1993). Consequently, programs for young children should emphasize functional, meaningful behaviors that will have many opportunities for practice across settings, people, and materials (Sandall, 1993). Settings should use natural activities, materials, and routines to promote generalization.

A preschool setting considered as a placement for a child with disabilities should be evaluated according to these factors. For example, are all the children responsible for putting away toys, setting the table for lunch, and dressing themselves for recess (all functional behaviors)? Are the children encouraged to play with each other, to verbalize their needs, to engage in group activities (vital for socialization)? Do children take part in regularly scheduled activities such as hand washing, story time, outdoor play, and snack time (routines)?

THE PHYSICAL ENVIRONMENT

The preschool environment should foster security and trust by being safe, warm, inviting, secure, and predictable (Bailey & Wolery, 1992). Personal identity, opportunities to develop control over their physical surroundings, and a rich and stimulating environment should also be a part of preschool designs (Bailey & Wolery, 1992). The environment should contain child-sized furniture, child-centered displays of their own work, personal storage spaces, and a shelter for escaping from overstimulation. Numerous activity areas should be available for arts and crafts, reading, sand and water play, housekeeping and dramatic play, woodworking, and outdoor exercise.

Different areas of a room may be more conducive to specific behaviors and routines or specialized instruction. For example, noisy block play should be located away from language activities where a therapist is working on the production of specific speech sounds. A one-way mirror could be located conveniently so that parents may observe instruction or evaluation without distracting a child. Finally, traffic patterns may have to be arranged to accommodate orthopedic equipment such as standing tables or wheelchairs. For some children, it may be necessary to adapt access to playground equipment.

MATERIAL ADAPTATIONS

A variety of supports and resources are needed to help adapt activities for individual children (Sandall, 1993). These include access to specialists and technical assistance and availability of specialized materials to accommodate for sensory, motor, health, or other specialized needs. In addition, all services should be delivered at locations close to the family.

For example, specialized feeding equipment, such as a nonslip plate with a lip to catch food, a built-up spoon handle, and a cutaway cup might allow a child to self-feed at lunch with other children. Therapy mats and bolsters should be a part of the classroom furnishings so that physical therapy can be provided without removing a child from the classroom. When not used for therapy, the equipment might make a nice obstacle course for all children. A computer with a touch screen could be used to help a child with severely limited movement to demonstrate cognitive skills and also for art activities or games with the other children.

DATA COLLECTION AND EVALUATION

A necessary component of any preschool program is a set of procedures for collecting and using data to monitor the effects of program efforts (Sandall, 1993). Data should be collected regularly and systematically and used in making daily, ongoing, educational decisions. Such data might be collected through direct observation of specific child behaviors, through the use of developmental checklists, through permanent product samples, such as videotapes or audiotapes, and through family reporting. Regardless of the method, it is critical that data be linked to a child's goals or program and used to adjust program activities in accordance with changes (or a lack of progress) in a child's development.

For example, a goal for Courtney, a child with Down syndrome, is to increase verbal interactions with peers. Her preschool teacher decides to observe Courtney on the playground and record how often she asks to play with other children during the daily 15 minutes of outdoor play. The teacher quickly discovers that across a week, Courtney initiated requests to play an average of only once a day, and in every case, the peers failed to accept her as a playmate. The teacher then devises a strategy to verbally prompt and praise such requests and to praise peers who play with Courtney. Further data collection shows that requests to play have risen to an average of five per day. Now the teacher can fade out her prompting while continuing to praise interactions with all children.

ASSISTIVE TECHNOLOGY

Finally, when determining the appropriateness of a placement setting, one should consider technological interventions that may benefit young children. Technology can allow young children opportunities for play, socialization, language, and manipulation of the environment (Sandall, 1993). For example, some simple electronic switches can be activated with as little as an eye blink or a puff of air to operate toys that teach cause and effect. Augmentative communication devices, such as an electronic board that speaks when a child touches a picture, allow children who have no capacity for speech or signing to interact with others in a variety of settings. Many preschool language programs are now available on personal computers and can be used with groups of children to stimulate language skills.

IDEA requires that IEP teams must consider what assistive technology is appropriate as a supplementary aid or intervention (Lahm & Nickels, 1999). Such devices include high and low technology which is defined as: "any item, piece of equipment, or product system, whether acquired commercially off the shelf, modified, or customized, that is used to increase, maintain, or improve functional capabilities of a child with a disability" (Lahm & Nickels, 1999, p. 57). Assistive technology service is also encouraged. These services can help evaluate needs; purchase or lease devices; select, design, fit, customize, adapt, maintain, or replace devices as needed; train a child or the child's family, and train professional staff who work with a child.

SUPPLEMENTARY AIDS AND SERVICES

Assistive technology is only one part of a full range of aids and services that may enable a student to benefit from an educational program without significant disruption (Etscheidt & Bartlett, 1999). The IEP team should discuss aids in terms of several dimensions: the physical, instructional, social-behavioral, and collaborative. The physical dimension includes factors such as mobility, room arrangement, lighting, acoustics and seating. The instructional dimension involves factors related to lesson planning, methodology, and assessment. The social-behavioral dimension relates to services or aids that would reduce disruptive behavior. The collaborative dimension addresses how multiple personnel are coordinated and how time for collaboration is arranged.

In summary, all these factors—experiences and activities, instructional methods, generalization, physical environment, material adaptations, data collection and evaluation, and technology—should influence the design of a preschool program. The critical piece of any IEP is the shared goal of enhancing the child's development and learning (Sandall, 1993). This outcome is reached only through the careful planning of instructional objectives, the deliberate selection of special education and related services that support those objectives, and the appropriate placement of the child in the least restrictive setting that will promote the child's involvement and progress.

CHALLENGING BEHAVIOR

Challenging behavior is behavior that interferes with children's learning and development, and/or is harmful to the child or to others (Bailey & Wolery, 1992). Self-injury, negative peer interaction, disruptive behavior, tantruming, and noncompliance are examples of challenging behavior (Chandler, Dahlquist, Repp, & Feltz, 1999). IDEA requires that appropriate strategies, including positive behavioral interventions and supports, be identified in the IEP. A functional behavioral assessment must be conducted when developing behavioral intervention plans for a student with challenging behavior. A functional assessment assists educators and others working with a child to understand the factors that produce and support challenging behavior by determining the relationship between events in a person's environment and the occurrence of the behaviors (Rogers, 1998). The result of this analysis is a clear definition or description of the behaviors, predictions as to the times and situations in which the behavior might happen, and identification of the function the behavior serves for the child; that is, one child might tantrum to escape a demanding situation while another might tantrum to get adult attention.

Take for example, Frank, who was a 3-year-old, developmentally delayed child, whose parents were both also developmentally delayed. Frank was referred for a functional assessment for the following behavioral concerns:

At school, Frank appeared "unmotivated" and stood apart from activities that took place; he held his hands clasped behind his back and refused to participate. Teachers reported that at times he would engage in these behaviors for as long as 1 hour, 45 minutes. The only activity he joined in was snack time. At home, the parents reported that they were frustrated by Frank's behavior; he would scream, throw objects, bite, kick, hit, bang his head against objects, the floor, and the wall, and he would refuse to follow his parents' directions. (Rogers, 1998, p. 32)

Frank's team completed a functional assessment in his home. First, the team interviewed family members and caregivers about their concerns regarding Frank's behavior. They asked questions about the frequency, intensity, and duration of his inappropriate behaviors. The team also asked about strategies that had been used to control the behavior, situations in which the behaviors were seen, the child's preferences, the child's means of communication, and relevant background such as his medical condition.

Next, the team undertook a motivation assessment. Parents, caregivers, teachers, and other service providers rated each specific behavior and identified the situations where it was likely to occur. This interview was followed by a setting-event checklist that asked about situations that occurred immediately prior to tantrums and seemed to set the stage for the behaviors. For example, if Frank missed a morning nap, would he be more likely to whine to get mother's attention?

Finally, direct observations were made of Frank under several different circumstances. The team found that, at school, Frank's behavior was used to escape activities; at home he misbehaved to get attention or tangible items he wanted and to escape demands made by his parents. Interventions could then be designed to change the environmental variables that contributed to his challenging behavior and to provide support for appropriate behavior that achieved the same function as the challenging behavior (Chandler et al., 1999). Interventions were designed so that Frank could escape tasks or request attention and tangibles through more acceptable means (such as signing "all done" when he wanted to leave an activity or raising his hand when he wanted attention).

There are several advantages to functional assessments (Chandler et al., 1999). A functional assessment:

1. Is a proactive approach, teaching children what they should do, rather than punishing children for engaging in challenging behavior
2. Focuses on prevention as well as remediation by arranging antecedents and consequences that may be related to appropriate behavior
3. Provides team members from a variety of disciplines with a common language and approach for addressing challenging behavior
4. Provides teams with a method of assessment that works for any child's challenging behavior, regardless of age, disability, or setting
5. Provides teams with consistent methods for selecting interventions for behavior

CREATING QUALITY IEPS

Bateman (1995) outlined practices that support the development of sound IEPs. The first step is for the school to provide an appropriate time and a comfortable place for the meeting to occur, keeping in mind that this should be mutually agreeable with the parents. The focus of an IEP meeting must be on the special needs of a student and how those will be addressed. She suggested a strategically placed photo of the youngster to keep participants from wandering off that topic. Members should be aware of their enormous power to arrange for services that are needed; they should not limit themselves to fitting the child into existing school services if those really don't suffice. All of the student's needs must be addressed, not just cognitive ones.

Bateman (1995) recommended starting with a blank piece of paper rather than letting a required form drive the discussion. The team should pretend they are "describing the student to a volunteer who has never met the student and is going to take him or her camping for a week." Next, the team should complete the statement: "We are individualizing Johnny's program because _____." This will help identify the child's unique needs. At the same time, the team may be detailing each need in terms of the child's present level of performance. Enough information should be provided so that the present level is readily understandable and the information is precise enough to allow the team to measure later progress. When words don't seem to be enough, a work sample might be provided. The team should address social–emotional–behavioral areas as well.

The next question the team asks is, "What will the district do about this?" for each need described. The team should be "as creative, flexible, innovative, and often inexpensive as the team's brainstorming and combined wisdom allow"

(Bateman, 1995). The answer to this question will include identifying special education services and related services the child needs. It will also include how teachers, other professionals, and paraprofessionals who will be working with the child can be prepared and will identify any modifications that will need to be made for participation in integrated education settings.

Bateman (1995) suggested approaching goals and objectives by asking, "If the service we are providing is effective, what will we see in Todd's behavior that tells us so?" It is important when stating goals and objectives to remember that one should be checking to see whether the student actually reaches them.

Kroeger, Leibold, and Ryan (1999) suggested recognizing that everyone on an IEP team is a significant stakeholder in the process. The team's job is to set a vision for that student, keeping in mind the child's gifts, abilities, and strengths. This process starts with a listing of all the positives a student may possess, a "list in progress" of strengths that may lead the group toward interventions best suited to that child. What follows this is identification of specific concerns, brainstorming about how to intervene in areas of need, and a specific plan of action. It is essential that each participant be invited to express his or her viewpoint on all the concerns so that information is complete and decisions are made collaboratively.

What are the quality indicators of an exemplary IEP meeting? Consider the following descriptors (Beach Center on Families and Disabilities, 1999):

◆ The process is ongoing, dynamic, and individualized.
◆ Family-initiated goals and objectives are given priority.
◆ Meetings and documents are jargon-free and use clear explanations.
◆ There is a mutually respectful relationship between families and professionals.
◆ Families are a part of the collaborative process and share equal decision-making responsibilities.
◆ Current best practices are discussed and a range of service settings are considered.

BEST PRACTICES IN PRESCHOOL INTERVENTION

Since the late 1960s, programs for young children with disabilities have proliferated (Karnes & Stayton, 1988). A model program may be defined as one in which the content and operational strategies are clearly conceptualized and defined in a manner that assures internal consistency and coherence (Peterson, 1987). A number of early intervention models have been developed that capture the best of what is known about how to serve young preschool children with disabilities. These models can be characterized by the following (Thurman & Widerstrom, 1990):

1. **Integrated:** Typical children and children with disabilities are served in the same settings; there is supported placement in generic early childhood service sites.
2. **Comprehensive:** A full array of professional services is offered through a transdisciplinary approach and using direct instruction for generalized responding.

Case Study INTEGRATING JOSH: INTERVIEW WITH AMY FINKEL

Getting Josh integrated into a regular classroom was a real battle. The only way that he could be successful in a regular classroom was with one of his own aides. In other words, someone from my home therapy program. Expressive language has always been the main focus that we have been after for Josh. Learning prepositions, learning math, and so on, was all great, but I wanted him to have functional speech. An untrained aide, or someone who didn't have a significant amount of hours with him here in the home, would have no clue what he was trying to say, because at that time, a lot of the words he said were really gross approximations of words. Unless you were pretty familiar with his speech patterns, you would have no idea what he was trying to say.

The first year, the school district refused to pay for a private aide, let alone hire someone from my home program. They said that was a conflict of interest, which we felt was ridiculous. So, we actually paid out of our own funds and got them to agree to let one of our home team members accompany Josh to school. He was only in school two afternoons a week at that time.

The next year, I decided, wait a minute! We were paying $30,000 a year for 40 hours of instruction a week; what's the school going to pay for? It just so happened that there were several landmark cases that had just been won by parents here in Washington state that year. I got the transcripts of the cases and I presented them, along with a financial argument to the school district. I pointed out that legally my son is entitled to a free appropriate education (FAPE), therefore, they should be paying for everything. All we were asking the school district to do was to pay for the Educational Aide at school. I negotiated with them that we would continue to pay for the home program; we just wanted the dis-

trict to pay for the little piece of the pie that served Josh in school. I said, "If you don't, then we certainly have the option to come back and ask you to pay for everything Josh is entitled to under FAPE." It was a subtle threat.

I prepared for that IEP meeting for months. I went without sleep for weeks at a time and I walked into that meeting with stacks of case law, quotes from professionals all across the country who talked about the need for 40-hour a week programs for children with autism. The school district agreed to our request.

Here we are today where Josh does have his own classroom aide, someone from my home program, someone he has a rapport with, someone who knows what his skill levels are on a daily basis. So when he is in the school setting, he is always required to perform to the level he is capable of, so there is no regression or backsliding. Most importantly the aide is there to immediately reinforce expressive language.

Josh also attends the extended school year (ESY) summer program. That was another interesting battle. Josh starts the ESY program the Monday after the regular school year lets out and goes right up until the Friday before the next regular school year begins. Schools traditionally use regression/recoupment formulas to qualify children for ESY (which means that data must be collected which prove that the children lose skills over the summer that they don't readily recover in the fall). I feel these formulas are illegal because they don't take into consideration each child's unique needs. With autism, once regression has occurred, you've lost valuable time. With autism, you can't have one set of standards in one place and another set of standards in another setting; intervention needs to be constant, year round. There are quite a few studies and a number of professionals that have written on the necessity for 12-month schooling for children with autism.

Again, that was another killer IEP meeting and I had to threaten due process. I said, "My son will be in ESY. Regression/recoupment formulas are illegal because they don't take into account my son's unique needs. Also with autism, there is a limited developmental window of opportunity. ESY is not going to do him any good when he is 12 years old. He needs every bit of intervention he can get now." I won ESY on those three points.

I don't anticipate that it will be a problem keeping him in regular education because the language in PL 105-17, IDEA, is so clear on that. However, I'm sure that as he gets older Josh will need to be pulled out of the regular classroom from time to time. My biggest fear for him is when he reaches junior high and high school and the peer stuff starts. On one hand, I want him to progress as much as he can, but on the other hand, if he progresses only to a point where he is still naive about his condition that might save him from some pain.

My fears are about how he'll be treated by peers. We already had an incident last year where there was a little girl who didn't want to sit next to Josh on the bus, and she was making fun of him. "He's such a pain!" she said. It starts early and kids can be cruel. No kids want to be different, they all want to fit in.

I went to a conference where an adult man with autism talked about his experiences. He had several suicide attempts because he was recovered enough that he was painfully aware of his peers teasing him and how different he was. I think that would be the hardest part. That's why it is so important, now while he's little, that's he's in an integrated classroom.

There already are three or four peers who really like Josh and that he gets along well with. Hopefully, as they grow up together in public

Josh playing during school recess.

school, there will always be a couple of "watchdog" kids that will be his friends and companions.

Josh's older brother David and I are going to go into Josh's classroom to give presentations later this month. One thing that is really cool to a kindergartner is a second grader, like David. So David can talk to them about his brother Josh and relieve some of their fears and tensions. We'll use a classic example where you hold up a can of vegetables that most kids don't like, such as spinach, but we'll have cleaned out the can and filled it with candy that the kids don't see. We'll ask, "Do you want any?" and of course the kids will say, "Icky, no!" Then we'll show them what is inside, and teach them that you can't tell a book by its cover.

We'll also do a felt board activity where we have a whole bunch of different shapes hodge podge on the felt board. But we'll show them how to put the shapes together to make this neat train. Even though everybody is different, if you all come together, you can really go places.

3. **Normalized:** Instruction is stressed across a number of settings, age-appropriate materials and strategies are used, contrived reinforcement and aversive control is avoided, and parents are supported.
4. **Adaptable:** Flexible procedures are employed within noncategorical models; emphasis is on the functionality of behavior rather than its developmental form or sequence.
5. **Peer and family referenced:** The curriculum is validated in reference to the child, family, and community; parents are full partners in decision making.
6. **Outcome-based:** There is an emphasis on development of skills for future usefulness; transition is carefully planned.

SUCCESSFUL INCLUSION

Drinkwater and Demchak (1995) described meaningful preschool inclusion of children with disabilities as involving all children in age-appropriate groups and activities that their peers are enjoying. All the children should follow the same schedule, use the same materials, and participate as fully as possible. This does not eliminate adaptation or assistance, but does so in a manner that minimizes the differences between children and maximizes the peer interaction. Teachers in these settings use the least-intrusive natural prompts and contingencies they can to help children actively participate. Drinkwater and Demchak (1995) use an example of a child who cannot walk to circle time being encouraged to get there as independently as possible, even if it means using a walker, rather than being carried to circle. Another example they provide: Though other children are expected to cover the entire paper with finger paint, a child with motor disorders might be allowed to make any marks on paper he can.

Meaningful inclusion also encourages social and communicative reciprocity (Drinkwater & Demchak, 1995). Teachers can do this by training nondisabled peers to initiate play activities, share toys, and respond to their disabled peer's initiations. Teachers must also make sure that a child with disabilities has some means of communicating, either by using signs, gesturing, or pointing to pictures. Nondisabled peers may need to be taught to recognize these communication attempts. When scheduling, teachers can make sure some activities require cooperation, such as bouncing objects with a parachute where everyone holds on to some part of the parachute to make it go up and down. It also helps if the child with a disability is given responsibilities, such as being a line leader or passing out snacks.

Another factor to consider is the appearance of a child with a disability (Drinkwater & Demchak, 1995). Unpleasant characteristics such as being dirty, being messy at snack, or wearing diapers may influence staff and other children negatively. Teaching grooming skills, using a napkin, and having a private changing area could do much to reduce a child's stigma and to encourage interaction.

At the same time, meaningful inclusion also addresses the goals and objectives identified in a child's IEP. Teachers need to look at the basic instructional strategies they are using to be sure they are facilitating growth (Thompson et al., 1993). Questions to ask might include:

◆ Is there a range of appropriate materials for the age group and learning tasks?

◆ Is the child positioned, handled, and moved in a way that is functional and age-appropriate?

◆ Are materials cues, contingencies, and fading of prompts used appropriately?

◆ Is a child's attention span accommodated and is enough practice provided?

◆ Are positive methods used to deal with problem behavior?

◆ Are IEP goals and objectives embedded in functional, naturally occurring activities?

IN CONCLUSON

The purpose of early childhood special education is the provision of appropriate intervention services that will ultimately assist all children with disabilities. Four fundamental assumptions support this purpose:

1. Children who have disabilities or are at risk for having disabilities need and have a right to specialized services to enhance their development and the likelihood of success.

2. Families of children with disabilities often experience special needs and stresses.

3. The earlier children's needs are identified and services provided, the more effective these services will be in achieving optimal outcomes.

4. Because of the unique characteristics, needs, and resources of each child and family, no one curriculum or set of services could be expected to meet the needs of all. An individualized approach to service planning and delivery, therefore, is essential. (Bailey & Wolery, 1992, p. 34)

Given these beliefs, several basic service goals for early intervention are apparent (Bailey & Wolery, 1992). First, it is essential that families are supported in achieving their own goals; professionals must serve children in ways that are consistent with family structures, values, needs, and functions. Assisting children in their development requires the promotion of child engagement, independence, and mastery across all the key domains; the final measure of a child's development is successful interaction within a great variety of physical and social environments. Special education must always recognize the primary goal of helping children live lives that are as normal as possible, incorporating all children and their families into mainstream settings and activities. Finally, early intervention must address the prevention of new disabilities or future problems.

Beyond these primary goals for children with disabilities, each early childhood professional must also accept responsibility for pursuing goals important for the culture as a whole (Bailey & Wolery, 1992). The services mandated through IDEA are very new in the history of this society and as such must be protected and supported if they are to be maintained. It is important that special educators continue to increase the public's awareness and acceptance of people with disabilities and their need for early intervention. It is essential that special educators continually and consistently attempt to improve the quality of early intervention services through research and evaluation. Finally, professionals must be active in communicating best practices and disseminating professional knowledge to others in order to promote the availability of quality services. Early childhood professionals must advocate not only for the children and families in their direct care but also for future populations who will face the same, if not new, challenges.

REAUTHORIZATION OF IDEA

THE PRESIDENT'S COMMISSION ON EXCELLENCE IN SPECIAL EDUCATION

The reauthorization process for IDEA was initiated under George W. Bush's administration with his establishment of the Commission on Excellence in Special Education in October 2001(President's Commission on Excellence in Special Education, 2002). The task of this commission was to study issues related to federal, state, and local special education. The commission was charged with holding open hearings and meetings across the country and interviewing expert witnesses, parents, teachers, students with disabilities, and members of the public for feedback on IDEA provisions. This information was used in making recommendations regarding the revision of IDEA legislation before it went forward for reauthorization by Congress.

The President's Commission (2002) noted a number of concerns with the current IDEA regulations raised by special education consumers, experts, and the public. Some of these were particularly relevant to early intervention and preschool special education:

> The process involved in complying with complex regulations often takes precedence over providing quality services. Excessive paperwork consumes time and effort that might be better applied to effective instruction and intervention.
>
> The current system uses a model that waits for children to fail, instead of emphasizing prevention and early intervention. Students are not given help early when such help could be most effective.
>
> Minority children continue to be overrepresented in special education, especially in high incidence categories (such as learning disabilities) that rely on intelligence testing, which may be culturally biased.
>
> When a child fails to make progress in special education, parents don't have adequate options and little recourse. They don't feel empowered when the system fails them.
>
> Litgation is too frequent and often diverts attention and energy from the public school's mission to educate every child.
>
> Many methods for identifying children as eligible for special education lack validity and, as a result, many children are misidentified and others not identified early enough.
>
> Children with disabilities need highly qualified teachers with better preparation, support, and professional development than is currently offered.

Research in special education needs enhanced rigor and long-term co-ordination. Often, intervention does not make use of evidence-based practices.

The recommendations that came out of the President's Commission on Excellence in Special Education (2002) focused on three main areas:

1. Place emphasis on performance results for children rather than litigation, process, regulation, and confrontation, which interfere with service delivery.
2. Embrace a model of prevention with early identification and intervention using evidence-based instruction rather than a model that requires failure before services begin.
3. Consider children with disabilities as part of general education first rather than as part of a separate system of special education. Provide flexibility in funding and teacher training so students can be appropriately educated in all settings.

In regard to very young children with disabilities, specific suggestions were made to reduce regulations so more attention would be given to direct services. It was suggested that paperwork could be reduced by simplifying the IEP, perhaps by eliminating the requirement of short-term objectives and simply listing special services related to annual outcomes. Services to infants and toddlers (currently provided by networks of multiple agencies and monitored differently in different states) should be better coordinated and streamlined, allowing families to maximize earlier services for their children. Services to children should be seamless from birth through 21, without the major transition between early intervention and public school programs that is now present. Finally, agencies providing early childhood services must be more accountable for documenting and demonstrating child-performance progress.

For preschool children with special needs, there should be earlier identification of learning and behavioral difficulties. Eligibility for services should be based on a child's response to intervention, not just on test results. Instead of listing 13 different categories of disabilities and assessing children to determine in which category they belong, identification for special services should be based on broader definitions of disorders: sensory disabilities, physical and neurological disabilities, and developmental disabilities. All young children should be a part of universal screening so children with special needs are not overlooked for early treatment. Time and money spent on reassessments every 3 years should be eliminated and replaced with brief and frequent progress monitoring and reporting. Intelligence testing (to determine discrepancies between IQ and achievement) should not be required for determining learning disabilities. However, parents should always have the right to request an evaluation more often.

A great deal of testimony was brought to the President's Commission on behalf of greater parent empowerment, particularly in terms of parent options and choice in educational placement. One recommendation for increasing choice was to allow special education funds to follow students to schools their families choose, especially when parents choose to leave failing public schools where their children do not make progress. The Commission recommended that families should be able to chose charter schools or other options, even if these offer relatively restrictive environments, as long as those programs can appropriately serve the student.

Finally, the President's Commission recommended increased funding both for Part B (mandated school services) and for Part C (services to infants and toddlers). The total estimated spending to educate students with disabilities was approximately $78.3 billion in the 1999–2000 school year. When IDEA was first passed in 1975, Congress estimated that the cost of special education was about twice that of general education and determined that federal monies should provide for up to 40% of that cost. This 40% figure has come to be known as the "full funding" target, but federal funding has, in fact, fallen far short of 40%. Though most children in special education have mild disabilities, increasing numbers of children with severe disabilities now survive birth and require highly specialized services that can cost more than $100,000 per student per year. These are extraordinary educational costs that many school districts find difficult to meet. The President's Commission calls for more flexibility in how districts use their special education funds to support all their children with special needs.

OTHER INPUT

The President's Commission was not the only group articulating preferences for how IDEA should be revised. The Center on Education Policy published its comments in *A Timely IDEA: Rethinking Federal Education Programs for Children with Disabilities* (2002). Its report also emphasized the importance of accountability for outcomes for students, increased assistance and support to schools for implementing IDEA, and reduction of paperwork

Many organizations responded to a January 2002 announcement in the *Federal Register* requesting public comment or to a version of IDEA passed by the House of Representatives (for example: Consortium for Citizens with Disabilities, July, 2002; Council for Exceptional Children, April, 2002). Many of the suggestions made mirrored the President's Commission report. Accountability for child progress was frequently mentioned as a priority but the input also encouraged flexibility and choice, allowing schools to work with students to customize services and placements; emphasized the need for early intervention and preschool programs; and urged that adequate (increased) funding be made available.

PUBLIC DEBATE

When the House of Representatives passed its version of IDEA reauthorization in April 2003, many of the changes were hotly debated and disability advocates rallied their organizations to give input before the Senate negotiated a final version of the reauthorization (for example: American Association of People with Disabilities, June, 2003; Autism National Committee, May, 2003; National Association of School Psychologists, June, 2003; National Association of Social Workers, June 2003; United Cerebral Palsy, June, 2003). Numerous advocates felt their earlier input had been misrepresented or that new provisions did not adequately address the needs of children with disabilities.

A rally was held in Washington, DC where children with disabilities teemed the Senate halls and chanted, "Don't Leave Us Behind." Opposition rose from national parent organizations because of proposed changes in due process grievance procedures that would involve voluntary binding arbitration as a substitute for traditional IDEA dispute resolution. Advocates fought against revised discipline procedures, which would eliminate the requirement of functional assessments to determine appropriate treatment for children with behavior disorders. Many disability organizations were upset by a provision that would allow 10 states to suspend IDEA regulations in order to pilot approaches to special education that might be more efficient. Some objected to the institution of 3-year IEPs (rather than annual IEPs) and the elimination of regular reassessments. Professional preparation programs and parents objected to the elimination of the words "highly qualified" in reference to personnel who could provide treatment to children with disabilities. Others fought for more direct language protecting a continuum of service placements in settings that are most appropriate for the child, as determined by the parent and the individualized family service team.

SUMMARY

At the time of this writing, the final IDEA reauthorization bill had not been released. It was not clear whether the concerns raised by advocates for the disabled would be addressed. What was certain, however, was that evidence-based practice would be emphasized in the treatment of children with disabilities and measurable performance outcomes would be required. As practitioners come to rely on data-based approaches, an attitude of science becomes essential.

Professionals in early intervention have to become adept at understanding research, and at the same time be skilled in developing positive relationships with families and colleagues; respecting individual and cultural differences; and providing appropriate, high-quality, personalized services. Achieving this integration of skills and attitudes is a challenge, but those who work in early intervention have the awesome opportunity to touch a life in its earliest days. This unequalled opportunity comes with tremendous responsibility for providing the best available treatment and education and continuous advocacy and support.

STUDY GUIDE QUESTIONS

1. What issues exist in respect to working with families of preschool children with disabilities?
2. What should professionals do to ease the transition to preschool special education?
3. What are the essential components of an IEP?
4. Generate an original example of a clear statement of present levels of performance.
5. Develop a good objective to describe communication targets for a 4-year-old child with moderate retardation. Be sure to include the behavior, the conditions, and the criterion.

6. Look carefully at the objective just written, what guidelines for an instructional objective does it already address? How could it be improved it to meet the remaining guidelines?
7. What are the critical characteristics of specially designed instruction?
8. Describe how one might ensure the generalization of conversational skills for a 3-year-old child.
9. Describe three specialists who might provide related services to a preschooler (and family) with a hearing impairment. What kinds of support might they provide?
10. Sometimes the same setting is least restrictive for one child but not for another. Give an example of a child for whom a self-contained preschool program for hearing impaired children might be most appropriate and an example of a child for whom it is not.
11. What is the purpose of a functional behavioral assessment? How might it be carried out?
12. Briefly describe how a teacher-directed program might be different from a child-directed one. What would be the possible advantages and disadvantages of each?
13. What are three recommendations that came out of the President's Commission on Excellence in Special Education?

REFERENCES

American Association of People with Disabilities. (June, 2003). Update on IDEA reauthorization. Retrieved June 26, 2003 at *http://www.aapd-dc.org/docs/ updateideareauth.html*

Ask the Expert. (1999). Barbara Bateman & Mary Anne Linden answered your questions on Writing Effective IEPs. Retrieved September 9, 1999 from *http://www. ldonline.org/ld_indepth/iep/iep.html*

Autism National Committee. (May, 2003). AUTCOM action alert! Save IDEA. Retrieved June 26, 2003 from *http://www.autcom.org/PACER_IDEA.htm*

Bailey, D. B., & Wolery, M. (1992). *Teaching infants and preschoolers with disabilities* (2nd ed.). New York: Macmillan.

Bateman, B., & Linden, M. A. (1998). *Better IEPs: How to develop legally correct and educationally useful programs* (3rd ed.). Longmont, CO: Sopris West Educational Services.

Bateman, B. D. (1995). Writing Individualized Education Programs (IEPs) for success. *Secondary Education and Beyond*. Learning Disabilities Association. Retrieved September 9, 1999 from *http:// www.ldonline.org/ ld_indepth/iep/success_ieps.html*

Beach Center on Families and Disabilities. (1999). *Quality indicators of exemplary IFSP/IEP development.* Retrieved September 9, 1999 from *http://www.lsi. ukans.edu/Beach/html/9i.htm*

Brown, W., & Rule, S. (1993). Personnel and disciplines in early intervention. In W. Brown, S. K. Thurman, & L. F. Pearl (Eds.), *Family-centered early intervention with infants and toddlers: Innovative cross-disciplinary approaches* (pp. 245–268). Baltimore: Paul H. Brookes.

Center on Education Policy. (2002). *A timely IDEA: Rethinking federal education programs for children with disabilities.* Washington, DC: Author.

Chandler, L. K., Dahlquist, C. M., Repp, A. C., & Feltz, C. (1999). The effects of team-based functional assessment on the behavior of students in classroom settings. *Exceptional Children, 66*(1), 101–122.

Consortium for Citizens with Disabilities. (July, 2002). *CCD responds to "Rethinking Special Education."* Retrieved July 10, 2003 from *http://www.c-c-d.org/ Fordhamresponse.htm*

Council for Exceptional Children. (April, 2002). *IDEA reauthorization recommendations.* Retrieved July 10, 2003 at *http://www.connsensebulletin.com/up052302*

D'Angelo, A., & Adler, C. R. (1991). Chapter 1: A catalyst for improving parent involvement. *Phi Delta Kappan, 72*(5), 350–354.

Drinkwater, S., & Demchak, M. (1995). The preschool Checklist: Integration of children with severe disabilities. *Teaching Exceptional Children, 28*(1), 4–8.

Epstein, J. L. (1992). *School and family partnerships*. Baltimore, MD: Johns Hopkins University Center on Families, Communities, Schools, and Children's Learning.

ERIC Clearinghouse on Disabilities and Gifted Education. (1999). What are your rights, as a parent, in the special education process? ED419326 98 Rights and Responsibilities of Parents of Children with Disabilities. *ERIC Digest #E567*. Retrieved September 10, 1999 from *http://www.ed.gov/databases/ERIC_Digests/ed419326.html*

Etscheidt, S. K., & Bartlett, L. (1999). The IDEA amendments: A four-step approach for determining supplementary aids. *Exceptional Children, 65*(2), 163–174.

Heward, W. L., & Orlansky, M. D. (1992). *Exceptional children* (4th ed.). New York: Macmillan.

Hurder, A. J. (1997). The Individuals with Disabilities Education Act and the right to learn. *Human Rights, 24*(1), 16–17.

Karnes, M. B., & Stayton, V. D. (1988). Model programs for infants and toddlers with handicaps. In J. B. Jordan, J. J. Gallagher, P. L. Hutinger, & M. B. Karnes (Eds.), *Early childhood special education: Birth to three* (pp. 67–108). Reston, VA: Council for Exceptional Children.

Kroeger, S. D., Leibold, C. K., & Ryan, B. (1999). Creating a sense of ownership in the IEP process. *Teaching Exceptional Children, 32*(1), 4–9.

Kroth, R. L., & Edge, D. (1997). *Strategies for communicating with parents and families of exceptional children* (3rd ed.). Denver: Love Publishing.

Lahm, E. A., & Nickels, B. L. (1999). Assistive technology competencies for special educators. *Teaching Exceptional Children, 32*(1), 56–63.

LD OnLine. (1999). *Individualized Education Program: The process*. Retrieved August 9, 1999 from *http://www.ldonline.org/ld_indepth/iep/iep_process.html*

Mager, R. F. (1962). *Preparing instructional objectives*. Belmont, CA: Fearon.

National Association of School Psychologists. (June, 2003). NASP legislative update. Retrieved June 26, 2003 from *http://www.asponline.org/advocacy/legisup061303_print.html*

National Association of Social Workers. (May, 2003). Government relations action alert: Senate will act soon on IDEA reauthorization. Retrieved June 26, 2003 from *http://www.naswdc.org/advocacy/alerts/052903.asp*

National Association of State Directors of Special Education. (1997). *Comparison of key issues: Current law and 1997 IDEA amendments*. Washington, DC: Author.

Noonan, M. J., & McCormick, L. (1993). *Early intervention in natural environments, methods and procedures*. Pacific Grove, CA: Brooks/Cole.

Pacer Center. (1999). Pacer Center looks at IDEA '97. Retrieved August 9, 1999 from *http://www.pacer.org/idea/pacer_idea97.htm*

Peterson, N. L. (1987). Early intervention for handicapped and at-risk children: *An introduction to early childhood special education*. Denver, CO: Love.

President's Commission on Excellence in Special Education. (2002). *A new era: Revitalizing special education for children and their families*. Retrieved July 3, 2003 from *http://www.ed.gov/inits/commissionsboards/whspecialeducation/reports.html*

Pruitt, P., Wandry, D., & Hollums, D. (1998). Listen to us! Parents speak out about their interactions with special educators. *Preventing School Failure, 42*(4), 161–167.

Rogers, E. L. (1998). Functional assessment in the home. *Preventing School Failure, 43*(1), 31–33.

Sandall, S. R. (1993). Curricula for early intervention. In W. Brown, S. K. Thurman, & L. F. Pearl (Eds.), *Family-centered early intervention with infants and toddlers: Innovative cross-disciplinary approaches* (pp. 129–151). Baltimore: Paul H. Brookes.

Stokes, T. F., & Baer, D. M. (1977). An implicit technology of generalization. *Journal of Applied Behavior Analysis, 10*, 349–367.

Strickland, B. B., & Turnbull, A. P. (1990). *Developing and implementing individualized education programs* (3rd ed.). Upper Saddle River, NJ: Merrill/Prentice Hall.

Thompson, B., Wickham, D., Wegner, J., Ault, M., Shanks, P., & Reinertson, B. (1993). *Handbook for the inclusion of young children with severe disabilities*. Lawrence, KS: Learner Managed Designs.

Thurman, S. K., & Widerstrom, A. H. (1990). *Infants and young children with special needs, a developmental and ecological approach* (2nd ed.). Baltimore: Paul H. Brookes.

Turnbull, A. P., & Turnbull, H. R. (1997). *Families, professionals, and exceptionality: A special partnership*. Upper Saddle River, NJ: Prentice Hall.

United Cerebral Palsy. (June, 2003). Public Policy: House passes IDEA reauthorization. *Washington Watch, 1*(4). Retrieved June 10, 2003 from *http://www.ucp.org/ucp-generaldoc.cfm/1/8/33/11873–11974/4767*

Yell, M. L. (1998). The legal basis of inclusion. *Educational Leadership, 56*(2), 70–73.

GLOSSARY

abduction: limbs move outward, away from the body

abruptio placenta: separation of placenta from the walls of the uterus prior to delivery

absence seizure: momentary interruption of ongoing activity with a brief, blank stare

accommodation (visual): the process by which the eye adjusts to focus on near objects

acidotic: high levels of blood acid

active listening: attentiveness to a speaker on multiple levels: hearing, interpreting, sorting, and analyzing

acute stressors: events that place strain on a family and occur as periodic incidents related to a child's disability

adaptive reflexes: mature reflexes such as sucking and swallowing

adaptive skills: self-help, problem solving, responding appropriately to environmental demands

adduction: limbs move in toward the body

adolescent stage: time starting at about 10 to 16 years of age, depending on physical maturity, and extending to adulthood

adventitious: aquired after birth

advocacy: favoring and supporting the needs or cause of another

albinism: a congenital condition characterized by a lack of the pigment that gives color to skin, hair, and eyes

alleles: one of two alternative versions of a gene with complementary alleles residing on each of the two chromosomes in a pair

alpha-fetoprotein (AFT) screening: a blood test on a pregnant woman to detect neural tube deficits in her fetus

alveoli: tiny airsacs in the lungs which permit normal exchange of oxygen and carbon dioxide

amblyopia: dimness of vision not due to organic defect or refractive errors

amniocentesis: a procedure in which fluid is removed from the sac surrounding the fetus to determine if the fetus carries a genetic anomaly

amniotic sac: the membrane that surrounds the fetus and contains fluid that protects the fetus from physical shocks and maintains a constant temperature

anemia: a condition in which the amount of oxygen-carrying hemoglobin is below normal in the blood

anencephaly: a congenital malformation in which the brain does not develop and the skull, which would normally cover the brain, is absent

antibodies: a protein produced by the body in response to the presence of an antigen (chemical substance that causes the body to produce specific antibodies) and is capable of combining specifically with the antigen

antiviral: a group of drugs used to treat infection by a virus

apnea: breathing pauses due to immature central nervous system

asphyxia: loss of consciousness from interruption of breathing as in suffocation or drowning

associative play: individual children play with other children engaging in similar or even identical activities

astigmatism: a visual defect caused by unequal curvatures of the refractile surfaces (cornea, lens) of the eye, resulting in light rays from a point not coming to focus at a point on the retina

asymmetrical tonic neck reflex (ATNR): a primitive reflex in which the limbs are extended on the side of the body toward which the head is turned but flexed on the opposite side; also called "fencer's reflex"

asymptomatic: showing no symptoms

at risk: used to refer to that class of infants who have been exposed to any one of a number of medical or environmental factors that may contribute to later developmental delay

ataxic cerebral palsy: cerebral damage that causes difficulty with coordination and balance

athetosis: variable muscle tone caused by noncortical cerebral damage, producing slow, writhing, and excessive movement

atonic seizure: sudden reduction in muscle tone, slumping

attachment: emotional bonding to another person

attention deficit hyperactivity disorder (ADHD): a combination of characteristics including inattention, impulsivity, and hyperactivity

attitude of science: the use of parsimony and empirical research to determine what is true

auditory nerve: vehicle of transmission of electrical energy from the ear to the temporal area of the brain

augmentative or alternative communication: using appliances or non-speech systems to enhance a child's natural communication skills

axon: the nerve-cell process that carries impules away from the nerve-cell body; any long nerve-cell process

babble: a combination of consonant and vowel sounds uttered by infants at about 4 months of age as they gain oral-motor control

Babinski reflex: a reflex in which stimulation applied to the sole of an infant's foot results in the infant spreading his or her toes

bacteria: a large group of typically one-celled, microscopic organisms widely distributed in air, water, soil, and the bodies of living plants and animals

behavioral assessment: examination of factors that govern children's behavior under given conditions

best practice: instructional and collaborative procedures based on current research and knowledge

binding communications: habits of interaction that generally close or diminish the probability of continued conversation

biological agents: microorganisms that cause damage to human cells by either living on cells or by causing inflammation of the cells and that travel throughout the body via the blood stream or lymphatic system

biological/medical risks: medical conditions that threaten to compromise a child's health, particularly perinatally, and are predictive of later delays

blended families: families including stepchildren and stepparents

bonding: attachment between infant and caregiver

bound morphemes: morphemes that cannot stand alone in meaning (-ed, -ing, etc.)

bronchopulmonary dysplasia (BPD): chronic lung disease resulting from respiratory distress syndrome

cardiovascular system: organ system including heart, veins, and arteries

carrier: individual who possesses a gene for a trait but does not express the characteristics

cataract: clouding or opacity of the lens of the eye

center-based programs: programs in which children are served in a central location

central nervous system (CNS): the brain and spinal cord

cephalo-caudal: the sequence of growth and development of motor skills that is progressively downward from head, to neck, to trunk, to hips, to legs, to feet, to toes

cerebral palsy: a nonprogressive neuromuscular condition affecting muscle tone, movement, reflexes, and posture

cerebrospinal fluid: a clear, colorless, odorless fluid that resembles water and is produced from blood through secretion and diffusion between the vascular system and the choroid plexuses in the brain; protects the nervous system from injury by acting as a shock absorber

chancre: a lesion at the site of contact with an infected person

child abuse: the willful behavior by parents or guardians that harms a child in their care

child-directed instruction: flexible instruction that follows a child's lead in terms of interests and motivation

chorionic villus sampling (CVS): testing a small tissue sample from the chorion, or outer sac that surrounds the fetus, to determine if the fetus carries a genetic anomaly

chorioretinitis: inflammation of the retina and choroid

chromosome disorders: disorders caused by whole chromosomes or chromosome segments rather than a single gene or combination of genes

chromosomes: the basic genetic units that stay constant within a species and across generations (For example, normal human cells contain a complement of 46 chromosomes or 23 pairs.)

chronic stressors: constant pressure or strain on a family caused by concerns related to a child's disability

cirrhosis: interstitial inflammation of an organ, particularly the liver

cleft lip: a split in facial tissue that affects the lip and gum and may extend upward into the nose and may occur with a cleft palate

cleft palate: a split in facial tissue that affects the hard or soft palate (roof of mouth) and may occur with a cleft lip

clonic seizure: alternate contraction and relaxation of muscles

cochlea: the portion of the inner ear associated with the reception of sound waves, which lies in a cavity in the temporal bone and is shaped like a snail shell

cognition: thinking, mental processes

cognitive-developmental approach: a theory about how children learn that recognizes a natural, fixed sequence in which thinking processes emerge

collaboration: an interactive process that enables teams of people with diverse expertise to generate creative solutions to mutually defined problems

collaborative teaming: members agree to work together collectively to achieve common goals

communication: the ability of two or more people to send and receive messages; the most necessary skill of both parents and childhood educators

complex sentence: a sentence that contains at least one independent clause and at least one subordinate or dependent clause

compound sentence: a sentence that contains more than one independent clause and combines two or more ideas in a single sentence by using conjunctions, relative pronouns, or other linguistic linkages

computerized axial tomography (CAT or CT): a procedure that uses X rays to view several plains of the body at one time to produce a three-dimensional image of body tissue

conceptual system: a set of principles that articulate a body of knowledge

concrete assistance: providing help acquiring basic needs such as food and housing

concrete operations: the stage of cognitive development (at age 7–11 years) when children can use real objects to logically solve problems

conduction: heat loss to unwarmed surfaces (such as a mattress), evaporation (heat loss through fluid loss through skin)

conductive hearing loss: disruption of mechanical conduction of sound as it is transferred from the outer ear through the middle ear

congenital: present at birth

consequate: to follow, contingent upon a specific behavior

consolidation: when disorganized behavior is replaced by more advanced developmental skills

contractures: a condition in which muscles and tendons shorten, causing rigidity and joint immobility

convection: heat loss with the delivery of unwarmed gases such as oxygen

conversational postulates: subtle conversational rules that allow humans to converse in a reciprocal manner (i.e., initiating, turn taking, questioning, repairing a breakdown in conversation, maintaining interactions, and closing a conversation)

consensus building: guiding groups in decision making based on group agreement

cooing: vowel sound production that requires little motor control or use of the articulators (tongue, lips, palate, and teeth), which usually occurs in infants during the perlocutionary stage

cooperative play: children engage in organized play activities

cornea: the transparent epithelium (tissue covering internal and external surfaces) and connective tissue membrane that covers the anterior portion of the eye, which refracts light rays and channels that light through the fluid-filled anterior chamber

corrected gestational age: age adjusted to reflect premature delivery

cortical visual impairments: a condition in which eye physiology is not impaired, yet there is a loss of visual ability caused by damage to the optic nerve or the cerebral tissue within the occipital portion of the brain

crawl: coordination of arms and legs to move across a surface on the abdomen

cruising: a child's movement by stepping sideways while holding on to furniture or some structure for support

cultural competence: knowledge of and respect for diverse beliefs, interpersonal styles, attitudes, and behaviors

culturally sensitive: awareness of different values and practices of divergent ethnic and cultural groups

cyanosis: a blue-tinged color to the skin, which can occur when blood bypasses the lungs, resulting in decreased oxygen being available to cells

cytomegalic inclusion viral infection (CMV): one of the family of herpes viruses that is common and produces no symptoms in adults but can cause malformations and brain damage to an unborn child

demographics: statistical characteristics of human populations

dentition: the development of teeth

deoxyribonucleic acid (DNA): a nucleic acid compound that carries the chemical coding needed to transmit genetic information from generation to generation

development: occurs when the complexity of a child's behavior increases

developmental delay: delayed progress experienced by infants and toddlers in one or more developmental areas: communication, physical development, adaptive behavior (feeding, dressing, toileting, etc.), cognition, and social/emotional development

developmental instruction: instruction that matches a child's abilities and interests according to age, skills, and cognitive level

developmental milestones: major indexes of development identified across developmental areas and across years and used to measure developmental progress

diabetes: any disorder characterized by excessive urine excretion, usually caused when the pancreas produces insufficient insulin

diplegia: cerebral palsy affecting all four extremities of the body, with greater involvement of the legs than of the trunk and arms

discretionary programs: allowed but not required by law

dominant gene: a gene that possesses sufficient genetic information for a characteristic to be expressed when only one allele carries the gene

dyskinesia: a condition caused by noncortical cerebral damage (See athetosis.)

early childhood stage: time from 3 years to 6 years of age

early intervention: period from birth to age 3 when services are delivered to infants and toddlers with developmental delays or at-risk conditions

ecological approach to assessment: evaluations focus on children, their environment, and the interaction between the two

electroencephalography (EEG): a procedure that measures electrical potentials on the scalp to produce an analysis of brain activity

embedding: a process in which children add clauses internally to sentences (develops at 4 to 13 years of age)

embryonic stage: begins in the 3rd week of pregnancy when cell differentiation permits the emergence of the central nervous system and circulatory system and is completed by the 8th week of gestation

emotional support: eliciting and listening to a person's needs while encouraging positive attitudes and actions

empirical: relying on observation and experimentation

empowerment: encouraging individual reliance on self and providing understandable and practical information that can be used by families

encephalitis: inflammation of the brain

environmental risks: environmental conditions, such as poverty or abuse, that place infants and toddlers at-risk for developmental delays

epilepsy: a condition of recurrent seizures

equilibrium reflex: the reflex that involuntarily causes the body to realign its trunk to a vertical posture after the body moves or is moved out of midline

established risks: diagnosed conditions that give infants and toddlers high probability of later delays in development

ethical conduct: action that is responsible and respectful of professional rules

ethical standards for conduct: accepted professional guidelines for appropriate behavior toward others

eustachian tube: a continuous passage from the middle ear to the throat that acts as a safety tube, equalizing internal and external air pressure on the tympanic membrane

exocrine glands: glands that secrete substances onto an inner surface of an organ or outside the body, such as salivary or sweat glands

exosystem: societal structures, such as local and state agencies or advocacy groups, that affect a child's life

expressive language: coded output message emitted by a child or adult

extension: the straightening of a joint that changes the angle between bones that meet in the joint; the opposite of flexion

external ear: the part of the ear responsible for collecting sound waves, consisting of the auricle, auditory canal, and tympanic membrane

extrapyramidal: outside the pyramidal nerve group; used to refer to noncortical cerebral damage

extremely low birth weight: less than 750 g (1 lb 10 oz)

failure to thrive: delay in physical and neurological growth in infancy and early childhood due to organic or environmental causes

family hardiness: a constellation of three dimensions: (1) control: the ability to influence events, (2) commitment: active involvement in events, and (3) challenge: viewing changes as opportunities for growth and development

family systems model: approaches families as complex organizations in which internal and external variables affect all members

Fetal Alcohol Effects (FAE): moderate birth defects caused by prenatal exposure to alcohol

Fetal Alcohol Syndrome (FAS): serious birth defects caused by prenatal exposure to alcohol

fetal blood sampling: a blood sample withdrawn from the umbilical cord to determine if the fetus carries a genetic anomaly

fetal stage: the stage of pregnancy from the 9th week through the 9th month

flexion: the bending of a joint; the opposite of extension

formal operations: the stage of cognitive development (at age 11 years and older) when humans develop abstract thinking; can classify and sort

freeing statements: habits of interaction that actually encourage expanded dialogue

functional assessment: manipulation of environmental conditions in order to determine their effects the observed behavior

functional skills: of immediate or future usefulness in the environment, such as self-feeding or mobility

functionality: degree to which skills are needed to operate as independently as possible in daily activities

gametes: the cells involved in reproduction (A sperm is a male gamete, and an ovum is a female gamete.

These germ cells have one half the number of chromosomes, one from each chromosome pair. When a sperm and ovum join during conception, the resultant cell has a full set of chromosomes, one of each chromosome pair from each parent.)

gastrointestinal system: the part of the digestive system that consists of the mouth, esophagus, stomach, and intestine

gastrostomy tube: a tube or a gastric button through which feedings can be given directly into the stomach, bypassing the esophagus

generalization: transfer of skills to other settings, other caregivers, and other appropriate situations

generalized seizure: caused by activation of the entire brain; involves the whole body

genes: regions of a chromosome made up of molecules that collectively define a particular trait

genetic mapping: a process of learning the genetic code of humans by charting the relationships between specific genes and individual chromosomes

genotype: the combination of alleles inherited for a particular trait within an individual (The genotype can only be determined through cellular testing since the trait determined by the genotype may or may not be expressed.)

gestation: the period of intrauterine fetal development

gestational diabetes: acquisition of diabetes during pregnancy

glaucoma: a condition characterized by a buildup of pressure in the anterior chamber of the eye

gravida: the medical term for a pregnant woman; often used with a number to indicate the number of pregnancies a woman has had (a 3-gravida)

group B streptococcus: a group of bacteria from the streptococcus family

group process: reflection by a group to determine what actions should be continued and what group behaviors should be changed in order to make collaborative efforts more effective

growth retardation: very small for age, weight less than the 10th percentile

handling: therapeutic preparation for movement and positioning

hematoma: bruise or swelling filled with blood

hemiplegia: cerebral palsy affecting one side of the body

herpes: infection with the herpes simplex virus, causing small, painful blisters on the skin

heterozygote: when an individual has two different alleles for a particular trait (For example, a child who receives a normal gene from one parent and a gene for cystic fibrosis from the other parent will not express the disease from this heterozygote pair since the gene for cystic fibrosis is not dominant.)

homozygote pair: when an individual has identical alleles for a certain trait (For example, when the gene for cystic fibrosis is inherited from both mother and father, the alleles form a homozygote pair and the child will express the disease.)

hydrocephalus: a condition in which there is an excessive accumulation of cerebrospinal fluid in the ventricles of the brain, causing the head to increase in size beyond two standard deviations above the mean on the standard growth chart

hyperopia: farsightedness; a condition in which parallel light rays come to focus beyond the retina because the refractile system is too weak or the eyeball is flattened

hypertonia: high muscle tone that limits joint movement

hypoglycemia: a condition in which there is a decreased amount of glucose available for use by cells

hypothermia: low body core temperature

hypotonia: low muscle tone that allows excessive joint movement

hypoxia: decreased oxygen flow

imitation: copy another's behavior or language

inclusion: to participate in the same activites as non-disabled peers

Individualized Education Program (IEP): an intervention plan developed by a team for a child (age 3–21 years) with a disability; includes a report of current performance, annual goals, instructional objectives, special education and related services, and an evaluation proposal

Individualized Family Service Plan (IFSP): an intervention plan developed by a team for an infant or toddler (birth to age 3) with a disability and for the child's family; includes identification of strengths and needs, a statement of expected outcomes, intervention and support services, and evaluation proposals for the child and the family

Individuals with Disabilities Education Act (IDEA): current federal legislation regarding the education of children with disabilities; provides for a free, appropriate education for all children with disabilities ages 3 to 21 and encourages services to infants and toddlers with disabilities or at-risk for developmental delay

infancy: time from 30 days to 12 months of age

inflammation: redness, swelling, heat, and pain in tissue caused by injury or infection

inner ear: a fluid-filled chamber located in the temporal bone medial to the middle ear, containing the cochlea, the vestibule, and the semicircular canals

instructional objectives: expected outcomes of educational intervention within a short-term timeframe; should state the observable behavior, the conditions, or situation under which the behavior is expected, and the criterion, or how well the child must perform the behavior

integumentary system: organ system including skin, nails, hair, glands, muscles, ligaments, tendons, and fat tissue

Interagency Coordinating Council (ICC): agencies at the federal, state, and local levels that provide administration and service delivery for infants and toddlers with special needs

interdisciplinary: the combination of expertise from several disciplines for evaluating, planning, and implementing intervention; a group whose members perform related tasks independently but interact collaboratively to meet goals

intracranial bleeding: bleeding in the brain; stroke

intraventricular hemorrhage: bleeding in the brain

invasive: a procedure that penetrates the body (such as surgery)

involvement: degree to which a child is affected motorically; ranges from mild to severe

ischemia: death of cells/tissue due to decreased blood flow and oxygen supply

karyotype: the number and configuration of chromosomes

kin: immediate and extended family

kinship care: child care, housing, and so on, provided by members of the immediate or extended family other than the parents

late visual bloomers: those children who, like children with motor, language, and social developmental delays, experience maturational delays in visual ability, appearing to be blind at birth and during their first months of life, but usually developing normal visual ability by 18 months to 3 years of age

least restrictive environment: the most appropriate setting in which a child with a disability can be with typical peers to the greatest extent possible and still meet individual needs

lens: transparent convex structure of the eye just behind the pupil, whose curvature can be altered to focus on near or far objects

low birth weight: less than 2,800 g (6 lb 3 oz) at birth

low vision: visual acuity at or less than 20/70 in the better eye with correction

macrosystem: the cultural and legislative/judicial contexts that affect a child, for example, IDEA legislation

magnetic resonance imaging (MRI): a procedure that uses magnetic force to draw ions to the edges of an internal organ to produce an image of normal and abnormal tissues

mandated: required by law

maturation: the universally observed sequence of biological changes as one ages; permits the development of psychological functions to evolve

Mean Length Utterance (MLU): an index of the sophistication of a child's language, acquired by measuring the frequency of morphemes in children's utterances

meconium: the thick, sticky, greenish-black feces passed by infants during the first day or two after birth

meconium aspiration syndrome: when the dark sticky mucous in the intestine of a fetus is expelled before birth and inhaled as the infant takes its first breaths

meiosis: cell division that produces sex cells, in which chromosomes divide and produce half the complement of 46 chromosomes in each of the resulting gametes

meninges: the covering that consists of three layers (arachnoid, dura mater, and pia mater) and surrounds the brain and spinal cord

meningitis: a condition in which infection occurs as the result of the entry of bacteria, producing inflammation of the meninges, which is the covering that surrounds the brain and spinal cord

meningocele: a neural tube defect that involves a soft tissue mass that is covered by skin, and does not contain nerves or nerve roots

mesosystem: relationships among microsystems in which a child sometimes spends time, for example, the relationship between teacher and parent

microbes: germs that are so small that they can only be seen through a microscope

microcephaly: very small head and brain; head circumference that falls at least two standard deviations below the mean on a standard growth chart for age

micropremature infant: an infant born at less than 600 g (1 lb 5 oz) or less than 25 weeks gestation

microsystem: the immediate environment in which a child spends the majority of time, for example, the child-care center

middle childhood stage: time from about 6 to 10 years of age

middle ear: a small air-filled chamber medial to the tympanic membrane containing three tiny bones: the malleus (hammer), incus (anvil), and stapes (stirrup)

milestones: behavioral markers or accomplishments of development

mitosis: cell division that produces two identical daughter cells, each containing the full set of 46 chromosomes; occurs in all body cell reproduction in which chromosomes replicate and the cell divides once to create two identical cells, as in the regeneration of skin cells

mitral valve: valve between the left atrium and the left ventricle; permits the left ventricle to contract and pump blood out the aorta without regurgitation of blood back into left atrium

mobility: degree to which individual is able to move around her or his environment independently, with or without adaptive equipment

monoplegia: cerebral palsy affecting one extremity of the body

morbidity: diseased; pertaining to disease

moro reflex: a symmetrical abduction and extension of the arms followed by an adduction when a child's head is suddenly dropped backwards (as if the child were embracing something)

morpheme: the smallest part of a word that possesses meaning

morphological development: evolution of word structure and word parts

mortality: the death rate; the ratio of total number of deaths to the total number in the population

mosaicism: a portion of cells have 46 chromosomes and another percentage of the cells have a deletion or an extra chromosome

multidisciplinary: a group of professionals from several different disciplines who work independently but meet to exchange information and to present goals and progress reports

multifactored diagnostic evaluation: administration of more than one test to determine the presence of a disability; tests should be administered in all areas relevant to a child's perceived needs

myelin sheath: lipid material with protein arranged in layers around many axons to increase efficiency of electrical transmission during neural activity; gives white matter in the brain its color

myelinization: production of myelin around an axon

myelomeningocele: a condition in which both the spinal cord and its covering, the meninges, push through a spinal defect to the surface

myoclonic seizure: brief, shock-like muscle contractions

myopia: nearsightedness; a condition in which parallel light rays come to focus in front of the retina because the refractile system is too strong or the eyeball is elongated

natal: pertaining to birth—before, during, and immediately after

natural routines: activities that normally take place in the daily routine of infants and toddlers and their families

negative sentences: statements using "no," "not," "can't," and so on

neonatal: time from birth to 30 days of age

neonate: an infant during the first 4 weeks after birth

neural tube defects: disorders in the development, closure, and formation of the neural groove, the vertebral column (which houses the spinal cord), or other soft tissue structures surrounding the nerves

neurological system: organ system including, brain, spinal cord, and nerves

neurons: cells responsible for receiving and sending messages

noncontingent helping: providing assistance without effort or request from the recipient

nondisjunction during meiosis: an incomplete detachment of the pairs of cells occurring during cell division to create either an ovum or sperm

noninvasive: a procedure that does not involve penetrating the body (such as ultrasonography)

nonorganic: without specific physical cause

normal development: a sequence of changes across time that is very similar for all children

norms: statistically determined age levels for developmental milestones

nystagmus: rapid involuntary oscillations or tremors of the eyeball; may be horizontal, vertical, or rotary

object permanence: the understanding that objects continue to exist even when they are out of sight

occipital lobe: the back section of the head

optic nerve: transmits visual image from the eye to the brain

organic: specific physical causation

organism: a total living form; one individual

orientation: conceptual, perceptual, sensory, and body awareness of space and environment

ostomy: an opening made from an internal tube to an external source, allowing for passage of urine or stool from the body (usually to a collection pouch)

otitis media (middle ear disease): an inflammatory disease of the middle ear; may be acute otitis media or serous otitis media

overextension: children's language usage that commonly occurs due to a limited repertoire of words or when categories are defined too broadly; for example, referring to all men as "Daddy"

ovum: an unfertilized female sex cell; egg

parachute reflex: extension of arms and legs toward the surface that results when an infant is held in a horizontal position and prone, and then lowered toward the floor

parallel play: children play independently even though they are near other children and engaged in similar activities

paraphrasing: the practice of the listener restating the heart of the conversation in order to confirm and clarify what was meant

paraplegia: cerebral palsy affecting the lower extremities of the body

paraprofessionals: staff who assist licensed or certified intervention specialists

parity: number of live births delivered by a woman

parsimony: the adoption of the simplest assumption in the formulation of a theory or the interpretation of data

partial complex seizure: seizures that commence from one cerebral hemisphere of the brain

patent ductus ateriosis (PDA): when the opening between the aorta and the pulmonary artery, which permits blood to bypass the lungs prenatally and normally closes shortly after birth, stays open after birth and diminishes flow from the aorta

pathogenic: capable of causing disease

perception checks: when a listener checks his or her perception or understanding of what was said in the course of a conversation in order to open up and clarify the communication

perinatal: relating to the period just before or just after birth

periventricular leukomalacia (PVL): development of cysts or fluid-filled holes in the brain

phenotype: refers to the observable expression, or appearance, of a genetically inherited characteristic in an individual

phonology: the study of speech sounds

placenta: a fleshy mass made up of villi or projectiles that insert themselves into the lining of the uterus to nurture a developing fetus

placenta previa: a condition in which the placenta implants itself near the cervix rather than the top of the uterus

plasticity: the quality of being plastic, or capable of being molded; in regard to neural function

positioning: treatment of postural and reflex abnormalities by careful, symmetrical placement and support of the body

positron emission tomography (PET): used to view tumors, seizures, etc.

postnatal: occurring after birth, with reference to the newborn

postural reflexes (adaptive reflexes): involuntary responses that supplement movement while preventing injury

predictive utility: providing accurate forecasts about what will happen

preexisting diabetes: diabetes that developed prior to pregnancy

premature labor: prior to 37 weeks of gestation

premature rupture of membranes: membranes of the water sac surrounding the fetus break prior to 37th week of pregnancy

prematurity: when a developing fetus is born prior to the 37th week of gestation

prenatal: preceding birth

preoperational stage: stage during which children reason through linguistic input and personal knowledge

present levels of performance: use of current evaluation information to summarize skills and abilities

presuppositions: judgments made about the listener in a conversation that allow one to modify the content and style of the communication (These judgments include assessment of social status, educational or developmental level, closeness of relationships, etc.)

preventive intervention: a variety of therapeutic services that build interaction skills between parents and their children

primary social supports: informal support network comprised of close family, friends, and neighbors

primitive reflexes: involuntary motor responses to specific stimuli that interfere with movement if persistent

proactive stance: working to influence others positively toward a particular position

procedural safeguards: rights guaranteed to families of children eligible for services under IDEA

prolapse of umbilical cord: baby presses on the umbilical cord during delivery and decreases or stops blood flow (and oxygen supply)

promotion: strategies that support healthy relationships between parents and their children

prone: lying on the tummy

protective extension: reaching an arm out to prevent falling when pushed out of midline, either from sitting or standing position

protozoan: a member of the phylum comprising the simplest forms of the animal kingdom; a unicellular organism

proximal-distal: sequence of development that progresses from the center of the body outward toward the extremities

psychometric approach: assessment comparing a child to normal standards of development, intelligence, or achievement in order to determine performance discrepancies

psychotherapy: professional assistance helping a person understand how past experience has affected current psychological conflicts

pyramidal tract: the motor cortex and spinal cord

quadriplegia: cerebral palsy affecting all four extremities of the body

qualitative–developmental assessment: assessment in which a child's skills, as well as the child's approach to people and tasks, are evaluated according to a developmental sequence

radiation: heat loss through dissipation from the body into the air

range of motion: the degrees of movement for a limb or body part

range of normalcy: lower and upper limits of age at which developmental milestones are attained

receptive language: understanding of a message sent by another individual

recessive gene: a gene that does not possess sufficient genetic information for the characteristic to be expressed unless the gene is carried on both alleles

refinement: sequence of development that progresses from large muscle control to small muscle control

reflex integration: the disappearance of involuntary reflexes to allow for normal motor development

reinforcement: a change in stimulus, contingent upon a response, that results in an increase in the probability of that response

related services: additional support services that allow children to benefit from their educational experiences

relative clauses: a part of a sentence that describes a subject, for example, "I want a doll that wets."

renal system: organ system including kidneys and bladder

replicate: to demonstrate again with the same results

residual vision: visual ability remaining to an individual with a visual loss

respiratory distress syndrome (RDS): collapse of alveoli in the lungs due to lack of surfactant production in premature infants

respiratory system: organ system including lungs and airways

retina: the innermost layer of the eye; the neural layer containing the receptors for light

Retinopathy of Prematurity (ROP): overgrowth of connective tissue in the eyes due to excess oxygen given to premature infants; oxygenation that causes damage to the blood vessels supplying the retina and, in severe cases, detachment of the retina

Rh sensitization: blood-type incompatibility of mother and fetus that causes a buildup of antigens in mother's blood

rooting reflex: occurs when an infant's cheek is lightly stroked and, in response, infant's head turns toward the stimulus

rubella: commonly called German measles; caused by a virus that usually produces only mild upper respiratory symptoms and a rash in the infected individual; can cause severe damage to a fetus and can result in spontaneous abortion

savant: an individual shows extreme aptitude in one area (e.g., music or mathematics)

scoliosis: spinal curvature of the lower back

screening: a relatively quick preliminary evaluation used to determine if a child should be referred for more in-depth assessment

secondary social supports: formal sources of support, such as health care providers, educators, and therapists, that are usually more temporary than primary social supports

seizure: abnormal electrical discharges in the brain that cause the body to tremor, lose consciousness, or move in uncontrollable ways

self-help skills: independent care including eating, dressing, toileting, and other personal responsibilities

self-stimulation: sensory input from personal tactile, visual, auditory, or other physical activity that ignores other people or objects in the environment (such as hand-flapping, lip smacking, biting, etc.)

semantic relationship: combinations of two or more words that possess more meaning than any one of the words uttered in isolation

semicircular canals: three canals in the temporal bone that lie approximately at right angles to one another, containing receptors for equilibrium, specifically for rotation

sensorimotor stage: takes place from birth to age 2; represents children's primitive exploration of their environment, wherein children attempt to integrate sensory information with their own movement

sensorineural hearing loss: results from damage to the cochlea or auditory nerve

service coordinator: person assigned to family of a child with special needs who is responsible for seeing that family and child receive all the services for which they are eligible under Part H of IDEA

sex-linked disorders: transmitted through the parents on a sex chromsome (X or Y) so that it is common for individuals of only one gender to express the disorder

shunting: procedure that requires the surgical placement of a soft pliable plastic tube between the ventricle and either the heart or the peritoneal cavity in the abdomen to drain off excess cerebral spinal fluid

sickle cell crisis: in persons with sickle cell disease, frequent and severe painful episodes

social–affective play: interaction between adult and child that elicits pleasure responses from the child

socioeconomic: relating to income and social factors

solitary play: a child is involved with his or her own play and does not interact with others

spastic cerebral palsy: cerebral damage in which the muscles tighten and resist efforts to move

special education: specially designed instruction that includes adaptations that are significantly different from modifications normally made for typical students and are necessary to offset or reduce the adverse effects of the child's disability

spectator play: a young child observes the play of others but does not attempt to join them

speech acts: the speaker's intentions or purposes for communicating

spina bifida: refers to an incomplete spinal column and the relationship of the spinal cord and contents to the defect

spina bifida occulta: a defect in the vertebrae covering the spinal cord, with no exposure of the neural membranes or any evidence of nerve tissue in the defect

spinal tap: a procedure in which a hollow needle is used to draw cerebrospinal fluid from the spinal canal

stage theory response: the naming and sequential ordering of complex emotions that are normal under a given set of circumstances

startle reflex: occurs when a sudden noise or movement causes a child to throw its arms away from the body and then back toward the midline

status epilepticus: a prolonged seizure of 15 minutes or more that is a life-threatening condition

stepping reflex: step-like response that occurs when a child is held in a vertical position so that its feet touch a surface

strabismus: a condition in which the optical axes of the two eyes are not parallel; cross-eyed

supine: lying on the back

surfactant: a chemical agent needed for independent breathing that is not produced in sufficient quantity until the 32nd to 33rd week of pregnancy

syntax: rules that govern structural patterns of language utterances and sentences

systemic: pertaining to or affecting the body as a whole

teacher-directed instruction: highly structured instruction planned in advance and guided by the teacher

temperament: characteristic emotional response

teratogen: any agent or factor that causes physical defects in a developing embryo

term pregnancy: gestational period of at least 38 weeks

tertiary: third in order, as in tertiary service delivery in which a professional serves a parent who, in turn, serves a child

tertiary services: indirect services that benefit children or their families (For example, when service providers enable parents to implement activities to assist in the development of their children, the child is receiving tertiary services from the professional.)

toddler stage: time from 1 year to 3 years of age

tonic-clonic seizure: rigid muscular contraction and rapid alternation of contraction and relaxation of muscles

total communication: a combination of manual signing with oral methods of communication

toxin: a poison

toxoplasmosis: a protozoan that is acquired by humans from contact with the feces of infected cats or birds and from the ingestion of raw or partially cooked meat; may result in premature delivery or spontaneous abortion

tracking: ability to follow moving objects with the eyes in several directions (vertically and horizontally)

transdisciplinary model: a group whose members share roles and combine assessment and treatment tasks so that they may be carried out by one professional

transition: change in growth and development that may result in unpredictable behavior or regression

transition plan: formal written plan that indicates activities and responsibility for those activities that will make the move from one program to the next as smoothly as possible

transition stressors: pressure on a family related to a child's disability and occurring at significant milestones in life

translocation: the existence of extra chromosomal material, which has become attached to another chromosome, varying in size from a piece of one arm to an entire chromosome

transplancental: substance crosses from maternal to fetal bloodstream, or vice versa, via the placenta

trimester: a period of 3 months, usually pertaining to gestational periods; for example, second trimester

triplegia: cerebral palsy affecting three extremities of the body

trisomy 21: the presence of an extra number 21 chromosome, which causes Down syndrome

ultrasonography or ultrasound: a procedure that uses high-frequency sound waves to produce an image of an internal organ

umbilical cord: the cord that joins the bloodstream of the fetus at the abdomen to the bloodstream of the mother via the uterine lining

underextension: children's language usage that occurs when categories are defined too narrowly (For example, a young child may use the word "chair" when referring to a high chair or table chair, but not include the rocking chair or kitchen stool in the category.)

unidisciplinary: trained from the perspective of one professional discipline

vaccines: consist of either active viral replications with decreased virulence or an inactive virus introduced into the human being to activate the immune system to produce antibodies, preventing an acute infection

varicella-zoster: a virus related to herpes responsible for chicken pox and shingles

ventricles: fluid-filled sacs that occupy space within and around the brain mass

very low birth weight: less than 1,500 g (3 lb 5 oz)

vestibule: a small cavity or space at the entrance to a canal, such as that in the inner ear

viable: the age at which the fetus has the potential to live outside of the womb, about 26 to 28 weeks

viruses: the smallest known types of infectious agent that invade cells, take over, and make copies of themselves

visual acuity: acuteness of vision; the power of the visual apparatus to distinguish visual detail, such as recognizing a letter of the alphabet

vitreous humor: the colorless, transparent gel filling the cavity of the eye behind the lens

X rays: a form of invisible electromagnetic energy that allows a view of the size, shape, and movement of organs

Author Index

Stullenbarger, B., 344, 386
Stump, C.S., 143, 153
Subramanian, K.N.S., 234, 247, 251, 252, 253, 254, 255, 257, 258, 259, 272
Sudhalter, V., 350, 386
Sulmont, V., 369, 387
Summers, C.R., 151
Summers, C.R. & Summers, 137
Summers, M., 151
Summerville, M.B., 185, 228
Supama, N., 194, 204, 228
Susman, E., 263, 264, 272
Sutton, L.N., 314, 323
Swank, P.R., 180, 228
Swick, K.J., 104, 153
Sykanda, A.M., 440
Sylvester, K., 101

Tager, I.B., 271
Tager-Flusberg, H., 201, 227
Talbert-Johnson, C., 21, 48
Tallal, P., 203, 229
Tam, D.A., 326
Tanguay, S., 327
Tanner-Halverson, P., 262, 272
Taylor, G., 271, 307
Taylor, H.G., 326
Taylor, R., 19, 20, 49
Temple, C.M., 363, 387
Temple, W.E., 327
Templin, T., 262, 263, 271
Teplin, S.W., 405, 440
Tessier, A., 57, 99, 113, 150
Thomas, A., 178, 230, 239
Thomas, D., 419, 440
Thomas, J.D., 272
Thomas, L., 261, 271
Thommessen, M., 289, 326
Thompson, H., 171, 228, 331, 334, 335, 337, 359
Thompson, L., 481
Thompson, M.W., 387
Thompson, R.J., 387
Thomsen, P.H., 325
Thomson, E., 24, 49
Thorndike, E.L., 65, 101
Thornton, A.R.D., 394
Thousand, J.S., 140, 153
Thurman, K.S., 94, 95, 101, 458, 465, 467, 481, 501, 502, 511
Thurston, L.P., 104, 151
Tiedje, L.B., 236, 237, 272
Tielsch, J.M., 266, 271
Tietze, W., 90, 101

Tocci, L., 448, 480
Tolan, P., 24, 47
Tompkins-McGill, P., 477, 479
Toral, J.C., 247, 272
Tordjman, S., 369, 387
Torup, E., 371, 387
Tosteson, T.D., 271
Tout, K., 72, 99
Traustadottir, R., 110, 153
Trivette, C., 30, 47, 450, 477, 478, 480
Trohanis, P.L., 445, 481
Troutman, A.C., 4, 6
Tucker, B.P., 470, 481
Turbiville, V.P., 153
Turnbull, A.P., 46, 49, 295, 490
Turnbull, J.D., 27, 30, 104, 109, 110, 113, 114, 133, 136, 139, 153, 326, 476, 484
Turnbull, R., 27, 30, 49, 76, 78, 79, 101, 104, 109, 113, 114, 133, 136, 139, 153, 326, 476, 484
Turner, E., 21, 350, 352, 353
Turner, G., 387
Tutty, S., 306, 326

Ulleland, C.N., 260, 271
Umansky, W., 81, 99, 442, 473, 474, 475, 481
Urbano, R.C., 349, 386
Uslan, M., 400, 440

Vacha, E.F., 184, 229
Vadasy, P.F., 110, 152
Vaillancourt, J.M.R., 384
Van Beneden, C.A., 413, 440
Van Loan, M.D., 361, 385
Vandell, D.L., 180, 230
Vanderas, A.P., 379, 387
Vanderslice, V., 104, 153
Vargha-Khadem, F., 291, 326
Varner, M.W., 264, 271
Vellet, S., 180, 228
Ventura, S.J., 443, 481
Ver der Werf, S., 291, 326
Vergason, G.A., 113, 150
Viera, A., 359, 385
Villa, R., 140, 153
Villani, S., 185, 230
Vinter, A., 291, 324
Visser, G.H.A., 271
Vitale, A., 385
Vollero, H., 324
Volpe, J., 316, 326
Voydanoff, P., 39, 49

Vunakis, H.V., 271
Vygotsky, L.S., 171, 230

Waaland, P.K., 307, 326
Wachtel, T.J., 347, 387
Wade, S.L., 307, 308, 309, 326
Wagner, M., 479
Wake, S., 350, 387
Wakefield, P., 38, 48
Walker, D., 38, 48
Walkup, J.T., 372, 373, 387
Walling, A.D., 247, 255, 272
Walther-Thomas, C., 23, 49
Wandry, D., 139, 152, 484
Wands, J., 438
Warger, C., 64, 101
Watson, J.B., 65, 101
Weatherston, D.J., 107, 108, 153
Wehman, T., 481
Wehrly, B., 21, 49
Wei, L.F., 181, 228
Weil, M., 22, 48
Weiner, L., 260, 272
Weintraub, Z., 263, 272
Weismer, S.E., 205, 229
Weiss, S.T., 271
Wellington, J., 319, 324
Wells, S.A., 25, 49
Wen, S.W., 267, 272
Werner, E., 114, 153
Wesley, J., 56, 101
Wesley, P.W., 30, 46
Wetzstein, C., 24, 49
Whaley, D.L., 5, 49, 432, 440
White, J.F., 60, 101, 347, 384
White, K., 45, 49
White-Williams, C., 343, 344, 387
Whitley, R., 422, 440
Whitman, B., 305, 326
Whitney, C.G., 413, 440
Widerstrom, A.H., 458, 481, 501, 502, 511
Wildin, S.R., 245, 273
Wilens, T.E., 327
Willard, H.F., 331, 334, 335, 337, 387
Williams, A.L., 149, 152, 262, 362, 363
Williams, B., 17, 23, 25, 49, 56, 57, 61, 62, 63
Williams, B.F., 271, 306, 327
Williams, B.T., 49
Williams, J.K., 387
Williams, L.R., 101
Williams, R.L., 306, 327

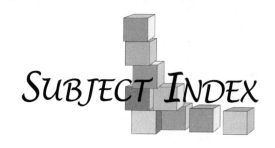

SUBJECT INDEX